MOTOCOURSE

The World's Leading MotoGP and Superbike Annual

REVOLUTIONARY

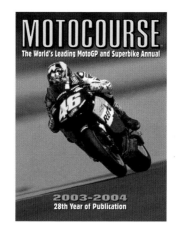

MOTOCOURSE
2003–2004

This edition published in 2003
by Motorbooks International,
an imprint of MBI Publishing
Company, Galtier Plaza,
Suite 200, 380 Jackson Street,
St. Paul, MN 55101-3885 USA

Produced and published in the
United Kingdom by
Hazleton Publishing Ltd,
5th Floor, Mermaid House,
2 Puddle Dock, London,
EC4V 3DS.

Colour reproduction by
Radstock Repro,
Midsomer Norton, Somerset, England

Printed in England by
Butler and Tanner Ltd,
Frome, Somerset, England

Hazleton Publishing Ltd is a member
of Profile Media Group Plc.

The information in this book is true and
complete to the best of our knowledge.
All recommendations are made without
any guarantee on the part of the
author or Publisher, who also disclaim
any liability incurred in connection with
the use of this data or specific details.

We recognize that some words, model
names and designations, for example,
mentioned herein are the property of
the trademark holder. We use them for
identification purposes only. This is not
an official publication.

Motorbooks International titles are also
available at discounts in bulk quantity
for industrial or sales-promotional use.
For details write to Special Sales
Manager at Motorbooks International
Wholesalers & Distributors, Galtier
Plaza, Suite 200, 380 Jackson Street,
St. Paul, MN 55101-3885 USA.

ISBN: 1 903135 30 3

MOTORBOOKS
INTERNATIONAL

Dust-jacket photograph:
**MotoGP World Champion Valentino Rossi
on the Repsol Honda V5**
Photograph: Mark Wernham

Title page photograph:
**World Superbike Champion Neil Hodgson
on the works Ducati**
Photograph: Gold & Goose

CONTENTS

Acknowledgements

The Editor and staff of MOTOCOURSE wish to thank the following for their assistance in compiling the
2003–2004 edition: Marc Petrier (FIM), Paul Butler (IRTA), Nick Harris and Eva Jirsenska (Dorna),
Chuck Aksland, Jerry Burgess, Carlo Fiorani, Ali Forth, Hamish Jamieson, Iain Mackay, Randy
Mamola, Tom O'Kane, Martin Port, Stuart Shenton, Garry Taylor, Bob Toomey, Debbie van Zon,
Rupert Williamson, Warren Willing, Jan Witteveen, as well as riders, friends and colleagues too
numerous to list.

Photographers

Photographs published in MOTOCOURSE 2003–2004 have been contributed by: Gold & Goose,
Mark Wernham, Dave Collister, Ducati Corse, Kel Edge, John McKenzie, Dave Purves, Tom Riles.

editor
MICHAEL SCOTT

director
ROBERT YARHAM

managing editor
IAN PENBERTHY

art editor
STEVE SMALL

business development manager
PETER MERCER

sales promotion
LAURA FELL

results and statistics
KAY EDGE

chief photographers
GOLD & GOOSE
MARK WERNHAM

www.motocourse.com

Dedication
BARRY SHEENE 1950

CINZA
GRAND
onington P

500 cc World

Donington Park 2000 – the ever-popular Barry
Sheene takes centre stage on the rostrum. Kenny
Roberts Jr, Valentino Rossi and Jeremy
McWilliams (and family) join the applause.
Photograph: Gold & Goose

to 2003

In 1976, *MOTOCOURSE* was born. The date is significant. It was the same year that Barry Sheene won his first 500 cc World Championship. He was already a household name.

Without his success and star quality, motor cycle racing probably would have remained a minority interest, especially in Britain. It is unlikely that *MOTOCOURSE* would have been published.

Sheene won the championship again the next year, and his distinctive figure was on the cover of the second issue of the racing annual as well.

This is the 28th edition of *MOTOCOURSE*. What started around Barry Sheene has grown ever since.

It is dedicated to the man who changed motor cycle racing.

To Barry Sheene.

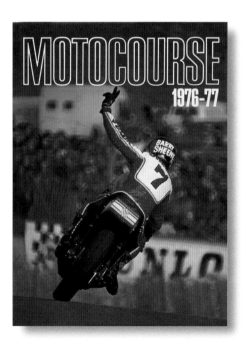

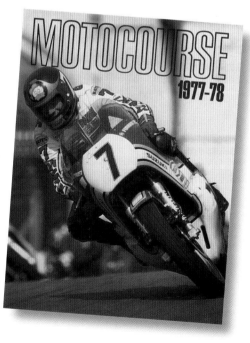

Champion 1976 & 1977

Honda triple-decker – Rossi found the competition tougher in 2003. Here he is sandwiched between leader Biaggi and Gibernau.
Photograph: Mark Wernham

ROLLER-COASTER RIDE

WHAT a whirligig season it was. Ups and downs, topsy-turvy. Craziness and laughter and excitement. And sudden death. This is motor cycle racing.

MotoGP's second year was simply a marvel. Never mind that Rossi dominated. He did so with variety and humanity, and breathtaking talent. He defeated the strongest, closest and most varied field in history, which included the awe-inspiring new Ducatis. Then he danced a jig to switch from his thrice-victorious Honda to serially defeated Yamaha.

The 125s prospered too – closely linked with the Spanish flavour imparted by Dorna. The same influence reaches into the 250 class, but that gave signs in 2003 of gradually fading away. The quarter-litre class is playing out its last.

Over at Superbikes, Englishman Neil Hodgson stepped into the shoes vacated by serial winner Carl Fogarty to bring the production-based championship back to its spiritual home.

But all was not well in the Flammini camp, the organisers at loggerheads with manufacturers and tyre companies after their bold decision to reinvent the whole series – taking it closer to its street-bike roots. The manufacturers obligingly decamped *en masse*. A controversial move to compulsory Pirelli tyres was still facing legal challenges even as testing began for 2004.

The short-term fall-out will benefit both British and American national championships – two series that were already enjoying a significant revival of interest and importance. For 2004, the factories will divert attention from World Superbikes to these championships.

This represents a further realignment of world racing, the national championships being more closely integrated with the ultimate MotoGP class – with or without a stop-over in World Superbikes on the way.

Motor cycle racing remains a high-risk pastime. This is part of its power – to excite, to enthral, and to devastate.

There were too many high-level reminders in a sad season – although in fact only two out of four significant deaths occurred on the track.

The first racing victim was Daijiro Kato, fatally injured in the opening GP. Honda's hope for Japan's first premier-class champion, he was just 26.

The next two shocks followed mid-season. The modern giant of the Isle of Man, David Jefferies, was killed instantly in a horrific high-speed crash during TT practice week. He had just set the fastest lap of the fortnight when he hit spilled oil at close to his Suzuki's top speed.

Then Steve Hislop, troubled but immaculate scientist of the British Superbike series, died when the helicopter he was piloting crashed soon after take-off.

The greatest impact, however, had struck before the racing even began, with the premature death of Barry Sheene, aged only 52. London-born Barry, who subsequently had emigrated to Australia, succumbed to a battle with cancer that had begun half-way through the previous year. He was still an icon of bike racing more than 25 years after his two world championships, and the sadness at his loss was felt worldwide.

Sheene was racing's first natural superstar, and he changed the face of grand prix racing. He wrote the first ever World Champion's Foreword for the first edition of *MOTOCOURSE*. This year, as a mark of respect and gratitude, we have replaced that traditional feature with a dedication to Barry Sheene.

He probably wouldn't give a monkey's…

Michael Scott
Wimbledon
November 2003

TRIPLE CENTURY

MICHELIN IN GRAND PRIX MOTOR CYCLE RACING

Above: Mick Doohan poses with a special Michelin tyre, cut to celebrate his five consecutive 500 cc World Championships.

Above centre: Champions all in the premier class of motor cycle racing. Barry Sheene (7) on his Suzuki in the 1977 French GP, Freddie Spencer on his number 3 Honda at Misano in 1983; Wayne Rainey leading team-mate Eddie Lawson on their Marlboro Yamahas in 1990 and Kevin Schwantz aboard the Lucky Strike Suzuki in 1994.

Top right: Sete Gibernau powers his Honda to Michelin's 300th premier class win at the 2003 Dutch TT.

RECENT MICHELIN WORLD CHAMPIONSHIP VICTORIES

500 cc Grands Prix

1992	Wayne Rainey	(Yamaha)
1993	Kevin Schwantz	(Suzuki)
1994	Mick Doohan	(Honda)
1995	Mick Doohan	(Honda)
1996	Mick Doohan	(Honda)
1997	Mick Doohan	(Honda)
1998	Mick Doohan	Honda)
1999	Alex Crivillé	(Honda)
2000	Kenny Roberts	(Suzuki)
2001	Valentino Rossi	(Honda)

MotoGP

2002	Valentino Rossi	(Honda)
2003	Valentino Rossi	(Honda)

World Superbike

1994	Carl Fogarty	(Ducati)
1995	Carl Fogarty	(Ducati)
1996	Troy Corser	(Ducati)
1997	John Kocinski	(Honda)
1998	Carl Fogarty	(Ducati)
1999	Carl Fogarty	(Ducati)
2000	Colin Edwards	(Honda)
2001	Troy Bayliss	(Ducati)
2002	Colin Edwards	(Honda)
2003	Neil Hodgson	(Ducati)

SETE Gibernau marked another milestone for Michelin at the Dutch TT on 28 June 2003, winning the company's 300th premier-class grand prix victory. This landmark emphasised the French company's leadership in the world's fastest, most technically challenging motor cycling world championship.

Michelin has been a growing force in bike racing ever since it entered the grand prix arena in the early seventies. Australian Jack Findlay (Suzuki TR500) became the first man to win a premier-class GP for the French concern when he took victory in the British round of the 1973 500 World Championship on the Isle of Man. Three years later, the late, great Barry Sheene (Suzuki RG500) secured Michelin's first 500 World Championship. And the very next year, Michelin scored the first of many grand slams, with success in the 500, 350, 250, 125 and 50 cc World Championships.

Following those across-the-board successes, Michelin now focuses its attention on the big-bike classes to cement its reputation as world leader in high-performance motor cycle tyre technology. The company has remained undefeated in the premier world championship over the past 11 seasons, and continues to reign in World Superbike, lifting the last nine titles. In all, Michelin has won more than 70 world championships in every class going.

Michelin took to the tracks in 1973 with its PZ road tyres, which quickly made an impression because their more rounded profile gave a greater contact patch for improved grip. Kent Andersson won Michelin's first world championship, the 1974 125 title, and two years later Barry Sheene gained that first 500 crown.

Initially, Sheene used a PZ2 treaded front tyre with one of the new slicks on the rear of his RG500. 'To start with, slicks weren't a massive leap forward because we didn't understand them,' he explained. 'I remember looking at one and thinking, "Wouldn't it work better with lots of nice tread?"'

Sunshine or rain, Michelin quickly became the tyre to be seen with. 'They gave their new wets to five or so riders when it rained at Spa in '78, and no one could believe how good they were,' added Sheene. 'The radial transformed racing... You could never really step the back out on crossplies because you'd have to be lucky to catch it. I couldn't believe what the radial would let me get away with. If the tyre started to slide, you just kept the throttle on and it would slide until it stopped sliding, then go straight.'

Michelin had been working on its first radial motor cycle tyres since the late seventies, much development work having been carried out by American genius Freddie Spencer, who gained Michelin's first radial 500 GP success (with a rear radial only) in 1984. Radials made a huge difference to Spencer, Mamola and other 500 stars – reducing heat build-up and prolonging performance, and improving handling and steering through a reduction in weight. Radials also offered a crucial improvement in feel for rear-wheel steering – by the mid-eighties, most riders were sliding the rear out of corners.

'From a tyre standpoint, the radial was the biggest improvement in my career,' says Spencer, who won the 1983 and '85 500 crowns, plus the '85 250 title with Michelin.

While the radial tyre revolutionised motor cycle performance, Michelin continued to work on other aspects of tyre design. 'Developments in tyre dimensions and compounds...triggered significant changes in motor cycle architecture,' says Aime Chatard, now head of Michelin's rally department. 'And developments in tyre casing technology brought changes in drive characteristics, promoting the emergence of different riding techniques. And by fine adjustment of relative front and rear tyre profiles, we were able to achieve a slight oversteer in response to the rider lightly rolling off the throttle...this is now known to be a significant safety factor.'

Horsepower outputs spiralled from the eighties into the nineties, during which time Michelin increased its grip on the premier 500 class. Eddie Lawson (Yamaha YZR500/Honda NSR500), Wayne Gardner (Honda NSR500), Wayne Rainey (Yamaha YZR500) and Kevin Schwantz (Suzuki RGV500) all won the 500 crown, followed by Mick Doohan (Honda NSR500). The Australian took five back-to-back 500 titles, all with Michelin.

Following Doohan's retirement, Michelin's engineers triggered another major advance in motor cycle tyre performance – the 16.5-inch rear slick, which dramatically raised the 500 pace from the 2000 season and into the new MotoGP era.

The current S4 MotoGP tyres, introduced in 2002 to cope with the massive horsepower outputs of the new four-strokes, are a development of the 16.5, which scored its first GP win in 1994 with Schwantz, but wasn't universally adopted until 2000.

'We started development for the four-strokes using the same 16.5 rim size,' explains Nicolas Goubert, Michelin's chief of motor cycling competition since 1997, 'but the four-stroke tyre has a bigger centre diameter, giving a different profile to increase the contact patch and thus reduce running temperature. The new profile also offers improved edge grip, because the four-strokes have more torque available when the riders start to open the throttle at full lean, and more traction, because you need a lot of acceleration grip when you've got more horsepower.'

MICHELIN PREMIER-CLASS WINNERS

1973 (500 GP)
- TT, Isle of Man — Jack Findlay (Suzuki)

1975 (500 GP)
- Dutch — Barry Sheene (Suzuki)
- Swedish — Barry Sheene (Suzuki)

1976 (500 GP)
- French — Barry Sheene (Suzuki)
- Austrian — Barry Sheene (Suzuki)
- Italian — Barry Sheene (Suzuki)
- Dutch — Barry Sheene (Suzuki)
- Swedish — Barry Sheene (Suzuki)
- Finnish — Pat Hennen (Suzuki)

1977 (500 GP)
- Venezuelan — Barry Sheene (Suzuki)
- Austrian — Jack Findlay (Suzuki)
- German — Barry Sheene (Suzuki)
- Italian — Barry Sheene (Suzuki)
- French — Barry Sheene (Suzuki)
- Dutch — Wil Hartog (Suzuki)
- Belgian — Barry Sheene (Suzuki)
- Swedish — Barry Sheene (Suzuki)
- Finnish — Johnny Cecotto (Yamaha)
- Czech — Johnny Cecotto (Yamaha)
- British — Pat Hennen (Suzuki)

1978 (500 GP)
- Venezuelan — Barry Sheene (Suzuki)
- Spanish — Pat Hennen (Suzuki)
- Dutch — Johnny Cecotto (Yamaha)
- Belgian — Wil Hartog (Suzuki)
- Swedish — Barry Sheene (Suzuki)
- Finnish — Wil Hartog (Suzuki)
- German — Virginio Ferrari (Suzuki)

1979 (500 GP)
- Venezuelan — Barry Sheene (Suzuki)
- German — Wil Hartog (Suzuki)
- Dutch — Virginio Ferrari (Suzuki)
- Swedish — Barry Sheene (Suzuki)
- Finnish — Boet van Dulmen (Suzuki)
- French — Barry Sheene (Suzuki)

1980 (500 GP)
- Dutch — Jack Middelburg (Yamaha)
- Finnish — Wil Hartog (Suzuki)
- German — Marco Lucchinelli (Suzuki)

1981 (500 GP)
- French — Marco Lucchinelli (Suzuki)
- Dutch — Marco Lucchinelli (Suzuki)
- Belgian — Marco Lucchinelli (Suzuki)
- San Marino — Marco Lucchinelli (Suzuki)
- British — Jack Middelburg (Suzuki)
- Finnish — Marco Lucchinelli (Suzuki)
- Swedish — Barry Sheene (Yamaha)

1982 (500 GP)
- Austrian — Franco Uncini (Suzuki)
- French — Michel Frutschi (Sanven-ero)
- Italian — Franco Uncini (Suzuki)
- Dutch — Franco Uncini (Suzuki)
- Belgian — Freddie Spencer (Honda)
- Yugoslav — Franco Uncini (Suzuki)
- British — Franco Uncini (Suzuki)
- Swedish — Takazumi Katayama (Honda)
- San Marino — Freddie Spencer (Honda)

1983 (500 GP)
- South African — Freddie Spencer (Honda)
- French — Freddie Spencer (Honda)
- Italian — Freddie Spencer (Honda)
- Spanish — Freddie Spencer (Honda)
- Yugoslav — Freddie Spencer (Honda)
- Swedish — Freddie Spencer (Honda)

1984 (500 GP)
- Italian — Freddie Spencer (Honda)
- German — Freddie Spencer (Honda)
- French — Freddie Spencer (Honda)
- Yugoslav — Freddie Spencer (Honda)
- Dutch — Randy Mamola (Honda)
- Belgian — Freddie Spencer (Honda)
- British — Randy Mamola (Honda)
- San Marino — Randy Mamola (Honda)

1985 (500 GP)
- South African — Eddie Lawson (Yamaha)
- Spanish — Freddie Spencer (Honda)
- German — Christian Sarron (Yamaha)
- Italian — Freddie Spencer (Honda)
- Austrian — Freddie Spencer (Honda)
- Yugoslav — Eddie Lawson (Yamaha)
- Dutch — Randy Mamola (Honda)
- Belgian — Freddie Spencer (Honda)
- French — Freddie Spencer (Honda)
- British — Freddie Spencer (Honda)
- Swedish — Freddie Spencer (Honda)
- San Marino — Eddie Lawson (Yamaha)

1986 (500 GP)
- Spanish — Wayne Gardner (Honda)
- Italian — Eddie Lawson (Yamaha)
- German — Eddie Lawson (Yamaha)
- Austrian — Eddie Lawson (Yamaha)
- Yugoslav — Eddie Lawson (Yamaha)
- Dutch — Eddie Lawson (Yamaha)
- Belgian — Randy Mamola (Yamaha)
- French — Eddie Lawson (Yamaha)
- British — Wayne Gardner (Honda)
- Swedish — Eddie Lawson (Yamaha)
- San Marino — Eddie Lawson (Yamaha)

1987 (500 GP)
- Spanish — Wayne Gardner (Honda)
- German — Eddie Lawson (Yamaha)
- Italian — Wayne Gardner (Honda)
- Austrian — Wayne Gardner (Honda)
- Yugoslav — Wayne Gardner (Honda)
- Dutch — Eddie Lawson (Yamaha)
- British — Eddie Lawson (Yamaha)
- Swedish — Wayne Gardner (Honda)
- Czech — Wayne Gardner (Honda)
- Portuguese — Eddie Lawson (Yamaha)
- Brazilian — Wayne Gardner (Honda)
- Argentine — Eddie Lawson (Yamaha)

1988 (500 GP)
- Japanese — Kevin Schwantz (Suzuki)
- US — Eddie Lawson (Yamaha)
- Portuguese — Eddie Lawson (Yamaha)
- Italian — Eddie Lawson (Yamaha)
- German — Kevin Schwantz (Suzuki)
- Austrian — Eddie Lawson (Yamaha)
- Dutch — Wayne Gardner (Honda)
- Belgian — Wayne Gardner (Honda)
- Yugoslav — Wayne Gardner (Honda)
- French — Eddie Lawson (Yamaha)
- Swedish — Eddie Lawson (Yamaha)
- Czech — Wayne Gardner (Honda)
- Brazilian — Eddie Lawson (Yamaha)

1989 (500 GP)
- Japanese — Kevin Schwantz (Suzuki)
- Australian — Wayne Gardner (Honda)
- Spanish — Eddie Lawson (Honda)
- Austrian — Kevin Schwantz (Suzuki)
- Yugoslav — Kevin Schwantz (Suzuki)
- Belgian — Eddie Lawson (Honda)
- French — Eddie Lawson (Honda)
- British — Kevin Schwantz (Suzuki)
- Swedish — Eddie Lawson (Honda)
- Czech — Kevin Schwantz (Suzuki)
- Brazilian — Kevin Schwantz (Suzuki)

1990 (500 GP)
- Japanese — Wayne Rainey (Yamaha)
- US — Wayne Rainey (Yamaha)
- Spanish — Wayne Gardner (Honda)
- Italian — Wayne Rainey (Yamaha)
- German — Kevin Schwantz (Suzuki)
- Austrian — Kevin Schwantz (Suzukin)
- Yugoslav — Wayne Rainey (Yamaha)
- Dutch — Kevin Schwantz (Suzuki)
- Belgian — Wayne Rainey (Yamaha)
- French — Kevin Schwantz (Suzuki)
- British — Kevin Schwantz (Suzuki)
- Swedish — Wayne Rainey (Yamaha)
- Czech — Wayne Rainey (Yamaha)
- Hungarian — Michael Doohan (Honda)
- Australian — Wayne Gardner (Honda)

1991 (500 GP)
- Spanish — Michael Doohan (Honda)
- Italian — Michael Doohan (Honda)
- Austrian — Michael Doohan (Honda)

1992 (500 GP)
- Japanese — Michael Doohan (Honda)
- Australian — Michael Doohan (Honda)
- Malaysian — Michael Doohan (Honda)
- Spanish — Michael Doohan (Honda)
- Italian — Kevin Schwantz (Suzuki)
- European — Wayne Rainey (Yamaha)
- German — Michael Doohan (Honda)
- Dutch — Alex Crivillé (Honda)
- French — Wayne Rainey (Yamaha)
- British — Wayne Gardner (Honda)
- Brazilian — Wayne Rainey (Yamaha)
- South African — John Kocinski (Yamaha)

1993 (500 GP)
- Australian — Kevin Schwantz (Suzuki)
- Spanish — Kevin Schwantz (Suzuki)
- Austrian — Kevin Schwantz (Suzuki)
- German — Daryl Beattie (Honda)
- Dutch — Kevin Schwantz (Suzuki)
- San Marino — Michael Doohan (Honda)
- US — John Kocinski (Cagiva)
- FIM — Alex Barros (Suzuki)

1994 (500 GP)
- Australian — John Kocinski (Cagiva)
- Malaysian — Michael Doohan (Honda)
- Japanese — Kevin Schwantz (Suzuki)
- Spanish — Michael Doohan (Honda)
- Austrian — Michael Doohan (Honda)
- German — Michael Doohan (Honda)
- Dutch — Michael Doohan (Honda)
- Italian — Michael Doohan (Honda)
- French — Michael Doohan (Honda)
- British — Kevin Schwantz (Suzuki)
- Czech — Michael Doohan (Honda)
- Argentine — Michael Doohan (Honda)

1995 (500 GP)
- Australian — Michael Doohan (Honda)
- Malaysian — Michael Doohan (Honda)
- Japanese — Daryl Beattie (Suzuki)
- Spanish — Alberto Puig (Honda)
- German — Daryl Beattie (Suzuki)
- Italian — Michael Doohan (Honda)
- Dutch — Michael Doohan (Honda)
- French — Michael Doohan (Honda)
- British — Michael Doohan (Honda)
- Argentine — Michael Doohan (Honda)
- European — Alex Crivillé (Honda)
- Australian — Wayne Gardner (Honda)

1996 (500 GP)
- Malaysian — Luca Cadalora (Honda)
- Indonesian — Michael Doohan (Honda)
- Japanese — Norifumi Abe (Yamaha)
- Spanish — Michael Doohan (Honda)
- Italian — Michael Doohan (Honda)
- French — Michael Doohan (Honda)
- Dutch — Michael Doohan (Honda)
- German — Luca Cadalora (Honda)
- British — Michael Doohan (Honda)
- Austrian — Alex Crivillé (Honda)
- Czech — Alex Crivillé (Honda)
- Imola — Michael Doohan (Honda)
- European — Carlos Checa (Honda)
- Brazilian — Michael Doohan (Honda)
- Australian — Loris Capirossi (Yamaha)

1997 (500 GP)
- Malaysian — Michael Doohan (Honda)
- Japanese — Michael Doohan (Honda)
- Spanish — Alex Crivillé (Honda)
- Italian — Michael Doohan (Honda)
- Austrian — Michael Doohan (Honda)
- French — Michael Doohan (Honda)
- Dutch — Michael Doohan (Honda)
- Imola — Michael Doohan (Honda)
- German — Michael Doohan (Honda)
- Brazilian — Michael Doohan (Honda)
- British — Michael Doohan (Honda)
- Czech — Michael Doohan (Honda)
- Catalan — Michael Doohan (Honda)
- Indonesian — Tadayuki Okada (Honda)
- Australian — Alex Crivillé (Honda)

1998 (500 GP)
- Japanese — Max Biaggi (Honda)
- Malaysian — Michael Doohan (Honda)
- Spanish — Alex Crivillé (Honda)
- Italian — Michael Doohan (Honda)
- French — Alex Crivillé (Honda)
- Madrid — Carlos Checa (Honda)
- Dutch — Michael Doohan (Honda)
- German — Michael Doohan (Honda)
- Czech — Max Biaggi (Honda)
- Imola — Michael Doohan (Honda)
- Catalan — Michael Doohan (Honda)
- Australian — Michael Doohan (Honda)
- Argentine — Michael Doohan (Honda)

1999 (500 GP)
- Malaysian — Kenny Roberts Jr (Suzuki)
- Japanese — Kenny Roberts Jr (Suzuki)
- Spanish — Alex Crivillé (Honda)
- French — Alex Crivillé (Honda)
- Italian — Alex Crivillé (Honda)
- Catalan — Alex Crivillé (Honda)
- Dutch — Tadayuki Okada (Honda)
- British — Alex Crivillé (Honda)
- German — Kenny Roberts Jr (Suzuki)
- Czech — Tadayuki Okada (Honda)
- San Marino — Alex Crivillé (Honda)
- Valencia — Régis Laconi (Yamaha)
- Australian — Tadayuki Okada (Honda)
- South African — Max Biaggi (Yamaha)
- Brazilian — Norick Abe (Yamaha)
- Argentine — Kenny Roberts (Suzuki)

2000 (500 GP)
- South African — Garry McCoy (Yamaha)
- Malaysian — Kenny Roberts (Suzuki)
- Japanese — Norick Abe (Yamaha)
- Spanish — Kenny Roberts (Suzuki)
- French — Alex Crivillé (Honda)
- Italian — Loris Capirossi (Honda)
- Catalan — Kenny Roberts (Suzuki)
- Dutch — Alex Barros (Honda)
- British — Valentino Rossi (Honda)
- German — Alex Barros (Honda)
- Czech — Max Biaggi (Yamaha)
- Portuguese — Garry McCoy (Yamaha)
- Valencia — Garry McCoy (Yamaha)
- Rio — Valentino Rossi (Honda)
- Pacific — Kenny Roberts (Suzuki)
- Australian — Max Biaggi (Yamaha)

2001 (500 GP)
- Japanese — Valentino Rossi (Honda)
- South African — Valentino Rossi (Honda)
- Spanish — Valentino Rossi (Honda)
- French — Max Biaggi (Yamaha)
- Italian — Alex Barros (Honda)
- Catalan — Valentino Rossi (Honda)
- Dutch — Max Biaggi (Yamaha)
- British — Valentino Rossi (Honda)
- German — Max Biaggi (Yamaha)
- Czech — Valentino Rossi (Honda)
- Portuguese — Valentino Rossi (Honda)
- Valencia — Sete Gibernau (Suzuki)
- Pacific — Valentino Rossi (Honda)
- Australian — Valentino Rossi (Honda)
- Malaysian — Valentino Rossi (Honda)
- Brazilian — Valentino Rossi (Honda)

2002 (MotoGP)
- Japanese — Valentino Rossi (Honda)
- South African — Tohru Ukawa (Honda)
- Spanish — Valentino Rossi (Honda)
- French — Valentino Rossi (Honda)
- Italian — Valentino Rossi (Honda)
- Catalan — Valentino Rossi (Honda)
- Dutch — Valentino Rossi (Honda)
- British — Valentino Rossi (Honda)
- German — Valentino Rossi (Honda)
- Czech — Max Biaggi (Yamaha)
- Portuguese — Valentino Rossi (Honda)
- Brazilian — Valentino Rossi (Honda)
- Pacific — Alex Barros (Honda)
- Malaysian — Max Biaggi (Yamaha)
- Australian — Valentino Rossi (Honda)
- Valencia — Alex Barros (Honda)

2003 (MotoGP)
- Japanese — Valentino Rossi (Honda)
- South African — Sete Gibernau (Honda)
- Spanish — Valentino Rossi (Honda)
- French — Sete Gibernau (Honda)
- Italian — Valentino Rossi (Honda)
- Catalan — Loris Capirossi (Ducati)
- Dutch — Sete Gibernau (Honda)
- British — Max Biaggi (Honda)
- German — Sete Gibernau (Honda)
- Czech — Valentino Rossi (Honda)
- Portuguese — Valentino Rossi (Honda)
- Brazilian — Valentino Rossi (Honda)
- Pacific — Max Biaggi (Honda)
- Malaysian — Valentino Rossi (Honda)
- Australian — Valentino Rossi (Honda)
- Valencia — Valentino Rossi (Honda)

1 VALENTINO ROSSI

IT would be impudent to put anybody else at the top of the list. An impudence that might strike a chord with Rossi. Because during the year, the growing-up boy wonder rediscovered how to find life, racing and everything amusing once again.

The burden of his rampant success had grown wearisome by the start of the season. Not even the challenge of the Ducatis, nor that of new Honda rider Sete Gibernau, who beat him fair and square in South Africa, France and most especially Germany, were enough to lift the gloom that had settled on his shoulders.

Then suddenly the old Rossi was back – cracking jokes in the paddock and press conferences, acting out the old pre-planned pantomimes after race wins, Technicolor hair changes… And winning races, with the simple old/new tactic that 'instead of thinking about it, any time anybody passes me, I will pass them back at the next corner.'

Rossi played mischief also with HRC, and with his rivals. Holding racing in the palm of his hand, he embarked on a bit of playful juggling.

His eventual decision to move to Yamaha shows courage and a sporting spirit to be admired, very reminiscent of Mike Hailwood. Although one must believe Rossi thinks that he (and virtually his whole nine-times-victorious HRC crew) can make a winning bike out of the perennially nearly-there M1.

Having conquered 125s, 250s and 500s as well as the MotoGP monsters; having won 59 GPs in all classes; having assembled a season with 12 new lap records (and retained two existing records), nine pole positions, nine wins and a record points score, Rossi's move puts him in line for another slice of history. If his quest to take the title on a Yamaha is successful, he will be only the fourth rider to win the top class on different makes of motor cycle. The others are all legends: Geoff Duke, Giacomo Agostini and Eddie Lawson. Not even Hailwood managed that.

Repsol Honda Team

2003 World Championship: 1st (MotoGP)

Race wins: 9

Pole positions: 9

Career GP wins: 59 (20 MGP, 13 500 cc, 14 250 cc, 12 125 cc)

World Championships: 5 (2 MGP, 1 500 cc, 1 250 cc, 1 125 cc)

Born: 16 February 1979, Urbino, Italy

TOP TEN RIDERS OF 2003

2 LORIS CAPIROSSI

DID the Desmosedici flatter Loris Capirossi, or was it the other way around? Certainly they made a marriage that was successful from the start. Manifestly powerful, the Ducati at full stretch wriggled and writhed and bounced off the kerbs, wheels seldom in line except at its imposing top speed. Just the way Capirossi seemed to like it.

Ducati Marlboro Team
2003 World Championship: 4th (MotoGP)
Race wins: 1
Pole positions: 3
Career GP wins: 23 (1 MGP, 2 500 cc, 12 250 cc, 8 125 cc)
World Championships: 3 (1 250 cc, 2 125 cc)
Born: 4 April 1973, Bologna, Italy

Capirossi fought the bike every lap and every corner – every inch of the way – and seldom stopped grinning. Exuberance on wheels. His small stature not only belies his strength, but also his importance as a motor cycle racer.

Loris's extensive portfolio includes a season riding for Wayne Rainey's factory Yamaha 500 team, and he had reason to thank his former employer for the dirt-track training that came with the deal. He needed those techniques to get the best out of the Duke.

Capirossi has had a chequered career, and has been around so long – always at or near the top – that he might be taken for granted. Not so in 2003, when he stepped confidently into the leading role in a bright red melodrama.

Loris was rewarded with one victory during the season, and threatened more. He sat on pole position three times too. It was a dream debut for the Ducati, and if team-mate Bayliss fairly frequently demonstrated that Loris wasn't the only person who could ride it fast, Capirossi came out on top. It was an all-Italian marvel, in the same colours as Ferrari. The former 125 and 250 champion may be in Rossi's shadow, but he is still a giant.

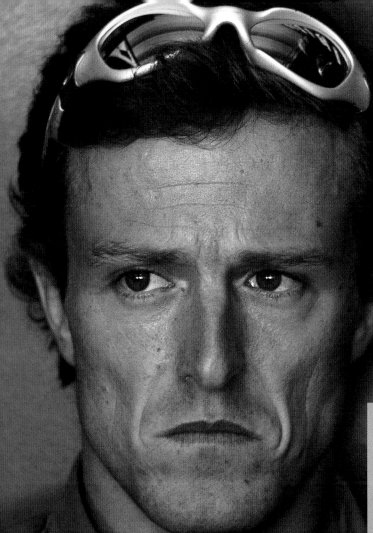

3 SETE GIBERNAU

SETE Gibernau came of age in 2003. It was the culmination of a long roller-coaster ride. In spite of his family motor cycle racing connections, Sete had to make his own way to the top of the sport. Now, after factory 500-class rides for Yamaha, Honda and Suzuki, he and sponsors Telefónica MoviStar had moved back to Honda, and found a machine with the race-winning potential that Sete was ready to use.

There is one other crucial aspect: an unwitting knack of (as he puts it) being in the right place at the wrong time. Sometimes this worked against him – moving to Suzuki just as they slumped. With uncanny frequency, however, he happened to be rider-in-waiting when serious injuries struck a series of top factory riders.

When Takuma Aoki was crippled in a pre-season testing crash, Sete was given his factory V-twin. In 1999, when Mick Doohan was terminally injured, Gibernau took over his top-dog NSR.

And in 2003, when Sete's new and illustrious team-mate, Kato, was tragically killed in the first GP of the year, he took his first four-stroke win at the next round in South Africa on a production Honda. Directly thereafter, he was given the ex-Kato HRC factory machinery.

He used it to superb effect, claiming three more wins, twice narrowly outfoxing Rossi. In Germany, his victory was classic Sete: aggressive, opportunistic and very determined. He's also to be much feared whenever the conditions are difficult.

What's more, Sete emerged as an articulate and multi-lingual spokesman for racing, particularly on matters of safety following Kato's crash.

It was a remarkable year for the grandson of the founder of Bultaco motor cycles.

Team Telefónica MoviStar Honda
2003 World Championship: 2nd (MotoGP)
Race wins: 4
Pole positions: 1
Career GP wins: 5 (4 MGP, 1 500 cc)
World Championships: 0
Born: 15 December 1972, Barcelona, Spain

Photograph: Mark Wernham

4 MAX BIAGGI

SAD-EYED Max found himself at the far edge of the HRC security blanket on his return from Yamaha, but to be fair he didn't complain too long and hard of real or imagined deficiencies in his stock bike, compared with the factory machines like Rossi's.

Max also missed out on Kato's factory bike, but gradually things improved, and by the latter part of the season, he was technically almost on a par with Rossi and Hayden. Even then, with the Pons team technical guru Antonio Cobas off ill for most of the year, he had to wait until Motegi for HRC technicians to find the abstruse electronic combination that at last made the bike work to his taste.

Camel Pramac Pons Honda
2003 World Championship: 3rd (MotoGP)
Race wins: 2
Pole positions: 3
Career GP wins: 41 (4 MGP, 8 500 cc, 29 250 cc)
World Championships: 4 (250 cc)
Born: 26 June 1971, Rome, Italy

Max had left Honda with some bad blood four years before. Was this evidence of a long shadow? Or wraiths of his imagination? Either way, for the most part, Max smiled and kept his comments carefully worded, saying at the start of the season, 'If I am a good boy, then maybe later I will get some cake.'

Some say Max is doomed to frequent the lower steps of the rostrum more often than the top, because he spent too long on a 250. His high-corner-speed style is graceful and turns very fast laps. When it comes to racing, his critics say he fails to adapt his style to suit close combat.

Max remains a formidable competitor. Even as the goal of the championship seems to remain for ever just out of his reach, he is still riding superbly.

Photograph: Mark Wernham

5 NICKY HAYDEN

HAYDEN'S world is a cuss-free zone: 'Dang' is about the strongest language you'll ever hear. This is indicative. The AMA champion, still a young 22 years old, has brought with him to GP racing a down-home Kentucky freshness and innocence.

In no way does his casual attitude and ready smile conceal the more important facet that made him Rookie of the Year, in a season when his fellow rookies included two former world champions. Nicky has heaps of natural talent, allied to a clarity of purpose. Everything he does takes him sauntering closer to the goal he has held since he was a teenager – the World Championship.

All year, Hayden has been safe, reliable and with ever improving results. At the end of the season, his strength and confidence were such that when Rossi vacated the other half of the HRC pit garage, few people had much trouble in imagining Hayden taking over as top dog.

What happened as the year wore on was simple. Hayden found a way to relax and be himself on the bike. The RCV is so good that it responds to a wide variety of styles. The combination started to become very fast.

And spectacular. Ex-oval-tracker Hayden (at 12, his professional nickname was 'Mr Dirt') showed his confidence by muscling the V5 around, sideways under brakes and with the power on. He knows he'll need to refine that somewhat, but this rookie was doing something more than just hanging on for the ride. He was already fighting for rostrum positions.

Hayden must be considered a title contender for 2004.

Repsol Honda Team	
2003 World Championship: 5th (MotoGP)	
Race wins:	0
Pole positions:	0
Career GP wins:	0
World Championships:	0
Born: 30 July 1981, Owensboro, USA	

Photograph: Mark Wernham

6 TROY BAYLISS

BAYLISS brought more with him to GP racing than a big reputation and gung-ho enjoyment. He was largely responsible for Rossi reassessing his riding tactics. The Australian had shown him another way – that as soon as anybody gets by you, you pass them straight back at the very next corner, and worry about the consequences later.

Nobody gets to this level without a certain analytical ability, yet Bayliss exudes more inspiration than science when he rides, and in this way regularly raced better than he qualified. More than once, he found himself leading.

This might have seemed a trifle impetuous, but only if one forgot that not only was Bayliss coming to tracks where the Ducati had never run before, in most cases he hadn't seen them either. He had an awful lot to learn in his learning year. He never forgot about racing hard while he was doing it either.

Ducati Marlboro Team	
2003 World Championship: 6th (MotoGP)	
Race wins:	0
Pole positions:	0
Career GP wins:	0
World Championships:	1 (World Superbike)
Born: 30 March 1969, Taree, Australia	

Of course, it's a big help having a bike of such quality. Contrast his season and results with those of his old Superbike rival, Colin Edwards. Bayliss appears like a shining hero; Edwards something of an also-ran. Of course, it's never that simple.

All the same, Bayliss made a great start to his GP career, and was another who clearly enjoyed the experience. And he was never less than thrilling to watch.

Photograph: Mark Wernham

7 JEREMY McWILLIAMS

THE Old Man of the Grid may have become a bit more grizzled, but he certainly didn't get any slower in his 11th season, on the brink of turning 40.

Once again, both Proton riders put up heroic performances, on the two-strokes in the earlier part of the season and on the four-strokes that finished the year, having achieved impressive reliability. In both cases, they were always at a disadvantage.

Nobody relishes this position as much as McWilliams. It brings out the best of his fighting spirit – always an impressive spectacle. The continual improvement of the new Proton V5 added another essential ingredient.

McWilliams isn't so much a circuit specialist as a corner specialist. This is by inclination as well as necessity, on a bike significantly down on top speed. As a result, certain tracks suit him better, and none so well as the magnificent Phillip Island circuit.

That was a landmark race – not only because it gave him his best four-stroke result of the year. It was also the first time the four-stroke had gone faster than the old 500 triple – which he had already made the fastest two-stroke ever around the Australian track.

One can only imagine what McWilliams might achieve on a fast, friendly Honda with genuine race-winning potential. Or would he find that just too easy?

Proton Team KR	
2003 World Championship: 18th (MotoGP)	
Race wins: 0	
Pole positions: 0	
Career GP wins: 1 (250 cc)	
World Championships: 0	
Born: 4 April 1964, Carnmoney, Northern Ireland	

Photograph: Gold & Goose

8 TONI ELIAS

CONSISTENTLY the most exciting 250 rider, Elias seems to do everything right – except win championships. When he was on a 125, there were dark tales of skul-duggery and sabotage. On the 250 this year, he made the errors for himself.

Significantly, though, they were very seldom errors of not trying hard enough, going fast enough or not having enough talent.

Elias is still free with his toothy grin, but as he gains maturity, the always conspicuous sense of purpose has gained an impressive focus.

He won more races than anyone else in the class – five to champion Poggiali's four – and took a string of five poles in a row at the end of the year. But he had some injury problems at various times, and twice failed to score, retiring in Japan and crashing out after taking the final-lap lead in Rio. But for that last indiscretion in particular, he might easily have been champion.

Elias can fall back on that old racing cliché – that it's easier for a fast rider to learn how to stop falling off than for a slow, safe rider to learn how to go fast. But he has not made his task easier for next year, switching from Aprilia to Honda, where he will ride alongside Rolfo.

Team Repsol Telefónica MoviStar Aprilia	
2003 World Championship: 3rd (250 cc)	
Race wins: 5	
Pole positions: 5	
Career GP wins: 8 (6 250 cc, 2 125 cc)	
World Championships: 0	
Born: 26 March 1983, Manresa, Spain	

Photograph: Mark Wernham

9 ROBERTO ROLFO

LUPINE logo notwithstanding, Rolfo was more St Bernard than wolf during 2003. After a troubled first Honda season on the hard-to-handle, ex-Kato twin-crank NSR, the works effort was downgraded to a factory-kitted version of the single-crank RS250 production machine.

It was not enough against the hordes of Aprilias. But in a year when talent was spread rather thinly in the class, Rolfo took a measured approach and produced a season of exemplary consistency. He was the only rider in the class to score points in every round.

That alone is not enough to earn a place in the Top Ten. What made his season special was that when the going got tough, or at circuits where his horsepower deficit was not so telling, Rolfo really made the most of every opportunity.

In this way, Rolfo claimed six rostrum finishes – two of them wins and three more second places. And pushed Poggiali, who had a significantly faster motor cycle, all the way to the last round before the title was decided.

Fortuna Honda	
2003 World Championship: 2nd (250 cc)	
Race wins: 2	
Pole positions: 0	
Career GP wins: 2 (250 cc)	
World Championships: 0	
Born: 23 March 1980, Turin, Italy	

Multi-lingual and with scholarly hobbies, Rolfo is an unusual character in the racing paddock. He is also an accurate and intelligent racer. It makes a very complete package. There is surely more to come – and one day perhaps a MotoGP future.

Photograph: Mark Wernham

10 MAKOTO TAMADA

MANY riders on both sides of the fence will agree that the Honda is a flattering bike. Tamada was one who excelled, albeit rather erratically. But the ex-All Japan Superbike rider – a GP beginner at the no longer tender age of 26 – had a good excuse. As well as being new to world travel, and to the variety of new tracks, he was the only Honda rider on Bridgestone tyres.

This, in itself, makes his performance difficult to assess, because he couldn't be measured directly against his peer group on Michelins. It was obvious, however, that the tyres worked in his favour at some tracks, especially in hot conditions.

Equally obvious was the absence of any hint of being overawed by the quality of the competition. His background was reflected in a hard-braking style and a willingness to attempt overtaking moves.

In the end, this facet worked against him. Race officials thought that he might have been more respectful of Gibernau at Motegi, and he was disqualified from a hardfought and impressive home-race rostrum.

Not everyone agreed with their opinion. Least of all Tamada. He'll be back next year, and with a bit of circuit knowledge plus his willingness to push, he will surely be on the rostrum more than once.

Team Pramac Honda	
2003 World Championship: 11th (MotoGP)	
Race wins: 0	
Pole positions: 0	
Career GP wins: 0	
World Championships: 0	
Born: 4 November 1976, Ehime, Japan	

Photograph: Gold & Goose

TRUE DRAMA
By MICHAEL SCOTT

Above: Faster, more furious, louder — and closer than ever. Biaggi leads Capirossi, Rossi and the rest in a MotoGP field of quality and variety.

Facing page, centre left: Alice were a welcome, if fleeting, non-tobacco sponsor for Aprilia.

Facing page, centre right: Cigarette companies took advantage of every branding opportunity.

Facing page, bottom: Kawasaki also ran in plain factory colours in their chastening debut year.
All photographs: Mark Wernham

Boom or bust? Hopefully not the latter for the thriving MotoGP series. The show became bigger, brighter and better in 2003 – and more expensive. Which is fine, as long as somebody is prepared to pay for it. The looming spectre of the banishment of the tobacco companies – still the providers of a huge proportion of backing for most major teams – was forgotten for the moment in a wave of optimism.

In its second season, the move to 990 cc four-strokes proved a resounding success. As well as attracting two more full-time factories, Ducati and Kawasaki (the first alone a considerable draw), it enlisted Team Roberts, who built an adventurously independent Proton KR V5 of their own.

The public responded in kind. Not only were the races pulling ever increasing crowds to the circuits, but also making much more impact among a wider audience. Media exposure was boosted everywhere, especially TV. In Britain, both factors were significant: crowds at the Donington Park GP were almost four times bigger than three years ago, while the TV coverage switched from Channel Five's small-time operation to the BBC's main 'Grandstand' programme (although few races were shown live).

The overall cost of machines and racing had risen by three or four times, yet there were still factories prepared to swallow the expense in the absence of major sponsors – Suzuki and Kawasaki. Again, this was encouraging in the short term for the series, if not for the accountants back in Japan.

And there were still others clamouring to join in. Ducati wanted another team, as did Aprilia. There were continuing rumours about BMW's interest (although with the exposure they get through their pace and race-control cars, and with the BMW cup, they are already well served). The independent Austrian firm KTM were on the way, with places reserved for their debut in 2005. Even the name Triumph kept coming up – in the more optimistic circles.

This faction suffered a blow, however, when KTM announced the cancellation of their MotoGP project. Staff had already been hired and prototype V4 motors had been nearing completion halfway through the year. Then, at the Sachsenring, came the surprise announcement from factory envoy Heinz Kinigadner. A fresh look at the soaring costs, set against a down-turn in income because of the falling dollar (a big proportion of the Austrian firm's sales comes from the USA), had led them to decide that it wasn't worth spending that much money, 'just to get beaten by Honda for the first three or four years'. Since parts had been ordered already, five

motors would be built, however. These, or derivatives, might yet emerge in another guise.

If this eddy carried foreboding of chill winds to follow, the summer-long heat wave helped everyone ignore it. There was an air of confidence emanating from Dorna's massive mobile field headquarters and reflected in the ever growing paddock. Not least because of an influx of glass-fronted hospitality suites, which replaced the old-style, chummy open-sided tents. In this way, the paddock main street took on something of the look and atmosphere of a post-sixties new town, purpose-built to house insurance company head offices – but at least the air conditioning worked throughout the blazing summer.

The question of tobacco may have receded, but it's not fair to say that Dorna and their cohorts were in denial. In fact, plans are already well under way to follow the lead set by car racing. In F1, there had been a voluntary agreement with the EU to relinquish all tobacco sponsorship by the end of 2006. Then the European Parliament wrong-footed the deal by voting to bring the deadline forward by a year. Car racing chiefs declared the whole agreement null and void, and looked for ways of carrying on arm in arm with the tobacco lobby. At a corporate gathering to celebrate Schumacher's world championship, backers Marlboro let slip that they plan to continue to sponsor Ferrari until at least 2010.

One solution is to move the racing out of Europe to smoker-friendly venues – China and the Middle East in particular. It is no coincidence that Qatar is on the MotoGP calendar for next year – another place where the motor cycles can run in full livery.

This will leave Europe with the problem of what to do about the branded TV images. At this stage, it remains a decision for the individual broadcasters. Technology is available that will block out the branding on the moving vehicles and trackside signage alike. This is already compulsory in France for print media – after losing a test case, motor cycle racing magazines, such as *Moto Journal* and *Moto Revue*, are obliged to 'wash' logos off images before they print them.

And it leaves another problem. While going to Qatar and Bahrain might suit the likes of Marlboro, Fortuna, Gauloises etc, it may not necessarily be very attractive to important and valued non-tobacco sponsors such as Telefónica MoviStar and Repsol.

The conundrum remains, while future legislation is also very uncertain. No wonder most people preferred to live in the present.

In the hurly-burly of the season, there was one major issue that overshadowed even fears for the future – safety. That concern was

Left: **Kenny Roberts Jr and Suzuki ran without major sponsorship.**

Below: **FIM President Francesco Zerbi lobbies the Italian press at Jerez. His intervention surprised many in 2003.**
Both photographs: Mark Wernham

triggered by the tragic events at Suzuka, where Daijiro Kato sustained fatal injuries in a crash that defied immediate explanation.

The accident was certainly of an unexpected type. Kato lost control under braking from high speed and was still travelling at more than 105 mph. But instead of following the usual trajectory – more or less in the previous direction of travel – both bike and rider turned sharp left.

This was unusual, although an acceptable explanation was provided by an independent commission of enquiry appointed by HRC, which analysed all the available data over a period of months. Much to the company's relief, the commission ruled out mechanical failure and described a plausible scenario.

Kato, trying hard, had been faster than before through the preceding bends and arrived at the braking zone with more lean than usual. The consequent greater slide under braking turned into a mini-highsider, and that flipped Kato out of the seat. From that point, he was out of control, and his pressure on the handlebars as he tried to get back into position not only exacerbated the bike's weaving instability, but also made it turn.

There was no mystery about the consequences. As the commission revealed, Kato and his bike hit the tyre barrier, clad in conveyor belt, at an angle, the rider on the left of the machine. But the tyre barrier was not continuous. After a distance, there was a small gap, then a different type of barrier began – foam rubber, wider than the tyres. Kato went into it head first and pivoted at the neck as it flipped him over in the air. This, the commission believed, was the fatal impact. Kato died because of a lack of run-off area and a break in the barrier.

Suzuka is a special case: space restrictions mean that the sort of generous run-off found at new tracks like Sepang or Catalunya simply isn't available. The difficulty of making the classic figure-eight circuit safe for motor cycles is such that it will not be ready for 2004, and possibly never. But it is far from being the only track with such obstructions by braking zones. Suzuka may have broken a few rules, but so too did Kato's crashing Honda.

The fear of similar accidents – that this was a new characteristic of the heavier and faster MotoGP bikes – led to action on all sides. As ever, that of the riders was the most prominent as they convened for a series of meetings at the next event at Welkom.

There have been such meetings before. What was remarkable about these was the lack of acrimony. In the past, riders have railed against officials who didn't seem to care about their safety. In 2003, that feeling had been eliminated. Rather, riders said that officials needed to acknowledge new problems, and to look for solutions. In short order, an informal floating committee was created to meet with Race Direction after practice at every event. The angry rebels of earlier times can congratulate themselves on their contribution to the progress made in safety. That said, before too much self-congratulation is allowed, it remains to be seen how many of the riders' suggestions will be implemented.

There was a backlash, however, when Race Direction decided that it was their turn to remind the riders that the 990s are big, heavy, fast and dangerous, and not to be trifled with, and that their behaviour also plays a part in safety. They did so by disqualifying Tamada from third place in the Pacific GP and John Hopkins from the next event (he had eliminated himself at Motegi by crashing), both for dangerous riding.

This was very severe punishment for what many other riders and racing folk saw as simple racing incidents. As McWilliams said, 'Close racing is why people like this sport.' But it represented something else: a flexing of muscles by Race Direction, a four-man committee made up of a representative of Dorna, Javier Alonso, FIM safety officer Claude Danis, Race Director and IRTA chief executive Paul Butler and IRTA safety delegate Franco Uncini. It was clear that not all four had agreed on the punishment, but it was equally obvious that they had decided to present a united front and remind the riders just who was boss.

The make-up of Race Direction suggests a close working partnership between the FIM, Dorna and IRTA. In 2003, FIM president Francesco Zerbi surprised everybody by playing something of a lone hand, and rather exceeding what, to MotoGP, was envisaged as a largely ceremonial role. Rather than following the accepted method of discussion between the parties, Zerbi convened a special meeting on his own account, inviting both MotoGP and Superbike management to submit suggestions on possible formula changes to make the sport safer.

Many thought he was showboating, or at least jumping on the safety bandwagon. In truth, the technical rules are devised by the manufacturers' association, the MSMA, then ratified by the various groups involved in management, including the FIM. At the time, the MSMA were already speculating about the possibility of reducing engine size, or looking for another way to limit top speeds, which were surging well beyond 200 mph.

This is something for the future, although some kind of restrictive

action seems more than likely – following the F1 precedent; even Rossi is prepared to debate the matter.

Zerbi's role, however, left many scratching their heads.

But it was not the only evidence during the year that, having leased both their major road-racing world championships to commercial partners, the FIM in general, and Zerbi in particular, still felt the desire to stir the pot.

For example, Zerbi had become personally involved in the controversy over the legality of the WCM MotoGP prototype. Rightly so, one might think, as FIM president. But there was a hint of mischief here.

Within MotoGP, nobody cared one way or the other about the machine's legality. The bike was no threat to any of the other participants, and it was in everybody's interest that the WCM two-rider franchise be preserved. And the prototype's early Suzuka form was only a transitory stage. Dorna had been prepared to turn a blind eye to the production cylinder heads and crankcases, as had everybody else. One difficulty with the case was the vague wording of the rules, which included such ill-defined terms as 'original design', whatever that might be; and 'industrial production' rather than 'series production', making it far from clear whether even a genuine factory prototype like Yamaha's M1 was fully legal.

The complaint had come from the beleaguered Superbike series, anxious that their rights to race modified road bikes were being infringed. This was clear from a leaked minute from a February FIM management committee meeting.

Of course, everybody was acting within their rights. But there was an uncomfortable feeling that Dorna were under some sort of attack from an all-Italian faction, where Superbike rights holders the Flammini Group were acting hand in hand with the FIM.

The Flammini Group certainly needed all the friends they could muster by the end of a landmark year. By then, they had lost the support of all the manufacturers and all but one of the major racing tyre suppliers. For the second year running, they had also lost

their world champion, Hodgson following the previous two, Edwards and Bayliss, to MotoGP.

The row with the manufacturers had been brewing for a while and concerned the ever changing approach to technical rules.

There had been a precedent. In 2000, a system had been devised whereby factories would be obliged to make works-spec kits available to all competitors. According to the MSMA's first statement, issued in July, the factories 'had already incurred the costs of development, manufacturing and ordering components' when the rules were 'suddenly changed only half a year before implementation. The companies suffered a great deal of damage on that occasion, but had come to believe promises that the same thing would never happen again.'

Accordingly, over the next two years, the MSMA and the Flammini Group had discussed and agreed the rule changes that came into force for 2003, whereby four-cylinder motor cycles could grow from 750 cc to 1000 cc (like the twins), using inlet restrictors to reduce power. Only Suzuki were actually racing a machine to this specification, but again, according to the statement, other companies had invested in research and preparations for competition in 2004.

Only to have the rule changed summarily with six months to go. The restrictor regulation was abandoned, and the Flammini Group began courting opinion on how to find other ways of levelling the competition without increasing costs.

Apparently, the Flammini view was that restrictors led to expensive technology that heavily favoured the factories over privateers, and that, in spite of promises to the contrary from the MSMA, not all of them did actually intend returning for 2004. Either way, this mid-year sea change was the last straw for the MSMA.

They announced their withdrawal from the SBK Commission (where rule changes were to be discussed) and from the series as a whole. 'We feel that this sudden change does not conform with the quality and status of a World Championship, and does not meet basic requirements for technical rules, such as enabling large numbers of teams and companies to compete under fairer conditions', read the statement.

At the same time, the unexpected announcement at Laguna Seca that both SBK and World Supersport championships would be switching to the compulsory use of Pirelli tyres (for which all teams would have to pay the Flammini Group) came as a shock to all. Especially the major suppliers, Dunlop and Michelin.

The same principle applied – the status of a world championship. This was not something that should have been for sale to a single tyre company. And if this principle of fair and open competition was to be abandoned by the FIM, then fair trading demanded that at least the series should be open to tender to all companies, whereas the Pirelli deal had been done behind closed doors.

Michelin took up the case directly with the FIM; Dunlop filed a complaint with the EU Directorate General for Competition, claiming an infringement by the FIM and FGSport under the EU treaty. At the time *MOTOCOURSE* went to press, there had been no resolution in either case. Testing of the new Pirellis, however, had already begun.

The Flammini line was positive, and not without merit. Their whole thrust for the future of Superbike racing was to level the playing field. One brand of tyres was a significant step in that direction. Planned changes to the technical rules likewise. Superbike racing was going back to its roots, and the resulting lack of factory involvement was a plus point.

At the same time, the 600 Supersport class seemed set to flourish, with or without tyre control. The manufacturers may have pulled out of the bigger class, but this near-production series is too important to be ignored, and it is in common cause that the likes of Ten Kate Honda operate in close co-operation with the factory.

It remains to be seen just what level the new-generation World Superbike Championship will find, and how long that will take.

MOTOGP TECHNICAL REVIEW

BETTER BY DESIGN

By NEIL SPALDING

WITH the Honda supreme at the end of 2002 and Yamaha making significant advances, there seemed every reason to believe that 2003, with its crop of new entrants and bikes, would see an even more competitive season.

Suzuki debuted their second bike; Kawasaki had built a super Superbike, and Proton were coming with a V5 from the Formula 1 belt in England. World Superbike rulers Ducati were going to try an all-new (to them) 90-degree V4 that had been developed during 2002, and Aprilia had found two top riders in Haga and WSB Champion Edwards. This competition gave 2003 all the signs of being a really close-fought battle.

It didn't work out like that. Honda upped their show just enough to stay in front, Ducati came out like an angry prize-fighter intent on landing at least one good punch, and at Yamaha they fell on their faces; the rest simply seemed to have got it all horribly wrong.

So how can it be that the cream of the world's motor cycle manufacturers have been so comprehensively beaten by Honda and a little upstart from Italy? It's not as if they all haven't made really good bikes in the past, and this MotoGP thing cannot be that difficult, can it?

Initially, you might think that there is little difference in overall power and size between the old 500 two-strokes and these new bikes. It is now obvious that MotoGP requires something more than a bigger Superbike. Designing machines that will produce good usable power and race effectively while dealing with the massively increased demands of the bulk, weight and heat of the larger four-stroke engines and their associated airboxes, exhausts, fuel tanks and electronics is proving to be a quite serious test of designers' capabilities. You just have to look at the results of this first full four-stroke year to see who can and who cannot, at least for now.

The rules encourage variety, differing weights being applied to differing engine configurations: 135 kg two- or three-cylinder; 145 kg four- or five-cylinder; and 155 kg for a six. Oval pistons add a 10-kg penalty. There are very few other restrictions, but tellingly the original maximum fuel capacity of 24 litres is scheduled to be reduced to 22 litres in 2005.

Just like the old Superbike regulations, these rules treat the engines simply as air pumps. As power comes from burning a combustible mixture, the more an engine pumps through and burns, the more power it should produce. The rules, therefore, assume that to make as much power as possible, an engine needs to obtain as many revs as possible. All other things being equal, a greater number of lighter pistons will allow higher revs and make the most power.

So why haven't we got a grid full of six-cylinder screamers?

Largely because this game is about more than just peak power. It's about getting the right balance of power and controllability for the rider to set the fastest lap – consistently. History is full of lower-powered motor cycles that lapped quicker than their more powerful contemporaries, but all the bikes that did so had other, significant advantages: low weight, smaller frontal area, etc. Under the current rules, however, no one has yet made a powerful bike that takes full advantage of the lower weights allowed for simpler engines.

The fastest bikes have peak power levels currently around 250 bhp, and at the moment no one has decided that they need, or can deliver, much more than that, although the nature of racing says it's just going to be a matter of time.

Motor cycle design is about compromise. More than even in Formula 1, there are restrictions on space. Dynamically, a motor cycle is far more difficult to understand than a car, there being no easy mathematical models to explain a bike's behaviour, particularly once the rider's weight is added into the equation. So what other considerations should be taken into account when looking at each team's answer to the rule makers' latest and largest ever challenge?

Size matters. Small frontal areas assist high speeds, but the smaller the frontal area, the less room behind it for the rider and acceptable packaging of engine, chassis, fuel and airbox. Worse, the more aerodynamic the bodywork for high speed, the more likely it is to have problems in corners. More to the point, a 990 cc four-stroke will need to be bigger than a 500 two-stroke, a lot bigger.

Weight matters. The wheel-rim rule hasn't changed, so the tyres are restricted to the same sizes as the old 131-kg 500 two-strokes; a contact patch the size of a credit card needs to be used very sparingly. Every kilo of weight on the bike reduces the potential maximum cornering speed, increases the braking distance and lowers the maximum power you can use on corner exits.

Dynamics matter. The heavier and higher-revving the crankshaft, the greater its gyro-scopic effect on the handling of the bike. Gyros provide stability. Arguably, on a race-track, too much stability is a problem; bikes need to be flickable to get through the corners well. So should some of the effect of the other gyroscopes on the bike – like the wheels, clutch and gearbox – be counteracted by turning the engine over backward? Judging from 2003, the jury is still out. Might there be other down-sides from a counter-rotating crank?

Handling matters. How stiff does a bike chassis really have to be to handle 250 bhp? How flexible must it be to make up for the fork stiction when leaned right over in corners? What can be done to prevent the engine braking from unsettling the suspension and grip going into corners?

Tyres matter. Even restricted to the same sizes as were allowed on the 500 GP bikes, Michelin and Dunlop are improving grip and controllability. Given the rim size restrictions, who has the best solution to the new levels of power and torque they are being asked to put on to the track?

And back to the engines. Power quality matters. A seamless, glitch-free power curve lets the rider load up his tyres and take them to their limits. Any flat spots or power jumps will disturb the balance of grip and traction. Fuel economy also matters; as the revs and power rise, the law of diminishing returns has a more pronounced effect. With more cylinders, there are higher levels of internal friction, using more fuel, but making more power – perhaps we will see more car technology in bike engines; bores are getting bigger and strokes reducing to allow revs to rise. Formula 1 car engines are at the leading edge of the development of high bore-and-stroke ratios. How to fill the cylinder, then make the mixture burn fast and effectively across big bores in the very short time these revs allow is the holy grail of the competition engine business.

We can be sure of many future changes, both in technology and appearance. We can also be sure that whatever the MotoGP bikes of the future look like, they will be different to what we see now. We just have to hope that the inevitably large bills will not mean that the rules are restricted before motor cycling has moved on from the powered bicycle era. The arrival of MotoGP may have finally kicked off the next golden age of motor cycle design.

So, with the undoubted benefit of 20:20 hindsight, let's have a look at the various solutions used in 2003.

Photograph: Kyrit Wernham

APRILIA

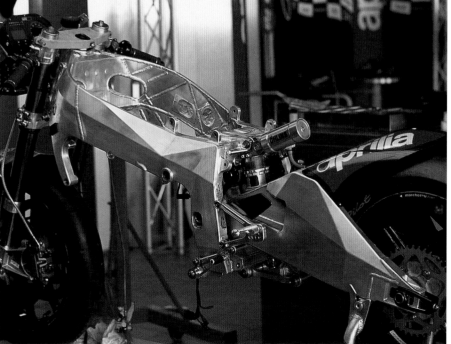

The real experiment. Last year, Aprilia joined forces with Cosworth to build an advanced-spec triple. Using F1-style pneumatic valve springs and a dry sump, the design is clearly influenced by Cosworth's F1 engines. A triple needs a balancer to counteract the large rocking couple from its crankshaft design. In the Aprilia, this does double duty as a jackshaft to allow the engine to rotate backward. The engine's car origins can be seen in its 'semi-pre-unit' design; the gearbox casing is part of the sump casting and is bolted to the back of the engine block for extra rigidity. It would appear that the original design brief was to encourage a pro-squat tendency, the chain run pulling the bike down under acceleration. It is almost as if the bike was designed to be a high-powered drag racer, jetting from corner to corner.

During 2003, the engine's peak power was slowly reduced and the mid-range improved to make it more rideable; the bike ended up with a peak of around 220 bhp, but with a much smoother power delivery and enhanced mid-range. On Colin Edwards's bikes, the chassis was redesigned to raise the front of the engine, but it seems now that the bike needs at least a new gearbox casting to allow a more conventional chassis to match its new-found, more conventional power output. Weight is still an issue; the bike is claimed to be only 8 kg over its class limit, but the whole point of the triple is the low weight limit.

If that new engine, gearbox and chassis design also allows the team to get down to its limit, 2004 will be a very different year for Aprilia.

One of the advantages of a vee-configuration is that the crankshaft is short (it has long been held in US dirt-track racing that a bike with its rotating weight near the centre-line is easier to turn), so the gyro effect is not as strong as other engine designs. Another aspect is that the overall engine is narrower, easing some packaging problems, but leaving the difficulty of managing the space requirement of a second bank of cylinders. This has led to all of the vee-engine manufacturers bar Suzuki using a new space-saving swingarm and rear shock absorber layout. In this, the rear shock is completely isolated from the frame with a linkage to the bottom mount and the top attached to the underside of the swingarm. This has freed space above the swingarm for the back of the fuel tank. It is unlikely that the suspension design is any more efficient than a conventional layout, but the space provided is invaluable on something as compact and crowded as a MotoGP bike.

Left: Aprilia RS³ Cube: packed tight with power, Formula 1 style.

Below left: Aprilia Cube chassis shows painstakingly crafted internal bracing (note welds) and origami-like appearance.

Below: Ducati Desmosedici combines factory's established practice with high adventure.
All photographs: Mark Wernham

DUCATI

The surprise of the season. Domenicali's men have kept as much of the construction and design of their bike as simple as possible. The chassis resembles a heavy-duty version of the frame debuted on the Supermono in 1993, and the overall layout is clearly based on their very successful range of Superbikes.

Some things are very different, though. The Desmosedici is capable of revs far more in line with current F1 practice, and can be expected to be employing very advanced combustion-chamber and lubrication technology. Using a 90-degree V4 layout with their preferred desmodromic valve gear, Ducati have clearly mixed their in-house technologies with F1 influences. The desmo arrangement allows Ducati to open and close valves very quickly, much like pneumatic springs, but where pneumatic springs add drag all the time the valve is off its seat, the desmo only suffers energy losses during the actual lifting and closing phases. We can expect the bore-and-stroke ratio to be quite radical and more in line with F1 practice.

The logical reason for Honda's choice of a V5 instead of a V4 is to allow them to use more revs, but Ducati are clearly revving their bike to at least another 1,000 rpm. A V4 has less internal friction and, therefore, it should be more economical; not normally a consideration on a race bike, but it will become more of a concern when the fuel limit drops for 2005. Over the 2003 season, the Ducati became slightly more controllable, but still clearly had more peak power than any other, spinning its rear tyre with alarming ease.

HONDA

The original five. Honda built a very subtle motor cycle to start their MotoGP adventure. A 75.5-degree V5 with the front three cylinders sufficiently forward in the chassis to allow the upper frame spars to pass over the front cylinders and around the rear pair, the bike is a masterpiece of understated and effective packaging. Honda had to raise their game a little to combat the threat from Ducati in 2003. While the engine looked identical to the 2002 version, the power had been increased to around 240 bhp, a 15-per-cent increase. Honda won't talk revs, but do say that the design is capable of a further 15 per cent. Currently still using a conventional valve-spring arrangement, the Honda revs high, but nowhere near as high as modern technology could allow.

Honda's greatest strength is in the core design. A V5 presents very special balancing problems. The use of the five-into-three exhaust system mid-way though 2003 gave away some of the solution to those difficulties. Making the centre cylinder in the front bank exhaust on its own confirms that it is not equally spaced for exhaust purposes. This means that the engine is using an un-equally-spaced single cylinder to even out the inherent imbalances of the V5 layout, without the need for a power sapping balancer.

At the end of 2002, the Honda demonstrated that its back torque limiter (slipper clutch) was pretty close to its limit, Honda have added an ECU controlled tick-over adjuster. This comprises a solenoid operated air bleed to the inlet manifold, which, in turn, triggers the secondary fuel injector in each port to deliver just enough mixture to prevent any drag from the engine under closed throttles, thus easing the load on the slipper clutch. Honda have also admitted using traction control and launch control, but say they dispensed with the latter after the riders expressed a desire to look after themselves during starts.

All RC211Vs are not the same, however. Rossi, Ukawa and Gibernau seemed to have higher-spec slipper clutches with turbine-like air scoops hidden behind the cosmetic outer cover for cooling. Moreover, most, but not all, of the Honda riders had frames with modified swingarm pivot positions to help stability under braking fitted to one of their two bikes by the end of the main European season.

KAWASAKI

Kawasaki has paid an inordinate price for the temporary loss of their chief test rider, Akira Yanegawa, in a crash at the Motegi GP in 2002. The prototype for their across-the-frame in-line four was an overbored 750 Superbike; the MotoGP bike was supposed to be a logical extension, but judging by the results, something went wrong in the translation.

The Kawasaki engine is a very conservative across-the-frame four. Where it is special is in its construction, using cast head and barrels, and crankcases exquisitely machined from solid. To look at, though, the Kawasaki's motor is like a standard, old-style Superbike engine, sitting very upright in the chassis. It is unusual in its flat-slide, dual-injector fuel injection system. The transmission includes a Suter slipper clutch, just like the ones Kawasaki has used on its 750 Superbikes for years. To give it some help, a stepper motor on the throttle linkage gives the engine differing tick-over levels depending on engine revs and the gear selected.

The chassis, with its substantial cast sections, is larger than any other bike in the paddock. Kawasaki have stayed with their normal aluminium twin-spar design passing around the outside of the cylinder heads. The air intake, though, is through the centre of the cast headstock, unlike the very successful 750 Superbikes, which had their air intakes through the side spars, making the chassis much more flexible at that point. The result is a wide and stiff chassis that simply seems to refuse to hook up on corner exits, appears to be inordinately sensitive to bumps while leaned over, and is very reluctant to change direction at speed.

At the start of 2003, several different set-ups were being used by three different riders, and chaos reigned. With the arrival of crew chief Hamish Jamieson, some order returned to the operation. Kawasaki have been testing a radically different ultra-short-wheelbase bike for 2004, apparently with the same basic engine. It will be interesting to see how this compares.

Above: Proton KR V5 was compact, but relatively conventional in its first form. More innovation will surely follow.

Above right: Experimental Suzuki ridden by Ryo at Motegi followed remote-rear-shock fashion to make more room for another exhaust loop. Other bikes had the silencer on the opposite side.

Right: WCM took street-bike design to full-race spec with their R1-based special.

All photographs: Mark Wernham

PROTON TEAM KR

The bravest effort of the season. Kenny Roberts's small Proton organisation built its own bike from the ground up. A new V5-engined machine was debuted in practice at Le Mans; the very first corner it turned was at its first race meeting. After that, it was a case of developing the bike in the full glare of the race season.

Employing a 60-degree vee-angle and a balancer shaft, the Proton was designed not only to allow the team to produce good horsepower, but also to make it possible to build the engine into a great-handling chassis. The 60-degree layout means that the engine is shorter than the Honda, but that the main beams on its quite conventional aluminium chassis have to be very wide to pass around the front cylinder head. That condemns the team to a machine with a higher frontal area than the otherwise similar Honda.

Examination of the engine castings, however, reveals areas at the rear of the gearbox where what appear to have been swingarm support lugs have been machined off. Clearly, the engine has been designed to allow substantial further chassis development.

Tuned by Kawasaki guru Rob Muzzy, the engine clearly has more to offer than was on show during 2003. What can be seen is an engine architecture that uses shim-and-bucket valve adjusters, a cassette gearbox and gear-driven cams. The bike is equipped with a slipper clutch from sponsors FCC.

The team have also taken on the services of some very experienced F1 veterans: designer John Barnard and ex-Cosworth chief engineer Stuart Banks. What is certain is that, with their input, Proton have a far greater opportunity to move motor cycle racing technology forward than anyone else, especially as they are not constrained by marketing considerations of what their bike should look like. It may not be obvious now, but the real technical advances in the next few years are more likely to come from this team than any other for that reason alone.

SUZUKI

Suzuki surprised even their own team with a new 65-degree counterbalanced V4 XRE1 engine for 2003 and a prototype 'Ride by Wire' system. The bike arrived late; first testing was at Jerez, where the bikes were so new that they did not even have proper fuel tanks, making do with carbon fibre dummies for their first test. From the looks on the team's faces, they were completely baffled by the 'Ride by Wire' technology. It was as if they hadn't been sent the operating manual!

The 2003 bike was a major change from the 2002 version, having a chassis that was clearly influenced by Honda's pioneering RCV. The swingarm length was much greater, making it the longest in the paddock, although the wheelbase was a little shorter than the Honda's.

As well as constant development, there were some major personnel changes during the year; the new team leader, Yasuo Kamomiya, confirmed in Estoril that Suzuki was in 'full attack'. Unfortunately, the package hadn't yet come together.

The new 'Ride by Wire' system had been produced in conjunction with Mitsubishi and was a first from one of the Japanese manufacturers. Programming the basic system produced problems, and on several occasions the riders had entirely unexpected results from their throttle input. A purely electrical system, the throttle control seeks to produce a throttle setting that generates a linear response from an engine that has anything but a linear power output.

The main difficulty, however, is the lag in throttle response. We don't now how much there is, but clearly it is more than the riders can deal with. Progress is rarely smooth, and Suzuki is gaining a lot of information on 'Ride by Wire', a technology that will become much more important in MotoGP over the next few years.

This difficulty of control was compounded by an engine that, initially at least, simply didn't seem to have enough power. The motor appears conventional, with DOHC per bank and bucket-

and-shim valve adjustment. The balance shaft is between the cylinder banks and drives the water pump at one end. The engine is very compact and is tilted back in the frame, both cylinder banks appearing to be equally off vertical. It is also thought that different crank phasing was tried – using a 180-degree crank – on at least one bike.

Over the year, several different exhaust systems were used, the final version being muffled to match the back pressure of the system fitted to the test team's bike in Japan. This alone sorted out one injection mapping problem suffered in MotoGP, but not apparently by the test team.

WCM

WCM had an extraordinary year. They only learned that they had lost their big-money sponsors late in 2002, so their planned Moriwaki-framed RCV Hondas had to be dropped and a credible bike found to allow them to race and maintain their franchise. The initial attempt employed standard Yamaha R1 castings, albeit modified. These were quickly outlawed under the technical regulations after a very unusual flying visit by the FIM technical committee.

WCM manager Peter Clifford felt sure of his ground and presented his bikes for racing at all the rounds until the Court of Arbitration for Sport rejected his legal appeal in late June. At the first opportunity thereafter, the team was back on track, but with 500 two-strokes out of team owner Bob MacLean's museum. At Brno, however, the new four-strokes were being assembled in the garage with their own cylinder-head and crankcase castings, and by Estoril they were racing.

The new engine is a 990 cc, across-the-frame water-cooled four with four valves per cylinder, based fairly closely on a Yamaha R1. However, the castings are unique. Built on a Harris alloy-beam chassis with Öhlins suspension, the bike is very conventional. Full use was made of the aftermarket, the fuel injection and alternator being lifted straight off a GSX-R1000. A cassette gearbox from Hewland completes the tech spec. It was relatively reliable considering the rushed development.

WCM have built a good privateers' tool, but it is shackled to compromises of the base design – the road-going R1. This means that the bore-and-stroke ratio is in the 1.4–1.5 range. It is unlikely that such a ratio would ever allow the engine to be tuned to any more than mid-field power levels. That should not detract from the team's achievement in simply being 'on track' though.

Above: Melandri's Yamaha M1 shows 'arched deltabox' chassis and earlier swinging arm.

Right: Yamaha's in-line four is a compact design, but looks massive.

Both photographs: Mark Wernham

MOTOGP ENGINES

Manufacturer	Aprilia	Ducati	Honda	Kawasaki	Proton
Model	Cube	Desmosedici	RC211V	ZX-RR	KR5
Engine type	990 cc Triple 4v	990 cc 90° V4 4v	990 cc 75.5° V5 4v	990 cc In-line 4 4v	990 cc 60° V5 4v
Bore and stroke	95 x 46.6 mm	86 x 42.6 mm	76 x 43.7 mm	84 x 44.7 mm	78 x 41.5 mm
Bore-and-stroke ratio	2.04	2.02	1.74	1.88	1.88
BMEP	12.8 psi	13.5 psi	14 psi	12.5 psi	12.5 psi
Max rpm	16,250	16,900	15,800	15,000	15,200
Piston speed	25.2 m/s	22.4 m/s	23 m/s	22.4 m/s	21 m/s
Peak power*	230 bhp	252 bhp	245 bhp	208 bhp	210 bhp
Crank rotation	Reverse	Forward	Forward	Forward	Forward

Manufacturer	Suzuki	WCM	Yamaha	N/A	BMW
Model	GSV-R	WCM	M1	Mini F1	F1 '03
Engine type	990 cc 65° V4 4v	990 cc In-line 4 4v	990 cc In-line 4 5v	990 cc Triple 4v	2998 cc V10 4v
Bore and stroke	80 x 49.2 mm	76 x 54.7 mm	82 x 47 mm	98 x 43.8 mm	98 x 39.8 mm
Bore-and-stroke ratio	1.625	1.39	1.745	2.235	2.46
BMEP	12.8 psi	12.4 psi	13.8 psi	14 psi	14 psi
Max rpm	15,000	14,000	15,000	17,250	18,800
Piston speed	24.5 m/s	25.5 m/s	23.5 m/s	25.2 m/s	25.2 m/s
Peak power*	211 bhp	192 bhp	230 bhp	267 bhp	890 bhp
Crank rotation	Forward	Forward	Reverse	Forward	–

* Crankshaft horsepower; rear-wheel power would be expected to be about 15 per cent less.

This chart gives estimated engine specs and power outputs of current MotoGP engines. Theoretically, the shorter the stroke, the higher the revs a motor can achieve – an average of 25 m/s is considered quite high!

Bore-and-stroke ratio is exactly what it says. I include a guesstimate of the current F1 top dog, the BMW, along with a theoretical three-cylinder 990 cc derivative for comparison.

BMEP is Brake Mean Effective Pressure and is a measure of the efficiency of the engine. A BMEP of 12 psi should be easy for a modern manufacturer, but levels of up to 14 psi are exceptional, especially as it is difficult to maintain efficiency as the revs rise.

YAMAHA

Yamaha are still reeling from the shock of Honda's supremacy after their apparently very successful pre-season testing. At the IRTA tests, Barros was fastest. They also had an additional specialist test team debuting a twin-shock chassis development racer.

For most of the year, Yamaha employed a second-generation M1 that featured simplified rear-wheel back torque control and an 'arched deltabox' chassis. The works bikes were fuel injected, although Nakano at least was still using carburettors at the start of the year. The bike was based on a narrow, over-the-engine chassis design, which offered the facility of a movable engine, allowing each rider to tailor the weight distribution to his preference. At the IRTA tests, it was fitted with the original rounded bodywork.

For the final race of the year at Valencia, a new bike with revised upper engine mountings and an 'upside-down', massively under-braced swinging arm was on track. Clearly intended to mimic the RC211V's front chassis section, the bike won immediate praise from riders Checa and Abe. The modified bike also featured a lowered top shock mount to make room for a revised fuel tank. Another bike also sported a new raised air intake designed to allow more air into the radiator.

The engine remained the same tiny, across-the-frame, five-valve in-line four with a combination of chain and gears driving the cams. This engine has a marked forward bias, probably the same as their new R1 street bike at 40 degrees. What is different is that the crankshaft in the Yamaha GP engine appears to turn backward, while a jackshaft runs across the engine behind the cylinder barrels. The gearbox is a, now normal, vertically stacked removable cassette type.

After testing through the winter with the 2002 bodywork, new more streamlined panels were fitted to the team leader's bikes at Suzuka; the muffler had also disappeared. External evidence of the effort Yamaha was expending came with new fuel tanks and airboxes, which appeared mid-year. The latest fuel tank allowed the retrofitting of previous smaller airboxes, making this the first bike whose power delivery is changed by fitting airboxes with different volumes.

Frustratingly for the works team, Nakano on the oldest Yamaha was consistently faster than their bikes until Brno, which saw a sea change in their machines' performances. Later, the team agreed that Checa had been running new engine parts at that round – top speeds were up, but the bike remained very sensitive to set-up. Reportedly, the Yamaha did not suffer the difficulty in changing direction that plagued the Kawasaki; most likely, the reverse-turning crank helped in this respect, but it has to be possible that the funny sensations the Yamaha riders reported from the front end were a result of the different torque reactions created by that same counter-rotating crankshaft.

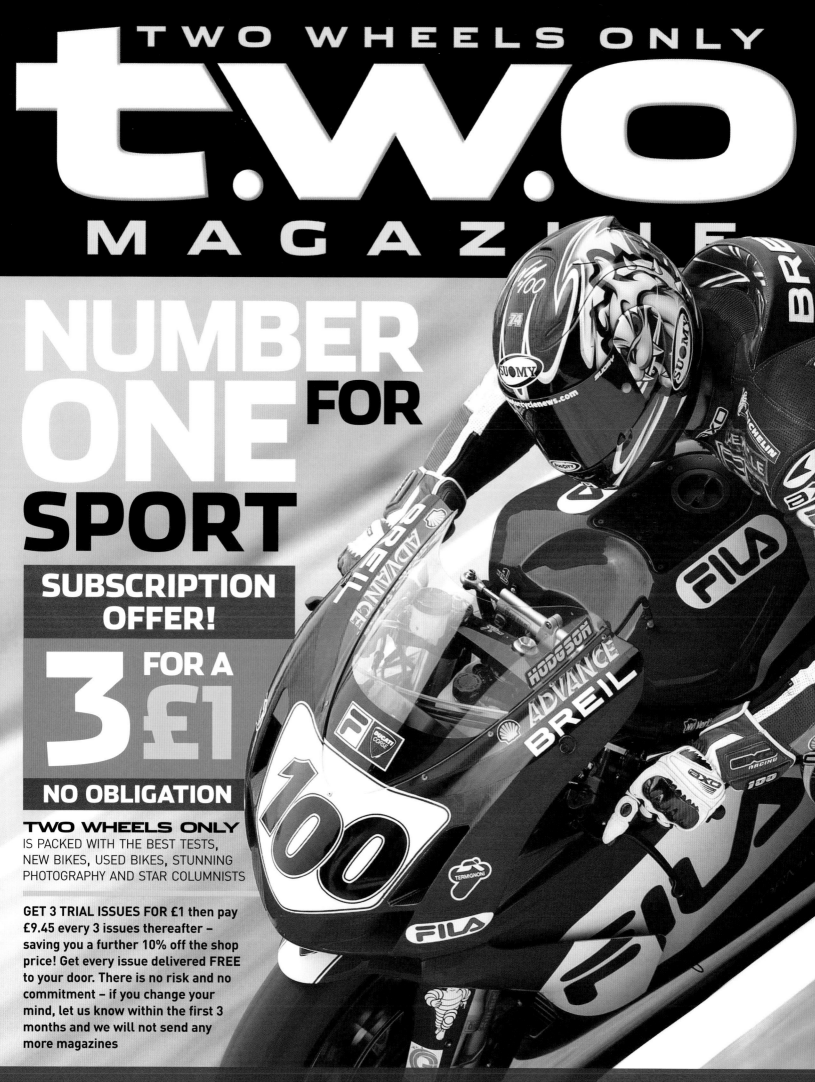

THE RISE OF DUCATI

GIANT KILLERS

By KEVIN CAMERON

DUCATICORSE

DUCATI rivets our attention because this small company is the only maker whose MotoGP bike actually competes with the top Hondas. During 2003, Ducati's first season in MotoGP, Loris Capirossi won one race outright and finished on the podium many times after duelling with the top four or five Hondas. The other makes generally brought up the rear in a separate race of their own. This dashed the idea that cash equals success in racing.

Ducati was one of many companies that switched to producing small motor bikes after World War 2. As Yamaha had originally produced propellers and Honda had made piston rings, so Ducati's product had been radio equipment. Why switch to motor bikes? After food and shelter, flexible transportation is a basic need, and little capital is required to begin motor bike production – far less than for cars and trucks.

Once established in the market, Ducati entered competitions to show that their products were just as good as those of the classic Italian builders Benelli, Gilera and Moto Guzzi. Their first bike, the four-stroke Cucciolo, was designed by Aldo Farinelli. Fabio Taglioni had studied engineering until the war intervened, but he resumed his education in 1948 and joined Ducati thereafter. Post-war design turned to higher rpm as a means of increasing power, but valve-spring quality could not keep up. Even mighty Gilera was plagued with spring breakage. In response, Taglioni developed an idea that dated back at least to World War 1 – desmodromic valve drive. In this arrangement, paired, but complementary, cam forms are used – one cam lobe to open the valve, the other to close it by means of a forked lever. Desmo valve drive eliminated spring failures by eliminating the springs.

Taglioni was not the only one interested in desmo valve drive. Mercedes-Benz would employ it on their 1954 W-196 grand prix car, and Norton would build and test a desmo head for their Manx 500 racing single. In the same period, Ferrari resorted to hairpin springs, and NSU would test a disc rotary valve. All were attempts to eliminate spring problems.

Ducati engines with Taglioni's desmo valve drive could rev higher than their competition, bringing the company a taste of GP success just as the Italian motor cycle industry was being overshadowed by rising auto production in the late 1950s.

So began a lean time, during which no Italian maker would thrive. While Japanese machines evolved from basic transportation into sports and recreation bikes for a world market, Italian firms remained small and starved of capital. Ducati produced a variety of sporting singles and stayed afloat by making industrial engines. As the US market in the late 1960s swung past British twins toward higher performance, Ducati planners sensed a commercial opportunity. What high-performance engine should they build? Bigger singles hit a dead end in the 450, whose vibration broke parts. Two attempts at a parallel twin ('Surely we can do better than the English!') produced bikes that, idling on their centre stands, vibrated steadily across the pavement. It was from this vibration crisis that Ducati's second signature feature arose – the 90-degree twin engine layout.

Legend has it that Dr Taglioni had designed a 90-degree 250 twin at university, but when asked about this, Ducati's present most senior engineer, Gianluigi Mengoli, shrugged and pouted his lips, saying that the idea was obvious and had been known for years. And it's true – the peripatetic Giuseppe Salmaggi had designed a 90-degree engine for Lambretta's beautiful, but never raced, 250 GP bike, and there had been others before that. The basic truth is that two cylinders at 90 degrees to each other, served by connecting-rods pivoting on the same crankpin and with a suitable crank counterweight, produce zero primary imbalance. Could this be a key to the US market? British parallel twins, when enlarged to meet that market's power demand, vibrated terribly. The

Japanese chose the in-line four design of Gilera's classic racers, requiring tooling that only their large scale could justify. Taglioni's insight was that a self-balancing 90-degree design would allow Ducati to use two of its already proven singles to make a smooth, high-performance twin.

A good product is never enough. The sword Excalibur, without its legend, is just a big knife. Part of Ducati's legend was created by their early whiff of grand prix success, part came from the unique desmo valve system, and more would arise from enthusiasts in the US and elsewhere, hungry for an alternative to Japanese commodity sameness. Most important of all, however, was a second racing gamble that paid off.

A 200-mile road race was scheduled for spring 1972, at Imola, patterned on the Daytona 200. At the last moment, Ducati entered two of their new desmo 750 90-degree twins, one for factory tester Bruno Spaggiari, the other for English star Paul Smart. In the race, Agostini led many laps on a shaft-driven 750 MV. When he slowed, Smart and Spaggiari finished 1-2. This sensational victory by an Italian company recharged and expanded Ducati's legend. The American magazine *CYCLE*, personified by its editors Cook Neilson and Phil Schilling, took on the task of telling and retelling the Ducati legend.

A good product and a legend can still fail without capital. Japanese companies took all the chips they'd won building stepthroughs to place a new bet. They gambled that convenient, modern motor cycles would become essential toys in the US and other prosperous countries. This was impossible in Europe, where the post-war motor cycle market had faded too early, leaving companies like Ducati chronically under-capitalised.

Ducati had attracted a devoted following of insiders who appreciated the special qualities of the machines. This was a means of survival, but it was not a large market. Japanese design gained sophistication through the 1970s, while two-valve Ducatis – despite their exotic aura – were approaching obsolescence. Imola had given the flywheel of Ducati's reputation a useful kick, but coasting is dangerous.

Change was fermenting – by the 1980s, Ducati engineering had split into two camps. In one were Dr Taglioni and his supporters, dedicated to the Norton-like, two-valve, hemispheric combustion chamber of classic type, and to chassis stabilised almost to the point of fixity by antique steering geometry. Always beware when you are told a machine 'steers as if on rails'. Locomotives, which do run on rails, cannot be steered at all. In the other camp were Massimo Bordi, Mengoli and the younger engineers, who appreciated that design had moved on in both areas, and that Ducati had to do the same.

In the mid-sixties, Englishman Keith Duckworth had changed the paradigm of the four-stroke racing engine. Rejecting both the classic two-valve hemi head and Honda's wide-valve-angle, pent-roof four-valve designs of the 1960s, he opted for an almost flat, narrow-valve-angle four-valve chamber, which burned the mixture rapidly and efficiently. Small, light valves permitted float-free, high-rpm valve action, while long slender valve stems made room for steep, nearly straight ports. Duckworth's innovations instantly dominated F1, then fostered a long trend toward shorter strokes, increased revs and higher specific power. Bordi and his men sought to incorporate these advanced features into a new Ducati twin. Taglioni opposed the idea.

This situation is common in the sciences, where the prestige of a senior researcher can be so great that the dissenting views of younger workers cannot even be published. Tension within Ducati was electric. Finally, management acted, sending Dr Taglioni as a consultant to Russia, thereby permitting Bordi and his group to test their work. This was the first time a Ducati engine had exceeded the 100-bhp mark. Although Taglioni had achieved a great

Facing page, main photograph and inset top: **Ducati Corse made a return to GP racing in 2003 after three decades away.** Both photographs: Mark Wernham

Facing page, insets bottom, left to right: **Factory racing Cucciolo 125 of 1948; Fabio Taglioni (second from right) shares Imola 200 trophy with Spaggiari and winner Paul Smart in 1972; the first desmo Dukes were 125s, here at TT.**

Bottom, left to right: **500 cc GP V-twin of 1971 was rolling test-bed for trade-mark V-twin concept; the same bike clothed; Phil Read taking it to fourth in the 1971 Italian GP.**

Below: **Ducati's racing return. Bruno Spaggiari's V-twin leads Agostini's MV Agusta at the crucial 1972 debut. Ducati finished first and second.** All photographs: Ducati Corse

Top: Smart and the victorious virgin Ducati at Imola. The win made Ducati's name and established their V-twin dedication.
Photograph: Ducati Corse

Above: Ducati honed their racing skills with serial Superbike success – Carl Fogarty, Ducati's most decorated World Superbike Champion, leads the field at Monza in 1999.
Photograph: Gold & Goose

deal, he found himself uncomfortable in a new frame of reference. We honour him for his work, but it was time to incorporate the discoveries of a new engineering era and move on.

In later prototype testing, Ducatis were unable to break through to lower lap times, despite their increased horsepower. Now a second confrontation occurred. Two chassis were prepared – one with the traditional rearward weight bias, raked-out front fork and large trail; the other with more forward weight distribution and steep, modern steering geometry. The latter was decisively faster. Once again, the views of the younger engineers had been vindicated. A way to the future was open.

Now began Ducati's intense period of V-twin development through Superbike racing, beginning with the 851. This activity would transform the company into a source of unmatched engine and chassis sophistication. Through Ducati's devotion to ceaseless track testing, and the detailed and constant evolution of the V-twin, an ability was developed to identify and solve problems quickly. This would not have been the case had the company done the usual thing and designed a completely new engine every few years.

In the process of this development, desmodromic valve drive was transformed from a relic of the 1950s into a modern system able to compete with any other. Any valve drive using either metal or gas springs must not only accelerate and decelerate its valves, but also bear the friction of the heavy restoring force of those springs. A desmo system, by contrast, involves only the forces required to move the valves – something that should appeal to producers of economy car engines. At maximum rpm, the power consumption of spring and desmo systems is probably similar, but at lower speeds, a desmo system generates lower friction.

The coming of highly defect-free spring steels in the late 1960s provided a valve drive solution that was satisfactory to other makers. But by the late 1980s, metal valve springs had again become an obstacle to progress in F1 engine design. The problem was that the sharp, impact-like accelerations needed to open valves at high rpm excite end-to-end wave action in the valve springs. Making the springs stiffer in an attempt to suppress valve 'float' often just increases this wave action. Waves travelling back and forth in the spring not only quickly fatigue and break the metal, but also cause moment-to-moment variations in the pressure available to move the valve. This permits irregular valve action. Palliatives exist – spring dampers, clever cam mathematics, ever higher spring stress – but in the extreme F1 environment, they had been used up.

Renault's answer to this was their *distribution pneumatique*. This substituted compressible gas for metal springs. These pneumatic springs became the new orthodoxy in F1 valve-drive design because they eliminated spring dynamics.

When Ducati decided to compete in MotoGP, there were pressures to adopt this 'exotic' system. After consideration, however, they rejected it. Why pay dearly for a new technology when your own system, which you understand intimately, is at least as good?

To understand why, consider the following analogy. Think of the valve and its tappet as a motocross bike, and the cam lobe as a hill in the path of the bike. The valve spring is gravity – the force holding the bike down on the track. At low speed, the bike drives up one side of the hill and down the other, its wheels always on the ground. This is normal valve-train action. But at some higher speed, the bike will rise off the ground as it reaches the top of the hill. This is valve float – the condition in which the cam is turning too fast for the tappet and valve to follow it. Such float is okay on an MX bike, but it's death to valve-train components – the impact of landing against a steel cam lobe damages parts.

Valve float can be prevented in a couple of ways. First, we can make the hill less steep by making it wider. This is the equivalent of lengthening the valve timing. Or we can make the hill less steep at the original width by reducing its height. This is the equivalent of reducing the valve lift. In either case, our bike can now travel over the hill without float at a higher speed than before.

Now an objection. Because of the engine's need for air, we may not want either to extend the valve timing or reduce the valve lift. The first increases top-end power, but reduces bottom-end torque. Reducing the valve lift restricts airflow into the cylinder, reducing engine torque.

So we try a third approach. We increase the downward force on our MX bike with a bigger spring. One end presses the bike down against the track; the top is jammed under a flat ceiling that we build above our track. With the extra downward pressure, we can now ride much faster over the hill without float. But there's a problem. The extra load of the spring is squashing the tyres almost flat, creating extra friction – so it takes more power to move the bike, and it may be less reliable than before. This is the equivalent of extra friction between cam and tappet, and of higher stress on the lubricant film between them – caused by increased valve-spring force. With a strong spring in place, we can go really fast over our

hill without float, but we can't do it many times without suffering a flat tyre or a bent frame. As we add spring pressure to make our system work at higher speeds, it becomes less reliable.

Now let's see what the bike-and-hill analogy looks like if we convert to desmodromic operation. What's different is that we build a curved ceiling over our track, which is a constant height above it at all points. As the hill rises, so does the ceiling. This curved ceiling is the equivalent of the desmo system's closing cam. Our bike is given an extra wheel on top, just high enough to touch the ceiling. This is the equivalent to the desmo system's closing lever. Now as we drive over the hill at low speed, there is no heavy spring to squash our tyres. This is the analogue of low friction and good cam/tappet lubrication.

We increase speed, but there is no float because our third wheel and curved ceiling force the bike to follow the hill perfectly. We go faster and faster, and still there is no float. Stress on our tyres does increase as a result of inertia – at high speed, it takes a lot of force to make the bike follow the hill without float. Even so, these forces are less than they were when a spring was used instead of a curved ceiling. The only forces acting are inertia forces – there is no spring adding to them.

Because of the reduced forces acting in the second system, it offers more flexibility than does the spring system – we can make the hill a bit taller or less wide and still have a reliable system. This is the equivalent of having more valve lift or less valve-open duration – useful in combining good cylinder filling and a wide power band. These are the very qualities required in a MotoGP engine.

More flexibility is attractive to engineers because it allows them a wider variety of responses to engine needs or special problems. Thus Ducati elected to employ their own desmodromic valve drive and their own unique experience of its use in racing.

By 1980, Ducati production had fallen to only a few thousand, and failure seemed imminent. Outdated methods kept production costs high, and suppliers were not paid regularly. A 1984 joint venture with the Castiglioni brothers, creators of Cagiva, saved the company. Twelve years later, the US Texas-Pacific Group acquired a large interest. TPG specialises in buying under-valued companies, injecting necessary new capital and management, then reselling them once the acquisition's valuation has risen satisfactorily. This provided the capital necessary for Ducati to modernise and expand production. Classics like Massimo Tamburini's 916 attract attention, and racing exploits add cachet, but Ducati's bread and butter has been sales of its more utilitarian Monster. The new Terblanche styled 999 is the first Ducati to have been planned with manufacturing ease as a major design element.

DESMOSEDICI

Back to the question: how did tiny Ducati – even revitalised as they have been – design a MotoGP bike that was instantly competitive with the world's best? When this was put to Filippo Preziosi, Ducati Corse technical director, he replied, 'The machine designs itself.' Wheels and tyres of the current sizes are drawn in, together with their suspension units, at a wheelbase that is workable. The rider is put in the position that racing experience shows to be necessary. The remaining space defines the limits of engine size and shape.

Claudio Domenicali, Corse's managing director, revealed that work had been done to evaluate a twin as the possible power unit, but to reach the revs necessary for the required power, its cylinder dimensions would have been outside Ducati's experience. Therefore, a pair of 90-degree twins were combined as a V4. Questions of front/rear weight bias and other mass properties were simplified by computer predictions of the weights and centres-of-mass of complex parts. The machine is dense – Preziosi says, 'There is not even room for air.'

When other companies have increased bore and shortened stroke, as Ducati have done repeatedly and successfully to raise the revs of their Superbike twin, they have often failed to achieve the horsepower of the previous model. The problem is combustion, which tends to slow as the stroke is shortened. When asked how his engineers have avoided this pitfall, Domenicali replied that in-cylinder turbulence studies were made, using simple equipment, and intake port diameter and port downdraught angle were varied to generate the turbulence level necessary for quick, efficient combustion. These are well-known techniques, so we must conclude that manufacturers who have failed to make their short-stroke engines work have neglected these methods.

Domenicali also said that the D16's bore-and-stroke ratio was extreme, indicating a bore and stroke in the order of 85 x 43.5 mm, which in turn suggests operation at 16,000 rpm, with more to come from development. Power? Clearly, as much as the

Honda, for which 240 bhp was the season's hot rumour. More important was smooth delivery off the bottom, allowing riders to apply early throttle with confidence that every degree of throttle rotation corresponded to a proportional increase in thrust. This is 'throttle connection', without which riders are all but helpless to match power to tyre grip. Top power is useful at the far end of the straight, but early acceleration adds speed that shortens entire straights.

In the Desmosedici engine, a train of large-diameter spur gears carries the drive to the desmo camshafts from the two-crankpin, 360-degree crank. As the rear suspension attaches to the engine alone, the only chassis is a steel-tube trellis that joins the steering head to the engine. An unseen technology here is that both the double-sided swingarm and the forward part of the vestigial chassis form parallelograms, able to act as lateral springs. This lateral flexibility absorbs small, high-frequency bumps that the normal suspension cannot handle when the machine is at a high lean angle in turns. The trick is to make the structure flexible laterally, but stiff enough torsionally to assure straight-line stability.

The original design of a racing motor cycle is a beginning, but the intimate matching of the vehicle to its purpose requires a partnership between riders and engineers. Ducati decided four years ago to put engineers at trackside, compelling them to learn all the essential, but non-academic, truths that ensure success in racing. Why not continue to rely on the cadre of experienced trackside technicians? The reason is that a barrier existed between the trackside group, whose language was based on practice, and the

engineers, whose language was that of Isaac Newton. For trackside information to exert a useful effect on future design, it had to be translated correctly at this barrier. For speed and accuracy, the barrier had to go.

Ducati Corse is small – there are 16 engineers. This eliminates long-winded meetings and makes it impossible for responsibility to be lost in a maze of corridors. It is possible to achieve what Winston Churchill called 'action today'.

This may be the most essential aspect of MotoGP – more important than design, more important than corporate size. Ducati Corse is effective in rapid development because its engineers understand racing and have first-hand access to essential information. Everyone has a brain and is responsible for using it. This contrasts with a 'brontosaurus' model of R & D management, in which there is only one (often rather small) brain at the head, communicating through a long neck to a ponderous body.

Filippo Preziosi notes that the most important elements of the motor cycle's performance are beyond the manufacturer's control and are equally available to all. These are the rider, the tyres and the suspension. Therefore, a winning margin of superiority must be sought in smaller matters. This makes it all the more important to identify cause and effect, and to control the result. The task at Ducati now is to combine the company's accumulated experience with more formal understandings. The goal is to pass more directly from concept to achieved performance. The instant competitiveness of the Desmosedici makes it clear that this can be done.

RIDERS FOR HEALTH
ON A MISSION
BY BARRY COLEMAN

Top: Randy and Kevin on bikes in Lesotho 1992.
Photograph: Gold & Goose

YEARS ago, I was out riding cross-country with Jim Schwantz, Kevin's dad. I'm slow and Jim's smart, so we are both pretty careful with our weary bones. We were standing up as I recall, going faster than we really wanted to, certainly too fast to take in much of the otherwise breathtaking mountain scenery of Lesotho. We weren't a bit surprised when the proper motor cycle guys went by. Thump – that was Randy. Another thump and a howl – Kevin, on his way to the hills beyond. Yet another whoomph – right on Kevin's wheel, that would be, er, Mohale Moshoeshoe.

How exactly do you pronounce that. The name, that is, of the little bloke apparently hanging in with Randy and Kevin while Jim and I are about ready to take a nap? Muharly Musheshwe. It means 'Chief of Thanes Shaving-noise'. 'Shaving-noise' was the interesting honorific name given to his ancestor, King Moshoeshoe I, founder of the Basutho nation, after he returned from a full and frank discussion with Shaka's upstart Zulus. The warriors and their thanes had brought home almost everything the Zulus had – cattle, wives, all that. 'Wow, chief, you really shaved those guys – and they are pretty tough guys. As a matter of fact, from now on, that's what we are going to call you and your descendants. Mmsheshwey. See, like a shaving noise. And then people will always want to hear about the great king and how he built this nation.'

As always in the magnificent tradition of African songs, stories, poetry and history, it was a tale intended to be told forever. And, so far, it's working. Here we are telling it again – for a very good reason – 180 years later in a classy motor cycle racing annual. Would Moshoeshoe's fledgling Basuto of Thaba Busiu have foreseen that? Well, yes and no. Certainly they believed in the power of stories, and so do we. Stories, after all, shape how we see ourselves and how others see us. And that really matters to us in motor cycle racing, especially in the UK and the US. We are always worrying about how others see us. And we do try to tell good stories about ourselves. 'There was an Italian kid called Valentino', for example, or how Ducati came from nowhere and so on. Let's tell them too about our very own development movement, Riders for Health. There's a man in it called Shaving-noise. And another called Loris, who could usually do with a shave, one called Sete, who needs a decent haircut, and a thousand others – Ngwarati, Rossi, Ngozi, Kenny, Olesegun. All with stories.

Here's another story, one used by the remarkable American philanthropist Ann Lurie to explain the intended impact of her innovative campaign against HIV/AIDS as it affects the Maasai in Kenya. It may shed some light on Riders. A boy was sitting on a beach next a huge pile of starfish thrown up by a freak tide. Painstakingly, he was throwing them back, one at a time, but the pile was still huge. An older, and therefore wiser, person arrived on the scene. 'You know,' he said, 'that you are never really going to make a difference here. There are too many.'

The child threw another starfish back into the sea. 'Well,' he said, 'I sure as hell made a difference to that one.'

You may know the story of Riders for Health. It was like this. The papers were mean to Randy (circa 1980–84) and often called him nasty names, and Andrea (Coleman) and he worked on telling them the now well-established truth about the freckly (now bald) kid. He loved children, he supported Save the Children, and he and I eventually went to Somalia (my job to keep him half-sane, the best we could hope for in those days), and we saw a lot of motor cycles intended for health care deliveries all broken down after a few hundred kilometres. There was something horribly wrong, and no health care was being delivered at all. He went back to racing, I worked on virtual vehicle maintenance systems in Africa, and Andrea worked on raising the money and building the organisation and organisational profile that every year brings you Day of Champions (from an original idea by Kenny Roberts Snr), and the rest of us close to nervous breakdown.

Andrea used to race. There are stories about that too. Several now-grey survivors happily recall the most glamorous racer of her time ('Long, flowing black hair all down her back, none on her head,' Dave Johnson used to say) hurtling across the grass at places like Cadwell to T-bone them with spectacular, military precision. But apart from all that, she had, if I may say so, a wonderful profile. Dear, sweet Leslie Nicholl was always writing about her in the *Express*, and every now and then they would run a picture of her in a bubble-bath or doing a naughty décolletage thing with her leathers. I was looking at one of these pictures the other day and thinking how very much harder it has been for her to get people to take serious notice of Riders for Health (nothing sexy about routinely changing air filters by the shores of the Zambezi) and how amazing it is that she has pulled the world around to seeing it our way. The president of Ducati, Federico Minoli, sits on our board of trustees, and the other day Honda gave us 75 motor cycles for the work in Africa. We are the official charity of MotoGP.

Andrea's grandfather founded motor cycle sport in Britain – a London-to-Edinburgh 'rally', which he later won. Up in Bradford, they called him not 'Chief Organiser Revving-noise' but Tommy Bullus. He was also famous for shooting a rampaging bull in a shop in Bradford with his service revolver. I hope it was a china shop. It's a story. Our sport is alive with stories. Tommy's son, also Tommy, rode for NSU out of Germany before that rather unfortunate war took place, and his daughter, Thora, married Jack Williams, one of the very brightest of Britain's motor cycle engineers. His 7R entered the language. It was called the 'Boy Racer'. Not many motor cycles enter the language. Jack and Thora's daughter is at work, turning the unlikely sport of motor cycle racing to face the need that it, and it alone apparently, can address – creating a predictable mechanical platform for the delivery of health services throughout Africa – or saving the world in fact, since if the rest of us don't do our part in helping Africa to sort itself out fairly soon, the whole world is going to be very sorry. Certainly, without this transport platform, it simply will not be possible to deliver adequate health care across that mighty continent. One of the most senior people in the World Health Organisation told us recently that without Riders for Health, the WHO campaign to eradicate polio in Africa just wasn't going to work. 'We need you,' he said. 'Simple as that.' Neither Shaving-noise nor Revving-noise would have predicted that, exactly. Although they would have understood it.

Since *MOTOCOURSE* is the journal of record, let me now put on the record what Riders actually do. Although I personally once made front-page headlines in the then soon-to-be-defunct weekly *Motor Cycle* just because I slightly strangled the then editor of *Motor Cycle News* with the (I thought) all-too-reasonable intention of squeezing the last drop of breath from his body, I have learned to love *MCN*. I think Adam Duckworth is a great bloke and I definitely did not run into him one afternoon in the Scottish National Art Galley in Edinburgh; I love Matt Birt; Richard Fairbairn is the most diamond of geezers, and I think Marc Potter is an absolute sweetheart. Led by Field Marshal Robin Miller (rtd) from his now lofty height, they support Riders through thick and thin, and that's not the only reason I love them. Jenipher Mutede, one of the environmental technicians who is supported by Riders in Zimbabwe, was *MCN* Motorcyclist of the Year in 2002. You just can't get more and better support than that. But there continues to be just the teeniest, weeniest niggling little hint that they haven't yet quite distilled into a word or two exactly what we do. Like most people, *MCN* say that Riders for Health buy motor cycles for doctors to take drugs to remote areas of Africa. Close, but no we don't.

What we do is change air filters.

Please hold that thought while I present a slightly more complicated picture. Well-intentioned development organisations – shall we pick on Unicef –, buy motor cycles to help with health care and general development in Africa. Back in Copenhagen, somebody who knows nothing at all about motor cycles, except that his granny used to ride one in the land army, gets out the office procurement pin and sticks it in a list. Fortunately, the list is pruned enough not to include ZZR1100s or we would be in even worse trouble. But it does include mopeds and completely inappropriate small-capacity street bikes, and off they are sent in their thousands to the bush. With no training, no replacement parts and no budget for running them.

No one has shared the useful information that spark plugs have to be replaced, that motor cycles have chains that stretch and sprockets that wear out. No one knows about filters and seals, although a lot of people do seem to have clocked that sooner or later tyres wear out. The more advanced procurers send something called ten-per-cent spares (ten per cent of the value of the order), which includes crankshafts, left-handed grooling-arms and traditional woogling-sprockets, guaranteed to gather dust in northern Burkina Faso for a lifetime – yours and mine at least.

This will not do. It doesn't work. The motor cycles break, very quickly. And so do four-wheeled vehicles (of which we now manage hundreds) and generators (of which we haltingly manage quite a lot), and goodness knows what else.

So, we change air filters, because someone has to. But getting the right kind of air filter to distant places in Africa and having a trained technician handy to fit it properly is, I have to say, quite difficult. It takes a lot of doing and it takes a lot of highly-trained, highly systematic behaviour. It calls for finely honed supply lines all the way from Japan to Chiredze or Bansang, and it calls for endless system improvement and system management. Then there is the matter of rider and driver training – not just in riding and driving, but in daily maintenance routines and, sometimes, in

monthly maintenance. Then there is the matter of managing what we call 'outreach maintenance', whereby our own Riders technicians go out to agreed points (clinics mainly) at agreed times and meet the riders (health workers) for routine maintenance (at least once a month). It calls for schedules, lists, software, software management, hardware, IT managers and so on.

We have policies and we have strategies. Among our policies is that all the people who manage the programmes in Africa must be nationals of the countries in which we work. That's because it's their problem. They have to solve it. We'll help. That's the nature of co-operation. On the wall of the reception area of our office in Zimbabwe, there is a picture of what appears to be a large red and yellow chicken riding a racing motor cycle and holding an Italian flag. This picture (and those of Little Kenny, Marco Melandri, Olivier Jacque and the others who have visited the programme) speaks of a kind of co-operation, but it doesn't mean that Valentino Rossi is going to come and change your spark plug. We all have roles to play, and his is to show up at Day of Champions and sign things – which he does, as you know, with his usual affable charm. What a kid.

The central aim of our strategy is to set up transport resource management programmes in a number of key countries to show what can be done in the field of efficient vehicle management, no matter how difficult the conditions. That, theoretically, comes easily to us. We are from an environment in which a human being will routinely ride a motor cycle at the absolute edge of a two-wheeled machine's capability in this part of the known universe. That is what we call a difficult environment. And yet (unlike the poor example set for four-wheeled vehicles elsewhere in motorsport), the motor cycles of Max, Sete and pals do not break down. So why would we expect a 9-bhp motor cycle to break down in Africa just because it's a bit hot or a bit dusty? We don't. And as well as showing how zero-breakdown management can be done, we have established a school, the International Academy of Vehicle Management, to share our skills and information with the rest of the development community. If you build it, they will come. And they do.

Another story, an important one. We have recently carried out a comparative survey of two adjacent districts in Zimbabwe, both of which are seriously affected by malaria. One of them, Binga, happens to have a full complement (16) of completely reliable motor cycles so that every health worker is mobile. The other, Gokwe North, has just three motor cycles (also reliable, also Riders maintained). The news is that malaria deaths have fallen in Binga by 20 per cent, but in Gokwe they have risen. Can anyone now doubt the importance of well-maintained motor cycles in Africa? We'll see.

And does anyone doubt what this sport of ours can do? People in government all over the world now know about Riders, as do people in the World Bank, the UN, in entertainment and in industry. Bill Gates knows about Riders for Health, Bono knows about us and has given us one of his own Ducatis to auction. We should get a good story out of that.

Mohale Moshoeshoe, motor cyclist extraordinary, former public health worker who changed Africa for ever by running 47 motor cycles in the ultra-tough country of Lesotho for seven years without a break-down, is now operations director of Riders for Health. A few years ago, the South African army invaded Lesotho (gee thanks, Nelson) and, among other things, attempted to requisition Mohale's lovingly restored veteran Mazda pick-up. A man with a machine-gun stood a few yards away to carry out the deed. Mohale, small and polite, but clear about his intentions, advised the soldier's colleague to encourage him to move.

'But he will shoot you,' said the other soldier. 'We want your car.'

'No, he will not shoot me, and you will most certainly not have my car,' said Mohale. 'But I will run him over unless he moves.'

No movement from the machine-gun guy, and finally Mohale slammed the door and slammed his foot down. The soldier dived into the weeds.

I often think about this story and I am very pleased that we have an operations director with such a clear sense of the way ahead. I often think of the time he whizzed by with Kevin and Randy. And I wonder whether Mohale drove at the soldier because he is a motor cyclist or because he is a Moshoeshoe, a close-shaver of dangerous opponents. But what the hell, what's the difference? Mike Hailwood, Kenny Roberts and Valentino did not achieve great things without shaving a few guys once in a while. In fact, I think there should be a passing manoeuvre in racing officially called a Moshoeshoe. And maybe another shaped by sheer, dogged don't-let-the-buggers-grind-you-down determination called a Riders. I shall speak to Julian and Toby. I think they'll like it.

Below: HRH Princess Anne at Donington 2003 chats with Bayliss.
Pphotograph: Gold & Goose

Above centre: Abe in Zimbabwe 1999.

Above: Mamola and Schwantz with kids in South Africa 1992.
Both photographs: Gold & Goose

BARRY SHEENE

Barry Sheene won the 500 cc title in 1976 and 1977, but he remained the most instantly recognisable world champion long after his retirement. As well as racing talent, Sheene had star quality. His popularity with the fans remained undimmed, at home in Britain and in his new adopted homeland, Australia.

In March 2003, Sheene lost a short but spirited fight against cancer. His death resounded around the world of racing.

Steve Parrish, five-times World Truck Champion, was Sheene's Suzuki team-mate in the seventies, and the pair became inseparable friends. This is his tribute.

I am still finding it hard to come to terms with the fact that a vile, disgusting disease like cancer can take away such a strong and vibrant person like Barry. I thought he was immortal.

I am sure many others in this industry are constantly being asked, 'Who will be the next Barry Sheene?' Well, unless we have a reincarnation, don't hold your breath. The UK currently has some great talent competing – and most are mates of mine. But there will never be another Barry Sheene.

I know people often used to comment that 'Stavros is in Barry's slipstream again'; off the track more than on, I would say. It was a right good tow, I can tell you.

Going out with Barry, it would be like going into Alice's Wonderland, but they were not all called Alice. The man had a special magic with people that I can assure you I studied assiduously, but was never able to replicate. He was unique.

His star status obviously came from his supreme riding abilities, and possibly the uncanny televised crashes – but he was just a natural celebrity. Most of Barry's incredible success came from his self-belief. He just knew that whatever decision he made was right, and

even if it wasn't, he would still make it work. Especially when it came to setting up bikes.

He would come in from a practice session and get his crew to change a load of stuff, then come over to me and say, 'Stavros, you need this spring, that shock setting,' etc, etc. I would go out and the bike would be unrideable – but he would go a second faster.

As to him using anyone else's settings, I can still hear his favourite saying: 'You must be joking. He couldn't sort out a chest of drawers.'

Barry really didn't suffer fools gladly. I was perhaps the exception! It seems selfish, but I really thought I was going to grow old with Bazza, to be able to sit and giggle about the mad, bad crazy things that went on.

I would love to tell you some of them, but I daren't...

As I said, whatever Barry did, he felt was right, and I am still expecting a fax to come through: 'Stavros, you want to get yourself up here ace. It's hot and sunny, and there's loads of crumpet.' I am sure he has got me an adjoining suite already arranged.

Along with many others – I miss you mate.

Main photograph: Gold & Goose

DAIJIRO KATO

Daijiro Kato suffered fatal injuries in a crash on the third lap of the Japanese GP. The former 250 champion was embarking on his first full MotoGP season. A reticent and private father of two, Kato was Honda's and Japan's hope for a first premier-class world champion. Japanese journalist Shigehiro Kondo wrote this appreciation.

He was a highly talented rider, as his achievements make obvious. But although he already had a world championship under his belt, Daijiro was still regarded as a future property. He was destined, many thought, to become a greater figure.

The other thing often said about the tiny world champion was that his character was hard to understand. More than just through his lack of any European language, Daijiro was a mystery.

Honestly speaking, my relationship with Daijiro Kato was that between a superb rider and an average journalist. We spoke in the paddock, and I interviewed him several times. But nothing personal, never at the same dining table. Now I will never have the chance to know him better. Even so, I will try to explain as much as I can.

Let me remind you why Kato counted as an exception among the world's highest riders. In his second season, Daijiro became 250 cc World Champion, defeating the experienced Tetsuya Harada. Long before then, the quiet Japanese was known to GP racing, twice winning as a Suzuka GP wild card. To be the best in the hard-fought middle class is itself an achievement many riders only dream of. In Kato's case, it was regarded merely as a passing point. It was not only because Daijiro was then just 24 years old.

Daijiro had many reasons to be thought of as a MotoGP contender. In winter tests before 2002, when he first rode the 500 NSR Honda, Kato was as fast as Valentino Rossi, just crowned the 500 cc champion. That left the world-beating Italian superstar wondering about the wisdom of switching to the then under-developed four-stroke machine. It wasn't the first time one of Daijiro's competitors had to rethink the situation on their first meeting. When Daijiro arrived, few riders could ignore his existence. That Rossi was no exception is more evidence of the depth of Kato's unmeasured talent.

Kato's short and quiet figure had something that made other riders feel uneasy. That was the case for the leading Japanese racers, who met him in the national championship. Usually, when a lucky young rider lands a ride for a mighty factory like Honda, rivals say they could be as fast, given the same-quality motor cycle. That wasn't the case with Daijiro. Many riders, more than one GP winner among them, chose the same word to describe him: 'different'. There was unwilling admiration in it. It wasn't his lap times, nor his race results, but the Difference that they could not explain. I wonder how the top European riders felt when they first met Daijiro.

Daijiro's character, which seemed so mysterious to many, is equally hard to explain.

I believe his shy and introverted manner may have been superficial.

There was a very rich humanity, as Fausto Gresini discovered. More evidence was the magnitude of emotion and sadness shown by those few people who knew him well. His friends, mainly riders, enjoyed his company without any condition. The depth of their grief was hard even to see. Many of them who rode with the number 74 on their bike did so purely spontaneously.

But why did so few touch Daijiro's lovely humanity? It may be because he was under the control of such a huge organisation like Honda from his teenage years. Honda-contracted riders seem to fall into two categories. Some are always bright and clear, with highly diplomatic speech. They seem open, but tell you nothing more than the official press release. Others give you few words and look rather private. They often seem afraid of journalists. Even Rossi, once a charming skinny boy, is no longer found in the media centre, in long chats with the Italian journalists.

Mick Doohan was often criticised for his stubborn character and limited responses to the media. I believe it was more than just the pressure of racing, and that might be the same case for Daijiro Kato. He was so quiet – not because he had little to say, but because he wasn't diplomatic enough to speak without giving too much away.

We will never know the truth. We have lost that chance forever.

It is especially saddening to recall that Kato was under extra pressure before his final outing. My last interview with Kato, before that fateful Japanese GP, was different. For the first time, he gave away his target for the coming race. Usually, he would simply say, 'I don't know.' His reply to my last question was an exception. 'I am going to win the race,' he said. He'd never said that before. I suspect this was a sign of a highly stressed situation.

About six months beforehand, at Motegi, I witnessed just how much pressure was upon our young, small rider. His potential as a Japanese MotoGP champion was unique. When he stopped with a mechanical problem, an employee of a promotional company alongside me hung his head at the TV monitor. But this wasn't the reaction of a Japanese racing fan. He explained that they had planned a grand ceremony to celebrate Kato's first MotoGP win. Now it was just a loss to his company.

You can hardly imagine how it must feel to be on a starting grid, knowing that a maiden win at your home track is considered an obligation. The late Daijiro Kato had been bearing such outrageous pressure on his small figure. You may understand why he looked mysterious to most of us, regardless of our nationality.

The loss to Japanese racing is great. The loss to his family, to his wife and two children is incalculable.

STEVE HISLOP

Defending British champion and TT hero Steve Hislop was poised to rejoin his title winning bike at Oulton Park, after yet another career crisis. Instead, he lost his life while piloting a private helicopter near his home town of Hawick. *MCN* race reporter Gary Pinchin wrote this memorial.

Photograph: Dave Purves

It had been a desperately sad year for motor cycle racing, with the deaths of Daijiro Kato, Barry Sheene and David Jefferies. The sport was still coming to terms with such devastating losses when Steve Hislop was killed in a helicopter accident.

I was lazing on a sun kissed beach with the family late on that fateful Wednesday afternoon when I heard. That morning, I'd filed my Oulton Park preview story to *MCN*. Our double-page preview focused on Hizzy's eagerly anticipated BSB comeback.

After his sacking from the Virgin Yamaha team, he'd been snapped up by ETI Ducati boss Alastair Flanagan, and was to be reunited with his 2002 title-winning 998R Testastretta.

Hizzy at Oulton on a Ducati was something to relish. It was one of his favourite circuits, and almost everyone in BSB expected him to be back to his best, rolling down the pit lane on Friday to set one of his bench-mark fast laps that everyone else would chase down through qualifying. He had a point to prove.

I'd spoken to him the previous Sunday, after Shakey Byrne had won the first WSB race at Brands – and his team-mate-to-be, Sean Emmett, had just finished fifth. Hizzy was bubbling over with enthusiasm for Shakey's success and also heartened by Emmett's ride. He said how much he was looking forward to racing with him and ETI at Oulton.

Suddenly, all that was wiped out, and the pages were ripped up to be replaced by his obituary. And I – along with thousands of his fans – had to come to terms with the fact that one of the best British racers of the last decade would not be around any more.

Hizzy and I went back a long way in professional terms, which meant spending many hours in pit garages with him. The conversation was always captivating. But most of all, it was fun. When he was happy, no one was more animated than Hizzy.

He'd talk you through a hot lap – even a full 37.73-mile lap of the TT if you asked him to – with throttle blips and engine noises thrown in. You'd get every last little detail of throttle position, rpm, gearchanges, how the suspension was working, what he needed to make it even better. His enthusiasm never stopped bubbling over.

Hizzy had won the British 250 title in 1990 and was the BSB champion in 1995 – but that year, his closest rival, James Whitham, had to sit out the final races of the season while he fought cancer. Hizzy had been leading the points when Whitham was sidelined, but he was never as comfortable with his title celebrations as he should have been.

At least Hizzy was able to enjoy his 2002 glory, especially as he had proven, beyond any shadow of doubt, his world-class ability. He had come so close to winning the previous year, only to be robbed by a serious leg injury after crashing at Rockingham. In 2002, he was at his unbeatable best – especially on the technical tracks like Oulton, Cadwell and the Brands GP circuit, all of which he loved so much.

Not for him the flat modern facilities with featureless hairpins. Hizzy was at his best on the fast, undulating, challenging traditional courses, and his technical ability allowed him to cut incredible one-off fast laps. He didn't necessarily need a qualifying tyre to do it either. Just look back at the races where he'd jump out of the gate and build a one-second lead on the first lap.

He also loved the technical aspect of racing – almost as much as racing itself. A lot of riders discuss how a bike feels, then leave it to the technicians to sort out the changes. Hizzy became another member of the technical staff.

Hizzy's career was full of spectacular highs. His smooth style and technical ability helped him to win 11 TTs, and he was a master at endurance racing, so much so that he could lap as fast in the dark as most of his rivals could in daylight.

But there were also some desperate lows. Hizzy was never easy to work with. He demanded so much. And he was not the first rider in the sport to under-achieve with a less-than-perfect bike. He knew what he wanted, but if he couldn't find it, things just went downhill – like in 2003 with the Virgin Yamaha.

He was always so transparent when things weren't working out – and told it straight, good day or bad. He'd explain exactly what was wrong, which didn't always go down well with his backers.

It was just such tough times that often led to the controversial, headline grabbing sackings that everyone remembers so well.

And that's the pity because, on his day, Hizzy was a world-class racer.

The sadness of Hizzy's death is compounded because we, like Steve and his new team, were eagerly anticipating him and his 2002 title bike being reunited at Oulton. Just to see what he could do. The chemistry was so right for him to end his season on a winning note, and hold his head high once more.

DAVID JEFFERIES

When David Jefferies died during practice on 29 May, the TT races lost the very man who had lifted them out of the doldrums of the nineties. Mac McDiarmid pays tribute.

At no other circuit is the lap record so prized as over the Mountain Course, nor is a rider's mettle gauged quite so closely by the stop-watch. For much of the nineties, no rider came close to matching the time set by Carl Fogarty on an ill-handling Yamaha in 1992. Yet once DJ found the circuit's measure, he spent three glorious years smashing race and lap records for fun. And 'fun' was the operative word. Watch DJ lift off his lid after a lap of the course, and you'd probably see him unveil the biggest, toothiest of racers' grins. Talk to him about the experience of lapping faster than any man before, and you'd get the same.

'I learn tracks pretty quick,' he enthused in 2002, 'and really enjoy riding ordinary road bikes on public roads, so this place really suits me. And it's awesome. Like at Bishopscourt, where you hit top gear and it just comes up on the back wheel. You just don't get that feeling at any other circuit.'

At fast corners – and the TT is about fast corners – DJ was visibly quicker than anyone else. It was as if he hated to brake. Big and ungainly off the bike, he was the embodiment of speed on it – precise, but frighteningly fast. In 2002, he lapped the Mountain Circuit at 127.29 mph, a feat for which 'awesome' is too slight a description.

Yet the son of Tony Jefferies, twice a TT winner, and nephew of Nick, who won once, might never have raced on the Island at all. Unlike many professional racers, DJ loved to ride bikes on public roads. As a teenager, he made a habit of epic journeys in all weathers, many on a 50 cc moped. If this made him a natural for racing on closed public-road circuits, his parents were opposed initially. 'Over my dead body,' was his father's first reaction.

DJ himself said, 'I always said I'd never come here, you had to be a nutter to race at this place. But my dad reckoned my style would suit the place, and after a few good results at the North-West and Scarborough, I decided to give it a try.' It was also true that big Dave had a natural handicap when it came to racing short circuits. Although he competed at the top level in World Championship grands prix and World Superbike events, his size and bulk – he stood at 6 foot, 2 inches and weighed in at 14 stone – were always against him. Nonetheless, he scored a number of successes in British championships, notably in 1996, when he took both the British Powerbike Production and the Triumph Speed Triple titles. Three years ago, he added the British Superstock championship to his tally.

So in 1998, DJ entered his first TT meeting, claiming the best newcomer's award. 'My first lap,' he recalled, 'wearing an orange bib. I just went touring. Didn't even tuck in. Just enjoyed myself and shut off anywhere I wasn't sure of.' By the end of the week, he was lapping at 113 mph on a stock 600 and knew that if he wanted to go quicker he needed a faster bike.

The following year, he missed the Manx races through injury, but returned in 1999 to win no fewer than three TT races for Yamaha, a remarkable achievement in only his second year. Over the next two TTs – 2000 and 2002 (the 2001 races were cancelled due to the foot-and-mouth epidemic) – he scored two further triples, a feat unique in the event's long history.

For all his speed, he wasn't reckless. 'I've had no real big moments – no "Omigod" moments – touch wood,' he explained once.

'And I know why,' he added with the quiet authority that distinguishes the best exponents of the Mountain Course, "cos I'll still back it off if I'm not sure or if the bike isn't up to it.'

But if the bike was up to it, he put the circuit on notice. 'I know I can do it – it's just a question of whether the bike can too,' he said after his opening qualifying session of the 2002 TT on the TAS Suzuki GS-R1000. The subject? Flat out – pinned to the stop in top gear. The place? Bray Hill, that giddy, twisting plunge through suburban Douglas. Most riders spend a career, on bikes they know intimately, without once quite managing that. On an unfamiliar bike, DJ had needed just 600 metres to get up to that speed.

Without DJ, TT 2003 was, to put it bluntly, a contest between also-rans. No winner seriously imagined that they'd have beaten him if he'd been around. That's an inestimable loss to the races, and to the fans, to whom his appeal, much like Joey Dunlop's, was his lack of star ego. Invariably breezy and cheerful, DJ was a down-to-earth guy who loved riding motor cycles, just like them. His loss was felt deeply, and nowhere more so than at the site of his death, which became a place of sombre pilgrimage throughout TT week and beyond. One of many moving tributes read, 'Good lad, DJ. Say hello to the others.'

Photograph: Dave Collister Photography

2003
GRAND PRIX
TEAMS
& RIDERS

MOTOGP

TWO new factory teams – from Ducati and Kawasaki – demonstrated how much of a transition 2002 had been for the new MotoGP formula. Now it was rapidly coming up to full strength. And if there were still a couple of two-strokes at most races for the first half of 2003, they had been firmly banished to history by the end of it.

Equally impressive – perhaps even more so – was an influx of new riders. Of seven class rookies, no fewer than four had previously won at least one world championship: Troy Bayliss and Colin Edwards in World Superbike, Andrew Pitt in World Supersport, and Marco Melandri in the 250 GP. Nicky Hayden was American Superbike champion; Makoto Tamada a World Superbike race winner. Only British hopeful Chris Burns was an international-level beginner.

The departure of Max Biaggi from Yamaha, and the loss of expected replacement Nicky Hayden – also to Honda – changed the profile at the top somewhat. To a large extent, Honda had taken their choice from the cream of the crop; Yamaha and the rest were left to pick over the remainder.

The second year of the franchise system led to some shuffling among the holders. At the end of 2002, some existing teams were without sponsorship, while other would-be entrants had no franchises. By the start of the new season, they had sorted themselves out, and come away with a full grid. Almost.

In this way, while Team Pons managed to acquire sufficient backing from Camel and Pramac to survive, Team d'Antin were able to lease out one of their franchise places for the season to (again) Pramac, who fielded an independent one-rider team on Bridgestone tyres.

The loser, for the first half of the year, was the independent WCM team. After being deprived of Red Bull sponsorship, and with it both riders (Hopkins and McCoy) as well as the prospect of Moriwaki-Honda four-strokes, and rather than becoming a bargaining counter in all the deals and counter-deals, they opted to go it alone, commissioning their own R1 Yamaha-based racer. Accumulated delays meant they were still running a modified stock engine at the start of the year, and they were disqualified from race after race. They returned finally at the British GP and contested three races with stop-gap 500 two-strokes before all the new parts were in place to make the Harris WCM a genuine prototype in the eyes of the FIM.

The Pramac deal meant that Honda gained what they had been fighting Dorna to achieve – a seventh entry; while Dorna retained the 24-place grid to which they had committed themselves when the franchise system had been instituted.

As a result, Honda were the most dominant marque by two bikes. They had seven RC211V V5s; Yamaha five M1s. The rest – Aprilia, Ducati, Kawasaki, Proton, Suzuki and WCM – had the compulsory two-rider teams envisaged by Dorna's original scheme.

Tyre loyalties were loaded heavily in favour of Michelin. The French leaders of the class serviced all but one of the seven Hondas, including the top Rossi/Repsol squad, all of the Yamahas, Aprilia, Ducati and Suzuki. Bridgestone, in their second year in the top class, supplied Proton Team KR and Tamada's Honda. Dunlop had lost Aprilia, but had gained Kawasaki and WCM.

Left: Noriyuki Haga.
Photograph: Mark Wernham

APRILIA

A lot of change at Aprilia – except for the motor cycle. Two new riders replaced 2002's lone entry, Regis Laconi; the Dunlop tyres gave way to Michelin rubber.

One rider was from the highest level – Texan Colin Edwards (29 at the first race), twice Superbike champion and on the rebound after Honda had disbanded his SBK team, but failed to come up with an acceptable MotoGP offer (he was unwilling to ride on Bridgestones, having spent a career working very closely with Michelin). Edwards brought long-time crew chief Adrian Gorst with him.

Japanese ex-Yamaha rider Noriyuki Haga (28) was back in GPs for a second season, after a year in Superbikes.

Based in Italy, the team was headed again by Dutch engineer Jan Witteveen, Aprilia's director of racing.

DUCATI MARLBORO TEAM

MotoGP racing's biggest prize – the cream of World Superbikes – was to live up to all its preceding fanfares. With shapely bodywork painted in the coveted Marlboro colours, just like Ferrari, and sounding like a close relative, Ducati returned to GP racing after spending some three decades away from it.

Their potential had been unclear in 2002, but the renowned factory had little trouble in attracting the interest of riders.

In the end, they settled for Loris Capirossi (30), three times a champion in the smaller classes, but a four-stroke virgin. Loris had come close to signing for Kawasaki: a lucky escape.

Ducati drew his team-mate from their own ranks: 2001 World Superbike champion and 2002 runner-up Troy Bayliss (34) made his full-time GP debut after a single 250 race in 1997.

The team was run by Ducati Corse, and managing director Claudio Domenicali was present frequently at the track. The technical director was Corrado Cecchinelli.

HONDA

Twice decorated with the title over the past two seasons, the seniority of HRC's main Repsol Honda factory team was not in dispute. They retained their chief rider – Italian demi-god Valentino Rossi (24), who had two premier-class titles to his credit, as well as 250 and 125 crowns. With Rossi came his full ex-Doohan pit crew, led by the renowned Jerry Burgess.

Rossi's 2002 team-mate, Ukawa, had been moved elsewhere to make room in the other side of the pit for recruit Nicky Hayden (21), fresh from victory in the AMA Superbike series and ready to learn. He inherited Ukawa's experienced crew chief, Trevor Morris.

First with any works upgrades – Rossi especially – this team was run under the watchful eye of the factory, operating out of HRC's base in Belgium. The managing director was Koiji Nakajima.

The other five Hondas were spread among three independent teams. There was no specific seniority, although two of them had riders placed by HRC.

For Honda Camel Pramac Pons, that was Tohru Ukawa (30). The Barcelona-based team had ended 2002 in a rather familiar situation, losing sponsors West as well as both riders, Capirossi and Barros. With a little help from his friends, owner Sito Pons had managed to attract Camel and Pramac backing, and put together a top-level team once again.

Top: High-level rookie Colin Edwards.

Above: Tohru Ukawa.
Both photographs: Gold & Goose

Max Biaggi came with Pramac – the 31-year-old Roman's contract was actually with that Italian company rather than Pons. Sensationally, four-times 250 champion Biaggi had been 'let go' by Yamaha at the end of 2002, after four years.

HRC steered Ukawa from the factory squad to take the second slot. It was the Japanese former 250 rider's second year in the class.

Antonio Cobas remained as Team Pons technical director, although the renowned Barcelona engineer and former constructor missed most of the year through serious illness.

Former 125 champion Fausto Gresini had lost Fortuna to Yamaha at the end of 2002, but backing for the Italian-based team was promptly secured from Telefónica MoviStar, who switched from Suzuki. They brought Sete Gibernau (30) with them, the Spaniard in his seventh season in the top class.

Gresini's second rider, fully backed by HRC, was as last year – Daijiro Kato (26). After his fatal accident at Suzuka, Kato's works-spec bike was allotted by HRC to Gibernau. The factory also nominated his replacement, a young GP rookie from the All Japan 600 Supersport series, Ryuichi Kiyonari (21).

The third supply team, with just one rider, was Pramac. At the end of 2002, the importers of Honda industrial engines – having the will and the budget to race, plus rider Biaggi – had been left high and dry after a single season on a short-term franchise. Although effectively they had to lend Max to Team Pons, they did secure a further year's lease, on half of d'Antin's franchise. With that, and hand in hand with Bridgestone, they entered ex-All Japan Superbike star Makoto Tamada (26), SBK winner at Sugo in 2002, for a first GP season.

The small team was operated out of the Netherlands by manager Gianluca Montiron.

KAWASAKI RACING TEAM

The newest Japanese factory MotoGP team, back after Kawasaki had quit the top class at the end of 1982, was a straightforward carry-over from their Superbike team. Although reporting directly to the factory race department, it was run out of Germany by ex-racer Harald Eckl, Kawasaki's long-time SBK team owner and boss.

Garry McCoy (30), five times a GP winner, was recruited after the end of the 2002 season, having been released from his WCM/Red Bull team contract when they didn't know whether or not they'd be racing in 2003. A second Australian made up the strength – former Supersport champion Andrew Pitt (27) was already on call, after a handful of wild-card rides at the end of 2002.

Kawasaki also had a full-time test rider and regular wild card in Alex Hofmann (22), who will be joined by Nakano in 2004.

During the season, the team recruited Hamish Jamieson, an experienced crew chief who had been with McCoy at Red Bull, to oversee machine development, working mainly with tester Hofmann. The team also employed the engineering skills of Foggy Petronas builder Eskil Suter, particularly for an alternative test chassis.

PROTON TEAM KR

The same riders and, for the start of the year, the same motor cycles for the all-independent team owned by a legend and based in the heart of England's F1 belt. But Kenny Roberts had already commissioned his own four-stroke, and it was to arrive soon after the start of the European season.

The team retained Ulsterman Jeremy McWilliams (39) and Japanese Nobuatsu Aoki (31) for a second year running, after each had impressed on the outclassed two-stroke during 2002. They also had another season with the Bridgestone tyres they had helped pioneer that year.

In addition to the existing team, which included engine designer John Magee and race engineers Nick Davis and Tom O'Kane, Roberts hired talent from F1. Among others were noted designer John Barnard (McLaren and Ferrari), Stuart Banks as engine project manager (from Cosworth, where he had filled the same role for the Aprilia project) and chief mechanic Les Jones.

TEAM SUZUKI

The third Japanese stalwart of the grid, Suzuki, had lost not only Gibernau, but also their Telefónica MoviStar sponsorship, which they had enjoyed for four years. Unable to find a replacement backer, they raced for the year in factory colours.

The team did profit from the Red Bull fall-out, however, gaining young Anglo-American (his parents were British) John Hopkins (19) after an impressive two-stroke rookie year for WCM.

California-resident Hopkins joined American son of a legend and 2000 World Champion Kenny Roberts Jr (29), in his fifth year with the team and his eighth in the top class.

Based in England, Team Suzuki's personnel remained as before. Long-standing manager Garry Taylor was in control, while Bob Toomey and Stuart Shenton were in charge of machines for Roberts and Hopkins respectively.

YAMAHA

The factory Yamaha team, having moved from Amsterdam to Belgarda SpA in Milan, replaced Marlboro sponsorship with that from Spanish cigarette brand Fortuna, a happy marriage with their incumbent Spanish rider, Carlos Checa (30), who started his fifth season with the marque.

Foiled in the attempt to replace Biaggi with Hayden, instead Yamaha put 2002 250 champion Marco Melandri (20) on their second bike. The Italian faced a year spoiled at the start and finish by injuries.

Working hand in hand with the factory technicians, the team was run by managing director Lin Jarvis. Antonio Jiminez was Checa's chief mechanic; Melandri's was the veteran Fiorenzo Fanali.

The second established team retained Gauloises sponsorship, and at the start of the year were congratulated for winning a big prize – in place of Nakano, they had signed veteran Brazilian Alex Barros (33), the most experienced rider in this or any class; by the end of the year, he had clocked up 225 GP starts. Fresh from two four-stroke Honda wins, and very fast in testing, Barros's status as one of the favourites was severely dented by a series of crashes (21 in all), starting at the first race.

The second rider was former 250 champion Olivier Jacque (29), in his third year in the class and his first full four-stroke season.

Team owner Hervé Poncharal retained Guy Coulon as crew chief for Jacque, while Gilles Bigot filled the same role for Barros. The well-established team with the French flavour was based on the Côte d'Azur.

The final Yamaha was run for Shinya Nakano (25) in the d'Antin Yamaha team. The Japanese rider was in his third season, all of them with Yamaha.

Based in Madrid and owned by former racer Luis d'Antin, this effort represented another exercise in survival for the franchise holder. The pay-off is expected in 2004, when d'Antin will regain his second leased-off franchise, and will run the second Ducati team with Neil Hodgson and Ruben Xaus.

WCM

The year was an exercise in survival for the independent team. Backed by American racing benefactor Bob MacLean, and operating out of Austria, the team had neither motor cycles nor riders at the end of 2002. Team manager Peter Clifford shopped around, mainly in Britain, for a chassis, obtaining one from Harris. The engine was a Yamaha R1 modified to prototype specification. It was not until late in the season that the engine had enough home-made parts to pass scrutiny under the rules.

The team had suffered another setback shortly before the season began, when one of their two riders, ex-250 star Ralf Waldmann, withdrew from the project after the first test. By then, young English rider Chris Burns (22) had already signed for a first season, fresh from British Superbikes. With a little help from Dorna, David de Gea (25), formerly with Modenas, was signed as a replacement for Waldmann.

Above, clockwise from top left: **Randy de Puniet, Manuel Poggiali, Sebastian Porto, Fonsi Nieto.**

Below, left to right: **Sylvain Guintoli, Naoki Matsudo, Anthony West, Chaz Davies.**
All photographs: Mark Wernham

250 cc Class

The French-based Scrab squad retained Hugo Marchand (21) for a second year, plus rookie Erwan Nigon (19). Martinez owned and ran another, lower-level team with a patchwork fairing of small sponsors. He had two Spanish riders, ex-125 junior Joan Olive (18) and Hector Faubel (19), in his second season. The Italian Team Matteoni fielded Alex Baldolini (18), in his first year.

Aprilia Germany had German rider Dirk Heidolf (26), in his second season, as well as class rookie Chaz Davies (16), the Welsh schoolboy up from a promising first year in the 125 class on a bike that fitted his fast growing frame rather better.

THE traditional quarter-litre junior class lost ground in world racing, Britain joining Australia in abandoning the category for national racing, and the USA following suit at the end of the 2003 season. The deleterious effect was felt at GP level too. There was a continued reduction of interest from the Japanese factories, Honda withdrawing the full factory twin-crank NSR to concentrate on developing power-up kit parts for the production RS machine. Yamaha took little more than a token interest in the class. Which left Aprilia sitting pretty, able to follow suit by cutting back on factory machinery while still prevailing in the class.

The Italian V-twin certainly dominated on numbers. Including the single full factory entry, there were no fewer than 15 Aprilias, the remaining 25 entries made up by eight Honda and just two Yamaha efforts.

APRILIA

For 2003, Aprilia had just one full factory entry again – for Manuel Poggiali (20). The nervous-looking youth from San Marino was up from the 125 class, where over two years he had won seven races on the works Gilera and taken the championship title in 2001. Now he took over from the departed champion Melandri, again sponsored by MS, the technical side run by veteran factory technician Rossano Brazzi.

The rest of the Aprilias filled that characteristic grey area of mix-and-match and factory favour, ranging from factory spec to basic production, although most of those had bits and pieces handed down from the works in one way or another.

The top echelon, machine-wise, was dominated by the main Telefónica MoviStar team, where Fonsi Nieto (24 – Angel's nephew) and 20-year-old fellow-Spaniard Toni Elias, in his second 250 season, were team-mates again. This strong team was run by former 80/125 cc multi-champion Jorge 'Aspar' Martinez, with Angel Nieto a major presence, especially on the pit wall.

Also on a factory machine was French bright hope Randy de Puniet (22), in his third season in the class, who had taken over from Stoner (down to 125s) in the Safilo Oxydo team, run by rider-manager Lucio Cecchinello, a very busy man.

Year-old factory bikes were supplied to Anthony West (21) and Franco Battaini (30). West, a former factory Honda 250 rider, had been unemployed in 2002, but had found a good way back with the Italian Zoppini Abruzzo team. His team-mate, Johan Stigefelt (27), had been in a similar position. Battaini, starting his seventh season, was in the multi-coloured Campetella livery, along with fast improving Frenchman Sylvain Guintoli (20).

HONDA

Roberto Rolfo (23) was in a one-rider team, backed by Fortuna and run by ex-racer Dani Amatriain. In 2002, the same team had run a factory bike, and Rolfo had finished third overall. At the start of his sixth season, the former Aprilia rider had finished second seven times, but had not won a race.

The second RS250-W was also in Telefónica MoviStar colours, although in a separate 'Junior' team, run by 500 GP winner Alberto Puig, encroaching from his power base in the 125 class. The rider was the Argentine Sebastian Porto (24), who had won his first GP in 2002 on a Yamaha.

Six privateer Hondas made up the numbers.

Molenaar Racing, run by former rider Arie, employed Dutch rookie Henk van de Lagemaat (at 34, the oldest rider in the class) and German woman racer Katja Poensgen (26), back after an absence for a second try. For the last few races, she was replaced by Czech rider Jakub Smrz (19), who had started the year on an Elit Honda.

German rookie Christian Gemmel (22) rode for the new Kiefer Castrol team; the Czech-based Elit squad began the season with Jakub Smrz, but dropped him before the finish in favour of Jaroslav Hules (28), who had come from Team Yamaha Kurz.

Spanish pair Alex Debon (27) and Eric Bataille (21) were together for the first time in the BQR team.

YAMAHA

Team Yamaha Kurz retained the services of Naoki Matsudo (29) for a second year, the Japanese rider's fifth. Initially, his team-mate had been the Czech Jaroslav Hules, but in a mid-season shuffle he was replaced by young team test rider Lukas Pesek (17).

125 cc Class

Far left: Steve Jenkner

Left: Dani Pedrosa.

Below left: Andrea Dovizioso.

Below: Arnaud Vincent.

Below centre: Max Sabbatani.

Bottom, left to right: Lucio Cecchinello, Hector Barbera, Youichi Ui, Mirko Giansanti.

All photographs: Mark Wernham

B Y contrast, the smallest class thrived in 2003, two new manu-facturers taking part to bring the total to six, almost rivalling MotoGP. When you realise that the Derbi and Gilera machines were identical, however, the number drops to five.

The newcomers were the Austrian firm KTM and Italian scooter manufacturers Malaguti, each fielding a two-rider team.

The franchise system applied only to the MotoGP class, and rules for stable year-long entries were enforced less strictly in the small-est class. This was necessary to allow for a generally more volatile situation, both in terms of the young riders and the small-scale teams involved.

The most important mid-season switch affected the new Austrian team. KTM had recruited World Champion Arnaud Vincent (28) for their effort, but friction between rider and team started early on, and grew to such an extent that he asked to be released from his contract after the German GP. Vincent returned later, on an Aprilia, taking the place of Youichi Ui in the Italian Sterilgarda team.

He was promptly replaced at KTM by fast Finn Mika Kallio (20), but his former Ajo Motosports team objected strongly, and legal action was still threatened at the end of the year. Kallio was replaced for the final races by former full-timer Andrea Ballerini (29), who only went and won in Australia!

Two British riders didn't see out the season. Cash-strapped Leon Camier (16) gave up the unequal struggle after failing to get anywhere near the points on an outclassed machine. National champion Chris Martin (22) lasted much less time, having fallen out with his Seedorf Racing team (owned and backed by soccer legend Clarence Seedorf) early in the season. He was replaced from the Catalan GP onward by the only Dane in any class, Robbin Harms (21).

Aprilia dominated a 33-strong entry list with 17 machines. Next came Honda with eight bikes, then two each for KTM, Derbi, Gilera and Malaguti.

Among the notables on Aprilias was Australian hope Casey Stoner (17), down from the 250 class with the same team run by fellow rider Lucio Cecchinello (33). The oldest man in the class, Cecchinello retired at the end of the season to concentrate on team management.

Other leading lights were Stefano Perugini (28), thrusting teen Alex de Angelis (19) – in his fourth season – the experienced Mirko Gi-ansanti (26) and Gino Borsoi (29), all from Italy; Spaniards Pablo Nieto

(22) and, in his second season, Hector Barbera (16); and the seasoned little German rider Steve Jenkner (26). At the start of the year, ex-Derbi rider Youichi Ui (30) was also on an Aprilia, although by the Portuguese GP he had been drafted back by his old employers, albeit wearing Gilera leathers this time.

Honda's troops were led by the formidable and precociously tal-ented Dani Pedrosa (17) in the Telefónica MoviStar Junior team. Masao Azuma (32) rode a Honda in his last season, and Swiss hope Thomas Luthi (16) in his first. Italian Andrea Dovizioso (17), in his sec-ond year, was another Honda man.

Spanish former champion Emilio Alzamora (29) was to have an undistinguished run-out season, on a Derbi for the first time and out-classed by Majorcan team-mate Jorge Lorenzo (15), in his second year. Stefano Bianco (17) rode the Gilera and was joined by Ui toward the end of the season.

Frenchman Vincent's team-mate at KTM was 2000 champion Roberto Locatelli (28), from Italy. The new Malagutis were campaigned by a pair of rookies, Spaniard Julian Simon (15) and Italian Fabrizio Lai (24).

GRANDS PRIX
2003

FIM WORLD CHAMPIONSHIP • ROUND 1

JAPANESEGP
SUZUKA

Main photograph: The big wheel keeps on turning and...
Photograph: Mark Wernham

Inset below left: ...Rossi keeps on winning...
Photograph: Gold & Goose

Inset far left: ...but Capirossi, on the rostrum after the Desmosedici's first race, was just one harbinger of change.

Left: Ill-fated home hero – Daijiro Kato in action at Suzuka.
Photographs: Mark Wernham

IN an image both vivid and poignant, Sete Gibernau conjured up the last moments of his team-mate, Kato: 'If you can imagine a flock of birds, wheeling in the sky. They all turn together, moving together. Suddenly, one bursts off in another direction. But you can't watch it. You have to go with the others.'

Kato crashed on the third of 21 laps of the classic figure-eight track, first used for a GP in 1963. Riding the only fully unsilenced factory RCV211, he was holding on to the leaders – seventh on lap one, one place higher on lap two. He fell, inexplicably, on the new section of track, just where they start braking heavily for the revised chicane. At well over 130 mph, his injuries proved fatal – the first in a GP race for almost 15 years.

It was inexplicable, because it seemed to be a new type of accident. Ukawa, directly behind, thought he might have collided with Bayliss. Later, he apologised for this 'imprudent' comment, which had only been his impression, apparently mistaken. Although photographic evidence showed only the aftermath, the bike badly damaged, a blurred privately shot video shows Kato alone, the bike flicking violently, first right, then left, maybe again, before somehow gripping and turning sharp left. In keeping with Suzuka's tight confines, and acceptable in that this was a freak accident at such a place, there was a concrete barrier a short distance from the track, lined with a tyre wall clad with conveyor belt. At that speed and with that sort of impact, Kato sustained effectively fatal injuries, including a broken neck. His heart was restarted in the ambulance, and he remained on life support for almost two weeks before finally succumbing. It had been ten years since the last GP fatality, his countryman Nobuyuki Wakai, in a pit-lane collision in 1993; the last in a race Ivan Palazzese in 1989.

The rider is remembered elsewhere in *MOTOCOURSE*; and of course the emotions were running high at the time, and for several weeks afterward. Not least because of a confusion of information. Some hours after the event, HRC issued an official bulletin saying that Kato had been taken to Mei hospital in Yokkaichi City suffering from 'concussion and breathing difficulties', which rather understated the case. Much later still, race director Paul Butler and medical director Claudio Macchiagodena released a brief, but more factual, report, which confirmed details and gave a bleak prognosis. In the meantime, the ever-indiscreet and always emotional Dr Costa had been painting a grim picture, at great length, to his fellow Italians in the press room.

The Japanese had lost a true hero, racing an enigmatic character who had shown true genius on a 250 and was still just starting on big bikes. His wife and two children, one barely a week old, lost far more. It was a time of great sadness. But questions had been raised by the incident, and they required immediate action and answers.

Gibernau again demonstrated compassion and articulacy: 'There is no gain in looking for somebody to blame. We are all in this together. We have to learn, and take action, so this never happens again. The bikes are much faster now, the tyres are better, the suspension...everything. But we are still racing on the same old circuits.'

The first questions were simply how and why a rider of Kato's calibre could have lost control so comprehensively in such an unexpected manner.

First thoughts were of mechanical failure – perhaps a carbon front disc had been damaged by contact in the first-lap scramble and had shattered, locking the front wheel. Or had his throttle jammed open? Nicky Hayden had crashed in practice when using some highly-secret throttle-off software, which may not have fitted the rather loose description of 'fly by wire'. Kato was said to be using similar experimental software. Perhaps something else had broken. Or maybe he was just not strong enough to cope with a 230-hp motor cycle.

Two weeks later, Max Biaggi suggested that the way the big four-strokes fish-tail under braking could have been responsible: 'With a two-stroke, if you made a mistake, you'd go straight on and crash in the gravel. With a four-stroke, three things could happen. You might go straight on. Or turn left. Or turn right. There can be more accidents like this, and track organisers will need to look at making more safety around braking areas.' Other riders concurred; Rossi also said his piece: 'I'd like never to come back to Suzuka. It is a shame for me to say this. It is an HRC track, and one of my favourites. I have won here for the last three years.' The future of the track was looking very doubtful.

HRC's prompt response, as well as properly honouring their fallen hero with public ceremonies, was to appoint an independent panel of enquiry, led by Professor Ichiro Kageyama of Nihon University's College of Industrial Technology, an experienced accident investigator. It was hoped that this would unearth the truth – that the crash had been caused (as HRC believed) by rider error. Comfortingly, if there had been a mechanical problem, the findings would not be released for at least 12 months. In the meantime, HRC president Suguru Kanezawa categorically denied that Kato had been using 'fly-by-wire', while Gibernau (having seen the data from the bike) confirmed that the throttle had been closed. The mystery remained.

Another urgent question was why the race had not been stopped. Following riders, who had seen all the debris, including one of Kato's boots, strewn over the track, expected a red flag. 'When we came past on the next lap and there was nothing, I thought, "Thank god, he must have walked away,"' said Gibernau.

That was some two minutes later, and since the track had indeed been cleared and Kato rapidly removed on a stretcher, there hadn't been any technical reason to stop the race. But this begged another question: Why had such a badly injured man (or indeed any injured man) been bundled on to the stretcher with such shockingly rough haste? The Japanese have a reputation for taking better care of crashed motor cycles than riders, but in the case of possible spinal injuries, it would have been more usual to keep the victim immobile and resuscitate him where he had fallen. The decision, however, had come from the track medical director, who had ordered him into an ambulance as quickly as possible to restart his heart, *MOTOCOURSE* was told.

But the biggest question concerned the track itself. Even if Kato's crash had been impossible to predict, there were many other places at Suzuka where the barriers were simply too close for comfort, as Yamaha riders Marco Melandri and Alex Barros had amply demonstrated.

Both had fallen at the fast right-hander between the hairpin and the Spoon Curve, and both had slammed into the barrier there, along with their bikes. Melandri's crash came during his first Friday laps, ruining the 250 champ's class debut with fractures of his right leg and ankle. Barros, a favourite for the year to come, had his chances spoiled in race-morning warm-up. Badly knocked about, but free from fractures, he raced anyway, in severe pain. Just to underline the point, there was a death-defying last-lap lucky escape in the 125 race.

It all put an edge on the much-vaunted start of what had been tipped as the best ever season of GP racing. Even without all this trouble, it hadn't gone exactly to plan. The Ducati debut was highly impressive; but everyone else apart from Honda was feeling the pace: Yamaha shipping in a new chassis as well as a new fairing on race weekend; Suzuki still at the start of what would prove to be a very long battle with a comprehensive package of electronics that behaved as if it had a virus; Aprilia having taken a step forward, only to find out how much farther there was to go. The Protons still had their two-stroke; the Harris WCM ran out of engines (or so they said). And Kawasaki, short of chassis, manageable horsepower and tyre grip, were just miles away.

Right and below: Rookies with high-level history. Ex-Superbike World Champion Troy Bayliss (right) and Colin Edwards (below), chased by AMA champion Nicky Hayden.
Both photographs: Gold & Goose

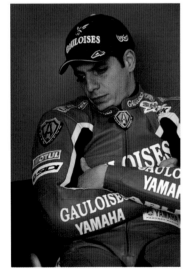

Above: Barros in pensive mood. The crashes that spoiled his season started here.

Right: Thirty years since the marque's last GP, a Ducati rejoins at the front. Capirossi leads Rossi and Biaggi. Checa is losing ground, then come Bayliss, Gibernau, Ukawa and the rest. Kato is among them, working his way forward.
Both photographs: Mark Wernham

MOTOGP RACE – 21 laps

A weather lottery – dry for the first untimed session, then variously dampish for the rest. The fast times all came in a window during Friday's first timed hour, except for McWilliams, left unqualified, who managed to go quicker in the wet on Saturday. He probably needn't have bothered: the organisers waived qualification rules for the smaller classes when six riders, including Elias, did not qualify.

All had tested here the week before, settling gearing etc, and there were not too many surprises in spite of the time constraints: Rossi on pole from Biaggi and Ukawa, then Checa's Yamaha. Tamada led row two from Gibernau (fast in the wet) and Roberts: 'Right time, right tyres,' he said drily. Kato was on row three; the Ducatis missed the window (although Capirossi had been fastest in the dry untimed, and Suzuka first-timer Bayliss second in the wet) and were 13th and 15th, sandwiching Abe on Melandri's Yamaha: he'd started the week-end on the experimental flexi-frame M6. The wild-card Moriwaki Honda, originally earmarked for the WCM team, was on row four; Burns had qualified their own R1 racer 22nd, but it was withdrawn from the race, elevating practice crasher Hayden, Pitt and McWilliams by its absence.

The race began by demonstrating a fact that would become increasingly obvious during the year. Those Ducatis aren't just fast at top speed, they're also very quick off the line. Checa led into turn one, then Biaggi took over briefly, but Capirossi had come flying off the fourth row in a red blur and assumed the lead first time down the straight. At the end of the lap, he was followed by Biaggi, Rossi, Checa and Roberts, quick off the line, but very uncomfortable in such fast company and soon to fade.

By lap three, the Suzuki was behind Kato, who was striving to close on Bayliss. His catastrophe was waiting, and although shocked following riders had to pick their way through the debris, the race was not otherwise affected.

Rossi was ahead of Biaggi, the first three gradually gapping Bayliss. Then Capirossi faltered on the chicane exit, and both the Hondas took over up front, Rossi pulling away gradually with apparent ease. Biaggi was to come under pressure from Capirossi, and it might have been more severe, but for a run across the grass at the chicane for the Ducati. Even so, Capirossi closed again to within 1.5 seconds after half-distance, and was not much farther behind at the end. A rostrum for Ducati in the first GP for 30 years was a remarkable achievement; while Bayliss was fifth, quipping afterward to his crew, 'What time's the second race? I've thought of a few things I want to do to the bike.'

As Roberts disappeared backward, Checa was also dropping, behind Bayliss and Ukawa by lap three, the pair trading blows. Then they almost clashed at the hairpin – perhaps Ukawa hadn't expected such fierce resistance from a class rookie. The Japanese rider ran straight on to head-butt the foam barrier, quickly remounting to rejoin at the back.

Gibernau had got ahead of them all, and then Bayliss as well on lap six: as others before him, he had taken to the Honda at once. Tamada followed him past the Ducati, only to fall with nine laps to go.

Behind Bayliss, Checa had become swamped by a mid-field brawl. Edwards came past him first, then Hayden, through from the back row; next came Nakano and the pain-stricken Barros. Edwards narrowly won out from his impressive compatriot rookie, Barros hanging on grimly close behind. Then Nakano, and Checa a distant tenth, ahead of former Suzuka winner Abe.

Some way behind, the Suzukis had run together, Hopkins tailing Roberts until the former champion nudged the kill switch while trying to select a different ECU map, letting the younger rider past. They remained in formation. 'It didn't matter who was ahead,' said Hopkins. 'We were both riding the machine to the maximum, and we were real close.'

Both were blitzed on the last lap by Haga. He'd worked his way up to tenth, then crashed, hastily remounting to charge through to 12th.

Lacklustre Jacque took the last point, with the Kawasakis of McCoy and Pitt more than six seconds behind. Wild-card team-mate Yanagawa was next, then Serizawa on the Moriwaki.

Neither of the last of the two-strokes made it to the end: McWilliams crashed out on lap seven while 16th and aiming for the points; Aoki retired with the chain jumping on the sprocket. 'Maybe I could have finished, but I thought the gearbox was going to seize,' he said.

Above: Oh joy, oh rapture. New team-mates Biaggi and Ukawa reflect on the thrill of the MotoGP class.
Photograph: Gold & Goose

Right: Nicky Hayden managed to smile most of the time.

Far right: Haga, returned to GPs, mimics the photographer.

Below: All the Duke's men: technical director Corrado Cecchinelli and Ducati Corse boss Claudio Domenicali could hardly have hoped for a better start to their campaign.
All photographs: Mark Wernham

250 cc RACE – 19 laps

The 250s were hit hard by the weather, with fallers (two among many) Poggiali 23rd and Elias 27th and unqualified, along with Chaz Davies and four others. All were allowed to start, while the wild cards made the most of it: Aoyama's Honda on pole, Nakasuga's Yamaha alongside, then Debon and Rolfo.

Porto came bursting through from the second row and pulled out a second a lap over the next four. Even more impressively, West had taken a flier off the fifth, forcing past Aoyama and Takahashi as well as Nieto, and now he started to close up gradually.

But there was somebody else going even faster – Poggiali, from right near the back. 'It's like a dream to ride a bike so much faster than the others on the straight,' he beamed afterward. By lap nine, he had tagged on behind West, who was just over a second adrift of Porto, with Nieto losing ground farther back to the Japanese pair.

On lap 12, having powered past West, Poggiali did the same to Porto, taking a lead that gradually grew until he slowed again on the final lap.

West had also passed Porto in a storming return after a full year away, but on lap 16 he suffered one big slide too many, crashing to earth in the Esses. He'd come back full of fight, in spite of painful back injuries from a pre-season test crash.

This left Takahashi and Aoyama battling it out in spirited fashion, with Porto close behind.

Battaini was fifth, ten seconds adrift; then Nieto narrowly holding off Rolfo and Matsudo, who had been near the front early on, but had run off the track.

With Nakasuga another of seven to crash out, the field was spread – not a good omen for the year to come. Elias, meanwhile, had made an impressive charge through the field up to sixth after 14 laps, but then his motor had gone sour and he retired to the pits.

125 cc RACE – 18 laps

De Angelis put his Aprilia half a second ahead of Pedrosa's Honda, with Cecchinello and Giansanti alongside. Pedrosa took the early lead, headed briefly on the first lap by Stoner, but there was something of a gang, with Dovizioso and de Angelis joined by Cecchinello, Jenkner and Giansanti.

At the end of the first lap, the returned Perugini was 11th, but he was flying and took eighth off Ui two laps later. Then he started to chew away at the gap to the group ahead.

Circumstances whittled away their number. De Angelis had been up to second; however, after seven laps, he crashed out, taking Dovizioso into the dirt – not down, but definitely out of contention.

Then it was Pedrosa's turn, but he managed to save it in a spectacular run across the dirt at the Spoon Curve. There were just four left for an epic last lap.

It came to a head on the main straight, at close to top speed (the fastest 125s were clocking 145 mph), when Perugini veered wildly across the pack and collided with Cecchinello. The veteran team owner/rider found himself on the grass, steering flapping lock to lock. By a miracle, he recovered, rejoining at the back of the group as they ran to the hard braking area before the last chicane. Here he discovered that his brake lever had been broken off in the collision. At barely diminished speed, he took a second trip across the grass, once

again surviving to regain the track farther along, running slower now, but still reaching the chequered flag before Perugini, Giansanti and Jenkner, who were as close as paint.

A 30-second penalty for the second short-cut would have put him eighth, behind Pedrosa, who had rejoined in arrears. Cecchinello protested, and race direction relented, instead rather arbitrarily giving him fourth.

It was Perugini's first win since 1996, and it survived a final attack from the hapless Cecchinello. He protested successfully that Perugini had passed him under a yellow flag, but the winner was given a fine rather than being handed a time penalty.

Dovizioso was eight seconds back, followed by Ui, Nieto and Pedrosa. Teenage rookie Luthi had won a big battle for ninth – an impressive start; the new KTMs found it harder, Vincent retiring on lap three, and Locatelli coming home 23rd.

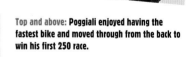

Top and above: Poggiali enjoyed having the fastest bike and moved through from the back to win his first 250 race.

Left: Perugini leads the surviving 125 front-runners to take the win.

All photographs: Mark Wernham

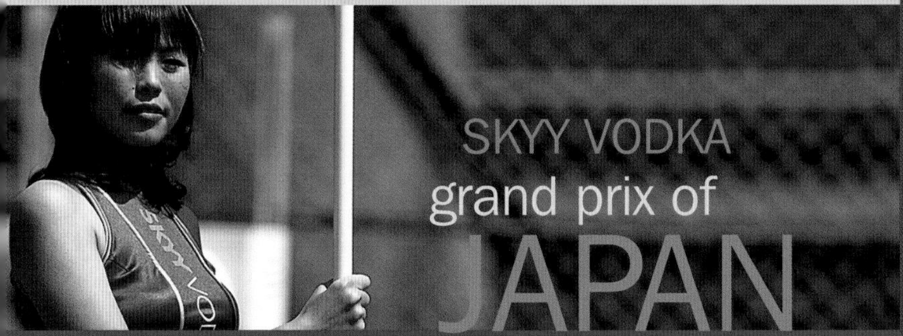
SKYY VODKA
grand prix of
JAPAN
Photograph: Mark Wernham

SKYY VODKA grand prix of JAPAN

6 APRIL 2003

SUZUKA RACING CIRCUIT

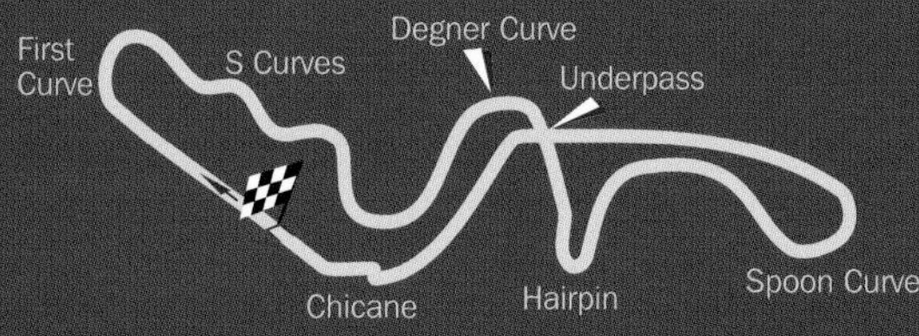
First Curve
S Curves
Degner Curve
Underpass
Chicane
Hairpin
Spoon Curve

CIRCUIT LENGTH: 3.619 miles/5.824 km

MotoGP

21 laps, 75.999 miles/122.304 km

Pos.	Rider (Nat.)	No.	Machine	Laps	Time & speed
1	Valentino Rossi (I)	46	Honda	21	44m 13.182s 103.116 mph/ 165.949 km/h
2	Max Biaggi (I)	3	Honda	21	44m 19.627s
3	Loris Capirossi (I)	65	Ducati	21	44m 21.391s
4	Sete Gibernau (E)	15	Honda	21	44m 26.391s
5	Troy Bayliss (AUS)	12	Ducati	21	44m 36.281s
6	Colin Edwards (USA)	45	Aprilia	21	44m 42.222s
7	Nicky Hayden (USA)	69	Honda	21	44m 42.308s
8	Alex Barros (BR)	4	Yamaha	21	44m 43.708s
9	Shinya Nakano (J)	56	Yamaha	21	44m 46.629s
10	Carlos Checa (E)	7	Yamaha	21	44m 53.382s
11	Norick Abe (J)	17	Yamaha	21	44m 57.972s
12	Noriyuki Haga (J)	41	Aprilia	21	45m 16.540s
13	John Hopkins (USA)	21	Suzuki	21	45m 17.132s
14	Kenny Roberts (USA)	10	Suzuki	21	45m 17.267s
15	Olivier Jacque (F)	19	Yamaha	21	45m 23.172s
16	Garry McCoy (AUS)	8	Kawasaki	21	45m 29.754s
17	Andrew Pitt (AUS)	88	Kawasaki	21	45m 30.562s
18	Akira Yanagawa (J)	48	Kawasaki	21	45m 36.787s
19	Tamaki Serizawa (J)	25	Moriwaki	21	45m 48.641s
20	Tohru Ukawa (J)	11	Honda	21	46m 10.310s
	Makoto Tamada (J)	6	Honda	12	DNF
	Nobuatsu Aoki (J)	9	Proton KR	7	DNF
	Jeremy McWilliams (GB)	99	Proton KR	6	DNF
	Daijiro Kato (J)	74	Honda	2	DNF
	Chris Burns (GB)	35	Harris WCM		DNS

Fastest lap: Rossi, 2m 04.970s, 104.248 mph/167.771 km/h (record).

Previous circuit record: Valentino Rossi, I (Honda), 2m 19.105s, 93.606 mph/ 150.645 km/h (2002).

Event best maximum speed: Capirossi, 196.7 mph/316.5 km/h (race).

Qualifying: 1 Rossi, 2m 06.838s; 2 Biaggi, 2m 07.092s; 3 Ukawa, 2m 07.298s; 4 Checa, 2m 07.426s; 5 Tamada, 2m 08.103s; 6 Gibernau, 2m 08.251s; 7 Roberts, 2m 08.389s; 8 Barros, 2m 08.670s; 9 Edwards, 2m 08.785s; 10 Nakano, 2m 08.930s; 11 Kato, 2m 09.104s; 12 Hopkins, 2m 09.141s; 13 Bayliss, 2m 09.147s; 14 Abe, 2m 09.162s; 15 Capirossi, 2m 09.325s; 16 Serizawa, 2m 09.416s; 17 Haga, 2m 09.690s; 18 Yanagawa, 2m 09.934s; 19 Aoki, 2m 10.120s; 20 McCoy, 2m 11.514s; 21 Jacque, 2m 11.924s; 22 Burns, 2m 13.074s; 23 Hayden, 2m 13.588s; 24 Pitt, 2m 13.871s; 25 McWilliams, 2m 14.011s.

Fastest race laps: 1 Rossi, 2m 04.970s; 2 Biaggi, 2m 05.169s; 3 Capirossi, 2m 05.329s; 4 Tamada, 2m 05.631s; 5 Gibernau, 2m 05.638s; 6 Bayliss, 2m 06.078s; 7 Ukawa, 2m 06.123s; 8 Kato, 2m 06.451s; 9 Hayden, 2m 06.646s; 10 Edwards, 2m 06.649s; 11 Nakano, 2m 06.731s; 12 Checa, 2m 06.735s; 13 Haga, 2m 06.736s; 14 Barros, 2m 06.893s; 15 Hopkins, 2m 07.265s; 16 Abe, 2m 07.404s; 17 Roberts, 2m 07.520s; 18 Yanagawa, 2m 07.630s; 19 Jacque, 2m 07.913s; 20 McWilliams, 2m 07.923s; 21 Aoki, 2m 08.057s; 22 McCoy, 2m 08.445s; 23 Serizawa, 2m 08.521s; 24 Pitt, 2m 08.636s.

World Championship: 1 Rossi, 25; 2 Biaggi, 20; 3 Capirossi, 16; 4 Gibernau, 13; 5 Bayliss, 11; 6 Edwards, 10; 7 Hayden, 9; 8 Barros, 8; 9 Nakano, 7; 10 Checa, 6; 11 Abe, 5; 12 Haga, 4; 13 Hopkins, 3; 14 Roberts, 2; 15 Jacque, 1.

Left: Rossi ran out of gas after the finish and hitched a ride home on Haga's Aprilia.
Photograph: Mark Wernham

250 cc

19 laps, 68.761 miles/110.656 km

Pos.	Rider (Nat.)	No.	Machine	Laps	Time & speed
1	Manuel Poggiali (RSM)	54	Aprilia	19	41m 36.284s 99.159 mph/ 159.581 km/h
2	Hiroshi Aoyama (J)	92	Honda	19	41m 37.657s
3	Yuki Takahashi (J)	72	Honda	19	41m 37.780s
4	Sebastian Porto (ARG)	5	Honda	19	41m 37.984s
5	Franco Battaini (I)	21	Aprilia	19	41m 48.055s
6	Fonsi Nieto (E)	10	Aprilia	19	41m 49.504s
7	Roberto Rolfo (I)	3	Honda	19	41m 49.781s
8	Naoki Matsudo (J)	8	Yamaha	19	41m 50.311s
9	Tekkyu Kayo (J)	68	Yamaha	19	42m 00.830s
10	Sylvain Guintoli (F)	50	Aprilia	19	42m 19.006s
11	Alex Debon (E)	6	Honda	19	42m 19.530s
12	Erwan Nigon (F)	36	Aprilia	19	42m 24.155s
13	Joan Olive (E)	11	Aprilia	19	42m 45.689s
14	Johan Stigefelt (S)	16	Aprilia	19	42m 46.063s
15	Jakub Smrz (CZ)	96	Honda	19	42m 57.332s
16	Eric Bataille (F)	34	Honda	19	42m 58.072s
17	Jaroslav Hules (CZ)	13	Yamaha	19	43m 11.822s
18	Chaz Davies (GB)	57	Aprilia	19	43m 14.773s
19	Henk vd Lagemaat (NL)	18	Honda	19	43m 17.791s
20	Katja Poensgen (D)	98	Honda	18	42m 40.020s
	Hector Faubel (E)	33	Aprilia	18	DNF
	Christian Gemmel (D)	15	Honda	17	DNF
	Alex Baldolini (I)	26	Aprilia	17	DNF
	Anthony West (AUS)	14	Aprilia	15	DNF
	Toni Elias (E)	24	Aprilia	14	DNF
	Katsuyuki Nakasuga (J)	71	Yamaha	10	DNF
	Randy de Puniet (F)	7	Aprilia	4	DNF
	Dirk Heidolf (D)	28	Aprilia	0	DNF
	Tomoyoshi Koyama (J)	67	Yamaha	0	DNF
	Hugo Marchand (F)	9	Aprilia	0	DNF

Fastest lap: Aoyama, 2m 09.839s, 100.338 mph/161.479 km/h (record).

Previous circuit record: Osamu Miyazaki, J (Yamaha), 2m 25.896s, 89.249 mph/ 143.633 km/h (2002).

Event best maximum speed: Poggiali, 166.3 mph/267.7 km/h (race).

Qualifying: 1 Aoyama, 2m 17.930s; 2 Nakasuga, 2m 18.105s; 3 Debon, 2m 18.274s; 4 Rolfo, 2m 19.990s; 5 Matsudo, 2m 20.018s; 6 Porto, 2m 20.285s; 7 Takahashi, 2m 20.998s; 8 Guintoli, 2m 22.111s; 9 Nieto, 2m 22.457s; 10 Smrz, 2m 22.464s; 11 Baldolini, 2m 22.811s; 12 Kayo, 2m 22.869s; 13 Stigefelt, 2m 23.476s; 14 Marchand, 2m 23.717s; 15 Hules, 2m 24.348s; 16 Battaini, 2m 24.692s; 17 West, 2m 25.134s; 18 Faubel, 2m 25.496s; 19 Heidolf, 2m 26.008s; 20 de Puniet, 2m 26.560s; 21 Nigon, 2m 26.613s; 22 Koyama, 2m 26.730s; 23 Poggiali, 2m 26.748s; 24 Gemmel, 2m 27.509s; 25 vd Lagemaat, 2m 28.804s; 26 Poensgen, 2m 28.988s; 27 Elias, 2m 29.111s; 28 Bataille, 2m 31.048s; 29 Davies, 2m 32.767s; 30 Olive, 2m 33.222s.

Fastest race laps: 1 Aoyama, 2m 09.839s; 2 Elias, 2m 09.848s; 3 Takahashi, 2m 10.039s; 4 Porto, 2m 10.155s; 5 Poggiali, 2m 10.227s; 6 West, 2m 10.312s; 7 Battaini, 2m 10.429s; 8 Nieto, 2m 10.622s; 9 Matsudo, 2m 11.181s; 10 Rolfo, 2m 11.229s; 11 Nakasuga, 2m 11.401s; 12 Kayo, 2m 11.581s; 13 de Puniet, 2m 11.815s; 14 Guintoli, 2m 12.117s; 15 Nigon, 2m 12.382s; 16 Faubel, 2m 12.514s; 17 Debon, 2m 12.602s; 18 Baldolini, 2m 12.754s; 19 Olive, 2m 13.254s; 20 Stigefelt, 2m 13.632s; 21 Bataille, 2m 13.986s; 22 Gemmel, 2m 14.296s; 23 Smrz, 2m 14.340s; 24 Hules, 2m 14.528s; 25 vd Lagemaat, 2m 15.051s; 26 Davies, 2m 15.126s; 27 Poensgen, 2m 19.966s.

World Championship: 1 Poggiali, 25; 2 Aoyama, 20; 3 Takahashi, 16; 4 Porto, 13; 5 Battaini, 11; 6 Nieto, 10; 7 Rolfo, 9; 8 Matsudo, 8; 9 Kayo, 7; 10 Guintoli, 6; 11 Debon, 5; 12 Nigon, 4; 13 Olive, 3; 14 Stigefelt, 2; 15 Smrz, 1.

125 cc

18 laps, 65.142 miles/104.832 km

Pos.	Rider (Nat.)	No.	Machine	Laps	Time & speed
1	Stefano Perugini (I)	7	Aprilia	18	40m 53.083s 95.595 mph/ 153.845 km/h
2	Mirko Giansanti (I)	6	Aprilia	18	40m 53.120s
3	Steve Jenkner (D)	17	Aprilia	18	40m 54.116s
4	Lucio Cecchinello (I)	4	Aprilia	18	40m 59.784s
5	Andrea Dovizioso (I)	34	Honda	18	41m 01.677s
6	Youichi Ui (J)	41	Aprilia	18	41m 02.023s
7	Pablo Nieto (E)	22	Aprilia	18	41m 02.166s
8	Daniel Pedrosa (E)	3	Honda	18	41m 16.076s
9	Thomas Luthi (CH)	12	Honda	18	41m 26.791s
10	Gino Borsoi (I)	23	Aprilia	18	41m 27.317s
11	Mika Kallio (SF)	36	Honda	18	41m 27.363s
12	Simone Corsi (I)	24	Honda	18	41m 28.328s
13	Max Sabbatani (I)	11	Aprilia	18	41m 28.901s
14	Gabor Talmacsi (H)	79	Aprilia	18	41m 29.028s
15	Gioele Pellino (I)	42	Aprilia	18	41m 29.390s
16	Fabrizio Lai (I)	32	Malaguti	18	41m 36.047s
17	Masao Azuma (J)	8	Honda	18	41m 36.146s
18	Alvaro Bautista (E)	19	Aprilia	18	41m 44.609s
19	Julian Simon (E)	31	Malaguti	18	41m 50.963s
20	Toshihisa Kuzuhara (J)	65	Honda	18	41m 51.212s
21	Marco Simoncelli (I)	58	Aprilia	18	41m 51.495s
22	Mike di Meglio (F)	63	Aprilia	18	42m 09.161s
23	Roberto Locatelli (I)	10	KTM	18	42m 10.247s
24	Imre Toth (H)	25	Honda	18	42m 14.223s
25	Christopher Martin (GB)	14	Aprilia	18	42m 14.467s
26	Leon Camier (GB)	21	Honda	18	42m 49.084s
27	Akio Tanaka (J)	67	Honda	17	41m 14.483s
	Shuhei Aoyama (J)	66	Honda	17	DNF
	Peter Lenart (H)	78	Honda	15	DNF
	Casey Stoner (AUS)	27	Aprilia	8	DNF
	Stefano Bianco (I)	33	Gilera	7	DNF
	Jorge Lorenzo (E)	48	Derbi	7	DNF
	Alex de Angelis (RSM)	15	Aprilia	6	DNF
	Arnaud Vincent (F)	1	KTM	2	DNF
	Emilio Alzamora (E)	26	Derbi	2	DNF
	Hector Barbera (E)	80	Aprilia	1	DNF
	Sadahito Suma (J)	68	Honda	1	DNF
	Cheung Way On (CHN)	64	Honda		DNS

Fastest lap: Perugini, 2m 14.282s, 97.019 mph/156.137 km/h (record).

Previous circuit record: Stefano Bianco, I (Aprilia), 2m 30.798s, 86.348 mph/ 138.964 km/h (2002).

Event best maximum speed: de Angelis, 144.0 mph/231.8 km/h (warm-up).

Qualifying: 1 de Angelis, 2m 15.417s; 2 Pedrosa, 2m 15.881s; 3 Cecchinello, 2m 16.732s; 4 Giansanti, 2m 16.884s; 5 Perugini, 2m 16.918s; 6 Sabbatani, 2m 16.959s; 7 Stoner, 2m 16.961s; 8 Dovizioso, 2m 16.975s; 9 Barbera, 2m 17.224s; 10 Bianco, 2m 17.308s; 11 Nieto, 2m 17.569s; 12 Aoyama, 2m 17.804s; 13 Jenkner, 2m 17.990s; 14 Alzamora, 2m 18.126s; 15 Simoncelli, 2m 18.428s; 16 Vincent, 2m 18.710s; 17 Luthi, 2m 19.062s; 18 Ui, 2m 19.308s; 19 Bautista, 2m 19.646s; 20 Borsoi, 2m 19.711s; 21 Lai, 2m 19.766s; 22 Pellino, 2m 20.130s; 23 Talmacsi, 2m 20.253s; 24 Simon, 2m 20.298s; 25 Kuzuhara, 2m 20.452s; 26 Suma, 2m 20.487s; 27 Locatelli, 2m 20.572s; 28 Corsi, 2m 21.133s; 29 Lorenzo, 2m 21.361s; 30 Azuma, 2m 21.446s; 31 Toth, 2m 21.730s; 32 Martin, 2m 21.920s; 33 di Meglio, 2m 22.906s; 34 Kallio, 2m 23.591s; 35 Lenart, 2m 24.088s; 36 Camier, 2m 24.229s; 37 Way On, 2m 29.504s; 38 Tanaka, 2m 54.091s.

Fastest race laps: 1 Perugini, 2m 14.282s; 2 Giansanti, 2m 14.743s; 3 Jenkner, 2m 14.851s; 4 Pedrosa, 2m 14.915s; 5 Cecchinello, 2m 14.919s; 6 Dovizioso, 2m 15.037s; 7 de Angelis, 2m 15.196s; 8 Nieto, 2m 15.228s; 9 Stoner, 2m 15.241s; 10 Ui, 2m 15.480s; 11 Sabbatani, 2m 16.109s; 12 Kallio, 2m 16.133s; 13 Luthi, 2m 16.155s; 14 Corsi, 2m 16.459s; 15 Borsoi, 2m 16.461s; 16 Talmacsi, 2m 16.890s; 17 Aoyama, 2m 17.054s; 18 Azuma, 2m 17.094s; 19 di Meglio, 2m 17.129s; 20 Pellino, 2m 17.218s; 21 Vincent, 2m 17.266s; 22 Bautista, 2m 17.278s; 23 Bianco, 2m 17.279s; 24 Lai, 2m 17.444s; 25 Kuzuhara, 2m 17.916s; 26 Lorenzo, 2m 18.029s; 27 Simoncelli, 2m 18.036s; 28 Simon, 2m 18.070s; 29 Locatelli, 2m 18.911s; 30 Martin, 2m 19.207s; 31 Toth, 2m 19.647s; 32 Camier, 2m 20.087s; 33 Lenart, 2m 20.433s; 34 Alzamora, 2m 20.573s; 35 Tanaka, 2m 22.030s; 36 Barbera, 2m 24.079s; 37 Suma, 2m 32.236s.

World Championship: 1 Perugini, 25; 2 Giansanti, 20; 3 Jenkner, 16; 4 Cecchinello, 13; 5 Dovizioso, 11; 6 Ui, 10; 7 Nieto, 9; 8 Pedrosa, 8; 9 Luthi, 7; 10 Borsoi, 6; 11 Kallio, 5; 12 Corsi, 4; 13 Sabbatani, 3; 14 Talmacsi, 2; 15 Pellino, 1.

FIM WORLD CHAMPIONSHIP • ROUND 2

SOUTH AFRICAN

WELKOM

Top: Bayliss (12), Rossi (46), Biaggi (3) and Capirossi (65) into the first corner – behind them mayhem as Edwards tumbles across the track at the back of the pack.

Above: The aftermath – McWilliams hits the dirt as unscathed Edwards looks around in amazement at his escape.

Right: Kato's team leads a minute of silence in remembrance. His spirit was with them.

Centre right: Gibernau won a fine race and after gestured emotionally to his lost team-mate.

Far right: WCM team boss Peter Clifford faced the first of a series of disqualifications. His problems were just beginning.

All photographs: Mark Wernham

GP

MOTOR cycle racing is certainly the most human and personal of motor sports. It must follow that it is also the most spiritual.

Thus when riders talk about being 'pushed from above', we may dispute whether the push comes from within or without, but there is no denying the advantage it yields. I recall the same phrase used by Kazuto Sakata and obliquely by Tetsuya Harada, after each had won a GP on the weekend that compatriot Wakai had died. Gibernau used it again after qualifying on pole at a dry, twisty, slippery and still somewhat bumpy Welkom, in spite of full resurfacing. 'It fell to me to lead the tribute we all wish to offer to Kato,' he said. But he added, 'It was not a coincidence…we've had good tests, and we continue to work hard.' In fact, he'd been on pole here before, in 2000, on the factory V4 NSR Honda. This tight track favours aggression and courage, qualities that Gibernau has aplenty, as he has proved more than once in the wet.

He used the phrase again following the race, after a heart-in-the-mouth duel with King Rossi had gone in Sete's favour, by a few feet. It was an exceedingly fine victory by any standards. And certainly the finest tribute to his fallen team-mate.

In the intervening three weeks, the Japanese rider had succumbed to his injuries and been laid to rest with a private funeral, attended by the entire Gresini team. The highveld air was rich with his memory. All the Honda riders and some others wore black armbands; Gibernau was one of several to mount a little reproduction number 74 on his fairing and on his leathers. Outside the team pit garage was a sign that read, 'DAI-CHAN. YOU WILL BE IN OUR HEARTS FOREVER. THANK YOU.'

The other significant reaction was a meeting of the MotoGP riders – the other classes weren't invited – during which some straight talking saw Friday's first discussion become Saturday's concrete plan, designed to avoid the pitfalls that had seen other rider safety movements run out of steam. Four elder statesmen of the grid – Roberts, Rossi, Gibernau and Aoki – were appointed, and one or more of them would discuss safety issues at each track on a race-by-race basis. Roberts said, 'It's not as though the situation was bad. Personally, I've found Franco [Uncini – Dorna safety officer] has always responded to any problems I've raised. What's needed is a complete review of the safety. The whole evolution of what these new bikes do needs to be examined.'

The business of racing went on. And the danger. There was a discomfortingly narrow escape at the start of the main event, when Colin Edwards's power-crazed Aprilia turned sideways on the start line and launched him across the field. Bikes were already swerving and bunching because Nakano had bogged on the second row. Edwards, on the same row, shot across at a diagonal. It was a recipe for catastrophe.

'I got it under control,' recounted Edwards, 'but by then I was going 4 or 5 mph slower than everyone else. I saw a gap, but then I got hit.' It was Hopkins, who mashed his clutch lever on to his left hand, leaving him with a painful race. Edwards fell under the wheels of the pack.

Team-mate Haga took avoiding action, hit the dirt and crashed. He rejoined, only to retire. McWilliams had even fewer options, with Edwards on the ground directly in front of him. 'No matter how hard you brake, you can't slow down as fast as a sliding rider,' he said. 'It's every rider's nightmare.' He did hit Edwards, but only a glancing blow on the helmet, then he too fell off on the dirt. Disaster had been averted by mere inches.

Every opportunity for tragicomedy had been taken by the hapless Roberts, meanwhile. He had been growing impatient at the slow development of the ill-behaved and under-powered Suzuki, then his mount had sprung a massive oil leak on the warm-up lap. At first, the cause was given as a burst oil pipe, but it turned out to have been a failed O-ring on the oil filter. The consequence was a serious quantity of oil spilled over much of the lap, and a delay of almost an hour while it was laboriously cleaned up.

Another drama fell into the same category. The problems of the WCM team had started at Suzuka, but they came to a head at Welkom. The private team, backed by American racing benefactor Bob MacLean, and already suffering the loss of sponsorship, bikes and riders, became the sparking point of a row much bigger than themselves.

The team's intentions had been good. They had planned to start with the R1 Yamaha and use the overall design (such as shaft centres) as the basis for an all-new, purpose-built racing engine. As well as a different bore and stroke, it would vary from the original in having a four-valve cylinder head, purpose-cast crankcases for a cassette-style gearbox, and a dry clutch. Even so, it would be a loophole special, although in a great tradition of successful racers developed from road bikes, not least by the Japanese factories themselves (Suzuki's and Kawasaki's 750s of the seventies are but two examples; the BSA Gold Star another). In the fullness of time, they hoped it might become a production standard for other private teams.

In retrospect, it all seems insanely optimistic. Not even Roberts, with his own engineering works, could manage to get a bike ready to a similar schedule. The chassis side was no problem, and Harris turned out a very workmanlike racer, reminiscent of an updated Formula One bike. The biggest hurdle was building the engine: far from being ready for the beginning of the season, they were still awaiting crankcases and cylinder heads three months after it had started. And after they had gone through every legal process, had still been disqualified.

The technical regulations framed by the MSMA rule out parts obtained from 'industrial production' and require 'original design'. Both terms are rather vague, but they are specific in naming two key components – crankcases and cylinder heads. Team boss Clifford admitted that they knew well beforehand that they would be stuck with Yamaha production cases and five-valve heads as the season began. At the Barcelona tests, he explained this to Dorna boss Ezpeleta, who offered to turn a blind eye for the first couple of races, after which the new parts were expected to be on stream. Nobody within GP racing would object, since the engine was only in interim form and would hardly pose a threat to their handcrafted, pure-bred racers. People outside GP racing, however, were not so amenable. Minutes of a February FIM committee meeting record a decision to appoint an internal commission of enquiry into the proposed WCM GP machine, 'following a complaint from the commercial partner of the Superbike World Championship'. At the time, that was Octagon, but now the beleaguered SBK series was back in the hands of the Flammini group, who could say, with a clear conscience, that they had nothing to do with it.

According to Clifford, the first sign of trouble came at Suzuka, with a query from the FIM. On the advice of Ezpeleta, he withdrew from that race, citing a shortage of engines as the reason. 'It was almost true,' he said later. The FIM's heavy guns arrived at Welkom: FIM Technical Commission president Oriol Puig Bulto and vice-president Fabio Fazi. They examined the Harris WCM and concluded that the motor cycle was 'not in conformity with…the regulations'.

Riders Chris Burns and David de Gea (Dorna's nominated replacement for Ralf Waldmann, who had pulled out unexpectedly on the eve of the first race) settled down for the first of many weekends with nothing to do but spectate enviously; the team started the long and ultimately fruitless legal battle. Somewhere far away, the SBK world might have celebrated a small victory; in Geneva, the FIM rubbed their hands in glee at the prospect of once again being able to exercise their own particular brand of autocratic blue-blazer authority, in spite of having sold off (actually leased) the family jewels.

MOTOGP RACE – 28 laps

The twisty Phakisa Freeway puts less emphasis on sheer speed than Suzuka, handing something back to the racers. Times were close: the first 14 riders within one second. Gibernau's pole came by just over a tenth from Rossi, who complained of flu after unexpectedly aborting his second end-of-session fast lap. Biaggi was third, followed by Capirossi, who had crashed one of his Dukes, ridden it back to the pits, then leapt on his spare for this fruitful gallop. The high altitude of Welkom may blunt the horsepower of even the big 990s, but the Duke was showing it still had plenty, squirming and wriggling as the riders fought with wheelspin.

The Ducati riders would face a different problem in the race – sheer heat. The Desmosedici was pouring out so much that it melted rubber components in the Öhlins rear shock, as well as part of one of Dorna's on-board cameras – and cooked both riders almost to crisps.

The warm-up lap was a false dawn, since Roberts's Suzuki sprayed oil for almost a third of a lap, starting at the second corner, before he became aware of it. The magnitude of the cleaning job delayed the start by 50 minutes.

Once again, the Duke's speed off the line paid dividends: Bayliss piled through from row three to lead the first lap and stay there for the first ten. Gibernau was also fast away, but unable to find a way past – until Bayliss slid wide off the clean line, giving Sete the opening he needed.

Biaggi had been losing ground; Rossi was in position close behind, waiting for his hard tyre choice to come good. The pair caught Bayliss on lap 13, when Biaggi managed to get past and clear, but Rossi found his hands unexpectedly full with the ex-Superbike champion. Later, he would say, 'I found out that every time you pass Bayliss, in the next corner he passes you back.' This happened four times on lap 14 alone, and it was not until lap 19 that Rossi finally got clear. He set the lap record as he rapidly closed a two-second gap on Biaggi, who subsequently complained of the return of a power loss he'd experienced in practice: 'I couldn't fight properly, especially when the tyres had gone away.'

Accordingly, he ran wide and Rossi nipped inside, now with a 2.44-second gap on Gibernau, with five laps to go. He needed half a second a lap, and he was getting it; Gibernau started to look a little flustered. It must have been at this point that the spirit of Kato intervened.

They started the last lap less than six-tenths apart, but Gibernau held an immaculate pace, and Rossi never came close enough to mount a serious challenge. He was 0.36 second behind at the flag. 'I chose the hardest possible tyre, and it was consistent,' said Rossi. 'Consistently bad. I never felt comfortable, but I did my best. Maybe…one more lap I can beat him. I'm not sure. But if I had to lose any race, this was the best one.' Gibernau is one of a handful of racers who have beaten Rossi in a straight fight, a fine reward for a rider rapidly showing that he'd actually come of age some time before.

A heated battle for fifth behind Bayliss lasted much of the race. Ukawa had led Abe, again on Melandri's bike, then Checa, Hayden and Barros swapping positions, Jacque at the back of the group. Abe took over with ten laps left, but Barros was getting faster all the time, taking the place on lap 22. Abe, meanwhile, ran into a last-lap misfire. He lost two places to Ukawa and a happy Hayden, who 'went to school on these riders'.

Checa, still queasy about the Yamaha's handling, was ninth; Jacque was three seconds adrift. Nakano recovered from his dud getaway to 11th, fending off the Phakisa-friendly two-stroke Proton for much of the race. 'I was waiting for him to make a mistake,' said Aoki. 'Unfortunately, he didn't.'

Hopkins came in next; Tamada was another 11 seconds down, but ahead of Roberts, who said succinctly, 'This bike is unrideable for me.'

The Kawasakis were worse off, Pitt ahead of McCoy, but still a long way back. McCoy had been lapped, and was last, at a track where he had claimed his first win in 2000. A dreadful afternoon – and not the last.

Capirossi was in all sorts of trouble: off the track on the second corner, rejoining near the back, then running off again before retiring, the Ducati leaking water or oil, according to following riders.

Main photograph: Gibernau leads Biaggi and Rossi (Bayliss is out of shot). He proved plenty in a first fighting four-stroke win.

Inset top: A mechanic makes a study in concentration.

Inset centre: First-timer Pitt was out of the points, but ahead of Kawasaki team-mate McCoy, a former Phakisa winner.

Inset above: Biaggi was finding that life on a Honda wasn't necessarily that easy.

Right: Abe took over the injured Melandri's Yamaha again.

All photographs: Mark Wernham

250 cc RACE – 26 laps

De Puniet took his second pole by less than a tenth from Poggiali, while Battaini and Nieto made it an all-Aprilia front row. The Honda RS250-Ws of Porto and Rolfo straddled row two, Elias and West in between. When the race ended, 68.53 miles later, Poggiali would become the first 250 rookie in history to win the opening two rounds.

From the start, de Puniet and Nieto squabbled, the Frenchman being ahead by the end of lap one, and Elias second, Battaini fourth, then Poggiali, who was on a charge. He followed Battaini to de Puniet's rear wheel, and on lap six moved cleanly into second to engage the Frenchman. Their spirited battle would last all the way to the flag, Poggiali always in front, but de Puniet tenacious to the last, trading fastest laps (the record went to Poggiali by nine-thousandths) and mounting one last desperate attack on the final lap.

Battaini hung on grimly until the closing stages, but was comfortably clear of any threat from behind as the pursuers fought it out between themselves.

Nieto had led the group for the first half, from Elias, West, Rolfo and Porto. Then Rolfo started to move through, passing West and Elias in one lap, but taking four more to get ahead of Nieto. Elias was done. A heavy crash in practice had fractured his left thumb and he was riding with difficulty.

Now Porto also began to push, passing Nieto and West, then Rolfo on lap 18, the pair pulling away somewhat. West led the pursuit, but a lack of fitness (he was still recuperating from pre-season back injuries) meant that he had to let the Hondas go.

Elias was fading fast at the end, being only three seconds clear of Guintoli, Matsudo and Faubel. Smrz crashed out; Debon was black-flagged after missing his stop-and-go for a jumped start.

125 cc RACE – 24 laps

An on-form Ui dominated practice, with Nieto second, from Dovizioso and de Angelis. Pedrosa was hunting for power, and seventh.

Ui led away from a tight six-pack that stayed together to the end, leaving the rest ever farther behind. He resisted sustained attacks from the fast and aggressive Dovizioso, while Pedrosa also made it to second for a couple of laps; Jenkner looked strong toward the closing stages.

Then came Ui's last-lap heartbreak, so familiar it seemed inevitable. First, Pedrosa dived under Dovizioso, then with equal aggression outbraked Ui a couple of corners later to take ultimate control.

More was to follow as Dovizioso forced past Ui into second in the last corner. Ui tried to tough it out, but ran wide into the dirt, letting Jenkner through to take the last podium position. Nieto was only inches behind, de Angelis just off the group.

Kallio tightened up on Cecchinello to lead the next trio over the line, Azuma following closely. Stoner was four seconds adrift by the finish, under threat from Borsoi and Vincent – giving the new orange KTM its first points – ahead of Barbera, Corsi and Giansanti. Title leader Perugini retired with a dead engine after completing a single lap.

Top: De Puniet in the lead from Battaini, Poggiali and the rest.
Photograph: Gold & Goose

Above: Pedrosa's first win of 2003 was an omen.
Photograph: Mark Wernham

Right: Furious 125 racing: long-time leader Ui has no respite from Pedrosa, Dovizioso, Nieto, Jenkner and de Angelis.
Photograph: Gold & Goose

ARNETTE'S
AFRICA'S
grand prix

27 APRIL 2003

PHAKISA FREEWAY
RACING CIRCUIT

CIRCUIT LENGTH:
2.636 miles/4.242 km

Photograph: Mark Wernham

MotoGP

28 laps, 73.808 miles/118.776 km

Pos.	Rider (Nat.)	No.	Machine	Laps	Time & speed
1	Sete Gibernau (E)	15	Honda	28	44m 10.398s 100.246 mph/ 161.331 km/h
2	Valentino Rossi (I)	46	Honda	28	44m 10.761s
3	Max Biaggi (I)	3	Honda	28	44m 15.471s
4	Troy Bayliss (AUS)	12	Ducati	28	44m 23.004s
5	Alex Barros (BR)	4	Yamaha	28	44m 29.328s
6	Tohru Ukawa (J)	11	Honda	28	44m 29.511s
7	Nicky Hayden (USA)	69	Honda	28	44m 30.554s
8	Norick Abe (J)	17	Yamaha	28	44m 31.268s
9	Carlos Checa (E)	7	Yamaha	28	44m 32.523s
10	Olivier Jacque (F)	19	Yamaha	28	44m 35.616s
11	Shinya Nakano (J)	56	Yamaha	28	44m 46.301s
12	Nobuatsu Aoki (J)	9	Proton KR	28	44m 49.656s
13	John Hopkins (USA)	21	Suzuki	28	45m 00.628s
14	Makoto Tamada (J)	6	Honda	28	45m 11.839s
15	Kenny Roberts (USA)	10	Suzuki	28	45m 14.540s
16	Andrew Pitt (AUS)	88	Kawasaki	28	45m 33.481s
17	Garry McCoy (AUS)	8	Kawasaki	27	44m 26.964s
	Noriyuki Haga (J)	41	Aprilia	12	DNF
	Loris Capirossi (I)	65	Ducati	8	DNF
	Colin Edwards (USA)	45	Aprilia	0	DNF
	Jeremy McWilliams (GB)	99	Proton KR	0	DNF

Fastest lap: Rossi, 1m 33.851s, 101.108 mph/162.717 km/h (record).

Previous record: Tohru Ukawa, J (Honda), 1m 34.834s, 100.059 mph/ 161.030 km/h (2002).

Event best maximum speed: Capirossi, 170.6 mph/274.5 km/h (qualifying practice no. 2).

Qualifying: 1 Gibernau, 1m 33.174s; 2 Rossi, 1m 33.370s; 3 Biaggi, 1m 33.386s; 4 Capirossi, 1m 33.408s; 5 Nakano, 1m 33.548s; 6 Ukawa, 1m 33.586s; 7 Checa, 1m 33.662s; 8 Edwards, 1m 33.697s; 9 Bayliss, 1m 33.756s; 10 Barros, 1m 33.765s; 11 Hayden, 1m 33.838s; 12 Jacque, 1m 33.917s; 13 McWilliams, 1m 33.938s; 14 Abe, 1m 34.152s; 15 Aoki, 1m 34.269s; 16 Hopkins, 1m 34.306s; 17 Roberts, 1m 34.646s; 18 Tamada, 1m 34.670s; 19 Haga, 1m 34.731s; 20 Pitt, 1m 35.128s; 21 McCoy, 1m 35.566s.

Fastest race laps: 1 Rossi, 1m 33.851s; 2 Gibernau, 1m 34.068s; 3 Biaggi, 1m 34.180s; 4 Bayliss, 1m 34.279s; 5 Ukawa, 1m 34.379s; 6 Barros, 1m 34.492s; 7 Capirossi, 1m 34.493s; 8 Hayden, 1m 34.501s; 9 Checa, 1m 34.655s; 10 Abe, 1m 34.664s; 11 Jacque, 1m 34.738s; 12 Nakano, 1m 34.775s; 13 Aoki, 1m 35.159s; 14 Hopkins, 1m 35.673s; 15 Tamada, 1m 35.705s; 16 Pitt, 1m 35.980s; 17 Roberts, 1m 35.997s; 18 Haga, 1m 36.388s; 19 McCoy, 1m 37.414s.

World Championship: 1 Rossi, 45; 2 Gibernau, 38; 3 Biaggi, 36; 4 Bayliss, 24; 5 Barros, 9; 6 Hayden, 8; 7 Capirossi, 16; 8 Abe and Checa, 13; 10 Nakano, 12; 11 Edwards and Ukawa, 10; 13 Jacque, 7; 14 Hopkins, 6; 15 Aoki and Haga, 4; 17 Roberts, 2; 18 Tamada, 2.

250 cc

26 laps, 68.536 miles/110.292 km

Pos.	Rider (Nat.)	No.	Machine	Laps	Time & speed
1	Manuel Poggiali (RSM)	54	Aprilia	26	42m 14.305s 97.350 mph/ 156.670 km/h
2	Randy de Puniet (F)	7	Aprilia	26	42m 14.920s
3	Franco Battaini (I)	21	Aprilia	26	42m 19.946s
4	Sebastian Porto (ARG)	5	Honda	26	42m 26.452s
5	Roberto Rolfo (I)	3	Honda	26	42m 27.272s
6	Anthony West (AUS)	14	Aprilia	26	42m 33.874s
7	Fonsi Nieto (E)	10	Aprilia	26	42m 37.385s
8	Toni Elias (E)	24	Aprilia	26	42m 41.601s
9	Sylvain Guintoli (F)	50	Aprilia	26	42m 44.492s
10	Naoki Matsudo (J)	8	Yamaha	26	42m 45.752s
11	Hector Faubel (E)	33	Aprilia	26	42m 45.816s
12	Alex Baldolini (I)	26	Aprilia	26	42m 53.616s
13	Eric Bataille (F)	34	Honda	26	42m 54.514s
14	Johan Stigefelt (S)	16	Aprilia	26	43m 01.061s
15	Chaz Davies (GB)	57	Aprilia	26	43m 09.138s
16	Jaroslav Hules (CZ)	13	Yamaha	26	43m 16.928s
17	Erwan Nigon (F)	36	Aprilia	26	43m 23.470s
18	Christian Gemmel (D)	15	Honda	26	43m 31.196s
19	Henk vd Lagemaat (NL)	18	Honda	25	42m 37.988s
	Hugo Marchand (F)	9	Aprilia	11	DNF
	Katja Poensgen (D)	98	Honda	10	DNF
	Jakub Smrz (CZ)	96	Honda	9	DNF
	Dirk Heidolf (D)	28	Aprilia	8	DNF
	Joan Olive (E)	11	Aprilia	3	DNF
	Alex Debon (E)	6	Honda	6	EXC

Fastest lap: Poggiali, 1m 36.649s, 98.180 mph/158.006 km/h (record).

Previous record: Marco Melandri, I (Aprilia), 1m 36.828s, 97.999 mph/ 157.714 km/h (2001).

Event best maximum speed: Poggiali, 148.6 mph/239.1 km/h (race).

Qualifying: 1 de Puniet, 1m 36.247s; 2 Poggiali, 1m 36.344s; 3 Battaini, 1m 36.523s; 4 Nieto, 1m 36.770s; 5 Porto, 1m 37.063s; 6 Elias, 1m 37.231s; 7 West, 1m 37.398s; 8 Rolfo, 1m 37.426s; 9 Matsudo, 1m 37.675s; 10 Faubel, 1m 37.822s; 11 Guintoli, 1m 37.864s; 12 Debon, 1m 37.934s; 13 Bataille, 1m 37.999s; 14 Stigefelt, 1m 38.010s; 15 Baldolini, 1m 38.086s; 16 Smrz, 1m 38.357s; 17 Marchand, 1m 38.514s; 18 Nigon, 1m 38.528s; 19 Heidolf, 1m 38.614s; 20 Davies, 1m 38.627s; 21 Olive, 1m 38.751s; 22 Gemmel, 1m 39.341s; 23 Hules, 1m 39.584s; 24 vd Lagemaat, 1m 41.087s; 25 Poensgen, 1m 42.759s.

Fastest race laps: 1 Poggiali, 1m 36.649s; 2 de Puniet, 1m 36.658s; 3 Battaini, 1m 37.052s; 4 Porto, 1m 37.178s; 5 Rolfo, 1m 37.278s; 6 West, 1m 37.459s; 7 Elias, 1m 37.490s; 8 Matsudo, 1m 37.534s; 9 Nieto, 1m 37.562s; 10 Faubel, 1m 37.677s; 11 Guintoli, 1m 37.867s; 12 Baldolini, 1m 38.144s; 13 Bataille, 1m 38.153s; 14 Stigefelt, 1m 38.407s; 15 Davies, 1m 38.533s; 16 Nigon, 1m 38.758s; 17 Debon, 1m 38.771s; 18 Heidolf, 1m 38.984s; 19 Hules, 1m 39.007s; 20 Marchand, 1m 39.216s; 21 Smrz, 1m 39.336s; 22 Gemmel, 1m 39.524s; 23 vd Lagemaat, 1m 41.102s; 24 Poensgen, 1m 43.603s; 25 Olive, 1m 46.014s.

World Championship: 1 Poggiali, 50; 2 Battaini, 27; 3 Porto, 26; 4 Aoyama, de Puniet and Rolfo, 20; 7 Nieto, 19; 8 Takahashi, 16; 9 Matsudo, 14; 10 Guintoli, 13; 11 West, 10; 12 Elias, 8; 13 Kayo, 7; 14 Debon and Faubel, 5; 16 Baldolini, Nigon and Stigefelt, 4; 19 Bataille and Olive, 3; 21 Davies and Smrz, 1.

125 cc

24 laps, 63.264 miles/101.808 km

Pos.	Rider (Nat.)	No.	Machine	Laps	Time & speed
1	Daniel Pedrosa (E)	3	Honda	24	40m 46.694s 93.080 mph/ 149.797 km/h
2	Andrea Dovizioso (I)	34	Honda	24	40m 47.050s
3	Steve Jenkner (D)	17	Aprilia	24	40m 47.242s
4	Youichi Ui (J)	41	Aprilia	24	40m 47.448s
5	Pablo Nieto (E)	22	Aprilia	24	40m 47.533s
6	Alex de Angelis (RSM)	15	Aprilia	24	40m 48.659s
7	Miko Kallio (SF)	36	Honda	24	41m 00.691s
8	Lucio Cecchinello (I)	4	Aprilia	24	41m 01.484s
9	Masao Azuma (J)	8	Honda	24	41m 03.484s
10	Casey Stoner (AUS)	27	Aprilia	24	41m 07.343s
11	Gino Borsoi (I)	23	Aprilia	24	41m 08.503s
12	Arnaud Vincent (F)	1	KTM	24	41m 08.709s
13	Hector Barbera (E)	80	Aprilia	24	41m 10.508s
14	Simone Corsi (I)	24	Honda	24	41m 10.565s
15	Mirko Giansanti (I)	6	Aprilia	24	41m 11.480s
16	Gioele Pellino (I)	42	Aprilia	24	41m 26.259s
17	Thomas Luthi (CH)	12	Honda	24	41m 28.974s
18	Fabrizio Lai (I)	32	Malaguti	24	41m 29.073s
19	Gabor Talmacsi (H)	79	Aprilia	24	41m 37.839s
20	Marco Simoncelli (I)	58	Aprilia	24	41m 37.880s
21	Stefano Bianco (I)	33	Gilera	24	41m 40.010s
22	Mike di Meglio (F)	63	Aprilia	24	41m 41.947s
23	Emilio Alzamora (E)	26	Derbi	24	41m 43.646s
24	Jorge Lorenzo (E)	48	Derbi	24	41m 43.729s
25	Alvaro Bautista (E)	19	Aprilia	24	41m 44.803s
26	Christopher Martin (GB)	14	Aprilia	24	41m 45.316s
27	Julian Simon (E)	31	Malaguti	24	41m 51.730s
28	Roberto Locatelli (I)	10	KTM	24	41m 58.368s
29	Peter Lenart (H)	78	Honda	24	42m 22.502s
	Max Sabbatani (I)	11	Aprilia	10	DNF
	Leon Camier (GB)	21	Honda	7	DNF
	Imre Toth (H)	25	Honda	2	DNF
	Stefano Perugini (I)	7	Aprilia	1	DNF

Fastest lap: Pedrosa, 1m 41.006s, 93.946 mph/151.191 km/h (record).

Previous record: Manuel Poggiali, RSM (Gilera), 1m 42.605s, 92.481 mph/ 148.834 km/h (2002).

Event best maximum speed: Pedrosa, 130.1 mph/209.3 km/h (race).

Qualifying: 1 Ui, 1m 40.834s; 2 Nieto, 1m 40.908s; 3 Dovizioso, 1m 41.449s; 4 de Angelis, 1m 41.655s; 5 Perugini, 1m 41.658s; 6 Jenkner, 1m 41.699s; 7 Pedrosa, 1m 41.793s; 8 Kallio, 1m 41.813s; 9 Giansanti, 1m 41.849s; 10 Talmacsi, 1m 41.973s; 11 Cecchinello, 1m 42.290s; 12 Azuma, 1m 42.348s; 13 Barbera, 1m 42.501s; 14 Vincent, 1m 42.634s; 15 Borsoi, 1m 42.639s; 16 Corsi, 1m 42.654s; 17 Bianco, 1m 42.700s; 18 Simoncelli, 1m 42.766s; 19 Stoner, 1m 42.773s; 20 Lorenzo, 1m 42.775s; 21 Alzamora, 1m 42.980s; 22 Luthi, 1m 43.043s; 23 Sabbatani, 1m 43.121s; 24 Pellino, 1m 43.277s; 25 Lai, 1m 43.524s; 26 Bautista, 1m 43.556s; 27 Simon, 1m 43.646s; 28 Martin, 1m 43.697s; 29 Locatelli, 1m 43.819s; 30 di Meglio, 1m 44.024s; 31 Toth, 1m 44.772s; 32 Camier, 1m 44.884s; 33 Lenart, 1m 46.204s.

Fastest race laps: 1 Pedrosa, 1m 41.006s; 2 de Angelis, 1m 41.260s; 3 Jenkner, 1m 41.267s; 4 Dovizioso, 1m 41.276s; 5 Nieto, 1m 41.292s; 6 Borsoi, 1m 41.313s; 7 Ui, 1m 41.341s; 8 Giansanti, 1m 41.684s; 9 Azuma, 1m 41.710s; 10 Vincent, 1m 41.720s; 11 Stoner, 1m 41.753s; 12 Kallio, 1m 41.759s; 13 Cecchinello, 1m 41.794s; 14 Barbera, 1m 41.981s; 15 Corsi, 1m 41.985s; 16 Sabbatani, 1m 42.124s; 17 Talmacsi, 1m 42.149s; 18 Luthi, 1m 42.231s; 19 Simoncelli, 1m 42.296s; 20 Pellino, 1m 42.445s; 21 Bianco, 1m 42.526s; 22 Lai, 1m 42.867s; 23 Martin, 1m 42.951s; 24 di Meglio, 1m 43.005s; 25 Alzamora, 1m 43.107s; 26 Simon, 1m 43.115s; 27 Lorenzo, 1m 43.230s; 28 Bautista, 1m 43.231s; 29 Locatelli, 1m 43.819s; 30 Lenart, 1m 44.687s; 31 Camier, 1m 44.813s; 32 Toth, 1m 56.171s; 33 Perugini, 2m 19.292s.

World Championship: 1 Pedrosa, 33; 2 Jenkner, 32; 3 Dovizioso, 31; 4 Perugini, 25; 5 Ui, 23; 6 Cecchinello and Giansanti, 21; 8 Nieto, 20; 9 Kallio, 14; 10 Borsoi, 11; 11 de Angelis, 10; 12 Azuma and Luthi, 7; 14 Corsi and Stoner, 6; 16 Vincent, 4; 17 Barbera and Sabbatani, 3; 19 Talmacsi, 2; 20 Pellino, 1.

FIM WORLD CHAMPIONSHIP • ROUND 3

SPANISHGP

JEREZ

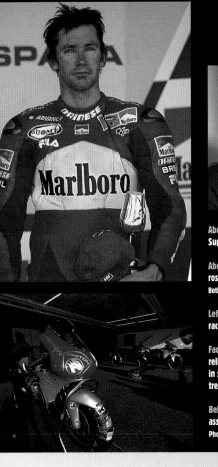

Above: Wide-eyed, Kiyonari stepped from a 600 Supersport Honda to a 990 monster.

Above left: Bayliss clearly found his first GP rostrum an imposing experience.
Both photographs: Mark Wernham

Left: Proton two-strokes came out for another last race. Not for the last time.

Facing page, above left and right: Jerez fans reliably celebrate the start of the European season in style: heroic home winner Elias got the treatment.

Below: The ever expanding MotoGP paddock assembled for the first time in Europe in 2003.
Photographs: Gold & Goose

IF this was the time to put the horrors and near misses of the fly-aways behind us, nobody told the fates. Jerez provided another chilling reminder: Motor Cycle Racing Is Dangerous.

It came on the warm-up lap. The Ducatis had qualified side by side at the front of the grid – a dream European debut. In response to the heat build-up problems, they sported a triple row of holes in the front of the fairing. Ducati Corse boss Domenicali had a typically elegant comment on the fact that they'd cooked Dorna's camera: 'We have to find a new solution…of where to put the camera.'

Bayliss practised his start, as always, and by the time he got to the back straight, he seemed to be miles ahead. 'Everyone else was going so slowly,' he said. Reluctant to spend too long heating up still further on the grid, he explained, 'I rolled over to the left-hand two-thirds of the track and held a constant throttle and held my brake on down the straight, at about 100 mph, to warm up the brake. Everyone came past me, then someone must have aimed at me, then pulled out at the last minute.' It was one of the Gauloises bikes; behind that was Capirossi, tucked in tight behind the screen, doing maybe 60 mph more. He managed to swerve sufficiently that it was only a glancing blow, gouging Bayliss's leg and bending his own handlebar. Had he been an inch or two farther across, the consequences don't bear thinking about.

The start of the European season was a big occasion, with sunshine blazing on a capacity crowd of some 130,000 excited fans.

The trailer park that assembled in the reworked Jerez paddock was similarly boosted, with ever larger hospitality units squeezing out such incidentals as tyre manufacturers to the far corner and riders to what had been a car park farther up the hill. The paddock made an impressive display: Western-style Bedouins, with a growing penchant for glass-clad gin palaces. Mirrored windows at the new Camel Pons facility, at Aprilia's extensive trattoria and bar, at the new Kawasaki unit and elsewhere contrasted sharply with the old-style open-sided tents, and put a physical barrier between the various factions of the sport: the 'them-and-us' attitude, which had been casual and implied in the past, had become explicit and much more divisive as a result. But the food was plentiful, and most of it was better than ever.

It was time for HRC and Gresini's Telefónica MoviStar team to get back to business. One question hanging in the air concerned the fate of Kato's full factory bikes. In South Africa, Max had been asked whether he hoped to inherit them. He had been discreet. 'I must be a good boy. Then perhaps some time I will get some cake,' he had smiled. He had been good, but Gibernau had been an even better boy, and the bikes stayed with the same team, the Spaniard taking the biscuit. Four times in the past, Gibernau had inherited factory machines: Harada's 250 Yamaha in 1996, the ex-Capirossi YZR500 Yamaha in 1997, injury victim Takuma Aoki's factory V-twin Honda in 1998, and finally Doohan's YZR500 after the Australian crashed at Jerez in 1999. The grandson of Bultaco founder Don Paco Bulto, sensitive to criticism about average results following his serial good fortune, was anxious to prove himself worthy. Too anxious, crashing out of the front battle early in the race – but he would have other chances to shine.

This left a supply-team machine going begging, and HRC had a surprise delegate. Ryuichi Kiyonari, aged just 20, had won the Japanese 600 Supersport championship and was fresh from second place in the recent World Championship round at Sugo. Now, without warning, he'd been plucked off the production racer and lined up for a seat on the fastest racing bike in the world. Wide-eyed and speaking through an interpreter, he admitted some misgivings about his ability to get the best out of the world's top GP bike. His compatriot, Tamada, had told him the RCV was 'monstrous'. Was this also a worry? Kiyonari laughed, and also the interpreter. 'No. He likes that,' he said. He would make his debut at Le Mans.

Both of Honda's oldest rivals were feeling the pressure. Yamaha had ditched work on the M1 replacement, code-named M3, and the twin-shock flexi-framed M6 to concentrate on the M1. Management changes came too, the head of the racing department, Hiroshi Ohsumi, stepping aside in favour of Masao Furusawa, while the department had been merged with R&D to put more engineers on the project. This approach was the same as that taken by Honda in developing the RCV.

Suzuki were testing after the GP, and had drafted in former off-road superstar and ex-GP racer Jean Michel Bayle to join the team regulars. Bayle now races for the successful Suzuki Endurance Racing Team (SERT) in 24-hour events, and with his GSX1000-R mechanics also coming along, it was hoped that he could provide a different overview to the so far frustrating battle to get the chassis and electronics to behave well enough to let the riders use the limited power to the full. 'When you're racing, you are only concerned with developing the bike for the next five minutes,' he said.

But all was not well at HRC, coming under pressure from Ducati. Hayden crashed out of the race after his engine seized – believed to be a first for the V5. They cancelled their own planned tests for the coming week and went back to base to investigate, later revising mileage schedules for various components.

Race direction was kept busy. The WCM team presented their bikes again for scrutineering, and although technical director Mike Webb had okayed them previously – only to be overruled by Bulto – this time, he felt obliged to stick with the FIM precedent and repeated their South African disqualification. Like Bulto, Webb had asked for a clarification of the rules, but so far none had been forthcoming. More than two months later, he was still waiting…

Proton had wondered out loud if the South African GP would be the last showing for their two-strokes. Sadly, their new four-stroke engine now added oil control and surging problems to a tendency to seize and break crankshafts. Rapid progress was being made in all these areas, but not rapid enough for a Jerez debut, and during the weekend planned tests for the days after the GP were also cancelled.

MOTOGP RACE – 27 laps

In spite of the new surface, Jerez showed the same sensitivity to temperature as ever, with times in the cool of the morning for free training well inside last year's pole, but only just nudging it in the afternoons. Ducati went double top, Capirossi on pole, almost nudged out by Bayliss but for a slip on his fast lap; then came the two Camel bikes of Biaggi and Ukawa. This pushed Rossi and Gibernau on to the second row: the factory-bike first-timer had been fastest on the first day. And there too was Aoki's two-stroke!

The changing conditions caught out plenty of people, although without serious consequences: Bayliss and Barros each fell twice, while Ukawa, Biaggi, Hopkins, Pitt and Jacque were content with just one crash apiece.

Bayliss led away, but was behind Capirossi and Gibernau by the end of lap one, with Hopkins fourth after a flying start, then Biaggi, Checa and Rossi. Several tangles in the following pack had shuffled them up: Hayden working out how to ride with a bent brake lever, and Aoki right at the back.

With South Africa fresh in his mind, Rossi had no intention of letting anyone get too far ahead. He had sliced through to second by the end of the next lap, poised on the sliding back wheel of Capirossi. On lap four, he pounced into the last hairpin, set a new lap record next time around, and from then on pulled away steadily. He was riding superbly.

Capirossi was using a lot of road, the Honda definitely a better all-round package at this very technical track, and both Gibernau and Biaggi got by next lap. Bayliss was tucked in behind his team-mate.

Gibernau was 1.3 seconds behind Rossi as they started the sixth lap. His victory in South Africa had put an estimated 20,000 on the gate, and he intended to give them their money's worth. 'I didn't want to settle for second in front of this great crowd,' he said, after slipping off at the second corner while trying to fend off a determined Biaggi. Heartbroken, he had slumped to his knees in the gravel.

From here on, the front of the race became somewhat processional. Biaggi was less than two seconds adrift, but the gap stretched by a few tenths every lap, with the Ducatis losing to Biaggi at a similar rate behind. Then Capirossi

crashed out, losing the front, at least partly because of the pre-race collision and subsequent derangement.

The next group were having a fine old time. Hopkins was at the back, but staying close as Barros, Ukawa and Tamada battled back and forth, the Bridgestone-shod rookie Tamada displaying some demon late braking to lead the group toward the finish, his tyres working well in hot conditions. At the end, Ukawa had crept ahead of Barros, complaining of a bad set-up, then came Tamada and a fading Hopkins, whose race had been even harder than the lacklustre prior performance of the Suzuki might have suggested. Not only had a big hole blown out of the exhaust, spoiling power, but also a footrest-hanger bolt had sheared, and he had had to hold the peg in place with his foot while shifting gear.

Another big gang behind had finally debouched Nakano, who had closed on Hopkins, but couldn't find a way past.

At half-distance, Haga had led the group from Jacque, Aoki, McWilliams and Melandri, the youngster not yet fully fit and succumbing to fatigue with a run into the gravel soon afterward. Then McWilliams found a false neutral at the hairpin and lost touch. But team-mate Aoki was on fire. With a 'perfect' race set-up, though a too-soft tyre choice of the heat-friendly Bridgestones, he caught up quickly, but had to wait until the closing stages before he could attack. He picked off Haga and Jacque within two laps, while McWilliams recovered to push Haga hard to the finish.

Two former world champions were locked in a lowly battle behind them. Edwards had his Aprilia 'fly-by-wire' throttle system go haywire, and he was obliged to watch as even Aoki's two-stroke got past while he coped with a machine that was driving him into the corners when he was trying to slow it down. Roberts had been complaining of similar problems for some time. Now, after a tentative early race, he found himself battling with his old teenage AMA 250 rival, and this time he won out.

A long way back, Pitt managed to beat Hofmann in a private Kawasaki battle for the last point. Melandri cruised in more than 20 seconds behind, then McCoy, a lap down and entertaining the crowd with his wild style. 'I don't want to get used to finishing at the back like this,' he said.

Hayden crashed out with a seized engine after just eight laps; Checa had retired five laps earlier with a dead engine.

Above: Ezpeleta and Rossi, a frequent dialogue.

Top right: Spanish sponsors made this a home race for the Italian-based Fortuna Yamaha team. Melandri was back for this race.

Above centre: Nakano was smiling at Jerez. As everywhere else.
Photographs: Gold & Goose

Above right: Roberts was coming to terms with the fact that the all-new Suzuki was at the bottom of the points table.

Right: McCoy seemed to be having fun, but hated coming last. The crowd loved him anyway.
Photographs: Mark wernham

Below: Chasing Roby – 250s in full flow, with Nieto, West and Battaini in formation behind Rolfo, while Porto and Elias are just out of touch. Elias came through to win.

Bottom left: Wily veteran Cecchinello celebrates his sixth GP win. The team owner would win once more in a career spanning almost 150 starts.

Bottom right: Dovizioso (34) and Stoner (27) would prove only a temporary hold-up to Jenkner (17) in his run for glory.
All photographs: Gold & Goose

250 cc RACE – 26 laps

The 250s were still slower than Kato's pole-winning time of two years before, with de Puniet taking the second pole in a row from Poggiali, Battaini and Rolfo. Nieto led row two from Elias, still troubled by his hand, then West and Porto on the second Honda.

Battaini and Rolfo disputed the early lead, but both Nieto and de Puniet displaced the Honda and were harrying Battaini when his engine went sick and he dropped out of contention.

Poggiali had also been moving through, and although he took two attempts to pass de Puniet, he began hunting down Nieto and took the lead on lap four. The first nine riders were still running within a second at this point, West in the group as well as Elias, who was soon to fade. Poggiali immediately opened up a lead – 1.3 seconds on lap six – as Nieto held up the pursuit. When de Puniet, Rolfo and West got by the Spaniard, they began closing up again.

West was on a charge, diving under Rolfo on lap ten and setting his sights on de Puniet and second, only to discover that he was already at the limit. 'The harder I tried, the more I spun up and slowed down,' he said. Rolfo passed him back next time around and started to pull clear to reel in the leaders.

After half-distance, de Puniet took to the front for nine laps or so, Rolfo harrying Poggiali from behind. At the same time, Elias had found his second wind, carving past Nieto and Porto in the same lap, then rapidly closing a gap of less than 1.5 seconds on West to blow past easily. Inspired, he was with the leaders with four laps to go, turning the three-way fight into an even more torrid quartet. They were about to engage in one of the best 250 battles to be seen for several years.

Elias took the lead for the first time as they started the final lap. At the far Dry Sack hairpin, de Puniet ran wide trying to regain the front and dropped to fourth. The next attack came from Rolfo, ahead in the first of the penultimate double right-handers, only for Elias to shove straight past again in the second. The crowd went wild.

All four were still locked together as they hit the brakes for the last hairpin. All made it around, with Elias hanging on grimly to the lead and Rolfo narrowly holding back de Puniet, Poggiali less than a tenth behind. What a finish. What a triumph for 20-year-old home hero Elias. 'My hand was painful, but when I saw victory was possible, I put it out of my mind,' he grinned.

West was 12 seconds back at the end, but two clear of Porto; Nieto was next, Matsudo a long way behind in a lonely eighth; Battaini was back in 11th. Guintoli, Faubel and Stigefelt crashed out, the last most spectacularly, yet unhurt. Poggiali took fastest lap, but was still nearly half a second off Kato's 2001 record.

125 cc RACE – 23 laps

Nieto, Cecchinello and de Angelis put Aprilias in the top three positions in practice, with Pedrosa a close fourth on the Honda. The last-named led away and held on for seven laps, fast starter Dovizioso dropping out of contention as Nieto, Cecchinello, Perugini and de Angelis stayed close and threatening.

Jenkner had started badly from the head of row two and was 11th at the end of lap one, trading blows with Stoner, Ui and Barbera. By lap six, he was heading that group, with the leaders five seconds clear. Riding smoothly and immaculately, he began to work on closing up.

Up front, Nieto had taken the lead, while Pedrosa had been dropped to fourth by Cecchinello and de Angelis, then to fifth by Perugini on lap ten, the Italian already having set a new record. And back to fourth – Nieto had slowed abruptly to retire with his engine overheating.

Jenkner had been gaining steadily as they went back and forth for the lead, and by lap 17 was just a second adrift. One lap later, he had caught Perugini and was soon to pass him to put his name in the frame for the win.

De Angelis stepped up the pace, taking the lead on lap 21 and moving ahead slightly. Only Cecchinello and Jenkner had the wherewithal to go with him for a final battle royal.

At the start of the last lap, de Angelis still led, then Jenkner took over for the middle part. But Cecchinello is both wily and aggressive, and he seized control with a couple of corners to go, the first three over the line within less than four-tenths of a second. Pedrosa held off Perugini close behind.

Ten seconds away, Stoner won out after a race-long tussle from Barbera and Ui; Dovizioso was a further seven seconds behind, holding Giansanti at bay. A little way back, Azuma did the same to Luthi at the head of a big gang going for the last points.

CIRCUITO DE JEREZ

Peluqui

Expo 92

Angel Nieto

Michelin

Ducados

Dry Sack

CIRCUIT LENGTH:
2.748 miles/4.423 km

MARLBORO SPANISH grand prix

Photograph: Mark Wernham

11 MAY 2003

MotoGP

27 laps, 74.196 miles/119.421 km

Pos.	Rider (Nat.)	No.	Machine	Laps	Time & speed
1	Valentino Rossi (I)	46	Honda	27	46m 50.345s 95.055 mph/ 152.976 km/h
2	Max Biaggi (I)	3	Honda	27	46m 56.678s
3	Troy Bayliss (AUS)	12	Ducati	27	47m 02.422s
4	Tohru Ukawa (J)	11	Honda	27	47m 06.531s
5	Alex Barros (BR)	4	Yamaha	27	47m 08.975s
6	Makoto Tamada (J)	6	Honda	27	47m 14.498s
7	John Hopkins (USA)	21	Suzuki	27	47m 21.304s
8	Shinya Nakano (J)	56	Yamaha	27	47m 21.563s
9	Nobuatsu Aoki (J)	9	Proton KR	27	47m 26.347s
10	Olivier Jacque (F)	19	Yamaha	27	47m 27.911s
11	Noriyuki Haga (J)	41	Aprilia	27	47m 34.098s
12	Jeremy McWilliams (GB)	99	Proton KR	27	47m 34.239s
13	Kenny Roberts (USA)	10	Suzuki	27	47m 39.236s
14	Colin Edwards (USA)	45	Aprilia	27	47m 42.473s
15	Andrew Pitt (AUS)	88	Kawasaki	27	47m 58.524s
16	Alex Hofmann (D)	66	Kawasaki	27	47m 58.717s
17	Marco Melandri (I)	33	Yamaha	27	48m 21.355s
18	Garry McCoy (AUS)	8	Kawasaki	26	46m 57.072s
	Loris Capirossi (I)	65	Ducati	12	DNF
	Nicky Hayden (USA)	69	Honda	8	DNF
	Sete Gibernau (E)	15	Honda	6	DNF
	Carlos Checa (E)	7	Yamaha	3	DNF

Fastest lap: Rossi, 1m 42.788s, 96.256 mph/154.909 km/h (record).

Previous record: Valentino Rossi, I (Honda), 1m 42.920s, 96.132 mph/154.710 km/h (2002).

Event best maximum speed: Hayden, 173.7 mph/279.6 km/h (free practice no. 2).

Qualifying: 1 Capirossi, 1m 41.983s; 2 Bayliss, 1m 41.993s; 3 Biaggi, 1m 42.124s; 4 Ukawa, 1m 42.258s; 5 Rossi, 1m 42.276s; 6 Gibernau, 1m 42.285s; 7 Hopkins, 1m 42.579s; 8 Aoki, 1m 42.609s; 9 Jacque, 1m 42.643s; 10 Checa, 1m 42.711s; 11 Edwards, 1m 42.761s; 12 Tamada, 1m 42.827s; 13 Nakano, 1m 42.906s; 14 McWilliams, 1m 42.985s; 15 Barros, 1m 42.988s; 16 Melandri, 1m 43.020s; 17 Roberts, 1m 43.026s; 18 Haga, 1m 43.269s; 19 Hayden, 1m 43.474s; 20 Pitt, 1m 43.889s; 21 Hofmann, 1m 44.702s; 22 McCoy, 1m 44.945s.

Fastest race laps: 1 Rossi, 1m 42.788s; 2 Biaggi, 1m 43.157s; 3 Gibernau, 1m 43.349s; 4 Tamada, 1m 43.509s; 5 Capirossi, 1m 43.575s; 6 Checa, 1m 43.631s; 7 Bayliss, 1m 43.776s; 8 Barros, 1m 43.798s; 9 Melandri, 1m 43.834s; 10 Ukawa, 1m 43.956s; 11 Jacque, 1m 43.984s; 12 Haga, 1m 44.006s; 13 Hopkins, 1m 44.195s; 14 Aoki, 1m 44.201s; 15 Nakano, 1m 44.258s; 16 Hayden, 1m 44.265s; 17 McWilliams, 1m 44.440s; 18 Edwards, 1m 44.451s; 19 Roberts, 1m 44.552s; 20 Pitt, 1m 44.909s; 21 Hofmann, 1m 45.463s; 22 McCoy, 1m 46.489s.

World Championship: 1 Rossi, 70; 2 Biaggi, 56; 3 Bayliss, 40; 4 Gibernau, 38; 5 Barros, 30; 6 Ukawa, 23; 7 Nakano, 20; 8 Hayden, 18; 9 Capirossi, 16; 10 Hopkins, 15; 11 Abe, Checa and Jacque, 13; 14 Edwards and Tamada, 12; 16 Aoki, 11; 17 Haga, 9; 18 Roberts, 6; 19 McWilliams, 4; 20 Pitt, 1.

---

250 cc

26 laps, 71.448 miles/114.998 km

Pos.	Rider (Nat.)	No.	Machine	Laps	Time & speed
1	Toni Elias (E)	24	Aprilia	26	46m 10.793s 92.841 mph/ 149.413 km/h
2	Roberto Rolfo (I)	3	Honda	26	46m 11.314s
3	Randy de Puniet (F)	7	Aprilia	26	46m 11.332s
4	Manuel Poggiali (RSM)	54	Aprilia	26	46m 11.400s
5	Anthony West (AUS)	14	Aprilia	26	46m 22.841s
6	Sebastian Porto (ARG)	5	Honda	26	46m 24.997s
7	Fonsi Nieto (E)	10	Aprilia	26	46m 33.256s
8	Naoki Matsudo (J)	8	Yamaha	26	46m 48.633s
9	Alex Debon (E)	6	Honda	26	46m 53.613s
10	Joan Olive (E)	11	Aprilia	26	46m 59.614s
11	Franco Battaini (I)	21	Aprilia	26	47m 02.978s
12	Alex Baldolini (I)	26	Aprilia	26	47m 05.497s
13	Eric Bataille (F)	34	Honda	26	47m 06.882s
14	Christian Gemmel (D)	15	Honda	26	47m 08.501s
15	Dirk Heidolf (D)	28	Aprilia	26	47m 14.226s
16	Jaroslav Hules (CZ)	13	Yamaha	26	47m 19.737s
17	Jakub Smrz (CZ)	96	Honda	26	47m 28.993s
18	Chaz Davies (GB)	57	Aprilia	26	47m 29.194s
19	Alvaro Molina (E)	40	Aprilia	26	47m 35.991s
20	Henk vd Lagemaat (NL)	18	Honda	25	46m 31.317s
21	Luis Castro (E)	39	Yamaha	25	47m 57.898s
	Johan Stigefelt (S)	16	Aprilia	22	DNF
	Sylvain Guintoli (F)	50	Aprilia	14	DNF
	Hugo Marchand (F)	9	Aprilia	14	DNF
	Hector Faubel (E)	33	Aprilia	5	DNF
	Erwan Nigon (F)	36	Aprilia	2	DNF
	Katja Poensgen (D)	98	Honda		DNQ

Fastest lap: Poggiali, 1m 45.350s, 93.915 mph/151.141 km/h.

Lap record: Daijiro Kato, J (Honda), 1m 44.444s, 94.729 mph/152.452 km/h (2001).

Event best maximum speed: Poggiali, 154.4 mph/248.5 km/h (warm-up).

Qualifying: 1 de Puniet, 1m 44.723s; 2 Poggiali, 1m 44.897s; 3 Battaini, 1m 44.899s; 4 Rolfo, 1m 45.688s; 5 Nieto, 1m 45.836s; 6 Elias, 1m 45.968s; 7 West, 1m 46.119s; 8 Porto, 1m 46.122s; 9 Guintoli, 1m 46.246s; 10 Matsudo, 1m 46.307s; 11 Bataille, 1m 46.364s; 12 Stigefelt, 1m 46.404s; 13 Marchand, 1m 46.586s; 14 Nigon, 1m 46.622s; 15 Gemmel, 1m 46.758s; 16 Debon, 1m 47.021s; 17 Faubel, 1m 47.096s; 18 Davies, 1m 47.358s; 19 Olive, 1m 47.571s; 20 Heidolf, 1m 47.669s; 21 Hules, 1m 48.102s; 22 Smrz, 1m 48.117s; 23 Baldolini, 1m 48.191s; 24 Molina, 1m 48.667s; 25 vd Lagemaat, 1m 49.063s; 26 Castro, 1m 51.459s; 27 Poensgen, 1m 52.287s.

Fastest race laps: 1 Poggiali, 1m 45.350s; 2 de Puniet, 1m 45.573s; 3 Elias, 1m 45.747s; 4 West, 1m 45.916s; 5 Rolfo, 1m 45.934s; 6 Nieto, 1m 45.996s; 7 Battaini, 1m 46.001s; 8 Porto, 1m 46.256s; 9 Matsudo, 1m 46.490s; 10 Bataille, 1m 46.754s; 11 Guintoli, 1m 46.762s; 12 Debon, 1m 47.058s; 13 Stigefelt, 1m 47.067s; 14 Olive, 1m 47.322s; 15 Faubel, 1m 47.430s; 16 Marchand, 1m 47.464s; 17 Baldolini, 1m 47.518s; 18 Gemmel, 1m 48.021s; 19 Heidolf, 1m 48.025s; 20 Hules, 1m 48.212s; 21 Davies, 1m 48.411s; 22 Smrz, 1m 48.557s; 23 Nigon, 1m 48.608s; 24 Molina, 1m 48.697s; 25 vd Lagemaat, 1m 50.191s; 26 Castro, 1m 52.610s.

World Championship: 1 Poggiali, 63; 2 Rolfo, 40; 3 de Puniet and Porto, 36; 5 Elias, 33; 6 Battaini, 32; 7 Nieto, 28; 8 Matsudo, 22; 9 West, 21; 10 Aoyama, 20; 11 Takahashi, 16; 12 Guintoli, 13; 13 Debon, 12; 14 Olive, 9; 15 Baldolini, 8; 16 Kayo, 7; 17 Bataille, 6; 18 Faubel, 5; 19 Nigon and Stigefelt, 4; 21 Gemmel, 2; 22 Davies, Heidolf and Smrz, 1.

---

125 cc

23 laps, 63.204 miles/101.729 km

Pos.	Rider (Nat.)	No.	Machine	Laps	Time & speed
1	Lucio Cecchinello (I)	4	Aprilia	23	41m 52.177s 90.583 mph/ 145.779 km/h
2	Steve Jenkner (D)	17	Aprilia	23	41m 52.265s
3	Alex de Angelis (RSM)	15	Aprilia	23	41m 52.555s
4	Daniel Pedrosa (E)	3	Honda	23	41m 53.562s
5	Stefano Perugini (I)	7	Aprilia	23	41m 53.684s
6	Casey Stoner (AUS)	27	Aprilia	23	42m 03.579s
7	Hector Barbera (E)	80	Aprilia	23	42m 03.673s
8	Youichi Ui (J)	41	Aprilia	23	42m 07.754s
9	Andrea Dovizioso (I)	34	Honda	23	42m 10.781s
10	Mirko Giansanti (I)	6	Aprilia	23	42m 11.074s
11	Masao Azuma (J)	8	Honda	23	42m 15.709s
12	Thomas Luthi (CH)	12	Honda	23	42m 15.777s
13	Gino Borsoi (I)	23	Aprilia	23	42m 15.987s
14	Marco Simoncelli (I)	58	Aprilia	23	42m 16.385s
15	Jorge Lorenzo (E)	48	Derbi	23	42m 17.316s
16	Mika Kallio (SF)	36	Honda	23	42m 17.407s
17	Alvaro Bautista (E)	19	Aprilia	23	42m 19.919s
18	Emilio Alzamora (E)	26	Derbi	23	42m 20.688s
19	Gabor Talmacsi (H)	79	Aprilia	23	42m 21.213s
20	Gioele Pellino (I)	42	Aprilia	23	42m 52.170s
21	Simone Corsi (I)	24	Honda	23	42m 54.676s
22	Arnaud Vincent (F)	1	KTM	23	42m 54.722s
23	Fabrizio Lai (I)	32	Malaguti	23	42m 55.018s
24	Max Sabbatani (I)	11	Aprilia	23	42m 55.223s
25	Sergio Gadea (E)	70	Aprilia	23	43m 03.541s
26	Imre Toth (H)	25	Honda	23	43m 03.630s
27	Ismael Ortega (E)	81	Aprilia	23	43m 03.870s
28	Mike di Meglio (F)	63	Aprilia	23	43m 12.475s
29	Ruben Catalan (E)	71	Aprilia	23	43m 27.052s
30	Leon Camier (GB)	21	Honda	23	43m 27.112s
	Roberto Locatelli (I)	10	KTM	12	DNF
	Pablo Nieto (E)	22	Aprilia	9	DNF
	Stefano Bianco (I)	33	Gilera	3	DNF
	Christopher Martin (GB)	14	Aprilia	1	DNF
	David Bonache (E)	69	TSR	1	DNF
	Julian Simon (E)	31	Malaguti	1	DNF
	Peter Lenart (H)	78	Honda	0	DNF

Fastest lap: Perugini, 1m 47.766s, 91.809 mph/147.753 km/h (record).

Previous record: Masao Azuma, J (Honda), 1m 48.385s, 91.285 mph/146.909 km/h (2001).

Event best maximum speed: Ui, 136.6 mph/219.8 km/h (race).

Qualifying: 1 Nieto, 1m 47.711s; 2 Cecchinello, 1m 48.059s; 3 de Angelis, 1m 48.269s; 4 Pedrosa, 1m 48.319s; 5 Jenkner, 1m 48.482s; 6 Ui, 1m 48.655s; 7 Barbera, 1m 48.904s; 8 Dovizioso, 1m 48.909s; 9 Giansanti, 1m 48.942s; 10 Simoncelli, 1m 49.075s; 11 Stoner, 1m 49.079s; 12 Perugini, 1m 49.082s; 13 Talmacsi, 1m 49.175s; 14 Kallio, 1m 49.267s; 15 Borsoi, 1m 49.279s; 16 Bautista, 1m 49.535s; 17 Azuma, 1m 49.583s; 18 Sabbatani, 1m 49.600s; 19 Vincent, 1m 49.743s; 20 Luthi, 1m 49.756s; 21 Corsi, 1m 49.832s; 22 Lorenzo, 1m 50.017s; 23 Alzamora, 1m 50.071s; 24 Bianco, 1m 50.201s; 25 Pellino, 1m 50.662s; 26 Lai, 1m 50.688s; 27 Martin, 1m 51.001s; 28 Toth, 1m 51.147s; 29 Simon, 1m 51.198s; 30 Locatelli, 1m 51.296s; 31 Ortega, 1m 51.372s; 32 di Meglio, 1m 51.379s; 33 Gadea, 1m 51.854s; 34 Catalan, 1m 53.234s; 35 Bonache, 1m 53.346s; 36 Camier, 1m 53.710s; 37 Lenart, 1m 54.196s.

Fastest race laps: 1 Perugini, 1m 47.766s; 2 Nieto, 1m 48.029s; 3 de Angelis, 1m 48.031s; 4 Pedrosa, 1m 48.062s; 5 Cecchinello, 1m 48.181s; 6 Jenkner, 1m 48.214s; 7 Ui, 1m 48.482s; 8 Stoner, 1m 48.774s; 9 Barbera, 1m 48.840s; 10 Dovizioso, 1m 48.995s; 11 Luthi, 1m 49.044s; 12 Giansanti, 1m 49.061s; 13 Alzamora, 1m 49.109s; 14 Simoncelli, 1m 49.172s; 15 Bautista, 1m 49.194s; 16 Kallio, 1m 49.250s; 17 Borsoi, 1m 49.292s; 18 Lorenzo, 1m 49.300s; 19 Azuma, 1m 49.364s; 20 Talmacsi, 1m 49.779s; 22 Sabbatani, 1m 50.059s; 23 Corsi, 1m 50.295s; 24 Bianco, 1m 50.367s; 25 Vincent, 1m 50.455s; 26 Lai, 1m 50.583s; 27 Gadea, 1m 50.905s; 28 di Meglio, 1m 50.950s; 29 Ortega, 1m 51.066s; 30 Toth, 1m 51.233s; 31 Camier, 1m 51.825s; 32 Locatelli, 1m 51.929s; 33 Catalan, 1m 52.350s; 34 Martin, 2m 03.542s; 35 Bonache, 2m 03.970s; 36 Simon, 2m 04.075s.

World Championship: 1 Jenkner, 52; 2 Cecchinello and Pedrosa, 46; 4 Dovizioso, 38; 5 Perugini, 36; 6 Ui, 31; 7 Giansanti, 27; 8 de Angelis, 26; 9 Nieto, 20; 10 Stoner, 16; 11 Borsoi and Kallio, 14; 13 Azuma and Barbera, 12; 15 Luthi, 11; 16 Corsi, 6; 17 Vincent, 4; 18 Sabbatani, 3; 19 Simoncelli and Talmacsi, 2; 21 Lorenzo and Pellino, 1.

FRENCHGP
LE MANS

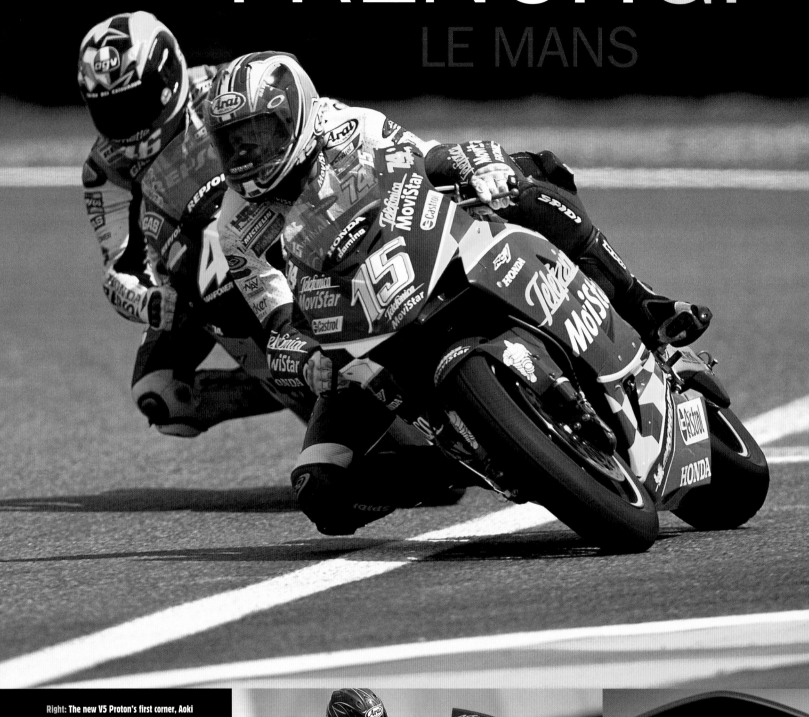

Right: The new V5 Proton's first corner, Aoki feeling his way around.
Photograph: Mark Wernham

Centre right: Kenny Roberts pricks his ears for the distinctive howl – another lap completed.
Photograph: Gold & Goose

Far right: McWilliams ponders the rain. Back on the two-stroke, he equalled the marque's highest ever placing, in sixth.
Photograph: Mark Wernham

Left: Eyes wide open. Again, Gibernau and Rossi were hard at it. Again, Gibernau won.
Photograph: Gold & Goose

Below: Michelin wets – the tyre of choice for the rostrum gang.
Photograph: Mark Wernham

THE 2002 French GP had been cut short by rain and had triggered a major rethink of the rules. There were two main articles of faith: that TV schedules must suffer minimum disruption; and that fans must see the scheduled number of laps. Even if a race was stopped on the penultimate lap, it would restart – although dangerous one-lap wonders were to be avoided with a minimum of three laps for the second leg.

Over the winter, a new system – Race Neutralisation – was devised. If rain struck, a pace car would usher the riders back to the pits, where tyres or even bikes could be changed, then the car would lead them out for two slow laps, in single file in the finishing order of the first race, before pulling off for a 'rolling' restart. A trial run pre-season at Catalunya was predictably rather shambolic, and universally unpopular, not least because of the safety issues involved – tyres and brakes losing temperature as the field trailed the car for the restart. The only advantage seemed to be TV time for BMW cars.

Arguments went back and forth until, at Jerez, it was announced that the system itself was to be neutralised, without ever having been used. Le Mans gave an immediate chance to try the replacement scheme, when rain struck after 15 laps of the 28-lap main event.

The latest plan was actually quite like the old one, in that riders pitted of their own accord when the new neutralisation flag (white with a red cross) was shown, made changes as quickly as possible, then lined up on the grid in the finishing order of the first leg. At Le Mans, this was achieved in well under 30 minutes, and the second sprint race made the waiting worthwhile. It also gave Gibernau the chance to display his full aggression in difficult conditions (something of a hallmark), to justify his factory bike and to vindicate his Jerez blunder, with a second straight defeat of Rossi, which put him equal on victories so far in the season. It was by inches, and the lead had changed hands four times in the last corners alone.

It was certainly a welcome relief from the prospect of a traffic jam of pace car and single-file motor cycles, but there remained one hangover from the aborted plan. It would be fairer, thought some, to award half points for each leg of the race, rather than discounting the first altogether. This would have meant that Rossi's three-second lead in the first leg actually meant something, and would have compensated Ukawa, Haga, Roberts and others whose work during the first period was undone when they gambled on the wrong tyres. But, as Rossi said, 'All the riders agreed. And it was very good for the show.'

The French GP was the 600th in the top class since the first had been won (on the Isle of Man, of course) by Harold Daniell (on a Norton, of course). The changes since then have been comprehensive; the core, thankfully, has remained the same – talented daredevils, intelligent enough to know better, stretching themselves, their equipment and their engineers to ever new limits. Norton are long gone: back then, nobody would have taken seriously the notion that they, along with Velocette and the rest, would be replaced by names like Honda, Yamaha and Suzuki. Ducati are the latest in a line of Italian flames that have burned with blinding brightness at times, and always kept the embers glowing. The last non-Japanese win was by Kocinski's Cagiva, in 1994.

The last British winner was Godfrey Nash's Norton, in 1969. It may be a long time before the next one, but the practice-only debut of the new Proton KR V5 at Le Mans made that at least a possibility.

Strictly speaking, the new bike is international – driven by American Kenny Roberts, funded by Proton in Malaysia. Roberts also hinted that the engine's internal design might owe something to Japan. 'Take one of [Rob] Muzzy's 750 Kawasaki Superbikes, add another cylinder, and that's what we have,' he said. But the conception had taken place in Banbury, at the much extended Team Roberts headquarters, the engine being drawn up by Belfast engineer John Magee, the chassis tailored around it by the team's established engineers. And the original thinking all came from there too.

The biggest impression the new bike made at Le Mans was aural. It differs from Honda's V5 in one crucial aspect. The latter's lack of a balance shaft condemns it to a fixed firing order and intervals. The Proton has a balancer, and engineers can dispose the crankpins more or less as they please. They wouldn't reveal where they were for the first version, but they got the sound right. Even among the louder 2003 bikes, the multi-layered rasping howl stood out.

Whether this was a real or a false dawn chorus remained to be seen. The new V5s ran only in practice and suffered teething troubles, but they were not unimpressive, and in the streaming wet McWilliams was tenth fastest. (He was also fastest on the two-stroke.) The first impression was a great deal better than that of the three-cylinder two-stroke Modenas in 1997 – especially since this new bike had only run in a straight line at airfields until now.

History and mystique aside, Le Mans is a prosaic circuit upon which to race the fastest motor cycles in the world. Sharing only name, (magnificent) pit buildings and a few hundred metres of tarmac with the 24-hour car circuit, the Bugatti short circuit wasn't much admired when new in 1969. And now, like anything left out in the weather for too long, it is showing its age.

The bumps were one thing, and to be fair no worse than at several other tracks. The surface was the real problem. Acceptably grippy over the newer revised sections – from after the pit straight to the exit of the first corner – it went to polished pot for the rest of the lap. Lucio Cecchinello: 'There are even places on the straight where you have to back off to avoid going spinning.' This on a 125!

And then it rained – for almost all of Saturday, and then half-way through the MotoGP race. There were 34 crashes. The worst victim was Hopkins, who (like 125 man de Angelis) fell three times in the weekend, finally in the race, and was lucky that he was only severely bashed about. Several others, including Checa, crashed twice. Conditions notwithstanding, the track needs resurfacing.

The factory Hondas had been given a new nose to the fairing, the earpiece ram-air intakes having been moved inward to become nostrils. Biaggi complained, since he still had the old-style bodywork, both underlining an obvious truth and fulfilling the predictions of Rossi and his camp followers.

How to cut out this incessant grumbling? The shriek of the two-strokes; the orchestral four-strokes? And the intrusive noise of yet another good crowd (75,000 on Sunday), treating their MotoGP fever with plenty of rock music, revving and shouting? The biggest noise came from Kenny's new Proton, the quietest place was his son's new purpose-built motorhome. Forbiddingly charcoal and mounted on a truck chassis, this was totally soundproofed to secure silent slumber in the paddock on race eve. 'I've wanted this for years,' said Junior.

MOTOGP RACE – 13 laps (restarted)

Friday times settled everything when Saturday was drenched. Barros had led, but Rossi blitzed him by almost a second at the end, and the Brazilian fell off trying to match the time. It was still a return to form for the Suzuka injury victim, and for the similarly afflicted Melandri, who was fourth for a first front row, on the far side of Capirossi, the Ducati better after 'we found something' in testing.

Biaggi led row two from Checa and Gibernau, all three of them also crashing in the process.

Had the riders known that the purpose of the first race was only to establish the grid for the second, they might not have made such a go of it. Capirossi led away, Barros taking over before the end of lap one, Rossi passing Abe for third. Over the next laps, Melandri and Biaggi also went by the Japanese wild card; a little way back, Checa had just passed Ukawa for eighth on lap three when he crashed out.

Two more early absentees were Aoki, whose Proton two-stroke seized on lap six, and Bayliss, who crashed out on the same lap; meanwhile, Capirossi dropped back with quick-shifter problems before retiring.

Barros's lead was under severe threat, and sure enough Rossi dived under him at the last corner and began pulling away steadily, three- to five-tenths a lap. Biaggi had closed on Barros too, Gibernau right behind him. Then a charging Ukawa arrived. He was ahead of both and leaning on Barros when the race was stopped.

Haga was sixth, pulling clear of Abe and the fading Melandri, then Nakano, Jacque and a gang led by Roberts, from McWilliams, Edwards and Tamada.

The restart was a total tyre gamble. The track was drying and there were even patches of blue sky at the start line. Tyres went on and off as riders tried to second-guess conditions and each other. Then the warm-up lap revealed that the back of the track was still streaming.

The second race only had ten real participants – the riders on full wet tyres – but it took a lap or two to sort out. Ukawa, Biaggi and Jacque started from the pit lane: the last two had pitted after the warm-up laps to fit wet tyres, Ukawa had pushed off the grid with 'suspension problems'.

Tyres made a huge difference. On the first flying lap, Barros was fastest at 1m 54.947s, while Roberts was slowest on his intermediates at 2m 27.535s. This spaced out the field rather rapidly.

Barros led Gibernau and Rossi away at a demon pace. Haga, heading the rest, was 12.5 seconds adrift after just four laps. Meanwhile, the leading trio gave a display of high-class close racing on a skating-rink surface. Barros led

for eight laps, then both Gibernau and Rossi pushed past. The Yamaha man was a close, but never quite threatening, third from then on.

Gibernau led for two laps, then Rossi took the block-pass inside line at the last corner. Now it was back to business as usual, it seemed. But Gibernau was not for giving up and held on for a stunning last-lap showdown.

Barros closed again as Gibernau tried first one side, then the other to push past Rossi. He succeeded at Museum, the long 180-degree left, but there was no respite. Rossi attacked at the third-from-last corner, diving beneath under braking, only to run wide and let the blue Honda ahead once more. Around the left and into the final right, and Rossi made another dive underneath. But again he ran wide, and Gibernau forced his way back inside. Both drifted to the kerb on the exit, Rossi right on the dirt. As they crossed the line, he was just 0.165 second behind.

Had they taken the first race into account, Rossi's three-second margin would have meant a comfortable win, but he was gracious enough to accept the narrowest of defeats.

Barros was less than two seconds adrift; another 30 seconds down came a good mid-field battle. Haga had lost fourth to McWilliams when Jacque arrived from the back, passing both and moving ahead steadily. Biaggi was also coming through, only slightly slower than the home hero, pushing past Edwards, a happy McCoy enjoying by far his best ride of the season so far, and Haga as the last laps came. He took McWilliams on the final lap and might have had Jacque as well had there been another.

Sixth equalled the Modenas/Proton's best ever finish, in what seemed certain to be the two-stroke triple's last GP. 'It was a horrible race – like riding on marbles. But it was a good way to say goodbye to the two-stroke,' said McWilliams.

Ukawa was close, passing Haga on the last lap, with McCoy adrift at the end, although handsomely ahead of Edwards.

The rest were merely surviving on their treacherous tyres. Abe was a lap down, then came Hayden, who led GP first-timer Kiyonari over the line. It had been an impressive debut for the ex-600 Supersport rider in his first ride on the RCV. Nakano was another lap adrift, with Melandri taking the last point; Roberts was way behind him, the last finisher.

Bayliss, Capirossi, Checa and Aoki had not finished the first leg; Hopkins had been caught out by the notoriously unpredictable Suzuki for a third time and crashed out painfully. Pitt and Tamada also crashed out.

There were winners and losers, but the final verdict was that the neutralisation procedure had been a success, or at least a major improvement over any previous system or any other proposed new scheme.

250 cc RACE – 26 laps

Poggiali's first 250 pole came by less than a tenth from Battaini, with de Puniet barely a hundredth slower. Nieto was only a couple of tenths down, and hopes for better racing in the class after an exciting Jerez seemed well founded. Not for the struggling Katja Poensgen, however, who failed to qualify for a second race in succession.

A close race was to follow – but it was not for first place. That went for a second time in succession to Elias, and by a comfortable margin as Poggiali blundered to his first non-finish of the season.

Elias led away from the second row, shadowed by de Puniet, as Nieto was passed by Porto and then Poggiali. By the fourth lap, to a great cheer, de Puniet had firmly seized the lead and pulled away by almost a second.

On lap six, Poggiali reinforced his reputation for ruthless recklessness when he ran into the back of Porto's Honda, sending them both looping into the gravel. Porto was furious. 'His bike's faster than mine. Why didn't he pass me on the straight?' he fumed. In his defence, Poggiali said that Porto had missed his line, slowed, then cut across in front of him, leaving him nowhere to go.

By now, Nieto was out of touch, while Elias was feeling more comfortable as the tyres started to slide and was beginning to close relentlessly. He caught de Puniet on lap 15 and dived straight underneath him into the first tight corner with a typically aggressive attack, trading paint as they touched. He'd made his point and pulled steadily away to the end. De Puniet had little choice but to settle for second.

Nieto had fallen among fast company, not only Battaini closing and passing, but also his inspired junior team-mate, Guintoli, who was having the race of his life at home. The 20-year-old was promoted to third when Battaini ran off into the dirt, lying almost two seconds ahead of the battling Rolfo, Nieto and Matsudo with ten laps to go. But experience will out: the trio caught up with two laps to go, whereupon the youngster ran wide and all three of them went by at the final corner.

Nieto was in front as they started the last lap, but was forcefully displaced in the final brawl by Rolfo; Matsudo and Guintoli were close.

West had started badly, lacking confidence and dropping to 15th at the end of lap three, but then he picked up the pace and was through to seventh by the end. Debon was five seconds back, narrowly heading Gemmel and Olive.

Davies retired after 22 laps near the back; the remounted Battaini was a distant 18th.

125 cc RACE – 24 laps

Thirty-year-old Ui, second fastest, spoiled an all-teen front rank, Dovizioso being on his first pole, with Lorenzo and Stoner filling the row. Pedrosa was on row two; Jenkner back on the fifth.

Ui led lap one, but Pedrosa took over on the second to pull away at a remarkable rate, anxious to avoid becoming mixed up in the pack. He was more than seven seconds ahead as the finish approached, comfortably able to cruise to a second win of the year by less than three.

A gang of four disputed second, Dovizioso, Cecchinello and de Angelis exchanging blows almost all the way to the finish. Ui had left the party after colliding with hapless British rookie Leon Camier as they lapped him, bending his brake lever.

Cecchinello prevailed on the last lap, with de Angelis crashing out and Dovizioso third.

Stoner led the next group to a career-best fourth, repassing Nieto at the end. Ui was close; Perugini, Jenkner and the impressive young Luthi trailed in at almost equal intervals.

Top: Pedrosa totally dominated the 125s.

Above: Chasing the uncatchable – Dovizioso, de Angelis and Ui pursue the disappearing Pedrosa.

Below: Guintoli (50) was prepared to try adventurous moves in his battle for third place. Here Nieto leads Rolfo and Matsudo around the tight line.

All photographs: Mark Wernham

My blue heaven. Barros takes a champagne shower from double winner Gibernau.
Photograph: Mark Wernham

LE MANS – BUGATTI CIRCUIT

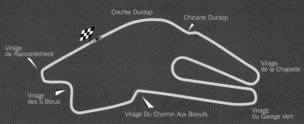

CIRCUIT LENGTH: 2.597 miles/4.180 km

POLINI
FRENCH
grand prix

25 MAY 2003

Photograph: Mark Wernham

MotoGP

13 laps, 33.761 miles/54.340 km

Pos.	Rider (Nat.)	No.	Machine	Laps	Time & speed
1	Sete Gibernau (E)	15	Honda	13	24m 29.665s 82.709 mph/ 133.107 km/h
2	Valentino Rossi (I)	46	Honda	13	24m 29.830s
3	Alex Barros (BR)	4	Yamaha	13	24m 31.458s
4	Olivier Jacque (F)	19	Yamaha	13	24m 59.577s
5	Max Biaggi (I)	3	Honda	13	25m 01.158s
6	Jeremy McWilliams (GB)	99	Proton KR	13	25m 03.611s
7	Tohru Ukawa (J)	11	Honda	13	25m 05.112s
8	Noriyuki Haga (J)	41	Aprilia	13	25m 05.896s
9	Garry McCoy (AUS)	8	Kawasaki	13	25m 20.919s
10	Colin Edwards (USA)	45	Aprilia	13	25m 31.467s
11	Norick Abe (J)	17	Yamaha	12	26m 15.843s
12	Nicky Hayden (USA)	69	Honda	12	26m 26.764s
13	Ryuichi Kiyonari (J)	23	Honda	12	26m 27.017s
14	Shinya Nakano (J)	56	Yamaha	11	25m 45.705s
15	Marco Melandri (I)	33	Yamaha	11	25m 54.740s
16	Kenny Roberts (USA)	10	Suzuki	11	26m 37.515s
	Andrew Pitt (AUS)	88	Kawasaki	3	DNF
	John Hopkins (USA)	21	Suzuki	2	DNF
	Makoto Tamada (J)	6	Honda	1	DNF
	Troy Bayliss (AUS)	12	Ducati		DNS
	Loris Capirossi (I)	65	Ducati		DNS
	Carlos Checa (E)	7	Yamaha		DNS
	Nobuatsu Aoki (J)	9	Proton KR		DNS

Fastest lap: Gibernau, 1m 50.358s, 84.728 mph/136.356 km/h.

Lap record: Valentino Rossi, I (Honda), 1m 36.846s, 96.549 mph/ 155.380 km/h (2002).

Event best maximum speed: Capirossi, 186.5 mph/300.1 km/h (qualifying practice no. 1).

Qualifying: 1 Rossi, 1m 35.208s; 2 Barros, 1m 35.985s; 3 Capirossi, 1m 36.019s; 4 Melandri, 1m 36.161s; 5 Biaggi, 1m 36.169s; 6 Checa, 1m 36.240s; 7 Gibernau, 1m 36.314s; 8 Ukawa, 1m 36.402s; 9 Nakano, 1m 36.512s; 10 Abe, 1m 36.617s; 11 Hopkins, 1m 36.673s; 12 McWilliams, 1m 36.720s; 13 Hayden, 1m 36.773s; 14 Bayliss, 1m 36.782s; 15 Tamada, 1m 36.868s; 16 Jacque, 1m 36.962s; 17 Roberts, 1m 37.033s; 18 Haga, 1m 37.122s; 19 Edwards, 1m 37.239s; 20 Aoki, 1m 37.515s; 21 Pitt, 1m 37.647s; 22 McCoy, 1m 38.956s; 23 Kiyonari, 1m 39.263s.

Fastest race laps: 1 Gibernau, 1m 50.358s; 2 Barros, 1m 50.452s; 3 Rossi, 1m 50.510s; 4 Biaggi, 1m 51.362s; 5 Ukawa, 1m 51.755s; 6 Jacque, 1m 52.727s; 7 Haga, 1m 53.633s; 8 McWilliams, 1m 53.701s; 9 McCoy, 1m 54.808s; 10 Edwards, 1m 55.643s; 11 Kiyonari, 1m 59.266s; 12 Hayden, 1m 59.437s; 13 Abe, 2m 00.420s; 14 Nakano, 2m 07.657s; 15 Melandri, 2m 08.306s; 16 Pitt, 2m 14.753s; 17 Roberts, 2m 18.802s; 18 Hopkins, 2m 20.848s; 19 Tamada, 2m 35.170s.

World Championship: 1 Rossi, 90; 2 Biaggi, 67; 3 Gibernau, 63; 4 Barros, 46; 5 Bayliss, 40; 6 Ukawa, 32; 7 Jacque, 26; 8 Hayden and Nakano, 22; 10 Abe and Edwards, 18; 12 Haga, 17; 13 Capirossi, 16; 14 Hopkins, 15; 15 McWilliams, 14; 16 Checa, 13; 17 Tamada, 12; 18 Aoki, 11; 19 McCoy, 7; 20 Roberts, 6; 21 Kiyonari, 3; 22 Melandri and Pitt, 1.

---

250 cc

26 laps, 67.522 miles/108.680 km

Pos.	Rider (Nat.)	No.	Machine	Laps	Time & speed
1	Toni Elias (E)	24	Aprilia	26	43m 55.538s 92.243 mph/ 148.450 km/h
2	Randy de Puniet (F)	7	Aprilia	26	43m 59.278s
3	Roberto Rolfo (I)	3	Honda	26	44m 00.100s
4	Fonsi Nieto (E)	10	Aprilia	26	44m 00.510s
5	Naoki Matsudo (J)	8	Yamaha	26	44m 00.660s
6	Sylvain Guintoli (F)	50	Aprilia	26	44m 01.638s
7	Anthony West (AUS)	14	Aprilia	26	44m 25.210s
8	Alex Debon (E)	6	Honda	26	44m 30.423s
9	Christian Gemmel (D)	15	Honda	26	44m 30.551s
10	Joan Olive (E)	11	Aprilia	26	44m 31.097s
11	Hector Faubel (E)	33	Aprilia	26	44m 41.100s
12	Johan Stigefelt (S)	16	Aprilia	26	44m 50.493s
13	Alex Baldolini (I)	26	Aprilia	26	44m 50.587s
14	Hugo Marchand (F)	9	Aprilia	26	44m 51.332s
15	Eric Bataille (F)	34	Honda	26	44m 51.721s
16	Jaroslav Hules (CZ)	13	Yamaha	26	44m 52.924s
17	Erwan Nigon (F)	36	Aprilia	26	45m 22.889s
18	Franco Battaini (I)	21	Aprilia	26	45m 32.135s
19	Jakub Smrz (CZ)	96	Honda	25	44m 17.899s
20	Henk vd Lagemaat (NL)	18	Honda	25	44m 17.956s
	Chaz Davies (GB)	57	Aprilia	22	DNF
	Dirk Heidolf (D)	28	Aprilia	9	DNF
	Sebastian Porto (ARG)	5	Honda	5	DNF
	Manuel Poggiali (RSM)	54	Aprilia	5	DNF
	Samuel Aubry (F)	45	Honda	2	DNF
	Vincent Eisen (F)	44	Honda		DNQ
	Katja Poensgen (D)	98	Honda		DNQ

Fastest lap: de Puniet, 1m 40.356s, 93.172 mph/149.946 km/h.

Lap record: Marco Melandri, I (Aprilia), 1m 39.648s, 93.834 mph/ 151.011 km/h (2002).

Event best maximum speed: Poggiali, 159.3 mph/256.4 km/h (qualifying practice no. 1).

Qualifying: 1 Poggiali, 1m 39.229s; 2 Battaini, 1m 39.324s; 3 de Puniet, 1m 39.341s; 4 Nieto, 1m 39.570s; 5 Elias, 1m 39.802s; 6 Porto, 1m 39.936s; 7 Guintoli, 1m 40.835s; 8 Matsudo, 1m 40.948s; 9 Rolfo, 1m 41.073s; 10 West, 1m 41.168s; 11 Nigon, 1m 41.275s; 12 Marchand, 1m 41.447s; 13 Olive, 1m 41.609s; 14 Stigefelt, 1m 41.642s; 15 Faubel, 1m 41.767s; 16 Davies, 1m 41.890s; 17 Debon, 1m 41.934s; 18 Bataille, 1m 41.942s; 19 Heidolf, 1m 41.980s; 20 Smrz, 1m 42.109s; 21 Hules, 1m 42.295s; 22 Gemmel, 1m 42.355s; 23 Baldolini, 1m 42.827s; 24 vd Lagemaat, 1m 44.180s; 25 Aubry, 1m 45.613s; 26 Eisen, 1m 46.396s; 27 Poensgen, 1m 46.421s.

Fastest race laps: 1 de Puniet, 1m 40.356s; 2 Elias, 1m 40.483s; 3 Rolfo, 1m 40.556s; 4 Battaini, 1m 40.666s; 5 Matsudo, 1m 40.713s; 6 Guintoli, 1m 40.746s; 7 Nieto, 1m 40.796s; 8 Poggiali, 1m 40.986s; 9 West, 1m 41.140s; 10 Porto, 1m 41.181s; 11 Debon, 1m 41.569s; 12 Gemmel, 1m 41.594s; 13 Nigon, 1m 41.963s; 14 Olive, 1m 41.999s; 15 Faubel, 1m 42.087s; 16 Stigefelt, 1m 42.266s; 17 Baldolini, 1m 42.278s; 18 Bataille, 1m 42.372s; 19 Marchand, 1m 42.381s; 20 Davies, 1m 42.575s; 21 Hules, 1m 42.645s; 22 Smrz, 1m 44.475s; 23 Heidolf, 1m 44.593s; 24 vd Lagemaat, 1m 44.866s; 25 Aubry, 1m 56.871s.

World Championship: 1 Poggiali, 63; 2 Elias, 58; 3 de Puniet and Rolfo, 56; 5 Nieto, 41; 6 Porto, 36; 7 Matsudo, 33; 8 Battaini, 32; 9 West, 30; 10 Guintoli, 23; 11 Aoyama and Debon, 20; 13 Takahashi, 16; 14 Olive, 15; 15 Baldolini, 11; 16 Faubel, 10; 17 Gemmel, 9; 18 Stigefelt, 8; 19 Bataille and Kayo, 7; 21 Nigon, 4; 22 Marchand, 2; 23 Davies, Heidolf and Smrz, 1.

---

125 cc

24 laps, 62.328 miles/100.320 km

Pos.	Rider (Nat.)	No.	Machine	Laps	Time & speed
1	Daniel Pedrosa (E)	3	Honda	24	41m 58.500s 89.014 mph/ 143.399 km/h
2	Lucio Cecchinello (I)	4	Aprilia	24	42m 00.837s
3	Andrea Dovizioso (I)	34	Honda	24	42m 00.927s
4	Casey Stoner (AUS)	27	Aprilia	24	42m 09.778s
5	Pablo Nieto (E)	22	Aprilia	24	42m 10.314s
6	Youichi Ui (J)	41	Aprilia	24	42m 11.092s
7	Stefano Perugini (I)	7	Aprilia	24	42m 17.430s
8	Steve Jenkner (D)	17	Aprilia	24	42m 23.706s
9	Thomas Luthi (CH)	12	Honda	24	42m 27.971s
10	Masao Azuma (J)	8	Honda	24	42m 32.410s
11	Hector Barbera (E)	80	Aprilia	24	42m 42.879s
12	Mirko Giansanti (I)	6	Aprilia	24	42m 43.037s
13	Gino Borsoi (I)	23	Aprilia	24	42m 53.718s
14	Simone Corsi (I)	24	Honda	24	42m 57.273s
15	Roberto Locatelli (I)	10	KTM	24	42m 57.462s
16	Gabor Talmacsi (H)	79	Aprilia	24	43m 06.303s
17	Mike di Meglio (F)	63	Aprilia	24	43m 16.104s
18	Max Sabbatani (I)	11	Aprilia	24	43m 18.640s
19	Emilio Alzamora (E)	26	Derbi	24	43m 39.257s
20	Julian Simon (E)	31	Malaguti	24	43m 42.408s
21	Christopher Martin (GB)	14	Aprilia	24	43m 48.278s
22	Peter Lenart (H)	78	Honda	23	42m 14.304s
23	Imre Toth (H)	25	Honda	23	42m 14.558s
24	Leon Camier (GB)	21	Honda	23	42m 27.843s
25	Jimmy Petit (F)	74	Honda	23	43m 08.123s
	Alex de Angelis (RSM)	15	Aprilia	23	DNF
	Fabrizio Lai (I)	32	Malaguti	18	DNF
	Alvaro Bautista (E)	19	Aprilia	16	DNF
	William Gautier (F)	73	Honda	13	DNF
	Gregory Lefort (F)	86	Aprilia	11	DNF
	Xavier Herouin (F)	85	Honda	10	DNF
	Alexis Masbou (F)	72	Honda	9	DNF
	Marco Simoncelli (I)	58	Aprilia	4	DNF
	Gioele Pellino (I)	42	Aprilia	3	DNF
	Arnaud Vincent (F)	1	KTM	0	DNF
	Mika Kallio (SF)	36	Honda	0	DNF
	Jorge Lorenzo (E)	48	Derbi	0	DNF
	Stefano Bianco (I)	33	Gilera		DNS

Fastest lap: Pedrosa, 1m 43.837s, 90.048 mph/144.919 km/h (record).

Previous record: Masao Azuma, J (Honda), 1m 44.259s, 89.684 mph/ 144.332 km/h (2002).

Event best maximum speed: Pedrosa, 135.9 mph/218.8 km/h (qualifying practice no. 1).

Qualifying: 1 Dovizioso, 1m 43.565s; 2 Ui, 1m 43.743s; 3 Lorenzo, 1m 43.947s; 4 Stoner, 1m 44.203s; 5 de Angelis, 1m 44.315s; 6 Pedrosa, 1m 44.437s; 7 Cecchinello, 1m 44.510s; 8 Vincent, 1m 44.522s; 9 Barbera, 1m 44.570s; 10 Luthi, 1m 44.638s; 11 Bianco, 1m 44.883s; 12 Giansanti, 1m 44.891s; 13 Borsoi, 1m 44.945s; 14 Kallio, 1m 44.963s; 15 Azuma, 1m 45.031s; 16 Perugini, 1m 45.326s; 17 Talmacsi, 1m 45.480s; 18 Nieto, 1m 45.541s; 19 Jenkner, 1m 45.554s; 20 Corsi, 1m 45.576s; 21 Sabbatani, 1m 45.700s; 22 Alzamora, 1m 46.007s; 23 Lai, 1m 46.229s; 24 Bautista, 1m 46.363s; 25 Pellino, 1m 46.503s; 26 Simoncelli, 1m 46.624s; 27 Simon, 1m 46.929s; 28 di Meglio, 1m 46.973s; 29 Locatelli, 1m 46.994s; 30 Masbou, 1m 47.588s; 31 Petit, 1m 47.616s; 32 Toth, 1m 47.709s; 33 Gautier, 1m 48.321s; 34 Martin, 1m 48.478s; 35 Lefort, 1m 48.500s; 36 Lenart, 1m 49.165s; 37 Herouin, 1m 49.522s; 38 Camier, 1m 50.678s.

Fastest race laps: 1 Pedrosa, 1m 43.837s; 2 Dovizioso, 1m 44.085s; 3 de Angelis, 1m 44.102s; 4 Cecchinello, 1m 44.164s; 5 Ui, 1m 44.290s; 6 Nieto, 1m 44.438s; 7 Perugini, 1m 44.560s; 8 Stoner, 1m 44.628s; 9 Jenkner, 1m 44.777s; 10 Azuma, 1m 44.834s; 11 Luthi, 1m 45.051s; 12 Barbera, 1m 45.190s; 13 Bautista, 1m 45.475s; 14 Borsoi, 1m 45.491s; 15 Giansanti, 1m 45.622s; 16 Corsi, 1m 45.810s; 17 Locatelli, 1m 45.856s; 18 di Meglio, 1m 46.462s; 19 Sabbatani, 1m 46.467s; 20 Talmacsi, 1m 46.795s; 21 Lai, 1m 47.080s; 22 Toth, 1m 47.642s; 23 Alzamora, 1m 47.687s; 24 Lenart, 1m 47.842s; 25 Simon, 1m 47.979s; 26 Pellino, 1m 47.997s; 27 Martin, 1m 48.256s; 28 Simoncelli, 1m 48.306s; 29 Masbou, 1m 48.576s; 30 Camier, 1m 48.952s; 31 Lefort, 1m 49.107s; 32 Gautier, 1m 49.208s; 33 Petit, 1m 49.463s; 34 Herouin, 1m 51.291s.

World Championship: 1 Pedrosa, 71; 2 Cecchinello, 66; 3 Jenkner, 60; 4 Dovizioso, 54; 5 Perugini, 45; 6 Ui, 41; 7 Giansanti and Nieto, 31; 9 Stoner, 29; 10 de Angelis, 26; 11 Azuma and Luthi, 18; 13 Barbera and Borsoi, 17; 15 Kallio, 14; 16 Corsi, 8; 17 Vincent, 4; 18 Sabbatani, 3; 19 Simoncelli and Talmacsi, 2; 21 Locatelli, Lorenzo and Pellino, 1.

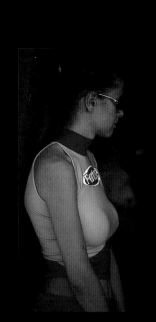

FIM WORLD CHAMPIONSHIP • ROUND 5

ITALIANGP
MUGELLO

IN 2002, Mugello joined the 200-mph club. Previously only recorded at the now defunct Hockenheimring, the speed went first to Laconi's Aprilia, before Ukawa's Honda went even faster in the race.

This year, the fastest track of the year was a measure of real progress in the MotoGP bikes – at least in the brute-force department. If you weren't clocking more than 200 mph (321.8688 km/h in MotoGP speak), you were hanging around in the kitchen rather than joining in the party. Fifteen of 23 entries broke the barrier; the Hondas of Tamada and Gibernau were just a shade too slow, likewise Roberts's Suzuki and all three Kawasakis (Hofmann was back for another race). The all-new Protons were almost 20 mph slower.

Fittingly, in the heartland of their much vaunted Passion (not to mention at their major test track, with many laps completed), the Ducatis led the way and set the pace. In the end, though, the big prizes remained just out of their reach, but it was a triumphant home debut for the five-race-old Desmosedicis. The highest speed of the weekend was recorded by Capirossi, who exceeded his practice record in the race with an ungodly 206.54 mph (332.4 km/h).

Fears that the big bikes might become dangerously unwieldy as they lofted the front wheel over the hump at the end of Mugello's long and undulating straight proved groundless – narrowly. But it was an exciting place to go and hang over the rail all the same, to watch the different ways the riders, as well as the engine-management systems, dealt with the problem of having to shed not only much of that speed, but also three gears at the same time, without locking the rear wheel. There are many ways to skin a cat, and not all of them reliable.

The progress in speed must have come from engine power rather than aerodynamics, judging from several retrograde steps in the airflow management business. The rows of small holes in the fairing nose had not entirely solved the Ducati's heat problems, as a sweltering European summer gathered momentum. For this race, the front mudguard had been ditched, as had that of the Proton, which had been specially designed for better penetration at the same time as improving flow to the radiators. Aerodynamicists were confused when both bikes ran cooler without it as temperatures soared to 34 degrees C on race day, the track surface a baking 47 degrees C.

Not much cooler, however, and the heat was very punishing for the Proton's first full race, an infant bike already suffering teething troubles after completing only one full day of testing after Le Mans. Now it added colic to its ailments, to be followed by fits of projectile vomiting. The colic related to fuel delivery, mainly blamed on pumps that couldn't stand the heat, and was bad enough in Aoki's case to keep him in the pits for more time than he was out. Both riders were short of gearing choices, the requisite sets simply not having been made in time, which, along with the modest power levels, contributed to the relatively low top speed. Neither bike made the finish. That said, McWilliams had qualified in front of two out of three Kawasakis and had been eyeing the points when he retired. Perhaps it wasn't a dream race debut, but as a second shake-down test, it was mighty impressive.

Rossi was in bad odour for his home GP – with officialdom, because he had been the one noticeable absentee at a special meeting with the Italian president, during a gala evening attended by such luminaries as Agostini and Ubbiali as well as the full panoply of modern riders; and with HRC, because he had gone public as he opened negotiations for 2004's contract, and it had leaked out that he was asking for an unprecedented eight million euros. HRC president Suguru Kanezawa was on hand and said, with a smile, 'It's too much.' A battle of wills was getting under way.

But the smell hadn't affected Rossi's popularity, which had far outstripped that of Capirossi and Biaggi, in spite of a groundswell of Ducati fervour for the former. Valentino's army packed the hillsides, but any potential repeat of last year's track invasion was forestalled when the MotoGP bikes cut straight back to the pits from the end of the finish straight. A notable police and security presence kept unusual order at an event that had become explosive, and for the first time in years the engine-revving contests from opposite sides of the valley were banned.

WCM went through their ritual disqualification, while the Desmosedici two-seater made its first appearance. One of Randy Mamola's first passengers was a beaming Luca Cadalora, who said, 'That was great. You need to place total trust in the rider, which was difficult, because it was Randy.'

Suzuki had a dreadful weekend, their bike's erratic engine management playing the nastiest of tricks on the smooth and rhythmical one-gear to-and-fro track. 'You never know what will happen when you close the throttle,' said Roberts. Smarting under criticism for his obvious unwillingness to take risks, and even less happy at being outqualified and outridden by his gung-ho new team-mate, Hopkins, he decided to throw caution to the wind. Battling to stay in the top 15 on the third lap, he was behind Hopkins, and both had just been passed by Edwards's Aprilia.

'I had speed over John and I wanted to stay with Colin,' recalled Roberts. He got a better exit from the previous bend, but 'as I shifted from third to second, the bike immediately went sideways like I had the back brake on.' Fighting to regain control, he flew straight into the side of his team-mate, putting both bikes out of the race, and himself out for the next three.

A cameo in the pit building, as practice began, provided a reminder of just how young you can be to race for world championships on the same tracks and even at the same time as the big boys. Welsh teenager Chaz Davies was in his second year as a world travelling GP racer, but he had to miss practice to finish off the GCSE exams he'd been taking under Italian invigilation all week. Sadly, he was without essential maps of Wales and feared that he hadn't done well in geography. If only they'd asked questions about Jacarepagua and Motegi instead...

Above: A Japanese affair in Italy: an on-form Nakano leads hard charging Tamada and Ukawa.
Photograph: Mark Wernham

Top right: Tamada took fourth, his best so far.

Centre right: Melandri was trying to make up for lost time – here with veteran race engineer Fiorenzo Fanali (right).

Right: Unholy trinity: the Italians disputing the lead gave their fans good value. Here Capirossi holds off Biaggi and Rossi.
Photographs: Gold & Goose

MOTOGP RACE – 23 laps

This was the Very Italian Grand Prix. The top three riders of that nation fought hard and fiercely. And one of the motor cycles, a candidate for victory from start to finish, was an all-red Ducati Desmosedici.

In qualifying, Capirossi had set a blistering top-speed target and was sitting on pole position. Until Rossi's final charge, a single lap with 'only a few mistakes' and faster than Loris by three-hundredths of a second. Nakano found the rhythm to be best Yamaha, nudging the third Italian, Biaggi, to the far end of the front row. The Japanese rider would remain close all weekend, but was not quite in the same frame.

The race started in blistering heat, Capirossi leading the explosion of sound (enriched now by the distinctive Proton wail) down the straight and into the first looping corner. Biaggi was second, then Nakano, Rossi, Gibernau...

By lap three, Nakano had taken second from Biaggi for a short run, while Gibernau had been joined by Checa and was pressing Rossi. Not far behind, another Yamaha – but Melandri was losing touch, with an erratic clutch, soon to be passed by Bayliss on the second Duke.

This was a crucial lap in the top-ten scramble. Barros had cause to regret his front tyre choice after being the first to crash out. Later on the same lap, the Suzukis collided, a blue-on-blue disaster. Bayliss lasted a while longer, up to sixth before his pace proved too ambitious.

Two laps later, leader Capirossi ran wide, the Ducati using lots of track as it slewed under braking and slithered under power. This let Biaggi through, but Capirossi held Rossi back for a couple more corners before the Honda's neater cornering allowed Rossi to slip past. Nakano couldn't follow, however, and was soon to lose touch as the Ducati stayed close and threatening while Rossi started to push and probe at Biaggi, to the delight of whole hillsides of fans.

The leading trio stretched away, then on lap 13 Rossi finally made his move under braking for the first corner to slip to the front. Capirossi then set about Biaggi, the pair bashing together at the top of the hill, giving Valentino a little more space. Four laps later, his lead was almost two seconds, while the other pair went back and forth, the battle being resolved in the Ducati's favour when Biaggi narrowly saved a costly front-wheel slide.

With six laps left, Capirossi shaved away at the gap, closing to within 1.4 seconds at the finish.

The battle for fourth was engaging, Nakano holding Gibernau at bay, with Ukawa closing up on the fading Checa. The fastest mover was Tamada, up from 18th on lap one. Later, he said, 'There were no tactics, but lots of overtaking.' His Bridgestones showed well in the hot conditions, and he went all the way with Ukawa as the factory rider closed on and overtook Gibernau. All three Hondas were jostling Nakano, heading for a last-lap battle of closely matched riders on closely matched bikes. Just like 125s. And Tamada, aggressive in a company of hard men, won the brawl from Nakano, Ukawa and Gibernau, all covered by one second.

Checa was a lonely eight seconds adrift by the end, well clear of Edwards and the ill-handling Aprilia (Haga had lost his personal battle, crashing out early on). Then came Jacque and Melandri, close, but far away, while Hayden was another ten seconds farther back, never at ease with the front-wheel wash-away feeling of this difficult track. Kiyonari, in his second race since jumping off a 600 Supersport machine, was closing on the American at the finish.

Hofmann was top Kawasaki again, with McCoy fighting his different chassis into the turns and 30 seconds back for the final point. He only got that after McWilliams had pulled out with five laps of the Proton's first GP remaining, succumbing to fuel supply problems that had already sidelined Aoki. Pitt was another 14 seconds adrift, the last finisher.

Rossi's third win in five races was a typical master-stroke – but it would be his last for a while.

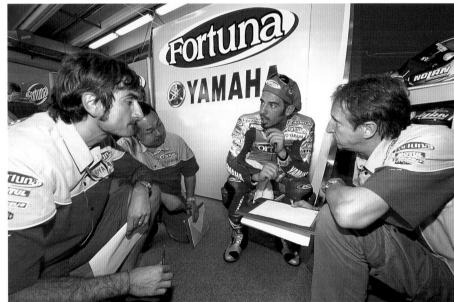

250 cc RACE – 20 laps (shortened)

A start-line shambles as Nieto stalled on the front row; the lights hadn't gone yet, but in the confusion some of the riders behind took off at full speed. Luckily, there were no collisions.

The race was shortened by a lap and restarted forthwith; Elias jumped into the lead from the second row, but Poggiali took over firmly before the end of the lap. Pole-starter de Puniet chased hard, and Nieto closed for the first five or six laps, before dropping away again once tyre wear started to tell.

De Puniet battled on until after half-distance, never far from Poggiali and frequently trying to attack. Then it all went wrong, the front tucking under as the track climbed the hill for the first time. He scrambled back on board, now mixed up in an almost race-long scrap for third between Battaini, Rolfo and Guintoli.

It took the Frenchman two laps to get to the front of this gang, Rolfo dropping to the back with a phenomenal save. With the lone Nieto less than four seconds in front and four laps to go, de Puniet had a slender hope of catching him. Enough to tempt him to a second crash, this time damaging his bike too badly to continue.

Battaini was closing on Nieto by the finish, Rolfo chasing hard, Guintoli dropping back. With Poggiali a massive 22 seconds clear, it had been a rather processional race. And rather slow: de Puniet's fastest lap was half a second short of Nakano's from 2000.

Sixth-placed Elias, who had crashed heavily in practice, had dropped quickly out of contention with handling problems, to be passed by Porto, before the Argentine also ran into trouble, falling back again to be nabbed by Matsudo at the finish. West had been ahead of the Japanese Yamaha rider, but couldn't stay with him once the order had been reversed. Olive was a distant tenth.

Chaz Davies avenged his geography teacher with his best result so far, 13th and three points. The misfortunate Katja Poensgen had failed to qualify for a third race in succession. Baldolini and Nigon crashed out, the latter rejoining; Stigefelt broke down on the first lap.

125 cc RACE – 20 laps

For a second year in succession, Mugello brought heartbreak and fractures to hard charging Australian teenager Casey Stoner. He had claimed a first ever pole position and was well up in the ten-strong battle for the lead, with quarter of a lap to go, when disaster struck. This time, he'd done nothing wrong, except to be in the way when Steve Jenkner crashed and slid straight into him.

It was a typically epic race, Cecchinello taking over from Stoner on lap two to do most of the leading. Perugini challenged, Pablo Nieto actually took over for more than a lap, Pedrosa carefully held his place in the group. Seven were still together on the last lap, reduced to five when Jenkner skittled Casey; and Cecchinello retained enough of an advantage to win his second GP of the year by seven-tenths.

Pedrosa's tactics netted him second when it mattered, with Nieto third and Dovizioso a close fourth. De Angelis had lost a little ground by the finish.

A surging last few laps put Ui up to sixth, narrowly ahead of Perugini and Borsoi, while Barbera led the next trio a long way back.

Briton Chris Martin retired from what would prove to be his last race for the Seedorf team; Leon Camier soldiered on second from last and a lap down.

Above: De Puniet and Poggiali battle for control of the first half of the race. The chasing Frenchman then crashed, twice.

Right: Poggiali took a third win in five races.

Below: Casey Stoner driving the train. Pablo Nieto leads the hot pursuit.
All photographs: Mark Wernham

AUTODROMO INTERNAZIONALE
DEL MUGELLO

CINZANO
ITALIAN
grand prix

8 JUNE 2003

Photograph: Mark Wernham

CIRCUIT LENGTH: 3.259 miles/5.245 km

MotoGP

23 laps, 74.957 miles/120.635 km

Pos.	Rider (Nat.)	No.	Machine	Laps	Time & speed
1	Valentino Rossi (I)	46	Honda	23	43m 28.008s 103.471 mph/ 166.520 km/h
2	Loris Capirossi (I)	65	Ducati	23	43m 29.424s
3	Max Biaggi (I)	3	Honda	23	43m 32.584s
4	Makoto Tamada (J)	6	Honda	23	43m 41.218s
5	Shinya Nakano (J)	56	Yamaha	23	43m 41.419s
6	Tohru Ukawa (J)	11	Honda	23	43m 41.674s
7	Sete Gibernau (E)	15	Honda	23	43m 42.261s
8	Carlos Checa (E)	7	Yamaha	23	43m 50.819s
9	Colin Edwards (USA)	45	Aprilia	23	44m 01.064s
10	Olivier Jacque (F)	19	Yamaha	23	44m 06.890s
11	Marco Melandri (I)	33	Yamaha	23	44m 06.985s
12	Nicky Hayden (USA)	69	Honda	23	44m 16.647s
13	Ryuichi Kiyonari (J)	23	Honda	23	44m 18.191s
14	Alex Hofmann (D)	66	Kawasaki	23	44m 22.221s
15	Garry McCoy (AUS)	8	Kawasaki	23	44m 51.289s
16	Andrew Pitt (AUS)	88	Kawasaki	23	45m 05.292s
	Jeremy McWilliams	99	Proton KR	18	DNF
	Nobuatsu Aoki (J)	9	Proton KR	14	DNF
	Troy Bayliss (AUS)	12	Ducati	10	DNF
	Noriyuki Haga (J)	41	Aprilia	7	DNF
	Alex Barros (BR)	4	Yamaha	2	DNF
	John Hopkins (USA)	21	Suzuki	2	DNF
	Kenny Roberts (USA)	10	Suzuki	2	DNF

Fastest lap: Capirossi, 1m 52.623s, 104.177 mph/167.656 km/h.

Lap record: Tohru Ukawa, J (Honda), 1m 52.601s, 104.197 mph/ 167.689 km/h (2002).

Event best maximum speed: Capirossi, 206.5 mph/332.4 km/h (race).

Qualifying: 1 Rossi, 1m 51.927s; 2 Capirossi, 1m 51.954s; 3 Nakano, 1m 51.986s; 4 Biaggi, 1m 52.021s; 5 Ukawa, 1m 52.027s; 6 Gibernau, 1m 52.153s; 7 Checa, 1m 52.290s; 8 Jacque, 1m 52.333s; 9 Barros, 1m 52.439s; 10 Tamada, 1m 52.513s; 11 Bayliss, 1m 52.644s; 12 Melandri, 1m 52.687s; 13 Edwards, 1m 52.767s; 14 Hopkins, 1m 52.969s; 15 Hofmann, 1m 53.146s; 16 Haga, 1m 53.149s; 17 Hayden, 1m 53.190s; 18 Roberts, 1m 53.399s; 19 McWilliams, 1m 53.813s; 20 McCoy, 1m 54.052s; 21 Pitt, 1m 54.345s; 22 Kiyonari, 1m 55.315s; 23 Aoki, 1m 56.394s.

Fastest race laps: 1 Capirossi, 1m 52.623s; 2 Rossi, 1m 52.700s; 3 Tamada, 1m 52.779s; 4 Biaggi, 1m 52.836s; 5 Checa, 1m 52.840s; 6 Ukawa, 1m 52.915s; 7 Bayliss, 1m 53.022s; 8 Gibernau, 1m 53.054s; 9 Nakano, 1m 53.104s; 10 Jacque, 1m 53.329s; 11 Edwards, 1m 53.355s; 12 Barros, 1m 53.397s; 13 Melandri, 1m 53.502s; 14 Haga, 1m 53.775s; 15 Hofmann, 1m 54.314s; 16 Kiyonari, 1m 54.398s; 17 Hayden, 1m 54.432s; 18 Roberts, 1m 54.502s; 19 Hopkins, 1m 54.626s; 20 McWilliams, 1m 55.325s; 21 McCoy, 1m 55.335s; 22 Pitt, 1m 56.021s; 23 Aoki, 1m 56.550s.

World Championship: 1 Rossi, 115; 2 Biaggi, 83; 3 Gibernau, 72; 4 Barros, 46; 5 Ukawa, 42; 6 Bayliss, 40; 7 Capirossi, 36; 8 Nakano, 33; 9 Jacque, 32; 10 Hayden, 26; 11 Edwards and Tamada, 25; 13 Checa, 21; 14 Abe, 18; 15 Haga, 17; 16 Hopkins, 15; 17 McWilliams, 14; 18 Aoki, 11; 19 McCoy, 8; 20 Kiyonari, Melandri and Roberts, 6; 23 Hofmann, 2; 24 Pitt, 1.

250 cc

20 laps, 65.180 miles/104.900 km

Pos.	Rider (Nat.)	No.	Machine	Laps	Time & speed
1	Manuel Poggiali (RSM)	54	Aprilia	20	38m 40.038s 101.142 mph/ 162.773 km/h
2	Fonsi Nieto (E)	10	Aprilia	20	39m 02.483s
3	Franco Battaini (I)	21	Aprilia	20	39m 03.484s
4	Roberto Rolfo (I)	3	Honda	20	39m 04.470s
5	Sylvain Guintoli (F)	50	Aprilia	20	39m 11.717s
6	Toni Elias (E)	24	Aprilia	20	39m 19.875s
7	Naoki Matsudo (J)	8	Yamaha	20	39m 24.870s
8	Sebastian Porto (ARG)	5	Honda	20	39m 24.943s
9	Anthony West (AUS)	14	Aprilia	20	39m 42.423s
10	Joan Olive (E)	11	Aprilia	20	39m 46.058s
11	Hugo Marchand (F)	9	Aprilia	20	39m 51.235s
12	Alex Debon (E)	6	Honda	20	39m 51.295s
13	Chaz Davies (GB)	57	Aprilia	20	39m 58.002s
14	Jakub Smrz (CZ)	96	Aprilia	20	40m 01.611s
15	Hector Faubel (E)	33	Aprilia	20	40m 05.332s
16	Christian Gemmel (D)	15	Honda	20	40m 06.818s
17	Erwan Nigon (F)	36	Aprilia	20	40m 15.244s
18	Henk vd Lagemaat (NL)	18	Honda	19	39m 00.258s
19	Christian Pistoni (I)	29	Aprilia	19	39m 11.496s
	Randy de Puniet (F)	7	Aprilia	16	DNF
	Alex Baldolini (I)	26	Aprilia	10	DNF
	Johan Stigefelt (S)	16	Aprilia	0	DNF
	Eric Bataille (F)	34	Honda		DNS
	Jaroslav Hules (CZ)	13	Yamaha		DNS
	Katja Poensgen (D)	98	Honda		DNQ

Fastest lap: de Puniet, 1m 54.994s, 102.029 mph/164.199 km/h.

Lap record: Shinya Nakano, J (Yamaha), 1m 54.462s, 102.503 mph/ 164.963 km/h (2000).

Event best maximum speed: Poggiali, 170.0 mph/273.6 km/h (qualifying practice no. 2).

Qualifying: 1 de Puniet, 1m 53.586s; 2 Poggiali, 1m 53.832s; 3 Nieto, 1m 54.676s; 4 Battaini, 1m 54.984s; 5 Elias, 1m 55.639s; 6 Rolfo, 1m 55.969s; 7 Porto, 1m 56.163s; 8 Guintoli, 1m 56.452s; 9 Matsudo, 1m 56.585s; 10 Nigon, 1m 56.939s; 11 Stigefelt, 1m 57.112s; 12 Olive, 1m 57.117s; 13 West, 1m 57.252s; 14 Faubel, 1m 57.352s; 15 Debon, 1m 57.646s; 16 Marchand, 1m 57.657s; 17 Davies, 1m 58.225s; 18 Gemmel, 1m 58.576s; 19 Bataille, 1m 58.582s; 20 Baldolini, 1m 58.677s; 21 Smrz, 1m 59.503s; 22 Hules, 2m 00.025s; 23 vd Lagemaat, 2m 01.161s; 24 Pistoni, 2m 01.203s; 25 Poensgen, 2m 03.163s.

Fastest race laps: 1 de Puniet, 1m 54.994s; 2 Poggiali, 1m 55.048s; 3 Nieto, 1m 55.268s; 4 Rolfo, 1m 56.062s; 5 Battaini, 1m 56.150s; 6 Guintoli, 1m 56.264s; 7 Elias, 1m 56.681s; 8 Porto, 1m 57.006s; 9 Matsudo, 1m 57.321s; 10 West, 1m 57.448s; 11 Nigon, 1m 57.766s; 12 Baldolini, 1m 57.866s; 13 Olive, 1m 57.894s; 14 Debon, 1m 58.291s; 15 Smrz, 1m 58.405s; 16 Marchand, 1m 58.438s; 17 Davies, 1m 58.484s; 18 Faubel, 1m 59.044s; 19 Gemmel, 1m 59.079s; 20 vd Lagemaat, 2m 01.520s; 21 Pistoni, 2m 02.213s.

World Championship: 1 Poggiali, 88; 2 Rolfo, 69; 3 Elias, 68; 4 Nieto, 61; 5 de Puniet, 56; 6 Battaini, 48; 7 Porto, 44; 8 Matsudo, 42; 9 West, 37; 10 Guintoli, 34; 11 Debon, 24; 12 Olive, 21; 13 Aoyama, 20; 14 Takahashi, 16; 15 Baldolini and Faubel, 11; 17 Gemmel, 9; 18 Stigefelt, 8; 19 Bataille, Kayo and Marchand, 7; 22 Davies and Nigon, 4; 24 Smrz, 3; 25 Heidolf, 1.

125 cc

20 laps, 65.180 miles/104.900 km

Pos.	Rider (Nat.)	No.	Machine	Laps	Time & speed
1	Lucio Cecchinello (I)	4	Aprilia	20	40m 01.738s 97.702 mph/ 157.236 km/h
2	Daniel Pedrosa (E)	3	Honda	20	40m 02.468s
3	Pablo Nieto (E)	22	Aprilia	20	40m 02.539s
4	Andrea Dovizioso (I)	34	Honda	20	40m 02.548s
5	Alex de Angelis (RSM)	15	Aprilia	20	40m 03.192s
6	Youichi Ui (J)	41	Aprilia	20	40m 09.394s
7	Stefano Perugini (I)	7	Aprilia	20	40m 09.440s
8	Gino Borsoi (I)	23	Aprilia	20	40m 09.446s
9	Hector Barbera (E)	80	Aprilia	20	40m 23.442s
10	Gioele Pellino (I)	42	Aprilia	20	40m 23.870s
11	Mirko Giansanti (I)	6	Aprilia	20	40m 23.946s
12	Simone Corsi (I)	24	Honda	20	40m 36.064s
13	Mika Kallio (SF)	36	Honda	20	40m 36.172s
14	Masao Azuma (J)	8	Honda	20	40m 36.231s
15	Thomas Luthi (CH)	12	Honda	20	40m 36.617s
16	Gabor Talmacsi (H)	79	Aprilia	20	40m 36.773s
17	Marco Simoncelli (I)	58	Aprilia	20	40m 47.090s
18	Casey Stoner (AUS)	27	Aprilia	20	40m 47.810s
19	Andrea Ballerini (I)	50	Gilera	20	40m 48.166s
20	Roberto Locatelli (I)	10	KTM	20	40m 48.174s
21	Arnaud Vincent (F)	1	KTM	20	40m 48.353s
22	Michele Conti (I)	87	Honda	20	40m 54.691s
23	Max Sabbatani (I)	11	Aprilia	20	40m 55.076s
24	Mattia Angeloni (I)	60	Honda	20	41m 05.848s
25	Robbin Harms (DK)	88	Aprilia	20	41m 05.924s
26	Alessio Aldrovandi (I)	62	Malaguti	20	41m 12.797s
27	Imre Toth (H)	25	Honda	20	41m 18.460s
28	Alvaro Bautista (E)	19	Aprilia	20	41m 18.568s
29	Michaele Pirro (I)	61	Aprilia	20	41m 24.553s
30	Leon Camier (GB)	21	Honda	19	40m 01.937s
31	Peter Lenart (H)	78	Honda	19	40m 19.387s
	Steve Jenkner (D)	17	Aprilia	19	DNF
	Jorge Lorenzo (E)	48	Derbi	19	DNF
	Fabrizio Lai (I)	32	Malaguti	11	DNF
	Julian Simon (E)	31	Malaguti	10	DNF
	Emilio Alzamora (E)	26	Derbi	9	DNF
	Christopher Martin (GB)	14	Aprilia	7	DNF
	Mike di Meglio (F)	63	Aprilia	0	DNF

Fastest lap: Borsoi, 1m 58.969s, 98.620 mph/158.713 km/h (record).

Previous record: Lucio Cecchinello, I (Aprilia), 1m 59.184s, 98.442 mph/ 158.427 km/h (2002).

Event best maximum speed: Ui, 147.2 mph/236.9 km/h (qualifying practice no. 1).

Qualifying: 1 Stoner, 1m 58.914s; 2 Perugini, 1m 58.977s; 3 de Angelis, 1m 59.012s; 4 Nieto, 1m 59.043s; 5 Jenkner, 1m 59.115s; 6 Cecchinello, 1m 59.143s; 7 Dovizioso, 1m 59.251s; 8 Ui, 1m 59.406s; 9 Borsoi, 1m 59.433s; 10 Pedrosa, 1m 59.608s; 11 Vincent, 1m 59.790s; 12 Barbera, 1m 59.934s; 13 Pellino, 2m 00.044s; 14 Talmacsi, 2m 00.140s; 15 Simoncelli, 2m 00.155s; 16 Giansanti, 2m 00.303s; 17 Corsi, 2m 00.404s; 18 Lorenzo, 2m 00.617s; 19 Sabbatani, 2m 00.739s; 20 Locatelli, 2m 00.949s; 21 Luthi, 2m 00.970s; 22 Azuma, 2m 01.042s; 23 Alzamora, 2m 01.236s; 24 Kallio, 2m 01.334s; 25 Toth, 2m 01.377s; 26 Conti, 2m 01.443s; 27 Ballerini, 2m 01.575s; 28 Angeloni, 2m 01.681s; 29 Aldrovandi, 2m 01.699s; 30 di Meglio, 2m 01.815s; 31 Harms, 2m 02.077s; 32 Lai, 2m 02.482s; 33 Pirro, 2m 02.728s; 34 Simon, 2m 03.129s; 35 Bautista, 2m 03.285s; 36 Martin, 2m 04.082s; 37 Camier, 2m 04.142s; 38 Lenart, 2m 05.490s.

Fastest race laps: 1 Borsoi, 1m 58.969s; 2 Dovizioso, 1m 58.987s; 3 Jenkner, 1m 59.039s; 4 de Angelis, 1m 59.063s; 5 Pedrosa, 1m 59.082s; 6 Stoner, 1m 59.156s; 7 Ui, 1m 59.271s; 8 Perugini, 1m 59.296s; 9 Nieto, 1m 59.302s; 10 Giansanti, 1m 59.397s; 11 Cecchinello, 1m 59.445s; 12 Pellino, 1m 59.775s; 13 Barbera, 1m 59.791s; 14 Luthi, 1m 59.837s; 15 Kallio, 2m 00.011s; 16 Corsi, 2m 00.087s; 17 Lorenzo, 2m 00.108s; 18 Azuma, 2m 00.338s; 19 Vincent, 2m 00.354s; 20 Talmacsi, 2m 00.355s; 21 Simoncelli, 2m 00.558s; 22 Locatelli, 2m 01.131s; 23 Conti, 2m 01.143s; 24 Alzamora, 2m 01.201s; 25 Ballerini, 2m 01.369s; 26 Sabbatani, 2m 01.386s; 27 Aldrovandi, 2m 01.758s; 28 Harms, 2m 01.927s; 29 Angeloni, 2m 01.929s; 30 Pirro, 2m 02.168s; 31 Bautista, 2m 02.237s; 32 Toth, 2m 02.489s; 33 Lai, 2m 02.489s; 34 Camier, 2m 04.736s; 35 Simon, 2m 04.773s; 36 Martin, 2m 05.147s; 37 Lenart, 2m 05.314s.

World Championship: 1 Cecchinello and Pedrosa, 91; 3 Dovizioso, 67; 4 Jenkner, 60; 5 Perugini, 54; 6 Ui, 51; 7 Nieto, 47; 8 de Angelis, 37; 9 Giansanti, 36; 10 Stoner, 29; 11 Borsoi, 25; 12 Barbera, 24; 13 Azuma, 19; 15 Kallio, 17; 16 Corsi, 12; 17 Pellino, 7; 18 Vincent, 4; 19 Sabbatani, 3; 20 Simoncelli and Talmacsi, 2; 22 Locatelli and Lorenzo, 1.

CATALANGP

BARCELONA

Top: Capirossi leads Rossi, Gibernau (15), Biaggi (3), Barros (4) in the early stages. Jacque behind Biaggi, Checa (7), Hayden (69), Nakano (56) are close, Bayliss (12) and Hopkins (21) also prominent.

Above: Schwantz, here with Suzuki man Howard Plumpton, was hoping to help his old team.

Far left: Capirossi made history for Ducati.

Above left: The crowd gasped as the big screens showed Rossi dirt-tracking.

Centre left: Yanagawa lasted only to the first corner.

Left: Swiss 125 rider Thomas Luthi, just 16, could hardly believe he was on the podium.

Right: Hopkins, battered and bruised, kept on trying to tame the unpredictable Suzuki.
All photographs: Mark Wernham

KEVIN Schwantz, hero of the two-stroke golden age, had ridden the Suzuki V4 at the end of 2002, but this was his first visit to a four-stroke race. He loyally defended the 500s, suggesting that he preferred their subtler noise to the ear-damaging orchestra of the 990s. He also pointed out that while a lot of people could ride the four-strokes near to the limit, making for closer racing and more particularly qualifying, that special edge was hard to find, even for the very best riders. 'You can't force the new bikes by your own will. You could over-ride a 500 and get away with stuff. I guess that makes the 500s more of a rider's bike,' he said.

Unless, as we would all see, the rider is Rossi at a self-professed 120 per cent.

Schwantz was there in Suzuki uniform, to observe and advise, hoping to help his old team. Not that there was much he could do, except confirm what lone rider John Hopkins was saying – he noted that the kid was having trouble wrestling the bike into the turns and was later than all the others opening the throttle on the way out. A punishing combination.

Only Hopkins, because while a downcast Roberts was present on Friday, it was just to show his bruises and announce that he was going back to the USA for treatment to a hatful of painful and debilitating internal chest and shoulder injuries. 'It'd have been better if my collar-bone had broken,' he opined. He took responsibility for the crash at Mugello, yet stopped short of actually apologising to Hopkins. Another little patch of darkness for the beleaguered team, who had also enlisted the analytical skills of Jean Michel Bayle to join tests in the days after the GP, along with factory rider Akiyoshi. Ticking off the bike's list of problems proved rather easier than solving them, although one experiment proved interesting. Erratic engine management, especially back-shifting into the corners, had plagued both riders. They unplugged all the gizmos so that Bayle could ride it just like an ordinary motor bike. And it worked pretty well, they said, but only up to the point where it started to need the electronics to improve toward a competitive lap time. Catch 22.

The Aprilia riders had been wrestling much the same sort of electro-mechanical issues with their own 'fly-by-wire' system, but at least they were able to report progress in the other direction. New parts and especially electronic mapping had been tested successfully by the factory's evergreen rider Marcellino Lucchi, serving to smooth out the triple's prodigious power and make it more predictable. Edwards was fast in practice from the start, but better was still not good enough to stay up top when it mattered.

Kawasaki fielded a different wild card, Yanagawa, riding yet another version of the disappointing super-Superbike – nobody was quite sure to what purpose. And it all went bad in the race, when Pitt sent not only McWilliams flying, but also Yanagawa, in a green-on-green replay of Suzuki's Italian misfortune. Yanagawa suffered internal injuries.

Proton had been flat out in the intervening week, with new fuel pumps and careful application of heat shielding for the bike's second race, which was run in even hotter conditions than Italy (it was the continuation of a notable Europe-wide heat wave). This took them to the next teething problems, one being a lack of cornering clearance. They raised McWilliams's bike as much as they could, and he was still dragging the fairing at full lean. He qualified on row five, only to be sent flying in the first-corner crash. Aoki achieved a first race finish for the V5, one place and just 16 seconds out of the points.

That was how the losers were trying to work their way forward. Unfortunately for them, the winners were doing the same thing. The most significant change was over at Honda, where

Rossi's crew chief, Jerry Burgess, had long been proud of having not just the winningest bike, but also the quietest. Making noise was for 16-year-olds, he would opine. Now Honda had their own new noise maker, for Rossi only. There was a package of secret improvements, probably including different camshaft profiles, and certainly revised electronics and a raised rev ceiling, all to liberate more power. Also new was a considerably raspier and louder exhaust system, with a two-into-one for the outer cylinder pairs and a single long megaphone for the central front cylinder. They started it up during the weekend, but reserved track time for testing after the race. It was a sign that HRC were feeling Ducati breathing down their neck, and an ominous confirmation of the fact that there was still more to come from what was already the most harmonious motor cycle on the grid.

Ducati technical boss Corrado Cecchinelli was working through something of a conundrum – that Michelin's latest tyres could stand plenty of wheelspin without losing too much drive, or even suffering from serious wear, to the extent that Capirossi frequently used softer rear race tyres than the others. They may only have been rediscovering what McCoy had demonstrated a couple of years before, but the Italian rider enjoyed the liberty to the full, backing into the turns and laying black lines out of them. 'I slide because I have to. I prefer not,' he said, confirming that those occasions when the tail-out entry could translate seamlessly into a wheel-spinning exit were more myth than reality. 'It is not a rally car. You have to get it settled,' he explained.

The race brought Ducati's first GP victory since 1959, when Mike Hailwood had beaten Gary Hocking's two-stroke MZ at the Ulster 125 cc GP, and their first ever in the premier class. Obviously, this was an emotional moment for all concerned. A well-earned triumph for the machine, and for Capirossi, who confounded those who had hinted he might be better at single fast laps than race distance. They all deserved to treasure the moment.

But there was another winner, even though he only came second. Rossi had a red-letter day, proving in the space of some 20 minutes firstly that he was only human, and secondly that when he throws caution to the wind and unleashes the full scope of his talent, he touches divinity.

The blunder came when he was paying too much attention to his instruments and not enough to race leader Capirossi, inches in front, and he was taken by surprise by the Ducati's slow entry into Turn Four, where they drop off the hill for the first time. 'I looked up, and all I could see was exhaust pipes,' Rossi said later.

He narrowly missed the collision and ran off the outside of the track into the dirt, dropping to sixth in a race that had plenty of close pursuit. Now he demonstrated the truth of Schwantz's assertion – about getting the last few per cent out of the bikes. With almost nine seconds to make up in as many laps, and with the best of the rest between him and the lead, Rossi broke the record twice as he made Nakano, Checa, Gibernau and Biaggi look as though they were in a lesser class. Only Biaggi tried to fight back. It was proof, unseen for a while, of just why Rossi is a giant of motor cycle racing.

Giants come and go, of course, and they don't always have the obvious physical stature or mind-set that goes with it. Not at first anyway. Swiss 16-year-old Thomas Luthi was the latest precocious talent to be thrown up by the 125 class, leading the race on the last lap and coming within inches of winning. On the rostrum afterward, wide-eyed, he could only say, 'I've seen these riders only on TV before. I still can't believe I was racing them.'

Left: Deep-end man Kiyonari was unobtrusive, but an impressive 11th.

Below: Jacque started from the front row, but ended in the gravel.
Both photographs: Mark Wernham

Below centre: Gibernau was feeling the heat for his home race.
Photograph: Gold & Goose

Left: MotoGP snake. Capirossi leads Gibernau, Biaggi, Barros, Jacque, Checa, Nakano, Melandri and Ukawa as they chase after Rossi.
Photograph: Mark Wernham

Right: Rossi 'at 120 per cent' was a genuinely awesome spectacle.
Photograph: Gold & Goose

MOTOGP RACE – 25 laps

Just like the previous week at Mugello, Capirossi's bid for pole was beaten in the closing minutes by Rossi, who had unwittingly given Jacque's Yamaha a tow for the Frenchman's first four-stroke front row, pushing Gibernau to the far end. Times were close, and all were finding the track slippery in the heat.

It was barely cooler on race day (42 degrees C track temperature), and the need to conserve tyres kept the first half of the race close and the pace reasonable. Capirossi led away, but by the end of the lap, Rossi was in front, with Gibernau third and Biaggi fourth, up from the third row. Two out of three Kawasakis and one of two Protons had been eliminated when Pitt left his braking too late into the first turn. 'I asked if he thought he was going to win the race in the first corner from the back row,' said an angry McWilliams, after watching Yanagawa being stretchered off.

Barros was fifth, but again had chosen a bad tyre and spent the rest of the afternoon 'surviving, not racing'. Jacque was behind him, and the Gauloises pair served to cost Checa and Nakano time, before they could find their way past to continue their almost race-long battle to be top Yamaha. Ukawa was starting to close on the fading Barros, followed by Hayden and Bayliss, moving through steadily from 14th on lap one.

Now Rossi upped the pace, and although Capirossi went with him, Biaggi was left behind. There wasn't much to choose between them, but Rossi was trying and ran wide on lap 15, letting the Ducati through. Half a lap later, his momentary lapse of attention led to a wild grass-tracking ride, and Capirossi was alone, in the lead.

Biaggi was less than a second away, but was fully occupied with Gibernau, who finally got past on lap 20, only to slow the pair up. Checa and Nakano were close behind. Then, five seconds away at the end of lap 17, came Rossi, the fastest man on the track.

At the end of lap 22, Rossi had closed the gap, breaking the lap record in the process. The massacre began at once. He outbraked Nakano into the first corner, sized up Checa to dive inside him at Turn Five, the tight downhill hairpin, then four corners later did the same thing to Biaggi into the stadium section. Biaggi passed him straight back, but Rossi was not to be denied and got by again going into the next corner.

Only Gibernau remained, and Rossi outbraked him also into Turn One next time around. In just over a lap, he had gone from sixth to second, past some of the finest riders in the world.

Capirossi was some three seconds ahead, and although Rossi did essay one more lap below 1m 46s, it was a hopeless task. As it was, he had already done more than anyone might have expected.

There was one more drama for Biaggi, entering the stadium two laps from the end. He tried to outbrake Gibernau to chase Rossi, but was too fast and slid off, clobbering the barrier before falling. Luckily, the engine was still running, allowing him to clamber back on and still finish in the points.

With Gibernau third, then Checa managing to fend off Nakano, Ukawa was a lacklustre sixth. Next came Tamada, another strong ride, who finished the first lap 15th, but moved steadily through to the top ten before two-thirds distance, finally picking off Barros and Hayden for seventh.

Bayliss was tenth after an off-track excursion lost him four places on lap 17. Then came the unobtrusive, but not unimpressive, Kiyonari, who had left Haga and Melandri behind him, the pair scrapping to the end. Biaggi was another two seconds away. Hopkins took the last point, still stiff and sore from Mugello.

Aoki was losing power at the end, but still running and ahead of McCoy on the surviving Kawasaki, again entertaining the crowd with wild tyre-smoking slides. 'It wasn't helping me go fast, but they seemed to enjoy it,' he said.

Jacque crashed out after dropping back for the last 12 laps; Edwards had already pitted with an electronic component failure – 'a 50-cent piece of wire' – which had caused the engine to cut in and out, dropping him to almost last before he retired.

Far left: Holier than thou. Loris Capirossi speeds the Desmosedici toward his historic win.

Left and below: Tension in the pit as the laps ticked away was followed by champagne for all after Ducati's first GP win since 1958.
Photographs: Mark Wernham

Left: The Desmosedici's trim tail, exhaust heat shrouding clearly visible.
Photograph: Mark Wernham

Elias had closed to within two seconds at the finish, following a storming ride from last place after stalling the engine on the line. He set third-fastest lap as he charged through the field.

The rest trailed in, Matsudo free of Battaini, who held Porto at bay. Guintoli was just four seconds off after another impressive ride, well clear of a disappointed Rolfo, who had fallen back among the mid-fielders with an overheating engine in the early stages and could do no better than ninth. Then came Olive, Debon and substitute rider Klaus Nöhles; Stigefelt, Nigon and Gemmel took the last points.

Chaz Davies was an early retirement with a power-valve failure; Marchand and Smrz crashed out.

Poggiali's second no-score in three races put some life back into the title chase, but the lap times showed this had not been a vintage year. The San Marinan had set fastest lap before retiring, but it was an amazing nine-tenths slower than Rossi's 1998 lap record.

125 cc RACE – 22 laps

Nieto was on pole, but second-fastest Dovizioso led from Hector Barbera by the end of the first lap. Cecchinello was right there, also Ui and Pedrosa, while Stoner was ninth and Luthi 12th. The wide and flowing circuit lends itself to brawling, and there was plenty of that to come as the front group took shape.

Cecchinello did most of the leading over the first eight laps, with Stoner taking a single lap up front; Dovizioso was very much present, then de Angelis, Jenkner, Pedrosa, Nieto and Barbera. Luthi was making his way through to join by half-distance.

It was all very close and scary, and two laps later Stoner paid the price when Dovizioso missed a gear on a corner exit. The Australian had to pick up, running fast across the dirt until he baled out just before the barrier, hitting it hard head-on.

A lap later, Cecchinello also ran off the track to avoid a collision, rejoining at the back of the group, only to retire. Then, on lap 15, Dovizioso and Barbera crashed out together.

Now de Angelis had a spell up front, until Pedrosa started the end-game on lap 20, taking the lead and trying to escape. The increased pace did for Nieto, who slid out one lap later. Now there were four.

Luthi's moment of glory came as they crested the hill for the first time on the final lap – he found himself leading a GP in his debut season. Pedrosa was in control, however, getting a better run on to the short back straight and sweeping through to take the lead into the tight left at the end, entering the stadium section. Luthi was only inches behind, then de Angelis, content with third.

Jenkner had been left a little way back by the flag; next came Perugini, almost 20 seconds adrift. Lorenzo and Kallio led the following group, battling for sixth, three seconds behind.

Top left and right: Unemployed in 2002, Anthony West 'rode the wheels off' his Aprilia to claim a first Australian 250 rostrum in 21 years.

Above: Guintoli heads the mid-field 250 pack.

Right: Luthi leads a pack of riders he'd 'only seen before on TV'.
All photographs: Mark Wernham

250 cc RACE – 23 laps

De Puniet claimed a third successive pole on a Friday time, with Poggiali second and Elias third. West led the third row.

Poggiali got the jump, but a spirited de Puniet was in front by the end of the lap, with Porto up to second and Nieto fourth. Battaini was next, then frequent fast starter Debon, ahead of West.

Porto was down on speed and split the leaders, letting Nieto, de Puniet and Poggiali escape. Battaini and Matsudo were delayed, but West was in determined mood and had passed all of them by lap five, the gap to the leading group now almost two seconds.

Nieto had led briefly, but now appeared to be struggling to stay in touch. It was only their own back-and-forth battling that slowed de Puniet and Poggiali enough for the gap to shrink again by half-distance. Soon, it seemed, Poggiali would start his run and draw out a lead to the finish. But he was already troubled with gearshift problems and overheating. Then, on lap 13, a terminal electronic failure meant his race was over.

The first three continued to close toward the finish, and they started the last lap with Nieto shadowing the Frenchman, West less than a second behind. De Puniet had the scent of a first victory in his nostrils and forced the pace. Nieto had a fishier smell – a pit signalling mix-up led him to believe that there were two laps left. He seemed poised to attack into the stadium section for the crucial showdown. Amazingly, he held back – dumbstruck to see the chequered flag as they crossed the line.

West was content with third place, the first Australian on a 250 rostrum since Graeme McGregor in 1982. 'The bike wasn't perfect, but I could ride around the problems. I'd been getting confused with set-up, so we took it back to what we had at the first race and I felt confident again. I rode the wheels off the thing,' he said.

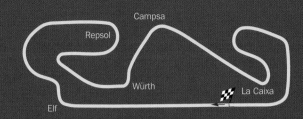

MARLBORO CATALAN grand prix

15 JUNE 2003

Campsa
Repsol
Würth
Elf
La Caixa

Photograph: Mark Wernham

CIRCUIT LENGTH: 2.937 miles/4.727 km

MotoGP

25 laps, 73.425 miles/118.175 km

Pos.	Rider (Nat.)	No.	Machine	Laps	Time & speed
1	Loris Capirossi (I)	65	Ducati	25	44m 21.758s 99.314 mph/ 159.830 km/h
2	Valentino Rossi (I)	46	Honda	25	44m 24.833s
3	Sete Gibernau (E)	15	Honda	25	44m 26.102s
4	Carlos Checa (E)	7	Yamaha	25	44m 26.693s
5	Shinya Nakano (J)	56	Yamaha	25	44m 26.761s
6	Tohru Ukawa (J)	11	Honda	25	44m 42.345s
7	Makoto Tamada (J)	6	Honda	25	44m 44.740s
8	Alex Barros (BR)	4	Yamaha	25	44m 46.747s
9	Nicky Hayden (USA)	69	Honda	25	44m 48.917s
10	Troy Bayliss (AUS)	12	Ducati	25	44m 52.134s
11	Ryuichi Kiyonari (J)	23	Honda	25	44m 54.951s
12	Noriyuki Haga (J)	41	Aprilia	25	45m 02.201s
13	Marco Melandri (I)	33	Yamaha	25	45m 02.203s
14	Max Biaggi (I)	3	Honda	25	45m 04.083s
15	John Hopkins (USA)	21	Suzuki	25	45m 10.417s
16	Nobuatsu Aoki (J)	9	Proton KR	25	45m 26.479s
17	Garry McCoy (AUS)	8	Kawasaki	25	45m 58.672s
	Olivier Jacque (F)	19	Yamaha	12	DNF
	Colin Edwards (USA)	45	Aprilia	6	DNF
	Akira Yanagawa (J)	48	Kawasaki	0	DNF
	Andrew Pitt (AUS)	88	Kawasaki	0	DNF
	Jeremy McWilliams (GB)	99	Proton KR	0	DNF

Fastest lap: Rossi, 1m 45.472s, 100.254 mph/161.343 km/h (record).

Previous record: Valentino Rossi, I (Honda), 1m 45.594s, 100.138 mph/ 161.156 km/h (2002).

Event best maximum speed: Capirossi, 202.5 mph/325.9 km/h (qualifying practice no. 1).

Qualifying: 1 Rossi, 1m 43.927s; 2 Capirossi, 1m 44.333s; 3 Jacque, 1m 44.358s; 4 Gibernau, 1m 44.366s; 5 Barros, 1m 44.642s; 6 Nakano, 1m 44.672s; 7 Edwards, 1m 44.708s; 8 Checa, 1m 44.790s; 9 Biaggi, 1m 44.848s; 10 Tamada, 1m 44.922s; 11 Ukawa, 1m 45.039s; 12 Bayliss, 1m 45.128s; 13 Hopkins, 1m 45.516s; 14 Melandri, 1m 45.804s; 15 Haga, 1m 46.108s; 16 Yanagawa, 1m 46.170s; 17 McWilliams, 1m 46.173s; 18 Hayden, 1m 46.216s; 19 McCoy, 1m 46.647s; 20 Kiyonari, 1m 46.950s; 21 Aoki, 1m 47.037s; 22 Pitt, 1m 47.473s.

Fastest race laps: 1 Rossi, 1m 45.472s; 2 Biaggi, 1m 45.558s; 3 Capirossi, 1m 45.632s; 4 Nakano, 1m 45.681s; 5 Checa, 1m 45.832s; 6 Gibernau, 1m 45.851s; 7 Jacque, 1m 45.993s; 8 Edwards, 1m 46.002s; 9 Ukawa, 1m 46.008s; 10 Bayliss, 1m 46.179s; 11 Melandri, 1m 46.200s; 12 Barros, 1m 46.230s; 13 Hayden, 1m 46.301s; 14 Tamada, 1m 46.468s; 15 Haga, 1m 46.773s; 16 Hopkins, 1m 46.820s; 17 Kiyonari, 1m 46.863s; 18 Aoki, 1m 47.941s; 19 McCoy, 1m 48.542s.

World Championship: 1 Rossi, 135; 2 Gibernau, 88; 3 Biaggi, 85; 4 Capirossi, 61; 5 Barros, 54; 6 Ukawa, 52; 7 Bayliss, 46; 8 Nakano, 44; 9 Checa and Tamada, 34; 11 Hayden, 33; 12 Jacque, 32; 13 Edwards, 25; 14 Haga, 21; 15 Abe, 18; 16 Hopkins, 16; 17 McWilliams, 14; 18 Aoki and Kiyonari, 11; 20 Melandri, 9; 21 McCoy, 8; 22 Roberts, 6; 23 Hofmann, 2; 24 Pitt, 1.

250 cc

23 laps, 67.551 miles/108.721 km

Pos.	Rider (Nat.)	No.	Machine	Laps	Time & speed
1	Randy de Puniet (F)	7	Aprilia	23	41m 59.893s 96.513 mph/ 155.322 km/h
2	Fonsi Nieto (E)	10	Aprilia	23	42m 00.137s
3	Anthony West (AUS)	14	Aprilia	23	42m 02.534s
4	Toni Elias (E)	24	Aprilia	23	42m 04.222s
5	Naoki Matsudo (J)	8	Yamaha	23	42m 07.789s
6	Franco Battaini (I)	21	Aprilia	23	42m 11.325s
7	Sebastian Porto (ARG)	5	Honda	23	42m 11.776s
8	Sylvain Guintoli (F)	50	Aprilia	23	42m 15.654s
9	Roberto Rolfo (I)	3	Honda	23	42m 24.163s
10	Joan Olive (E)	11	Aprilia	23	42m 29.263s
11	Alex Debon (E)	6	Honda	23	42m 31.984s
12	Klaus Nöhles (D)	30	Aprilia	23	42m 34.841s
13	Johan Stigefelt (S)	16	Aprilia	23	42m 44.152s
14	Erwan Nigon (F)	36	Aprilia	23	42m 46.277s
15	Christian Gemmel (D)	15	Honda	23	42m 59.660s
16	Lukas Pesek (CZ)	52	Yamaha	23	43m 36.190s
17	Katja Poensgen (D)	98	Honda	22	42m 37.758s
18	Henk vd Lagemaat (NL)	18	Honda	22	42m 51.541s
	Jakub Smrz (CZ)	96	Honda	22	DNF
	Manuel Poggiali (RSM)	54	Aprilia	12	DNF
	Hector Faubel (E)	33	Aprilia	10	DNF
	Alex Baldolini (I)	26	Aprilia	10	DNF
	Hugo Marchand (F)	9	Aprilia	5	DNF
	Christophe Rastel (F)	31	Honda	5	DNF
	Chaz Davies (GB)	57	Aprilia	3	DNF
	Eric Bataille (F)	34	Honda	1	DNF

Fastest lap: Poggiali, 1m 48.483s, 97.471 mph/156.865 km/h.

Lap record: Valentino Rossi, I (Aprilia), 1m 47.585s, 98.285 mph/ 158.174 km/h (1998).

Event best maximum speed: Poggiali, 170.3 mph/274.0 km/h (warm-up).

Qualifying: 1 de Puniet, 1m 47.117s; 2 Poggiali, 1m 47.284s; 3 Elias, 1m 47.551s; 4 Battaini, 1m 47.904s; 5 Porto, 1m 48.022s; 6 Nieto, 1m 48.122s; 7 Matsudo, 1m 48.133s; 8 Rolfo, 1m 48.891s; 9 West, 1m 48.892s; 10 Guintoli, 1m 49.126s; 11 Marchand, 1m 49.294s; 12 Nöhles, 1m 49.404s; 13 Stigefelt, 1m 49.442s; 14 Olive, 1m 49.708s; 15 Nigon, 1m 49.713s; 16 Faubel, 1m 49.824s; 17 Debon, 1m 49.832s; 18 Bataille, 1m 49.906s; 19 Gemmel, 1m 50.546s; 20 Davies, 1m 50.712s; 21 Smrz, 1m 50.787s; 22 Pesek, 1m 50.974s; 23 Baldolini, 1m 51.534s; 24 vd Lagemaat, 1m 52.995s; 25 Poensgen, 1m 53.222s; 26 Rastel, 1m 53.927s.

Fastest race laps: 1 Poggiali, 1m 48.483s; 2 Nieto, 1m 48.485s; 3 Elias, 1m 48.609s; 4 de Puniet, 1m 48.755s; 5 West, 1m 48.867s; 6 Battaini, 1m 49.053s; 7 Matsudo, 1m 49.178s; 8 Guintoli, 1m 49.299s; 9 Porto, 1m 49.431s; 10 Rolfo, 1m 49.495s; 11 Nöhles, 1m 49.866s; 12 Olive, 1m 49.894s; 13 Debon, 1m 50.042s; 14 Stigefelt, 1m 50.178s; 15 Nigon, 1m 50.495s; 16 Faubel, 1m 50.746s; 17 Marchand, 1m 50.751s; 18 Gemmel, 1m 50.880s; 19 Smrz, 1m 51.317s; 20 Pesek, 1m 51.343s; 21 Baldolini, 1m 51.424s; 22 vd Lagemaat, 1m 53.151s; 23 Davies, 1m 53.397s; 24 Rastel, 1m 54.329s; 25 Poensgen, 1m 54.557s; 26 Bataille, 1m 59.540s.

World Championship: 1 Poggiali, 88; 2 de Puniet, Elias and Nieto, 81; 5 Rolfo, 76; 6 Battaini, 58; 7 Matsudo, Porto and West, 53; 10 Guintoli, 42; 11 Debon, 29; 12 Olive, 27; 13 Aoyama, 20; 14 Takahashi, 16; 15 Baldolini, Faubel and Stigefelt, 11; 18 Gemmel, 10; 19 Bataille, Kayo and Marchand, 7; 22 Nigon, 6; 23 Davies and Nöhles, 4; 25 Smrz, 3; 26 Heidolf, 1.

125 cc

22 laps, 64.614 miles/103.994 km

Pos.	Rider (Nat.)	No.	Machine	Laps	Time & speed
1	Daniel Pedrosa (E)	3	Honda	22	41m 16.672s 93.927 mph/ 151.161 km/h
2	Thomas Luthi (CH)	12	Honda	22	41m 16.809s
3	Alex de Angelis (RSM)	15	Aprilia	22	41m 16.987s
4	Steve Jenkner (D)	17	Aprilia	22	41m 18.261s
5	Stefano Perugini (I)	7	Aprilia	22	41m 36.546s
6	Jorge Lorenzo (E)	48	Derbi	22	41m 39.232s
7	Mika Kallio (SF)	36	Honda	22	41m 39.319s
8	Gino Borsoi (I)	23	Aprilia	22	41m 39.528s
9	Gabor Talmacsi (H)	79	Aprilia	22	41m 39.588s
10	Roberto Locatelli (I)	10	KTM	22	41m 40.087s
11	Gioele Pellino (I)	42	Aprilia	22	41m 48.487s
12	Mirko Giansanti (I)	6	Aprilia	22	41m 51.520s
13	Mike di Meglio (F)	63	Aprilia	22	41m 57.610s
14	Arnaud Vincent (F)	1	KTM	22	41m 57.835s
15	Simone Corsi (I)	24	Honda	22	41m 58.077s
16	Marco Simoncelli (I)	58	Aprilia	22	41m 58.560s
17	Pablo Nieto (E)	22	Aprilia	22	42m 08.002s
18	Andrea Ballerini (I)	50	Gilera	22	42m 08.665s
19	Fabrizio Lai (I)	32	Malaguti	22	42m 08.961s
20	Imre Toth (H)	25	Honda	22	42m 11.036s
21	Max Sabbatani (I)	11	Aprilia	22	42m 24.799s
22	Masao Azuma (J)	8	Honda	22	42m 26.440s
23	Sergio Gadea (E)	70	Aprilia	22	42m 39.466s
24	Julian Simon (E)	31	Malaguti	22	42m 49.344s
25	Jordi Carchano (E)	82	Honda	22	42m 57.179s
26	Peter Lenart (H)	78	Honda	22	42m 57.276s
27	Leon Camier (GB)	21	Honda	22	42m 57.402s
28	Alvaro Bautista (E)	19	Aprilia	17	41m 45.481s
	Andrea Dovizioso (I)	34	Honda	15	DNF
	Hector Barbera (E)	80	Aprilia	15	DNF
	David Bonache (E)	69	Honda	14	DNF
	Lucio Cecchinello (I)	4	Aprilia	13	DNF
	Youichi Ui (J)	41	Aprilia	11	DNF
	Emilio Alzamora (E)	26	Derbi	10	DNF
	Casey Stoner (AUS)	27	Aprilia	9	DNF
	Christopher Martin (GB)	14	Aprilia	7	DNF

Fastest lap: Stoney, 1m 51.190s, 95.098 mph/153.046 km/h (record).

Previous record: Youichi Ui, J (Derbi), 1m 51.443s, 94.882 mph/ 152.698 km/h (2002).

Event best maximum speed: Pedrosa, 147.7 mph/237.7 km/h (race).

Qualifying: 1 Nieto, 1m 51.043s; 2 Dovizioso, 1m 51.220s; 3 Cecchinello, 1m 51.281s; 4 Barbera, 1m 51.349s; 5 de Angelis, 1m 51.417s; 6 Pedrosa, 1m 51.453s; 7 Ui, 1m 51.686s; 8 Jenkner, 1m 51.977s; 9 Perugini, 1m 52.011s; 10 Stoner, 1m 52.076s; 11 Lorenzo, 1m 52.295s; 12 Talmacsi, 1m 52.386s; 13 Pellino, 1m 52.954s; 14 Luthi, 1m 52.994s; 15 di Meglio, 1m 53.052s; 16 Corsi, 1m 53.111s; 17 Vincent, 1m 53.122s; 18 Borsoi, 1m 53.148s; 19 Kallio, 1m 53.160s; 20 Giansanti, 1m 53.168s; 21 Lai, 1m 53.387s; 22 Simoncelli, 1m 53.464s; 23 Locatelli, 1m 53.494s; 24 Azuma, 1m 53.511s; 25 Alzamora, 1m 53.600s; 26 Ballerini, 1m 53.648s; 27 Gadea, 1m 53.744s; 28 Simon, 1m 53.875s; 29 Bautista, 1m 54.044s; 30 Toth, 1m 54.246s; 31 Bonache, 1m 55.148s; 32 Camier, 1m 55.493s; 33 Sabbatani, 1m 56.270s; 34 Martin, 1m 56.835s; 35 Carchano, 1m 56.934s; 36 Lenart, 1m 57.152s.

Fastest race laps: 1 Stoner, 1m 51.190s; 2 de Angelis, 1m 51.379s; 3 Luthi, 1m 51.441s; 4 Nieto, 1m 51.490s; 5 Jenkner, 1m 51.588s; 6 Pedrosa, 1m 51.641s; 7 Talmacsi, 1m 51.798s; 8 Cecchinello, 1m 51.801s; 9 Perugini, 1m 51.808s; 10 Ui, 1m 51.870s; 11 Dovizioso, 1m 51.872s; 12 Barbera, 1m 51.894s; 13 Borsoi, 1m 52.275s; 14 Locatelli, 1m 52.476s; 15 Giansanti, 1m 52.578s; 16 Lorenzo, 1m 52.615s; 17 Pellino, 1m 52.653s; 18 Kallio, 1m 52.732s; 19 Azuma, 1m 52.892s; 20 Simoncelli, 1m 53.155s; 21 di Meglio, 1m 53.184s; 22 Vincent, 1m 53.322s; 23 Corsi, 1m 53.349s; 24 Ballerini, 1m 53.649s; 25 Toth, 1m 53.672s; 26 Gadea, 1m 53.877s; 27 Sabbatani, 1m 53.929s; 28 Lai, 1m 53.973s; 29 Bonache, 1m 54.206s; 30 Alzamora, 1m 54.339s; 31 Simon, 1m 54.453s; 32 Bautista, 1m 55.245s; 33 Lenart, 1m 55.642s; 34 Camier, 1m 55.690s; 35 Carchano, 1m 55.816s; 36 Martin, 1m 56.782s.

World Championship: 1 Pedrosa, 116; 2 Cecchinello, 91; 3 Jenkner, 73; 4 Dovizioso, 67; 5 Perugini, 65; 6 de Angelis, 53; 7 Ui, 51; 8 Nieto, 47; 9 Giansanti, 40; 10 Luthi, 39; 11 Borsoi, 33; 12 Stoner, 29; 13 Kallio, 26; 14 Barbera, 24; 15 Azuma, 20; 16 Corsi, 13; 17 Pellino, 12; 18 Lorenzo, 11; 19 Talmacsi, 9; 20 Locatelli, 7; 21 Vincent, 6; 22 di Meglio and Sabbatani, 3; 24 Simoncelli, 1.

DUTCH TT
ASSEN

Above: Gibernau and Biaggi battle out the race. In the end, the Spaniard was more determined.
Photograph: Gold & Goose

Right and far right: Superbike champions reigning and elect, Colin Edwards and...
Photograph: Gold & Goose

...paddock visitor Neil Hodgson.
Photograph: Mark Wernham

Centre right: Hayden found the conditions far from cool, but managed to get the better of Ukawa.
Photograph: Gold & Goose

Below: West made history for a second race in a row, taking a maiden victory.
Photograph: Gold & Goose

Below centre: For Yukio Kagayama, the Dutch TT was one of eight consecutive weekends of racing on three different types of Suzuki.
Photograph: Mark Wernham

ASSEN remains the cathedral of motor cycle racing, 2002's track changes having slipped seamlessly into history. It endures as the classic inquisition of riders and motor cycles, testing every weapon in the human arsenal, from courage to intelligence, and closely scrutinising chassis integrity, machine balance and engine power.

How ironic that more often than not the weather plays the decisive card.

So it was again this year, when deceptively benign practice conditions gave way on race Saturday to typical Assen weather, always threatening a downpour, and several times making good. All three races were wet, the MotoGP event being delayed when it rained again on the warm-up lap. As a happy consequence, with the emphasis thrown on to riding skill (and tyre choice), the smaller classes came up with two first-time winners, Anthony West in the 250s and Steve Jenkner in the 125s.

How much of a surprise was it that Rossi didn't win the MotoGP race? Quite a big one, obviously, although Gibernau was not a first-timer. He outrode Biaggi to equal Rossi's three wins so far this year. At the same time, Rossi was moving into a mid-season bad patch (for him), with third place falling short of expectations. This trend would continue, for one reason or another.

It's natural to concentrate on the winners in racing. At Assen, there was an interloper whose track record put the pampered lives of the big stars into some kind of perspective. Nowadays, GP riders compete only in GPs, 16 races a year – the days of big-money internationals and the odd endurance race are long gone. Not for Yukio Kagayama, a sometime former GP racer and Suzuki factory tester, and in 2003 a popular British Superbike contender. He took Roberts's GSV-R at Assen, for the third of an amazing eight consecutive weekends of racing. The previous two had been at World Superbikes at Silverstone (fifth) and in British Superbikes at Brands, on the Rizla Crescent Suzuki GSX1000-R. The weekend after Assen, he would compete in BSB again, then the British GP, another BSB round, followed directly by the Suzuka Eight-Hour. Finally, another BSB round. A cheerful soul, Kagayama found it all rather amusing; rather less so the fact that while the GSX is very competitive, the GSV-R is well short of the pace. In some circumstances, the more manageable production-based racer might even be faster. He laughed at the notion: 'That's a secret.'

At the other end of the grid came the first public evidence that Honda were becoming rattled by Ducati – a single power-up version of the RCV for Rossi, distinguished by a three-pipe exhaust system that produced a much louder and pleasingly raspy sound. Rossi had tested it at Catalunya after the grand prix. At Assen, he practised it, then parked it. He found the excess noise distracting, and the power advantage unimportant at the Dutch circuit, where corner flow and smoothness mean speed. But the bike would return, and in greater numbers, at faster tracks to come.

Princess Anne caused a minor flutter in the paddock, being there to support the Riders for Health charity and attend a gala dinner on the eve of practice. The Princess visited the Proton KR pit (they carry Riders for Health stickers) and seemed to enjoy the experience, but she didn't stay for the race. Nor did she witness a little cameo in practice, when Aoki's V5 came out of the chicane in a plume of smoke, a small fire developing nicely in the belly pan. He stopped just past the pits and gave the bike a kick, whereupon it flared up even more and he ran away. It was an oil fire and soon extinguished, for the sustained fast sections of Assen had found another weakness in the still-new engine, and sundry oil leaks were to keep the team hard at work.

The axe finally fell on the Harris WCM during practice, when the team received the final judgement of the independent Court of Arbitration for Sport. It went against them, ending a long trail that had begun at Suzuka. Now team boss Peter Clifford had to discover a way to keep racing or risk losing his franchise. This meant finding 500 cc two-strokes, with a two-race deadline. Dorna had been prepared to wait, said boss Carmelo Ezpeleta, 'until the legality of the machine was finally established. But the franchise contract is that they have to race. They must enter at Donington Park or, if that is not possible, the next round in Germany.'

Another British hope had bitten the dust when ex-125 champion Chris Martin split with his team, sponsored by Dutch footballer Clarence Seedorf, after Catalunya. Martin had been chafing at the new team's uncompetitive machinery; they, in turn, at his resultant abrasive mien. He was replaced by Danish youngster Robbin Harms.

Neil Hodgson was a visitor, happy to articulate his GP hopes at the track where later he would tie up the Superbike title. And also to oblige a fan, who failed to recognise him while he was chatting to Mamola and handed him his camera to take a snap of himself with the American. Luckily, Hodgson has a sense of humour.

The fun stopped on race day, when conditions were atrocious. For Hayden, schooled in the AMA, where rain means a postponed race, the conditions were deeply disturbing. 'I've never raced when it was that hard to see. It wasn't cool,' he said.

Edwards is seasoned to European ways, but also was eloquent, describing how, since it had been impossible to see ahead, he had been going down the front straight looking sideways at the pit wall and judging his peel-off point from that. His official Aprilia press statements appeared to have been translated into Italian, then back into English, using an internet program along the way. This turned the highly articulate and entertaining Texan into a sort of rambling racing buffoon. Here he explains the vision problems: 'Since half the race, I was unable to see the track. The visor was dimmed and all the little parts and the insects coming from the other riders turned off my light.'

Insects there may have been, but again there were no flies on Alex Hofmann, Kawasaki's nightmare wild card, who once more comprehensively beat dispirited regulars Pitt and McCoy. There may have been more to this than met the eye, but a top ten in the wet at Assen turned the German into a hot property.

MOTOGP RACE – 19 laps

One year older and wiser, and enjoying benign weather, the four-stroke riders showed how much faster they were this year than last, the top 15 qualifying inside last year's pole time. On top was Capirossi, for the second time in the Desmosedici's short racing career. Biaggi was second, 0.0023 second ahead of Rossi, and all three had broken the two-minute barrier. Checa completed the front row, scotching his own gloomy prognostication of handling problems with the Yamaha after switching to last year's chassis in a search for corner confidence. An on-form Jacque led row two.

The agreeable weather didn't last. Race day was black and blustery, and both earlier races disrupted. The skies loomed again as a nominated Dry Race got under way, only to be stopped half-way through the warm-up lap. A mercy to Capirossi, who had already pitted to change tyres, missing the warm-up lap and thus consigned to start from the pit lane. Now he took his place on pole, after 30 minutes of frantic indecision and flapping all round. The tyre choice would, of course, be crucial.

It was raining heavily for the restart. Rossi and Biaggi led a cloud of spray out of sight under the Dunlop bridge; Gibernau slipped inside into the first corner. He had chosen harder tyres than his rivals, which would pay off later on the drying track; at this point, it was his typical wet-weather daring that kept him in front. By the end of the lap, Jacque, on soft tyres, had pushed the similarly shod, but cautious, Rossi to fourth. Bayliss was leaning on the Honda; Barros and Edwards close. The ex-Superbike rivals were on a familiar track, for once.

Gibernau had some narrow squeaks as Biaggi reclaimed the lead, while Rossi was soon back ahead of Jacque, Bayliss following on. It took Bayliss three more laps to find a way past Rossi, the gap to the leading pair now two seconds. Bayliss never got the chance to close it down, running too deep into the first corner and sliding off right in front of Rossi as he fiddled with the switch for the troublesome quickshifter on the dash. 'It was cutting in and out. I'd been shifting manually. I haven't done that for years,' he said later. 'It was a pity. Everything else was going quite good in the wet.' He scrambled back in 16th and soon was picking his way forward again.

The crucial moment occurred at the end of lap nine, as the leaders came up to lap McCoy at the final chicane. Gibernau saw a gap and dived past; the less daring Biaggi was stuck behind. That opened up a second. With the track drying, Gibernau maintained the pressure, while Biaggi found a couple more backmarkers and was out of touch. By the end, the gap had stretched to ten seconds. Gibernau also claimed fastest lap, and Michelin's 300th GP win.

Rossi closed impressively in the final stages, but Biaggi had enough in hand to beat his rival for the first time on a Honda.

Lap nine also saw the battle for fourth take shape. Jacque was under pressure from Haga, who had passed Edwards among others, both getting ahead of Barros at the same time as he faded away with familiar tyre complaints. Soon afterward, he succumbed to Checa as well. Meanwhile, Capirossi had gained pace to join the group from behind.

By lap 13, Haga led from Checa, Jacque and Capirossi, Edwards now losing touch. Then Checa dived past Haga, spattering his visor with mud. He wiped it clean and crashed out in the process.

A long way back came Bayliss, whose last victim had been Hofmann, smooth in the wet for a personal-best tenth, Kawasaki's second top ten. Behind him was Hayden, wide-eyed at the conditions. He had eventually beaten a baffled off-form Ukawa, and fended off Nakano, through from a bad start. Ukawa also came under attack from Kagayama, until – foxed by Ukawa's slow corner speed – the wild card ran into the back of him and fell off.

A lap down, Pitt was 14th, ahead of Hopkins, finding the Suzuki's unpredictable electronics a handful. 'The wet is all about feel and smoothness,' he said. Seven seconds behind, Tamada was mortified at having been lapped; fellow Assen rookie and general new boy Kiyonari was a further three seconds adrift. Blame it on the Bridgestone wets: Aoki fell off his Proton on the sighting lap and again in the race; McWilliams also crashed, saying afterward, 'With hindsight, I'd have been better off not trying so hard…but that's not in me.' A depressed McCoy was 18th and last.

250 cc RACE – 18 laps

Poggiali claimed the pole by half a second from de Puniet, who had suffered a heavy fall on the second morning, then came Elias and Nieto. With the Hondas of Porto and Rolfo on row two, West's ex-factory Aprilia led row three.

The race brought many upsets in difficult conditions – damp, but lifting. The first was to Elias. 'The only time my bike went right was on the start straight,' he said. Then he was swallowed up, and one candidate for victory had gone.

Poggiali and Rolfo set the pace from the word go, but West had started brilliantly and was revelling in the conditions. He took the lead as they went into the chicane at the end of the first lap, and that was that. Smooth and very close to the limit, he was more than five seconds clear after four laps and never faltered all the way to the flag. It was the first in the class by an Australian since Gregg Hansford, more than 25 years before.

De Puniet crashed out after finishing the first lap tenth; one lap later, Poggiali lost second to Guintoli, also intent on exploiting his chances in the wet. His team-mate, Battaini, was right on Poggiali's tail; Rolfo tagged on behind.

The colourful Campetella riders were unstoppable, Battaini taking second and leading Guintoli away from Poggiali and Rolfo, who had been joined by Porto and Nieto. A long way back, rain specialist Matsudo was moving through fast, only to crash out before one-third distance.

Half-way through the race, Battaini was beginning to close on West, who later explained that he had been having trouble keeping his concentration on such a lonely ride. But he was still more than four seconds away when the Australian got the message, then he lost a knee slider, ending his distant challenge.

Guintoli was safe in third in what was becoming rather a procession. Nieto had left the party, his chain jumping off the sprocket; Poggiali was way back, focused only on finishing safely in his first wet race on a 250. Porto trailed in behind, then came Rolfo well to the rear, followed by a mixed bunch who filled the top ten: Nigon a career-best seventh ahead of Gemmel; Marchand narrowly beating Stigefelt. Elias was down in 13th.

A red-letter day for West, after his first rostrum in Catalunya, still had a down-side. 'I'd have preferred a dry race. Even if I didn't win, another rostrum in the dry would prove that I didn't just fluke it last week,' he said.

125 cc RACE – 17 laps

Jenkner had been threatening a win for some time. A proper shower for a fully wet race gave him his chance. On the front row, he led off the line, only Stoner going with him, and after two laps he was more than three seconds in front. The Australian was even farther ahead of the spray of the pack, but once again the teenager was racing in dubious medical circumstances. Unable to take the medication he needed for a viral infection, he was having trouble concentrating and couldn't read his pit board. On the third lap, he touched a white line and crashed out.

That left Jenkner almost 15 seconds ahead, and he preserved the gap to the finish, lapping consistently all the way. 'I've waited a long time, so I didn't want to give up,' he said.

Nieto had pushed through to lead the battle for second. Behind him, Kallio and Barbera were fighting, the Spaniard prevailing, but never close enough to challenge Nieto. They completed the rostrum.

By the half-way mark, Ui had taken fourth off Perugini and held on to it. Kallio was heading Pedrosa and Talmacsi, Luthi tagging on behind; de Angelis was charging through from the back – he'd fallen on the sighting lap, then had suffered a bad start.

If the first five were widely spread at the finish, the others were not. De Angelis narrowly beat Luthi for sixth; pole-starter Pedrosa was three seconds adrift, his hands full not only with Talmacsi, but also with the threat of another gang behind – Dovizioso ahead of Kallio, Corsi and Borsoi. Less than four seconds spanned eighth and 15th places.

Main photograph: Poggiali takes a couple of inches from the front-row competitors at the start of the 250 race.

Below: Jenkner's first GP victory was flawless.
Both photographs: Gold & Goose

Above: Alex Hofmann made the top ten.

Above right: Scotsman Hamish Jamieson, formerly McCoy's technical other half, had joined Kawasaki to oversee testing and development.
Both photographs: Mark Wernham

Right: McCoy needed all the help he could get – and, if possible, a different motor cycle.

Below: Rossi played it safe – third maintained a perfect record of rostrum finishes.
Both photographs: Gold & Goose

ASSEN TT RACING CIRCUIT

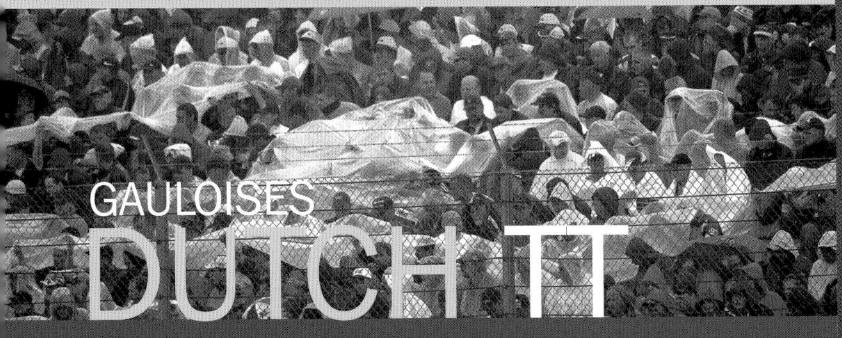

GAULOISES DUTCH TT

28 JUNE 2003

Photograph: Gold & Goose

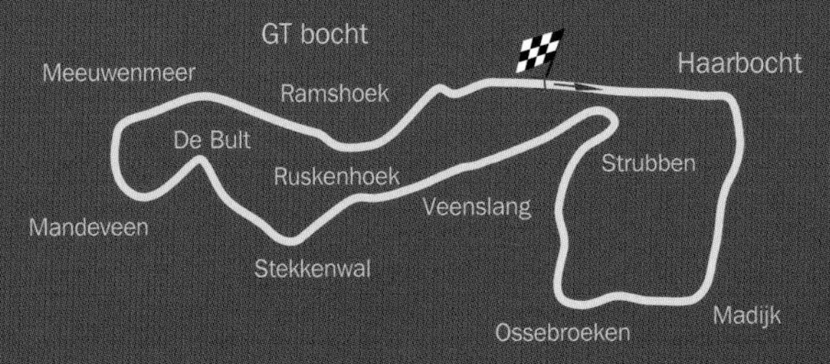
GT bocht
Meeuwenmeer
Ramshoek
Haarbocht
De Bult
Ruskenhoek
Strubben
Veenslang
Mandeveen
Stekkenwal
Ossebroeken
Madijk

CIRCUIT LENGTH: 3.745 miles/6.027 km

MotoGP

19 laps, 71.155 miles/114.513 km

Pos.	Rider (Nat.)	No.	Machine	Laps	Time & speed
1	Sete Gibernau (E)	15	Honda	19	42m 39.006s 100.100 mph/ 161.096 km/h
2	Max Biaggi (I)	3	Honda	19	42m 49.117s
3	Valentino Rossi (I)	46	Honda	19	42m 52.881s
4	Carlos Checa (E)	7	Yamaha	19	43m 15.984s
5	Olivier Jacque (F)	19	Yamaha	19	43m 19.351s
6	Loris Capirossi (I)	65	Ducati	19	43m 21.183s
7	Colin Edwards (USA)	45	Aprilia	19	43m 29.524s
8	Alex Barros (BR)	4	Yamaha	19	43m 38.029s
9	Troy Bayliss (AUS)	12	Ducati	19	44m 12.542s
10	Alex Hofmann (D)	66	Kawasaki	19	44m 15.409s
11	Nicky Hayden (USA)	69	Honda	19	44m 18.039s
12	Tohru Ukawa (J)	11	Honda	19	44m 21.404s
13	Shinya Nakano (J)	56	Yamaha	19	44m 22.696s
14	Andrew Pitt (AUS)	88	Kawasaki	18	43m 44.761s
15	John Hopkins (USA)	21	Suzuki	18	43m 48.247s
16	Makoto Tamada (J)	6	Honda	18	43m 55.348s
17	Ryuichi Kiyonari (J)	23	Honda	18	43m 58.430s
18	Garry McCoy (AUS)	8	Kawasaki	18	44m 51.345s
	Noriyuki Haga (J)	41	Aprilia	17	DNF
	Yukio Kagayama (J)	71	Suzuki	14	DNF
	Marco Melandri (I)	33	Yamaha	14	DNF
	Nobuatsu Aoki (J)	9	Proton KR	10	DNF
	Jeremy McWilliams (GB)	99	Proton KR	9	DNF

Fastest lap: Gibernau, 2m 11.805s, 102.287 mph/164.615 km/h.

Lap record: Valentino Rossi, I (Honda), 2m 00.973s, 111.446 mph/ 179.355 km/h (2002).

Event best maximum speed: Rossi, 187.1 mph/301.1 km/h (qualifying practice no. 1).

Qualifying: 1 Capirossi, 1m 59.770s; 2 Biaggi, 1m 59.941s; 3 Rossi, 1m 59.964s; 4 Checa, 2m 00.169s; 5 Jacque, 2m 00.294s; 6 Barros, 2m 00.501s; 7 Gibernau, 2m 00.553s; 8 Melandri, 2m 00.553s; 9 Edwards, 2m 00.579s; 10 Nakano, 2m 00.693s; 11 Ukawa, 2m 00.929s; 12 Hayden, 2m 00.998s; 13 Bayliss, 2m 01.147s; 14 Haga, 2m 01.188s; 15 Kagayama, 2m 01.601s; 16 Hopkins, 2m 01.715s; 17 Hofmann, 2m 02.172s; 18 Tamada, 2m 02.351s; 19 McWilliams, 2m 02.996s; 20 Pitt, 2m 03.371s; 21 McCoy, 2m 03.407s; 22 Kiyonari, 2m 03.707s; 23 Aoki, 2m 06.172s.

Fastest race laps: 1 Gibernau, 2m 11.805s; 2 Rossi, 2m 12.483s; 3 Biaggi, 2m 12.653s; 4 Capirossi, 2m 12.983s; 5 Checa, 2m 13.191s; 6 Haga, 2m 13.669s; 7 Bayliss, 2m 13.727s; 8 Edwards, 2m 13.747s; 9 Jacque, 2m 13.783s; 10 Barros, 2m 14.558s; 11 Nakano, 2m 14.668s; 12 Ukawa, 2m 15.158s; 13 Hofmann, 2m 15.680s; 14 Hayden, 2m 15.791s; 15 Kagayama, 2m 16.133s; 16 Melandri, 2m 17.022s; 17 Hopkins, 2m 17.590s; 18 Kiyonari, 2m 19.190s; 19 Tamada, 2m 19.361s; 20 Pitt, 2m 19.750s; 21 McWilliams, 2m 21.869s; 22 McCoy, 2m 22.297s; 23 Aoki, 2m 27.259s.

World Championship: 1 Rossi, 151; 2 Gibernau, 113; 3 Biaggi, 105; 4 Capirossi, 71; 5 Barros, 62; 6 Ukawa, 56; 7 Bayliss, 53; 8 Checa and Nakano, 47; 10 Jacque, 43; 11 Hayden, 38; 12 Edwards and Tamada, 34; 14 Haga, 21; 15 Abe, 18; 16 Hopkins, 17; 17 McWilliams, 14; 18 Aoki and Kiyonari, 11; 20 Melandri, 9; 21 Hofmann and McCoy, 8; 23 Roberts, 6; 24 Pitt, 3.

250 cc

18 laps, 67.410 miles/108.468 km

Pos.	Rider (Nat.)	No.	Machine	Laps	Time & speed
1	Anthony West (AUS)	14	Aprilia	18	41m 57.413s 96.399 mph/ 155.139 km/h
2	Franco Battaini (I)	21	Aprilia	18	42m 00.400s
3	Sylvain Guintoli (F)	50	Aprilia	18	42m 08.074s
4	Manuel Poggiali (RSM)	54	Aprilia	18	42m 11.573s
5	Sebastian Porto (ARG)	5	Honda	18	42m 24.030s
6	Roberto Rolfo (I)	3	Honda	18	42m 29.361s
7	Erwan Nigon (F)	36	Aprilia	18	43m 11.610s
8	Christian Gemmel (D)	15	Honda	18	43m 22.071s
9	Hugo Marchand (F)	9	Aprilia	18	43m 33.572s
10	Johan Stigefelt (S)	16	Aprilia	18	43m 33.683s
11	Alex Debon (E)	6	Honda	18	43m 53.662s
12	Jakub Smrz (CZ)	96	Honda	18	43m 54.392s
13	Toni Elias (E)	24	Aprilia	18	44m 00.640s
14	Alex Baldolini (I)	26	Aprilia	18	44m 00.934s
15	Klaus Nöhles (D)	30	Aprilia	17	42m 01.894s
16	Henk vd Lagemaat (NL)	18	Honda	17	42m 22.303s
17	Hector Faubel (E)	33	Aprilia	17	42m 40.729s
18	Katja Poensgen (D)	98	Honda	17	42m 50.355s
19	Jan Blok (NL)	46	Honda	17	43m 21.001s
20	Christian Pistoni (I)	29	Yamaha	17	43m 30.927s
21	Arie Vos (NL)	47	Yamaha	17	43m 30.976s
22	Hans Smees (NL)	48	Honda	17	43m 31.320s
23	Joan Olive (E)	11	Aprilia	16	42m 48.969s
24	Chaz Davies (GB)	57	Aprilia	16	42m 55.368s
	Fonsi Nieto (E)	10	Aprilia	6	DNF
	Naoki Matsudo (J)	8	Yamaha	4	DNF
	Randy de Puniet (F)	7	Aprilia	1	DNF
	Eric Bataille (F)	34	Honda	0	DNF
	Randy Gevers (NL)	49	Honda		DNQ

Fastest lap: Battaini, 2m 16.926s, 98.462 mph/158.459 km/h.

Lap record: Roberto Rolfo, I (Honda), 2m 04.824s, 108.008 mph/ 173.822 km/h (2002).

Event best maximum speed: Elias, 157.9 mph/254.1 km/h (warm-up).

Qualifying: 1 Poggiali, 2m 04.050s; 2 de Puniet, 2m 04.586s; 3 Elias, 2m 04.712s; 4 Nieto, 2m 04.866s; 5 Porto, 2m 04.920s; 6 Guintoli, 2m 05.190s; 7 Battaini, 2m 05.190s; 8 Rolfo, 2m 05.547s; 9 West, 2m 05.755s; 10 Matsudo, 2m 05.755s; 11 Bataille, 2m 06.330s; 12 Nigon, 2m 06.417s; 13 Olive, 2m 06.585s; 14 Nöhles, 2m 06.957s; 15 Faubel, 2m 07.040s; 16 Stigefelt, 2m 07.400s; 17 Marchand, 2m 07.529s; 18 Debon, 2m 07.545s; 19 Davies, 2m 07.719s; 20 Gemmel, 2m 08.125s; 21 Smrz, 2m 08.128s; 22 Baldolini, 2m 08.828s; 23 Vos, 2m 09.700s; 24 vd Lagemaat, 2m 09.713s; 25 Pistoni, 2m 11.106s; 26 Smees, 2m 11.845s; 27 Blok, 2m 12.104s; 28 Poensgen, 2m 12.716s; 29 Gevers, 2m 13.743s.

Fastest race laps: 1 Battaini, 2m 16.926s; 2 Poggiali, 2m 17.163s; 3 West, 2m 17.293s; 4 Guintoli, 2m 17.589s; 5 Rolfo, 2m 18.520s; 6 Porto, 2m 18.902s; 7 Nieto, 2m 20.206s; 8 Stigefelt, 2m 20.691s; 9 Elias, 2m 20.938s; 10 Nigon, 2m 21.070s; 11 Nöhles, 2m 21.072s; 12 Marchand, 2m 21.133s; 13 Smrz, 2m 21.276s; 14 Baldolini, 2m 21.567s; 15 Gemmel, 2m 21.904s; 16 Debon, 2m 22.220s; 17 Vos, 2m 23.473s; 18 Matsudo, 2m 24.359s; 19 vd Lagemaat, 2m 24.807s; 20 Faubel, 2m 25.531s; 21 Poensgen, 2m 26.274s; 22 Blok, 2m 29.421s; 23 Smees, 2m 29.459s; 24 Pistoni, 2m 29.836s; 25 Olive, 2m 30.298s; 26 Davies, 2m 30.739s; 27 de Puniet, 2m 39.792s.

World Championship: 1 Poggiali, 101; 2 Rolfo, 86; 3 Elias, 84; 4 de Puniet and Nieto, 81; 6 Battaini and West, 78; 8 Porto, 64; 9 Guintoli, 58; 10 Matsudo, 53; 11 Debon, 34; 12 Olive, 27; 13 Aoyama, 20; 14 Gemmel, 18; 15 Stigefelt, 17; 16 Takahashi, 16; 17 Nigon, 15; 18 Marchand, 14; 19 Baldolini, 13; 20 Faubel, 11; 21 Bataille, Kayo and Smrz, 7; 24 Nöhles, 5; 25 Davies, 4; 26 Heidolf, 1.

125 cc

17 laps, 63.665 miles/102.459 km

Pos.	Rider (Nat.)	No.	Machine	Laps	Time & speed
1	Steve Jenkner (D)	17	Aprilia	17	42m 25.609s 90.035 mph/ 144.897 km/h
2	Pablo Nieto (E)	22	Aprilia	17	42m 36.798s
3	Hector Barbera (E)	80	Aprilia	17	42m 50.292s
4	Youichi Ui (J)	41	Aprilia	17	42m 56.029s
5	Stefano Perugini (I)	7	Aprilia	17	43m 12.048s
6	Alex de Angelis (RSM)	15	Aprilia	17	43m 27.335s
7	Thomas Luthi (CH)	12	Honda	17	43m 27.464s
8	Daniel Pedrosa (E)	3	Honda	17	43m 30.207s
9	Gabor Talmacsi (H)	79	Aprilia	17	43m 30.785s
10	Andrea Dovizioso (I)	34	Honda	17	43m 31.629s
11	Mika Kallio (SF)	36	Honda	17	43m 31.684s
12	Simone Corsi (I)	24	Honda	17	43m 32.028s
13	Gino Borsoi (I)	23	Aprilia	17	43m 32.483s
14	Fabrizio Lai (I)	32	Malaguti	17	43m 33.910s
15	Mirko Giansanti (I)	6	Aprilia	17	43m 33.912s
16	Lucio Cecchinello (I)	4	Aprilia	17	43m 44.587s
17	Julian Simon (E)	31	Malaguti	17	44m 11.359s
18	Adri den Bekker (NL)	75	Honda	17	44m 17.282s
19	Mike di Meglio (F)	63	Aprilia	17	44m 17.610s
20	Marco Simoncelli (I)	58	Aprilia	17	44m 31.511s
21	Emilio Alzamora (E)	26	Derbi	17	44m 33.119s
22	Max Sabbatani (I)	11	Aprilia	17	44m 57.548s
23	Imre Toth (H)	25	Honda	16	42m 37.939s
24	Jarno vd Marel (NL)	76	Honda	16	43m 24.747s
	Leon Camier (GB)	21	Honda	14	DNF
	Masao Azuma (J)	8	Honda	12	DNF
	Alvaro Bautista (E)	19	Aprilia	10	DNF
	Raymond Schouten (NL)	77	Honda	10	DNF
	Peter Lenart (H)	78	Honda	10	DNF
	Jorge Lorenzo (E)	48	Derbi	9	DNF
	Roberto Locatelli (I)	10	KTM	9	DNF
	Arnaud Vincent (F)	1	KTM	7	DNF
	Mark van Kreij (NL)	89	Honda	7	DNF
	Gioele Pellino (I)	42	Aprilia	7	DNF
	Casey Stoner (AUS)	27	Aprilia	2	DNF
	Stefano Bianco (I)	33	Gilera	0	DNF
	Robbin Harms (DK)	88	Aprilia		EXC

Fastest lap: Barbera, 2m 26.247s, 92.186 mph/148.359 km/h.

Lap record: Joan Olive, E (Honda), 2m 11.209s, 102.752 mph/ 165.363 km/h (2002).

Event best maximum speed: Ui, 138.3 mph/222.6 km/h (warm-up).

Qualifying: 1 Pedrosa, 2m 10.724s; 2 de Angelis, 2m 10.777s; 3 Jenkner, 2m 10.814s; 4 Perugini, 2m 11.052s; 5 Luthi, 2m 11.554s; 6 Stoner, 2m 11.632s; 7 Ui, 2m 11.700s; 8 Lorenzo, 2m 11.714s; 9 Barbera, 2m 11.741s; 10 Kallio, 2m 11.957s; 11 Nieto, 2m 12.000s; 12 Cecchinello, 2m 12.043s; 13 Borsoi, 2m 12.203s; 14 Lai, 2m 12.204s; 15 Simoncelli, 2m 12.267s; 16 Dovizioso, 2m 12.398s; 17 Talmacsi, 2m 12.467s; 18 Corsi, 2m 12.608s; 19 Giansanti, 2m 12.799s; 20 Bautista, 2m 13.007s; 21 Vincent, 2m 13.168s; 22 Azuma, 2m 13.420s; 23 Harms, 2m 13.505s; 24 Sabbatani, 2m 13.690s; 25 di Meglio, 2m 14.095s; 26 Toth, 2m 14.185s; 27 Bianco, 2m 14.345s; 28 Pellino, 2m 14.404s; 29 Simon, 2m 14.521s; 30 Locatelli, 2m 14.621s; 31 Schouten, 2m 14.715s; 32 Alzamora, 2m 14.912s; 33 vd Marel, 2m 15.604s; 34 Camier, 2m 16.036s; 35 Lenart, 2m 17.939s; 36 den Bekker, 2m 18.672s; 37 van Kreij, 2m 19.791s.

Fastest race laps: 1 Barbera, 2m 26.247s; 2 Jenkner, 2m 26.435s; 3 Nieto, 2m 26.582s; 4 Perugini, 2m 28.413s; 5 Ui, 2m 28.653s; 6 Luthi, 2m 29.229s; 7 Bautista, 2m 29.498s; 8 Lorenzo, 2m 29.639s; 9 Azuma, 2m 29.906s; 10 Vincent, 2m 30.011s; 11 Lai, 2m 30.018s; 12 Talmacsi, 2m 30.091s; 13 Harms, 2m 30.119s; 14 Corsi, 2m 30.179s; 15 Dovizioso, 2m 30.307s; 16 de Angelis, 2m 30.456s; 17 Borsoi, 2m 30.481s; 18 Giansanti, 2m 30.525s; 19 Locatelli, 2m 30.602s; 20 Cecchinello, 2m 30.761s; 21 Kallio, 2m 30.833s; 22 Simoncelli, 2m 30.932s; 23 Pedrosa, 2m 30.948s; 24 den Bekker, 2m 31.096s; 25 di Meglio, 2m 31.151s; 26 Simon, 2m 31.709s; 27 Camier, 2m 32.049s; 28 Schouten, 2m 32.318s; 29 Stoner, 2m 32.384s; 30 Sabbatani, 2m 33.147s; 31 Alzamora, 2m 33.857s; 32 Lenart, 2m 35.280s; 33 vd Marel, 2m 35.451s; 34 van Kreij, 2m 35.588s; 35 Toth, 2m 37.087s; 36 Pellino, 2m 39.027s.

World Championship: 1 Pedrosa, 124; 2 Jenkner, 98; 3 Cecchinello, 91; 4 Perugini, 76; 5 Dovizioso, 73; 6 Nieto, 67; 7 Ui, 64; 8 de Angelis, 63; 9 Luthi, 48; 10 Giansanti, 41; 11 Barbera, 40; 12 Borsoi, 36; 13 Kallio, 31; 14 Stoner, 29; 15 Azuma, 20; 16 Corsi, 17; 17 Talmacsi, 16; 18 Pellino, 12; 19 Lorenzo, 11; 20 Locatelli, 7; 21 Vincent, 6; 22 di Meglio and Sabbatani, 3; 24 Lai and Simoncelli, 2.

BRITISH GP
DONINGTON

Above: Rossi triumphant. Or so he thought. Crew chief Jerry Burgess peeks around the back. The bad news has yet to come.

Left: Rossi's British army got what they wanted.

Far left: Biaggi feels the heat, as Rossi and Gibernau fill the air with noise behind him.

Below: Jay Vincent was back, and knocking on the top ten in his only race of the year.
All photographs: Mark Wernham

Rules is rules, no matter what. Thus it was perfectly right and fair that Valentino Rossi was penalised by losing his race win, because of his clear and obvious infringement in passing Capirossi into Redgate Corner – Turn One – under yellow flags. Wasn't it? After all, British motor racing is surely the home of probity and fair play.

Or not. The offence was clear cut. The penalty a muddle. Most of all because of the timing. They didn't tell Rossi until after he'd climbed off the rostrum, already celebrating his return to winning form.

The reason Race Direction took so long to catch on was because they were still either rushing from their start-line posts to the control centre, or studying start-line videos for jump-starts. It happened at the beginning of the second lap: the luckless Ukawa had tumbled at the first corner, and they were still moving rider and debris as the pack came surging past the pits, led by Biaggi.

Even so, the delay seemed unconscionable – in F1, there is a three-lap window for such penalties to be applied; miss that, and he's got away with it. And the vagueness. Originally, Rossi was penalised 30 seconds, the notional time lost by a ten-second stop-and-go – the probable penalty had he been rumbled straight away. This was unfair, argued his team. If he'd known of such a penalty, he'd have been able to ride faster to make up for it. Since he was already at lap-record pace, this seems rather optimistic, but Race Direction gave in anyway, taking a wild guess that he'd have made up about a second a lap. They cut the penalty to ten seconds. This meant Rossi finished third rather than seventh.

And that Max Biaggi had won his first race on a Honda, without even having to arrive at the flag in front of Rossi. A further boost to his spirits, after he had also been supplied with the latest factory chassis upgrade. Nothing that made much difference, but an acknowledgment from above, with perhaps more to come. It was not a win in which to revel, but typically, Max found a personal angle on the incident: 'I can sympathise. The same thing happened to me in Barcelona in 1998. I won on the track, but was disqualified. The difference is that decision cost me the championship.' (Another difference was that Biaggi had persistently ignored not only stop-and-go flags, but the black flag as well.)

And Rossi? 'I didn't see the flags, and did nothing wrong intentionally to take advantage. But I can't argue with the law. I race on the track, not in the office.'

It was another embarrassment at a venue where there is plenty of reason for it. The crowds have come back to the British GP – 72,000, compared with 18,000 in 2000. But there is no air of prosperity with them. Compared with, say, Malaysia, Valencia, Assen – indeed, almost anywhere except Rio – the pit and paddock facilities are unprepossessing and down-at-heel, those for spectators of a similar quality, and even the approaches are wanting. The only good thing about Donington is that they have at least kept the race alive through the hard times – and that's certainly something.

The weekend began, as usual, with the Riders for Health Day of Champions, an extremely convivial affair that once again broke its own record, raising £117,000 to mobilise health-care workers in rural Africa. There was a dark cloud, however: not all those attending had charity in mind, and the theft of passports and money from an HRC truck (the documents were returned later cloak-and-dagger style) made many wonder how long the paddock could be thrown open in this way.

The two-strokes made a come-back at Donington, although not all were exactly fit and fighting. WCM had hurriedly assembled four assorted privateer Roc/Harris Yamahas, two from the defunct Sabre sports team, another from Clifford's home in New Zealand, and the fourth (arriving on the morning practice began) from team patron Bob MacLean's private collection in the USA. Clifford's bike had been campaigned between 1994 and 1997 by a succession of WCM riders: Niall Mackenzie, Neil Hodgson, James Haydon and Kirk McCarthy; MacLean's had finished third in the British GP back in 1993, ridden by Mackenzie.

The others were closer to the pace at this technical track, being at a disadvantage only in the point-and-squirt sections between the slow corners at the end of the lap. The doughty Proton KR3s were called in at the last minute after the team ran short of crankshafts for the four-stroke – they were still awaiting redesigned replacements. McWilliams persevered with his bike until race morning, the oil leaks not returning, before succumbing to the inevitable and going out to have some fun in the corners.

Out of mothballs came jobless 250 rider Jay Vincent, who only knew that he had a ride on the morning before practice began. He rushed off to get a medical; Padgetts dusted off an old Aprilia. Vincent qualified and finished 11th. He was missed from 2003's lacklustre 250 class, a talent wasted.

Two past masters provided notable history lessons. One came from John Surtees, a genuine giant with both two-wheel and four-wheel world championships to prove it. Inducted into the Hall of Fame, Surtees advised Rossi that if he wanted to move to cars, he'd better do it quickly. 'Everybody has a personal built-in rev-counter, and you have to make the change while you are still accelerating up your power curve,' said the 68-year-old legend. Other ex-motor cyclists, like Mike Hailwood and Johnny Cecotto, had left it too late, he opined.

Another came from former top privateer Jack Findlay, the first GP winner on Michelin tyres, at a gala party to celebrate the manufacturer's 300th, at Assen. Asked how he'd felt after his pioneering victory, he replied, 'I didn't think about it much…but then we didn't think much in those days.'

Above: The return of the good old days? The vast crowd thought so.
Photograph: Mark Wernham

MOTOGP RACE – 30 laps

The continuing heat wave ensured there was no rain, and also meant that there was none of the usual cold-tyre tumbles at the notorious Craner Curves. Rossi was always fast, only to be displaced by Gibernau and Melandri; his response was scotched by a cracked front wheel rim and a deflating tyre. By then, Biaggi had overtaken them both for his first pole of the year. Times were close and fast, the pole nearly a second quicker than last year. Bayliss was fractionally the faster of the Ducatis, on the second row, at another familiar circuit.

Barros missed the start, having pulled out of the pits in morning warm-up to be knocked flying by Kagayama, who was struggling with his Suzuki's braking, going into the first corner.

Biaggi led away from Gibernau, Capirossi, Melandri and Bayliss; Rossi was slow off the line. Near the back, Edwards had an encounter with another rider, which bounced him into Ukawa, sending him off into the first-corner gravel trap and precipitating the situation that would spoil Rossi's day.

Rossi was up to fifth by the end of lap one, and third next time around, smashing the lap record. But he'd started the lap by diving inside Capirossi, intent on regaining ground rather than concentrating on the flags. And he carried on doing so, second to Biaggi by lap three and hounding his rival, waiting to pounce as his harder tyre choice started to pay dividends.

The others were still close, until lap five, when Melandri crashed in the middle of the chicane. He was lying fourth and broke up the pack as his bike slid back across the track, narrowly missing Capirossi and fast-starting Hayden. This gave the front trio a three-second breathing space.

Gibernau was struggling with the fast pace and lost a second on lap seven when he ran wide at the chicane. He was never a threat again.

When would Rossi pass Max? Could he do so? The pressure was on, but he was relieved of having to exert it when Biaggi braked too late and ran wide into the chicane. Just two hairpins later, Rossi was 1.6 seconds ahead, a gap that never became smaller until the last lap, when he played a bit with wheelies and slides for the crowd, finishing 1.2 seconds in the lead. Gibernau was another seven seconds adrift – still close enough to gain a place when Rossi received his ten-second penalty, and well clear of any threat from behind.

After Melandri's spin, the race formed into two groups. Capirossi was just clear of the first gang, from Checa, Jacque, Bayliss, Edwards and Hayden. By half-distance, Bayliss was ahead of Checa; four laps later, Jacque was aiming to follow on when he suffered a big highsider on the exit from the Melbourne hairpin. At about the same time, Edwards lost his right knee-slider – a major drawback at such a right-handed track – and when Haga closed from behind, he had no answer. The Japanese rider was still moving, taking Hayden with five laps left, then moving forward to challenge Checa for sixth, only to think better of it. 'My back tyre was almost finished, so I preferred not to make any stupid mistakes,' he said. He was just half a second adrift at the flag.

The next group had been led on lap seven by Hopkins, although as it warmed up he ran into handling problems, letting Haga through. Nakano and Kagayama were up close and Tamada was hanging on grimly – an all-Japanese posse. Nakano was past Hopkins at half-distance and moved up toward the next group, catching Edwards and dogging his back wheel for five laps before nipping past on the last one.

Then came Hopkins and Kagayama, with Tamada's Bridgestones for once not giving him a hot-weather edge, so he was five seconds back at the finish.

Kiyonari was next, finally getting clear of Aoki's hastily set up two-stroke when the older rider had clutch problems; the Kawasakis were a lap down.

Burns had crashed out on the second lap, breaking his collar-bone in his first two-stroke race; team-mate de Gea had started from the pit lane and returned there after nine laps. McWilliams had battled with his last-minute two-stroke, running off at the chicane after encountering backshifting problems on lap 13 and giving up the unequal struggle. 'I really wanted to be riding the four-stroke,' he said.

250 cc RACE – 27 laps

Donington is a bogey track for Poggiali, who crashed twice in practice, but still qualified second to Nieto, with Elias alongside, then Matsudo in Yamaha's first front row of the year. De Puniet led the second row; Vincent was 11th on his old Aprilia.

Elias grabbed a one-second lead on the first lap as Nieto took his time to get going, Rolfo chasing him all the way around. Poggiali was next and about to pass both of them on lap two, closing directly on to Elias, the pair drawing clear of Nieto by a couple of seconds as de Puniet got past Rolfo and started to push the Spaniard hard.

Nieto is often slower with a full tank, and before half-distance he was making life harder for the Frenchman, who ran straight on at the chicane on lap 12. The former was speeding up and soon after had closed the gap on the leaders, Poggiali now in front. His intervention inspired a flawed attack at Macleans by Elias, who dropped to third after running on to the dirt at the exit.

On lap 20, Nieto dived inside Poggiali at Melbourne and started to force the pace, with Elias losing touch. The Spaniard toughed it out to the finish, taking his first win of the year by a quarter of a second.

West was coming into the picture at this point, after a moment on the first lap had dropped him out of the top ten. By half-distance, he'd passed Porto and was fifth, chasing Rolfo, although when he tried to pass him at the chicane, he ran wide and dropped behind again. But Rolfo was closing on Elias, so the Australian followed on until they'd caught up, then dived inside the Honda at the hairpin.

Above: Poggiali finds the other side of the limit in practice.
Photograph: Clive Challinor Motorsport Photography

Below: Rolfo leads a determined West.
Photograph: Mark Wernham

Bottom: Nieto heads for his first win of the season, chased by de Puniet and Rolfo.
Photograph: Gold & Goose

Sanctuary from the madding crowd for Rossi. The
focus is total.
Photograph: Mark Wernham

Now he set about Elias, passing him for the first time at Melbourne on lap 23. Elias promptly reversed the positions at the next hairpin. On lap 25, West did it again, and this time he made it stick. With two laps left, the last-corners showdown was approaching fast.

Elias held off West's attack through Melbourne and dived inside into Goddards, the last corner. It should have been a clincher, but West had judged his speed perfectly and moved past again at the exit as Elias ran wide. He took a third successive rostrum by half a second.

Rolfo was a close fifth; Porto a way back in sixth, with Battaini close and de Puniet a little further adrift. Matsudo was never on the pace, a distant ninth. With Debon tenth, Vincent was 11th in his first race of the year; fellow-Briton Chaz Davies was two places back, just failing to pounce on Faubel. Wild card Desborough crashed out, Dickinson retired and Sawford failed to qualify by less than two-tenths.

125 cc RACE – 25 laps

Hector Barbera (16) became the third-youngest ever GP winner when he emerged the victor of an almost race-long five-bike battle, ahead of Andrea Dovizioso and Stefano Perugini. The big loser was points leader Dani Pedrosa (Telefónica MoviStar Honda), who was knocked flying in the second-to-last corner by Perugini.

Lucio Cecchinello (Aprilia) had earlier crashed out of the lead in a race of many spills, remounting to finish tenth. Four riders crashed out in the second lap alone.

Perugini took the pole ahead of Pedrosa, but it was Dovizioso who set off in the lead, chased by Barbera, Pedrosa, Cecchinello, Perugini and Ui. Jenkner and front-row first-timer Corsi were with them, but crashed out together at the Old Hairpin on lap one.

The crashing continued: Sabbatani, Lorenzo, Lai and Luthi on the second lap, the last-named remounting; then Ui four laps later, already out of touch with the front group.

They were back and forth on the swoops and hairpins; Barbera took the lead on lap five, then lost it to Cecchinello just before half-distance. The veteran started to stretch the pace, the rest hanging on grimly over the next three laps,

until Cecchinello pushed too hard into the last hairpin, losing the front wheel; he sprinted back to his bike to rejoin in 12th.

Barbera was in front again, but there were ten more dramatic laps. Next time around, luckless wild card Chester Lusk, about to be lapped, fell at the chicane, his bike skating across the track and almost taking down the leading group of four. Then Barbera found a quicker way past some more backmarkers to gain a little gap, only for the others to close it again.

He led for the whole of the last lap, but with no comfort. Perugini was pushing and nudging, until he ran wide at Macleans, short of brakes, and dropped to fourth. Now Pedrosa was third, then he slipped past Dovizioso before the chicane, only for the Italian to reverse the positions on the exit. Pedrosa tried again into Melbourne, but the bikes touched and he had to lift – just as Perugini was attacking on the outside line. They collided and Pedrosa went down.

Less than ten seconds back, de Angelis won a long battle with Stoner; Nieto had moved through a big mid-field gang for sixth. Five seconds behind, Kallio held off Vincent and Talmacsi – the Frenchman's eighth was KTM's best finish so far. Cecchinello was closing at the finish, bringing Giansanti and Pellino with him.

Barbera had turned 16 in the previous November, and the Majorcan seems set to be a potent force.

DONINGTON PARK

Old Hairpin
McLeans Corner
Craner Curves
Goddard's Corner
Coppice Corner
Redgate
The Esses
Melbourne Hairpin

CIRCUIT LENGTH: 2.500 miles/4.023 km

CINZANO BRITISH grand prix

13 JULY 2003

Photograph: Mark Wernham

MotoGP

30 laps, 75.000 miles/120.690 km

Pos.	Rider (Nat.)	No.	Machine	Laps	Time & speed
1	Max Biaggi (I)	3	Honda	30	46m 06.688s 97.581 mph/ 157.041 km/h
2	Sete Gibernau (E)	15	Honda	30	46m 13.826s
3	Valentino Rossi (I)	46	Honda	30	46m 15.482s
4	Loris Capirossi (I)	65	Ducati	30	46m 19.729s
5	Troy Bayliss (AUS)	12	Ducati	30	46m 22.957s
6	Carlos Checa (E)	7	Yamaha	30	46m 33.773s
7	Noriyuki Haga (J)	41	Aprilia	30	46m 34.350s
8	Nicky Hayden (USA)	69	Honda	30	46m 38.700s
9	Shinya Nakano (J)	56	Yamaha	30	46m 41.487s
10	Colin Edwards (USA)	45	Aprilia	30	46m 41.689s
11	John Hopkins (USA)	21	Suzuki	30	46m 54.853s
12	Yukio Kagayama (J)	71	Suzuki	30	47m 07.111s
13	Makoto Tamada (J)	6	Honda	30	47m 12.848s
14	Ryuichi Kiyonari (J)	23	Honda	30	47m 21.554s
15	Nobuatsu Aoki (J)	9	Proton KR	30	47m 36.979s
16	Garry McCoy (AUS)	8	Kawasaki	29	46m 08.643s
17	Andrew Pitt (AUS)	88	Kawasaki	29	46m 46.667s
	Olivier Jacque (F)	19	Yamaha	18	DNF
	Jeremy McWilliams (GB)	99	Proton KR	13	DNF
	David de Gea (E)	52	Sabre V4	9	DNF
	Marco Melandri (I)	33	Yamaha	4	DNF
	Chris Burns (GB)	35	Roc Yamaha	1	DNF
	Tohru Ukawa (J)	11	Honda	0	DNF
	Alex Barros (BR)	4	Yamaha		DNS

Fastest lap: Rossi, 1m 31.023s, 98.867 mph/159.111 km/h (record).

Previous record: Valentino Rossi, I (Honda), 1m 32.247s, 97.555 mph/ 157.000 km/h (2002).

Event best maximum speed: Jacque, 170.1 mph/273.8 km/h (race).

Qualifying: 1 Biaggi, 1m 30.740s; 2 Melandri, 1m 30.862s; 3 Melandri, 1m 30.926s; 4 Rossi, 1m 30.938s; 5 Checa, 1m 31.035s; 6 Bayliss, 1m 31.036s; 7 Capirossi, 1m 31.067s; 8 Jacque, 1m 31.241s; 9 Edwards, 1m 31.354s; 10 Ukawa, 1m 31.385s; 11 Nakano, 1m 31.614s; 12 Barros, 1m 31.776s; 13 Hayden, 1m 31.779s; 14 Haga, 1m 31.877s; 15 Hopkins, 1m 31.962s; 16 Tamada, 1m 32.526s; 17 Kagayama, 1m 32.573s; 18 McCoy, 1m 32.793s; 19 McWilliams, 1m 32.802s; 20 Kiyonari, 1m 33.288s; 21 Pitt, 1m 33.705s; 22 Aoki, 1m 34.364s; 23 Burns, 1m 34.400s; 24 de Gea, 1m 36.851s.

Fastest race laps: 1 Rossi, 1m 31.023s; 2 Checa, 1m 31.598s; 3 Biaggi, 1m 31.611s; 4 Capirossi, 1m 31.651s; 5 Gibernau, 1m 31.663s; 6 Melandri, 1m 31.822s; 7 Bayliss, 1m 31.826s; 8 Jacque, 1m 32.228s; 10 Hayden, 1m 32.373s; 11 Haga, 1m 32.499s; 12 Hopkins, 1m 32.528s; 13 Nakano, 1m 32.707s; 14 Tamada, 1m 32.835s; 15 Kagayama, 1m 32.866s; 16 Kiyonari, 1m 33.567s; 17 McWilliams, 1m 33.855s; 18 McCoy, 1m 34.078s; 19 Aoki, 1m 34.139s; 20 Pitt, 1m 34.907s; 21 de Gea, 1m 37.638s; 22 Burns, 1m 43.551s.

World Championship: 1 Rossi, 167; 2 Gibernau, 133; 3 Biaggi, 130; 4 Capirossi, 84; 5 Bayliss, 64; 6 Barros, 62; 7 Checa, 57; 8 Ukawa, 56; 9 Nakano, 54; 10 Hayden, 46; 11 Jacque, 43; 12 Edwards, 40; 13 Tamada, 37; 14 Haga, 30; 15 Hopkins, 22; 16 Abe, 18; 17 McWilliams, 14; 18 Kiyonari, 13; 19 Aoki, 12; 20 Melandri, 9; 21 Hofmann and McCoy, 8; 23 Roberts, 6; 24 Kagayama, 4; 25 Pitt, 3.

---

250 cc

27 laps, 67.500 miles/108.621 km

Pos.	Rider (Nat.)	No.	Machine	Laps	Time & speed
1	Fonsi Nieto (E)	10	Aprilia	27	42m 58.011s 94.250 mph/ 151.681 km/h
2	Manuel Poggiali (RSM)	54	Aprilia	27	42m 58.280s
3	Anthony West (AUS)	14	Aprilia	27	43m 00.569s
4	Toni Elias (E)	24	Aprilia	27	43m 00.944s
5	Roberto Rolfo (I)	3	Honda	27	43m 00.945s
6	Sebastian Porto (ARG)	5	Honda	27	43m 23.041s
7	Franco Battaini (I)	21	Aprilia	27	43m 25.674s
8	Randy de Puniet (F)	7	Aprilia	27	43m 29.602s
9	Naoki Matsudo (J)	8	Yamaha	27	43m 48.359s
10	Alex Debon (E)	6	Honda	27	43m 51.348s
11	Jay Vincent (GB)	23	Aprilia	27	43m 56.109s
12	Hector Faubel (E)	33	Aprilia	27	43m 58.061s
13	Chaz Davies (GB)	57	Aprilia	27	43m 58.261s
14	Jakub Smrz (CZ)	96	Honda	27	44m 08.366s
15	Dirk Heidolf (D)	28	Aprilia	27	44m 09.677s
16	Hugo Marchand (F)	9	Aprilia	27	44m 13.047s
17	Alex Baldolini (I)	26	Aprilia	27	44m 21.693s
18	Henk vd Lagemaat (NL)	18	Honda	26	43m 54.583s
19	Katja Poensgen (D)	98	Honda	26	44m 36.197s
	Joan Olive (E)	11	Aprilia	19	DNF
	Erwan Nigon (F)	36	Aprilia	19	DNF
	Lee Dickinson (GB)	58	Yamaha	12	DNF
	Johan Stigefelt (S)	16	Aprilia	8	DNF
	Phillip Desborough (GB)	60	Yamaha	5	DNF
	Eric Bataille (F)	34	Honda	4	DNF
	Christian Gemmel (D)	15	Honda	4	DNF
	Sylvain Guintoli (F)	50	Aprilia	1	DNF
	Andrew Sawford (GB)	59	Honda		DNQ

Fastest lap: Poggiali, 1m 34.558s, 95.171 mph/153.163 km/h.

Lap record: Daijiro Kato, J (Honda), 1m 34.096s, 95.638 mph/ 153.915 km/h (2001).

Event best maximum speed: Poggiali, 147.5 mph/237.4 km/h (warm-up).

Qualifying: 1 Nieto, 1m 33.859s; 2 Poggiali, 1m 34.215s; 3 Elias, 1m 34.386s; 4 Matsudo, 1m 34.398s; 5 de Puniet, 1m 34.572s; 6 Battaini, 1m 34.743s; 7 Rolfo, 1m 34.781s; 8 Porto, 1m 34.856s; 9 Guintoli, 1m 34.995s; 10 West, 1m 35.182s; 11 Vincent, 1m 35.591s; 12 Debon, 1m 35.730s; 13 Bataille, 1m 35.833s; 14 Stigefelt, 1m 35.937s; 15 Nigon, 1m 36.193s; 16 Faubel, 1m 36.249s; 17 Davies, 1m 36.290s; 18 Olive, 1m 36.390s; 19 Marchand, 1m 36.411s; 20 Baldolini, 1m 37.000s; 21 Smrz, 1m 37.021s; 22 Gemmel, 1m 37.083s; 23 Heidolf, 1m 37.105s; 24 vd Lagemaat, 1m 38.700s; 25 Desborough, 1m 39.587s; 26 Dickinson, 1m 39.718s; 27 Poensgen, 1m 40.088s; 28 Sawford, 1m 40.664s.

Fastest race laps: 1 Poggiali, 1m 34.558s; 2 Rolfo, 1m 34.697s; 3 Nieto, 1m 34.780s; 4 West, 1m 34.797s; 5 Elias, 1m 34.941s; 6 de Puniet, 1m 35.372s; 7 Battaini, 1m 35.732s; 8 Porto, 1m 35.851s; 9 Matsudo, 1m 36.356s; 10 Olive, 1m 36.379s; 11 Davies, 1m 36.784s; 12 Debon, 1m 36.798s; 13 Vincent, 1m 36.971s; 14 Faubel, 1m 37.018s; 15 Bataille, 1m 37.239s; 16 Smrz, 1m 37.288s; 17 Gemmel, 1m 37.363s; 18 Marchand, 1m 37.426s; 19 Heidolf, 1m 37.447s; 20 Nigon, 1m 37.485s; 21 Baldolini, 1m 37.589s; 22 Stigefelt, 1m 37.752s; 23 Dickinson, 1m 39.661s; 24 vd Lagemaat, 1m 40.248s; 25 Desborough, 1m 40.965s; 26 Poensgen, 1m 40.968s; 27 Guintoli, 1m 41.382s.

World Championship: 1 Poggiali, 121; 2 Nieto, 106; 3 Elias and Rolfo, 97; 5 West, 94; 6 de Puniet, 89; 7 Battaini, 81; 8 Porto, 74; 9 Matsudo, 60; 10 Guintoli, 58; 11 Debon, 40; 12 Olive, 27; 13 Aoyama, 20; 14 Gemmel, 18; 15 Stigefelt, 17; 16 Takahashi, 16; 17 Faubel and Nigon, 15; 19 Marchand, 14; 20 Baldolini, 13; 21 Smrz, 9; 22 Bataille, Davies and Kayo, 7; 25 Nöhles and Vincent, 5; 27 Heidolf, 2.

---

125 cc

25 laps, 62.500 miles/100.575 km

Pos.	Rider (Nat.)	No.	Machine	Laps	Time & speed
1	Hector Barbera (E)	80	Aprilia	25	41m 25.907s 90.502 mph/ 145.649 km/h
2	Andrea Dovizioso (I)	34	Honda	25	41m 26.512s
3	Stefano Perugini (I)	7	Aprilia	25	41m 28.504s
4	Alex de Angelis (RSM)	15	Aprilia	25	41m 35.077s
5	Casey Stoner (AUS)	27	Aprilia	25	41m 37.599s
6	Pablo Nieto (E)	22	Aprilia	25	41m 41.805s
7	Mika Kallio (SF)	36	Honda	25	41m 46.911s
8	Arnaud Vincent (F)	1	KTM	25	41m 47.663s
9	Gabor Talmacsi (H)	79	Aprilia	25	41m 48.119s
10	Lucio Cecchinello (I)	4	Aprilia	25	41m 49.549s
11	Mirko Giansanti (I)	6	Aprilia	25	41m 49.719s
12	Gioele Pellino (I)	42	Aprilia	25	42m 00.060s
13	Masao Azuma (J)	8	Honda	25	42m 01.459s
14	Alvaro Bautista (E)	19	Aprilia	25	42m 01.780s
15	Mike di Meglio (F)	63	Aprilia	25	42m 02.110s
16	Marco Simoncelli (I)	58	Aprilia	25	42m 10.250s
17	Imre Toth (H)	25	Honda	25	42m 17.427s
18	Julian Simon (E)	31	Malaguti	25	42m 32.286s
19	Gino Borsoi (I)	23	Aprilia	25	42m 32.879s
20	Peter Lenart (H)	78	Honda	25	42m 37.690s
21	Ismael Ortega (E)	81	Aprilia	25	42m 38.380s
22	Thomas Luthi (CH)	12	Honda	25	42m 52.050s
23	Paul Veazey (GB)	84	Honda	24	41m 41.200s
24	Midge Smart (GB)	50	Honda	24	41m 49.558s
25	Lee Longden (GB)	49	Honda	24	41m 50.412s
26	Chester Lusk (GB)	83	Honda	23	42m 16.106s
	Daniel Pedrosa (E)	3	Honda	24	DNF
	Emilio Alzamora (E)	26	Derbi	24	DNF
	Roberto Locatelli (I)	10	KTM	22	DNF
	Leon Camier (GB)	21	Honda	7	DNF
	Youichi Ui (J)	41	Aprilia	5	DNF
	Stefano Bianco (I)	33	Gilera	5	DNF
	Max Sabbatani (I)	11	Aprilia	1	DNF
	Jorge Lorenzo (E)	48	Derbi	1	DNF
	Fabrizio Lai (I)	32	Malaguti	1	DNF
	Steve Jenkner (D)	17	Aprilia	0	DNF
	Simone Corsi (I)	24	Honda	0	DNF
	Kris Weston (GB)	51	Honda		DNS

Fastest lap: Cecchinello, 1m 38.463s, 91.396 mph/147.088 km/h.

Lap record: Lucio Cecchinello, I (Aprilia), 1m 38.312s, 91.537 mph/ 147.314 km/h (2002).

Event best maximum speed: Pellino, 131.7 mph/212.0 km/h (race).

Qualifying: 1 Perugini, 1m 37.984s; 2 Pedrosa, 1m 38.078s; 3 Dovizioso, 1m 38.143s; 4 Corsi, 1m 38.370s; 5 Kallio, 1m 38.386s; 6 Barbera, 1m 38.417s; 7 Jenkner, 1m 38.609s; 8 Cecchinello, 1m 38.652s; 9 Stoner, 1m 38.680s; 10 de Angelis, 1m 38.752s; 11 Nieto, 1m 38.754s; 12 Borsoi, 1m 38.792s; 13 Luthi, 1m 38.845s; 14 Ui, 1m 38.889s; 15 Talmacsi, 1m 38.960s; 16 Pellino, 1m 38.999s; 17 Vincent, 1m 39.012s; 18 Bautista, 1m 39.037s; 19 Lorenzo, 1m 39.053s; 20 Giansanti, 1m 39.100s; 21 Sabbatani, 1m 39.118s; 22 Azuma, 1m 39.400s; 23 Lai, 1m 39.519s; 24 Simoncelli, 1m 39.879s; 25 Toth, 1m 40.009s; 26 di Meglio, 1m 40.120s; 27 Locatelli, 1m 40.396s; 28 Alzamora, 1m 40.783s; 29 Bianco, 1m 40.867s; 30 Simon, 1m 41.110s; 31 Camier, 1m 41.415s; 32 Ortega, 1m 41.736s; 33 Lenart, 1m 41.975s; 34 Veazey, 1m 42.634s; 35 Weston, 1m 42.956s; 36 Smart, 1m 43.809s; 37 Longden, 1m 43.835s; 38 Lusk, 1m 44.156s.

Fastest race laps: 1 Cecchinello, 1m 38.463s; 2 Perugini, 1m 38.676s; 3 Pedrosa, 1m 38.738s; 4 Barbera, 1m 38.824s; 5 Dovizioso, 1m 38.833s; 6 de Angelis, 1m 38.948s; 7 Stoner, 1m 39.140s; 8 Nieto, 1m 39.157s; 9 Vincent, 1m 39.203s; 10 Pellino, 1m 39.243s; 11 Giansanti, 1m 39.355s; 12 Kallio, 1m 39.383s; 13 Talmacsi, 1m 39.529s; 14 di Meglio, 1m 39.706s; 15 Borsoi, 1m 38.778s; 16 Azuma, 1m 39.920s; 17 Bautista, 1m 39.923s; 18 Simoncelli, 1m 40.064s; 19 Ui, 1m 40.076s; 20 Toth, 1m 40.400s; 21 Alzamora, 1m 40.698s; 22 Locatelli, 1m 40.804s; 23 Luthi, 1m 40.822s; 24 Simon, 1m 40.982s; 25 Lenart, 1m 41.081s; 26 Bianco, 1m 41.151s; 27 Ortega, 1m 41.200s; 28 Camier, 1m 42.054s; 29 Veazey, 1m 42.626s; 30 Smart, 1m 43.227s; 31 Longden, 1m 43.298s; 32 Lusk, 1m 44.552s; 33 Sabbatani, 1m 47.230s; 34 Lorenzo, 1m 47.525s; 35 Lai, 1m 47.531s.

World Championship: 1 Pedrosa, 124; 2 Jenkner, 98; 3 Cecchinello, 97; 4 Dovizioso, 93; 5 Perugini, 92; 6 Nieto, 79; 7 de Angelis, 76; 8 Barbera, 65; 9 Ui, 64; 10 Luthi, 48; 11 Giansanti, 46; 12 Kallio and Stoner, 40; 14 Borsoi, 36; 15 Azuma and Talmacsi, 23; 17 Corsi, 17; 18 Pellino, 16; 19 Vincent, 14; 20 Lorenzo, 11; 21 Locatelli, 7; 22 di Meglio, 4; 23 Sabbatani, 3; 24 Bautista, Lai and Simoncelli, 2.

GERMAN GP
SACHSENRING

Main photograph and insets: Head to head and nose to tail: for a third time in 2003, Gibernau beat Rossi fair and square. This time, Valentino took it seriously.
All photographs: Mark Wernham

IN retrospect, there was no question. The German GP was a pivotal race – for the championship, and for Rossi. It had been seven weeks and four races since his last win, but this defeat was different. In Catalunya, he'd erred, but had recovered with brilliance; in Assen, he'd been careful in the rain; in Britain, bamboozled by officials.

At the Sachsenring, he was out-thought, out-fumbled and outridden. He blamed the defeat on himself, of course, in that his last-lap tactics had gone wrong. The victor, Gibernau, responded in kind: 'I had no plan. If you have a plan and it doesn't work, then what do you do?'

Crew chief Burgess was dismayed for another reason – that earlier in the race Rossi had been leading by better than 2.5 seconds. And he'd let it all go. Rather than stretching his legs and sustaining the challenge, he'd let Gibernau catch up, to deal with him hand to hand. And lost.

The Italian press led the chorus over the ensuing race-less three weeks of a baking summer break, becoming ever more fanciful. Was Rossi finished? A burnt-out case at 24, even now living it large in Ibiza? Was he too rich? Gone soft and lazy? The comments certainly registered, as we would see from his direct response at Brno, where he dressed as a chain-ganger breaking a rock with a pickaxe. But Rossi was probably far harder on himself, and the real significance of his next-round, post-race pantomime was a deliberate return to his joking, mocking ways of old. The teenage funster was back, and deliberately so. Rossi turned a corner in Germany.

Honda had more power-up parts, including the three-pipe machine seen at Assen, for Gibernau and Rossi, and another mysterious spec for the silenced version. They were probably the same internally, with cam timing tickled and rev limit increased slightly; the noisier bike was said to be marginally faster. Both riders went loud for the race.

It was the climax to a weekend of explosive action. Literally. The first and most dramatic fireball could hardly have been bettered by a Hollywood stuntman, as Colin Edwards's Aprilia Cube started spewing petrol at high speed. The cause was simple – the filler cap was improperly fastened, and as Edwards hit the brakes at the bottom of the track's trade-mark fast roller-coaster swoop down the hill, it sloshed out. 'I thought it was raining,' he said, unaware that the droplets had already ignited in his wake (the Cube is prodigious with its backfiring) and he was about to be engulfed in a ball of flame.

He found out soon enough and was faced with a stark choice. Heroically, he didn't hesitate, leaping off the back of a machine doing well over 100 mph and tumbling through the gravel. He escaped with minor burns and scrapes; the motor cycle cartwheeled to its final funeral pyre, leaving a blazing puddle at each point it touched down.

Hardly less dramatic was Sunday morning's Ducati flame-out. Capirossi, on a fast lap, crashed, but all seemed well enough as he walked away. Four marshals went to carry the bike out of the gravel, but as they picked it up and took its weight, it too exploded. Orange-clad figures ran away, beating at flames on their clothing, as the Desmosedici burned merrily. Again, by extremely good luck, nobody was seriously burned. But the point was made. As well as being faster and more wayward under brakes than the old two-strokes, the four-strokes had another facet to their mean streak.

Roberts was back, ready to ride and willing to race – except that, at this stage, the Suzuki was making little progress in catching up. 'It's good to be back on the scene, but extremely frustrating not to be part of the action up front. I can't use my ability to make the bike do a better lap time. I can only sit on top of it and do what it wants to do,' he said.

Schwantz was in Germany as an observer and concurred: 'I can see how both riders have to get off the gas to change direction where you would want to keep the throttle open. It unsettles the bike, then they have to wait before they can open it again. I'd be asking for some chassis changes and engine position changes to try to get it out.' The man to ask was on hand: a new race department chief whose presence would later bear some fruit.

At the same time, Kawasaki were taking tentative steps forward, with some examples of a lighter crankshaft, although not used by McCoy. Equally important was a new Dunlop rear with a taller and flatter section, and consequent larger contact patch, offering more consistent grip levels, according to the Australian.

The news was all bad from KTM, who confirmed growing rumours that their MotoGP project had run out of steam – or at least the finances it would need to become competitive, after a slump in the dollar had seen their income from the lucrative off-road market drop. They admitted their budget estimates had been too small, and off-road hero Heinz Kinigadner explained to pressmen during practice that the project was on ice: 'We will finish building five engines, because we have ordered the parts, but we will not build chassis or set up a test team. At the moment, everybody is behind Honda, and we can't afford to spend 30 million euro a year to get blown away for three or four years.' The 125 project would continue, but the future was uncertain for specially hired engineers Harald Barol and Warren Willing, and for the 12-strong development team. Kinigadner's visit was cut short by tragedy, when his 21-year-old son, Hannes, was critically injured in a motocross accident.

Proton succumbed to circumstances (and a mischievous thought of the chance of a good result at a two-stroke-friendly track) by leaving the four-strokes at home in favour of the KR3 500 triple. These are in short supply, Aoki's spare arriving only on the second morning of practice, after many delays in retrieving it from the Proton stand at a motor show in Iran. It was the last race for the nimble three-cylinder two-strokes.

Troy Bayliss appeared shaven-headed – in sympathy with a team cook who had been forcibly shorn after appearing with an unpopular hair style; Hopkins sprouted computer ports on the hump of his leathers – an attempt to bring data collection into the human rather than just the mechanical realm; Erv Kanemoto was on hand, hoping to get a team going for next year; Marlboro introduced a forbidding new glassed-in hospitality suite, adding to the mirrored walls that are taking the paddock rapidly toward the impersonality complained about in F1.

But nobody cared too much. Because it was holiday time, and although this year's break would be bisected by the Czech Republic GP, it marked the end of a long haul.

Left: Bald-for-the-weekend Bayliss made the rostrum again.

Below: Obvious assets.

Below centre: McWilliams was relishing the corner speed of the 500 cc triple in the two-stroke's real last race.

Bottom: Checa and Jacque exchange paint in a close mid-points battle.
All photographs: Mark Wernham

Above: Ukawa laments his lacklustre season.
Photograph: Mark Wernham

Above right: The Japanese rider is sandwiched between Capirossi and Hayden.
Photograph: Gold & Goose

Right: They also serve who only squat and wash.
Photograph: Mark Wernham

MOTOGP RACE – 30 laps

Rossi and the Dukes led away, the rest sorting themselves out through the tight corners. By the (very short) time they came howling up the hill again, Gibernau had snatched third from Bayliss, with Melandri and McWilliams hard behind, the Proton rider for once fast off the line.

Rossi made the most of the clear track as Gibernau took a couple of laps to find his way past Capirossi, and finished lap four ahead by 2.568 seconds. Then the rot set in, Gibernau pegging him back one- or two-tenths at a time. By half-distance, the gap between the snarling three-pipe Hondas was three-quarters of a second, and shrinking. Two laps later, Gibernau dived inside Rossi under braking for the first corner.

Had Rossi let him through? Looked that way, as he loomed over his shoulder in familiar playful style, several times pulling alongside under braking at the bottom of the hill. He was waiting for the last lap.

The showdown occurred over the roller-coaster back straight. Rossi came out of the preceding right wide and fast, and got a better drive down the hill. He was ahead as he took a tight line into the penultimate left. This was his undoing. Both riders were fighting slides, but Gibernau had the better approach line to the last corner. Rossi tried to close the door, but ran wide on the exit as Gibernau opened the throttle earlier and inched alongside to win by a wheel, thanking Kenny Roberts and his dirt-track ranch for teaching him how to unload a sliding front wheel by opening the gas. A crestfallen Rossi explained that losing momentum in the penultimate corner had cost him the race. 'Sometimes this year I have been unlucky with the weather, or the rules. Today, I just made a mistake,' he said.

This all took place well clear of an up-and-down brawl, at a track where supposedly passing is almost impossible. Cautious starter Biaggi disproved it by dropping back to tenth as a charging Melandri took over third from Capirossi; then disproved it back the other way as he moved forward again.

Melandri was displaced by Bayliss on lap five; two laps later, Biaggi was also past, breaking the lap record as he closed rapidly on the

Australian. Typically, Bayliss proved hard to pass. On lap ten, Biaggi twice pushed ahead, only to be dropped firmly at the next bend. It took another three laps before he got by for keeps. Five corners later, pulling away, Biaggi pushed the front end at speed and crashed out. Bayliss had a safe rostrum after all.

Melandri was doggedly holding fourth, with a mixed bag of assailants crowding up behind him by half-distance: Capirossi, Checa, Ukawa, Hayden, Nakano and McWilliams in a pack. Checa was losing places until he ended up hounded by McWilliams's two-stroke. The Proton pulled aside every lap, 'but never enough to close the door on him'. But he already had fuelling problems, and they were to cripple McWilliams for the last five laps of what had been a blindingly fast last two-stroke ride.

Hayden was gaining speed and confidence, past Ukawa on lap 23 to lean on Capirossi who, in turn, closed on Melandri. With seven laps left, the pressured 250 champion missed a shift and slid off. The AMA champion kept at it, getting ahead of Capirossi on the second-to-last lap, only for the wily Italian to reverse the positions by inches on the last. It was still a fine result for the fast maturing young American.

Two seconds adrift, Ukawa fended off Nakano. Checa had fallen back, almost into the hands of Jacque, the mid-field intervals close as Abe, Aoki and McWilliams crossed the line within two seconds.

Tamada was a downbeat 13th; Edwards was battling a leaky spare bike, after another spill during morning warm-up, the Aprilia's erratic throttle response making the machine a real handful. Disillusion was setting in.

Roberts was another four seconds down, after succumbing to McCoy, then regaining the position in the later stages, his Michelins still hanging on while the Kawasaki's Dunlops were on the slide, McCoy 'getting big two-wheel drifts even going into the turns'. On the slow-down lap, Roberts had watched Jacque stop to do a burn-out, only to be highsided. 'That was the most fun I had all weekend,' he said grimly.

Hofmann was 17th, just ahead of Kiyonari; Pitt and de Gea were a lap down. Hopkins had gone out in an embarrassing cloud of engine smoke on lap 24; Haga and Barros both crashed unhurt.

250 cc RACE – 29 laps

For once, the Hondas were not simply out-powered and they took the first two places on the grid, Porto from Rolfo. Matsudo might have had some fun on the Yamaha too, but was one of five involved in a first-corner shambles, along with Gemmel, Faubel, Marchand and Olive, the last two rejoining. The muddle had shuffled the pursuit and gave the leaders a chance to escape.

Rolfo was in front, from Porto, Nieto, de Puniet, Battaini and Guintoli. Poggiali was tenth after a bad start; Elias was 14th after switching to his spare before the warm-up lap, starting from the back of the grid. It took only five laps for the first six to get well clear. De Puniet was now third, Poggiali seventh, pulling away from the lone West.

De Puniet was charging, and Porto started to drop away after he'd been relegated to third. Then to fourth by second Frenchman Guintoli, on fine form, as de Puniet took the lead. Battaini was losing touch; Nieto was having a typically eventful race, surviving a long, fast run across the grass on lap eight. Back under control, he rode out directly in front of Poggiali, who was obliged to brake hard to avoid a collision. No penalty was given for this clearly dangerous move.

The pair were closing on Battaini and passed him together to close on the front gang, Nieto setting the record on the way. By then, he was alone again, Poggiali also having run off on the grass and crashed at walking speed. He scrambled back on to rejoin a distant tenth behind Elias, who had worked through steadily. He was 20 seconds adrift, but the field was well spread.

Nieto passed Porto on lap 20, and one lap later he was with the front trio. Almost simultaneously, Guintoli slid off. Five laps left, three possible winners.

Now Rolfo looked for the chance to use his better handling, and found it around the last corners on lap 24. He led from there to the finish, under relentless pressure, to take his first GP win. The articulate Italian also turned the tide in the championship. 'The season starts here,' he said.

They'd started the last lap three abreast into the first hairpin, and Nieto emerged second. His attack was blunted by a slide half-way around, but he managed to stay clear of de Puniet, the trio crossing the line within three-tenths of a second.

Porto was five seconds away, then Battaini and a distant West. Poggiali had caught and passed Elias, only to be pushed wide in the final corners, losing seventh by less than a tenth.

Debon and Baldolini trailed in, then Heidolf got the better of Davies and Smrz for 11th.

125 cc RACE – 27 laps

A brawling first corner put Lorenzo and Mickan at the back; Barbera led a scrum, but had jumped the start, pitting for a stop-and-go on the fifth lap.

This left Perugini ahead of Stoner, Pedrosa and de Angelis, the quartet breaking away by half-distance. Dovizioso led the next trio from Ui and Cecchinello, Nieto joining and getting ahead on lap 23, as Ui crashed out.,

Up front, it was fierce. De Angelis led lap ten, then Stoner took over for a long spell. Pedrosa was as high as second, but generally fourth.

Then Perugini got the lead again with three laps to go, surviving a big slide or two as he hung on desperately. Stoner was poised to attack in the last corners, but instead found himself defending second from a determined de Angelis. Pedrosa, outgunned, was less than half a second behind.

Nieto was a lonely fifth; Talmacsi snatched sixth from Dovizioso, Cecchinello and Corsi right behind; Kallio prevailed over the next trio. Local hero Jenkner started badly and was tenth when he crashed on lap 18.

Above: Rolfo took his first win, using his Honda's handling to the full. Here he leads Porto, Nieto, de Puniet and Battaini in the early stages.

Right: Stoner, Perugini and de Angelis shared the 125 trophies.

Below right: The same three in action, Pedrosa (3) sandwiched between de Angelis (15) and Stoner.

All photographs: Mark Wernham

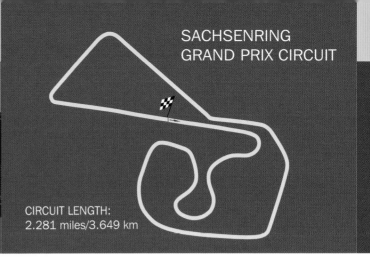

FIM WORLD CHAMPIONSHIP • ROUND 9

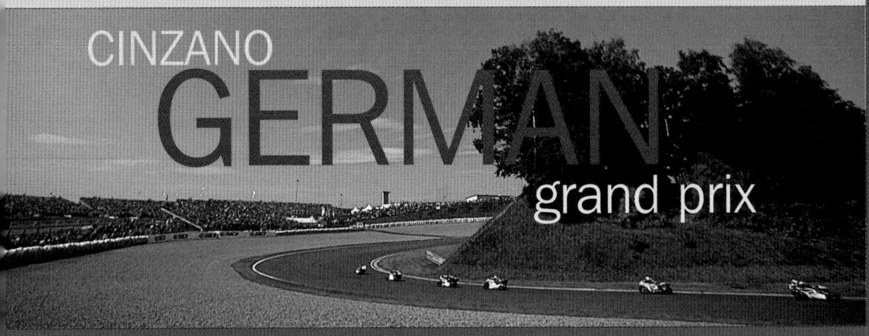

CINZANO GERMAN grand prix

27 JULY 2003

SACHSENRING GRAND PRIX CIRCUIT

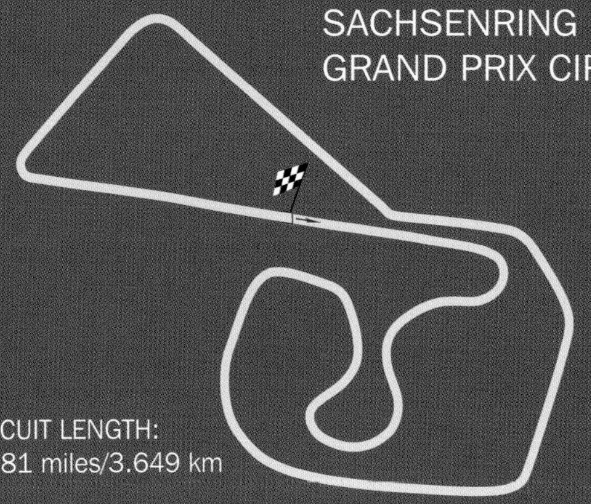

CIRCUIT LENGTH: 2.281 miles/3.649 km

MotoGP

30 laps, 68.430 miles/110.130 km

Pos.	Rider (Nat.)	No.	Machine	Laps	Time & speed
1	Sete Gibernau (E)	15	Honda	30	42m 41.180s 96.187 mph/ 154.798 km/h
2	Valentino Rossi (I)	46	Honda	30	42m 41.240s
3	Troy Bayliss (AUS)	12	Ducati	30	42m 54.387s
4	Loris Capirossi (I)	65	Ducati	30	42m 57.701s
5	Nicky Hayden (USA)	69	Honda	30	42m 57.743s
6	Tohru Ukawa (J)	11	Honda	30	42m 59.923s
7	Shinya Nakano (J)	56	Yamaha	30	43m 00.065s
8	Carlos Checa (E)	7	Yamaha	30	43m 07.345s
9	Olivier Jacque (F)	19	Yamaha	30	43m 09.461s
10	Norick Abe (J)	17	Yamaha	30	43m 10.339s
11	Nobuatsu Aoki (J)	9	Proton KR	30	43m 10.496s
12	Jeremy McWilliams (GB)	99	Proton KR	30	43m 11.607s
13	Makoto Tamada (J)	6	Honda	30	43m 30.760s
14	Colin Edwards (USA)	45	Aprilia	30	43m 34.624s
15	Kenny Roberts (USA)	10	Suzuki	30	43m 38.692s
16	Garry McCoy (AUS)	8	Kawasaki	30	43m 40.760s
17	Alex Hofmann (D)	66	Kawasaki	30	43m 46.420s
18	Ryuichi Kiyonari (J)	23	Honda	30	43m 46.528s
19	Andrew Pitt (AUS)	88	Kawasaki	29	42m 59.448s
20	David de Gea (E)	52	Sabre V4	29	43m 06.981s
	Marco Melandri (I)	33	Yamaha	23	DNF
	John Hopkins (USA)	21	Suzuki	23	DNF
	Alex Barros (BR)	4	Yamaha	15	DNF
	Max Biaggi (I)	3	Honda	13	DNF
	Noriyuki Haga (J)	41	Aprilia	7	DNF

Fastest lap: Biaggi, 1m 24.630s, 97.031 mph/156.157 km/h (record).

Previous circuit record: Valentino Rossi, I (Honda), 1m 26.226s, 96.091 mph/ 154.644 km/h (2002).

Event best maximum speed: Capirossi, 175.9 mph/283.2 km/h (qualifying practice no. 2).

Qualifying: 1 Biaggi, 1m 23.734s; 2 McWilliams, 1m 23.736s; 3 Capirossi, 1m 24.058s; 4 Rossi, 1m 24.253s; 5 Gibernau, 1m 24.287s; 6 Bayliss, 1m 24.405s; 7 Checa, 1m 24.423s; 8 Ukawa, 1m 24.492s; 9 Aoki, 1m 24.574s; 10 Nakano, 1m 24.592s; 11 Barros, 1m 24.745s; 12 Melandri, 1m 24.781s; 13 Edwards, 1m 24.794s; 14 Roberts, 1m 24.913s; 15 Hayden, 1m 24.961s; 16 Abe, 1m 24.981s; 17 Haga, 1m 25.008s; 18 Jacque, 1m 25.038s; 19 Tamada, 1m 25.360s; 20 McCoy, 1m 25.563s; 21 Hofmann, 1m 26.003s; 22 Hopkins, 1m 26.247s; 23 Kiyonari, 1m 26.296s; 24 Pitt, 1m 26.302s; 25 de Gea, 1m 26.727s.

Fastest race laps: 1 Biaggi, 1m 24.630s; 2 Rossi, 1m 24.698s; 3 Gibernau, 1m 24.862s; 4 Bayliss, 1m 24.893s; 5 Capirossi, 1m 25.246s; 6 Hayden, 1m 25.280s; 7 Melandri, 1m 25.300s; 8 Ukawa, 1m 25.343s; 9 Checa, 1m 25.343s; 10 Nakano, 1m 25.445s; 11 Jacque, 1m 25.451s; 12 McWilliams, 1m 25.499s; 13 Barros, 1m 25.549s; 14 Haga, 1m 25.611s; 15 Edwards, 1m 25.645s; 16 Abe, 1m 25.760s; 17 Aoki, 1m 25.839s; 18 Tamada, 1m 26.032s; 19 Kiyonari, 1m 26.133s; 20 McCoy, 1m 26.244s; 21 Roberts, 1m 26.393s; 22 Hofmann, 1m 26.593s; 23 Hopkins, 1m 26.853s; 24 Pitt, 1m 27.261s; 25 de Gea, 1m 28.385s.

World Championship: 1 Rossi, 187; 2 Gibernau, 158; 3 Biaggi, 130; 4 Capirossi, 97; 5 Bayliss, 80; 6 Ukawa, 66; 7 Checa, 65; 8 Nakano, 63; 9 Barros, 62; 10 Hayden, 57; 11 Jacque, 50; 12 Edwards, 42; 13 Tamada, 40; 14 Haga, 30; 15 Abe, 24; 16 Hopkins, 22; 17 McWilliams, 18; 18 Aoki, 17; 19 Kiyonari, 13; 20 Melandri, 9; 21 Hofmann and McCoy, 8; 23 Roberts, 7; 24 Kagayama, 4; 25 Pitt, 3.

250 cc

29 laps, 66.149 miles/106.459 km

Pos.	Rider (Nat.)	No.	Machine	Laps	Time & speed
1	Roberto Rolfo (I)	3	Honda	29	42m 06.199s 94.269 mph/ 151.711 km/h
2	Fonsi Nieto (E)	10	Aprilia	29	42m 06.349s
3	Randy de Puniet (F)	7	Aprilia	29	42m 06.486s
4	Sebastian Porto (ARG)	5	Honda	29	42m 11.504s
5	Franco Battaini (I)	21	Aprilia	29	42m 19.296s
6	Anthony West (AUS)	14	Aprilia	29	42m 24.488s
7	Toni Elias (E)	24	Aprilia	29	42m 27.080s
8	Manuel Poggiali (RSM)	54	Aprilia	29	42m 27.126s
9	Alex Debon (E)	6	Honda	29	42m 51.370s
10	Alex Baldolini (I)	26	Aprilia	29	42m 54.900s
11	Dirk Heidolf (D)	28	Aprilia	29	43m 03.277s
12	Chaz Davies (GB)	57	Aprilia	29	43m 03.467s
13	Jakub Smrz (CZ)	96	Honda	29	43m 03.658s
14	Erwan Nigon (F)	36	Aprilia	29	43m 23.666s
15	Max Neukirchner (D)	62	Honda	29	43m 35.338s
16	Lukas Pesek (CZ)	52	Yamaha	29	43m 35.537s
17	Joan Olive (E)	11	Aprilia	28	42m 25.652s
18	Katja Poensgen (D)	98	Honda	28	42m 44.555s
19	Vesa Kallio (SF)	66	Yamaha	28	42m 49.765s
	Tomas Palander (S)	63	Honda	28	DNF
	Henk vd Lagemaat (NL)	18	Honda	27	DNF
	Norman Rank (D)	65	Honda	25	DNF
	Eric Bataille (F)	34	Honda	24	DNF
	Sylvain Guintoli (F)	50	Aprilia	21	DNF
	Johan Stigefelt (S)	16	Aprilia	9	DNF
	Hugo Marchand (F)	9	Aprilia	3	DNF
	Christian Gemmel (D)	15	Honda	0	DNF
	Hector Faubel (E)	33	Aprilia	0	DNF
	Naoki Matsudo (J)	8	Yamaha	0	DNF
	Nico Kehrer (D)	64	Honda		DNQ

Fastest lap: Nieto, 1m 26.469s, 94.968 mph/152.836 km/h (record).

Previous circuit record: Marco Melandri, I (Aprilia), 1m 27.233s, 94.982 mph/ 152.859 km/h (2001).

Event best maximum speed: Poggiali, 148.7 mph/239.3 km/h (race).

Qualifying: 1 Porto, 1m 25.728s; 2 Rolfo, 1m 25.891s; 3 Battaini, 1m 25.944s; 4 Nieto, 1m 25.963s; 5 de Puniet, 1m 26.032s; 6 Poggiali, 1m 26.104s; 7 Matsudo, 1m 26.116s; 8 Guintoli, 1m 26.381s; 9 Elias, 1m 26.517s; 10 West, 1m 26.878s; 11 Olive, 1m 27.099s; 12 Baldolini, 1m 27.212s; 13 Debon, 1m 27.241s; 14 Nigon, 1m 27.281s; 15 Faubel, 1m 27.409s; 16 Marchand, 1m 27.482s; 17 Davies, 1m 27.512s; 18 Heidolf, 1m 27.568s; 19 Smrz, 1m 27.656s; 20 Stigefelt, 1m 27.768s; 21 Bataille, 1m 28.057s; 22 Neukirchner, 1m 28.458s; 23 Pesek, 1m 28.563s; 24 Gemmel, 1m 28.670s; 25 Palander, 1m 29.191s; 26 vd Lagemaat, 1m 30.214s; 27 Kallio, 1m 30.377s; 28 Rank, 1m 30.725s; 29 Poensgen, 1m 31.103s; 30 Kehrer, 1m 32.270s.

Fastest race laps: 1 Nieto, 1m 26.469s; 2 Rolfo, 1m 26.557s; 3 Poggiali, 1m 26.557s; 4 de Puniet, 1m 26.561s; 5 Guintoli, 1m 26.593s; 6 Porto, 1m 26.647s; 7 Battaini, 1m 26.658s; 8 Elias, 1m 26.810s; 9 West, 1m 27.022s; 10 Baldolini, 1m 27.754s; 11 Debon, 1m 27.933s; 12 Olive, 1m 28.122s; 13 Davies, 1m 28.169s; 14 Heidolf, 1m 28.317s; 15 Bataille, 1m 28.329s; 16 Nigon, 1m 28.388s; 17 Smrz, 1m 28.503s; 18 Pesek, 1m 28.619s; 19 Stigefelt, 1m 28.717s; 20 Palander, 1m 29.446s; 21 Neukirchner, 1m 29.564s; 22 Poensgen, 1m 30.678s; 23 vd Lagemaat, 1m 30.685s; 24 Marchand, 1m 30.792s; 25 Kallio, 1m 30.806s; 26 Rank, 1m 31.014s.

World Championship: 1 Poggiali, 129; 2 Nieto, 126; 3 Rolfo, 122; 4 Elias, 106; 5 de Puniet, 105; 6 West, 104; 7 Battaini, 98; 8 Porto, 87; 9 Matsudo, 60; 10 Guintoli, 58; 11 Debon, 47; 12 Olive, 27; 13 Aoyama, 20; 14 Baldolini, 19; 15 Gemmel, 18; 16 Nigon and Stigefelt, 17; 18 Takahashi, 16; 19 Faubel, 15; 20 Marchand, 14; 21 Smrz, 12; 22 Davies, 11; 23 Bataille, Heidolf and Kayo, 7; 26 Nöhles and Vincent, 5; 28 Neukirchner, 1.

125 cc

27 laps, 61.587 miles/99.117 km

Pos.	Rider (Nat.)	No.	Machine	Laps	Time & speed
1	Stefano Perugini (I)	7	Aprilia	27	40m 11.124s 91.956 mph/ 147.989 km/h
2	Casey Stoner (AUS)	27	Aprilia	27	40m 11.336s
3	Alex de Angelis (RSM)	15	Aprilia	27	40m 11.499s
4	Daniel Pedrosa (E)	3	Honda	27	40m 11.898s
5	Pablo Nieto (E)	22	Aprilia	27	40m 17.001s
6	Gabor Talmacsi (H)	79	Aprilia	27	40m 22.915s
7	Andrea Dovizioso (I)	34	Honda	27	40m 23.194s
8	Lucio Cecchinello (I)	4	Aprilia	27	40m 23.336s
9	Simone Corsi (I)	24	Honda	27	40m 23.769s
10	Mika Kallio (SF)	36	Honda	27	40m 27.493s
11	Mirko Giansanti (I)	6	Aprilia	27	40m 27.494s
12	Marco Simoncelli (I)	58	Aprilia	27	40m 27.949s
13	Gioele Pellino (I)	42	Aprilia	27	40m 32.746s
14	Hector Barbera (E)	80	Aprilia	27	40m 38.285s
15	Fabrizio Lai (I)	32	Malaguti	27	40m 52.152s
16	Robbin Harms (DK)	88	Aprilia	27	40m 56.255s
17	Gino Borsoi (I)	23	Aprilia	27	40m 56.501s
18	Roberto Locatelli (I)	10	KTM	27	41m 05.700s
19	Dario Giuseppetti (D)	90	Honda	27	41m 06.301s
20	Julian Simon (E)	31	Malaguti	27	41m 22.781s
21	Jorge Lorenzo (E)	48	Derbi	27	41m 33.877s
22	Peter Lenart (H)	78	Honda	27	41m 47.579s
23	Leon Camier (GB)	21	Honda	26	40m 14.758s
	Alvaro Bautista (E)	19	Aprilia	25	DNF
	Thomas Luthi (CH)	12	Honda	25	DNF
	Youichi Ui (J)	41	Aprilia	23	DNF
	Patrick Unger (D)	54	Honda	18	DNF
	Steve Jenkner (D)	17	Aprilia	17	DNF
	Masao Azuma (J)	8	Honda	14	DNF
	Jarno Müller (D)	52	Honda	14	DNF
	Jascha Buech (D)	91	Honda	12	DNF
	Stefano Bianco (I)	33	Gilera	11	DNF
	Arnaud Vincent (F)	1	KTM	9	DNF
	Manuel Mickan (D)	53	Honda	7	DNF
	Emilio Alzamora (E)	26	Derbi	7	DNF
	Mike di Meglio (F)	63	Aprilia	2	DNF
	Imre Toth (H)	25	Honda	2	DNF
	Max Sabbatani (I)	11	Aprilia		DNS

Fastest lap: Nieto, 1m 28.490s, 92.799 mph/149.345 km/h (record).

Previous circuit record: Steve Jenkner, D (Aprilia), 1m 29.486s, 92.591 mph/ 149.011 km/h (2002).

Event best maximum speed: Pedrosa, 129.7 mph/208.7 km/h (qualifying practice no. 2).

Qualifying: 1 Perugini, 1m 27.717s; 2 de Angelis, 1m 27.771s; 3 Barbera, 1m 28.022s; 4 Cecchinello, 1m 28.097s; 5 Stoner, 1m 28.223s; 6 Dovizioso, 1m 28.291s; 7 Pedrosa, 1m 28.355s; 8 Borsoi, 1m 28.392s; 9 Jenkner, 1m 28.457s; 10 Corsi, 1m 28.459s; 11 Giansanti, 1m 28.482s; 12 Kallio, 1m 28.536s; 13 Nieto, 1m 28.559s; 14 Ui, 1m 28.595s; 15 Luthi, 1m 28.620s; 16 Pellino, 1m 28.703s; 17 Talmacsi, 1m 28.766s; 18 Lai, 1m 28.820s; 19 Lorenzo, 1m 28.951s; 20 Simoncelli, 1m 29.055s; 21 Harms, 1m 29.600s; 22 Locatelli, 1m 29.657s; 23 Bautista, 1m 29.691s; 24 Vincent, 1m 29.723s; 25 Sabbatani, 1m 29.732s; 26 Simon, 1m 29.742s; 27 Toth, 1m 29.966s; 28 Mickan, 1m 30.252s; 29 Alzamora, 1m 30.336s; 30 Giuseppetti, 1m 30.351s; 31 Buech, 1m 30.405s; 32 di Meglio, 1m 30.830s; 33 Azuma, 1m 30.956s; 34 Bianco, 1m 31.237s; 35 Müller, 1m 31.395s; 36 Unger, 1m 31.764s; 37 Camier, 1m 31.784s; 38 Lenart, 1m 32.099s.

Fastest race laps: 1 Nieto, 1m 28.490s; 2 Talmacsi, 1m 28.551s; 3 Ui, 1m 28.643s; 4 Perugini, 1m 28.645s; 5 Pedrosa, 1m 28.682s; 6 de Angelis, 1m 28.692s; 7 Stoner, 1m 28.785s; 8 Barbera, 1m 28.785s; 9 Cecchinello, 1m 28.800s; 10 Dovizioso, 1m 28.802s; 11 Jenkner, 1m 28.874s; 12 Corsi, 1m 28.894s; 13 Giansanti, 1m 28.925s; 14 Simoncelli, 1m 28.965s; 15 Pellino, 1m 28.975s; 16 Bautista, 1m 28.979s; 17 Kallio, 1m 29.080s; 18 Luthi, 1m 29.104s; 19 Borsoi, 1m 29.174s; 20 Lai, 1m 29.922s; 21 Azuma, 1m 29.938s; 22 Harms, 1m 29.977s; 23 Vincent, 1m 30.270s; 24 Lorenzo, 1m 30.272s; 25 di Meglio, 1m 30.376s; 26 Giuseppetti, 1m 30.413s; 27 Buech, 1m 30.472s; 28 Simon, 1m 30.596s; 29 Locatelli, 1m 30.619s; 30 Bianco, 1m 31.105s; 31 Mickan, 1m 31.216s; 32 Lenart, 1m 31.263s; 33 Unger, 1m 31.857s; 34 Camier, 1m 31.934s; 35 Alzamora, 1m 32.172s; 36 Müller, 1m 32.371s; 37 Toth, 2m 04.076s.

World Championship: 1 Pedrosa, 137; 2 Perugini, 117; 3 Cecchinello, 105; 4 Dovizioso, 102; 5 Jenkner, 98; 6 de Angelis, 92; 7 Nieto, 88; 8 Barbera, 67; 9 Ui, 64; 10 Stoner, 60; 11 Giansanti, 51; 12 Luthi, 48; 13 Kallio, 46; 14 Borsoi, 36; 15 Talmacsi, 33; 16 Corsi, 24; 17 Azuma, 23; 18 Pellino, 19; 19 Vincent, 14; 20 Lorenzo, 11; 21 Locatelli, 7; 22 Simoncelli, 6; 23 di Meglio, 4; 24 Lai and Sabbatani, 3; 26 Bautista, 2.

CZECH GP
BRNO

BRNO came bang in the middle of the summer break rather than at the end of it. With the premature return came a pronounced spirit of renewal on almost all sides. This was so not only in a very fast-paced race, but especially in Rossi's race, a very narrow victory over Gibernau with a new record on the crucial last lap. It was a turning point, and the last of such close finishes. Rossi had turned his fortunes around, and his chain-gang clowning after the race was the proof.

Back from Ibiza with his hair dyed crimson, Rossi articulated a new resolve. 'After some stupid mistakes at the last two races from thinking too much, I changed my tactics…ride at 100 per cent, and if anyone comes past, attack immediately.' The result was his 54th career win, equalling Doohan's tally, although all the Australian's were in the premier class.

Renewal was visible also at Ducati, in evo form, with a package of changes ranging from revised chassis stiffness ratios and new large-diameter forks to upgraded bodywork and larger oil and water radiators. Revised internal airflow served the twin purpose of keeping the mechanical parts and the riders cooler after both had been suffering from the prodigious heat given off by this (and the other) four-strokes. The second-guess rows of holes in the fairing had been replaced with new intakes on each side of the oval, and enlarged outlets on the fairing flanks. The frontal area was more or less the same, and the drag possibly 'a tad less', according to team aerodynamicist Alan Jenkins.

Proton had less visible renewal after their two-race four-stroke break, but they had gained reliability, with cases machined for better oil seals and remachined crankshafts with revised radii to improve life. 'With the old crank, if it lasted on the dyno, it was usually okay on the track, but some of them would break after an hour on the bench,' said Roberts. There was also a small, but useful, mid-range power boost through simple gas-flow work. More significantly, they had much-improved engine braking software. It moved McWilliams to say, 'It's starting to feel like a real racing bike now.'

Suzuki had nothing much but a set of fresh promises from the new man in their garage. Masahito Imada had been with the old square-four project and now was back in racing after a management reshuffle; he pledged to restore the faster response and decision time that had prevailed in the old days, as well as deliver an improved engine spec before the year's end. Too little, too late, perhaps, given that we were already into the second half of the season, but certainly the start of finding a better direction.

Kawasaki had even longer-term promises, a rumour breaking cover of a V4 to replace their current in-line four some time during next season, and news that a fresh chassis had been commissioned in an attempt to find a better direction for development. And it was announced that Alex Hofmann had been signed for 2004, after his promising start as their test rider had seen other teams sniffing around. This needed to be forestalled, even at the cost of demotivating at least one of the current riders. It would turn out to be McCoy, already baffled by a bike that wouldn't respond to his style at all.

At the opposite end of the spectrum came Biaggi, seven times a winner at Brno in nine visits and now at last blessed with electronic upgrades to his Honda, taking him closer to Rossi and Gibernau's spec. Instead of the expected epiphany, Biaggi found the way darker, and it would take several races before he could get the bike settings to his liking, and for the upgrade actually to produce an improvement.

Fun and games in the paddock followed the Italian tradition of mid-August – gangs of youths prowling around with buckets of water, drenching selected targets. Rossi was a prominent gang leader, and as wet as anybody; luckily, his hair dye didn't run. Since the European heat wave was still in full sway, only a small number of the drowned rats actually objected.

Race Direction announced a new ruling on yellow-flag infringements in the wake of the Donington affair. From now on, riders would be promptly informed of such an infringement and the application of a ten-second penalty. All because of Rossi, and it would be the same pre-eminent rider who would suffer the first application of such a penalty, in Australia. But he had another beef about the officials, triggered by an accident on Saturday morning.

The victim was Nakano, who was violently highsided at an unusual spot and slammed the barrier head first. Briefly unconscious, he lay by the trackside for several minutes, attended by medical workers before being stretchered away and helicoptered to hospital. There, mercifully, all scans were negative, and he was back and ready to race the next day. Rossi and Capirossi both came upon this scene, close to the tarmac at a fast section, and both expected the session to be red-flagged. 'At our first safety meeting in South Africa, it was decided that when a rider was unconscious after an accident there should be an immediate red flag,' said Rossi later. But it wasn't done, and both he and Capirossi stopped at the entrance to the pit lane to remonstrate with officials. To no avail, but also without any immediate consequences either way. Just another few degrees of temperature all round.

Likewise in the smallest class, where an increasingly disillusioned champion Arnaud Vincent had agreed to split with the KTM team in the week after the German GP, following friction with technical leading light Warren Willing. KTM had immediately poached up-and-coming Finn Mika Kallio from Ajo Motorsport, who reacted by threatening legal action against both the rider and KTM. Kallio promptly gave KTM their best weekend yet, coming within one place of a spot on the rostrum. Ajo were to get their revenge later in the year, in Australia.

In the same class, the hapless Casey Stoner suffered another blow in his battle to get to the top. Leading the first practice session, he had yet another heavy crash – he seldom seems to have minor ones – and was flown to Italy to repair a broken collar-bone and scaphoid.

Midsummer madness drenched much of the paddock during practice. Rossi started it, and ended up as wet as anyone (right and bottom right). Except perhaps Gibernau (left) and a number of paddock ingénues. Somehow, Hayden and Honda team manager Tadayuki Okada (above) stayed dry.

All photographs: Mark Wernham

MOTOGP RACE – 22 laps

The second closest ever front row was led at the last gasp by Rossi, with fast times all round, and first to fourth covered by less than one-and-a-half tenths. Gibernau was alongside, then Biaggi and Capirossi. Checa was next, but four-tenths adrift at a track that might suit the Yamaha. One problem was a drive chain that had broken as he passed the pits, leaving him with a long push back in the heat. 'At least I'll be fit for the race,' he said grimly.

Bayliss was on the second row, but again demonstrated the speed of the Ducati by bursting through to lead into the first corner, from Rossi, Gibernau, Biaggi and Capirossi. The order stayed much the same as the leaders pulled clear, Rossi trying one attack out of the stadium, only to run wide and drop behind Gibernau, although he was ahead again within a couple of corners. Checa was losing tenths every lap as he tried to hang on – he was a full second adrift at one-third distance and also troubled by a persistent Hayden.

Rossi finally relieved Bayliss of his long lead after ten laps, only to be passed straight back again. But Rossi was in charge, and Bayliss's efforts only put him wide and vulnerable to Gibernau's prompt attack at the bottom of the hill. Biaggi and Capirossi were still close, also swapping positions briefly once. It was still anybody's race.

Lap 13 saw Biaggi done for, with a big slip that he only narrowly saved, losing fourth and then fifth as Checa came past. It seemed to knock the fight out of the Italian.

As the end came nearer, Capirossi began to play his hand, consigning Bayliss to fourth and starting to impose on Gibernau. Clearly a candidate for victory, instead, on lap 20, he slowed abruptly, his elbow flapping at the throttle as he tried to get some life out of an engine whose electronics had expired.

On the following lap, Gibernau pushed inside Rossi to lead. At the next bend, Rossi's attack almost ended in disaster, as he was forced out wide to avoid hitting Gibernau. As a result, he was four-tenths down as they started the last lap, Bayliss right behind him.

It was a Rossi masterpiece, breaking Kato's lap record by a massive seven-tenths as he slashed the gap to nothing, then flew straight past Gibernau with apparent ease. The Spaniard was close enough to almost hit Rossi in the final corner, and was practically alongside over the line, Bayliss a few feet adrift.

Checa had dropped Biaggi by the end for his best result so far; Hayden was two seconds off Biaggi and lucky to be able to save his place from Barros, who had taken much of the race to get away from Ukawa, but was attacking strongly at the end. 'If I had woken up earlier, I think I could have passed Max as well,' he said later.

Tamada was ten seconds adrift of Ukawa, blaming his bad start and a lack of rear grip, although he'd worked through the next group, where Melandri had also picked his way to the front, finishing just three-tenths ahead of Jacque. Edwards had led this group until half-distance, the full fuel load easing the Aprilia's persistent chatter. Haga was almost ten seconds behind after making a bad start. Nakano came straight out of hospital to finish 14th, with Kiyonari taking the last point.

The lesser Japanese factories battled for the no-score positions. McCoy had been in front, before dropping behind not only team-mate Pitt, but also Hopkins in the closing stages, his tyre grip a distant memory. Hopkins was dismayed, even flabbergasted, that his last-lap attack on Pitt's derided Kawasaki had been repulsed. This had never happened before. Nor perhaps the fate that his team-mate suffered – Roberts was 20th and last.

Both Protons retired, Aoki with fuel problems, McWilliams miles off the pace; likewise the WCM Yamaha of Burns. De Gea did not start in what would also be their two-strokes' last race.

125 cc RACE – 19 laps

Jenkner made the break from Pedrosa, Luthi and Talmacsi, with the last named soon to drop back as more and more riders joined the front pack, and pole qualifier de Angelis picked his way through to take the lead after eight laps. Cecchinello and Perugini had followed on his heels, although Jenkner was still second; Nieto and Dovizioso had tagged on behind Pedrosa and Luthi. All eight were swapping back and forth at almost every turn.

Then de Angelis slowed suddenly, his engine having expired temporarily. By the time it got going again, he was 13th and out of the picture.

The next excitement came after Cecchinello had taken the lead. Into the first corner, his engine seized and he flicked sideways to fall right under Jenkner's front wheel. He ploughed into the wreckage, and now there were five.

Pedrosa led, with Nieto threatening. He was poised into the last turn at the end of lap 11 when he slid off. Likewise, Swiss teenager Luthi was unable to avoid running into the machine, and he was sent looping several feet into the air, landing hard enough to fracture his pelvis.

With Dovizioso beginning to lose touch, this left Pedrosa up front, Perugini shadowing him threateningly. In the last two laps, the young Spaniard managed to creep ahead for the win.

Behind this, Barbera had been fending off the persistent Kallio, the new KTM rider, who had fractured a finger by falling in practice. With four laps left, they caught Dovizioso to make it a three-way scrap for the last rostrum position. But that was not all.

At the same time, de Angelis was charging through. He'd caught the trio at the end of lap 17 and straight away started cutting to the front. Kallio went with him, half a second adrift at the flag, Barbera shading Dovizioso behind. Eight seconds back, Giansanti pounced on Borsoi for seventh on the final lap, while Ui was a couple more seconds adrift.

Left: Squirming around on a wave of revs and horsepower, leader Bayliss paints stripes for Rossi and Gibernau to follow.

Below left: Biaggi got new factory parts for a favourite track, but remained in the dark as to how to make them work like Rossi.
Both photographs: Gold & Goose

Below: Frantic 125 racing was whittled away by crashes. Winner Pedrosa is shadowed by Perugini; Luthi and Nieto behind will soon collide catastrophically.

Bottom: Elias and Poggiali were so busy with one another that neither could prevent de Puniet from winning the 250 race.
Both photographs: Mark Wernham

250 cc RACE – 20 laps

Poggiali was on pole, but the last-minute rush on soft tyres was aborted when West fell with less than a minute remaining, bringing out the red flags.

The race again proved the breadth of the 250 field – a trio of front-runners moving clear away up front, the rest straggling at intervals. Thankfully, the front men were able to inject some life into the proceedings in the closing stages.

Elias led away from de Puniet and Poggiali, de Puniet taking over from the second to the eighth laps. Rolfo was hanging on behind, with a two-second gap to Nieto and Porto.

Rolfo lost touch with 'one little mistake', and the pace was too fast for him to catch up. Ahead, Poggiali took over just before half-distance, whereupon Elias nipped into second, then dived into the lead for a couple of laps, trying to escape.

To no avail – the others matched his charge, and they went on swapping to and fro for the rest of the race. At the end of lap 18, Elias led, with Poggiali third. Next time around, they reshuffled once more at the same corner after the stadium lefts, de Puniet in front as they started a hectic last lap.

Poggiali forced past through the early part of the lap. De Puniet regained the lead before the stadium. Now Elias pushed into second, and he and Poggiali were hand to hand for the rest of the lap, too busy with one another to be able to depose de Puniet as he headed for his second win. Elias won out, getting to the top of the hill first to block the last two corners before the finish.

Rolfo was less than five seconds adrift and all alone. Nieto had been fifth for most of the race, with Porto awaiting his chance right behind. It came with three laps left, and the Honda was half a second ahead at the flag.

Next came Battaini, managing to fend off team-mate Guintoli. They were almost 20 seconds away from Matsudo, who'd come through to head the battling Faubel and Marchand over the line.

Chaz Davies was 14th in the thick of the next group of privateers, in the points for a third successive race.

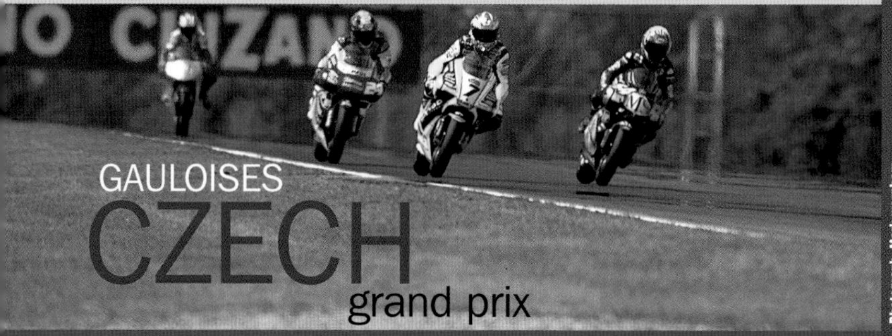

GAULOISES
CZECH grand prix

Photograph: Mark Wernham

17 AUGUST 2003

AUTODROM BRNO – CZECH REPUBLIC

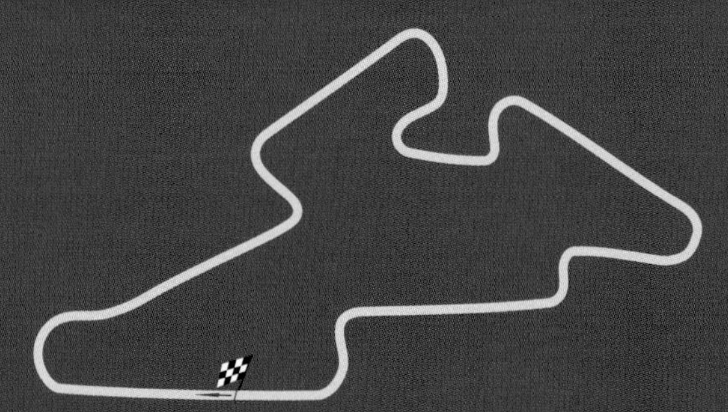

CIRCUIT LENGTH: 3.357 miles/5.403 km

MotoGP

22 laps, 73.854 miles/118.866 km

Pos.	Rider (Nat.)	No.	Machine	Laps	Time & speed
1	Valentino Rossi (I)	46	Honda	22	44m 18.907s 100.002 mph/ 160.937 km/h
2	Sete Gibernau (E)	15	Honda	22	44m 18.949s
3	Troy Bayliss (AUS)	12	Ducati	22	44m 19.575s
4	Carlos Checa (E)	7	Yamaha	22	44m 24.297s
5	Max Biaggi (I)	3	Honda	22	44m 27.636s
6	Nicky Hayden (USA)	69	Honda	22	44m 29.950s
7	Alex Barros (BR)	4	Yamaha	22	44m 30.346s
8	Tohru Ukawa (J)	11	Honda	22	44m 32.481s
9	Makoto Tamada (J)	6	Honda	22	44m 42.180s
10	Marco Melandri (I)	33	Yamaha	22	44m 45.311s
11	Olivier Jacque (F)	19	Yamaha	22	44m 45.592s
12	Colin Edwards (USA)	45	Aprilia	22	44m 49.635s
13	Noriyuki Haga (J)	41	Aprilia	22	44m 58.438s
14	Shinya Nakano (J)	56	Yamaha	22	45m 00.147s
15	Ryuichi Kiyonari (J)	23	Honda	22	45m 03.530s
16	Andrew Pitt (AUS)	88	Kawasaki	22	45m 14.406s
17	John Hopkins (USA)	21	Suzuki	22	45m 14.584s
18	Garry McCoy (AUS)	8	Kawasaki	22	45m 19.607s
19	Alex Hofmann (D)	66	Kawasaki	22	45m 27.037s
20	Kenny Roberts (USA)	10	Suzuki	22	45m 33.431s
	Loris Capirossi (I)	65	Ducati	19	DNF
	Jeremy McWilliams (GB)	99	Proton KR	12	DNF
	Nobuatsu Aoki (J)	9	Proton KR	11	DNF
	Chris Burns (GB)	35	Roc Yamaha	9	DNF
	David de Gea (E)	52	Sabre V4		DNS

Fastest lap: Rossi, 1m 59.966s, 100.746 mph/162.135 km/h (record).

Previous record: Daijiro Kato, J (Honda), 2m 00.605s, 100.212 mph/ 161.276 km/h (2002).

Event best maximum speed: Rossi, 186.7 mph/300.5 km/h (race).

Qualifying: 1 Rossi, 1m 58.769s; 2 Gibernau, 1m 58.899s; 3 Biaggi, 1m 58.908s; 4 Capirossi, 1m 58.916s; 5 Checa, 1m 59.295s; 6 Bayliss, 1m 59.373s; 7 Hayden, 1m 59.432s; 8 Ukawa, 1m 59.629s; 9 Barros, 1m 59.765s; 10 Tamada, 2m 00.145s; 11 Jacque, 2m 00.165s; 12 Edwards, 2m 00.627s; 13 Hopkins, 2m 00.740s; 14 Nakano, 2m 00.800s; 15 Kiyonari, 2m 00.862s; 16 Roberts, 2m 00.891s; 17 Melandri, 2m 00.892s; 18 Haga, 2m 01.303s; 19 McCoy, 2m 01.320s; 20 Hofmann, 2m 01.753s; 21 McWilliams, 2m 01.809s; 22 Pitt, 2m 01.994s; 23 Aoki, 2m 02.704s; 24 de Gea, 2m 04.638s; 25 Burns, 2m 05.083s.

Fastest race laps: 1 Rossi, 1m 59.966s; 2 Bayliss, 2m 00.069s; 3 Biaggi, 2m 00.154s; 4 Gibernau, 2m 00.197s; 5 Capirossi, 2m 00.234s; 6 Hayden, 2m 00.411s; 7 Checa, 2m 00.415s; 8 Ukawa, 2m 00.744s; 9 Barros, 2m 00.749s; 10 Jacque, 2m 00.764s; 11 Edwards, 2m 00.883s; 12 Tamada, 2m 01.161s; 13 Melandri, 2m 01.343s; 14 Haga, 2m 01.540s; 15 Nakano, 2m 01.867s; 16 Kiyonari, 2m 01.993s; 17 McCoy, 2m 02.064s; 18 Pitt, 2m 02.139s; 19 Roberts, 2m 02.351s; 20 Hopkins, 2m 02.352s; 21 Hofmann, 2m 02.563s; 22 McWilliams, 2m 03.239s; 23 Aoki, 2m 04.611s; 24 Burns, 2m 07.488s.

World Championship: 1 Rossi, 212; 2 Gibernau, 178; 3 Biaggi, 141; 4 Capirossi, 97; 5 Bayliss, 96; 6 Checa, 78; 7 Ukawa, 74; 8 Barros, 71; 9 Hayden, 67; 10 Nakano, 65; 11 Jacque, 55; 12 Tamada, 47; 13 Edwards, 46; 14 Haga, 33; 15 Abe, 24; 16 Hopkins, 22; 17 McWilliams, 18; 18 Aoki, 17; 19 Melandri, 15; 20 Kiyonari, 14; 21 Hofmann and McCoy, 8; 23 Roberts, 7; 24 Kagayama, 4; 25 Pitt, 3.

Left: The usual suspects – prison-capped Rossi flanked by happy Gibernau and Bayliss.
Photograph: Gold & Goose

250 cc

20 laps, 67.140 miles/108.060 km

Pos.	Rider (Nat.)	No.	Machine	Laps	Time & speed
1	Randy de Puniet (F)	7	Aprilia	20	41m 45.354s 96.482 mph/ 155.273 km/h
2	Toni Elias (E)	24	Aprilia	20	41m 45.881s
3	Manuel Poggiali (RSM)	54	Aprilia	20	41m 46.305s
4	Roberto Rolfo (I)	3	Honda	20	41m 50.846s
5	Sebastian Porto (ARG)	5	Honda	20	41m 55.761s
6	Fonsi Nieto (E)	10	Aprilia	20	41m 56.229s
7	Franco Battaini (I)	21	Aprilia	20	42m 00.632s
8	Sylvain Guintoli (F)	50	Aprilia	20	42m 00.919s
9	Naoki Matsudo (J)	8	Yamaha	20	42m 18.106s
10	Hector Faubel (E)	33	Aprilia	20	42m 21.521s
11	Hugo Marchand (F)	9	Aprilia	20	42m 21.962s
12	Eric Bataille (F)	34	Honda	20	42m 36.054s
13	Dirk Heidolf (D)	28	Aprilia	20	42m 37.653s
14	Chaz Davies (GB)	57	Aprilia	20	42m 38.224s
15	Christian Gemmel (D)	15	Honda	20	42m 38.417s
16	Joan Olive (E)	11	Aprilia	20	42m 44.257s
17	Lukas Pesek (CZ)	52	Yamaha	20	42m 53.547s
18	Vesa Kallio (SF)	66	Yamaha	20	43m 21.343s
19	Michal Filla (CZ)	74	Yamaha	20	43m 29.584s
20	Katja Poensgen (D)	98	Honda	20	43m 44.424s
21	Arie Vos (NL)	47	Yamaha	20	43m 47.153s
22	Gabor Rizmayer (H)	75	Honda	19	41m 54.862s
	Jakub Smrz (CZ)	96	Honda	19	DNF
	Johan Stigefelt (S)	16	Aprilia	13	DNF
	Henk vd Lagemaat (NL)	18	Honda	12	DNF
	Alex Baldolini (I)	26	Aprilia	6	DNF
	Anthony West (AUS)	14	Aprilia	3	DNF
	Erwan Nigon (F)	36	Aprilia	0	DNF
	Radomil Rous (CZ)	73	Aprilia	0	DNF
	Alex Debon (E)	6	Honda		DNS

Fastest lap: Elias, 2m 03.969s, 97.493 mph/156.900 km/h.

Lap record: Marco Melandri, I (Aprilia), 2m 03.836s, 97.598 mph/ 157.069 km/h (2001).

Event best maximum speed: Poggiali, 155.8 mph/250.8 km/h (race).

Qualifying: 1 Poggiali, 2m 03.872s; 2 de Puniet, 2m 03.920s; 3 Nieto, 2m 04.037s; 4 Elias, 2m 04.088s; 5 Battaini, 2m 04.233s; 6 Rolfo, 2m 04.413s; 7 Guintoli, 2m 04.663s; 8 West, 2m 04.771s; 9 Matsudo, 2m 04.909s; 10 Porto, 2m 05.054s; 11 Rous, 2m 05.157s; 12 Marchand, 2m 05.563s; 13 Debon, 2m 05.995s; 14 Faubel, 2m 06.018s; 15 Bataille, 2m 06.032s; 16 Gemmel, 2m 06.044s; 17 Heidolf, 2m 06.264s; 18 Stigefelt, 2m 06.859s; 19 Nigon, 2m 06.923s; 20 Davies, 2m 07.038s; 21 Smrz, 2m 07.182s; 22 Olive, 2m 07.493s; 23 Baldolini, 2m 07.598s; 24 Pesek, 2m 07.758s; 25 Kallio, 2m 08.225s; 26 Filla, 2m 08.960s; 27 Vos, 2m 09.654s; 28 Poensgen, 2m 10.193s; 29 Rizmayer, 2m 10.236s; 30 vd Lagemaat, 2m 10.740s.

Fastest race laps: 1 Elias, 2m 03.969s; 2 Poggiali, 2m 04.267s; 3 de Puniet, 2m 04.491s; 4 Rolfo, 2m 04.530s; 5 Porto, 2m 04.785s; 6 Nieto, 2m 04.996s; 7 Guintoli, 2m 05.077s; 8 Battaini, 2m 05.198s; 9 Matsudo, 2m 05.543s; 10 Marchand, 2m 05.919s; 11 Faubel, 2m 06.090s; 12 Bataille, 2m 06.100s; 13 Davies, 2m 06.566s; 14 Smrz, 2m 06.914s; 15 Gemmel, 2m 06.949s; 16 Heidolf, 2m 07.022s; 17 Baldolini, 2m 07.061s; 18 Stigefelt, 2m 07.065s; 19 Pesek, 2m 07.127s; 20 Olive, 2m 07.308s; 21 Kallio, 2m 08.602s; 22 Filla, 2m 09.264s; 23 Vos, 2m 10.360s; 24 Poensgen, 2m 10.380s; 25 vd Lagemaat, 2m 10.565s; 26 Rizmayer, 2m 11.094s; 27 West, 2m 11.223s.

World Championship: 1 Poggiali, 145; 2 Nieto, 136; 3 Rolfo, 135; 4 de Puniet, 130; 5 Elias, 126; 6 Battaini, 107; 7 West, 104; 8 Porto, 98; 9 Matsudo, 67; 10 Guintoli, 66; 11 Debon, 47; 12 Olive, 27; 13 Faubel, 21; 14 Aoyama, 20; 15 Baldolini, Gemmel and Marchand, 19; 18 Nigon and Stigefelt, 17; 20 Takahashi, 16; 21 Davies, 13; 22 Smrz, 12; 23 Bataille, 11; 24 Heidolf, 10; 25 Kayo, 7; 26 Nöhles and Vincent, 5; 28 Neukirchner, 1.

125 cc

19 laps, 63.783 miles/102.657 km

Pos.	Rider (Nat.)	No.	Machine	Laps	Time & speed
1	Daniel Pedrosa (E)	3	Honda	19	40m 59.354s 93.373 mph/ 150.269 km/h
2	Stefano Perugini (I)	7	Aprilia	19	41m 03.335s
3	Alex de Angelis (RSM)	15	Aprilia	19	41m 09.808s
4	Mika Kallio (SF)	36	KTM	19	41m 10.406s
5	Hector Barbera (E)	80	Aprilia	19	41m 11.705s
6	Andrea Dovizioso (I)	34	Honda	19	41m 12.322s
7	Mirko Giansanti (I)	6	Aprilia	19	41m 20.463s
8	Gino Borsoi (I)	23	Aprilia	19	41m 20.867s
9	Youichi Ui (J)	41	Aprilia	19	41m 24.195s
10	Gioele Pellino (I)	42	Aprilia	19	41m 34.296s
11	Gabor Talmacsi (H)	79	Aprilia	19	41m 34.567s
12	Jorge Lorenzo (E)	48	Derbi	19	41m 40.396s
13	Masao Azuma (J)	8	Honda	19	41m 40.716s
14	Marco Simoncelli (I)	58	Aprilia	19	41m 40.894s
15	Mike di Meglio (F)	63	Aprilia	19	41m 41.016s
16	Alvaro Bautista (E)	19	Aprilia	19	41m 41.867s
17	Roberto Locatelli (I)	10	KTM	19	41m 42.364s
18	Fabrizio Lai (I)	32	Malaguti	19	41m 42.422s
19	Robbin Harms (DK)	88	Aprilia	19	42m 01.835s
20	Stefano Bianco (I)	33	Gilera	19	42m 01.965s
21	Emilio Alzamora (E)	26	Derbi	19	42m 02.101s
22	Julian Simon (E)	31	Malaguti	19	42m 09.626s
23	Imre Toth (H)	25	Honda	19	42m 09.752s
24	Igor Kalab (CZ)	55	Honda	19	42m 19.512s
25	Marketa Janakova (CZ)	56	Honda	19	42m 30.447s
26	Luka Nedog (SLO)	57	Honda	18	41m 31.966s
	Vaclav Bittman (CZ)	92	Honda	18	DNF
	Andrea Ballerini (I)	50	Honda	16	DNF
	Pablo Nieto (E)	22	Aprilia	11	DNF
	Thomas Luthi (CH)	12	Honda	11	DNF
	Max Sabbatani (I)	11	Aprilia	10	DNF
	Lucio Cecchinello (I)	4	Aprilia	9	DNF
	Steve Jenkner (D)	17	Aprilia	9	DNF
	Simone Corsi (I)	24	Honda	8	DNF
	Peter Lenart (H)	78	Honda	7	DNF
	Casey Stoner (AUS)	27	Aprilia		DNS
	Hiroyuki Kikuchi (J)	39	Honda		DNS

Fastest lap: Cecchinello, 2m 07.836s, 94.544 mph/152.154 km/h (record).

Previous record: Lucio Cecchinello, I (Aprilia), 2m 08.903s, 93.761 mph/ 150.894 km/h (2002).

Event best maximum speed: de Angelis, 138.1 mph/222.3 km/h (race).

Qualifying: 1 de Angelis, 2m 08.100s; 2 Jenkner, 2m 08.330s; 3 Cecchinello, 2m 08.421s; 4 Pedrosa, 2m 08.562s; 5 Perugini, 2m 08.755s; 6 Nieto, 2m 08.817s; 7 Luthi, 2m 08.857s; 8 Talmacsi, 2m 09.253s; 9 Barbera, 2m 09.268s; 10 Dovizioso, 2m 09.322s; 11 Stoner, 2m 09.477s; 12 Giansanti, 2m 09.532s; 13 Borsoi, 2m 09.553s; 14 Lorenzo, 2m 09.602s; 15 Ui, 2m 09.702s; 16 Pellino, 2m 10.044s; 17 Lai, 2m 10.049s; 18 Kallio, 2m 10.089s; 19 Corsi, 2m 10.112s; 20 Azuma, 2m 10.235s; 21 Kikuchi, 2m 10.308s; 22 Bianco, 2m 10.836s; 23 di Meglio, 2m 10.863s; 24 Simoncelli, 2m 10.923s; 25 Simon, 2m 10.928s; 26 Harms, 2m 10.935s; 27 Locatelli, 2m 11.160s; 28 Alzamora, 2m 11.180s; 29 Sabbatani, 2m 11.213s; 30 Toth, 2m 11.270s; 31 Bautista, 2m 12.753s; 32 Ballerini, 2m 12.755s; 33 Kalab, 2m 12.792s; 34 Janakova, 2m 12.801s; 35 Bittman, 2m 13.192s; 36 Lenart, 2m 14.256s; 37 Nedog, 2m 14.903s.

Fastest race laps: 1 Cecchinello, 2m 07.836s; 2 Perugini, 2m 08.066s; 3 de Angelis, 2m 08.174s; 4 Nieto, 2m 08.340s; 5 Luthi, 2m 08.418s; 6 Pedrosa, 2m 08.518s; 7 Jenkner, 2m 08.603s; 8 Barbera, 2m 08.840s; 9 Dovizioso, 2m 08.904s; 10 Kallio, 2m 08.981s; 11 Ui, 2m 08.996s; 12 Giansanti, 2m 09.184s; 13 Borsoi, 2m 09.231s; 14 Locatelli, 2m 09.485s; 15 Pellino, 2m 09.580s; 16 Talmacsi, 2m 09.777s; 17 Corsi, 2m 09.867s; 18 Lai, 2m 09.913s; 19 di Meglio, 2m 10.023s; 20 Azuma, 2m 10.094s; 21 Simoncelli, 2m 10.237s; 22 Bautista, 2m 10.242s; 23 Lorenzo, 2m 10.281s; 24 Harms, 2m 10.438s; 25 Bianco, 2m 10.941s; 26 Alzamora, 2m 11.135s; 27 Simon, 2m 11.445s; 28 Toth, 2m 11.562s; 29 Ballerini, 2m 12.081s; 30 Kalab, 2m 12.156s; 31 Janakova, 2m 12.164s; 32 Bittman, 2m 12.557s; 33 Lenart, 2m 13.330s; 34 Sabbatani, 2m 13.581s; 35 Nedog, 2m 14.488s.

World Championship: 1 Pedrosa, 162; 2 Perugini, 137; 3 Dovizioso, 112; 4 de Angelis, 108; 5 Cecchinello, 105; 6 Jenkner, 98; 7 Nieto, 88; 8 Barbera, 78; 9 Ui, 71; 10 Giansanti and Stoner, 60; 12 Kallio, 59; 13 Luthi, 48; 14 Borsoi, 44; 15 Talmacsi, 38; 16 Azuma, 26; 17 Pellino, 25; 18 Corsi, 24; 19 Lorenzo, 15; 20 Vincent, 14; 21 Simoncelli, 8; 22 Locatelli, 7; 23 di Meglio, 5; 24 Lai and Sabbatani, 3; 26 Bautista, 2.

PORTUGUESE GP
ESTORIL

VALENCIA notwithstanding, after the forthcoming fly-away four, Estoril was the real end of the European season, and felt like it too, not least because the long hot summer was clearly and finally coming to an end. In Atlantic conditions that were cool and at first very windy, although mercifully not wet, the circuit looping on the flanks of the misty coastal hills came up with a fine close race, the top 14 finishing within a little more than 30 seconds. It had only been closer twice before – in Australia in 2001, the last all-two-stroke year (21.30 seconds), and in the rain-shortened French GP of 2002 (27.011 seconds).

It was another demonstration that Rossi had turned the corner and was rewriting the ground rules. There was, of course, a sense of *déjà vu*. Where, if he and his bike were that much better, was the challenge? Later, it became clear that the same question was troubling the former boy wonder.

One of HRC's occasional briefings underlined the point. Their RCV was already the best thing out there, albeit pushed a little by the Ducatis. But there was no need for radical change to maintain superiority in 2003, nor would it be difficult to take another significant step forward for 2004.

This was the message in a packed tent, where new RCV project leader Shogo Kanaumi revealed that the 2003 bike had been boosted by some 15 per cent to produce 240 horsepower, and at the same time made more easily managed in the equally crucial slowing-down phase with the overlay of engine-braking management software and revised rear suspension geometry. Intriguingly, the former was only half explained, diagrams revealing that a solenoid triggered by unrevealed parameters bled air into the throttle bodies at certain phases of deceleration. Honda's men declined to explain further, until general puzzlement and some published misunderstandings obliged them to call another meeting at Motegi, to add the vital second part of knowledge – that this, in turn, causes the ECU to inject a little fuel, effectively raising the idle speed without opening the throttle.

Extra power had been easily accomplished with the new exhaust system, along with different cam profiles and (for Rossi only) a very small increase in the rev ceiling. The exemplary RCV continued to prove the virtue of using tried and tested principles along with deeply considered clean-sheet design.

Before the exposition, HRC's affable president, Suguru Kanezawa, had found it necessary to deny persistent rumours that they were already testing a V6 for next year. 'There will be six Hondas next year, and all will be RCV V5s...not the V6 you are expecting,' he smiled. At the same time, HRC manager Koji Nakajima revealed that they expected to finalise their new contract with Rossi 'in the near future'. This, at least, was definitely not so.

Biaggi was given another upgrade here, his first time with the three-pipe Honda, showing that the pecking order in the Camel team had quietly been changed: team-mate Ukawa had started the year as the supposedly senior HRC-backed rider. It still wasn't enough to stop Biaggi complaining. Or for him to win the race, although he had a good stab at it for the first half.

Upgrades over at Yamaha too, where a new cylinder head boosted the M1 to the extent that, for much of practice, it set the highest top-speed figures down Estoril's rather long straight and challenged for the front row. In the end, Rossi shaded Jacque by less than 0.1 km/h, at 320.5 km/h, just a whisker outside the 200-mph club. And he hadn't even used qualifying tyres.

Qualifying tyres? Hadn't Michelin withdrawn them after 2000, on the grounds that they were irrelevant and a distraction to riders looking for valid race set-up? 'Now we have some competition, it is only natural we want to fight with the same weapons,' explained Nicolas Goubert, the French company's motor cycle competition chief. He meant not only Dunlop, although to be honest, even with qualifying tyres, their runners Kawasaki and WCM were hardly a threat, but also Bridgestone, making significant progress with Tamada (again, the Protons were not close enough to the pace). The latest generation of qualifiers was good for one or two laps and could be counted on to take at least a second off anybody's lap time.

Silence reigned at Suzuki, where the once pleasingly gruff GSV-R had gained a massive silencer slashing up the side. The reason was as complex as the engine's obtuse management system. When the GP machine is tested at the factory's Ryuyo facility, it must

comply with noise regulations. Then they'd realised that the can, rather than riding style, was the reason that tester Ryo did not complain of the same too-touchy throttle responses as the GP riders. The mufflers increased back pressure and improved the overall behaviour of the V4. Hopkins said that 'basically, it's a little smoother off the bottom, which helps at a tight track like this.' Team-mate Roberts was more cynical. 'It's to help me hear Rossi when he's coming up to lap me.' Another weekend of poor results rather bore him out.

The Suzukis did manage to get ahead of the Kawasakis at the end, and to defeat the improving Protons, the newest V5 claiming a first double finish. But there was a new candidate for slowest four-stroke – the WCM had returned with its own cylinder heads and crankcases, passed scrutineering and was out there running at last. Not too badly either. With 206 bhp claimed from Dutch-built engine parts, de Gea ran more than 304 km/h in practice, faster than both Protons. Nowhere near truly competitive, nonetheless it might prove a versatile privateer's tool. If there were any need for such a device in the factory-packed field.

The 125 riders' shuffle that began at Brno rustled on. Vincent was back after missing a race, taking over Ui's Aprilia, the displaced Japanese veteran moving back to Gilera (although the one he used to ride was called a Derbi), where Mike di Meglio was dumped. At the same time, old stager Andrea Ballerini became the permanent replacement for Kallio. Only one of these was to win a GP as the season wore on. And it was the rider least expected to...

Meantime, Stoner's crash-happy class debut continued. His scaphoid freshly stapled, he crashed again in practice, this time because his engine had seized. His recently broken collar-bone was displaced again, and the young Australian was out of another race.

Main photograph: **Last-time shine for the paddock village after a full summer.**
All photographs: Mark Wernham

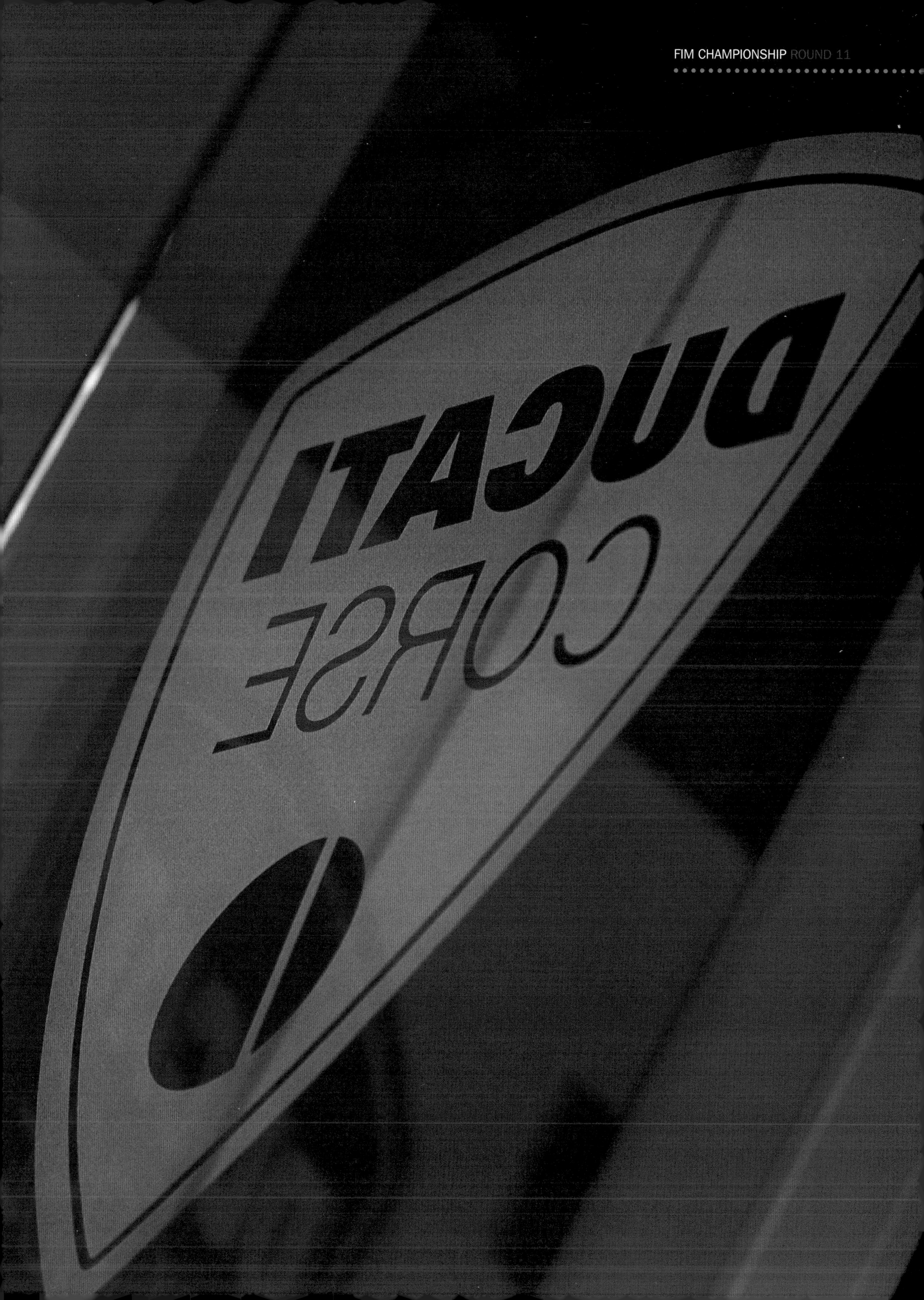
DUCATI
CORSE

Above: Having drafted past, Rossi dealt decisively with Biaggi.
Photograph: Mark Wernham

MOTOGP RACE – 28 laps

Four out of the top five qualifiers used the new soft tyres. 'It was incredible. I did the whole lap without wheelspin,' said Capirossi, taking the Desmosedici's third pole of the season. The exception was Rossi, and he slotted into third, between Biaggi and Gibernau on the front row, and arguably in much better condition for the race.

Estoril's start is on the long straight, followed by a first-gear scrum approached at very high speed. Biaggi aimed to avoid the danger by arriving first, and succeeded. In fact, all made it around without mishap, in a remarkable race with not a single crash.

Capirossi and Gibernau led Rossi at the end of lap one, but he passed them both next time around, then set a new record as he started to slash at Biaggi's one-second lead. From the fourth to the 14th laps, Rossi shadowed his old rival, nosing alongside often enough to look in total control. Sure enough, he drafted past cleanly opposite the pits and dived inside for the first corner. Their battle was over; Rossi now controlled it from the front.

Two seconds behind, Capirossi was using speed on the straight and sheer daring on the corners to stay ahead of Gibernau. On lap 12, the red bike ran wide into the first corner, and Gibernau took the opportunity to nip ahead – but he wasn't able to get away, and the last lap was a battle royal. Capirossi pushed inside at Turn One, only to run wide on the exit. They swapped again in the same way on the twists up the hill. Gibernau led into the last corner, a challenging swoop at ever increasing speed, but on the exit, Capirossi opened up the big Ducati and howled alongside to lead over the line by a hundredth. 'I used my bike's excellent engine to pass him,' grinned the Italian, on the rostrum for the fourth time after an absence of four races.

Bayliss had led the pursuit during the early laps as Nakano and Jacque dropped away, the first named troubled by his Brno shoulder injury and soon fading fast. Ukawa and Melandri were hard at it behind them, the 250 champion forcing the pace so that by lap ten they were all over Bayliss, Ukawa ahead of the young Yamaha rider. Both found a way past; Bayliss fought back, but while eventually he was able to force ahead of Melandri, he never did get close enough to Ukawa.

Barros was the next target for Checa, who had started badly, but soon caught up. It took another eight laps for him to get ahead of the Brazilian; at the same time, Hayden had been picking his way through, ahead of Nakano, Tamada and also Jacque shortly after half-distance. He took a while to pass Barros, but did so with four laps left to close right up on Checa as well. His last lap was his fastest; he was starting to relax and feel more casual on the bike, and it showed.

Tamada also passed Barros by the end; Nakano and Jacque were spaced out behind, Edwards a few seconds adrift after recovering from a bad start. Team-mate Haga was a long way off, but both had prevailed over the Suzukis. Roberts faced a bigger humiliation still, when rookie Kiyonari also got past. The 2000 champion stayed with him, but didn't have the wherewithal to overtake. Hopkins was losing ground behind him at the finish; Pitt had dropped away only toward the end. McWilliams had been between them until his engine started making 'strange noises', and he had to nurse it to the finish, Aoki right behind in not dissimilar circumstances. It was the first time that both four-stroke Protons had made it all the way.

De Gea never faltered, giving the WCM a first finish, one lap down; Burns didn't start after blowing a head gasket in morning warm-up and crashing on his own spray of spilt coolant. The engine was wrecked. Former winner McCoy retired with a water leak, and an increasingly glum expression.

knocked off line, all plans ruined. Not only did Poggiali escape his intended last-corner assault, but also de Puniet got ahead.

Thus Poggiali hung on, with de Puniet third and Rolfo half a second behind. Porto scrambled back on board to hold fifth by two-tenths from Battaini; Guintoli was another two seconds away, repassing Matsudo on the last lap, both having slipped past a troubled Nieto earlier on.

Nieto managed to hang on enough to stay clear of West, who had spent too long getting past the persistent Debon. 'I needed another corner to pass Nieto,' he said.

125 cc RACE – 23 laps

De Angelis finally took pole from Pedrosa, with Lorenzo third for his first front row, and led away at the first attempt. That was quickly red-flagged after Simoncelli and Ui collided on the third corner, leaving the latter briefly unconscious by the track, a bad start to his Gilera come-back.

Perugini led the restart, Pedrosa taking over soon afterward for a long spell, and a pack forming behind. Another first-lap crash had already eliminated Cecchinello and Borsoi.

Eight laps in, a pack of ten was led by de Angelis from Pedrosa, Perugini, Dovizioso, Jenkner, Barbera, Nieto, Talmacsi, Lorenzo and the returned Vincent, jousting furiously. Luthi had been there too, but had crashed two laps earlier.

Three laps later, de Angelis ran into brake problems, Barbera taking over and Nieto up to third. Then, on lap 14, Perugini crashed, taking Dovizioso off the track as he did so and delaying Vincent, Lorenzo and Talmacsi.

Barbera led as the last lap began, fending off a persistent Nieto. He was still in front on to the final straight, but Nieto had pushed him on the way in and timed the run out better, inching past to win his first GP in 75 starts and join the ranks of father-and-son GP winners at last (his father, Angel, is a living legend). Close behind, de Angelis managed to hold Pedrosa in fourth.

Vincent was a lonely fifth, then came Lorenzo and Talmacsi. The rejoined Dovizioso was next, leading Corsi and Giansanti.

After the race, 14th-placed Mika Kallio was disqualified for being 700 grams below the weight limit.

250 cc RACE – 26 laps

Pole-qualifier Elias was knocked off on Saturday morning, being hit so hard on the head by his bike that he wasn't able to go out in the afternoon. Still 'a bit dizzy' on race day, he defied caution and proved that he could win even when he couldn't really see where he was going.

De Puniet was second fastest, then Guintoli and Poggiali; but it was Porto away in the lead from the second row. By the end of lap one, Elias was ahead, Rolfo behind Porto, then de Puniet, Poggiali, Battaini and Debon. Katja Poensgen crashed heavily at the chicane on the first lap, landing in the middle of the track, but it was quickly cleared and there was no need for a red flag.

Soon, a five-rider group was outpacing Battaini, with Debon even farther adrift. Porto regained the lead on lap four as Elias dropped to third behind de Puniet, and Rolfo held Poggiali at bay, until the Honda rider suffered a huge slide, lucky not to be thrown off. This let Poggiali through to set a new record as he chased the leaders.

The front three were back and forth, de Puniet leading for a couple of laps before half-distance, then running wide to give Elias another chance. He seized it impressively, charging away to gain more than two seconds over the next six laps. And he carried on, able to showboat over the line and still win by five seconds, gaining second place in a title battle that was gaining strength.

De Puniet had fallen behind to fifth at the back of the pursuers by half-distance, then dropped away by a second. But he was saving his tyres for a fierce last-lap struggle.

Poggiali had just regained second from Rolfo as it began, Porto also passing the Italian and de Puniet closing up again. Rolfo repassed Porto before the chicane, only for the Argentine to hit him from behind, falling off. Rolfo was

Above: Rostrum-bound, Capirossi displays the Ducati's second-generation nose.

Right: Lots of hard work for just one point: Nitro Nori Haga's struggle with the Aprilia continued.
Both photographs: Mark Wernham

Above: De Gea never gave up trying on the heavily outpaced WCM four-stroke.

Right: Hopkins has a double struggle — with his Suzuki and with rookie Kiyonari's Honda.

Centre right: Cheeky monkey: Rossi's latest post-race partner was his favourite fluffy toy.
All photographs: Mark Wernham

FIM WORLD CHAMPIONSHIP • ROUND 11

ESTORIL CIRCUIT

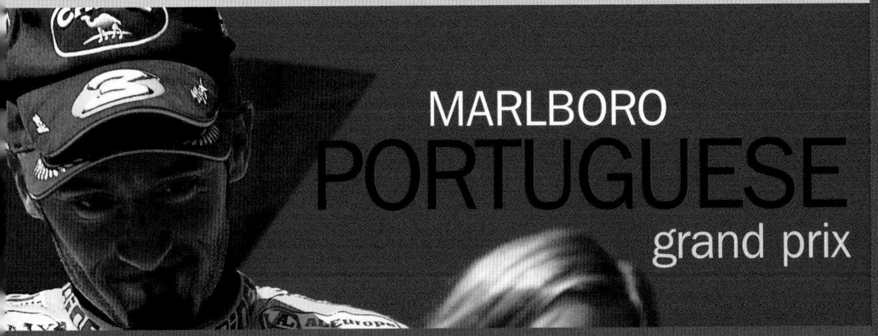

MARLBORO PORTUGUESE grand prix

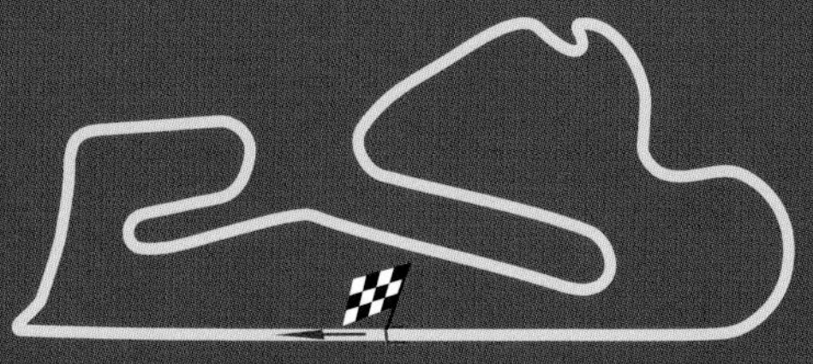

7 SEPTEMBER 2003

CIRCUIT LENGTH: 2.599 miles/4.182 km

MotoGP

28 laps, 72.772 miles/117.096 km

Pos.	Rider (Nat.)	No.	Machine	Laps	Time & speed
1	Valentino Rossi (I)	46	Honda	28	46m 48.005s 93.281 mph/ 150.122 km/h
2	Max Biaggi (I)	3	Honda	28	46m 50.099s
3	Loris Capirossi (I)	65	Ducati	28	46m 53.259s
4	Sete Gibernau (E)	15	Honda	28	46m 53.274s
5	Tohru Ukawa (J)	11	Honda	28	46m 58.586s
6	Troy Bayliss (AUS)	12	Ducati	28	47m 02.251s
7	Marco Melandri (I)	33	Yamaha	28	47m 04.148s
8	Carlos Checa (E)	7	Yamaha	28	47m 06.088s
9	Nicky Hayden (USA)	69	Honda	28	47m 06.289s
10	Makoto Tamada (J)	6	Honda	28	47m 09.820s
11	Alex Barros (BR)	4	Yamaha	28	47m 12.064s
12	Shinya Nakano (J)	56	Yamaha	28	47m 15.087s
13	Olivier Jacque (F)	19	Yamaha	28	47m 15.656s
14	Colin Edwards (USA)	45	Aprilia	28	47m 19.510s
15	Noriyuki Haga (J)	41	Aprilia	28	47m 45.123s
16	Ryuichi Kiyonari (J)	23	Honda	28	47m 49.417s
17	Kenny Roberts (USA)	10	Suzuki	28	47m 49.547s
18	John Hopkins (USA)	21	Suzuki	28	47m 54.606s
19	Jeremy McWilliams (GB)	99	Proton KR	28	47m 58.963s
20	Nobuatsu Aoki (J)	9	Proton KR	28	47m 59.528s
21	Andrew Pitt (AUS)	88	Kawasaki	28	48m 06.555s
22	David de Gea (E)	52	Harris WCM	27	46m 58.734s
	Garry McCoy (AUS)	8	Kawasaki	26	DNF
	Chris Burns (GB)	35	Harris WCM		DNS

Fastest lap: Rossi, 1m 39.189s, 94.313 mph/151.782 km/h (record).

Previous record: Loris Capirossi, I (Honda), 1m 40.683s, 92.914 mph/ 149.530 km/h (2001).

Event best maximum speed: Rossi, 199.1 mph/320.5 km/h (qualifying practice no. 2).

Qualifying: 1 Capirossi, 1m 38.412s; 2 Biaggi, 1m 38.718s; 3 Rossi, 1m 38.744s; 4 Gibernau, 1m 38.920s; 5 Jacque, 1m 39.042s; 6 Nakano, 1m 39.159s; 7 Checa, 1m 39.225s; 8 Bayliss, 1m 39.344s; 9 Tamada, 1m 39.368s; 10 Ukawa, 1m 39.541s; 11 Melandri, 1m 39.557s; 12 Barros, 1m 39.571s; 13 Edwards, 1m 39.837s; 14 Roberts, 1m 39.839s; 15 Hayden, 1m 40.069s; 16 McWilliams, 1m 40.325s; 17 Hopkins, 1m 40.766s; 18 Haga, 1m 40.779s; 19 Kiyonari, 1m 40.883s; 20 Pitt, 1m 41.020s; 21 de Gea, 1m 41.105s; 22 McCoy, 1m 41.485s; 23 Aoki, 1m 41.656s; 24 Burns, 1m 42.199s.

Fastest race laps: 1 Rossi, 1m 39.189s; 2 Gibernau, 1m 39.411s; 3 Capirossi, 1m 39.411s; 4 Biaggi, 1m 39.561s; 5 Ukawa, 1m 39.625s; 6 Bayliss, 1m 39.839s; 7 Barros, 1m 39.867s; 8 Melandri, 1m 39.881s; 9 Jacque, 1m 40.043s; 10 Hayden, 1m 40.298s; 11 Checa, 1m 40.327s; 12 Tamada, 1m 40.349s; 13 Nakano, 1m 40.521s; 14 Edwards, 1m 40.535s; 15 Roberts, 1m 40.869s; 16 Haga, 1m 41.409s; 17 Kiyonari, 1m 41.446s; 18 McWilliams, 1m 41.531s; 19 Pitt, 1m 41.590s; 20 Hopkins, 1m 41.674s; 21 Aoki, 1m 41.775s; 22 McCoy, 1m 42.396s; 23 de Gea, 1m 43.280s.

World Championship: 1 Rossi, 237; 2 Gibernau, 191; 3 Biaggi, 161; 4 Capirossi, 113; 5 Bayliss, 106; 6 Checa, 86; 7 Ukawa, 85; 8 Barros, 76; 9 Hayden, 74; 10 Nakano, 69; 11 Jacque, 58; 12 Tamada, 53; 13 Edwards, 48; 14 Haga, 34; 15 Abe and Melandri, 24; 17 Hopkins, 22; 18 McWilliams, 18; 19 Aoki, 17; 20 Kiyonari, 14; 21 Hofmann and McCoy, 8; 23 Roberts, 7; 24 Kagayama, 4; 25 Pitt, 3.

Top: Biaggi was becoming well practised at the rueful smile.

Left: Sete hunkers down to 240 Honda horsepower.

Both photographs: Mark Wernham

250 cc

26 laps, 67.574 miles/108.732 km

Pos.	Rider (Nat.)	No.	Machine	Laps	Time & speed
1	Toni Elias (E)	24	Aprilia	26	44m 37.770s 90.831 mph/ 146.179 km/h
2	Manuel Poggiali (RSM)	54	Aprilia	26	44m 42.501s
3	Randy de Puniet (F)	7	Aprilia	26	44m 43.757s
4	Roberto Rolfo (I)	3	Honda	26	44m 44.240s
5	Sebastian Porto (ARG)	5	Honda	26	45m 02.793s
6	Franco Battaini (I)	21	Aprilia	26	45m 03.043s
7	Sylvain Guintoli (F)	50	Aprilia	26	45m 05.561s
8	Naoki Matsudo (J)	8	Yamaha	26	45m 05.683s
9	Fonsi Nieto (E)	10	Aprilia	26	45m 20.817s
10	Anthony West (AUS)	14	Aprilia	26	45m 20.882s
11	Alex Debon (E)	6	Honda	26	45m 22.566s
12	Eric Bataille (F)	34	Honda	26	45m 48.535s
13	Hector Faubel (E)	33	Aprilia	26	45m 49.472s
14	Alex Baldolini (I)	26	Aprilia	26	45m 49.484s
15	Christian Gemmel (D)	15	Honda	26	45m 51.753s
16	Erwan Nigon (F)	36	Aprilia	26	45m 57.008s
17	Dirk Heidolf (D)	28	Aprilia	26	46m 14.285s
18	Vesa Kallio (SF)	66	Yamaha	25	44m 42.152s
19	Alvaro Molina (E)	40	Aprilia	25	44m 42.331s
20	Chaz Davies (GB)	57	Aprilia	25	44m 52.376s
21	Frederik Watz (S)	51	Yamaha	25	45m 08.780s
22	Miguel Praia (P)	41	Yamaha	25	45m 21.157s
23	Henk vd Lagemaat (NL)	18	Honda	25	45m 27.067s
	Hugo Marchand (F)	9	Aprilia	10	DNF
	Joan Olive (E)	11	Aprilia	5	DNF
	Jakub Smrz (CZ)	96	Honda	5	DNF
	Lukas Pesek (CZ)	52	Yamaha	2	DNF
	Katja Poensgen (D)	98	Honda	0	DNF
	Johan Stigefelt (S)	16	Aprilia		DNS

Fastest lap: Poggiali, 1m 42.215s, 91.521 mph/147.289 km/h (record).

Previous record: Daijiro Katoh, J (Honda), 1m 42.285s, 91.458 mph/ 147.188 km/h (2001).

Event best maximum speed: Poggiali, 170.7 mph/274.7 km/h (race).

Qualifying: 1 Elias, 1m 42.255s; 2 de Puniet, 1m 42.458s; 3 Guintoli, 1m 42.554s; 4 Poggiali, 1m 42.675s; 5 Porto, 1m 42.682s; 6 Battaini, 1m 42.892s; 7 Rolfo, 1m 42.902s; 8 Nieto, 1m 43.009s; 9 Matsudo, 1m 43.149s; 10 Debon, 1m 43.340s; 11 West, 1m 44.001s; 12 Bataille, 1m 44.272s; 13 Marchand, 1m 44.401s; 14 Davies, 1m 44.835s; 15 Gemmel, 1m 44.890s; 16 Baldolini, 1m 44.924s; 17 Olive, 1m 44.939s; 18 Heidolf, 1m 45.016s; 19 Stigefelt, 1m 45.171s; 20 Nigon, 1m 45.227s; 21 Faubel, 1m 45.494s; 22 Smrz, 1m 45.889s; 23 Pesek, 1m 46.021s; 24 Watz, 1m 46.243s; 25 Kallio, 1m 47.266s; 26 Molina, 1m 47.298s; 27 Praia, 1m 47.884s; 28 vd Lagemaat, 1m 48.126s; 29 Poensgen, 1m 48.181s.

Fastest race laps: 1 Poggiali, 1m 42.215s; 2 Elias, 1m 42.265s; 3 de Puniet, 1m 42.323s; 4 Rolfo, 1m 42.434s; 5 Porto, 1m 42.519s; 6 Battaini, 1m 42.927s; 7 West, 1m 43.178s; 8 Matsudo, 1m 43.225s; 9 Guintoli, 1m 43.316s; 10 Debon, 1m 43.355s; 11 Nieto, 1m 43.494s; 12 Bataille, 1m 44.354s; 13 Faubel, 1m 44.641s; 14 Baldolini, 1m 44.708s; 15 Davies, 1m 44.727s; 16 Gemmel, 1m 44.834s; 17 Nigon, 1m 44.886s; 18 Heidolf, 1m 44.989s; 19 Marchand, 1m 45.033s; 20 Olive, 1m 45.080s; 21 Molina, 1m 46.129s; 22 Kallio, 1m 46.134s; 23 Smrz, 1m 46.353s; 24 Watz, 1m 47.045s; 25 Pesek, 1m 47.221s; 26 Praia, 1m 47.614s; 27 vd Lagemaat, 1m 47.937s.

World Championship: 1 Poggiali, 165; 2 Elias, 151; 3 Rolfo, 148; 4 de Puniet, 146; 5 Nieto, 143; 6 Battaini, 117; 7 West, 110; 8 Porto, 109; 9 Guintoli and Matsudo, 75; 11 Debon, 52; 12 Olive, 27; 13 Faubel, 24; 14 Baldolini, 21; 15 Aoyama and Gemmel, 20; 17 Marchand, 19; 18 Nigon and Stigefelt, 17; 20 Takahashi, 16; 21 Bataille, 15; 22 Davies, 13; 23 Smrz, 12; 24 Heidolf, 10; 25 Kayo, 7; 26 Nöhles and Vincent, 5; 28 Neukirchner, 1.

125 cc

23 laps, 59.777 miles/96.186 km

Pos.	Rider (Nat.)	No.	Machine	Laps	Time & speed
1	Pablo Nieto (E)	22	Aprilia	23	41m 08.307s 87.170 mph/ 140.286 km/h
2	Hector Barbera (E)	80	Aprilia	23	41m 08.329s
3	Alex de Angelis (RSM)	15	Aprilia	23	41m 08.615s
4	Daniel Pedrosa (E)	3	Honda	23	41m 08.867s
5	Arnaud Vincent (F)	1	Aprilia	23	41m 11.633s
6	Jorge Lorenzo (E)	48	Derbi	23	41m 16.450s
7	Gabor Talmacsi (H)	79	Aprilia	23	41m 16.594s
8	Andrea Dovizioso (I)	34	Honda	23	41m 21.660s
9	Simone Corsi (I)	24	Honda	23	41m 21.881s
10	Mirko Giansanti (I)	6	Aprilia	23	41m 22.176s
11	Roberto Locatelli (I)	10	KTM	23	41m 33.186s
12	Fabrizio Lai (I)	32	Malaguti	23	41m 47.877s
13	Masao Azuma (J)	8	Honda	23	41m 54.930s
14	Stefano Bianco (I)	33	Gilera	23	41m 55.290s
15	Alvaro Bautista (E)	19	Aprilia	23	41m 55.483s
16	Mattia Angeloni (I)	60	Honda	23	41m 55.585s
17	Manuel Manna (I)	93	Aprilia	23	41m 55.921s
18	Sergio Gadea (E)	70	Aprilia	23	42m 30.702s
19	Emilio Alzamora (E)	26	Derbi	23	42m 33.321s
20	Ismael Ortega (E)	81	Aprilia	23	42m 33.840s
21	Max Sabbatani (I)	11	Aprilia	23	42m 34.783s
	Stefano Perugini (I)	7	Aprilia	13	DNF
	Andrea Ballerini (I)	50	Honda	13	DNF
	Steve Jenkner (D)	17	Aprilia	10	DNF
	Peter Lenart (H)	78	Honda	7	DNF
	Thomas Luthi (CH)	12	Honda	6	DNF
	Robbin Harms (DK)	88	Aprilia	5	DNF
	Gioele Pellino (I)	42	Aprilia	4	DNF
	Julian Simon (E)	31	Malaguti	4	DNF
	Imre Toth (H)	25	Honda	1	DNF
	Gino Borsoi (I)	23	Aprilia	0	DNF
	Lucio Cecchinello (I)	4	Aprilia	0	DNF
	David Bonache (E)	69	Honda	0	DNF
	Mika Kallio (SF)	36	KTM		DSQ
	Marco Simoncelli (I)	58	Aprilia		DNS
	Youichi Ui (J)	41	Gilera		DNS
	Casey Stoner (AUS)	27	Aprilia		DNS

Fastest lap: Barbera, 1m 46.225s, 88.066 mph/141.729 km/h (record).

Previous record: Youichi Ui, J (Derbi), 1m 46.329s, 87.980 mph/ 141.590 km/h (2001).

Event best maximum speed: Stoner, 148.8 mph/239.5 km/h (free practice no. 1).

Qualifying: 1 de Angelis, 1m 45.580s; 2 Pedrosa, 1m 46.106s; 3 Lorenzo, 1m 46.278s; 4 Perugini, 1m 46.323s; 5 Nieto, 1m 46.330s; 6 Simoncelli, 1m 46.414s; 7 Borsoi, 1m 46.449s; 8 Dovizioso, 1m 46.479s; 9 Jenkner, 1m 46.739s; 10 Talmacsi, 1m 46.793s; 11 Cecchinello, 1m 46.800s; 12 Ui, 1m 46.901s; 13 Vincent, 1m 46.913s; 14 Luthi, 1m 46.967s; 15 Azuma, 1m 47.009s; 16 Giansanti, 1m 47.055s; 17 Bianco, 1m 47.165s; 18 Corsi, 1m 47.186s; 19 Kallio, 1m 47.246s; 20 Simon, 1m 47.303s; 21 Bautista, 1m 47.386s; 22 Barbera, 1m 47.392s; 23 Locatelli, 1m 47.456s; 24 Angeloni, 1m 47.611s; 25 Lai, 1m 47.656s; 26 Stoner, 1m 47.805s; 27 Pellino, 1m 47.913s; 28 Ballerini, 1m 48.915s; 29 Manna, 1m 48.953s; 30 Sabbatani, 1m 49.008s; 31 Harms, 1m 49.149s; 32 Gadea, 1m 49.207s; 33 Alzamora, 1m 49.287s; 34 Bonache, 1m 49.516s; 35 Lenart, 1m 49.586s; 36 Toth, 1m 49.727s; 37 Ortega, 1m 50.983s.

Fastest race laps: 1 Barbera, 1m 46.225s; 2 Pedrosa, 1m 46.317s; 3 Dovizioso, 1m 46.330s; 4 Nieto, 1m 46.379s; 5 de Angelis, 1m 46.394s; 6 Jenkner, 1m 46.478s; 7 Luthi, 1m 46.634s; 8 Perugini, 1m 46.776s; 9 Talmacsi, 1m 46.785s; 10 Vincent, 1m 46.807s; 11 Lorenzo, 1m 46.928s; 12 Giansanti, 1m 46.935s; 13 Pellino, 1m 47.112s; 14 Corsi, 1m 47.141s; 15 Locatelli, 1m 47.217s; 16 Lai, 1m 47.334s; 17 Azuma, 1m 47.879s; 18 Angeloni, 1m 48.093s; 19 Kallio, 1m 48.102s; 20 Bautista, 1m 48.106s; 21 Bianco, 1m 48.146s; 22 Manna, 1m 48.205s; 23 Alzamora, 1m 49.154s; 24 Ballerini, 1m 49.231s; 25 Gadea, 1m 49.263s; 26 Sabbatani, 1m 49.828s; 27 Ortega, 1m 49.885s; 28 Simon, 1m 50.062s; 29 Lenart, 1m 50.122s; 30 Harms, 1m 51.714s; 31 Toth, 2m 56.066s.

World Championship: 1 Pedrosa, 175; 2 Perugini, 137; 3 de Angelis, 124; 4 Dovizioso, 120; 5 Nieto, 113; 6 Cecchinello, 105; 7 Barbera and Jenkner, 98; 9 Ui, 71; 10 Giansanti, 66; 11 Stoner, 60; 12 Kallio, 59; 13 Luthi, 48; 14 Talmacsi, 47; 15 Borsoi, 44; 16 Corsi, 31; 17 Azuma, 29; 18 Lorenzo, Pellino and Vincent, 25; 21 Locatelli, 12; 22 Simoncelli, 8; 23 Lai, 7; 24 di Meglio, 5; 25 Bautista and Sabbatani, 3; 27 Bianco, 2.

FIM WORLD CHAMPIONSHIP • ROUND 12

RIOGP

RIO DE JANEIRO

I N familiar style, Brazil's GP survived again by the skin of its teeth, while the participants attended with the usual mixed feelings. On the one hand, it's fun to be in Rio, in spite of the rampant crime and air of menace behind the gaiety (there were several stories of muggings and lucky escapes circulating behind the garages). On the other, the down-at-heel facilities and dubious surface emphasise the tenuous nature of the whole enterprise. What saves this sole American GP is the sheer scale of what otherwise might be a dull and sterile track. What look like tedious U-turns on the map are much faster and more challenging; nor does the layout reveal the width at the end of the straight, where groups of riders are able to sweep into the fast left-hander side by side. Bumps notwithstanding, this is a difficult technical challenge for riders and mechanics alike.

This year's event attracted a healthy crowd for the Saturday race, the weather clearing nicely from Thursday rain to hot sunshine. The main race fitted into the normal overall pattern of the latter half of the season, with a bit beside. That was a Honda clean sweep, taking the first five places, with (naturally enough) Rossi on the leading RCV. The Ducatis found the going tough over the constant bumps and ripples, and for Bayliss in tenth, the only good news of the day was that wife Kim had successfully delivered a third child, a boy called Oliver, on race eve. His team kept it secret until after the race.

Later, Rossi would say that it was only at Sepang that he started to think seriously about moving to Yamaha, but everybody else was doing so already. Now he was tight-lipped, and Yamaha were obliged to deny strong rumours that, in fact, they had already reached agreement with the Italian star. And there was more – a firm assertion that Marlboro had offered ten million euros to lure him to Ducati. 'This is bullshit,' said Jacques Gobet, the sponsorship chief for the munificent (but not that munificent) brand. 'I don't think the sport is ready to pay that much for a rider.'

Rio was where the speculation really started to gather momentum – not only about Valentino, who had continued his determined light-heartedness by turning up with his hair in Brazil's national colours, green and yellow. Rossi's importance is such that no other rider without an existing contract could really start to plan his own future until Valentino's had been decided. Rossi was playing the tune for this game of musical chairs, and he would keep the merry jig going a while longer.

Melandri made a stab at redrafting his own position, telling the Italian press that he hoped Rossi would join Yamaha, to give them some development direction, sadly lacking with the current two top men, Checa and Barros. 'One rider says it is a chassis problem, the other blames the engine,' commented the petulant youngster, rather unwisely for a class rookie whose injury-plagued first season had shown that an ability to turn a fast lap or two almost everywhere was not complemented by the knack of being able to finish races reliably. The same pressmen sought Rossi's opinion, who thought that Melandri might be better off concentrating on his own riding rather than that of companions who were ahead of him in the World Championship. His bosses' attention was elsewhere, and it passed simply as evidence of immaturity.

The race brought some interesting tyre variations. Michelin, almost completely dominant in the big class, regularly release a press bulletin just before the start of the race showing the tyre choices of each rider, in the rather broad categories of soft, medium and hard. For the first time, Rossi blocked his information. He wanted to keep his choice secret for as long as possible. And this may have been timely, because new rivals Bridgestone passed a milestone, Tamada taking third, their first rostrum. Thus the first direct shots were fired in a gathering tyre war, echoing that in F1.

Hopkins's first factory-bike season reached its lowest ebb at Rio, along with the general bad fortunes of his Suzuki team. New parts would come only at the next race in Japan; meantime, both riders were struggling with a bike that was ill-tempered and slow. The young Anglo-American's moment came when striving to get at least into the top 15 – the power snapped in hard in the middle of the last corner, and although he hung on for a wild rodeo ride, it was only to be thrown heavily. Nothing was broken, but plenty was battered, including both legs, his back and his left wrist. In view of the three consecutive races coming up in a fortnight, he pulled out, with a strong sense of relief.

The biggest class was fast approaching a foregone conclusion – Gibernau's points deficit was 46, with 125 left on the table over the next five races. Given the nature of things, he would need a miracle – or more likely a disastrous injury to Rossi – to be able to make it up. Mathematically, both Biaggi and Capirossi could also still win, but only mathematically.

The 125 class offered close racing, but Pedrosa was inching ahead of the rest because not only was he consistent, but also he had by far the best win rate in a season of 11 races and six different winners. He'd won four, with one non-finish; his nearest challenger, Perugini, had taken just two, with two no-pointers. He was already 38 points behind.

Things were different in the middle class, the top five 250 riders arriving for the first fly-away all within a spread of just 22 points. Elias's Estoril win had vaulted him up to second, 14 points adrift of Poggiali's factory Aprilia, pushing the more consistent Rolfo on the slower Honda to a close third. Two more Aprilias were within spitting distance: de Puniet and Nieto, two and five points adrift of Rolfo. The racing was seldom close in a class that had had the cream taken away, both rider-wise and technically, over the past couple of years, but this title would go to the wire.

MOTOGP RACE – 24 laps

A turn for the better in the weather, after a cool and damp start, considerably changed the amount of grip available. The qualifying tyres also applied radical revision in the closing minutes, Rossi taking the honours, fully 1.5 seconds faster than Biaggi's pole last year. Capirossi ended up second, Gibernau third, in spite of a looping crash while exercising his own qualifiers at the end. Biaggi completed the front row.

The powerful Ducati got to the first corner in the lead, but by the end of the lap, Gibernau was in front and Capirossi in third following Rossi; Biaggi, Hayden and Bayliss tucked in behind. For the most part, it was a rather processional race from then on, but not without some changes of fortune.

Seventh-placed Tamada was soon making progress through the pack, chasing Biaggi as the Italian got past countryman Capirossi, following him by one lap later. His Bridgestones were working well in the warmer conditions and the rider was unfazed by the sort of bumpy track he knew well from racing in Japan. Past Biaggi by half-distance, he quickly put a gap on him, the former complaining later that abrupt engine response had ruined his tyres. 'Passing Capirossi and Biaggi made me smile under my helmet,' said Tamada. He never did get higher than third, however, the front pair being out of reach.

By now, Rossi had grown tired of shadowing Gibernau and slipped past easily at the ess-bend before the straight, pulling away immediately at half a second a lap until he had a comfortable margin. He was in a class of his own at a difficult circuit. 'You need to be very gentle with the throttle because of the bumps and the low grip,' he explained, making it sound easy.

Capirossi's rookie problems weren't over yet: Hayden found his way past on lap 13 and set off after Biaggi, a good measure of his growing confidence. He pushed him hard, but never did get ahead, losing ground at the end with a

tyre vibration. 'I'm disappointed. I've had fifth before, and I thought a rostrum might have been possible today,' he said.

Two seconds behind Capirossi, Ukawa emerged the victor in a long battle with Nakano. He'd caught the Yamaha rider on lap 15, passing him and Bayliss on consecutive laps; Nakano trumped Bayliss with two laps to go. Checa had been gaining speed, and he too got ahead of the downcast Ducati rider before the finish.

Melandri had followed Checa for much of the race, but encountered grip problems, dropping away to finish ten seconds behind Bayliss and a similar distance ahead of Barros, whose dreams of home-race glory were slipping away on sliding tyres.

Edwards was a long way back. He'd made up time impressively in the early laps, having been slowed in a first-corner sandwich between Barros and McCoy. Then the Aprilia's serious chatter problem got worse and he slowed. 'I'm so shook up that even my vertebrae hurt,' he drawled.

Haga had similar problems, plus the bother of dealing with Kiyonari, who got his RCV ahead; Haga reclaimed the place on the last lap. McWilliams had been involved, until fading power saw him lose touch and any chance of a first four-stroke point for the Proton.

He still finished ahead of the Suzukis and Kawasakis, Roberts being able to shake off Pitt by the finish, but not go forward with Kiyonari. 'We're really struggling at the moment. I had to push pretty hard, with the risk of falling down pretty high, just to do 1:53,' he said. Rossi's pace was in the 1m 50s band.

The distant Pitt blamed a too-soft front tyre for his slowing pace, 13 seconds adrift. De Gea, a lap down again in the WCM's second race, was the only other finisher. Jacque had slipped off and out, while Burns and Aoki had retired to the pits, the latter in the points in the early stages before familiar fuel-pump gremlins brought his race to an end. McCoy also pitted after holding Roberts at bay for the first half of the race.

he crashed out. The young Spaniard ran back to the bike and remounted, eventually finishing 18th, fairing flapping. It was to prove a crucial error for his title hopes.

De Puniet and Rolfo were engaged in much the same way some ten seconds adrift. Rolfo demonstrated the correct tactics, starting the last lap behind the Frenchman and pushing past early in the lap, then keeping all the doors firmly closed to take what was now second place by six-hundredths of a second.

Guintoli, another 13 seconds adrift, had been engaged in holding off Matsudo, until he faded after half-distance, still safe in a distant fifth.

Faubel gained his best result so far in sixth, alone for much of the race, although a mid-field pack had closed to within two seconds at the end. By then, there were three of them, Olive narrowly beating West and Davies, who claimed his first top ten. Bataille was two seconds behind, with Debon following closely.

Nigon, Stigefelt, Heidolf and Hules took the last points; Poggiali the lap record, and a comforting increase in his points margin.

125 cc RACE – 21 laps

Pedrosa claimed a narrow second pole of the season from de Angelis, but got a dreadful start, finishing the first lap 12th. Fellow front-row starter Talmacsi led, from de Angelis, Barbera, Dovizioso and a huge pack.

Pedrosa picked his way through rapidly, and by lap four was third, Talmacsi still leading. The front three made a little ground, but Stoner was coming through and led the pack back up again. From the seventh lap almost to the end, there were nine bikes nose to tail through the bends, and three abreast at the end of the straight.

Pedrosa took over on lap five, de Angelis on lap ten. Two laps later, Lorenzo showed that the newest Derbi upgrades had given a good turn of speed, taking to the front down the straight and holding on for five laps. He said later that leading that way was already more than he had expected.

The last five laps saw the fighting become even more desperate. De Angelis took over the lead again, then Stoner drafted through from third to first and led the carnival for two more laps. Impressive, given that he was still suffering from injuries received at Brno and Estoril. Then de Angelis pushed past again as they started an epic last lap.

Pedrosa wasn't able to take a leading role: a piston ring had broken three laps earlier, and it was all he could do to hang on to the end.

Lorenzo was in full attack, sweeping past Pedrosa and Stoner early in the lap, drafting de Angelis down the straight, then narrowly squeaking past into the fast left at the end, the pair almost colliding.

From there to the end, the Majorcan teen held the rest at bay in most impressive style for a classic debut win, Derbi's first for two years. Stoner was two-tenths behind, heading straight off to Dr Costa for some urgent pain relief, de Angelis just one-tenth adrift of him. Pedrosa followed by a similar distance, trailed closely by Nieto and Dovizioso.

Perugini was still close in seventh, Talmacsi and Barbera losing touch only in the closing stages. Jenkner was a distant tenth.

Above: Majorcan teenager Jorge Lorenzo was another first-time 125 winner.

Below: Elias has the advantage for the moment in his race-long battle with Poggiali.
Both photographs: Gold & Goose

250 cc RACE – 22 laps

Elias claimed a second pole in succession, with Poggiali just a tenth down and Rolfo third. He was losing time conspicuously on the straight, but making it up again through the difficult medium-speed corners.

The Hondas got away first, former winner Porto ahead, but Rolfo was in control at the end of the first lap. Elias was third, followed by Poggiali, Nieto, de Puniet, Guintoli and Matsudo.

They were still brawling as Porto snatched the lead back on the next lap, only for both Poggiali and Elias to storm past down the straight. By the end of the lap, Rolfo was also ahead of the Argentine rider, with Nieto poised on his back wheel.

On lap three, Porto pushed too hard on the slippery stuff and he was down. Some way behind, Battaini also fell. One further lap and Nieto slowed abruptly, his engine dead.

Thus, by lap six, the race had taken on more or less its ultimate form: three pairs of riders miles ahead, each engaged in a private battle.

The struggle that mattered was for the lead, Elias and Poggiali scrapping furiously for almost the full distance. Poggiali was in front most often over the line, complaining afterward of his rival's aggressive tactics in the turns, which resulted in at least one collision. Given his own record, nobody paid much attention.

In any case, he was the stronger rider, at least tactically, as was proved at the end of the straight. Elias regained the lead just before the long run past the grandstands, leaving himself vulnerable to attack at the end. Sure enough, Poggiali held off the brakes and moved inside. Elias tried to hold him at bay, staying wide. But he was off the cleaned, scrubbed and rubber-coated line, and simply ran out of grip. The front wheel slipped away and

CINZANO

RIO
grand prix

20 SEPTEMBER 2003

CIRCUIT LENGTH: 3.065 miles/4.933 km

MotoGP

24 laps, 73.560 miles/118.392 km

Pos.	Rider (Nat.)	No.	Machine	Laps	Time & speed
1	Valentino Rossi (I)	46	Honda	24	44m 36.633s 98.943 mph/ 159.234 km/h
2	Sete Gibernau (E)	15	Honda	24	44m 39.742s
3	Makoto Tamada (J)	6	Honda	24	44m 43.931s
4	Max Biaggi (I)	3	Honda	24	44m 45.868s
5	Nicky Hayden (USA)	69	Honda	24	44m 47.798s
6	Loris Capirossi (I)	65	Ducati	24	44m 51.459s
7	Tohru Ukawa (J)	11	Honda	24	44m 53.994s
8	Shinya Nakano (J)	56	Yamaha	24	44m 57.872s
9	Carlos Checa (E)	7	Yamaha	24	44m 58.155s
10	Troy Bayliss (AUS)	12	Ducati	24	44m 59.604s
11	Marco Melandri (I)	33	Yamaha	24	45m 09.543s
12	Alex Barros (BR)	4	Yamaha	24	45m 16.769s
13	Colin Edwards (USA)	45	Aprilia	24	45m 30.732s
14	Noriyuki Haga (J)	41	Aprilia	24	45m 33.867s
15	Ryuichi Kiyonari (J)	23	Honda	24	45m 34.311s
16	Jeremy McWilliams (GB)	99	Proton KR	24	45m 42.702s
17	Kenny Roberts (USA)	10	Suzuki	24	45m 46.077s
18	Andrew Pitt (AUS)	88	Kawasaki	24	45m 59.096s
19	David de Gea (E)	52	Harris WCM	23	44m 54.808s
	Garry McCoy (AUS)	8	Kawasaki	14	DNF
	Nobuatsu Aoki (J)	9	Proton KR	11	DNF
	Chris Burns (GB)	35	Harris WCM	8	DNF
	Olivier Jacque (F)	19	Yamaha	7	DNF
	John Hopkins (USA)	21	Suzuki		DNS

Fastest lap: Rossi, 1m 50.453s, 99.905 mph/160.781 km/h (record).

Previous record: Tadayuki Okada, J (Honda), 1m 51.928s, 98.588 mph/ 158.662 km/h (1997).

Event best maximum speed: Rossi, 199.0 mph/320.2 km/h (qualifying practice no. 1).

Qualifying: 1 Rossi, 1m 49.038s; 2 Capirossi, 1m 49.340s; 3 Gibernau, 1m 49.808s; 4 Biaggi, 1m 49.876s; 5 Bayliss, 1m 50.042s; 6 Nakano, 1m 50.171s; 7 Hayden, 1m 50.679s; 8 Ukawa, 1m 50.684s; 9 Tamada, 1m 50.775s; 10 Checa, 1m 50.856s; 11 Barros, 1m 50.876s; 12 Edwards, 1m 51.007s; 13 McCoy, 1m 51.179s; 14 Jacque, 1m 51.385s; 15 Kiyonari, 1m 51.500s; 16 Melandri, 1m 51.566s; 17 Aoki, 1m 51.576s; 18 Hopkins, 1m 51.802s; 19 Roberts, 1m 51.839s; 20 Haga, 1m 51.870s; 21 McWilliams, 1m 52.180s; 22 Pitt, 1m 52.715s; 23 de Gea, 1m 53.373s; 24 Burns, 1m 54.667s.

Fastest race laps: 1 Rossi, 1m 50.453s; 2 Tamada, 1m 50.958s; 3 Biaggi, 1m 51.113s; 4 Capirossi, 1m 51.206s; 5 Gibernau, 1m 51.252s; 6 Bayliss, 1m 51.318s; 7 Hayden, 1m 51.357s; 8 Nakano, 1m 51.414s; 9 Melandri, 1m 51.606s; 10 Checa, 1m 51.618s; 11 Ukawa, 1m 51.675s; 12 Barros, 1m 52.060s; 13 Edwards, 1m 52.430s; 14 Jacque, 1m 52.743s; 15 Kiyonari, 1m 52.805s; 16 McWilliams, 1m 52.982s; 17 Haga, 1m 53.109s; 18 Aoki, 1m 53.154s; 19 McCoy, 1m 53.433s; 20 Pitt, 1m 53.519s; 21 Roberts, 1m 53.603s; 22 de Gea, 1m 55.981s; 23 Burns, 1m 56.612s.

World Championship: 1 Rossi, 262; 2 Gibernau, 211; 3 Biaggi, 174; 4 Capirossi, 123; 5 Bayliss, 112; 6 Ukawa, 94; 7 Checa, 93; 8 Hayden, 85; 9 Barros, 80; 10 Nakano, 77; 11 Tamada, 69; 12 Jacque, 58; 13 Edwards, 51; 14 Haga, 36; 15 Melandri, 29; 16 Abe, 24; 17 Hopkins, 22; 18 McWilliams, 18; 19 Aoki, 17; 20 Kiyonari, 15; 21 Hofmann and McCoy, 8; 23 Roberts, 7; 24 Kagayama, 4; 25 Pitt, 3.

250 cc

22 laps, 67.430 miles/108.526 km

Pos.	Rider (Nat.)	No.	Machine	Laps	Time & speed
1	Manuel Poggiali (RSM)	54	Aprilia	22	42m 09.055s 95.991 mph/ 154.482 km/h
2	Roberto Rolfo (I)	3	Honda	22	42m 21.956s
3	Randy de Puniet (F)	7	Aprilia	22	42m 22.020s
4	Sylvain Guintoli (F)	50	Aprilia	22	42m 34.372s
5	Naoki Matsudo (J)	8	Yamaha	22	42m 56.523s
6	Hector Faubel (E)	33	Aprilia	22	43m 04.749s
7	Joan Olive (E)	11	Aprilia	22	43m 07.319s
8	Anthony West (AUS)	14	Aprilia	22	43m 07.394s
9	Chaz Davies (GB)	57	Aprilia	22	43m 09.248s
10	Eric Bataille (F)	34	Honda	22	43m 11.661s
11	Alex Debon (E)	6	Honda	22	43m 12.555s
12	Erwan Nigon (F)	36	Aprilia	22	43m 18.959s
13	Johan Stigefelt (S)	16	Aprilia	22	43m 23.254s
14	Dirk Heidolf (D)	28	Aprilia	22	43m 23.425s
15	Jaroslav Hules (CZ)	13	Honda	22	43m 25.968s
16	Christian Gemmel (D)	15	Honda	22	43m 26.092s
17	Lukas Pesek (CZ)	52	Yamaha	22	43m 28.893s
18	Toni Elias (E)	24	Aprilia	22	43m 36.253s
19	Henk vd Lagemaat (NL)	18	Honda	21	42m 29.283s
	Alex Baldolini (I)	26	Aprilia	11	DNF
	Hugo Marchand (F)	9	Aprilia	4	DNF
	Fonsi Nieto (E)	10	Aprilia	3	DNF
	Sebastian Porto (ARG)	5	Honda	2	DNF
	Franco Battaini (I)	21	Aprilia	2	DNF
	Katja Poensgen (D)	98	Honda		DNS

Fastest lap: Poggiali, 1m 54.215s, 96.614 mph/155.485 km/h (record).

Previous record: Valentino Rossi, I (Aprilia), 1m 54.230s, 96.601 mph/ 155.465 km/h (1999).

Event best maximum speed: Elias, 167.0 mph/268.8 km/h (free practice no. 2).

Qualifying: 1 Elias, 1m 53.457s; 2 Poggiali, 1m 53.589s; 3 Rolfo, 1m 53.827s; 4 de Puniet, 1m 53.832s; 5 Nieto, 1m 53.872s; 6 Porto, 1m 53.876s; 7 Guintoli, 1m 54.017s; 8 Battaini, 1m 54.282s; 9 Matsudo, 1m 55.432s; 10 Faubel, 1m 55.502s; 11 Nigon, 1m 55.864s; 12 Marchand, 1m 55.865s; 13 Debon, 1m 56.205s; 14 Olive, 1m 56.212s; 15 Davies, 1m 56.227s; 16 West, 1m 56.305s; 17 Stigefelt, 1m 56.339s; 18 Baldolini, 1m 56.524s; 19 Bataille, 1m 56.539s; 20 Heidolf, 1m 56.640s; 21 Pesek, 1m 57.425s; 22 Hules, 1m 57.607s; 23 Gemmel, 1m 57.613s; 24 vd Lagemaat, 2m 00.061s; 25 Poensgen, 2m 00.167s.

Fastest race laps: 1 Poggiali, 1m 54.215s; 2 Elias, 1m 54.257s; 3 de Puniet, 1m 54.603s; 4 Rolfo, 1m 54.796s; 5 Matsudo, 1m 54.927s; 6 Guintoli, 1m 55.191s; 7 Nieto, 1m 55.270s; 8 Porto, 1m 55.574s; 9 Faubel, 1m 56.280s; 10 Battaini, 1m 56.554s; 11 West, 1m 56.679s; 12 Baldolini, 1m 56.758s; 13 Bataille, 1m 56.784s; 14 Heidolf, 1m 56.873s; 15 Olive, 1m 56.900s; 16 Davies, 1m 56.927s; 17 Stigefelt, 1m 57.076s; 18 Hules, 1m 57.089s; 19 Debon, 1m 57.158s; 20 Pesek, 1m 57.201s; 21 Gemmel, 1m 57.394s; 22 Nigon, 1m 57.466s; 23 Marchand, 1m 57.709s; 24 vd Lagemaat, 2m 00.061s.

World Championship: 1 Poggiali, 190; 2 Rolfo, 168; 3 de Puniet, 162; 4 Elias, 151; 5 Nieto, 143; 6 West, 118; 7 Battaini, 117; 8 Porto, 109; 9 Guintoli, 88; 10 Matsudo, 86; 11 Debon, 57; 12 Olive, 36; 13 Faubel, 34; 14 Baldolini, Bataille and Nigon, 21; 17 Aoyama, Davies, Gemmel and Stigefelt, 20; 21 Marchand, 19; 22 Takahashi, 16; 23 Heidolf and Smrz, 12; 25 Kayo, 7; 26 Nöhles and Vincent, 5; 28 Hules and Neukirchner, 1.

125 cc

21 laps, 64.365 miles/103.593 km

Pos.	Rider (Nat.)	No.	Machine	Laps	Time & speed
1	Jorge Lorenzo (E)	48	Derbi	21	41m 51.624s 92.263 mph/ 148.483 km/h
2	Casey Stoner (AUS)	27	Aprilia	21	41m 51.856s
3	Alex de Angelis (RSM)	15	Aprilia	21	41m 51.996s
4	Daniel Pedrosa (E)	3	Honda	21	41m 52.213s
5	Pablo Nieto (E)	22	Aprilia	21	41m 52.395s
6	Andrea Dovizioso (I)	34	Honda	21	41m 52.523s
7	Stefano Perugini (I)	7	Aprilia	21	41m 52.864s
8	Gabor Talmacsi (H)	79	Aprilia	21	41m 55.459s
9	Hector Barbera (E)	80	Aprilia	21	41m 55.741s
10	Steve Jenkner (D)	17	Aprilia	21	42m 06.892s
11	Marco Simoncelli (I)	58	Aprilia	21	42m 10.711s
12	Gino Borsoi (I)	23	Aprilia	21	42m 11.069s
13	Arnaud Vincent (F)	1	Aprilia	21	42m 11.208s
14	Mirko Giansanti (I)	6	Aprilia	21	42m 11.297s
15	Thomas Luthi (CH)	12	Honda	21	42m 12.090s
16	Alvaro Bautista (E)	19	Aprilia	21	42m 19.526s
17	Roberto Locatelli (I)	10	KTM	21	42m 19.616s
18	Lucio Cecchinello (I)	4	Aprilia	21	42m 24.351s
19	Mika Kallio (SF)	36	KTM	21	42m 27.762s
20	Stefano Bianco (I)	33	Gilera	21	42m 32.168s
21	Youichi Ui (J)	41	Gilera	21	42m 33.234s
22	Simone Corsi (I)	24	Honda	21	42m 41.604s
23	Robbin Harms (DK)	88	Aprilia	21	42m 41.760s
24	Fabrizio Lai (I)	32	Malaguti	21	42m 41.803s
25	Julian Simon (E)	31	Malaguti	21	42m 47.248s
26	Gioele Pellino (I)	42	Aprilia	21	42m 52.371s
27	Michele Danese (I)	28	Honda	21	43m 43.808s
	Andrea Ballerini (I)	50	Honda	16	DNF
	Mike di Meglio (F)	63	Honda	15	DNF
	Masao Azuma (J)	8	Honda	10	DNF
	Emilio Alzamora (E)	26	Derbi	6	DNF
	Max Sabbatani (I)	11	Aprilia	3	DNF
	Imre Toth (H)	25	Honda	1	DNF

Fastest lap: Pedrosa, 1m 58.121s, 93.419 mph/150.344 km/h (record).

Previous record: Mirko Giansanti, I (Honda), 1m 59.368s, 92.443 mph/ 148.773 km/h (2000).

Event best maximum speed: de Angelis, 144.2 mph/232.1 km/h (qualifying practice no. 2).

Qualifying: 1 Pedrosa, 1m 58.052s; 2 de Angelis, 1m 58.070s; 3 Dovizioso, 1m 58.092s; 4 Talmacsi, 1m 58.273s; 5 Lorenzo, 1m 58.352s; 6 Perugini, 1m 58.614s; 7 Barbera, 1m 58.644s; 8 Jenkner, 1m 58.675s; 9 Stoner, 1m 58.687s; 10 Borsoi, 1m 58.812s; 11 Vincent, 1m 58.827s; 12 Luthi, 1m 58.944s; 13 Cecchinello, 1m 58.945s; 14 Nieto, 1m 59.163s; 15 Giansanti, 1m 59.213s; 16 Simoncelli, 1m 59.469s; 17 Azuma, 1m 59.488s; 18 Lai, 1m 59.832s; 19 Corsi, 2m 00.101s; 20 Bautista, 2m 00.165s; 21 Locatelli, 2m 00.247s; 22 Ui, 2m 00.515s; 23 Kallio, 2m 00.528s; 24 Simon, 2m 00.593s; 25 Alzamora, 2m 00.598s; 26 Bianco, 2m 00.605s; 27 Toth, 2m 00.819s; 28 Ballerini, 2m 00.843s; 29 di Meglio, 2m 01.107s; 30 Harms, 2m 01.169s; 31 Pellino, 2m 01.275s; 32 Danese, 2m 02.290s; 33 Sabbatani, 2m 02.656s.

Fastest race laps: 1 Pedrosa, 1m 58.121s; 2 Barbera, 1m 58.712s; 3 de Angelis, 1m 58.729s; 4 Stoner, 1m 58.804s; 5 Nieto, 1m 58.892s; 6 Perugini, 1m 58.994s; 7 Lorenzo, 1m 59.012s; 8 Dovizioso, 1m 59.019s; 9 Azuma, 1m 59.105s; 10 Talmacsi, 1m 59.124s; 11 Jenkner, 1m 59.140s; 12 Kallio, 1m 59.199s; 13 Vincent, 1m 59.227s; 14 Luthi, 1m 59.349s; 15 Borsoi, 1m 59.430s; 16 Simoncelli, 1m 59.465s; 17 Giansanti, 1m 59.516s; 18 Cecchinello, 1m 59.562s; 19 di Meglio, 1m 59.760s; 20 Locatelli, 1m 59.897s; 21 Bautista, 2m 00.075s; 22 Bianco, 2m 00.111s; 23 Ui, 2m 00.273s; 24 Harms, 2m 00.363s; 25 Lai, 2m 00.580s; 26 Pellino, 2m 00.707s; 27 Ballerini, 2m 00.806s; 28 Corsi, 2m 01.030s; 29 Simon, 2m 01.044s; 30 Alzamora, 2m 01.749s; 31 Danese, 2m 03.458s; 32 Sabbatani, 2m 05.823s; 33 Toth, 2m 37.601s.

World Championship: 1 Pedrosa, 188; 2 Perugini, 146; 3 de Angelis, 140; 4 Dovizioso, 130; 5 Nieto, 124; 6 Barbera and Cecchinello, 105; 8 Jenkner, 104; 9 Stoner, 80; 10 Ui, 71; 11 Giansanti, 68; 12 Kallio, 59; 13 Talmacsi, 55; 14 Lorenzo, 50; 15 Luthi, 49; 16 Borsoi, 48; 17 Corsi, 31; 18 Azuma, 29; 19 Vincent, 28; 20 Pellino, 25; 21 Simoncelli, 13; 22 Locatelli, 12; 23 Lai, 7; 24 di Meglio, 5; 25 Bautista and Sabbatani, 3; 27 Bianco, 2.

Above: Erstwhile challenger Elias scrambles to pick up his bike.

Left: Poggiali dances the dance of a man with some sort of championship reprieve.

Photographs: Gold & Goose

129

PACIFICGP

MOTEGI

EVERY so often there is a weekend when off-track events overshadow the racing. Motegi was one such, for all the wrong reasons.

The weekend already had a sombre overlay, as the late Daijiro Kato was celebrated repeatedly, both in private and very much in public. A ceremony attended by a tableful of solemn-faced racing greats inducted the victim of Suzuka into the Hall of Fame; on race day, a grandstandful of special guests rather bodged the job of making a mosaic of his number 74, which was officially retired from the 250 class. And his father, Kashi Kato, was presented with a trophy on the rostrum by HRC luminaries. At each of these occasions, the seven-months bereaved Kato-San Senior gave a speech; his dignity throughout the ordeal honoured his son's memory more than any of the formalities.

The race was refreshingly different, thanks to one of Rossi's occasional indiscretions. Shadowing early leader Biaggi, Valentino had misjudged his braking for the first corner, and had to pick up and run right across the gravel trap at perilously high speed. He saved the crash, rejoined in ninth, then vindicated himself with another new record as he carved his way through to second. Biaggi, however, was out of reach for his first proper win on a four-stroke Honda.

And there'd been an uplifting ride from Tamada. Boosted by personal home-race fervour and a home track for the Bridgestones (much tested at Motegi), he'd just missed pole and been a factor throughout, culminating in a hard-nosed overtaking move on Gibernau three corners from the finish. Gibernau had tried to resist and came off worse, running into the gravel after they collided. His brake lever was trapped, locking the wheel briefly. He was lucky not to fall.

Then came the shattering news – Tamada had been disqualified, for riding 'in an irresponsible manner causing danger to…other riders'.

This penalty, imposed by Race Direction, found little support among observers. True, it had been a hard pass, and photographs showed he'd come across Gibernau on something of a collision course. They also indicated that Gibernau had been fighting back: when the bikes touched, there was still plenty of room between him and the white line. Arguably, it had been dangerous, and perhaps merited a time penalty. But disqualification?

There was little time to digest this before the second shock. John Hopkins was also disqualified, his offence being to ride 'irresponsibly' into the first corner. It had been a wild stunt, and the subsequent mayhem put Hopkins, Checa and Bayliss out, and ruined Edwards's afternoon too. Since Hopkins had not finished, the disqualification would have to apply to the next race, the Malaysian GP.

This future-shock penalty was unprecedented and extraordinary. Hopkins had definitely blundered, charging off the fourth row, then running up the inside of the pack with one foot already down. He admitted as much. 'I wanted the best start possible. Unfortunately, I ended up a big idiot. There was nowhere to go except into Checa. I deeply apologise to him…and to the other riders involved,' he said, immediately after the race.

Again, perhaps some punishment was appropriate, especially since (as Race Director Paul Butler said) they all felt it was time to remind the riders that the MotoGP bikes are fast, heavy and dangerous. But this was far from a one-off accident of this type. In fact, it was the third this year in the MotoGP class alone (South Africa, Catalunya). There might have been a case for an exemplary fine or the retrospective deduction of points, but disqualification was draconian enough to change the role of Hopkins from villain to hapless victim. Most riders accepted it as the sort of racing indiscretion that they'd all been guilty of. 'You have to laugh or cry. I prefer to laugh,' said a non-judgmental Bayliss. Ironically enough, one non-believer was Checa, hardly known for his calm and total control.

The highly artificial Motegi Twin Ring has never been a popular track, the stop-and-start layout putting emphasis on power rather than riding skill, but in some ways it seemed to be settling in to its role. Just as well. The week before there had been the news that Suzuka would not be ready for 2004 (possibly never), making Motegi Japan's only GP circuit by default. Bad news for racing heritage, for spectators and for riders who make high speed into an art form. Good news for safety, however.

Back to business, where Hayden got the latest three-pipe exhaust for his RCV, and the unfortunate backmarker factories all got something of a boost. For Suzuki, it was a revised engine spec, which really did seem to improve throttle response, although without providing the extra power the riders desperately needed. Factory tester Akira Ryo was also entered as a wild card, and he had a rather different machine – not only a motor with more bottom end, but also a remotely mounted rear shock (à la Honda and Proton), which freed up space for an extra loop of exhaust, the big Yoshimura silencer (also revised for this race) being on the left rather than the right of the bike.

Proton had also made some improvements before the fly-aways, a power-up engine spec significantly boosting the mid-range (as much as 20 bhp according to Aoki) with altered injection and mapping, and surprisingly a lower compression ratio. The reward was the four-stroke's first points, pleasingly in the heartland of the Japanese factory opposition.

Kawasaki had a more powerful engine, but sadly this meant going back to the heavier crankshaft that they had dumped earlier in the season, while the European-made lighter and more manageable chassis was also left behind. Encouragingly, they had found big improvements in recent tests of Bridgestone tyres, but this was all castles in the air to the increasingly disillusioned McCoy, and he was still fighting a chassis that was 'real heavy in changes of direction. In a lot of corners, you have to close the gas to make it turn. If you open it up, the bike just wants to go straight.' They had requested changes, 'but we haven't seen anything big coming from the factory,' he said.

Main photograph: Max unleashed made the most of Rossi's slip for a first proper RCV win.

Inset left: Positions reversed for once on the rostrum – Max and Valentino together again.

Insets far and centre left: Japanese beauties were in abundance.

Inset bottom left: Daijiro's father, Kashi Kato, speaks on the podium; Fausto Gresini and HRC president Suguru Kanezawa stand by.
All photographs: Mark Wernham

MOTOGP RACE – 24 laps

Tamada used soft race tyres rather than qualifiers to put his name at the top of the list at the end of practice, but Bridgestone were denied a first four-stroke pole because Biaggi was already half-way around a soft-tyre lap, enjoying a factory reset of his electronics to take pole by just a tenth, fully 1.3 seconds faster than Kato's pole last year. Rossi was third and Gibernau fourth.

Gibernau got the jump to lead Biaggi, Hayden, Rossi, Capirossi and Tamada. Close behind, Hopkins triggered mayhem, charging down the inside out of control and slamming into Checa, who had started well from row two. Bayliss ran into the wreckage; Edwards ended up in the dirt, although still on board. With all the marshals engaged in picking up debris, it fell to his old Superbike mate, Bayliss, to give a helpful push so he could regain the tarmac, miles behind. 'I almost wished he hadn't,' joked Edwards later.

Up front, Biaggi took over from Gibernau at the start of lap three, braking for the first turn. Rossi made the same move a lap later, and both were drawing clear when Rossi ran off at the start of lap seven, narrowly keeping control as he sped through the gravel.

Biaggi now led by a second, and he kept on eking it out until he was almost five seconds clear with three laps to go, able to win at his leisure. The electronics sorting and a race win had come together. 'At last, I am enjoying racing a motor cycle again,' he glowed afterward.

Gibernau was already feeling the pressure of Hayden when the pair were joined by Tamada on lap five. They battled together for the rest of the race, Tamada passing the American on lap eight and occasionally nosing ahead of Gibernau too. At the same time, Rossi was coming. He sliced past Melandri in one lap, Ukawa and Capirossi on the next. Then he set about Barros, who put up a token resistance that required a couple of attempts.

After ten laps, Rossi was fifth, four seconds behind Hayden. He swallowed that up within six laps, the last of them a new record, but next time around, he almost ran into his team-mate's rear wheel and had to swerve out wide again.

With six laps left, there was another shuffle, Hayden briefly in front, then Gibernau again. At the end of the next lap, Rossi outbraked Hayden at the bottom of the hill and pushed past Gibernau in the final esses. The others stayed close, but never enough to be a real threat. In any case, they were busy with one another.

Tamada was riding hard at the back of the gang, finally outbraking Hayden before the first underpass. There were two more laps, and Gibernau inched ahead. They started the last lap, Tamada eyeing the rostrum. His first attack before the underpass was repulsed. It left only the last hard braking area, before the second underpass. He used all his considerable late braking skills to prevail, and (according to officials) a little too much kamikaze-style contact and danger as well. Their view was backed by the FIM stewards, and Tamada's rostrum celebrations were all for nothing.

Hayden inherited the position, Gibernau getting back out of the gravel without falling for fourth.

Barros had led the next group until half-distance, when sliding tyres meant he succumbed to Melandri. Ukawa dropped away slightly; Capirossi lost touch completely for the second half of the race.

Nakano, Jacque and Ryo had been close until half-distance, when the wild card started to drop back, bamboozled by a too-soft front tyre. Then Jacque missed his braking and ran across the gravel on lap 15, losing six places before rejoining.

Behind, Haga was fending off Kyonari, who at least had some track knowledge and eventually got ahead for 11th, equalling his best result of the year. Both had passed Roberts, plugging on in uninspired fashion.

Jacque was gaining ground again and had picked up Aoki as they both closed on the Suzuki. Jacque made it by with four laps to go, Aoki two laps later, his handling improving as the fuel load lightened and his eye on the points. In fact, he got two of them after Tamada was disqualified, and Roberts was put back into the top 15. To his chagrin, the improvements to the Suzuki were too little and too late. 'If you're the sort of person who is happy to finish out of the top three, then there are things to be happy about. I'm not,' he said.

Pitt had been with Roberts and was just two seconds behind at the flag; Edwards was some way back after rejoining. Wild card Serizawa's Moriwaki Honda was even farther back; de Gea was his familiar one lap down, but still running. McCoy had retired, likewise Burns; McWilliams crashed out on lap three, his carbon brakes overheating within the Proton's fancy F1-inspired front-wheel shroud. This improved top speed marginally and fed the radiators better, but at the cost to McWilliams of not being able to make the corner.

250 cc RACE – 23 laps

Elias claimed a third pole by just over a tenth from Battaini; de Puniet was third, but crashed out when trying to improve, suffering some concussion. Poggiali was seventh, on row two.

Elias also led by the end of the first lap, after passing Porto, fast away from the other end of the front row. The Spaniard hardly saw another motor cycle, keeping his head down and setting fastest lap as he pulled steadily away, 3.5 seconds in front by half-distance, almost five with two laps to go. Only then did he reduce his pace and cruise in for a clear and dominant win. But who had he beaten? His best lap was an amazing 1.4 seconds slower than Nakano's year 2000 record.

The battle for second had been lively. Porto held it until half-distance, Rolfo crawling all over him and Poggiali closing, passing the fading de Puniet on lap six. Battaini had been following him, but crashed out.

These three were at it almost to the end, the positions all changing as first

Rolfo and then Poggiali passed the Argentine on lap 12. Poggiali got ahead of Rolfo, and the pair of them opened up a gap of a second. But Porto had more in him and had closed up to attack, when he highsided dramatically at the corner at the bottom of the steep hill.

It seemed that Poggiali's extra power gave him an edge, but Rolfo had the cases covered, and when he passed at the corner before the back straight on the penultimate lap, he was able to gain enough of a cushion to secure an impressive second.

The battered de Puniet had been easy meat for wild cards Takahashi and Aoyama, and they continued their fight to the very end, with Takahashi nipping past for the flag. Matsudo was a lone and distant seventh; an off-form Nieto likewise in eighth. Chaz Davies just missed the top ten, behind Debon and wild card Kameya.

Guintoli destroyed his Aprilia in a spectacular crash before half-distance, but walked away.

125 cc RACE – 21 laps

Pedrosa took off in the lead from pole, Barbera and the rest in close and threatening pursuit. Not for long, however: with a clear track and on top form, Pedrosa started to pull clear at a couple of tenths every lap, so that after half-distance his lead was more than four seconds. He seemed to have this one in the bag.

Talmacsi dropped out of a pack that was still eight-strong at half-distance, with Lorenzo picking his way through steadily. After challenging for pole, he'd been slow away, taking ten laps to regain the top ten and move up to sixth.

Four laps later, the picture changed. Pedrosa was in trouble, his steering damper coming loose and getting worse. The gap started to shrink rapidly.

Now Stoner was heading the pursuit, Barbera, Lorenzo and Dovizioso with him; Kallio, Perugini and Jenkner were close behind, de Angelis dropping away. Within two laps, Pedrosa was swamped. Stoner passed him at the bottom of the hill, ran wide and let Pedrosa straight back into the lead. But the end was inevitable, and Pedrosa was struggling just to stay with the group, losing places lap by lap.

With three laps left, the impressive Lorenzo suddenly left the quartet in a strange incident, grounding a footrest on the way through the final chicane and, instead of swinging right, continuing to go left to tumble in the dirt.

It was all down to the last lap, but in fact the order didn't change the whole way around: Barbera, Stoner, Dovizioso all covered by three-tenths. Perugini triumphed over the next group, from Jenkner, Pedrosa and Kallio. Nieto was six seconds adrift, followed by de Angelis, who managed to fend off Luthi and Giansanti past the flag.

TWIN RING MOTEGI

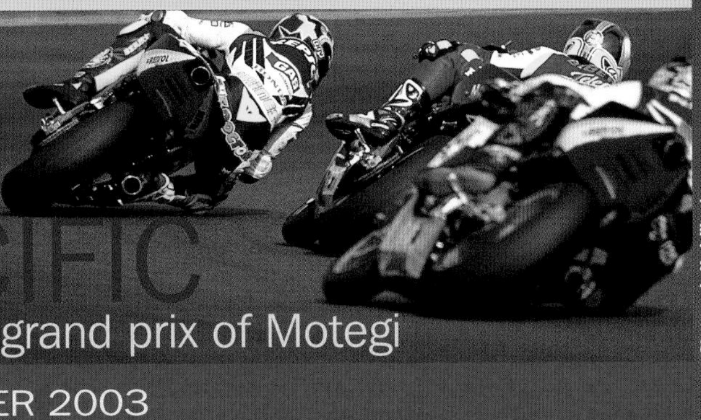

Photograph: Mark Wernham

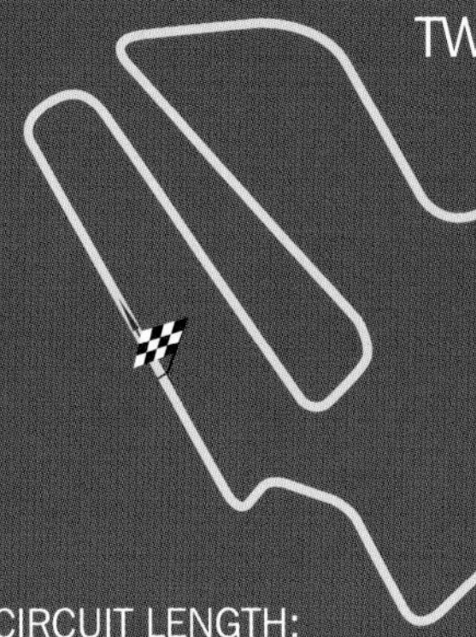

GAULOISES PACIFIC grand prix of Motegi

5 OCTOBER 2003

CIRCUIT LENGTH:
2.983 miles/4.801 km

MotoGP

24 laps, 71.592 miles/115.224 km

Pos.	Rider (Nat.)	No.	Machine	Laps	Time & speed
1	Max Biaggi (I)	3	Honda	24	43m 57.590s 97.721 mph/ 157.267 km/h
2	Valentino Rossi (I)	46	Honda	24	44m 01.344s
3	Nicky Hayden (USA)	69	Honda	24	44m 03.231s
4	Sete Gibernau (E)	15	Honda	24	44m 17.046s
5	Marco Melandri (I)	33	Yamaha	24	44m 17.499s
6	Alex Barros (BR)	4	Yamaha	24	44m 18.528s
7	Tohru Ukawa (J)	11	Honda	24	44m 19.897s
8	Loris Capirossi (I)	65	Ducati	24	44m 25.477s
9	Shinya Nakano (J)	56	Yamaha	24	44m 39.321s
10	Akira Ryo (J)	43	Suzuki	24	44m 47.696s
11	Ryuichi Kiyonari (J)	23	Honda	24	44m 50.804s
12	Noriyuki Haga (J)	41	Aprilia	24	44m 51.179s
13	Olivier Jacque (F)	19	Yamaha	24	45m 03.210s
14	Nobuatsu Aoki (J)	9	Proton KR	24	45m 05.125s
15	Kenny Roberts (USA)	10	Suzuki	24	45m 06.645s
16	Andrew Pitt (AUS)	88	Kawasaki	24	45m 09.123s
17	Colin Edwards (USA)	45	Aprilia	24	45m 25.173s
18	Tamaki Serizawa (J)	25	Moriwaki	24	45m 30.591s
19	David de Gea (E)	52	Harris WCM	23	44m 19.502s
	Garry McCoy (AUS)	8	Kawasaki	10	DNF
	Jeremy McWilliams (GB)	99	Proton KR	2	DNF
	Chris Burns (GB)	35	Harris WCM	1	DNF
	Troy Bayliss (AUS)	12	Ducati	0	DNF
	John Hopkins (USA)	21	Suzuki	0	DNF
	Carlos Checa (E)	7	Yamaha	0	DNF
	Makoto Tamada (J)	6	Honda		DSQ

Fastest lap: Rossi, 1m 48.885s, 98.631 mph/158.732 km/h (record).

Previous record: Alex Barros, BR (Honda), 1m 49.947s, 97.679 mph/ 157.199 km/h (2002).

Event best maximum speed: Hayden, 179.5 mph/288.8 km/h (warm-up).

Qualifying: 1 Biaggi, 1m 47.696s; 2 Tamada, 1m 47.804s; 3 Rossi, 1m 48.030s; 4 Gibernau, 1m 48.457s; 5 Hayden, 1m 48.618s; 6 Capirossi, 1m 48.695s; 7 Checa, 1m 48.767s; 8 Barros, 1m 48.780s; 9 Melandri, 1m 48.882s; 10 Bayliss, 1m 48.964s; 11 Ukawa, 1m 49.022s; 12 Nakano, 1m 49.123s; 13 Edwards, 1m 49.158s; 14 Ryo, 1m 49.404s; 15 Jacque, 1m 49.638s; 16 Hopkins, 1m 49.650s; 17 McWilliams, 1m 50.273s; 18 Aoki, 1m 50.421s; 19 Roberts, 1m 50.436s; 20 Kiyonari, 1m 50.480s; 21 McCoy, 1m 50.677s; 22 Pitt, 1m 51.008s; 23 Serizawa, 1m 51.112s; 24 de Gea, 1m 51.429s; 25 Haga, 1m 51.505s; 26 Burns, 1m 53.133s.

Fastest race laps: 1 Rossi, 1m 48.885s; 2 Tamada, 1m 49.164s; 3 Biaggi, 1m 49.404s; 4 Hayden, 1m 49.409s; 5 Gibernau, 1m 49.502s; 6 Melandri, 1m 49.534s; 7 Capirossi, 1m 50.002s; 8 Barros, 1m 50.041s; 9 Ukawa, 1m 50.230s; 10 Edwards, 1m 50.800s; 11 Nakano, 1m 50.833s; 12 Haga, 1m 50.895s; 13 Jacque, 1m 50.950s; 14 Ryo, 1m 50.963s; 15 Roberts, 1m 50.996s; 16 Kiyonari, 1m 51.177s; 17 McWilliams, 1m 51.336s; 18 Aoki, 1m 51.598s; 19 Pitt, 1m 52.041s; 20 McCoy, 1m 52.402s; 21 Serizawa, 1m 52.419s; 22 de Gea, 1m 53.639s; 23 Burns, 2m 02.922s.

World Championship: 1 Rossi, 282; 2 Gibernau, 224; 3 Biaggi, 199; 4 Capirossi, 131; 5 Bayliss, 112; 6 Ukawa, 103; 7 Hayden, 101; 8 Checa, 93; 9 Barros, 90; 10 Nakano, 84; 11 Tamada, 69; 12 Jacque, 61; 13 Edwards, 51; 14 Haga and Melandri, 40; 16 Abe, 24; 17 Hopkins, 22; 18 Kiyonari, 20; 19 Aoki, 19; 20 McWilliams, 18; 21 Hofmann, McCoy and Roberts, 8; 24 Ryo, 6; 25 Kagayama, 4; 26 Pitt, 3.

250 cc

23 laps, 68.609 miles/110.423 km

Pos.	Rider (Nat.)	No.	Machine	Laps	Time & speed
1	Toni Elias (E)	24	Aprilia	23	43m 57.125s 93.665 mph/ 150.740 km/h
2	Roberto Rolfo (I)	3	Honda	23	43m 58.608s
3	Manuel Poggiali (RSM)	54	Aprilia	23	43m 59.284s
4	Yuki Takahashi (J)	55	Honda	23	44m 03.143s
5	Hiroshi Aoyama (J)	92	Honda	23	44m 03.288s
6	Randy de Puniet (F)	7	Aprilia	23	44m 17.532s
7	Naoki Matsudo (J)	8	Yamaha	23	44m 23.063s
8	Fonsi Nieto (E)	10	Aprilia	23	44m 25.542s
9	Alex Debon (E)	6	Honda	23	44m 36.929s
10	Choujun Kameya (J)	70	Honda	23	44m 37.044s
11	Chaz Davies (GB)	57	Aprilia	23	44m 46.828s
12	Christian Gemmel (D)	15	Honda	23	44m 53.046s
13	Alex Baldolini (I)	26	Aprilia	23	44m 58.140s
14	Dirk Heidolf (D)	28	Aprilia	23	45m 00.512s
15	Masaki Tokudome (J)	69	Yamaha	23	45m 00.655s
16	Hugo Marchand (F)	9	Aprilia	23	45m 01.424s
17	Erwan Nigon (F)	36	Aprilia	23	45m 01.746s
18	Jakub Smrz (CZ)	96	Honda	23	45m 18.805s
19	Joan Olive (E)	11	Aprilia	23	45m 41.317s
20	Henk vd Lagemaat (NL)	18	Honda	22	44m 35.755s
	Sebastian Porto (ARG)	5	Honda	18	DNF
	Tomoyoshi Koyama (J)	67	Yamaha	11	DNF
	Sylvain Guintoli (F)	50	Aprilia	9	DNF
	Jaroslav Hules (CZ)	13	Honda	9	DNF
	Anthony West (AUS)	14	Aprilia	8	DNF
	Eric Bataille (F)	34	Honda	6	DNF
	Hector Faubel (E)	33	Aprilia	5	DNF
	Johan Stigefelt (S)	16	Aprilia	3	DNF
	Franco Battaini (I)	21	Aprilia	2	DNF
	Lukas Pesek (CZ)	52	Yamaha	1	DNF

Fastest lap: Elias, 1m 53.612s, 94.528 mph/152.128 km/h.

Lap record: Shinya Nakano, J (Yamaha), 1m 52.253s, 95.673 mph/ 153.970 km/h (2000).

Event best maximum speed: Elias, 157.5 mph/253.5 km/h (warm-up).

Qualifying: 1 Elias, 1m 52.849s; 2 Battaini, 1m 52.965s; 3 de Puniet, 1m 53.247s; 4 Porto, 1m 53.650s; 5 Guintoli, 1m 53.713s; 6 Aoyama, 1m 53.830s; 7 Poggiali, 1m 53.868s; 8 Matsudo, 1m 54.021s; 9 Koyama, 1m 54.132s; 10 Takahashi, 1m 54.141s; 11 Rolfo, 1m 54.385s; 12 Davies, 1m 54.641s; 13 Debon, 1m 54.680s; 14 Kameya, 1m 54.714s; 15 Nieto, 1m 55.095s; 16 Nigon, 1m 55.164s; 17 Faubel, 1m 55.300s; 18 Gemmel, 1m 55.450s; 19 Marchand, 1m 55.774s; 20 Tokudome, 1m 55.811s; 21 Bataille, 1m 55.949s; 22 Baldolini, 1m 56.174s; 23 West, 1m 56.231s; 24 Heidolf, 1m 56.343s; 25 Pesek, 1m 56.361s; 26 Smrz, 1m 56.370s; 27 Stigefelt, 1m 57.112s; 28 Olive, 1m 57.329s; 29 Hules, 1m 57.486s; 30 vd Lagemaat, 1m 58.941s.

Fastest race laps: 1 Elias, 1m 53.612s; 2 Rolfo, 1m 53.912s; 3 Aoyama, 1m 53.999s; 4 Poggiali, 1m 54.019s; 5 de Puniet, 1m 54.085s; 6 Takahashi, 1m 54.096s; 7 Porto, 1m 54.098s; 8 Koyama, 1m 54.478s; 9 Guintoli, 1m 54.517s; 10 Matsudo, 1m 54.558s; 11 Battaini, 1m 54.826s; 12 Nieto, 1m 54.837s; 13 Kameya, 1m 55.648s; 14 Debon, 1m 55.657s; 15 Davies, 1m 55.997s; 16 Faubel, 1m 56.082s; 17 Gemmel, 1m 56.152s; 18 Nigon, 1m 56.190s; 19 Baldolini, 1m 56.215s; 20 Marchand, 1m 56.230s; 21 Tokudome, 1m 56.319s; 22 Heidolf, 1m 56.383s; 23 Smrz, 1m 56.880s; 24 West, 1m 57.092s; 25 Hules, 1m 57.184s; 26 Bataille, 1m 57.230s; 27 Olive, 1m 58.146s; 28 vd Lagemaat, 2m 00.341s; 29 Stigefelt, 2m 00.485s; 30 Pesek, 2m 46.608s.

World Championship: 1 Poggiali, 206; 2 Rolfo, 188; 3 Elias, 176; 4 de Puniet, 172; 5 Nieto, 151; 6 West, 118; 7 Battaini, 117; 8 Porto, 109; 9 Matsudo, 95; 10 Guintoli, 88; 11 Debon, 64; 12 Olive, 36; 13 Faubel, 34; 14 Aoyama, 31; 15 Takahashi, 29; 16 Davies, 25; 17 Baldolini and Gemmel, 24; 19 Bataille and Nigon, 21; 21 Stigefelt, 20; 22 Marchand, 19; 23 Heidolf, 14; 24 Smrz, 12; 25 Kayo, 7; 26 Kameya, 6; 27 Nöhles and Vincent, 5; 29 Hules, Neukirchner and Tokudome, 1.

125 cc

21 laps, 62.643 miles/100.821 km

Pos.	Rider (Nat.)	No.	Machine	Laps	Time & speed
1	Hector Barbera (E)	80	Aprilia	21	41m 54.483s 89.692 mph/ 144.346 km/h
2	Casey Stoner (AUS)	27	Aprilia	21	41m 54.647s
3	Andrea Dovizioso (I)	34	Honda	21	41m 54.787s
4	Stefano Perugini (I)	7	Aprilia	21	41m 57.214s
5	Steve Jenkner (D)	17	Aprilia	21	41m 57.453s
6	Daniel Pedrosa (E)	3	Honda	21	41m 57.698s
7	Mika Kallio (SF)	36	KTM	21	41m 57.747s
8	Pablo Nieto (E)	22	Aprilia	21	42m 03.683s
9	Alex de Angelis (RSM)	15	Aprilia	21	42m 07.499s
10	Thomas Luthi (CH)	12	Honda	21	42m 07.678s
11	Mirko Giansanti (I)	6	Aprilia	21	42m 07.836s
12	Alvaro Bautista (E)	19	Aprilia	21	42m 14.331s
13	Masao Azuma (J)	8	Honda	21	42m 14.590s
14	Gabor Talmacsi (H)	79	Aprilia	21	42m 15.099s
15	Simone Corsi (I)	24	Honda	21	42m 17.885s
16	Stefano Bianco (I)	33	Gilera	21	42m 19.323s
17	Youichi Ui (J)	41	Gilera	21	42m 25.031s
18	Fabrizio Lai (I)	32	Malaguti	21	42m 41.491s
19	Arnaud Vincent (F)	1	Aprilia	21	42m 46.914s
20	Andrea Ballerini (I)	50	Honda	21	42m 47.158s
21	Shuhei Aoyama (J)	66	Honda	21	42m 51.950s
22	Robbin Harms (DK)	88	Aprilia	21	43m 06.177s
23	Hiroaki Kuzuhara (J)	59	Honda	21	43m 06.253s
24	Julian Simon (E)	31	Malaguti	21	43m 07.678s
25	Sadahito Suma (J)	94	Honda	21	43m 11.059s
26	Imre Toth (H)	25	Honda	21	43m 23.447s
	Roberto Locatelli (I)	10	KTM	20	DNF
	Jorge Lorenzo (E)	48	Derbi	19	DNF
	Gino Borsoi (I)	23	Aprilia	14	DNF
	Marco Simoncelli (I)	58	Aprilia	14	DNF
	Yuki Hatano (J)	95	Honda	12	DNF
	Mike di Meglio (F)	63	Honda	7	DNF
	Lucio Cecchinello (I)	4	Aprilia	5	DNF
	Michele Danese (I)	28	Honda	5	DNF
	Toshihisa Kuzuhara (J)	65	Honda	4	DNF
	Max Sabbatani (I)	11	Aprilia	4	DNF
	Emilio Alzamora (E)	26	Derbi	3	DNF
	Gioele Pellino (I)	42	Aprilia	3	DNF

Fastest lap: Lorenzo, 1m 58.545s, 90.594 mph/145.797 km/h.

Lap record: Daniel Pedrosa, E (Honda) 1m 58.354s, 90.741 mph/ 146.033 km/h (2002).

Event best maximum speed: Kallio, 136.7 mph/220.0 km/h (race).

Qualifying: 1 Pedrosa, 1m 57.736s; 2 Perugini, 1m 58.558s; 3 Lorenzo, 1m 58.662s; 4 Barbera, 1m 58.684s; 5 Dovizioso, 1m 58.988s; 6 Nieto, 1m 59.092s; 7 Cecchinello, 1m 59.219s; 8 de Angelis, 1m 59.286s; 9 Bianco, 1m 59.320s; 10 Stoner, 1m 59.360s; 11 Borsoi, 1m 59.378s; 12 Talmacsi, 1m 59.393s; 13 Kallio, 1m 59.437s; 14 Simoncelli, 1m 59.448s; 15 Luthi, 1m 59.520s; 16 Jenkner, 1m 59.620s; 17 Corsi, 1m 59.737s; 18 Bautista, 1m 59.756s; 19 Giansanti, 1m 59.866s; 20 Locatelli, 1m 59.916s; 21 Azuma, 2m 00.076s; 22 Vincent, 2m 00.381s; 23 Lai, 2m 00.616s; 24 Ui, 2m 00.849s; 25 Simon, 2m 01.198s; 26 di Meglio, 2m 01.340s; 27 T. Kuzuhara, 2m 01.564s; 28 Alzamora, 2m 01.596s; 29 Aoyama, 2m 01.614s; 30 Ballerini, 2m 01.618s; 31 Suma, 2m 02.058s; 32 Toth, 2m 02.131s; 33 Harms, 2m 02.294s; 34 Pellino, 2m 02.309s; 35 Sabbatani, 2m 02.495s; 36 H. Kuzuhara, 2m 02.569s; 37 Hatano, 2m 02.771s; 38 Danese, 2m 03.345s.

Fastest race laps: 1 Lorenzo, 1m 58.545s; 2 Dovizioso, 1m 58.555s; 3 Pedrosa, 1m 58.593s; 4 Stoner, 1m 58.788s; 5 Perugini, 1m 58.871s; 6 Kallio, 1m 58.901s; 7 Jenkner, 1m 58.948s; 8 Barbera, 1m 58.964s; 9 Giansanti, 1m 59.147s; 10 de Angelis, 1m 59.180s; 11 Nieto, 1m 59.227s; 12 Borsoi, 1m 59.275s; 13 Luthi, 1m 59.328s; 14 Simoncelli, 1m 59.348s; 15 Cecchinello, 1m 59.384s; 16 Azuma, 1m 59.395s; 17 Talmacsi, 1m 59.440s; 18 Bautista, 1m 59.610s; 19 Corsi, 1m 59.722s; 20 Bianco, 1m 59.795s; 21 Locatelli, 1m 59.901s; 22 Ui, 1m 59.979s; 23 Lai, 2m 00.486s; 24 di Meglio, 2m 00.728s; 25 Vincent, 2m 00.977s; 26 Ballerini, 2m 01.113s; 27 Aoyama, 2m 01.426s; 28 H. Kuzuhara, 2m 01.721s; 29 Harms, 2m 01.772s; 30 Suma, 2m 01.960s; 31 Hatano, 2m 02.061s; 32 Simon, 2m 02.090s; 33 Toth, 2m 02.546s; 34 T. Kuzuhara, 2m 03.101s; 35 Alzamora, 2m 03.189s; 36 Pellino, 2m 03.209s; 37 Danese, 2m 03.367s; 38 Sabbatani, 2m 04.411s.

World Championship: 1 Pedrosa, 198; 2 Perugini, 159; 3 de Angelis, 147; 4 Dovizioso, 146; 5 Nieto, 132; 6 Barbera, 130; 7 Jenkner, 115; 8 Cecchinello, 105; 9 Stoner, 100; 10 Giansanti, 73; 11 Ui, 71; 12 Kallio, 68; 13 Talmacsi, 57; 14 Luthi, 55; 15 Lorenzo, 50; 16 Borsoi, 48; 17 Azuma and Corsi, 32; 19 Vincent, 28; 20 Pellino, 25; 21 Simoncelli, 13; 22 Locatelli, 12; 23 Bautista and Lai, 7; 25 di Meglio, 5; 26 Sabbatani, 3; 27 Bianco, 2.

MALAYSIANGP
SEPANG

Giant with an earring. With two races to spare, Rossi completed a hat trick of top-class titles. He did it with a win.

Photograph: Mark Wernham

WITH contract turmoil pressing hard, not to mention the usual energy sapping heat and brain numbing humidity, Rossi did well to remain completely focused on racing. And he was faultless, narrowly shading his season-long adversary Gibernau for a seventh win, a fifth World Championship and the third premier-class title in a row. This job of winning, against tougher opposition than last year, on an upgraded 2003 RCV, was done. Time for the next one.

It was at this stage, he said later, that he started to think seriously about switching to Yamaha. In the public eye, matters seemed already to have gone farther. The European press had widely and confidently reported that he had signed for Yamaha – it was a done deal. In which case, the arrival of his manager, Gibo Badioli, at Sepang during the weekend, bearing a counter-proposal to HRC's final offer at Motegi, was just a charade. It mattered little, either way. What counted was his inner feeling that, having won two in a row with the dominant RCV, in the absence of something new from Honda, fresh stimulation would have to be sought elsewhere.

A side-effect of Rossi's indecision imposed a stasis on a number of other riders. If he was to leave HRC, that would open a highly desirable factory slot, and trigger a top-level reshuffle. Colin Edwards was one – his two-year Aprilia contract had a get-out clause, if he did not finish in the top ten of the championship. At the same time, although he'd given heart and soul to developing the bike, he'd realised that the technical responses from the cash-strapped company were too slow. It was time to look around – but until the King was in place, none of the courtiers was able to make any commitment.

The heat was oppressive, as always, at the track by the big international airport south of the steamy capital, Kuala Lumpur. The four-strokes, in any case, generate a fair few therms on their own account. Nobu Aoki's approach illustrated the problem. Inside his leathers, over his shins, he was wearing the same gold-finished, high-tech heat insulation used under the Proton's tank to protect the fuel from engine heat. It was only just enough to make riding barely tolerable, he said. Without that, he doubted that full race distance would be possible.

Gibernau was the trendsetter for a couple of other riders, wearing a back-pack water pouch with a drinking tube leading into his helmet – a system pioneered at the similarly hot and even more exhausting Suzuka Eight-Hour race. It was rather showy, and fitted well with Rossi's private new nickname for Sete – 'Hollywood'. This was the champion elect's response to the Barcelona rider's reported browbeating complaints to Race Direction about Tamada's Motegi move. (To *MOTOCOURSE*, Gibernau denied having complained, but was at pains to highlight the risks involved: 'I could have been in hospital. Then how would he have felt.')

In public, Rossi spoke for many riders when he said, 'I think it [the disqualification] was not right. It was the last lap, and the last braking area. Tamada was a little close to Gibernau, but Sete also moved towards the centre of the track.' Hopkins's enforced

absence (he'd left for Australia on Friday morning, unable to bear being trackside when the 990s fired up) was also a talking point. It was left to McWilliams to make the most pungent comment as he assembled a small group of riders to attend the regular Saturday safety meeting with Race Direction, to 'seek clarification as to what is and isn't permissible'. This after Checa, chief complainant of the previous weekend, had butt-packed team-mate Melandri in practice, putting both Fortuna Yamahas down in a heap. 'To ban someone from the podium in his home race after a normal racing incident is disgusting,' said McWilliams. 'And then to ban Hopkins adds insult to injury. Close racing is why people love this sport.'

Checa did a bit of insult-to-injury work himself: apart from taking Melandri down on Saturday, the day before he'd kicked out petulantly at a marshal who was trying to help him restart, after the first of three tumbles of the weekend. That merited a stern ticking-off from Race Director Butler, but he did not believe there was a case for disqualifying Checa for having endangered Melandri. 'There is a clear difference between somebody losing control in a corner, or Pitt's first-corner crash [at Catalunya] where somebody gets into the corner too hot, and the Hopkins case, when he was out of control 75 metres before, with his foot down and absolutely no possibility of making the corner. It was not deliberate, but it was out of order for a professional rider,' said Butler. Then he rather confirmed rumours of disagreement within the four-man committee on the action taken. 'You can argue with the severity of the punishment,' he agreed. 'I have no problem with that.'

A little bit of history came in the 250 class. Zhao Huang Shi and Xian He Zi were not the first Chinese riders to enter a GP, but the former was the first to qualify. Xian He Zi missed the cut by less than two-tenths; both rode Yamahas fielded by the d'Antin team and backed by Arlen Ness.

A moment to celebrate in the 125s came when the perpetually glum-faced Dani Pedrosa was seen to smile, after a close-to-perfect 125 campaign was rewarded with a clear and well-deserved first world championship. He was not to have long to celebrate.

Mid-way through three gruelling weeks of long-distance travel, snatched moments of leisure and intensive work at racing, King Kenny Roberts provided some welcome comedy. His KR V5 may have been designed and built in England, but the name and the major backing came from Malaysia, and he took to the high table in the briefing room for the pre-race press conference, along with Rossi, Biaggi, Edwards and Nakano. And had them and a roomful of press-men hooting with laughter.

Asked about the difficulties faced by his project, he explained what had hurt them most was just racing. 'We can't develop an engine and race,' he said. Then added, 'Our engine is very good…if you're looking for a boat anchor.' He agreed the project had been both laborious and expensive, but continued, 'The oil companies love us because our bike is so hard on oil.' Questions over, the host asked the top-table stars to stand up for the photographers. Kenny shot straight back, 'I am standing up.'

MOTOGP RACE – 21 laps

Rossi stated his intentions. 'I know I only have to finish behind Sete to be champion, but I love riding at this track. I will try to win,' he said. A distinct possibility too, as he took his seventh pole of the year, the qualifying tyres cutting fully two seconds off Barros's pole here in 2002. Rossi's final lap consigned erstwhile leader Tamada to an eventual third, with Checa a best-of-season second and Biaggi fourth; a relaxed Nakano led row two.

Heavy tropical rain on Saturday night left the track damp for morning warm-up, bamboozling those who had planned to use it for final tyre assessment. Worse than that, it washed off the track surface, changing grip levels for the race and leaving many riders wishing they'd chosen harder rubber even before the finish.

Checa led Gibernau into the first corner, all around safely. Not so the second. In the middle of the pack, an over-enthusiastic Barros touched one of the Suzukis and went down right in the middle. Luckily, nobody hit him, and he remounted at the back of the field.

Gibernau was quickly in front, and had a second over Checa when they came back around the hairpin to surge past the pits in front of sparsely populated grandstands. Capirossi was fourth, followed by Rossi, Biaggi and Hayden.

Rossi wasn't for hanging around, and next time they came to the hairpin, he was in second, Gibernau well within range. Behind Checa, Capirossi's struggle to find grip was causing him to lose touch with the leaders. As was Biaggi, stuck behind him. By the time he got by on the third lap, he was almost three seconds adrift.

Rossi was at record pace, leaning on Gibernau. On lap eight, he pounced, but didn't pull away more than a second or so, for his rival (still nursing a fever he'd developed before Motegi) kept up the pressure. No Hollywood now.

Checa was losing ground fast, Biaggi closing rapidly and ahead on the seventh lap. He was two seconds behind Gibernau, and although he whittled it away slightly before mid-race, it didn't last, and third was his final destiny.

This was one of the few tracks the Ducatis had visited before, but Capirossi was struggling, and by lap six he was under pressure from Hayden, who had already outpaced Bayliss. The pair closed on Checa, now losing speed as the tyres wore. On lap 13, Hayden finally succeeded in getting ahead of Capirossi, who lost touch as the rookie on the Honda joined battle with the veteran on the Yamaha. They changed places – sometimes twice a lap – before Hayden finally took control with two to go.

The next group was all Japanese: Nakano, Ukawa and Tamada at close quarters. The last-named had caught up from a poor start, then dropped away again after half-distance, his tyres shot. The other two were on top of Bayliss with five laps left, Ukawa getting past to gain a gap, Nakano taking a couple more laps, his former rival now out of reach.

Behind them, Melandri was struggling hard with Haga, the Aprilia fast in a straight line. Only toward the end did Haga's pace drop, the bike's difficult handling and chatter problems taking their toll, and Melandri was sure of 11th. Edwards had been losing ground behind them, troubled by an oil leak and bad handling – it transpired that a rear suspension link had been fitted the wrong way round.

He was lonely and disgruntled at the finish; likewise his old junior AMA sparring partner, Roberts, whose Suzuki had cut out unpredictably, the usual electronic glitchery. All the same, he gave fuel to critics of his lack of commitment, running his fastest lap on the last. This was to stay ahead of the remounted Barros, handlebars bent, but dander undented. Roberts was just three-tenths ahead at the flag.

The Brazilian's late return spoiled Pitt's hopes of points, and he was three seconds back. The Protons were behind this time, McWilliams struggling with a failed quick-shift mechanism. Aoki, with different gear-changing problems, had caught right up by the finish. McCoy had been slithering backward after a spirited first half; Ryo was more than 20 seconds away, also fading on sliding tyres after running with Roberts earlier. Kiyonari was last; neither of the WCMs made the finish, while Jacque did not start, suffering from concussion after crashing in practice.

Left: Checa versus Hayden: the bullish young American beat the veteran by less than a tenth.
Photograph: Mark Wernham

Below: Biaggi explores the laws of dynamic physics on the Honda.
Photograph: Gold & Goose

Right: Nieto did his best to get back in front of Poggiali at the flag, and so nearly succeeded.
Photograph: Mark Wernham

Above: Tiddler tearaways: Finn Kallio's KTM leads teenagers Luthi, Lorenzo and de Angelis.
Photograph: Gold & Goose

Right: World Champion at 18, Daniel Pedrosa essays an exploratory smile. Mentor Alberto Puig tries the same trick.
Photograph: Mark Wernham

250 cc RACE – 20 laps

Elias survived a first-day crash to dominate the front row by a massive margin – eight-tenths; points leader Poggiali was second. Nieto and Matsudo were next up.

Debon jumped the lights from the third row and led into the first tight complex, only to be passed first by Rolfo, then by Nieto, who was in front at the end of the first lap. Elias and Poggiali were also past Debon, de Puniet right behind. The early leader would soon be in the pits for a stop-and-go penalty.

Nieto took a second out of the pursuit on lap two, but now Elias was up to second, and by the end of the third, he'd caught up. Nieto had obligingly run wide to let his team-mate through – repayment of similar favours last year. Elias was on fire, setting four consecutive fastest laps and ultimately taking three-tenths off the previous record as he built up a commanding lead. It was more than five seconds after only seven laps, and still getting wider.

Nieto kept up his repayments, fending off every attack by Poggiali and apparently slowing him up. Then he went wide at the last hairpin at the end of lap seven, and Poggiali was through. But he neither made any impression on Elias nor escaped Nieto, who was biding his time, with more to come.

As they started the last lap, Nieto attacked, inside at Turn One, only to run wide at the exit. Half-way around, he was in front again. But his front tyre was close to ruin and failed him under the fierce braking for the final hairpin. He ran wide, Poggiali dived inside for the apex, and although Nieto tried everything to pull back alongside on the run to the line, using his higher exit speed, he failed by one-hundredth of a second.

A little way back, Rolfo had long since realised he couldn't match the pace of the leading Aprilias and was concentrating on keeping de Puniet behind him. On lap 12, this task was made all the easier when the Frenchman's engine lost power. He fell back steadily, although he was still two seconds clear of Battaini at the finish.

With Matsudo a lonely seventh, the rest of the race was rather mediocre. This was illustrated by Porto, who had started strongly with the leaders, then had been called in for a jump-start stop-and-go, had rejoined in 21st and finally had pulled through strongly, overtaking no less than 13 other riders. His last victim had been a peeved West, baffled by his bike's, or his, inability to match his practice lap times.

Baldolini defeated Heidolf for tenth; Davies triumphed over the next group. Elias had avenged his Rio mishap and was now equal on points with Rolfo, but 25 behind Poggiali. It was all still possible.

125 cc RACE – 19 laps

Lorenzo's late fast run snatched pole from Pedrosa; Kallio was third, the KTM's first front row, thanks to power-up exhausts that arrived mid-meeting. Stoner was fourth after yet another big crash in practice.

Pedrosa was on a mission and, with Lorenzo stuck behind Kallio's orange KTM, he pulled a second on each of the first two laps. It was the start of a perfect ride to the end of the championship trail.

His last remaining rival was Perugini, fourth at the end of the first lap. On the third, he slowed suddenly, coasted past the pits and U-turned into the exit lane, his engine seized.

By now, Lorenzo was second at the head of a huge gang, Stoner pushing through it impressively. By lap five, he was second, but three laps later he ran wide and dropped to sixth.

Mid-way, Lorenzo headed Kallio, Luthi and Azuma, then Stoner and de Angelis. The Australian set fastest lap as he cut through to fifth; a lap later, on a track with damp patches, another big highsider gave him a painful landing.

On lap 14, Kallio got to the front of the wheel-to-wheel five. With three laps left, de Angelis dropped away. Then Azuma got the worst of a mid-corner tussle and also lost touch.

Lorenzo was in second as they started the final lap, but by the end of it, Kallio had found his way past for his and the bike's best finish yet. Lorenzo was next, Luthi close.

Giansanti was a lonely seventh, then came Barbera, recovering from a bad start and poor early pace. Nieto was with him, Locatelli two seconds behind.

MARLBORO MALAYSIAN grand prix

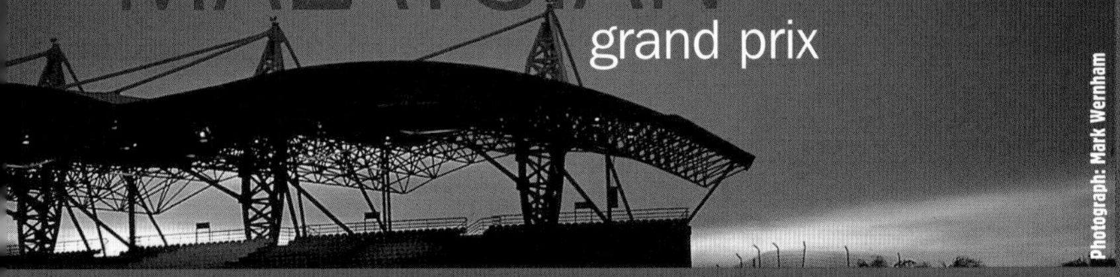

Photograph: Mark Wernham

SEPANG

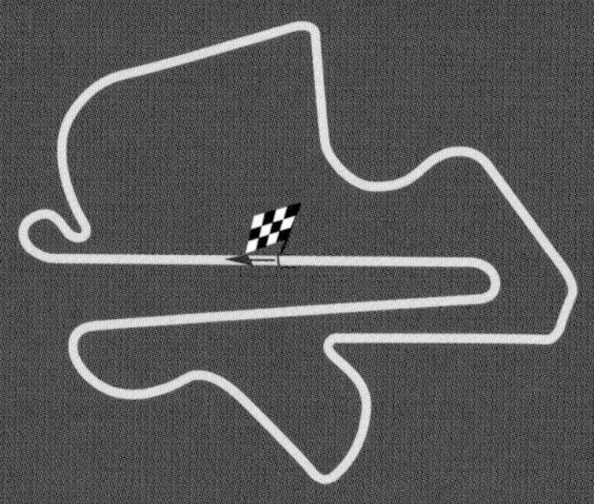

12 OCTOBER 2003

CIRCUIT LENGTH: 3.447 miles/5.548 km

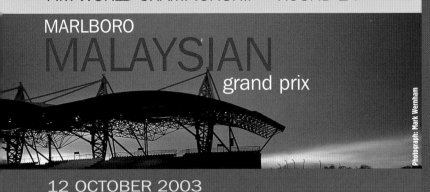

MotoGP

21 laps, 72.387 miles/116.508 km

Pos.	Rider (Nat.)	No.	Machine	Laps	Time & speed
1	Valentino Rossi (I)	46	Honda	21	43m 41.457s 99.418 mph/ 159.998 km/h
2	Sete Gibernau (E)	15	Honda	21	43m 43.499s
3	Max Biaggi (I)	3	Honda	21	43m 49.101s
4	Nicky Hayden (USA)	69	Honda	21	43m 55.190s
5	Carlos Checa (E)	7	Yamaha	21	43m 55.246s
6	Loris Capirossi (I)	65	Ducati	21	44m 02.024s
7	Tohru Ukawa (J)	11	Honda	21	44m 04.906s
8	Shinya Nakano (J)	56	Yamaha	21	44m 08.197s
9	Troy Bayliss (AUS)	12	Ducati	21	44m 13.606s
10	Makoto Tamada (J)	6	Honda	21	44m 22.013s
11	Marco Melandri (I)	33	Yamaha	21	44m 25.320s
12	Noriyuki Haga (J)	41	Aprilia	21	44m 26.070s
13	Colin Edwards (USA)	45	Aprilia	21	44m 36.124s
14	Kenny Roberts (USA)	10	Suzuki	21	44m 44.144s
15	Alex Barros (BR)	4	Yamaha	21	44m 44.463s
16	Andrew Pitt (AUS)	88	Kawasaki	21	44m 47.585s
17	Jeremy McWilliams (GB)	99	Proton KR	21	44m 52.373s
18	Nobuatsu Aoki (J)	9	Proton KR	21	44m 52.801s
19	Garry McCoy (AUS)	8	Kawasaki	21	44m 58.662s
20	Akira Ryo (J)	43	Suzuki	21	45m 22.772s
21	Ryuichi Kiyonari (J)	23	Honda	21	45m 30.551s
	David de Gea (E)	52	Harris WCM	18	DNF
	Chris Burns (GB)	35	Harris WCM	12	DNF
	Olivier Jacque (F)	19	Yamaha		DNS

Fastest lap: Rossi, 2m 03.822s, 100.228 mph/161.302 km/h (record).

Previous record: Max Biaggi, I (Yamaha), 2m 04.925s, 99.344 mph/ 159.878 km/h (2002).

Event best maximum speed: Rossi, 191.3 mph/307.9 km/h (qualifying practice no. 2).

Qualifying: 1 Rossi, 2m 02.480s; 2 Checa, 2m 02.885s; 3 Tamada, 2m 03.138s; 4 Biaggi, 2m 03.254s; 5 Nakano, 2m 03.342s; 6 Capirossi, 2m 03.376s; 7 Gibernau, 2m 03.381s; 8 Ukawa, 2m 03.559s; 9 Hayden, 2m 03.564s; 10 Roberts, 2m 03.936s; 11 Bayliss, 2m 04.000s; 12 Barros, 2m 04.050s; 13 Edwards, 2m 04.390s; 14 Melandri, 2m 04.832s; 15 Ryo, 2m 05.043s; 16 McCoy, 2m 05.084s; 17 Haga, 2m 05.150s; 18 McWilliams, 2m 05.365s; 19 Aoki, 2m 05.512s; 20 Pitt, 2m 06.112s; 21 Kiyonari, 2m 06.819s; 22 de Gea, 2m 06.941s; 23 Jacque, 2m 07.017s; 24 Burns, 2m 08.675s.

Fastest race laps: 1 Rossi, 2m 03.822s; 2 Checa, 2m 04.193s; 3 Biaggi, 2m 04.284s; 4 Gibernau, 2m 04.297s; 5 Capirossi, 2m 04.486s; 6 Hayden, 2m 04.575s; 7 Tamada, 2m 04.938s; 8 Bayliss, 2m 04.989s; 9 Ukawa, 2m 05.082s; 10 Nakano, 2m 05.175s; 11 Edwards, 2m 05.399s; 12 Melandri, 2m 05.594s; 13 Barros, 2m 05.774s; 14 Haga, 2m 05.789s; 15 Roberts, 2m 06.482s; 16 McWilliams, 2m 06.826s; 17 Pitt, 2m 06.886s; 18 Ryo, 2m 06.934s; 19 Aoki, 2m 07.280s; 20 McCoy, 2m 07.299s; 21 Kiyonari, 2m 08.903s; 22 de Gea, 2m 09.451s; 23 Burns, 2m 09.681s.

World Championship: 1 Rossi, 307; 2 Gibernau, 244; 3 Biaggi, 215; 4 Capirossi, 141; 5 Bayliss, 119; 6 Hayden, 114; 7 Ukawa, 112; 8 Checa, 104; 9 Nakano, 92; 10 Barros, 91; 11 Tamada, 75; 12 Jacque, 61; 13 Edwards, 54; 14 Melandri, 45; 15 Haga, 44; 16 Abe, 24; 17 Hopkins, 22; 18 Kiyonari, 20; 19 Aoki, 19; 20 McWilliams, 18; 21 Roberts, 10; 22 Hofmann and McCoy, 8; 24 Ryo, 6; 25 Kagayama, 4; 26 Pitt, 3.

250 cc

20 laps, 68.940 miles/110.960 km

Pos.	Rider (Nat.)	No.	Machine	Laps	Time & speed
1	Toni Elias (E)	24	Aprilia	20	43m 15.925s 95.615 mph/ 153.878 km/h
2	Manuel Poggiali (RSM)	54	Aprilia	20	43m 25.856s
3	Fonsi Nieto (E)	10	Aprilia	20	43m 25.867s
4	Roberto Rolfo (I)	3	Honda	20	43m 41.764s
5	Randy de Puniet (F)	7	Aprilia	20	43m 49.985s
6	Franco Battaini (I)	21	Aprilia	20	43m 51.929s
7	Naoki Matsudo (J)	8	Yamaha	20	44m 05.370s
8	Sebastian Porto (ARG)	5	Honda	20	44m 09.880s
9	Anthony West (AUS)	14	Aprilia	20	44m 13.090s
10	Alex Baldolini (I)	26	Aprilia	20	44m 19.625s
11	Dirk Heidolf (D)	28	Aprilia	20	44m 20.344s
12	Chaz Davies (GB)	57	Aprilia	20	44m 22.274s
13	Hugo Marchand (F)	9	Aprilia	20	44m 23.412s
14	Joan Olive (E)	11	Aprilia	20	44m 23.933s
15	Jaroslav Hules (CZ)	13	Honda	20	44m 34.105s
16	Christian Gemmel (D)	15	Honda	20	44m 37.567s
17	Katja Poensgen (D)	98	Honda	20	45m 24.135s
18	Henk vd Lagemaat (NL)	18	Honda	20	45m 29.418s
19	Zhao Huang Shi (CHN)	81	Yamaha	19	44m 23.347s
	Hector Faubel (E)	33	Aprilia	8	DNF
	Johan Stigefelt (S)	16	Aprilia	8	DNF
	Alex Debon (E)	6	Honda	8	DNF
	Lukas Pesek (CZ)	52	Yamaha	3	DNF
	Eric Bataille (F)	34	Honda	1	DNF
	Erwan Nigon (F)	36	Aprilia	0	DNF
	Sylvain Guintoli (F)	50	Aprilia		DNS
	Xian He Zi	82	CHN		DNQ

Fastest lap: Elias, 2m 08.566s, 96.530 mph/155.350 km/h (record).

Previous record: Fonsi Nieto, E (Aprilia), 2m 08.858s, 96.311 mph/ 154.998 km/h (2002).

Event best maximum speed: Nieto, 158.7 mph/255.4 km/h (race).

Qualifying: 1 Elias, 2m 07.535s; 2 Poggiali, 2m 08.419s; 3 Nieto, 2m 08.836s; 4 Matsudo, 2m 09.278s; 5 de Puniet, 2m 09.353s; 6 Battaini, 2m 09.380s; 7 Porto, 2m 09.407s; 8 Guintoli, 2m 09.687s; 9 West, 2m 09.827s; 10 Rolfo, 2m 10.231s; 11 Debon, 2m 10.604s; 12 Baldolini, 2m 10.764s; 13 Nigon, 2m 10.823s; 14 Marchand, 2m 10.985s; 15 Faubel, 2m 11.194s; 16 Bataille, 2m 11.316s; 17 Heidolf, 2m 11.351s; 18 Olive, 2m 11.412s; 19 Gemmel, 2m 11.691s; 20 Davies, 2m 12.024s; 21 Hules, 2m 12.248s; 22 Pesek, 2m 12.919s; 23 Stigefelt, 2m 13.210s; 24 Poensgen, 2m 15.004s; 25 Huang, 2m 16.107s; 26 vd Lagemaat, 2m 16.377s; 27 Zi, 2m 16.645s.

Fastest race laps: 1 Elias, 2m 08.566s; 2 Nieto, 2m 09.381s; 3 Poggiali, 2m 09.382s; 4 Porto, 2m 10.001s; 5 de Puniet, 2m 10.235s; 6 Rolfo, 2m 10.237s; 7 Battaini, 2m 10.609s; 8 Matsudo, 2m 11.275s; 9 West, 2m 11.581s; 10 Davies, 2m 11.875s; 11 Heidolf, 2m 11.969s; 12 Marchand, 2m 12.020s; 13 Baldolini, 2m 12.085s; 14 Olive, 2m 12.225s; 15 Debon, 2m 12.293s; 16 Hules, 2m 12.404s; 17 Gemmel, 2m 12.585s; 18 Faubel, 2m 12.833s; 19 Stigefelt, 2m 14.403s; 20 Poensgen, 2m 14.676s; 21 Pesek, 2m 14.759s; 22 vd Lagemaat, 2m 15.061s; 23 Shi, 2m 18.984s; 24 Bataille, 2m 21.224s.

World Championship: 1 Poggiali, 226; 2 Elias and Rolfo, 201; 4 de Puniet, 183; 5 Nieto, 167; 6 Battaini, 127; 7 West, 125; 8 Porto, 117; 9 Matsudo, 104; 10 Guintoli, 88; 11 Debon, 64; 12 Olive, 38; 13 Faubel, 34; 14 Aoyama, 31; 15 Baldolini, 30; 16 Davies and Takahashi, 29; 18 Gemmel, 24; 19 Marchand, 22; 20 Bataille and Nigon, 21; 22 Stigefelt, 20; 23 Heidolf, 19; 24 Smrz, 12; 25 Kayo, 7; 26 Kameya, 6; 27 Nöhles and Vincent, 5; 29 Hules, 2; 30 Neukirchner and Tokudome, 1.

125 cc

19 laps, 65.493 miles/105.412 km

Pos.	Rider (Nat.)	No.	Machine	Laps	Time & speed
1	Daniel Pedrosa (E)	3	Honda	19	43m 07.647s 91.125 mph/ 146.651 km/h
2	Mika Kallio (SF)	36	KTM	19	43m 10.305s
3	Jorge Lorenzo (E)	48	Derbi	19	43m 10.397s
4	Thomas Luthi (CH)	12	Honda	19	43m 10.653s
5	Masao Azuma (J)	8	Honda	19	43m 12.679s
6	Alex de Angelis (RSM)	15	Aprilia	19	43m 14.889s
7	Mirko Giansanti (I)	6	Aprilia	19	43m 17.196s
8	Hector Barbera (E)	80	Aprilia	19	43m 18.555s
9	Pablo Nieto (E)	22	Aprilia	19	43m 18.844s
10	Roberto Locatelli (I)	10	KTM	19	43m 20.521s
11	Marco Simoncelli (I)	58	Aprilia	19	43m 22.573s
12	Stefano Bianco (I)	33	Gilera	19	43m 23.090s
13	Andrea Dovizioso (I)	34	Honda	19	43m 23.223s
14	Gabor Talmacsi (H)	79	Aprilia	19	43m 30.536s
15	Alvaro Bautista (E)	19	Aprilia	19	43m 31.808s
16	Arnaud Vincent (F)	1	Aprilia	19	43m 31.913s
17	Fabrizio Lai (I)	32	Malaguti	19	43m 32.507s
18	Youichi Ui (J)	41	Gilera	19	43m 35.619s
19	Andrea Ballerini (I)	50	Honda	19	43m 55.460s
20	Gino Borsoi (I)	23	Aprilia	19	43m 56.259s
21	Robbin Harms (DK)	88	Aprilia	19	44m 06.095s
22	Mike di Meglio (F)	63	Honda	19	44m 06.121s
23	Emilio Alzamora (E)	26	Derbi	19	44m 33.169s
24	Imre Toth (H)	25	Honda	19	44m 33.207s
25	Julian Simon (E)	31	Malaguti	19	44m 33.528s
26	Michele Danese (I)	28	Honda	19	45m 18.144s
	Lucio Cecchinello (I)	4	Aprilia	15	DNF
	Casey Stoner (AUS)	27	Aprilia	12	DNF
	Steve Jenkner (D)	17	Aprilia	12	DNF
	Max Sabbatani (I)	11	Aprilia	4	DNF
	Stefano Perugini (I)	7	Aprilia	3	DNF
	Gioele Pellino (I)	42	Aprilia	3	DNF
	Simone Corsi (I)	24	Honda		DNS

Fastest lap: Stoner, 2m 14.932s, 91.976 mph/148.021 km/h.

Lap record: Lucio Cecchinello, I (Aprilia), 2m 13.919s, 92.671 mph/ 149.140 km/h (2002).

Event best maximum speed: Barbera, 139.1 mph/223.8 km/h (race).

Qualifying: 1 Lorenzo, 2m 14.403s; 2 Pedrosa, 2m 14.485s; 3 Kallio, 2m 14.541s; 4 Stoner, 2m 14.569s; 5 Jenkner, 2m 14.655s; 6 Luthi, 2m 14.844s; 7 Nieto, 2m 14.887s; 8 Dovizioso, 2m 14.980s; 9 Perugini, 2m 15.036s; 10 Bianco, 2m 15.052s; 11 Giansanti, 2m 15.065s; 12 Azuma, 2m 15.088s; 13 Lai, 2m 15.239s; 14 Barbera, 2m 15.410s; 15 Simoncelli, 2m 15.480s; 16 de Angelis, 2m 15.566s; 17 Talmacsi, 2m 15.579s; 18 Vincent, 2m 15.602s; 19 Locatelli, 2m 15.720s; 20 Borsoi, 2m 15.727s; 21 Bautista, 2m 15.869s; 22 Cecchinello, 2m 16.091s; 23 Ui, 2m 16.231s; 24 Ballerini, 2m 16.742s; 25 Pellino, 2m 17.128s; 26 di Meglio, 2m 17.512s; 27 Harms, 2m 17.851s; 28 Toth, 2m 18.055s; 29 Alzamora, 2m 18.064s; 30 Simon, 2m 18.285s; 31 Sabbatani, 2m 18.606s; 32 Danese, 2m 19.298s; 33 Corsi, 2m 19.706s.

Fastest race laps: 1 Stoner, 2m 14.932s; 2 Luthi, 2m 14.938s; 3 Lorenzo, 2m 14.982s; 4 Barbera, 2m 15.037s; 5 de Angelis, 2m 15.051s; 6 Kallio, 2m 15.068s; 7 Locatelli, 2m 15.118s; 8 Simoncelli, 2m 15.168s; 9 Giansanti, 2m 15.227s; 10 Azuma, 2m 15.263s; 11 Cecchinello, 2m 15.308s; 12 Jenkner, 2m 15.311s; 13 Pedrosa, 2m 15.325s; 14 Bianco, 2m 15.404s; 15 Talmacsi, 2m 15.437s; 16 Nieto, 2m 15.628s; 17 Vincent, 2m 15.717s; 18 Dovizioso, 2m 15.817s; 19 Ui, 2m 16.189s; 20 Bautista, 2m 16.332s; 21 Lai, 2m 16.357s; 22 Borsoi, 2m 16.920s; 23 Perugini, 2m 17.307s; 24 Ballerini, 2m 17.445s; 25 Harms, 2m 17.647s; 26 di Meglio, 2m 17.694s; 27 Toth, 2m 18.614s; 28 Alzamora, 2m 19.066s; 29 Simon, 2m 19.092s; 30 Danese, 2m 20.590s; 31 Sabbatani, 2m 23.273s; 32 Pellino, 2m 24.013s.

World Championship: 1 Pedrosa, 223; 2 Perugini, 159; 3 de Angelis, 157; 4 Dovizioso, 149; 5 Nieto, 139; 6 Barbera, 138; 7 Jenkner, 115; 8 Cecchinello, 105; 9 Stoner, 100; 10 Kallio, 88; 11 Giansanti, 82; 12 Ui, 71; 13 Luthi, 68; 14 Lorenzo, 66; 15 Talmacsi, 59; 16 Borsoi, 48; 17 Azuma, 43; 18 Corsi, 32; 19 Vincent, 28; 20 Pellino, 25; 21 Locatelli and Simoncelli, 18; 23 Bautista, 8; 24 Lai, 7; 25 Bianco, 6; 26 di Meglio, 5; 27 Sabbatani, 3.

AUSTRALIAN GP
PHILLIP ISLAND

Above: Bayliss tumbles out of the front pack after brushing Melandri.

Main photograph: Rossi was in a race of his own, even before he heard about the time penalty. Melandri, Hayden and Capirossi head Gibernau, Ukawa and the rest.
Both photographs: Gold & Goose

Left: Rossi and his improvised Sheene tribute.
Photograph: Mark Wernham

AS the absence of Kato had been felt at Motegi, so the presence of Barry Sheene prevailed at Phillip Island. In 2002, he'd been all over the place at the track, his farewell visit, already engaged in a losing battle with virulent cancer. This year, his memory was everywhere.

Celebrations of the adopted Australian's life were less formal than in Japan, starting with a 700-bike road convoy from upstate Victoria, a fine mix of machines from cruisers to supersports that finished off with a lap of the magnificent old circuit; and culminating in a rain soaked slow lap on race morning by Mick Doohan, on the Manx Norton used by Barry to win his last race. A small stand in the public area was selling metal pins in a limited edition – proceeds to an Australian cancer charity. But no reminders were necessary. As his one-time team manager, Garry Taylor, said, 'You keep expecting to bump into him round some corner in the pits.'

Rossi felt it too, and had already prepared, should he win the race, a banner bearing Sheene's number 7. 'When we came back here, I had a strange feeling, to realise he has gone. We made a flag using a sheet from the hotel. Sorry, hotel,' he explained. Because he had won the race, in a style that Sheene would have appreciated – against all the odds, and showing two fingers to officialdom.

Rossi's big chance came after his second yellow-flag infringement of the season triggered another administrative interference. Under new rules announced at Brno, it was a ten-second penalty, and he was informed in good time, on the tenth of 27 laps. He had a chance to do something about it.

He said later that it was the only time he had ridden at 100 per cent for the whole race all year. It gave him four consecutive fastest laps, each a new record. And it yielded interesting arithmetic. He was 15 seconds ahead of Capirossi on the surviving Ducati, enough to win the race. Significantly, he was another seven in front of the next best Honda. That

was ridden by heir apparent Nicky Hayden, who finally had defeated Gibernau on the last lap to earn a legitimate top-three rostrum. That's how much better Rossi was. In turn, Hayden was 16 seconds ahead of the best Yamaha, ridden this time by Jacque. Put Rossi on that Yamaha, and he would still have been ahead of the Hondas. As long as he rode it at 100 per cent all the time.

The flags were triggered by Bayliss, who crashed heavily at Honda Hairpin on lap four. He was disputing the lead and appeared to touch Melandri as they started braking. The Ducati began looping, the rider bouncing along beside it like a rag doll, already unconscious. Ultimately, he escaped injury, but he was still prone by the trackside when the pack came sweeping around again, and Rossi snitched past Melandri, one of three he passed that lap on his way to the front.

Bayliss might fairly be said to have been somewhat hyped up for his home race – this was his third crash of Sunday alone. The other two had happened during a morning session of sodden comedy, nine out of 24 riders falling victim to conditions so bad that there were fears the race might have to be called off if the rain didn't stop falling. The other fallers were Biaggi, Roberts, Barros (on his first lap out), Gibernau, Aoki, Melandri, Edwards and Haga. Fortunately, nobody was going fast, and nobody was hurt, so it was allowed to be funny.

In fact, the circuit's high speeds mean that accidents are to be taken very seriously, and the riders' committee had some questions about safety. 'It's not the track, but what's alongside the track,' said Rossi. Gibernau, for instance, was very lucky to escape with nothing worse than bruising after a high-speed chute at the daunting Turn One. At other places, however, the tyre wall is very close.

Gibernau's compatriot, Pedrosa, didn't crash at such speed, but with much worse consequences. First free practice had only been in progress for 15 minutes when he had a strange tumble over Lukey Heights, saying later that his foot had slipped off the peg. His bike turned hard left into the tyre barrier; Pedrosa landed heavily feet first, suffering fractures in both legs and ankles that required almost immediate surgery. He was taken to Melbourne by helicopter for a four-hour operation.

The absence of the chopper rebounded on Aoki, who also fell in free training after being put off line by Haga. He escaped serious injuries, but he had wrenched his neck painfully, and precautionary X-rays and scans were required to be certain that he had not suffered damage to his vertebrae. Now it became clear that the track X-ray equipment simply wasn't up to the job. Aoki had to be transported to Dandenong, more than an hour away by road, and by the time he'd been given a clean bill of health, he had missed the afternoon qualifying session altogether.

These cracks in the infrastructure came at a worrying time for this grand old circuit, which has hardly been improved since new pit buildings were set up in 1997. Standards are still reasonably high, but the track is currently on the market. It is far from certain that a buyer will be found who will preserve the circuit, rather than making some other use of an increasingly valuable swathe of prime seaside property. The days of the Assen of the South may be numbered.

A pity, for it is a fine track for underdogs. Like McCoy, back home without glory following his bad year on the green Kawasaki. Using all his sideways prowess during practice, he put it on the third row of the grid, then had to fend off suggestions that at last he was trying hard, only because he was in Australia. 'It's a normal day for me, just going flat out,' he said, before taking the best ever dry finish. And like McWilliams, whose pole winning performance last year remained the fastest ever two-stroke lap. He loves the track, and for the first time qualified faster on the V5 than he had on the old two-stroke triple. A landmark for the new bike.

MOTOGP RACE – 27 laps

Pole number eight of 2003 came in convincing style for the new world champion, dominant from the beginning of the session. The Ducatis were also going well at Phillip Island, the highest top speed (204.99 mph from Capirossi) making up for their wayward manners. Capirossi was second and Bayliss fourth, beyond Gibernau, who admitted to feeling a little dizzy after his heavy fall on the first day.

The first laps were desperately close, Biaggi leading away down to Turn One, only to run out wide, leaving Bayliss up front. He, in turn, had given way to Gibernau by the time they passed the pits for the first time. Melandri was close, as were Capirossi, Hayden, Rossi and Biaggi, all pushing and shoving, and blasting down the straight at 200 mph or more, with a fiendish noise.

Into Honda Hairpin for the second time, Melandri took advantage of a fairly cautious pace to dive into the lead. They stayed bunched, and it looked dangerous. It was lucky that when the crash came at the same spot two laps later, only Bayliss went down – although Biaggi was also taken on to the grass, where he slipped off, rejoining right at the back.

Hayden was the next leader – a first taste for him – but Rossi was up to fourth, and next time around he passed three riders to finish the lap first. The move on Melandri, however, had been made under the yellow flags.

Rossi kept pushing, seeking a comfort zone ahead of this perilously close action. Just as well, because it was another six laps before the flag was shown for his ten-second penalty, and he had already dealt with a third of it, 3.4 seconds clear of Melandri, Capirossi, Gibernau, Hayden, Ukawa and Checa. Barros had dropped off the back, pitting to retire with engine problems; Jacque and Nakano had lost touch, but were fully engaged with one another.

Rossi's first reaction was amazement. 'I thought, "F***, what's this?"' But at least his task was clear – he had to go absolutely flat out. It was a masterful display, although he did allow later, 'This is a special kind of race-track. It would not have been possible to do the same thing at Donington Park.'

Melandri had been holding off Capirossi, but then he crashed at the start of the last set of left-handers. The Ducati was never troubled again.

The next four were still very busy, until Checa ran on to the grass on lap 23. This left Gibernau in third place, and he was still there at the start of the final lap. Behind him, an aggressive Hayden and Ukawa had a minor collision, putting the Japanese rider out of contention. Now the rookie attacked Gibernau, who elected not to fight back – mindful of his championship points tally. Hayden passed Gibernau out of Siberia and crossed the line three-hundredths ahead of the Spaniard, with Ukawa only two-tenths away.

Jacque and Nakano were next; Checa had rejoined behind, but was losing ground. Then came Roberts, for his best finish of the year, although he was unimpressed by a mere top ten. 'We need people to crash in front of us for that. I still believe I am capable of winning these races. And Suzuki is too,' he said.

A great three-way scrap behind – McWilliams, Hopkins and McCoy – had been joined by Tamada, who moved through for tenth, one second ahead of McWilliams, who claimed his first four-stroke points.

Hopkins, three seconds farther back, said, 'McWilliams is an evil little rascal. Some of his moves were pretty heavy.' He had managed to out-fumble McCoy on the last lap, the Australian's rear tyre sliding badly. It was still the Kawasaki's best dry-weather finish.

Seven seconds away, Haga had finally caught Pitt's clutchless Kawasaki. The Australian narrowly held off a lacklustre Edwards, clearly tiring of the Aprilia's many problems.

Biaggi was 17th, having passed a troubled Aoki toward the end. Still in pain, the latter had hyperventilated mid-race, and he was a lap adrift and close to collapse at the finish.

Kiyonari was behind him, fazed by this fast track. Then came Burns on the WCM – team-mate de Gea had crashed out on the first lap.

Left: Melandri enjoyed an early lead, if only briefly. Gibernau, Bayliss, Capirossi, Hayden, Rossi and the Camel Hondas followed on.

Below: Checa dropped out of the fight for third with a trip across the grass.

Bottom: A fine battle. McCoy, McWilliams and Hopkins were trading blows at the back end of the points.

All photographs: Mark Wernham

Scenes from the Aprilia pits.

Above: Poggiali's 250 shows its holes.

Right and below: Gear cluster, with mechanic choosing the cogs.

All photographs: Mark Wernham

250 cc RACE – 25 laps

Elias's fifth successive pole flattered to deceive. He'd fallen heavily in practice, running off the track at speed and being obliged to abandon ship as he sped toward one of the tyre walls. He felt very second-hand. Porto was was next on the grid, then Battaini and de Puniet, with the other two title contenders on the second row – Poggiali seventh and Rolfo eighth.

It was still wet when they started, but drying. Then another shower sprinkled the track before the rain stopped altogether at half-distance. Difficult conditions, and while Guintoli was the first of 11 to fall victim, on the first lap, Rolfo made the most of them. Only Battaini was close at the end of lap one, then he also crashed.

By the end of lap two, the Italian had a full seven seconds over West, for whom home conditions could hardly have been better – he'd started on the third row and took just two laps to get to second, ahead of de Puniet.

Rolfo was flying, but after another two laps West started whittling away at a gap now better than eight seconds. At half-distance, he was still more than six-and-a-half seconds away. Then Rolfo ran a poor lap. 'I lost concentration for a time,' he said later, and West was less than four seconds behind.

He was pushing hard now, the pair trading fastest laps, and he closed in to within just over three seconds. Rolfo had more in hand, however, and finally West started to lose touch, eventually settling for second place, 14 seconds adrift at the end.

De Puniet and Nieto were back and forth for the last rostrum slot, the latter upping the pace toward the end. It did for de Puniet, who crashed out with two laps left.

Strange conditions made for a strange race. Battaini had scrambled straight back on and had pushed through the privateers, some surprised to find themselves in the top ten. His reward was fourth.

And Elias? He was in all sorts of trouble, his settings way off and his handling likewise. At one point, he was 18th, and it took a number of crashes to help him improve his position.

Porto went early, with a high-speed ride across wet grass from the first corner. He rejoined at the back and was up to fifth by lap six, only to crash out terminally. Davies slipped off, running strongly in the points; Pesek was ninth when he fell on the final lap.

Debon was fifth, just ahead of Matsudo, Nigon seventh. Hules, relishing the difficulty, set fastest lap on the last, in the process taking eighth from Poggiali, who was sliding around on a ruined rear tyre.

Stigefelt was delighted with tenth; Elias a downcast 11th, well out of touch. Then came Pesek (again!), heading Heidolf, Marchand and Davies, another to remount and be rewarded with a point.

The title balance was altered radically, with just one race left. Elias was out of the picture, now more than 25 points behind Poggiali. But Rolfo's brave and skilful win meant he would go to Valencia just seven behind.

125 cc RACE – 23 laps

With Pedrosa down and out, erstwhile rival Perugini won a big fight for pole position, from de Angelis, Kallio and Stoner, on full charge, despite suffering from painful hand injuries.

Practice had been dry; the race was very wet. Stoner led away, he and Perugini quickly gapping Barbera. Kallio led the pursuit, but Jenkner displaced him on lap five and started to close on Barbera.

Up front, Stoner manfully resisted Perugini's attentions, a home win being a powerful incentive. Instead, on lap six, he slid off at Lukey Heights, his 11th recorded crash.

Ballerini is an often overlooked 30-year-old veteran, only racing the Ajo Honda as a substitute for renegade Kallio, who crashed out after eight laps. The Italian was revelling in the conditions. He'd followed, then passed, Jenkner, going on to snatch second from Barbera. The track was drying, and both his and team-mate Azuma's Bridgestones were working well. Perugini was less than six seconds away and the gap was shrinking fast.

By lap 15, Ballerini had caught him. Next time down the front straight, he surged past. He gained a second on that lap, then Perugini slipped off, losing second overall in the process.

Azuma had been following on, some three seconds behind Ballerini and pushing hard. But, as he explained rather endearingly afterward on international live TV, 'He was f***ing so fast...'

Jenkner was alone in third, a strong mid-race threat from Locatelli having ended when the KTM rider fell – a fork leg had leaked.

Bautista got his best run of the year, right with Jenkner at the flag. The conditions favoured brave privateers – like wild card Joshua Waters (Honda), 11th before he retired on lap six.

Defending champion Arnaud Vincent had pushed through steadily to fifth, leaving Barbera six seconds behind. De Angelis got snagged behind Barbera; Lorenzo was a long way back. Talmacsi, Harms, Ui, Simon, Lai, Alzamora and Bianco took the rest of the points in a widely spread field.

Left: Conditions were perfect for West's home GP. He took second.

Below: Matsudo (Yamaha, 8) fights to hold off Battaini's Aprilia. The Italian had crashed and remounted, and was on his way to fourth.

Bottom: Unexpected 125 winner Andrea Ballerini took victory at his 53rd attempt.

All photographs: Mark Wernham

PHILLIP ISLAND

SKYY VODKA
AUSTRALIAN
grand prix

Photograph: Gold & Goose

19 OCTOBER 2003

CIRCUIT LENGTH:
2.764 miles/4.448 km

MotoGP

27 laps, 74.628 miles/120.096 km

Pos.	Rider (Nat.)	No.	Machine	Laps	Time & speed
1	Valentino Rossi (I)	46	Honda	27	41m 53.543s 106.880 mph/ 172.006 km/h
2	Loris Capirossi (I)	65	Ducati	27	41m 58.755s
3	Nicky Hayden (USA)	69	Honda	27	42m 05.582s
4	Sete Gibernau (E)	15	Honda	27	42m 05.613s
5	Tohru Ukawa (J)	11	Honda	27	42m 05.837s
6	Olivier Jacque (F)	19	Yamaha	27	42m 21.560s
7	Shinya Nakano (J)	56	Yamaha	27	42m 21.587s
8	Carlos Checa (E)	7	Yamaha	27	42m 33.655s
9	Kenny Roberts (USA)	10	Suzuki	27	42m 34.953s
10	Makoto Tamada (J)	6	Honda	27	42m 43.445s
11	Jeremy McWilliams (GB)	99	Proton KR	27	42m 44.803s
12	John Hopkins (USA)	21	Suzuki	27	42m 47.644s
13	Garry McCoy (AUS)	8	Kawasaki	27	42m 48.322s
14	Noriyuki Haga (J)	41	Aprilia	27	42m 55.063s
15	Andrew Pitt (AUS)	88	Kawasaki	27	42m 59.623s
16	Colin Edwards (USA)	45	Aprilia	27	43m 00.173s
17	Max Biaggi (I)	3	Honda	27	43m 07.546s
18	Nobuatsu Aoki (J)	9	Proton KR	26	41m 51.191s
19	Ryuichi Kiyonari (J)	23	Honda	26	42m 09.784s
20	Chris Burns (GB)	35	Harris WCM	26	42m 42.848s
	Marco Melandri (I)	33	Yamaha	14	DNF
	Alex Barros (BR)	4	Yamaha	9	DNF
	Troy Bayliss (AUS)	12	Ducati	3	DNF
	David de Gea (E)	52	Harris WCM	0	DNF

Fastest lap: Rossi, 1m 31.421s, 108.836 mph/175.154 km/h (record).

Previous record: Valentino Rossi, I (Honda), 1m 32.233s, 107.877 mph/ 173.612 km/h (2002).

Event best maximum speed: Capirossi, 205.0 mph/329.9 km/h (qualifying practice no. 2).

Qualifying: 1 Rossi, 1m 30.068s; 2 Capirossi, 1m 30.496s; 3 Gibernau, 1m 30.676s; 4 Bayliss, 1m 30.683s; 5 Hayden, 1m 30.863s; 6 Biaggi, 1m 30.993s; 7 Melandri, 1m 31.227s; 8 Ukawa, 1m 31.280s; 9 Checa, 1m 31.302s; 10 McWilliams, 1m 31.367s; 11 Nakano, 1m 31.444s; 12 McCoy, 1m 31.572s; 13 Hopkins, 1m 31.705s; 14 Roberts, 1m 31.742s; 15 Jacque, 1m 31.759s; 16 Barros, 1m 31.802s; 17 Tamada, 1m 31.806s; 18 Edwards, 1m 31.938s; 19 Haga, 1m 32.145s; 20 Aoki, 1m 32.460s; 21 Pitt, 1m 32.555s; 22 Kiyonari, 1m 33.900s; 23 de Gea, 1m 34.246s; 24 Burns, 1m 34.858s.

Fastest race laps: 1 Rossi, 1m 31.421s; 2 Capirossi, 1m 32.109s; 3 Checa, 1m 32.593s; 4 Hayden, 1m 32.618s; 5 Ukawa, 1m 32.697s; 6 Gibernau, 1m 32.762s; 7 Melandri, 1m 32.833s; 8 Nakano, 1m 33.011s; 9 Jacque, 1m 33.050s; 10 Biaggi, 1m 33.145s; 11 Roberts, 1m 33.509s; 12 Tamada, 1m 33.509s; 13 Barros, 1m 33.605s; 14 McWilliams, 1m 33.822s; 15 Bayliss, 1m 34.018s; 16 Haga, 1m 34.048s; 17 Edwards, 1m 34.059s; 18 McCoy, 1m 34.060s; 19 Pitt, 1m 34.093s; 20 Hopkins, 1m 34.176s; 21 Kiyonari, 1m 34.938s; 22 Aoki, 1m 35.416s; 23 Burns, 1m 36.353s.

World Championship: 1 Rossi, 332; 2 Gibernau, 257; 3 Biaggi, 215; 4 Capirossi, 161; 5 Hayden, 130; 6 Ukawa, 123; 7 Bayliss, 119; 8 Checa, 112; 9 Nakano, 101; 10 Barros, 91; 11 Tamada, 81; 12 Jacque, 71; 13 Edwards, 54; 14 Haga, 46; 15 Melandri, 45; 16 Hopkins, 26; 17 Abe, 24; 18 McWilliams, 23; 19 Kiyonari, 20; 20 Aoki, 19; 21 Roberts, 17; 22 McCoy, 11; 23 Hofmann, 8; 24 Ryo, 6; 25 Kagayama and Pitt, 4.

Left: Rolfo reheated the 250 title battle with his well-timed wet-weather win.
Photograph: Mark Wernham

250 cc

25 laps, 69.100 miles/111.200 km

Pos.	Rider (Nat.)	No.	Machine	Laps	Time & speed
1	Roberto Rolfo (I)	3	Honda	25	45m 14.993s 91.619 mph/ 147.447 km/h
2	Anthony West (AUS)	14	Aprilia	25	45m 29.033s
3	Fonsi Nieto (E)	10	Aprilia	25	45m 48.504s
4	Franco Battaini (I)	21	Aprilia	25	46m 09.245s
5	Alex Debon (E)	6	Honda	25	46m 21.888s
6	Naoki Matsudo (J)	8	Yamaha	25	46m 21.936s
7	Erwan Nigon (F)	36	Aprilia	25	46m 28.414s
8	Jaroslav Hules (CZ)	13	Honda	25	46m 37.112s
9	Manuel Poggiali (RSM)	54	Aprilia	25	46m 37.156s
10	Johan Stigefelt (S)	16	Aprilia	25	46m 40.296s
11	Toni Elias (E)	24	Aprilia	25	46m 56.584s
12	Lukas Pesek (CZ)	52	Yamaha	25	48m 04.675s
13	Dirk Heidolf (D)	28	Aprilia	24	45m 35.463s
14	Hugo Marchand (F)	9	Aprilia	24	45m 57.840s
15	Chaz Davies (GB)	57	Aprilia	24	46m 06.215s
16	Hector Faubel (E)	33	Aprilia	24	46m 34.738s
17	Henk vd Lagemaat (NL)	18	Honda	23	45m 56.097s
18	Joan Olive (E)	11	Aprilia	22	45m 50.129s
	Randy de Puniet (F)	7	Aprilia	23	DNF
	Christian Gemmel (D)	15	Honda	19	DNF
	Eric Bataille (F)	34	Honda	16	DNF
	Sebastian Porto (ARG)	5	Honda	5	DNF
	Katja Poensgen (D)	98	Honda	4	DNF
	Geoff Hardcastle (AUS)	79	Yamaha	4	DNF
	Alex Baldolini (I)	26	Aprilia	2	DNF
	Sylvain Guintoli (F)	50	Aprilia	0	DNF
	Mark Rowling (AUS)	77	Yamaha		DNQ
	Peter Taplin (AUS)	78	Honda		DNQ
	Rodney Camm (AUS)	80	Honda		DNQ
	Brett Underwood (AUS)	76	Yamaha		DNQ

Fastest lap: Hules, 1m 45.680s, 94.151 mph/151.521 km/h.

Lap record: Valentino Rossi, I (Aprilia), 1m 33.556s, 106.352 mph/ 171.157 km/h (1999).

Event best maximum speed: Nigon, 168.4 mph/271.1 km/h (qualifying practice no. 2).

Qualifying: 1 Elias, 1m 33.771s; 2 Porto, 1m 33.851s; 3 Battaini, 1m 33.999s; 4 de Puniet, 1m 34.085s; 5 Nieto, 1m 34.188s; 6 Guintoli, 1m 34.446s; 7 Poggiali, 1m 34.672s; 8 Rolfo, 1m 34.703s; 9 Matsudo, 1m 35.206s; 10 Hules, 1m 35.280s; 11 West, 1m 35.325s; 12 Nigon, 1m 35.508s; 13 Debon, 1m 35.738s; 14 Bataille, 1m 35.750s; 15 Davies, 1m 35.927s; 16 Faubel, 1m 36.031s; 17 Heidolf, 1m 36.086s; 18 Pesek, 1m 36.118s; 19 Marchand, 1m 36.188s; 20 Olive, 1m 36.220s; 21 Baldolini, 1m 36.326s; 22 Stigefelt, 1m 36.477s; 23 Gemmel, 1m 37.038s; 24 Poensgen, 1m 39.122s; 25 vd Lagemaat, 1m 39.350s; 26 Hardcastle, 1m 39.985s; 27 Rowling, 1m 40.714s; 28 Taplin, 1m 40.730s; 29 Camm, 1m 41.247s; 30 Underwood, 1m 43.552s.

Fastest race laps: 1 Hules, 1m 45.680s; 2 Rolfo, 1m 46.094s; 3 Matsudo, 1m 46.142s; 4 Debon, 1m 46.159s; 5 de Puniet, 1m 46.450s; 6 Nieto, 1m 46.561s; 7 Battaini, 1m 46.650s; 8 West, 1m 46.712s; 9 Stigefelt, 1m 47.475s; 10 Davies, 1m 48.087s; 11 Nigon, 1m 48.152s; 12 Elias, 1m 48.611s; 13 Pesek, 1m 48.941s; 14 Poggiali, 1m 48.962s; 15 Bataille, 1m 49.127s; 16 Marchand, 1m 49.583s; 17 Gemmel, 1m 50.125s; 18 Heidolf, 1m 50.939s; 19 Porto, 1m 51.424s; 20 Faubel, 1m 53.296s; 21 vd Lagemaat, 1m 55.878s; 22 Baldolini, 1m 57.412s; 23 Hardcastle, 1m 57.518s; 24 Poensgen, 1m 57.939s; 25 Olive, 1m 58.178s.

World Championship: 1 Poggiali, 233; 2 Rolfo, 226; 3 Elias, 206; 4 de Puniet and Nieto, 183; 6 West, 145; 7 Battaini, 140; 8 Porto, 117; 9 Matsudo, 114; 10 Guintoli, 88; 11 Debon, 75; 12 Olive, 38; 13 Faubel, 34; 14 Aoyama, 31; 15 Baldolini, Davies and Nigon, 30; 18 Takahashi, 29; 19 Stigefelt, 26; 20 Gemmel and Marchand, 24; 22 Heidolf, 22; 23 Bataille, 15; 24 Smrz, 12; 25 Hules, 10; 26 Kayo, 7; 27 Kameya, 6; 28 Nöhles and Vincent, 5; 30 Pesek, 4; 31 Neukirchner and Tokudome, 1.

125 cc

23 laps, 63.572 miles/102.304 km

Pos.	Rider (Nat.)	No.	Machine	Laps	Time & speed
1	Andrea Ballerini (I)	50	Honda	23	43m 41.886s 87.283 mph/ 140.469 km/h
2	Masao Azuma (J)	8	Honda	23	43m 50.735s
3	Steve Jenkner (D)	17	Aprilia	23	43m 56.073s
4	Alvaro Bautista (E)	19	Aprilia	23	43m 56.638s
5	Arnaud Vincent (F)	1	Aprilia	23	43m 58.273s
6	Hector Barbera (E)	80	Aprilia	23	44m 04.738s
7	Alex de Angelis (RSM)	15	Aprilia	23	44m 05.053s
8	Jorge Lorenzo (E)	48	Derbi	23	44m 21.096s
9	Gabor Talmacsi (H)	79	Aprilia	23	44m 27.774s
10	Robbin Harms (DK)	88	Aprilia	23	44m 30.386s
11	Youichi Ui (J)	41	Gilera	23	44m 49.359s
12	Julian Simon (E)	31	Malaguti	23	44m 50.385s
13	Fabrizio Lai (I)	32	Malaguti	23	45m 07.703s
14	Emilio Alzamora (E)	26	Derbi	23	45m 28.281s
15	Stefano Bianco (I)	33	Gilera	23	45m 32.731s
16	Thomas Luthi (CH)	12	Honda	22	43m 55.105s
17	Michele Danese (I)	28	Honda	22	44m 07.850s
	Imre Toth (H)	25	Honda	20	DNF
	Mirko Giansanti (I)	6	Aprilia	19	DNF
	Matthew Kuhne (AUS)	46	Honda	19	DNF
	Stefano Perugini (I)	7	Aprilia	17	DNF
	Gino Borsoi (I)	23	Aprilia	17	DNF
	Lucio Cecchinello (I)	4	Aprilia	14	DNF
	Pablo Nieto (E)	22	Aprilia	14	DNF
	Roberto Locatelli (I)	10	KTM	12	DNF
	Mika Kallio (SF)	36	KTM	9	DNF
	Max Sabbatani (I)	11	Aprilia	8	DNF
	Marco Simoncelli (I)	58	Aprilia	7	DNF
	Andrea Dovizioso (I)	34	Honda	6	DNF
	Casey Stoner (AUS)	27	Aprilia	5	DNF
	Joshua Waters (AUS)	44	Honda	5	DNF
	Mike di Meglio (F)	63	Honda	1	DNF
	Gioele Pellino (I)	42	Aprilia	1	DNF
	Simone Corsi (I)	24	Honda		DNS
	Brett Simmonds (AUS)	45	Honda		DNQ

Fastest lap: Ballerini, 1m 50.518s, 90.029 mph/144.888 km/h.

Lap record: Daniel Pedrosa, E (Honda), 1m 37.983s, 101.547 mph/ 163.424 km/h (2002).

Event best maximum speed: Kallio, 149.3 mph/240.3 km/h (qualifying practice no. 2).

Qualifying: 1 Perugini, 1m 37.342s; 2 de Angelis, 1m 37.455s; 3 Kallio, 1m 37.644s; 4 Stoner, 1m 37.787s; 5 Lorenzo, 1m 37.802s; 6 Barbera, 1m 37.824s; 7 Giansanti, 1m 37.828s; 8 Dovizioso, 1m 37.958s; 9 Jenkner, 1m 37.967s; 10 Cecchinello, 1m 38.038s; 11 Simoncelli, 1m 38.089s; 12 Luthi, 1m 38.125s; 13 Nieto, 1m 38.190s; 14 Talmacsi, 1m 38.268s; 15 Harms, 1m 38.291s; 16 Bautista, 1m 38.409s; 17 Azuma, 1m 38.641s; 18 Lai, 1m 38.835s; 19 Locatelli, 1m 38.919s; 20 Ui, 1m 39.039s; 21 di Meglio, 1m 39.048s; 22 Vincent, 1m 39.070s; 23 Ballerini, 1m 39.260s; 24 Borsoi, 1m 39.273s; 25 Bianco, 1m 39.303s; 26 Sabbatani, 1m 39.432s; 27 Alzamora, 1m 39.651s; 28 Simon, 1m 39.668s; 29 Toth, 1m 40.523s; 30 Waters, 1m 40.830s; 31 Danese, 1m 41.064s; 32 Pellino, 1m 41.455s; 33 Corsi, 1m 42.184s; 34 Kuhne, 1m 43.816s; 35 Simmonds, 1m 46.831s.

Fastest race laps: 1 Ballerini, 1m 50.518s; 2 Azuma, 1m 50.797s; 3 Bautista, 1m 51.418s; 4 Vincent, 1m 51.554s; 5 de Angelis, 1m 51.706s; 6 Perugini, 1m 51.893s; 7 Jenkner, 1m 52.570s; 8 Barbera, 1m 52.852s; 9 Harms, 1m 52.866s; 10 Giansanti, 1m 53.106s; 11 Lorenzo, 1m 53.134s; 12 Talmacsi, 1m 53.137s; 13 Borsoi, 1m 53.298s; 14 Locatelli, 1m 53.517s; 15 Nieto, 1m 53.864s; 16 Stoner, 1m 54.043s; 17 Cecchinello, 1m 54.047s; 18 Ui, 1m 54.203s; 19 Kallio, 1m 54.510s; 20 Lai, 1m 54.682s; 21 Alzamora, 1m 54.720s; 22 Simon, 1m 54.734s; 23 Danese, 1m 54.811s; 24 Bianco, 1m 55.026s; 25 Waters, 1m 55.806s; 26 Luthi, 1m 56.507s; 27 Simoncelli, 1m 56.532s; 28 Dovizioso, 1m 58.741s; 29 Kuhne, 1m 58.916s; 30 Toth, 2m 00.831s; 31 Sabbatani, 2m 01.347s; 32 di Meglio, 2m 11.972s; 33 Pellino, 2m 16.149s.

World Championship: 1 Pedrosa, 223; 2 de Angelis, 166; 3 Perugini, 159; 4 Dovizioso, 149; 5 Barbera, 148; 6 Nieto, 139; 7 Jenkner, 131; 8 Cecchinello, 105; 9 Stoner, 100; 10 Kallio, 88; 11 Giansanti, 82; 12 Ui, 76; 13 Lorenzo, 74; 14 Luthi, 68; 15 Talmacsi, 66; 16 Azuma, 63; 17 Borsoi, 48; 18 Vincent, 39; 19 Corsi, 32; 20 Ballerini and Pellino, 25; 22 Bautista, 21; 23 Locatelli and Simoncelli, 18; 25 Lai, 10; 26 Bianco, 7; 27 Harms, 6; 28 di Meglio, 5; 29 Simon, 4; 30 Sabbatani, 3; 31 Alzamora, 2.

VALENCIAGP
VALENCIA

THERE was a 250 title to be settled, but that fizzled out somewhat, at least for fans of the plucky year-long effort put up by Roby Rolfo, on a bike slower than the hordes of Aprilia rivals. Rolfo missed the boat in qualifying, and had early-race engine trouble on Sunday. Poggiali won the crown. Good job.

For the rest – perhaps most especially for recuperating wheelchair-bound 125 champion Dani Pedrosa, taken from his bed of pain to be paraded around in an open car – the Valencia GP was one race too many. It was something to be got out of the way, before dealing with the business of 2004.

The biggest story of all had to wait until 6 pm on Sunday, after the capacity crowd of more than 120,000 had gone home. Everyone knew what was coming, but nobody expected the public love-in between HRC and Valentino, in a joint announcement that he was leaving in search of what Honda could not give him – a new challenge. (Why, one wonders, did they not just offer to build him a slower bike?)

Rossi didn't mention the Y-word, but did ask Honda for 'one more favour' – that he should be allowed to test 'the other bike' before his contract expired at the end of December. Some time after the season, Honda were still withholding their permission. In cases like this, it is usually granted on a 'knock-for-knock' basis, but Rossi was special.

Everyone might have known Rossi was going, but it was only late on Sunday that the other part of the question was answered – the majority of the pit crew he had inherited from Mick Doohan would go with him. Most notably the man in charge, Jerry Burgess, veteran of nine titles, with Gardner, Doohan and Rossi. One of his great assets is a simple racing creed, avoiding unnecessary experiments, and concentrating on lap times and the task in hand. Another is the status and authority to be able to enforce this. In this way, HRC have been saved from the sorts of wild fancies that young engineers are prone to foist on winning teams and riders. Yet another strong suit is his communication with his riders. Add it all up, measure Yamaha's potential gain against Honda's loss, and it's clear that the longer Burgess, Rossi and the Yamaha could be kept apart, the better for HRC. Proving they at least took the challenge seriously.

By then, much else had already been arranged as a consequence. In the case of Edwards, off to join Gibernau in Gresini's Telefónica MoviStar team for 2004, it was shortly to be consummated, with first tests the following week in Catalunya. At the same time, factory tester Lucchi was to test new chassis parts for Aprilia, in preparation for 2004's riders (Haga was also leaving). Almost everyone else except Suzuki had tests scheduled, Yamaha also staying on in Spain, as well as Kawasaki and Proton, each with a development chassis to try. In fact, Yamaha's had been pressed into service in the race by Checa and Abe, substituting for the injured Melandri, who was recuperating from surgery on his dislocated shoulder from Australia.

Barros was in the hot seat to take over Rossi's slot; Melandri shuffled over to the Tech 3 team in his place. Suzuki's Roberts and Hopkins were to stay put, Hofmann was in the Kawasaki pit, and while McCoy definitely wasn't to stay as his team-mate, Pitt was hanging on to hopes. With Tamada due to take one of the Team Pons slots, leaving Biaggi alone, Ukawa looked set for unplanned retirement. At this stage, both McWilliams and Aoki hoped to stay with Proton, although there were many questions to be settled.

One of 2004's Aprilia riders was signed during the weekend – new BSB champion Shane Byrne. This was part two of a British double: new SBK champion Hodgson was also at the track, and it was confirmed officially that he and ex-Fila team-mate Ruben Xaus would be riding the satellite-team Ducatis run in 2004 by Luis d'Antin.

And it was goodbye to three 125-class veterans – Alzamora, Azuma and Cecchinello raced their last at the twisting Valencia autodrome.

Aside from all the meeting and greeting, there was something of a party atmosphere for the final race, reinforced when the huge crowd on the kilometre-long grandstands formed a world-record mosaic, spelling out a message against the Spanish and Valencian flags condemning violence. And emphasised still further by the loudest ever display of explosives after the race, fireworks being a local speciality.

There were presents – a BMW Z4 two-seater for Valentino Rossi, as a reward for setting the lowest aggregate qualifying lap times of the season to date, plus the Catalunya pre-season test times. Rossi was 4.769 seconds faster than Biaggi over the year, an average of 0.298 second on each of the 16 occasions.

There were distinguished guests, among them famed car engineer Gordon Murray, who won titles with Brabham and McLaren before designing the F1 road car and the Mercedes-McLaren SLR. A keen motor cyclist, Murray had plenty of old F1 contacts to look up, especially in the Proton pit – but all he really wanted to do was meet Valentino Rossi.

Antonio Cobas was back in the pits after missing most of the season for medical treatment – the Team Pons guru was a welcome sight, if a shadow of himself.

Rossi had one last bit of frippery on the Honda – on Saturday morning, he emerged with a specially painted fairing, with all the usual graphics in huge sixties-style balloon lettering, reflecting his Peace and Love theme. The design came from a competition in a Spanish magazine and had people craning their necks to try to make out what the hell it was all about.

Left: Injured 125 champion Dani Pedrosa took a lap of honour in an open car.

Above: Third place was enough for class rookie Manuel Poggiali to take the 250 title.
Both photographs: Mark Wernham

Above centre: MOTOCOURSE photographer David Goldman captures the moment as Nieto and Elias (right) hasten to greet the avid fans.
Photograph: Gold & Goose

Top and right: Peace, love and silly sixties wig – Rossi carried through the Austin Powers theme of his special last-race graphics.
Both photographs: Mark Wernham

MOTOGP RACE – 30 laps

Three Hondas and a Ducati filled the front row, but it was Rossi significantly on top for a ninth time in the season, and Gibernau his closest challenger. Checa was only just pushed off the front row, cheering up for almost the first time all year with good results from the latest chassis and rear suspension.

The Ducatis had made their public debut at Valencia a year before, when they were still testing the Twin-Pulse against the engine they eventually used. It's not the Desmosedicis' sort of track, with tight corners and just one reasonably long straight. But Capirossi had been quick in practice, and he seized the lead from Rossi in the second corner, a sharp left, and hung on for the rest of the lap.

That was enough for Rossi, however, and he grabbed it back as they started the second lap, a big gang all close and meaningful as they howled back and forth in the bowl overlooked by the packed hillsides and grandstands surrounding the looping circuit.

The first upset came on lap three. Hayden had been fighting off Gibernau, but hooked second gear by mistake in the tight second corner. Quick as a flash, his bike swapped ends. 'A rookie's mistake,' he said later. He scrambled back on and embarked on a charge through the backmarkers.

Gibernau made it to second on the fifth lap, when the top five (Checa briefly ahead of Biaggi) were covered by 1.7 seconds. Next time around, Capirossi ran wide. This gave the leaders a useful gap of more than a second, but on the twists they weren't able to do anything with it. Before ten laps had passed, Capirossi was back with them, Biaggi struggling to stay in touch and Checa failing to do so, his set-up on the new chassis lacking race-distance refinement.

At that point, Gibernau got a strong drive out of the crucial last turn and surged past Rossi on the straight, meeting with little resistance, and over the next lap the first four all closed up again. Rossi regained the lead without drama at the next opportunity, and from there he and Gibernau started to pull away, leaving Capirossi to the difficult task of blocking a persistent Biaggi.

At one point, Rossi looked over his shoulder, checking – he said later – to see where Capirossi was. Gibernau waved, he thought. 'He said, "Ciao," so I thought maybe he didn't want to come with me.' This was not the case, but it was all Gibernau could do to stay with Rossi, and with six laps left and yet another new record from Rossi, the local man settled for second, dropping 2.5 seconds behind with three laps remaining. Rossi slowed to celebrate, and came close to a classic blunder, with Gibernau just over half a second adrift over the line. Or was it once again just an example of his accurate judgement?

The first seven were spaced well out at the finish – Biaggi fourth, then Checa, Barros and Bayliss, who had picked through from tenth after a battle with Ukawa and Nakano, which ended abruptly when the latter collided with the former at turn two, and both crashed out.

Edwards had started his last Aprilia ride strongly, chasing Barros as the pair outpaced Bayliss. Then the American ran into short-lived, but frightening, brake problems, which lost him so much ground that Bayliss was able to get past and away. Abe closed on the Aprilia, but never got near enough.

The brawl in the mid-field had been led by Jacque, until Roberts took over on lap six. Then the Frenchman found himself embroiled in a close battle between McWilliams and Haga, with slow-starting Tamada joining in on lap eight.

The Honda rider picked his way through, and McWilliams went with him for a while. And now Hopkins joined the gang, the three closing again on McWilliams; Kiyonari also tagged on behind.

With three laps left, Jacque ran off, and McWilliams took a little gap for another strong Proton finish. Hopkins was next, outbraking Haga into Turn Two on the last lap, with Kiyonari also past the Aprilia at the line.

Hayden needed a couple more laps to get in the points; Aoki was next, passing both Kawasakis in the closing laps.

De Gea was a lap down; Burns did not start after breaking his collar-bone during practice.

Rossi had a record number of points, likewise runner-up Gibernau. Biaggi was safe in third. Hayden was fifth behind Capirossi, in spite of failing to score; Bayliss ended up just two points short of winning Rookie of the Year, in a year of remarkable rookies.

Main photograph: Air time – Capirossi cools the tyres on his Desmosedici.

Below left: Ukawa had a strong race until he was knocked off. Reluctantly, it may have been his last GP.

Below centre: McWilliams rides his tiger – the Proton KR V5.

Bottom left: Anonymous grid girl on one side, grid guru Doohan on the other – Hayden fell and failed to score, but was still Rookie of the Year by two points from Bayliss.

All photographs: Gold & Goose

Above: **At last, a 125 win for never-say-die Australian teenager Casey Stoner.**
Photograph: Gold & Goose

Below: **De Puniet survived an engine glitch to defeat home hero Elias in a close 250 finish.**
Photograph: Mark Wernham

250 cc RACE – 27 laps

The front row was close, covered by two-tenths, and on the far end of it, behind de Puniet, Elias and Guintoli, sat Poggiali, nursing a fever as well as a seven-point advantage. But he seemed intent on making it hard for himself, having collided twice with slower riders to crash, once at the end of the final session, and again in morning warm-up. The second time he was stretchered away, but was only winded.

It was not the sort of glimmer of hope Rolfo would have wanted, but he was desperate, having struggled with handling problems through practice, back on the third row.

De Puniet had galloped away, more than a second ahead by the time Elias had got past team-mate Nieto to chase after him. The gap grew bigger, Elias in turn stretching away from Nieto, now heading Debon and Poggiali. It took five laps for Poggiali to get into third, and by then he was more than four seconds behind Elias. He never did get any closer.

As they settled in, Elias managed to pick up his pace, setting a relatively slow fastest lap on the 14th time around. This allowed him to catch up to de Puniet, but that was all he could do. Then, on lap 21, the French rider suddenly sat up and slowed, Elias swerving past to lead. His engine had

died inexplicably for a second or less, then just as inexplicably started running again. Now he was the hare, and Elias the rabbit. With five laps to go, he had pounced, and although Elias challenged strongly on the last lap, the pair changing places both into and then again out of Turn Two, de Puniet managed to block all the way to the flag, weaving down the straight to make sure of it.

Poggiali was 12 seconds adrift, and World Champion.

The next man, another ten seconds away, was Guintoli, through from a slow start and finishing lap one in 12th. Ahead of Nieto and Debon by half-distance, he pulled away to the finish. West had been with him and got stuck behind this pair, but his thoughts of getting by and catching Guintoli again came to naught when his exhaust silencer came adrift on lap 14, and he toured noisily into the pits.

Porto was closing on Nieto at the flag. Rolfo had also picked up speed after being slowed by an unaccountable engine ailment in the early laps, and was seventh, ahead of Battaini. 'I don't know what caused the problem, but I tried my best, and I have to congratulate Poggiali,' he said.

Bataille was ninth, Debon dropping to tenth.

Poggiali's third place added 16 points to his total to finish on 249, 14 points clear of Rolfo on 235; Elias was third overall on 226. De Puniet's win secured fourth on 208 – he and Nieto had arrived in Valencia equal on points.

125 cc RACE – 24 laps

De Angelis finally won pole in the dying seconds from Nieto, with Simoncelli and Barbera completing the front row. Stoner was eighth.

Again, it was Stoner away first, chased by Barbera and Simoncelli. At a cracking pace, swapping back and forth, with Barbera and Stoner making most of the running, they had more than three seconds on the pursuit after ten laps. The field was stretched out somewhat, but among them was Jenkner, at full gallop.

Ninth on lap one, he was fourth by the tenth, Perugini and Dovizioso keeping him company, and slicing at a gap of just under four seconds. Jenkner set fastest lap during this pursuit, one-thousandth slower than his own record!

By lap 20, the leading group numbered six; again, Jenkner was the fastest man in it, pushing through to second for a last-lap challenge. Barbera made it three, and they had a little gap as they started on the final lap.

Stoner judged it perfectly for his first win, and when Barbera ran past outside of him in the last corner, he didn't flinch. Sure enough, the young Spaniard ran way wide on the exit, finishing a second down as Stoner headed Jenkner by a quarter of a second. 'I knew it was impossible, so when he went by, I kept it tight. I've been waiting a long time for this victory,' said Stoner, who was easily top rookie in an up-and-down season, and eighth overall.

Simoncelli was fourth, but Perugini and Dovizioso collided in their last-lap struggle, and although both rejoined, it left fifth place to Giansanti, just holding off an inspired Bautista. Dovizioso was eighth behind Nieto; Perugini 13th.

Pole-starter de Angelis crashed out on the second lap.

Thus, second overall went to de Angelis, by just two points from Barbera, with erstwhile title challenger Perugini dropped to fourth by his last-lap indiscretion.

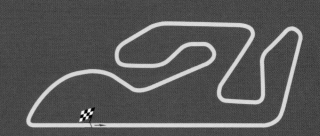

MARLBORO
VALENCIA
grand prix

Photograph: Gold & Goose

2 NOVEMBER 2003

CIRCUIT LENGTH: 2.489 miles/4.005 km

MotoGP

30 laps, 74.670 miles/120.150 km

Pos.	Rider (Nat.)	No.	Machine	Laps	Time & speed
1	Valentino Rossi (I)	46	Honda	30	47m 13.078s 94.867 mph/ 152.674 km/h
2	Sete Gibernau (E)	15	Honda	30	47m 13.759s
3	Loris Capirossi (I)	65	Ducati	30	47m 24.305s
4	Max Biaggi (I)	3	Honda	30	47m 29.371s
5	Carlos Checa (E)	7	Yamaha	30	47m 33.946s
6	Alex Barros (BR)	4	Yamaha	30	47m 43.929s
7	Troy Bayliss (AUS)	12	Ducati	30	47m 50.848s
8	Colin Edwards (USA)	45	Aprilia	30	47m 52.000s
9	Norick Abe (J)	17	Yamaha	30	47m 53.307s
10	Makoto Tamada (J)	6	Honda	30	47m 59.578s
11	Kenny Roberts (USA)	10	Suzuki	30	48m 14.574s
12	Jeremy McWilliams (GB)	99	Proton KR	30	48m 17.588s
13	John Hopkins (USA)	21	Suzuki	30	48m 18.269s
14	Ryuichi Kiyonari (J)	23	Honda	30	48m 19.090s
15	Noriyuki Haga (J)	41	Aprilia	30	48m 19.232s
16	Nicky Hayden (USA)	69	Honda	30	48m 24.510s
17	Nobuatsu Aoki (J)	9	Proton KR	30	48m 39.814s
18	Andrew Pitt (AUS)	88	Kawasaki	30	48m 40.094s
19	Garry McCoy (AUS)	8	Kawasaki	30	48m 40.528s
20	David de Gea (E)	52	Harris WCM	29	48m 02.194s
	Olivier Jacque (F)	19	Yamaha	28	DNF
	Tohru Ukawa (J)	11	Honda	4	DNF
	Shinya Nakano (J)	56	Yamaha	4	DNF

Fastest lap: Rossi, 1m 33.317s, 96.005 mph/154.505 km/h (record).

Previous record: Alex Barros, BR (Honda), 1m 33.873s, 95.436 mph/ 153.590 km/h (2002).

Event best maximum speed: Capirossi, 196.5 mph/316.2 km/h (qualifying practice no. 1).

Qualifying: 1 Rossi, 1m 32.478s; **2** Gibernau, 1m 33.148s; **3** Capirossi, 1m 33.275s; **4** Hayden, 1m 33.348s; **5** Checa, 1m 33.454s; **6** Biaggi, 1m 33.575s; **7** Edwards, 1m 33.984s; **8** Barros, 1m 34.247s; **9** Ukawa, 1m 34.286s; **10** Bayliss, 1m 34.398s; **11** Abe, 1m 34.467s; **12** Nakano, 1m 34.677s; **13** Tamada, 1m 34.742s; **14** McCoy, 1m 34.912s; **15** McWilliams, 1m 34.975s; **16** Pitt, 1m 35.125s; **17** Hopkins, 1m 35.178s; **18** Roberts, 1m 35.269s; **19** Aoki, 1m 35.439s; **20** Kiyonari, 1m 35.572s; **21** Jacque, 1m 35.816s; **22** Haga, 1m 36.524s; **23** de Gea, 1m 36.604s.

Fastest race laps: 1 Rossi, 1m 33.317s; **2** Gibernau, 1m 33.404s; **3** Checa, 1m 33.892s; **4** Capirossi, 1m 33.899s; **5** Biaggi, 1m 33.927s; **6** Hayden, 1m 34.244s; **7** Edwards, 1m 34.292s; **8** Barros, 1m 34.370s; **9** Bayliss, 1m 34.658s; **10** Tamada, 1m 34.996s; **11** Nakano, 1m 35.019s; **12** Abe, 1m 35.042s; **13** Haga, 1m 35.221s; **14** Jacque, 1m 35.222s; **15** Roberts, 1m 35.362s; **16** Ukawa, 1m 35.534s; **17** McWilliams, 1m 35.552s; **18** Pitt, 1m 35.747s; **19** Kiyonari, 1m 35.754s; **20** Hopkins, 1m 35.783s; **21** McCoy, 1m 35.878s; **22** Aoki, 1m 36.110s; **23** de Gea, 1m 37.912s.

Final World Championship points: See pages 156–157.

---

250 cc

27 laps, 67.203 miles/108.135 km

Pos.	Rider (Nat.)	No.	Machine	Laps	Time & speed
1	Randy de Puniet (F)	7	Aprilia	27	44m 01.924s 91.558 mph/ 147.349 km/h
2	Toni Elias (E)	24	Aprilia	27	44m 01.996s
3	Manuel Poggiali (RSM)	54	Aprilia	27	44m 14.734s
4	Sylvain Guintoli (F)	50	Aprilia	27	44m 24.420s
5	Fonsi Nieto (E)	10	Aprilia	27	44m 32.655s
6	Sebastian Porto (ARG)	5	Honda	27	44m 34.305s
7	Roberto Rolfo (I)	3	Honda	27	44m 37.471s
8	Franco Battaini (I)	21	Aprilia	27	44m 38.911s
9	Eric Bataille (F)	34	Honda	27	44m 40.596s
10	Alex Debon (E)	6	Honda	27	44m 43.672s
11	Naoki Matsudo (J)	8	Yamaha	27	44m 57.080s
12	Dirk Heidolf (D)	28	Aprilia	27	45m 05.041s
13	Chaz Davies (GB)	57	Aprilia	27	45m 09.942s
14	Jakub Smrz (CZ)	96	Honda	27	45m 19.965s
15	Radomil Rous (CZ)	73	Aprilia	27	45m 25.995s
16	Alvaro Molina (E)	40	Aprilia	27	45m 31.918s
17	Johan Stigefelt (S)	16	Aprilia	27	45m 34.395s
18	Henk vd Lagemaat (NL)	18	Honda	26	44m 59.502s
19	Lukas Pesek (CZ)	52	Yamaha	26	45m 17.395s
20	Patrick Lakerveld (NL)	83	Aprilia	25	44m 13.975s
	Erwan Nigon (F)	36	Aprilia	15	DNF
	Anthony West (AUS)	14	Aprilia	14	DNF
	Alex Baldolini (I)	26	Aprilia	13	DNF
	Hugo Marchand (F)	9	Aprilia	11	DNF
	Christian Gemmel (D)	15	Honda	8	DNF
	Jaroslav Hules (CZ)	13	Honda	2	DNF
	Hector Faubel (E)	33	Aprilia	1	DNF
	Joan Olive (E)	11	Aprilia	1	DNF
	Yves Polzer (A)	84	Honda		DNQ
	Gregory Leblanc (F)	42	Honda		DNQ

Fastest lap: Elias, 1m 36.840s, 92.512 mph/148.884 km/h.

Lap record: Shinya Nakano, J (Yamaha), 1m 36.398s, 92.937 mph/ 149.567 km/h (2000).

Event best maximum speed: Poggiali, 160.9 mph/258.9 km/h (qualifying practice no. 1).

Qualifying: 1 de Puniet, 1m 36.499s; **2** Elias, 1m 36.590s; **3** Guintoli, 1m 36.647s; **4** Poggiali, 1m 36.735s; **5** Debon, 1m 37.221s; **6** Battaini, 1m 37.327s; **7** Nieto, 1m 37.711s; **8** Matsudo, 1m 37.875s; **9** Porto, 1m 38.028s; **10** Rolfo, 1m 38.110s; **11** Faubel, 1m 38.313s; **12** Bataille, 1m 38.468s; **13** West, 1m 38.586s; **14** Hules, 1m 38.744s; **15** Davies, 1m 38.850s; **16** Smrz, 1m 38.935s; **17** Nigon, 1m 39.059s; **18** Heidolf, 1m 39.112s; **19** Rous, 1m 39.334s; **20** Gemmel, 1m 39.382s; **21** Stigefelt, 1m 39.489s; **22** Olive, 1m 39.498s; **23** Marchand, 1m 39.731s; **24** Baldolini, 1m 39.887s; **25** Pesek, 1m 40.040s; **26** Molina, 1m 40.098s; **27** vd Lagemaat, 1m 41.656s; **28** Lakerveld, 1m 42.534s; **29** Polzer, 1m 43.591s; **30** Leblanc, 1m 43.758s.

Fastest race laps: 1 Elias, 1m 36.840s; **2** de Puniet, 1m 36.928s; **3** Poggiali, 1m 37.479s; **4** Guintoli, 1m 37.687s; **5** Bataille, 1m 38.125s; **6** Debon, 1m 38.211s; **7** Nieto, 1m 38.237s; **8** Battaini, 1m 38.270s; **9** West, 1m 38.277s; **10** Rolfo, 1m 38.318s; **11** Porto, 1m 38.345s; **12** Matsudo, 1m 38.423s; **13** Davies, 1m 38.684s; **14** Heidolf, 1m 38.799s; **15** Nigon, 1m 39.290s; **16** Marchand, 1m 39.455s; **17** Rous, 1m 39.488s; **18** Baldolini, 1m 39.762s; **19** Smrz, 1m 39.980s; **20** Stigefelt, 1m 40.002s; **21** Molina, 1m 40.029s; **22** Hules, 1m 40.143s; **23** Gemmel, 1m 40.483s; **24** vd Lagemaat, 1m 41.446s; **25** Pesek, 1m 42.719s; **26** Lakerveld, 1m 44.015s; **27** Faubel, 2m 00.919s; **28** Olive, 2m 08.433s.

Final World Championship points: See pages 156–157.

---

125 cc

24 laps, 59.736 miles/96.120 km

Pos.	Rider (Nat.)	No.	Machine	Laps	Time & speed
1	Casey Stoner (AUS)	27	Aprilia	24	40m 27.662s 88.568 mph/ 142.537 km/h
2	Steve Jenkner (D)	17	Aprilia	24	40m 27.930s
3	Hector Barbera (E)	80	Aprilia	24	40m 28.763s
4	Marco Simoncelli (I)	58	Aprilia	24	40m 30.867s
5	Mirko Giansanti (I)	6	Aprilia	24	40m 36.422s
6	Alvaro Bautista (E)	19	Honda	24	40m 36.550s
7	Pablo Nieto (E)	22	Aprilia	24	40m 39.927s
8	Andrea Dovizioso (I)	32	Honda	24	40m 44.400s
9	Lucio Cecchinello (I)	4	Aprilia	24	40m 48.751s
10	Gino Borsoi (I)	23	Aprilia	24	40m 58.335s
11	Jorge Lorenzo (E)	48	Derbi	24	41m 00.509s
12	Gabor Talmacsi (H)	79	Aprilia	24	41m 00.616s
13	Stefano Perugini (I)	7	Aprilia	24	41m 01.011s
14	Robbin Harms (DK)	88	Aprilia	24	41m 02.551s
15	Masao Azuma (J)	8	Honda	24	41m 02.620s
16	Max Sabbatani (I)	11	Aprilia	24	41m 08.295s
17	Roberto Locatelli (I)	10	KTM	24	41m 13.340s
18	Fabrizio Lai (I)	32	Malaguti	24	41m 17.903s
19	Julian Simon (E)	31	Malaguti	24	41m 17.975s
20	Sergio Gadea (E)	70	Aprilia	24	41m 25.967s
21	Stefano Bianco (I)	33	Gilera	24	41m 25.977s
22	Imre Toth (H)	25	Aprilia	24	41m 50.971s
23	Ismael Ortega (E)	81	Aprilia	24	42m 01.293s
24	Emilio Alzamora (E)	26	Derbi	24	42m 06.704s
	Dario Giuseppetti (D)	90	Honda	20	DNF
	Michele Danese (I)	28	Honda	17	DNF
	Arnaud Vincent (F)	1	Aprilia	14	DNF
	Gioele Pellino (I)	42	Aprilia	9	DNF
	Mike di Meglio (F)	63	Honda	7	DNF
	Simone Corsi (I)	24	Honda	3	DNF
	Andrea Ballerini (I)	50	Honda	3	DNF
	Alex de Angelis (RSM)	15	Aprilia	1	DNF
	Mika Kallio (SF)	36	KTM	1	DNF
	Youichi Ui (J)	41	Gilera	1	DNF
	Thomas Luthi (CH)	12	Honda		DNS
	Manuel Hernandez (E)	43	Aprilia		DNS
	David Bonache (E)	69	Honda		DNS

Fastest lap: Jenkner, 1m 40.253s, 89.363 mph/143.816 km/h.

Lap record: Steve Jenkner, D (Aprilia), 1m 40.252s, 89.364 mph/ 143.817 km/h (2002).

Event best maximum speed: Perugini, 140.4 mph/225.9 km/h (qualifying practice no. 1).

Qualifying: 1 de Angelis, 1m 40.440s; **2** Nieto, 1m 40.551s; **3** Simoncelli, 1m 40.599s; **4** Barbera, 1m 40.723s; **5** Dovizioso, 1m 40.802s; **6** Perugini, 1m 40.911s; **7** Bautista, 1m 41.210s; **8** Stoner, 1m 41.240s; **9** Borsoi, 1m 41.354s; **10** Kallio, 1m 41.457s; **11** Giansanti, 1m 41.590s; **12** Vincent, 1m 41.606s; **13** Jenkner, 1m 41.642s; **14** Harms, 1m 41.862s; **15** Cecchinello, 1m 41.875s; **16** Ui, 1m 41.946s; **17** Lorenzo, 1m 42.056s; **18** Locatelli, 1m 42.146s; **19** Lai, 1m 42.216s; **20** Luthi, 1m 42.286s; **21** Talmacsi, 1m 42.335s; **22** Simon, 1m 42.398s; **23** Bianco, 1m 42.430s; **24** Sabbatani, 1m 42.452s; **25** di Meglio, 1m 42.543s; **26** Toth, 1m 42.551s; **27** Hernandez, 1m 42.827s; **28** Alzamora, 1m 42.996s; **29** Gadea, 1m 43.098s; **30** Giuseppetti, 1m 43.296s; **31** Azuma, 1m 43.420s; **32** Ballerini, 1m 43.426s; **33** Corsi, 1m 43.445s; **34** Bonache, 1m 44.590s; **35** Ortega, 1m 44.745s; **36** Pellino, 1m 45.123s; **37** Danese, 1m 45.780s.

Fastest race laps: 1 Jenkner, 1m 40.253s; **2** Perugini, 1m 40.253s; **3** Dovizioso, 1m 40.277s; **4** Barbera, 1m 40.387s; **5** Stoner, 1m 40.423s; **6** Nieto, 1m 40.424s; **7** Giansanti, 1m 40.480s; **8** Bautista, 1m 40.514s; **9** Simoncelli, 1m 40.549s; **10** Cecchinello, 1m 40.674s; **11** Sabbatani, 1m 40.886s; **12** Azuma, 1m 40.987s; **13** Borsoi, 1m 41.004s; **14** Lorenzo, 1m 41.286s; **15** Talmacsi, 1m 41.361s; **16** Harms, 1m 41.565s; **17** Vincent, 1m 41.597s; **18** Locatelli, 1m 41.603s; **19** Lai, 1m 42.057s; **20** Simon, 1m 42.145s; **21** Toth, 1m 42.223s; **22** Gadea, 1m 42.246s; **23** Giuseppetti, 1m 42.314s; **24** Bianco, 1m 42.366s; **25** di Meglio, 1m 42.708s; **26** Corsi, 1m 42.969s; **27** Ballerini, 1m 43.212s; **28** Ortega, 1m 43.754s; **29** Alzamora, 1m 43.854s; **30** Danese, 1m 44.691s; **31** Pellino, 1m 44.814s; **32** de Angelis, 1m 49.783s; **33** Kallio, 1m 51.625s; **34** Ui, 1m 52.788s.

Final World Championship points: See pages 156–157.

WORLD CHAMPIONSHIP POINTS 2003

MOTOGP

Position	Rider	Nationality	Machine	Japan	South Africa	Spain	France	Italy	Catalunya	Netherlands	Great Britain	Germany	Czech Republic	Portugal	Rio	Pacific	Malaysia	Australia	Valencia	Points total
1	Valentino Rossi	I	Honda	25	20	25	20	25	20	16	16	20	25	25	25	20	25	25	25	357
2	Sete Gibernau	E	Honda	13	25	–	25	9	16	25	20	25	20	13	20	13	20	13	20	277
3	Max Biaggi	I	Honda	20	16	20	11	16	2	20	25	–	11	20	13	25	16	–	13	228
4	Loris Capirossi	I	Ducati	16	–	–	–	20	25	10	13	13	–	16	10	8	10	20	16	177
5	Nicky Hayden	USA	Honda	9	9	–	4	4	7	5	8	11	10	7	11	16	13	16	–	130
6	Troy Bayliss	AUS	Ducati	11	13	16	–	–	6	7	11	16	16	10	6	–	7	–	9	128
7=	Carlos Checa	E	Yamaha	6	7	–	–	8	13	13	10	8	13	8	7	–	11	8	11	123
7=	Tohru Ukawa	J	Honda	–	10	13	9	10	10	4	–	10	8	11	9	9	9	11	–	123
9=	Alex Barros	BR	Yamaha	8	11	11	16	–	8	8	–	–	9	5	4	10	1	–	10	101
9=	Shinya Nakano	J	Yamaha	7	5	8	2	11	11	3	7	9	2	4	8	7	8	9	–	101
11	Makoto Tamada	J	Honda	–	2	10	–	13	9	–	3	3	7	6	16	–	6	6	6	87
12	Olivier Jacque	F	Yamaha	1	6	6	13	6	–	11	–	7	5	3	–	3	–	10	–	71
13	Colin Edwards	USA	Aprilia	10	–	2	6	7	–	9	6	2	4	2	3	–	3	–	8	62
14	Noriyuki Haga	J	Aprilia	4	–	5	8	–	4	–	9	–	3	1	2	4	4	2	1	47
15	Marco Melandri	I	Yamaha	–	–	–	1	5	3	–	–	6	9	5	11	5	–	–	–	45
16	Norick Abe	J	Yamaha	5	8	–	5	–	–	–	–	6	–	–	–	–	–	–	7	31
17	John Hopkins	USA	Suzuki	3	3	9	–	–	1	1	5	–	–	–	–	–	–	4	3	29
18	Jeremy McWilliams	GB	Proton KR	–	–	4	10	–	–	–	–	4	–	–	–	–	–	5	4	27
19=	Ryuichi Kiyonari	J	Honda	–	–	–	3	3	5	–	2	–	1	–	1	5	–	–	2	22
19=	Kenny Roberts	USA	Suzuki	2	1	3	–	–	–	–	–	1	–	–	–	1	2	7	5	22
21	Nobuatsu Aoki	J	Proton KR	–	4	7	–	–	–	–	1	5	–	–	–	2	–	–	–	19
22	Garry McCoy	AUS	Kawasaki	–	–	–	7	1	–	–	–	–	–	–	–	–	–	3	–	11
23	Alex Hofmann	D	Kawasaki	–	–	–	–	2	–	6	–	–	–	–	–	–	–	–	–	8
24	Akira Ryo	J	Suzuki	–	–	–	–	–	–	–	–	–	–	–	6	–	–	–	–	6
25=	Andrew Pitt	AUS	Kawasaki	–	–	1	–	–	–	2	–	–	–	–	–	–	–	1	–	4
25=	Yukio Kagayama	J	Suzuki	–	–	–	–	–	–	–	–	4	–	–	–	–	–	–	–	4

Position	Rider	Nationality	Machine	Japan	South Africa	Spain	France	Italy	Catalunya	Netherlands	Great Britain	Germany	Czech Republic	Portugal	Rio	Pacific	Malaysia	Australia	Valencia	Points total
1	Manuel Poggiali	RSM	Aprilia	25	25	13	–	25	–	13	20	8	16	20	25	16	20	7	16	249
2	Roberto Rolfo	I	Honda	9	11	20	16	13	7	10	11	25	13	13	20	20	13	25	9	235
3	Toni Elias	E	Aprilia	–	8	25	25	10	13	3	13	9	20	25	–	25	25	5	20	226
4	Randy de Puniet	F	Aprilia	–	20	16	20	–	25	–	8	16	25	16	16	10	11	–	25	208
5	Fonsi Nieto	E	Aprilia	10	9	9	13	20	20	–	25	20	10	7	–	8	16	16	11	194
6	Franco Battaini	I	Aprilia	11	16	5	–	16	10	20	9	11	9	10	–	–	10	13	8	148
7	Anthony West	AUS	Aprilia	–	10	11	9	7	16	25	16	10	–	6	8	–	7	20	–	145
8	Sebastian Porto	ARG	Honda	13	13	10	–	8	9	11	10	13	11	11	–	–	8	–	10	127
9	Naoki Matsudo	J	Yamaha	8	6	8	11	9	11	–	7	–	7	8	11	9	9	10	5	119
10	Sylvain Guintoli	F	Aprilia	6	7	–	10	11	8	16	–	–	8	9	13	–	–	–	13	101
11	Alex Debon	E	Honda	5	–	7	8	4	5	5	6	7	–	5	5	7	–	11	6	81
12	Joan Olive	E	Aprilia	3	–	6	6	6	6	–	–	–	–	–	9	–	2	–	–	38
13	Hector Faubel	E	Aprilia	–	5	–	5	1	–	–	4	–	6	3	10	–	–	–	–	34
14	Chaz Davies	GB	Aprilia	–	1	–	–	3	–	–	3	4	2	–	7	5	4	1	3	33
15	Hiroshi Aoyama	J	Honda	20	–	–	–	–	–	–	–	–	–	–	–	11	–	–	–	31
16=	Alex Baldolini	I	Aprilia	–	4	4	3	–	–	2	–	6	–	2	–	3	6	–	–	30
16=	Erwan Nigon	F	Aprilia	4	–	–	–	–	2	9	–	2	–	4	–	–	9	–	–	30
18	Yuki Takahashi	J	Honda	16	–	–	–	–	–	–	–	–	–	–	–	13	–	–	–	29
19	Eric Bataille	F	Honda	–	3	3	1	–	–	–	–	4	4	6	–	–	–	7	–	28
20=	Dirk Heidolf	D	Aprilia	–	–	1	–	–	–	–	1	5	3	–	2	2	5	3	4	26
20=	Johan Stigefelt	S	Aprilia	2	2	–	4	–	3	6	–	–	–	3	–	–	6	–	–	26
22=	Christian Gemmel	D	Honda	–	–	2	7	–	1	8	–	–	1	1	–	4	–	–	–	24
22=	Hugo Marchand	F	Aprilia	–	–	2	5	–	7	–	–	5	–	–	–	3	2	–	–	24
24	Jakub Smrz	CZ	Honda	1	–	–	2	–	4	2	3	–	–	–	–	–	–	–	2	14
25	Jaroslav Hules	CZ	Honda	–	–	–	–	–	–	–	–	–	–	1	–	1	8	–	–	10
26	Tekkyu Kayo	J	Yamaha	7	–	–	–	–	–	–	–	–	–	–	–	–	–	–	–	7
27	Choujun Kameya	J	Honda	–	–	–	–	–	–	–	–	–	–	–	–	6	–	–	–	6
28=	Klaus Nöhles	D	Aprilia	–	–	–	–	–	–	4	1	–	–	–	–	–	–	–	–	5
28=	Jay Vincent	GB	Aprilia	–	–	–	–	–	–	5	–	–	–	–	–	–	–	–	–	5
30	Lukas Pesek	CZ	Yamaha	–	–	–	–	–	–	–	–	–	–	–	–	–	–	4	–	4
31=	Max Neukirchner	D	Honda	–	–	–	–	–	–	–	–	1	–	–	–	–	–	–	–	1
31=	Radomil Rous	CZ	Aprilia	–	–	–	–	–	–	–	–	–	–	–	–	–	–	–	1	1
31=	Masaki Tokudome	J	Yamaha	–	–	–	–	–	–	–	–	–	–	–	–	1	–	–	–	1

Position	Rider	Nationality	Machine	Japan	South Africa	Spain	France	Italy	Catalunya	Netherlands	Great Britain	Germany	Czech Republic	Portugal	Rio	Pacific	Malaysia	Australia	Valencia	Points total
1	Daniel Pedrosa	E	Honda	8	25	13	25	20	25	8	–	13	25	13	13	10	25	–	–	223
2	Alex de Angelis	RSM	Aprilia	–	10	16	–	11	16	10	13	16	16	16	16	7	10	9	–	166
3	Hector Barbera	E	Aprilia	–	3	9	5	7	–	16	25	2	11	20	7	25	8	10	16	164
4	Stefano Perugini	I	Aprilia	25	–	11	9	9	11	11	16	25	20	–	9	13	–	–	3	162
5	Andrea Dovizioso	I	Honda	11	20	7	16	13	–	6	20	9	10	8	10	16	3	–	8	157
6	Steve Jenkner	D	Aprilia	16	16	20	8	–	13	25	–	–	–	–	6	11	–	16	20	151
7	Pablo Nieto	E	Aprilia	9	11	–	11	16	–	20	10	11	–	25	11	8	7	–	9	148
8	Casey Stoner	AUS	Aprilia	–	6	10	13	–	–	–	11	20	–	–	20	20	–	–	25	125
9	Lucio Cecchinello	I	Aprilia	13	8	25	20	25	–	–	6	8	–	–	–	–	–	–	7	112
10	Mirko Giansanti	I	Aprilia	20	1	6	4	5	4	1	5	5	9	6	2	5	9	–	11	93
11	Mika Kallio	SF	Honda/KTM	5	9	–	3	9	5	9	6	13	–	–	9	20	–	–	–	88
12	Jorge Lorenzo	E	Derbi	–	–	1	–	–	10	–	–	–	4	10	25	–	16	8	5	79
13	Youichi Ui	J	Gilera	10	13	8	10	10	–	13	–	–	7	–	–	–	–	5	–	76
14	Gabor Talmacsi	H	Aprilia	2	–	–	–	7	7	7	10	5	9	8	2	2	7	4	–	70
15	Thomas Luthi	CH	Honda	7	–	4	7	1	20	9	–	–	–	1	6	13	–	–	–	68
16	Masao Azuma	J	Honda	–	7	5	6	2	–	–	3	–	3	3	–	3	11	20	1	64
17	Gino Borsoi	I	Aprilia	6	5	3	3	8	8	3	–	–	8	–	4	–	–	–	6	54
18	Arnaud Vincent	F	KTM/Aprilia	–	4	–	–	–	2	–	8	–	–	11	3	–	–	11	–	39
19	Simone Corsi	I	Honda	4	2	–	2	4	1	4	–	7	–	7	–	1	–	–	–	32
20=	Alvaro Bautista	E	Aprilia	–	–	–	–	–	–	2	–	–	1	–	4	1	13	10	–	31
20=	Marco Simoncelli	I	Aprilia	–	–	2	–	–	–	–	–	–	4	2	–	5	–	5	13	31
22=	Andrea Ballerini	I	Honda	–	–	–	–	–	–	–	–	–	–	–	–	–	25	–	–	25
22=	Gioele Pellino	I	Aprilia	1	–	–	–	–	6	5	–	4	3	6	–	–	–	–	–	25
24	Roberto Locatelli	I	KTM	–	–	–	–	1	–	6	–	–	–	–	5	–	6	–	–	18
25	Fabrizio Lai	I	Malaguti	–	–	–	–	–	–	2	–	1	–	4	–	–	3	–	–	10
26	Robbin Harms	DK	Aprilia	–	–	–	–	–	–	–	–	–	–	–	–	–	–	6	2	8
27	Stefano Bianco	I	Gilera	–	–	–	–	–	–	–	–	–	–	–	–	2	–	4	1	7
28	Mike di Meglio	F	Honda	–	–	–	–	–	3	–	–	1	–	1	–	–	–	–	–	5
29	Julian Simon	E	Malaguti	–	–	–	–	–	–	–	–	–	–	–	–	–	–	4	–	4
30	Max Sabbatani	I	Aprilia	3	–	–	–	–	–	–	–	–	–	–	–	–	–	–	–	3
31	Emilio Alzamora	E	Derbi	–	–	–	–	–	–	–	–	–	–	–	–	–	–	2	–	2

Photograph: Gold & Goose

WORLD SUPERBIKES REVIEW

CHANGING TIMES

By GORDON RITCHIE

'**A**LL change at SBK central for next year and how many times have we heard that? Too many for some of the factories it appears in the short term, so roll on 2004.'

So went the sign-off from last year's MOTOCOURSE SBK intro, as a new era of stability beckoned – even if we had to get through 2003 first. Come mid-season, all those notions of a predictable future had been blasted away when the Octagon Group sold SBK back to its original owners, the Flammini brothers, in the shape of their FGSport Group.

Sudden volte-faces from all sides on the rules and numbers of participating factory teams for 2004 led to searing recriminations and contradictions, flowing like spiteful lava between FGSport, the MSMA, the FIM and the championship's three tyre suppliers.

It was a distracting and depressing backdrop to the season.

On track, 2002's Honda/Ducati fight was condensed into an all-Ducati battle for 2003, the lone regular Suzuki of Lavilla occasionally changing the engine note at the front of the pack.

With Troy Bayliss, Colin Edwards, Noriyuki Haga and Ben Bostrom all heading off to other series, the number of potential championship winners dropped to a realistic two – Neil Hodgson and Ruben Xaus.

There was, however, a new 900 cc triple, entered by the high-profile Foggy Petronas outfit, and it brought much needed Malaysian spice to an otherwise rather plain bowl of pasta and tofu. But not at the front of the pack.

The restricted 1000 cc, four-cylinder concept was proven to work just fine, with big numbers still being posted on the top-speed charts – yet only Suzuki joined in with a full-on factory Japanese effort. This was unquestionably a contributing factor in FGSport's nervousness and decision to change the whole precept of the championship again.

Sport for all was the new motto at season end, but this year at least there were a surprising number of participants with at least fleeting slots on the winning podium. And the racing was – unexpectedly – nothing short of brilliant on many occasions, even when Hodgson was winning at will.

Last year in SBK, there were only three race winners, this year there were five, three of them on Dunlops. Something for those quick to put down the 2003 season to consider.

NEW AND IMPROVED

UNLIKE any previous world champion outline it's been my privilege to undertake, no reference to the history books is needed for Neil Hodgson. First-hand accounts can be given, from his early British Championship campaigns to his rebirth as a win-monger at national and global Superbike level.

In effect, Hodgson has had two careers: the upwardly-mobile one under the guiding hand of his manager, Roger Burnett, and his second coming, again alongside Burnett, with the GSE Racing team and finally Davide Tardozzi's Fila Ducati outfit.

Seldom in the nineties did British riders enjoy the chances for promotion given to Hodgson, as he hopped from 125 GPs, to top privateer in 500 GPs, to the full factory Ducati team in SBK.

His meritorious rise was only rivalled in scale by the deleterious effects that a black hole of misery had on his confidence from that point on. Too insecure and inexperienced to make an impact alongside quirky Kocinski and derogatory Fogarty at Ducati; joining the Doubting Thomas Kawasaki squad in 1998, the worst year of development for the ZX-7RR; then finding himself the butt of jokes as he stumbled back into the British championship scene a year later, in a somewhat unconvincing fashion in his first season.

Then something changed. Samson lost his powers after a haircut, but the convict coiffure and glacial stares adopted by Hodgson in the 2000 season proved that he was in the mood to pull down a few temples.

His two wins in SBK events at Donington and Brands were proof of his psychological turn-around, even intimidating riders like Noriyuki Haga with his sheer guts and determination to win.

If there was one more secret to his success from then on, it was that he had to overcome becoming vilified by many sectors of the British racing scene. He had dared to beat people's champion Walker on the final day of term, after the latter's Suzuki suffered an engine failure.

Inexplicably, Hodgson was hated for it by thousands of his compatriots.

The old Neil would have been crushed by this lack of love and empathy, but the new improved Hodgson was first hardened, then tempered, by this unfair treatment.

Back in SBK, he went about work for his beloved GSE Racing Ducati team in single-minded fashion – easily the best non-factory rider outside the Edwards-Bayliss slug-out in 2002, even on Dunlops.

For some, suspicions of his fragility lingered when the call came in the winter of 2002/03 to rejoin a very different full factory, Michelin-supplied Ducati team from the one he had left in high dudgeon in '97.

He answered his critics by fighting his way past the front-end and tyre-selection problems on the 999 that crucified the early-season Ruben Xaus. Hodgson was consistently fast come race day, and proved his mettle by winning 13 races when it mattered – not merely after wins became 'only' shiny baubles, or the bike and tyre had been altered to suit his particular style.

So is Hodgson a worthy champion, given that 2003 was a weakened year of competition?

A ludicrous question, one that crumbles in the face of objective and statistical analysis. If Colin Edwards's 2002 championship season was an all-time lesson in self-belief, then Hodgson's longer-term reconstructive surgery on his once-doomed career can hardly be thought of as less.

Below: One eye on the title, the other on the MotoGP class, Hodgson came into his own in 2003.
Photograph: Gold & Goose

Gold & Goose

2003 TEAMS AND RIDERS

neil hodgson

Gold & Goose

ruben xaus

james toseland

Gold & Goose

regis laconi

gregorio lavilla

Gold & Goose

pierfrancesco chili

Mark Wernham

james haydon

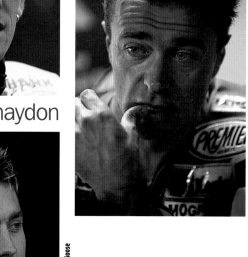

Mark Wernham

troy corser

chris walker

Gold & Goose

Gold & Goose

Facing page, centre: **Hodgson and his winning Fila Ducati crew at Assen.**

Below: **Davide Tardozzi** (right) **held sway once more at Ducati.**

Below centre: **GSE team boss Colin Wright.**

Bottom: **Carl Fogarty, motor cycle racing legend turned team owner.**
All photographs: Gold & Goose

Fila Ducati

The heaviest hitting Ducati squad on the block, and the only ones with a full works machine to play with, the Fila Ducati team featured the talents of favourite Neil Hodgson (29) and eventual runner-up Ruben Xaus (25).

Still overseen by Davide Tardozzi, the works effort nonetheless suffered the loss of many regular personnel to the MotoGP paddock, leaving Ernesto Marinelli as the head of technical operations (and Hodgson's crew chief), although he had to sit out half the year after breaking his leg badly.

Although in the shadow of Ducati's new MotoGP project, there was no drop-off in quality of performance or commitment to the outside world, and the close relationship with Michelin continued to deliver wins aplenty.

HM Plant Ducati

Sponsored by HM Plant, Darrell Healey's GSE Racing Team enjoyed another successful season, James Toseland (22) winning a race, and Chris Walker (30) securing multiple podiums, and a few injuries before and during the year.

Small in number, but organised – often with strict military precision – by Colin Wright, the GSE team was its usual impressive self. Stewart Johnstone, the team's experienced technical guru, was charged with caring for the year-old factory machines, and GSE were the only ones running ex-Bayliss-spec bikes (apart from the Dunlop tyres) in a satellite Ducati Corse team.

PSG-1 Ducati

Two men and a couple of year-old motor cycles, such was the make-up of the bright yellow perils in the PSG-1 Team. Pierfrancesco Chili (38) was co-owner of the new team and picked up several individual awards to go with a colossal number of non-finishes. The bikes' specs were almost two years old, but the results were beyond the sum of the parts involved. Dunlops graced the rims, Frankie's experience being a valuable tool for the tyre company.

Team Pedercini Ducati

A three-man team at season start – Lucio Pedercini (30), Serafino Foti (35) and Nello Russo (32) – became Pedercini, Lorenzo Mauri (26), Gianmaria Liverani (33) and Luca Pedersoli (28) on occasion. Pedercini is an immovable object in SBK and was destined to finish ninth overall, but ultimately all others would be overshadowed by the likes of Chili and the DFX hordes.

Team Caracchi NCR Nortel Networks Ducati

Regis Laconi (28) proved to be a superb signing for the NCR team, running fast all year. Stefano Caracchi's crew has the talents of the likes of Franco Farne to call on in the pit lane and workshop, but some bizarre pit work and mechanical woes contributed to an up-and-down season for Laconi. His team-mate, David Garcia (25), proved fast in flashes, but was prone to some incredible incidents and misfortune. He was replaced by Marco Masetti and Giancarlo De Matteis when he suffered some of his frequent injuries.

DFX Racing Team

Three riders were bankrolled by Pirelli once more, the team being a mobile test-bed for the latest generations of Italian rubber. Steve Martin (34) battled manfully on his 2003-spec 998RS, as did Marco Borciani (27). Juan Borja (33) had a season to forget in what was probably a swan-song year. One of the bigger and better pit presentations made the DFX team high-profile, Martin being the best of the true privateers, other than Chili.

JM SBK Team

Czech rider Jiri Mrkyvka (29) re-entered SBK after a miserable 2002 and, with a 998RS to play with, went more reliably round and round. He still tailed along at the back as normal, and qualification itself was always hard won.

WET Honda VTR1000

The machines were hardly ex-Colin Edwards spec, and the WET team signed up Italian Euro Superstock competitor Walter Tortoroglio (25) for a one-man assault on SBK. The Swiss team also ran Bertrand Stey when Tortoroglio was unavailable, but the results remained the same. The best points came for 'Tortorix' in the USA, which was a surprise to all.

Alstare Suzuki Team

A lone Gregorio Lavilla (29) contested all the races on a factory GSX-R, and he was joined in Francis Batta's team by the forceful Vittorio Ianuzzo (21) at some rounds, even if his particular machine was far from full works.

Taking on the twins on a fully competitive footing some weekends, the Alstare team were as visible and busy as ever, their image and marketing power challenged only by the Fila team and the upstarts at Foggy Petronas.

Prowess off track was occasionally matched by the aggressive Lavilla, but as one man against the Ducati masses, it was a hard season for all concerned.

MIR Suzuki

Sergio Fuertes (24) took out a very stock Suzuki for his first appearances in Superbike, his 163-bhp restricted GSX-R out-powered throughout. The fifth Spaniard in the championship, he came with sponsorship from the Valencia circuit.

Team Kawasaki Bertocchi

Mauro Sanchini (32) and Ivan Clementi (28) made up the two-man team. Sanchini went well for a 750 cc competitor and was a seasoned veteran of 77 starts (at the start of the season). In possession of ex-works bikes, Bertocchi were frequently outdone by the bigger private V-twins and the cramped scale of their operations in some areas. Perennials of the hardiest kind, they may produce the green shoots of further recovery with 1000 cc bikes in 2004.

UnionBike Gi Motorsports Yamaha

Giovanni Bussei (31) and Davide Messori started the season in the UnionBike colours, supposedly, but the team dropped to one rider after Messori left.

Alessandro Gramigni (34) was drafted in for Valencia and had other outings on his own R1. Bussei's eventual trip to America to ride for the Austin Ducati AMA squad put an end to his SBK season, but he was replaced by luckless Redamo Assirelli, then Gianmaria Liverani and finally Frédéric Protat in France.

Foggy Petronas Racing

Arguably the biggest presence in the paddock, a lot of preparation obviously went into the FPR effort, backed sufficiently, if not over-generously by their Malaysian sponsors and technical partners.

Headed in figure and spirit by four-times SBK Champion Carl Fogarty, the team also featured ex-Team Roberts man Nigel Bosworth as team manager and experienced chief engineer Steve Thomson. They were backed by a serious array of generally trade sponsors and, other than the Fila works Ducati squad, were the only team to run Michelins.

With Troy Corser (31) and James Haydon (29), the riding line-up was stronger than all bar one on paper. The oft-injured Haydon was replaced by Lorenzo Mauriat at Misano. However, he fell immediately and suffered a horrid leg injury. Haydon was let go at the end of his contract, but finished the 2003 season on the FP-1.

THE
BIKES
OF
2003

Top: **Rider's eye view of the GSE Ducati 998 F02.**

Above: **The 2003 factory Ducati – lighter, faster and touchier than before.**
Both photographs: Gold & Goose

Ducati 999 F03

Stiffer in chassis, lower in riding position, with more power from its revamped 104 x 58.8 mm bore and stroke engine, the 999 was a major change from the nine-season-old 998-series machines and, as such, has been the most important bike in Ducati's recent history.

Fed fuel and air by single-injector IWF1 throttle bodies, controlled by a Magneti Marelli MF5 processor, the 999 cc engine produced a claimed 189 bhp at 12,500 rpm. A useful tool for Hodgson and Xaus – but the chassis seemed to be another story altogether.

Even after Hodgson had won eight straight races on the 999, he was still remarking that it was more nervous than the previous breed and pushed the front more than was welcome. The low-rear/high-front riding sensation merely exacerbated this characteristic, and by Oschersleben a removable chassis spar, designed to give access for top-end work on the upright cylinder of the 90-degree V-twin, had been taken out to give more flex and, thus, more feel.

The double-sided swingarm was braced underneath to allow more space for the typical Ducati shock linkage.

The secret to getting the best out of it all, reckoned Hodgson, was to be smoother than on the old bike. If true, then that caused more early problems for the all-action Xaus than Hodgson, a theory the crash ratio bears out.

Extensive Michelin tyre tests developed new fronts to allow the Fila team to stay ahead of most of its rivals, and the bike ran pressurised Öhlins 42-mm forks, plus Öhlins rear shocks.

At 164 kg, the 999 was about 2.5 kg lighter than the previous factory 998. The two-into-one unitary silencer box on the bike's distinctive rear end alone weighed half as much as the previous two-into-one-into-two versions.

Ducati 998 F02

Same as Bayliss's machine for 2002, and only used by the GSE team, the 998 F02 shared the same 104 x 58.8 mm bore and stroke of the current factory models, but was not updated. It made a single claimed horsepower less, at the same 12,500-rpm mark.

Declared weight was the same at 164 kg, but the new bike was reckoned to need ballasting in any case.

The newer 42-mm Öhlins forks were also used by GSE.

Ducati 998RS

Significantly different in engine architecture from the Fila and GSE machines, the 998RS was nonetheless a Testastretta (narrow-head) design, which reduced frictional losses, increased revs and steepened valve angles compared to older motors. Although making around 175 bhp at lower revs (12,000 rpm) than the later versions, the customer Ducati was still an impressive piece of kit for any privateer to buy.

The 100 x 63.5 mm bore and stroke figures accounted for the major differences to the factory engines, and some teams went as far as claiming over 180 bhp from their own machines, and a 310-km/h top speed.

The NCR team dabbled with a two-into-one exhaust for a race or two, and some teams (Chili's most notably) preferred the tuneability of smaller silencer exits than the traditional huge orifices used by most. NCR also swapped around rear swingarms to put the power on the ground more effectively.

Petronas FP-1

Watered-down F1 technology in an aquamarine box, the FP-1 was the technological marvel of the year. Whatever its empirical abilities, the design touches on the cycle parts were exquisite, from the convoluted exhaust system to the carbon seat units of differing stiffness, bolted into the frame spars to alter overall chassis rigidity.

On a good day, the three-cylinder 899.5 cc FP-1 would make over 170 bhp at 13,600 rpm, with 78 lb/ft of torque from the reverse-head engine design – exhausts out the back, intake at the front.

The EFI was a custom Marelli MF4M system, working in conjunction with 55-mm double-injector throttle bodies mounted inside the airbox. The engine itself had major cooling and combustion-chamber blow-by problems from the outset, the latter only marginally controlled by a new head design for the last few races of the year.

The extravagant flame-outs from the carbon exhausts were caused by a mixture of oil and fuel igniting. The exhaust gases were escaping at over 1,000 degrees C on occasion, and this burned through the carbon silencers of the original machine, encouraging the adoption of titanium versions at the first opportunity.

Power-ups through the season also came through the adoption of serpent-head exhaust-header profiles, speeding up exhaust gas flow, but maintaining the overall three-into-one-into-two-into-three exhaust's tuned length.

Additional cooling rads and overflow bottles took the FP-1 over its 162-kg design mass, but in terms of cycle parts and finish, the rolling chassis was a minor work of the state of the art. At the front, 43-mm Öhlins were preferred to the 42-mm versions, and the chassis ran adjustable offsets, Corser tending to keep his trail figure at around 95 mm.

The aesthetics package was signed off by custom six-spoke OZ wheels, which were also lighter than most other options.

Suzuki GSX-R1000

The leading light in the new era of multi-cylinder SBK life, the GSX-R1000 was based on the newer K3 road bike, itself a small step ahead of the bike that had cleaned up in Superstock and Endurance all over the planet. The 1000 cc four-cylinders were the only engine configurations to run restrictors in 2003, and the GSX-R was required to have 32.5-mm intake orifices placed between throttle body and intake port on each combustion chamber.

Despite this encumbrance, the 73 x 59 mm bore and stroke of the Suzuki allowed a power output of 190 bhp, at 12,000 rpm, rising to nearly 200 bhp at season's end. Always one of the fastest through the speed traps, the GSX-R had problems exiting corners, its smaller intake throats making too

much power and the wrong kind of torque to drive the Dunlop tyres rather than spin them.

The 167-kg machine ran Showa suspension, but the ubiquitous Brembo braking components were in place.

Yamaha YZF1000R1

The UnionBike Gi Motorsport team found the R1 as amenable to tuning as they expected and largely overcame the effects of the engine restrictors by season's end. The handsome R1 wore WP forks and shocks, and Dunlop tyres.

Kawasaki ZX-7RR

Running largely ex-Kawasaki Eckl racing team machines, the main difference for the 750 cc (and thus unrestricted) in-line fours came from the adoption of Bitubo forks and shocks. The 45-mm front forks, whose preload was adjusted by an alteration of the volume of air above the oil, rather than the oil level itself, retained their trade-mark flat sections along the length of the fork to provide engineered-in levels of stiffness. The newest versions enjoyed a new form of black anti-stiction coating – although the Bitubo guys pointed out that it was not the same material as that used by Suzuki on some road bikes.

Nissin brakes ran on the ZX-7RR's wheels, Dunlops on the rims, and 41-mm Keihin carburettors fed the 75 x 44.7 bore and stroke engine, which was good for a claimed 172 bhp.

Honda VTR 1000SP-2

Around 170 bhp from the standard kitted SP-2 told the story of the WET team's season, the machine struggling to keep pace with all but the second-string Ducatis. With the 2002 factory engines used in the BSB series, it was all the Swiss enthusiasts could hope for.

Top left: The GSE team raced with Ducati's 2002 factory machines.

Top right: The Alstare Suzuki was the only 1000 cc multi, under new rules.

Centre left: Latest iteration of the 750 cc Kawasaki ZX-7RR was much as before.

Centre right: F1-inspired Foggy Petronas FP1 – gaining maturity.

Above: FP1 exhaust outlet is the back end of a serpentine system.

All photographs: Gold & Goose

Round 1
VALENCIA, Spain
2 March, 2.489-mile/4.005-km circuit

Race 1 23 laps, 57.247 miles/92.115 km

Pl.	Name	Nat.	Machine	No.	Time & gap	Laps
1	Neil Hodgson	GB	Ducati	100	36m 56.205s	23
					92.976 mph/149.631 km/h	
2	Ruben Xaus	E	Ducati	11	4.700s	23
3	Chris Walker	GB	Ducati	9	12.377s	23
4	James Toseland	GB	Ducati	52	12.682s	23
5	Regis Laconi	F	Ducati	55	24.068s	23
6	Steve Martin	AUS	Ducati	99	27.006s	23
7	Gregorio Lavilla	E	Suzuki	10	39.792s	23
8	Lucio Pedercini	I	Ducati	19	49.662s	23
9	Marco Borciani	I	Ducati	20	56.200s	23
10	David Garcia	E	Ducati	48	1m 06.328s	23
11	Ivan Clementi	I	Kawasaki	5	1m 09.139s	23
12	James Haydon	GB	Petronas	8	1m 09.541s	23
13	Nello Russo	I	Ducati	35	1m 14.450s	23
14	Juan Borja	E	Ducati	33	1m 14.712s	23
15	Sergio Fuertes	E	Ducati	16	1m 22.845s	23
16	Martin Isaac	E	Yamaha	71	1 lap	22

DNF: Pierfrancesco Chili, I (Ducati) 7, 20 laps; Giovanni Bussei, I (Yamaha) 15, 14 laps; Alessandro Gramigni, I (Yamaha) 39, 14 laps; Serafino Foti, I (Ducati) 28, 10 laps; Troy Corser, AUS (Petronas) 4, 9 laps; Walter Tortoroglio, I (Honda) 91, 9 laps; Mauro Sanchini, I (Kawasaki) 6, 4 laps.

Fastest lap: Hodgson, 1m 35.557s, 93.755 mph/150.804 km/h.

Race 2 23 laps, 57.247 miles/92.115 km

Pl.	Name	Nat.	Machine	No.	Time & gap	Laps
1	Neil Hodgson	GB	Ducati	100	36m 46.191s	23
					93.399 mph/150.311 km/h	
2	Ruben Xaus	E	Ducati	11	2.619s	23
3	James Toseland	GB	Ducati	52	13.468s	23
4	Chris Walker	GB	Ducati	9	23.426s	23
5	Steve Martin	AUS	Ducati	99	36.539s	23
6	Gregorio Lavilla	E	Suzuki	10	38.594s	23
7	Troy Corser	AUS	Petronas	4	42.969s	23
8	Juan Borja	E	Ducati	33	51.625s	23
9	Lucio Pedercini	I	Ducati	19	52.824s	23
10	Marco Borciani	I	Ducati	20	54.721s	23
11	Giovanni Bussei	I	Yamaha	15	1m 00.510s	23
12	David Garcia	E	Ducati	48	1m 02.114s	23
13	Mauro Sanchini	I	Kawasaki	6	1m 02.393s	23
14	Ivan Clementi	I	Kawasaki	5	1m 09.885s	23
15	Nello Russo	I	Ducati	35	1m 17.697s	23
16	Walter Tortoroglio	I	Honda	91	1m 28.520s	23
17	Martin Isaac	E	Yamaha	71	1 lap	22

DNF: Sergio Fuertes, E (Suzuki) 16, 16 laps; Pierfrancesco Chili, I (Ducati) 7, 13 laps; James Haydon, GB (Petronas) 8, 9 laps; Regis Laconi, F (Ducati) 55, 5 laps; Serafino Foti, I (Ducati) 28, 2 laps.

DNS: Alessandro Gramigni, I (Yamaha) 39.

Fastest lap: Hodgson, 1m 35.007s, 94.297 mph/151.757 km/h (record).

Superpole: Hodgson, 1m 34.863s, 94.441 mph/151.988 km/h.

Previous record: Ben Bostrom, USA (Ducati) 1m 35.306s, 94.002 mph/151.281 km/h (2002).

Championship points: 1 Hodgson, 50; 2 Xaus, 40; 3 Toseland and Walker, 29; 5 Martin, 21; 6 Lavilla, 19; 7 Pedercini, 15; 8 Borciani, 13; 9 Laconi, 11; 10 Borja and Garcia, 10; 12 Corser, 9; 13 Clementi, 7; 14 Bussei, 5; 15 Haydon and Russo, 4.

Right: Troy Corser showed promise in practice on the Petronas, but could only muster a seventh place in race two at Valencia.
Photograph: Gold & Goose

VALENCIA

WITH the emphasis of Ducati's race operations very much directed toward MotoGP, the first competitive outings of the new 999 Superbike models were, for some, almost a sideshow. Not for insiders though. The factory has dominated SBK racing for over a decade, and with a month to go before Suzuka, this was an important new machine.

Nonetheless, development had been limited. Virtually all testing had been carried out at Valencia; there was a creeping feeling of minimum application to important matters by Ducati.

Despite this, the Ducati Fila 999 F03 team, running Neil Hodgson and Ruben Xaus on Michelin tyres, were still operating at an advantage over their peer group – a lone Suzuki factory machine and a virtual gridful of 998-based Dukes. Plus the high-profile Foggy Petronas FP-1s.

Irrespective of the short gestation period of the 999 F03, and the fact that it was Neil Hodgson's first factory Ducati ride for six years, the Englishman cleaned up efficiently in Spain. He outpaced team-mate Xaus, although the Catalan continued the factory dominance and scored two seconds, to trail by only ten points.

The Fila fellas were strata above the rest, with Walker and Toseland swapping podium finishes, ahead of the restricted Suzuki and the now archaic remaining Ducatis.

Despite the added complication of a whipping and meandering wind, it was all very predictable, not to say processional – not to say uneventful. Even

Far left: Hodgson retained control in Australia.

Left: Chris Walker marked his first GSE race with a podium finish.
Both photographs: Gold & Goose

GSX-R1000s, we got Gregorio Lavilla's trick, but trickling, Alstare GSX-R, which posted seventh in race one and sixth in race two – almost 40 seconds behind the new twins.

The Petronas was down in even deeper debut dumps, with only one rider finishing each race – James Haydon 12th in the opener, and Troy Corser seventh in race two: a disappointment after Corser's front-row performances in regular and Superpole qualifying.

PHILLIP ISLAND

MAYBE it was the very nature of the flowing and rapid Phillip Island circuit; maybe it was the Ducati Fila crew coming to a new track with an all-new bike; maybe it was simply the human elements involved. Whatever the contributing factors, Phillip Island pointed the SBK happy highway away from the processions of Valencia.

The Victorian venue generally attracts one of SBK's most enthusiastic audiences, and they really appreciated an unpredictable weekend.

After a nightmarish qualifying experience for Ruben Xaus, who crashed three times in total and once on his Superpole lap, the big Spaniard dug into his considerable reserves of self-belief and sheer riding exuberance for the races. The fact that he could only manage a pair of second places behind team-mate Neil Hodgson was due to more than Xaus's backward eighth on the grid.

But Hodgson outperformed Xaus yet again, even if Australia became a game of inches, in race two at least.

The points leader was immaculate in his seven-second win in the PI opener, more tactically astute and better able to get behind the screen of the 999 than Xaus in his second-race 0.070-second squeak over the line.

Xaus, to give him credit, had some problems passing backmarkers in the opener, notably the NCR Ducati of David Garcia, some of whose lines were as eccentric as his experimental single-exhaust 998RS.

A veritable *feria* for the Spaniards had Garcia on the front row after Superpole, but arguably the star toreador was Lavilla, and the bike of the meeting his GSX-R1000. Three individual races into the season and Suzuki had the honour of taking a podium finish, with the competitive top speed of the biggest Gixxer proving that the 32.5-mm restrictors clogging up the air passages of its four intake ports were eminently surmountable handicaps after all. Lavilla's third in race one was also a vindication of the man, and of the new-construction Dunlop rear tyres; similarly, Steve Martin's Pirelli-shod fourth in race one. A former Aussie Superbike superstar and now a global mid-fielder for the DFX Ducati squad, Martin used the abrasive PI surface to good effect.

Laconi secured fourth in race two, sixth in the opener; but the hometown star once more was Troy Corser. The woes of Foggy Petronas seemed to be abating since he secured a front-row start and an outstanding fifth in race one – although eighth in race two was probably more of an accurate appraisal of the machine's abilities.

Two Valencia no-scores may have suggested that Pierfrancesco Chili really had ridden a season too far, but his immediate speed at Phillip Island, maintained all through practice, was to reap a tangible reward – even if Hodgson did rob him of the Breil watch for Superpole winner.

A DNF in race one was enough of a blood-boiler to pump 'Frankie' up to and beyond the limit of his two-year-old 998RS on Dunlops. His third place in race two was a corker of a result to open his score after three straight zeros. In a season already under threat from terminal boredom, Chili's podium took the total of riders to have accepted some colour of top-three silverware to six, in only four races.

On the evidence of Phillip Island, maybe this year wouldn't be so bad after all, even if Hodgson left Australia with 100 perfect points, and a gap of 20 on Xaus.

The parting thought as the packing cases were loaded for a skim across the Pacific Rim to Sugo was this: although there was no shortage of riders able to fight for lesser podium points, who among them could stop Hodgson from grinding inexorably toward the title?

Hodgson's new lap record of 1m 35.007s (in race two), and faster race time than Troy Bayliss in 2002, was somehow naturally expected of the new bike and MotoGP-derived Michelin tyres. Especially as he had managed to squeeze in five full Valencia race simulations over the winter months.

It was not that straightforward. Hodgson's new lap record came on lap ten of race two, proving that with no one else to really play with up front, he was still ballsy enough to push himself. The new 999 was also exhibiting some front-end peculiarities on braking and turn in, to the extent that he almost lost the front half a dozen times – a very un-998-like characteristic that was beginning to plague Xaus with even more malevolence.

Add in that Hodgson needed extensive pre-race painkilling injections to blot out the effects of his week-old crash-damaged ribs, and his showings on the first day of school became more hallowed than hollow.

A good day for Neil was not quite so promising for the new-look SBK series, the results simply stratifying downward from the Michelin/999 to the Dunlop- and Pirelli-shod 998 also-rans.

With the first four places filled by 2003 and 2002 Ducati factory machines, Regis Laconi secured fifth place (and a DNF) in his SBK return, working hard to hold off Pirelli-supported Steve Martin (DFX Ducati) who, in turn, scored a sixth and then a fifth. Pirelli make use of Valencia as their winter testing ground, and it showed.

Tyres were on the menu all round, new regulations limiting the number of rear tyres each team could use in practice to 13.

Valencia was the beginning of the all-new era of 1000 cc four-cylinder competition, but instead of a flood of new Yamaha R1s, Honda FireBlades and

Round 2

PHILLIP ISLAND, Australia
30 March, 2.762-mile/4.445-km circuit

Race 1 22 laps, 60.764 miles/97.790 km

Pl.	Name	Nat	Machine	No.	Time & gap	Laps
1	Neil Hodgson	GB	Ducati	100	34m 51.974s	22
					104.566 mph/168.283 km/h	
2	Ruben Xaus	E	Ducati	11	7.745s	22
3	Gregorio Lavilla	E	Suzuki	10	11.480s	22
4	Steve Martin	AUS	Ducati	99	17.968s	22
5	Troy Corser	AUS	Petronas	4	18.353s	22
6	Regis Laconi	F	Ducati	55	18.647s	22
7	Chris Walker	GB	Ducati	9	20.317s	22
8	David Garcia	E	Ducati	48	29.731s	22
9	Marco Borciani	I	Ducati	20	30.113s	22
10	Lucio Pedercini	I	Ducati	19	30.226s	22
11	Ivan Clementi	I	Kawasaki	5	30.530s	22
12	Juan Borja	E	Ducati	33	43.660s	22
13	Mauro Sanchini	I	Kawasaki	6	47.605s	22
14	Giovanni Bussei	I	Yamaha	15	47.624s	22
15	James Haydon	GB	Petronas	8	1m 05.711s	22
16	Nello Russo	I	Ducati	35	1m 29.603s	22
17	Jay Normoyle	AUS	Suzuki	78	1 lap	21
18	Steven Cutting	AUS	Suzuki	73	1 lap	21
19	Alistair Maxwell	AUS	Honda	75	1 lap	21

DNF: Walter Tortoroglio, I (Honda) 91, 15 laps; Pierfrancesco Chili, I (Ducati) 7, 4 laps.

DSQ: James Toseland, GB (Ducati) 52, 7 laps.

DNS: Davide Messori, I (Yamaha) 51.

Fastest lap: Hodgson, 1m 33.895s, 105.897 mph/170.424 km/h.

Race 2 22 laps, 60.764 miles/97.790 km

Pl.	Name	Nat.	Machine	No.	Time & gap	Laps
1	Neil Hodgson	AUS	Ducati	100	34m 44.425s	22
					104.945 mph/168.893 km/h	
2	Ruben Xaus	E	Ducati	11	0.070s	22
3	Pierfrancesco Chili	I	Ducati	7	6.308s	22
4	Regis Laconi	F	Ducati	55	6.409s	22
5	James Toseland	GB	Ducati	52	14.402s	22
6	Chris Walker	GB	Ducati	9	14.409s	22
7	Gregorio Lavilla	E	Suzuki	10	14.426s	22
8	Troy Corser	AUS	Petronas	4	28.645s	22
9	Steve Martin	AUS	Ducati	99	34.094s	22
10	Marco Borciani	I	Ducati	20	34.808s	22
11	Ivan Clementi	I	Kawasaki	5	34.920s	22
12	Mauro Sanchini	I	Kawasaki	6	35.667s	22
13	Nello Russo	I	Ducati	35	35.773s	22
14	Lucio Pedercini	I	Ducati	19	55.419s	22
15	Juan Borja	E	Ducati	33	1m 01.414s	22
16	James Haydon	GB	Petronas	8	1m 05.237s	22
17	Walter Tortoroglio	I	Honda	91	1m 27.781s	22
18	Steven Cutting	AUS	Suzuki	73	1 lap	21
19	Jay Normoyle	AUS	Suzuki	78	1 lap	21
20	Alistair Maxwell	AUS	Honda	75	1 lap	21

DNF: Davide Messori, I (Yamaha) 51, 3 laps; David Garcia, E (Ducati) 48, 2 laps; Giovanni Bussei, I (Yamaha) 15, 1 lap.

Fastest lap: Xaus, 1m 33.813s, 105.989 mph/170.573 km/h.

Superpole: Hodgson, 1m 33.030s, 106.881 mph/172.009 km/h.

Lap record: Troy Corser, AUS (Ducati), 1m 33.019s, 106.894 mph/172.029 km/h (1999).

Championship points: 1 Hodgson, **100; 2** Xaus, **80; 3** Walker, **48; 4** Lavilla, **44; 5** Martin, **41; 6** Toseland, **40; 7** Laconi, **34; 8** Corser, **28; 9** Borciani, **26; 10** Pedercini, **23; 11** Garcia, **18; 12** Clementi, **17; 13** Chili, **16; 14** Borja, **15; 15** Sanchini, **10.**

Round 3
SUGO, Japan
27 April, 2.322-mile/3.737-km circuit

Race 1 25 laps, 58.050 miles/93.425 km

Pl.	Name	Nat.	Machine	No.	Time & gap	Laps
1	Neil Hodgson	GB	Ducati	100	37m 57.829s	25
					91.748 mph/147.654 km/h	
2	Regis Laconi	F	Ducati	55	7.167s	25
3	James Toseland	GB	Ducati	52	14.853s	25
4	Ruben Xaus	E	Ducati	11	28.299s	25
5	Gregorio Lavilla	E	Suzuki	10	32.382s	25
6	Hitoyasu Izutsu	J	Honda	77	32.584s	25
7	Lucio Pedercini	I	Ducati	19	1m 00.615s	25
8	Atsushi Watanabe	J	Suzuki	76	1m 02.154s	25
9	James Haydon	GB	Petronas	8	1m 07.432s	25
10	Juan Borja	E	Ducati	33	1m 11.446s	25
11	Mauro Sanchini	I	Kawasaki	6	1m 17.354s	25
12	Giovanni Bussei	I	Yamaha	15	1m 18.970s	25
13	Marco Borciani	I	Ducati	20	1m 27.846s	25
14	Kenichiro Nakamura	J	Honda	74	1m 28.048s	25
15	Steve Martin	AUS	Ducati	99	1 lap	24

DNF: Walter Tortoroglio, I (Honda) 91, 18 laps; Noriyasu Numata, J (Ducati) 79, 16 laps; Ivan Clementi, I (Kawasaki) 5, 0 laps; Troy Corser, AUS (Petronas) 4, 0 laps; Chris Walker, GB (Ducati) 9, 0 laps; Pierfrancesco Chili, I (Ducati) 7, 0 laps.

Fastest lap: Hodgson, 1m 29.999s, 92.884 mph/149.482 km/h.

Race 2 25 laps, 58.050 miles/93.425 km

Pl.	Name	Nat.	Machine	No.	Time & gap	Laps
1	Neil Hodgson	GB	Ducati	100	37m 56.499s	25
					91.801 mph/147.740 km/h	
2	Gregorio Lavilla	E	Suzuki	10	0.818s	25
3	Pierfrancesco Chili	I	Ducati	7	1.470s	25
4	Ruben Xaus	E	Ducati	11	10.470s	25
5	James Toseland	GB	Ducati	52	11.133s	25
6	Hitoyasu Izutsu	J	Honda	77	21.604s	25
7	Regis Laconi	F	Ducati	55	21.953s	25
8	Ivan Clementi	I	Kawasaki	5	48.857s	25
9	Juan Borja	E	Ducati	33	1m 01.770s	25
10	Mauro Sanchini	I	Kawasaki	6	1m 05.289s	25
11	Giovanni Bussei	I	Yamaha	15	1m 09.325s	25
12	Troy Corser	AUS	Petronas	4	1m 15.284s	25
13	Marco Borciani	I	Ducati	20	1 lap	24
14	Kenichiro Nakamura	J	Honda	74	1 lap	24
15	Walter Tortoroglio	I	Honda	91	1 lap	24

DNF: Atsushi Watanabe, J (Suzuki) 76, 13 laps; Noriyasu Numata, J (Ducati) 79, 8 laps; James Haydon, GB (Petronas) 8, 7 laps; Steve Martin, AUS (Ducati) 99, 4 laps; Chris Walker, GB (Ducati) 9, 2 laps; Lucio Pedercini, I (Ducati) 19, 0 laps.

Fastest lap: Chili, 1m 30.146s, 92.732 mph/149.238 km/h.

Superpole: Laconi, 1m 30.064s, 92.817 mph/149.374 km/h.

Lap record: Makoto Tamada, J (Honda), 1m 29.108s, 93.812 mph/ 150.976 km/h (2002).

Championship points: 1 Hodgson, 150; 2 Xaus, 106; 3 Lavilla, 75; 4 Toseland, 67; 5 Laconi, 63; 6 Walker, 48; 7 Martin, 42; 8 Borciani, Chili, Corser and Pedercini, 32; 12 Borja, 28; 13 Clementi, 25; 14 Sanchini, 21; 15 Izutsu, 20.

SUGO

HODGSON, soaring high on a thermal of success and factory horsepower, had a new playmate or two in Sugo, his regular high-speed dance partner having a less-than-glorious weekend on a track strewn with apple-blossom petals. Sugo is traditionally a tough nut for Western riders to crack, and indeed until Hodgson pummelled his 999 to his third double in a row, only Colin Edwards had scored top marks in the preceding seven years at the track.

For once, Hodgson may have found little advantage in being on Michelins, as the local Dunlops are used almost exclusively in the Japanese championship. Even on qualifiers, he could do no better than fifth in Superpole, eased out by the combined Dunlop talents of Laconi, Chili, Lavilla and local Suzuki pilot Atsushi Watanabe.

The looming threat to Hodgson was not, for once, the wild cards. The number of would-be local winners was down, although Watanabe was in contention for a time. Superpole went to Laconi for the first time, and he went on to haunt Hodgson in race one. Neil finally disposed of him in the last few laps; a clutch problem would hold the Frenchman down in seventh in race two.

Next up from the Euro tag team was Lavilla in race two, proving to have a better package and more experience than Watanabe and his local Yoshimura machine.

Chili put in a trademark gritty ride to take third in the second 25-lapper. He was one of several to make stage-right exits after the first right-hander in race one. Clementi, Corser, Walker and Chili all fell, Lavilla and wild-card Honda rider Hitoyasu Izutsu being delayed by the human and mechanical debris. Quite what happened is something of a mystery, even with the benefit of repeat TV coverage, but Toseland and Corser were two participants in a chain of events that made four riders immediate non-finishers.

Toseland escaped and took third, only because Watanabe ran on, suffering from consistent problems under braking.

Xaus battled hard for his pair of fourth places, and dropped farther behind Hodgson in the championship – 44 points adrift after only six races. He'd toiled away in spite of inexact set-up and tyre choices, with the penalty of starting from the far end of the third row after qualifying 12th. Significantly, he was 28 and then ten seconds behind his team-mate, and even Hodgson was way down on the best race times set by 2002 winners Edwards and GP refugee Makoto Tamada.

One big surprise was the lack of showing from Hitoyasu Izutsu, on a full works VTR, on Michelins. He took a brace of sixths, not quite the result a recent double Sugo SBK race winner would have hoped for, especially on a similar bike to the one that had secured all four most recent victories.

Six down, six wins for Hodgson, and despite the sometimes close and exuberant on-track action, Sugo proved quite conclusively that in terms of rider and machine package, there was going to be only one season-long game in town. So far, Hodgson had played it immaculately.

The Ducati Cup, as its critics had cruelly, if understandably, dubbed it, was otherwise unpredictable and full of contrasts, with even the customer Ducatis and the top Suzukis in with a shout against the latest 104-mm-bore desmo missiles. An unexpected, but welcome, event.

MONZA

IN a season when there were already dark mutterings about the relevant potency of the championship in relation to years past, Neil Hodgson at least showed that whatever the level of competition, he would be racing current foes and phantoms from the past to the very best of his ability.

He even set a couple of records at Monza, that most majestic of mainland European venues, a shrine still tended lovingly by the angels of velocity, even if chicanes mean average lap speeds have fallen.

No rider had won eight straight races at the start of a season before, and after securing the race-one victory, Hodgson raised the total of Ducati wins in SBK to 200. A nice touch in Italy, especially when the odometer of dominance clicked on to 201 after race two. He also set a new Superpole and qualifying record of 1m 46.981s.

Hodgson's three-second lead in race one had shrunk to a mere 0.3 second advantage after 18 laps of perspiration and inspiration from his pursuers. Backmarkers had played a part in that, but Hodgson was maybe a tad fortunate to have the start/finish line so close to the final Parabolica corner.

He was also lucky to have a front Michelin hard enough to withstand the 44-degree C track temperatures, especially at such a fast circuit. The 999 was proving less than fully co-operative on braking and in terms of front-end feel for Hodgson and Xaus. Although the Spaniard's confidence and push for the title were being garrotted inexorably by this phenomenon, it also made Hodgson's job appreciably harder.

Second went to Laconi, in aggressive form in both races and, like most of his non-factory brethren, on Dunlop tyres, which certainly

earned their keep this weekend. Third in race one and second in race two were deservedly hoovered up by the restricted breathing passages of the increasingly competitive 1000 cc Suzuki of Lavilla, with Laconi number two in the opener.

Race two could have gone to any one of four riders, as Hodgson, Laconi, Lavilla and Chili gave each other's slipstreams a good testing for all 18 laps. Factory horsepower helped Hodgson overtake the lot on the run down the back straight for the final time, and he admitted so afterward. It was still the closest single race so far, Lavilla being only 0.044 second down, and all four top men within a second of each other.

The claimed 72,000 crowd loved it, and SBK in general left Monza with a heightened sense of self-respect. It was turning into a season after all.

Xaus's challenge wilted twice at Ascari. He clashed with Chris Walker in race one and ran off track, restarting last and finishing a cavalier and commendable seventh. Then he fell on a slip of his own making in race two. He had suffered concussion at pretty much the same spot on Saturday, was allowed to race, and clung on to second place overall by his fingernails.

Despite being part of the rolling maul in race two, Toseland missed out on both podiums, finishing fourth in race one and fifth in the second, due to some injudicious set-up changes between races. Walker, his team-mate, scored two sixths, still suffering from his Sugo beatings.

Chili accepted the plaudits of his local crowd with thanks and pride, finishing fifth in race one, but following up with a podium finish of third. Addicted to racing, Frankie may be; addicted to the rush of a top-three success at your home track – well, who would not be partial to a fix of that highball on an annual basis?

Round 4
MONZA, Italy
18 May, 3.600-mile/5.793-km circuit

Race 1 18 laps, 64.800 miles/104.274 km

Pl.	Name	Nat.	Machine	No.	Time & gap	Laps
1	Neil Hodgson	GB	Ducati	100	32m 38.264s	18
					119.113 mph/191.693 km/h	
2	Regis Laconi	F	Ducati	55	0.352s	18
3	Gregorio Lavilla	E	Suzuki	10	0.389s	18
4	James Toseland	GB	Ducati	52	0.396s	18
5	Pierfrancesco Chili	I	Ducati	7	1.617s	18
6	Chris Walker	GB	Ducati	9	24.138s	18
7	Ruben Xaus	E	Ducati	11	30.889s	18
8	Marco Borciani	I	Ducati	20	31.609s	18
9	Steve Martin	AUS	Ducati	99	32.877s	18
10	Lucio Pedercini	I	Ducati	19	35.902s	18
11	Alessandro Gramigni	I	Yamaha	39	41.700s	18
12	Vittorio Iannuzzo	I	Suzuki	31	45.872s	18
13	Troy Corser	AUS	Petronas	4	54.204s	18
14	Mauro Sanchini	I	Kawasaki	6	1m 13.406s	18
15	Serafino Foti	I	Ducati	28	1m 27.704s	18
16	Sergio Fuertes	E	Suzuki	16	1m 31.924s	18
17	Lorenzo Mauri	I	Ducati	82	1 lap	17
18	Marco Masetti	I	Ducati	50	1 lap	17

DNF: Ivan Clementi, I (Kawasaki) 5, 16 laps; James Haydon, GB (Petronas) 8, 14 laps; Giovanni Bussei, I (Yamaha) 15, 12 laps; Walter Tortoroglio, I (Honda) 91, 2 laps.

Fastest lap: Hodgson, 1m 47.715s, 120.304 mph/193.611 km/h.

Race 2 18 laps, 64.800 miles/104.274 km

Pl.	Name	Nat.	Machine	No.	Time & gap	Laps
1	Neil Hodgson	GB	Ducati	100	32m 41.366s	18
					118.924 mph/191.390 km/h	
2	Gregorio Lavilla	E	Suzuki	10	0.044s	18
3	Pierfrancesco Chili	I	Ducati	7	0.657s	18
4	Regis Laconi	F	Ducati	55	0.998s	18
5	James Toseland	GB	Ducati	52	6.379s	18
6	Chris Walker	GB	Ducati	9	27.289s	18
7	Steve Martin	AUS	Ducati	99	39.585s	18
8	Marco Borciani	I	Ducati	20	39.820s	18
9	Vittorio Iannuzzo	I	Suzuki	31	39.881s	18
10	Lucio Pedercini	I	Ducati	19	43.406s	18
11	Alessandro Gramigni	I	Yamaha	39	51.240s	18
12	Mauro Sanchini	I	Kawasaki	6	57.491s	18
13	Giovanni Bussei	I	Yamaha	15	57.503s	18
14	Serafino Foti	I	Ducati	28	1m 30.656s	18
15	Walter Tortoroglio	I	Honda	91	1m 41.410s	18
16	Marco Masetti	I	Ducati	50	1m 49.762s	18
17	Lorenzo Mauri	I	Ducati	82	1 lap	17

DNF: Ruben Xaus, E (Ducati) 11, 16 laps; Ivan Clementi, I (Kawasaki) 5, 15 laps; Troy Corser, AUS (Petronas) 4, 14 laps; Sergio Fuertes, E (Suzuki) 16, 14 laps; James Haydon, GB (Petronas) 8, 12 laps.

Fastest lap: Laconi, 1m 47.909s, 120.088 mph/193.263 km/h.

Superpole: Hodgson, 1m 46.981s, 121.129 mph/194.939 km/h.

Lap record: Troy Bayliss, AUS (Ducati), 1m 47.434s, 120.619 mph/194.117 km/h (2002).

Championship points: 1 Hodgson, 200; 2 Xaus, 115; 3 Lavilla, 111; 4 Laconi, 96; 5 Toseland, 91; 6 Walker, 68; 7 Chili, 59; 8 Martin, 58; 9 Borciani, 48; 10 Pedercini, 44; 11 Corser, 35; 12 Borja, 28; 13 Sanchini, 27; 14 Clementi, 25; 15 Izutsu, 20.

Facing page, top: Hodgson upset Sugo form with a rare non-Japanese double.

Facing page, centre: Laconi, Hodgson and Toseland rode three generations of Ducati to the Sugo race-one rostrum.

Facing page, bottom: Lavilla made second to prove the new Suzuki's strength in Japan.

All photographs: Gold & Goose

Above left: Close as paint at classic Monza – Laconi heads Lavilla and Hodgson.

Far left: Legs flailing, Xaus heads for the gravel after clashing with Walker in race one.

Left: Evergreen Frankie Chili pleased his home fans with a rostrum.

All photographs: Mark Wernham

Round 5
OSCHERSLEBEN, Germany
1 June, 2.279-mile/3.667-km circuit

Race 1 28 laps, 63.812 miles/102.676 km

Pl.	Name	Nat.	Machine	No.	Time & gap	Laps
1	Neil Hodgson	GB	Ducati	100	41m 29.894s	28
					92.245 mph/148.454 km/h	
2	Pierfrancesco Chili	I	Ducati	7	0.556s	28
3	James Toseland	GB	Ducati	52	12.965s	28
4	Regis Laconi	F	Ducati	55	16.630s	28
5	Chris Walker	GB	Ducati	9	16.754s	28
6	Steve Martin	AUS	Ducati	99	38.142s	28
7	Marco Borciani	I	Ducati	20	43.496s	28
8	Vittorio Iannuzzo	I	Suzuki	31	45.452s	28
9	Lucio Pedercini	I	Ducati	19	50.154s	28
10	Giovanni Bussei	I	Yamaha	15	51.218s	28
11	Mauro Sanchini	I	Kawasaki	6	1m 04.353s	28
12	Troy Corser	AUS	Petronas	4	1m 10.643s	28
13	Nello Russo	I	Ducati	35	1 lap	27
14	Serafino Foti	I	Ducati	28	1 lap	27
15	Jiri Mrkyvka	CZ	Ducati	23	1 lap	27
16	Sergio Fuertes	E	Suzuki	16	1 lap	27
17	Sundby Dag Steinar	(N)	Yamaha	36	1 lap	27

DNF: James Haydon, GB (Petronas) 8, 14 laps; Walter Tortoroglio, I (Honda) 91, 10 laps; Ruben Xaus, E (Ducati) 11, 9 laps; Juan Borja, E (Ducati) 33, 4 laps; Ivan Clementi, I (Kawasaki) 5, 1 lap; Gregorio Lavilla, E (Suzuki) 10, 0 laps.

Fastest lap: Chili, 1m 27.972s, 93.244 mph/150.061 km/h.

Race 2 28 laps, 63.812 miles/102.676 km

Pl.	Name	Nat	Machine	No.	Time & gap	Laps
1	James Toseland	GB	Ducati	52	41m 20.103s	28
					92.609 mph/149.040 km/h	
2	Neil Hodgson	GB	Ducati	100	7.416s	28
3	Chris Walker	GB	Ducati	9	15.314s	28
4	Regis Laconi	F	Ducati	55	19.277s	28
5	Ruben Xaus	E	Ducati	11	24.228s	28
6	Steve Martin	AUS	Ducati	99	43.648s	28
7	Juan Borja	E	Ducati	33	46.868s	28
8	Vittorio Iannuzzo	I	Suzuki	31	47.807s	28
9	Marco Borciani	I	Ducati	20	48.930s	28
10	Lucio Pedercini	I	Ducati	19	1m 02.514s	28
11	Pierfrancesco Chili	I	Ducati	7	1m 10.394s	28
12	Mauro Sanchini	I	Kawasaki	6	1m 12.686s	28
13	Ivan Clementi	I	Kawasaki	5	1m 13.019s	28
14	Troy Corser	AUS	Petronas	4	1m 27.387s	28
15	Serafino Foti	I	Ducati	28	1 lap	27
16	Sergio Fuertes	E	Suzuki	16	1 lap	27
17	Jiri Mrkyvka	CZ	Ducati	23	1 lap	27
18	Walter Tortoroglio	I	Honda	91	1 lap	27
19	Sundby Dag Steinar	N	Yamaha	36	1 lap	27

DNF: Gregorio Lavilla, E (Suzuki) 10, 16 laps; Nello Russo, I (Ducati) 35, 16 laps; Giovanni Bussei, I (Yamaha) 15, 5 laps.

DNS: James Haydon, GB (Petronas) 8.

Fastest lap: Hodgson, 1m 27.734s, 93.496 mph/150.468 km/h.

Superpole: Hodgson, 1m 26.907s, 94.386 mph/151.900 km/h.

Lap record: Colin Edwards, USA (Honda), 1m 26.549s, 94.777 mph/152.529 km/h (2002).

Championship points: 1 Hodgson, 245; 2 Toseland, 132; 3 Xaus, 126; 4 Laconi, 122; 5 Lavilla, 111; 6 Walker, 95; 7 Chili, 84; 8 Martin, 78; 9 Borciani, 64; 10 Pedercini, 57; 11 Corser, 41; 12 Borja, 37; 13 Sanchini, 36; 14 Clementi, 28; 15 Iannuzzo, 27.

OSCHERSLEBEN

THE Union Jack displaced the German tricolour at Oschersleben, five out of the six podium slots going to Britons on another landmark day in the SBK series. Only the outstanding contribution of Chili and his old customer Ducati looked set to deprive Hodgson of his ninth straight win of the season, but ultimately the attempt was to prove futile. The last-corner sort-out went the way of Hodgson, who played a more cunning final hand.

Ironically, the rides from Hodgson and even underdog Frankie were overshadowed by the fierce and fearless game of rollerball undertaken by James Toseland. Fast in qualifying, not quite there in Superpole, Toseland was pushed off the black stuff at the first corner by a crashing Lavilla, then had his dentistry rearranged as his suspension jack hammered at high speed across the run-off areas. He was spectacularly fortunate not to be hit as he crossed the lines of a high-speed armada of leaders, but could do nothing to alter his trajectory.

Recovering his composure, Toseland assaulted the rest of the race with vengeful pace, finishing third overall from dead last. Had there been no first-corner Supermoto simulation, he would have won by some distance, and ultimately was to become the second race winner of the year in race two.

Toseland and Hodgson had led the tightly bunched pack, and clanged into each other hard enough to temporarily dislodge Hodgson's clutch lever and rub his Fila stickers off the side. An accident, each said – entertainment said the crowd, which included a large contingent of visitors from the UK.

Those who had travelled to this featureless part of Germany saw something more unique than Toseland on top for the first time. Race two delivered the first ever all-British podium in SBK history – an incongruous statistic for a championship with such a mesmeric hold on the British racing psyche.

The final stripe of the union flag was painted in by Walker, making his first appearance in the top rank since the opening round.

A significant day for Dunlop too, long-term SBK majority supplier, who took a race win for the first time since Sugo 2002. This was no mean feat on the 48-degree C track surface and in the 30-degree C air temperature. It was hot and dusty work for all in two 28-lap races. A big difference from the torrential and long lived Saturday-morning thunderstorm, which prevented all track action for a while.

A seven-second margin of victory for Toseland, Dunlop and the 2002-spec factory Ducati told the story of Oschersleben in three small chapters.

Hodgson was master of the Superpole universe again, snuffing out Chili's dream gift of the watch for his wife. He was fast and consistent, but the Fila Ducati team had to work hard once more. The 999 rather flattered to deceive, with a whole new set of peculiarities that drove Hodgson and Xaus to choose from the rock-hard end of the range of Michelin front tyres.

Laconi put in two tough races to score a brace of fourths, but more tellingly Xaus dropped from second to third in the championship standings, after a fall in race one and a fifth in race two.

SILVERSTONE

A CLAIMED 83,000 souls were inflamed by SBK fever at Silverstone over a mid-June weekend, and as if to thank them, all the action was glowing cherry red, the temperature rising throughout. And to complete the local feel-good factor, British riders were pretty well to the fore during two outstandingly entertaining races.

With a less-than-laudable 2002 meeting behind them, the Silverstone organisers made a much better go of 2003's version, although one major problem proved to be an all-new development – the taming of awe-inspiring Woodcote corner, the fast and dangerous final bend. Chicanes generally attract criticism from purists, but the ridiculously slow and tight geometric stammer was vociferously panned by competitors in all classes. Featuring a ludicrous bump mid-apex of the first low-speed lunge, the obtusely-angled left-right was a design gaff.

However, the arrangement did help the ten-rider concertina in the first race to bunch up together after every lap of the circuit – but so would a well-designed chicane. A better version might also have offered passing opportunities, as opposed to preventing them.

It jarred on this full Silverstone track, a wondrous, sweeping high-speed serpent of a thing and – we hope because of this characteristic – the racing was the best of the year.

Lavilla's big Suzuki and the Rizla GSX-Rs of the local Crescent Racing BSB riders, John Reynolds and Yukio Kagayama, were right in the thick of the action against the hordes of Ducatis, including a far-from-mild wild card Michael Rutter (Renegade Ducati).

Given double the normal competition, and that the fast circuit was proving something of a leveller, Hodgson's double win was a twin peak of concentration and commitment. A full 12 races in, and Hodgson had only dropped five measly points overall.

The first race was the finer of two 20-lap cavalry charges, with five riders sometimes side by side along the straights, jostling for position and the silent embrace of the next slipstream.

Kagayama, trying every which way to slip by Hodgson in race one, was breathtaking to watch, especially into the right-hander of Bridge. His passes were seldom made to stick, as Hodgson slapped his name to the top of proceedings time after time.

There were five leaders of race one, four in race two, but one of those most frequently breaking the airstream, Gregorio Lavilla, lost the front on lap 17 of race one, which later saw Toseland and Xaus almost teetering off in the slow chicane as the field's hard nuts balanced full risk against determination on the very last lap.

Hodgson, Toseland, Xaus, Laconi, Kagayama, Reynolds, Chili, Rutter and Walker eventually crossed the first-race finish line within seven seconds – but they were frequently closer than that.

Race two was equally claustrophobic, with Hodgson, Lavilla, Xaus, Toseland, Kagayama, Laconi and Chili all separated by seven seconds.

Two thirds showed that Xaus had regained some front-end confidence, and thus form.

Twice fifth was the imported martial artisan Kagayama, who chopped himself off the track in race one, running at high speed across the grass and getting it all back on course in eloquent style. Laconi was far from happy, even with a fourth and sixth at an all-new track for him. Nothing beats factory – even year-old factory – horsepower, and Laconi's 998RS machine was left gasping.

Round 6
SILVERSTONE, Great Britain
15 June, 3.129-mile/5.036-km circuit

Race 1 20 laps, 62.580 miles/100.720 km

Pl.	Name	Nat.	Machine	No.	Time & gap	Laps
1	Neil Hodgson	GB	Ducati	100	38m 24.187s	20
					97.780 mph/157.362 km/h	
2	James Toseland	GB	Ducati	52	0.440s	20
3	Ruben Xaus	E	Ducati	11	0.599s	20
4	Regis Laconi	F	Ducati	55	0.943s	20
5	Yukio Kagayama	J	Suzuki	64	4.779s	20
6	John Reynolds	GB	Suzuki	61	5.085s	20
7	Pierfrancesco Chili	I	Ducati	7	5.942s	20
8	Michael Rutter	GB	Ducati	60	6.371s	20
9	Chris Walker	GB	Ducati	9	7.229s	20
10	Marco Borciani	I	Ducati	20	34.399s	20
11	Lucio Pedercini	I	Ducati	19	39.260s	20
12	Giovanni Bussei	I	Yamaha	15	43.387s	20
13	Mauro Sanchini	I	Kawasaki	6	45.266s	20
14	Ivan Clementi	I	Kawasaki	5	45.628s	20
15	Nello Russo	I	Ducati	35	46.388s	20
16	Troy Corser	AUS	Petronas	4	54.366s	20
17	Sergio Fuertes	E	Suzuki	16	57.282s	20

DNF: Gregorio Lavilla, E (Suzuki) 10, 16 laps; Vittorio Iannuzzo, I (Suzuki) 31, 12 laps; Serafino Foti, I (Ducati) 28, 11 laps; Sean Emmett, GB (Ducati) 62, 3 laps; Walter Tortoroglio, I (Honda) 91, 3 laps; Juan Borja, E (Ducati) 33, 1 lap; Steve Martin, AUS (Ducati) 99, 1 lap.

DNS: David Garcia, E (Ducati) 48.

Fastest lap: Lavilla, 1m 54.105s, 98.727 mph/158.885 km/h (record).

Race 2 20 laps, 62.580 miles/100.720 km

Pl.	Name	Nat.	Machine	No.	Time & gap	Laps
1	Neil Hodgson	GB	Ducati	100	38m 13.944s	20
					98.217 mph/158.065 km/h	
2	Gregorio Lavilla	E	Suzuki	10	0.493s	20
3	Ruben Xaus	E	Ducati	11	0.653s	20
4	James Toseland	GB	Ducati	52	3.435s	20
5	Yukio Kagayama	J	Suzuki	64	4.117s	20
6	Regis Laconi	F	Ducati	55	4.220s	20
7	Pierfrancesco Chili	I	Ducati	7	7.246s	20
8	Chris Walker	GB	Ducati	9	11.822s	20
9	Michael Rutter	GB	Ducati	60	12.399s	20
10	John Reynolds	GB	Suzuki	61	38.499s	20
11	Lucio Pedercini	I	Ducati	19	44.491s	20
12	Giovanni Bussei	I	Yamaha	15	48.029s	20
13	Marco Borciani	I	Ducati	20	48.803s	20
14	Mauro Sanchini	I	Kawasaki	6	48.994s	20
15	Vittorio Iannuzzo	I	Suzuki	31	49.342s	20
16	Ivan Clementi	I	Kawasaki	5	49.563s	20
17	Sergio Fuertes	E	Suzuki	16	1m 12.403s	20
18	Nello Russo	I	Ducati	35	1m 12.935s	20

DNF: Serafino Foti, I (Ducati) 28, 14 laps; Steve Martin, AUS (Ducati) 99, 8 laps; Troy Corser, AUS (Petronas) 4, 6 laps; Juan Borja, E (Ducati) 33, 6 laps; Sean Emmett, GB (Ducati) 62, 6 laps; Walter Tortoroglio, I (Honda) 91, 4 laps.

DNS: David Garcia, E (Ducati) 48.

Fastest lap: Lavilla, 1m 53.629s, 99.140 mph/159.551 km/h (record).

Superpole: Hodgson, 1m 52.875s, 99.803 mph/160.617 km/h.

Previous circuit record: Troy Bayliss, AUS (Ducati), 2m 02.145s, 93.290 mph/150.136 km/h (2002).

Championship points: 1 Hodgson, 295; 2 Toseland, 165; 3 Xaus, 158; 4 Laconi, 145; 5 Lavilla, 131; 6 Walker, 110; 7 Chili, 102; 8 Martin, 78; 9 Borciani, 73; 10 Pedercini, 67; 11 Corser and Sanchini, 41; 13 Borja, 37; 14 Bussei, 33; 15 Clementi, 30.

Facing page, top: Germany, and Toseland runs away from Hodgson to become the second person to win a race in 2003.

Facing page, bottom: Xaus on the grid at Oschersleben.

Above far left: Martial artisan Yukio Kagayama was a prominent Silverstone wild card.

Above left: Crescent Suzuki team-mate John Reynolds was another.

Left: Lavilla led in at Silverstone and achieved the 1000 cc Suzuki's best finish so far.

All photographs: Gold & Goose

Round 7
MISANO, Italy
22 June, 2.523-mile/4.060-km circuit

Race 1 25 laps, 63.075 miles/101.500 km

Pl.	Name	Nat.	Machine	No.	Time & gap	Laps
1	Ruben Xaus	E	Ducati	11	40m 22.423s	25
					93.728 mph/150.841 km/h	
2	James Toseland	GB	Ducati	52	0.760s	25
3	Regis Laconi	F	Ducati	55	1.711s	25
4	Gregorio Lavilla	E	Suzuki	10	10.933s	25
5	Chris Walker	GB	Ducati	9	20.487s	25
6	Steve Martin	AUS	Ducati	99	23.234s	25
7	Troy Corser	AUS	Petronas	4	27.083s	25
8	Lucio Pedercini	I	Ducati	19	32.026s	25
9	Mauro Sanchini	I	Kawasaki	6	36.701s	25
10	Ivan Clementi	I	Kawasaki	5	48.537s	25
11	Marco Borciani	I	Ducati	20	54.636s	25
12	Alessandro Gramigni	I	Yamaha	39	57.320s	25
13	Paolo Blora	I	Ducati	113	1m 01.084s	25
14	Serafino Foti	I	Ducati	28	1m 10.003s	25
15	Sergio Fuertes	E	Suzuki	16	1m 24.423s	25
16	Giuseppe Zannini	I	Ducati	29	1m 26.461s	25
17	Luca Pini	I	Suzuki	23	1m 33.879s	25

DNF: Pierfrancesco Chili, I (Ducati) 7, 24 laps; Vittorio Iannuzzo, I (Suzuki) 31, 15 laps; Giovanni Bussei, I (Yamaha) 15, 10 laps; Walter Tortoroglio, I (Honda) 91, 9 laps; Jiri Mrkyvka, CZ (Ducati) 23, 6 laps; Juan Borja, E (Ducati) 33, 3 laps; Neil Hodgson, GB (Ducati) 100, 1 lap; Nello Russo, I (Ducati) 35, 1 lap; Christian Zaiser, A (Aprilia) 70, 0 laps.

DNS: David Garcia, E (Ducati) 48.

Fastest lap: Xaus, 1m 36.158s, 94.448 mph/152.000 km/h.

Race 2 25 laps, 63.075 miles/101.500 km

Pl.	Name	Nat	Machine	No.	Time & gap	Laps
1	Ruben Xaus	E	Ducati	11	40m 17.321s	25
					93.926 mph/151.159 km/h	
2	Neil Hodgson	GB	Ducati	100	0.244s	25
3	Pierfrancesco Chili	I	Ducati	7	6.896s	25
4	Regis Laconi	F	Ducati	55	13.814s	25
5	Gregorio Lavilla	E	Suzuki	10	17.399s	25
6	Lucio Pedercini	I	Ducati	19	19.345s	25
7	Vittorio Iannuzzo	I	Suzuki	31	24.651s	25
8	Chris Walker	GB	Ducati	9	29.164s	25
9	Steve Martin	AUS	Ducati	99	32.310s	25
10	Troy Corser	AUS	Petronas	4	33.516s	25
11	Mauro Sanchini	I	Kawasaki	6	44.197s	25
12	Juan Borja	E	Ducati	33	52.247s	25
13	Ivan Clementi	I	Kawasaki	5	52.628s	25
14	Marco Borciani	I	Ducati	20	1m 01.445s	25
15	Alessandro Gramigni	I	Yamaha	39	1m 02.445s	25
16	Sergio Fuertes	E	Suzuki	16	1m 11.728s	25
17	Paolo Blora	I	Ducati	113	1m 17.352s	25
18	Giuseppe Zannini	I	Ducati	29	1m 29.848s	25
19	Luca Pini	I	Suzuki	96	1m 36.711s	25

DNF: James Toseland, GB (Ducati) 52, 14 laps; Jiri Mrkyvka, CZ (Ducati) 23, 11 laps; Nello Russo, I (Ducati) 35, 10 laps; Giovanni Bussei, I (Yamaha) 15, 2 laps; Serafino Foti, I (Ducati) 28, 2 laps; Walter Tortoroglio, I (Honda) 91, 1 lap.

DNS: Christian Zaiser, A (Aprilia) 70; David Garcia, E (Ducati) 48.

Fastest lap: Xaus, 1m 35.629s, 94.971 mph/152.841 km/h.

Superpole: Hodgson, 1m 34.586s, 96.018 mph/154.526 km/h.

Lap record: John Kocinski, USA (Ducati), 1m 34.296s, 96.313 mph 155.001 km/h (1996).

Championship points: 1 Hodgson, 315; 2 Xaus, 208; 3 Toseland, 185; 4 Laconi, 174; 5 Lavilla, 155; 6 Walker, 129; 7 Chili, 118; 8 Martin, 95; 9 Pedercini, 85; 10 Borciani, 80; 11 Corser, 56; 12 Sanchini, 53; 13 Borja, 41; 14 Clementi, 39; 15 Iannuzzo, 37.

Top right: Risk and benefit – Xaus claimed a pair of wins by inches at Misano.

Above right: Pirelli-shod Martin leads Pedercini, Walker and a distant Corser at Misano.

Both photographs: Gold & Goose

MISANO

THE unremitting 31-degree C heat and 71-per-cent humidity made Misano a steam bath on race day. Having started on the third row, Ruben Xaus might have been forgiven for riding with some degree of restraint at this popular testing circuit on the Adriatic coast.

Not so. Two wins – the first by 0.760 second over Toseland, the second by 0.244 second over Hodgson – gave him 30 points in his chase of the elder Englishman. And restored his second place in the championship.

However, he did not secure a new lap record, and neither was Troy Bayliss's old track best time beaten in qualifying, regardless of some sections having been resurfaced.

Xaus's cause was helped no end when Hodgson, the pole man once more, fell on lap two of race one, on the first significant left, Curva del Carro. Losing the front in an instant, he only lost the plot momentarily, returning for a superb joust with Xaus in race two. Finishing on the rough end of that one, nevertheless he courageously chose risk over restraint. Just like Xaus.

Arguably, the races were won and lost on the seemingly never-ending, long triple lefts on to the back straight, Xaus pulling off the remarkable trick of running inside the other riders, yet at a faster pace and with a superior exit speed.

Before the tyre melting races had even started, there was conflagration. Wild card Christian Zaiser's ride at Misano began badly when his Aprilia set itself ablaze on the start line; he hopped over the barrier to escape the seaside barbecue.

Once under way, the track action was a pleasing mix of telescoping fortunes, some riders starting well and fading, others coming into the game as the laps timed out.

The second-string Ducati machines got some good coverage for their sponsors, with Laconi, Chili and Toseland all taking the lead in one race or other, even if Frankie was to crash out of race one, suffering a good old-fashioned highsider.

A broken fuel line on Toseland's 998 F02 dropped him to third in the title race, as Xaus got motoring.

After some impressive recent postings, Lavilla was fourth and then fifth, suffering the after-effects of a hard crash in qualifying. He was almost eclipsed by another purple and yellow Alstare Suzuki, European Superstock Champion Vittorio Iannuzzo securing seventh on a far-from-factory GSX-R, albeit run by the factory team.

There were the usual dramas for the Petronas team. Haydon was hurt in a pre-race accident, and local rider Lorenzo Mauri, who took over for the weekend, suffered a horrible left tibial plate fracture in qualifying, blanching the complexions of the battle-hardened Clinica Mobile staff.

Corser, whose FP-1 was running at merely gas mark nine-point-five, thanks to myriad small steps in the cooling and exhaust systems, left Misano in great haste – seventh- and tenth-place finishes in his pocket – to be at the birth of his first child.

In the heat, Dunlop had proved to have some sort of solution again. But as far as tyre news was concerned, we'd heard nothing yet. That was coming at the next round, across the Atlantic horizon.

LAGUNA SECA

LAGUNA is at once revered and feared by the regular Superbike riders. The reverence is understandable, the 3.610-km circuit being one of the most intense riding experiences imaginable, and not just because of the breathtaking Corkscrew.

The fear is partly down to the circuit's reputation for incident, and partly to the strength of the local wild cards, led this time around by Mat Mladin and his Yoshimura Suzuki.

The wild cards, as it turned out, were all they could have been in qualifying, but not quite so formidable over the entire race distance. Tyres, fatigue, and the simple fact that the SBK regulars are a quick and tough bunch at any track took their toll on the American threat, which was blunted to the point that Mladin decided not to contest race two.

His favourite sport in qualifying had been Hodgson baiting, even if he did deny deliberately going out in company with the world champ elect and passing at will on almost any part of the track. Hodgson got his own back on race day, with two second places to Mladin's single fourth.

Xaus, again like Hodgson having dirt-bound dramas in qualifying, was the

convincing leader of race one, at least until he crashed. He blamed the fall on easing off, not pushing too hard, as once more he found he had to walk the tightrope of the 999's front tyre grip.

In race two, he reasserted his resurgence, running out the clear winner to make three full-pointers from four races.

Having slid away from Xaus, race one came under the influence of the two-year-old Ducati of 39-year-old Pierfrancesco Chili. His sixth podium of the year was the top step, but a matching six DNFs were completed in race two as he highsided out of contention. Frankie's form and his erratic machine reliability were holding him down in seventh overall, but the man himself was a potent threat to any and every podium.

Race day started with some expected Laguna slapstick, made sharper by the edge that only racing motor cycles can bring. Chili, Hodgson, Corser and Eric Bostrom (Kawasaki) were all sucked into a crash after Aaron Yates (Yoshimura Suzuki) fell at turn one. Yates clipped the apex, hit Chili, and the dominos started dropping. Bostrom was forced to withdraw with a dislocated right shoulder and a compressed thorax.

Four riders led the restart, although early pace man Laconi was to dip off the diving board, crashing on what he reckoned was fairing debris from the earlier carnage.

Lap speeds and race times were below those of 2002, race two being slower than race one. Track conditions played a part: 53-degree C temperature in the afternoon equalled the season high set at Misano.

Walker took fifth in race one and was an aggressive podium finisher in race two, making sure that the wild cards did not get a top three.

Hodgson had an eventful race two, after being passed decisively by a flying Toseland; he ran off the track to avoid his young compatriot's subsequent crash. Hodgson rejoined in fifth and fought through to second again.

Lavilla, a faller in race one, put 'tired' absentee Suzuki rider Mladin in an awkward position by finishing fifth in race two, beaten-up ribs and all.

Thankfully, the all-action heats at Laguna offered a potent distraction from the politics and recriminations that followed two major announcements. From within SBK, Paolo Flammini announced that Pirelli would be the one-make tyre supplier in 2004, to surprise and dismay. At the same time, the MSMA released a decree that none of the major Japanese factories, nor Aprilia, would be running their awesome new Superbikes in SBK in 2004.

This double strike would change everything from now on. Except the racing.

Round 8
LAGUNA SECA, USA
13 July, 2.243-mile/3.610-km circuit

Race 1 28 laps, 62.804 miles/101.080 km

Pl.	Name	Nat	Machine	No.	Time & gap	Laps
1	Pierfrancesco Chili	I	Ducati	7	40m 35.653s	28
					92.833 mph/149.401 km/h	
2	Neil Hodgson	GB	Ducati	100	3.068s	28
3	James Toseland	GB	Ducati	52	6.072s	28
4	Mat Mladin	AUS	Suzuki	66	12.322s	28
5	Chris Walker	GB	Ducati	9	21.605s	28
6	Aaron Yates	USA	Suzuki	120	21.891s	28
7	Giovanni Bussei	I	Ducati	15	27.068s	28
8	Troy Corser	AUS	Petronas	4	49.287s	28
9	Mauro Sanchini	I	Kawasaki	6	49.679s	28
10	Marco Borciani	I	Ducati	20	50.261s	28
11	Juan Borja	E	Ducati	33	1m 17.878s	28
12	Walter Tortoroglio	I	Honda	91	1 lap	27
13	Luca Pedersoli	I	Ducati	26	1 lap	27

DNF: Gregorio Lavilla, E (Suzuki) 10, 22 laps; Regis Laconi, F (Ducati) 55, 16 laps; Ruben Xaus, E (Ducati) 11, 11 laps; Steve Martin, AUS (Ducati) 99, 11 laps; Lucio Pedercini, I (Ducati) 19, 11 laps; David Garcia, E (Ducati) 48, 4 laps; Jiri Mrkyvka, CZ (Ducati) 23, 4 laps; James Haydon, GB (Petronas) 8, 1 lap; Ivan Clementi, I (Kawasaki) 5, 1 lap.

DNS: Eric Bostrom, USA (Kawasaki) 32.

Fastest lap: Laconi, 1m 26.023s, 93.874 mph/151.076 km/h.

Race 2 28 laps, 62.804 miles/101.080 km

Pl.	Name	Nat.	Machine	No.	Time & gap	Laps
1	Ruben Xaus	E	Ducati	11	40m 43.876s	28
					92.521 mph/148.898 km/h	
2	Neil Hodgson	GB	Ducati	100	11.565s	28
3	Chris Walker	GB	Ducati	9	13.064s	28
4	Regis Laconi	F	Ducati	55	15.560s	28
5	Gregorio Lavilla	E	Suzuki	10	16.354s	28
6	Giovanni Bussei	I	Ducati	15	19.685s	28
7	Juan Borja	E	Ducati	33	33.494s	28
8	Mauro Sanchini	I	Kawasaki	6	35.564s	28
9	Marco Borciani	I	Ducati	20	35.859s	28
10	Lucio Pedercini	I	Ducati	19	39.330s	28

DNF: Ivan Clementi, I (Kawasaki) 5, 27 laps; Aaron Yates, USA (Suzuki) 120, 24 laps; James Toseland, GB (Ducati) 52, 17 laps; Luca Pedersoli, I (Ducati) 26, 17 laps; Troy Corser, AUS (Petronas) 4, 14 laps; Jiri Mrkyvka, CZ (Ducati) 23, 4 laps; James Haydon, GB (Petronas) 8, 3 laps; Walter Tortoroglio, I (Honda) 91, 3 laps; David Garcia, E (Ducati) 48, 2 laps; Steve Martin, AUS (Ducati) 99, 0 laps; Pierfrancesco Chili, I (Ducati) 7, 0 laps.

DNS: Eric Bostrom, USA (Kawasaki) 32; Mat Mladin, AUS (Suzuki) 66.

Fastest lap: Xaus, 1m 26.451s, 93.409 mph/150.328 km/h.

Superpole: Mladin, 1m 25.561s, 94.381 mph/151.892 km/h.

Lap record: Noriyuki Haga, J (Aprilia), 1m 25.475s, 94.476 mph 152.044 km/h (2002).

Championship points: 1 Hodgson, 355; 2 Xaus, 233; 3 Toseland, 201; 4 Laconi, 187; 5 Lavilla, 166; 6 Walker, 156; 7 Chili, 143; 8 Martin, 95; 9 Borciani, 93; 10 Pedercini, 91; 11 Sanchini, 68; 12 Corser, 64; 13 Borja, 55; 14 Bussei, 52; 15 Clementi, 39.

Above far left: Chili took his private Ducati to his first win in race one at Laguna.

Above left: Chris Walker, rostrum bound again.

Left: Toseland took the lead off Hodgson and soon afterward fell at the Corkscrew. Hodgson's evasive action dropped him to fifth.
All photographs: Gold & Goose

Round 9
BRANDS HATCH, Great Britain
27 July, 2.608-mile/4.197-km circuit

Race 1 25 laps, 65.200 miles/104.925 km

Pl.	Name	Nat.	Machine	No.	Time & gap	Laps
1	Shane Byrne	GB	Ducati	67	36m 25.400s	25
					107.400 mph/172.843 km/h	
2	Neil Hodgson	GB	Ducati	100	5.799s	25
3	Chris Walker	GB	Ducati	9	5.918s	25
4	Regis Laconi	F	Ducati	55	6.808s	25
5	Sean Emmett	GB	Ducati	62	9.663s	25
6	James Toseland	GB	Ducati	52	9.926s	25
7	Gregorio Lavilla	E	Suzuki	10	10.370s	25
8	Michael Rutter	GB	Ducati	60	32.465s	25
9	Pierfrancesco Chili	I	Ducati	7	32.724s	25
10	Yukio Kagayama	J	Suzuki	64	36.218s	25
11	Dean Ellison	GB	Ducati	89	45.798s	25
12	Juan Borja	E	Ducati	33	52.302s	25
13	Ivan Clementi	I	Kawasaki	5	53.241s	25
14	Steve Martin	AUS	Ducati	99	54.176s	25
15	Mauro Sanchini	I	Kawasaki	6	1m 09.534s	25
16	Alessandro Gramigni	I	Yamaha	39	1m 11.592s	25
17	James Haydon	GB	Petronas	8	1m 30.467s	25
18	Giancarlo de Matteis	I	Ducati	38	1 lap	24
19	Luca Pedersoli	I	Ducati	26	1 lap	24

DNF: Troy Corser, AUS (Petronas) 4, 22 laps; Ruben Xaus, E (Ducati) 11, 15 laps; Marco Borciani, I (Ducati) 20, 13 laps; Leon Haslam, GB (Ducati) 90, 13 laps; John Reynolds, GB (Suzuki) 61, 11 laps; Sergio Fuertes, E (Suzuki) 16, 11 laps; Lucio Pedercini, I (Ducati) 19, 9 laps; Walter Tortoroglio, I (Honda) 91, 9 laps; Nick Medd, GB (Ducati) 40, 7 laps; Jiri Mrkyvka, CZ (Ducati) 23, 3 laps.

Fastest lap: Byrne, 1m 26.755s, 108.217 mph/174.159 km/h (record).

Race 2 25 laps, 65.200 miles/104.925 km

Pl.	Name	Nat.	Machine	No.	Time & gap	Laps
1	Shane Byrne	GB	Ducati	67	36m 25.639s	25
					107.388 mph/172.824 km/h	
2	John Reynolds	GB	Suzuki	61	0.539s	25
3	James Toseland	GB	Ducati	52	2.891s	25
4	Ruben Xaus	E	Ducati	11	4.862s	25
5	Neil Hodgson	GB	Ducati	100	5.804s	25
6	Gregorio Lavilla	E	Suzuki	10	9.493s	25
7	Pierfrancesco Chili	I	Ducati	7	16.049s	25
8	Regis Laconi	F	Ducati	55	17.771s	25
9	Yukio Kagayama	J	Suzuki	64	29.290s	25
10	Leon Haslam	GB	Ducati	90	31.484s	25
11	Alessandro Gramigni	I	Yamaha	39	1m 02.420s	25
12	Dean Ellison	GB	Ducati	89	1m 02.453s	25
13	Ivan Clementi	I	Kawasaki	5	1m 02.749s	25
14	Marco Borciani	I	Ducati	20	1m 03.308s	25
15	Mauro Sanchini	I	Kawasaki	6	1m 07.499s	25
16	Lucio Pedercini	I	Ducati	19	1m 16.220s	25
17	Sergio Fuertes	E	Suzuki	16	1 lap	24

DNF: Michael Rutter, GB (Ducati) 60, 21 laps; Juan Borja, E (Ducati) 33, 17 laps; Chris Walker, GB (Ducati) 9, 14 laps; Nick Medd, GB (Ducati) 40, 13 laps; Jiri Mrkyvka, CZ (Ducati) 23, 9 laps; Walter Tortoroglio, I (Honda) 91, 8 laps; Steve Martin, AUS (Ducati) 99, 7 laps; Luca Pedersoli, I (Ducati) 26, 7 laps; Sean Emmett, GB (Ducati) 62, 6 laps; Troy Corser, AUS (Petronas) 4, 3 laps; James Haydon, GB (Petronas) 8, 2 laps; Giancarlo de Matteis, I (Ducati) 38, 1 lap.

Fastest lap: Reynolds, 1m 26.767s, 108.202 mph/174.135 km/h.

Superpole: Reynolds, 1m 35.706s, 98.096 mph/157.871 km/h.

Previous circuit record: Troy Bayliss, AUS (Ducati), 1m 26.690s, 108.918 mph/175.287 km/h (2002).

Championship points: 1 Hodgson, 386; 2 Xaus, 246; 3 Toseland, 227; 4 Laconi, 208; 5 Lavilla, 185; 6 Walker, 172; 7 Chili, 159; 8 Martin, 97; 9 Borciani, 95; 10 Pedercini, 91; 11 Sanchini, 70; 12 Corser, 64; 13 Borja, 59; 14 Bussei, 52; 15 Byrne, 50.

Above right: Wild-card wonder. Kentishman Shane Byrne used track knowledge and sheer talent to claim two race wins at Brands. Fellow BSB racer John Reynolds was a close second in race two.

Photograph: Gold & Goose

BRANDS HATCH

ONE of the delights of Superbike racing at a global level is that national riders can join the party for the weekend. There is a long list of riders who have come to prominence at their home SBK round, and 2003 saw another name added to that roll of honour.

Kentishman Shane Byrne had enjoyed intimate home-track knowledge since his club racing days, while rain left the SBK regulars short of dry practice time. The Monstermob Ducati rider added wise tyre choices and ripped the SBK field asunder.

The cantankerous old circuit had changed a bit since Byrne was a novice, and for 2003 it shrank to 4.197 km after modifications at the renamed Sheene corner. The teeth had been drawn from the old Dingle Dell.

With the Xaus express derailed temporarily, and Hodgson second and then fifth, it was left to Toseland and Walker to salvage the regulars' pride with a third-place finish apiece.

The remaining podium slot, second in race two, went to the big Suzuki of John Reynolds, the only rider who looked like upsetting Byrne's apple-cart in front of another big Brands race-day attendance. Fewer on Saturday and Friday, but the weather behaved badly for the first couple of days.

Considering that Byrne had missed the Silverstone meeting, his double win was all the more unexpected. But he'd not needed to do any homework on the opposition, setting the new lap record of 1m 26.755s on lap 13 of the first leg.

In race one, Superpole winner and early leader Reynolds was in contention for second when his bike developed a fault, and he dropped away. In the second 25-lapper, Byrne was gently pressured by Reynolds all the way, winning by 0.5 second in an all-English summer afternoon.

Swapping results with team-mate Walker, Toseland scored third in the second outing, out-slugging a somewhat troubled Xaus. Mechanical retirement and then tyre problems were enough to keep him off the podiums, his mood not improved by being captive in the Three Lions' cage. Fighting Hodgson, Walker and Toseland every week was hard enough, even if most have a soft spot for the big brawling X-man.

After the ground-breaking appearance of three Brits on a podium at Oschersleben, the feat was repeated not once, but twice, at Brands: Byrne, Hodgson, Walker; Byrne, Reynolds, Toseland.

Hodgson's second in race one came from a level of nervous energy he normally reins in convincingly. Unquestionably, he felt pressured by talk of winning the title on home ground. He needn't have worried unduly, and it was a long shot anyway.

Laconi secured fourth in race one, despite the suspicion that he had jumped the start; in race two, Sean Emmett (ETI Ducati) did just that, getting his spon-

sors on TV for a time, before pulling out of the race to take his penalty. His pace was good for half a dozen laps in any case.

Lavilla scored sixth in an ultimately lonely second race, with Chili seventh, 16 seconds behind the leader.

Laconi, Yukio Kagayama and Leon Haslam seized the last places in the top ten, Kagayama perhaps simply being all raced out after his recent travails for Suzuki in three different series.

Byrne left Brands as the fifth race winner of the season, while Reynolds added his name to the Superpole list.

We were lucky to be racing in such good conditions, given the wet weather in qualifying and the paucity of dry testing time. The only problem was that as we left the UK for Assen, Hodgson had a 140-point lead over Xaus, with only a possible 150 points left in total, assuming Xaus won all the rest.

ASSEN

AFTER the overwhelming joy of becoming a father shortly before Assen, Hodgson's Dutch weekend away was not turning out according to his perfect pre-race plan. He awoke on race day disappointed to have lost out on what had seemed a sure pole position the day before, Chili having belied the odds against his level-three Ducati to score Superpole convincingly – with a time only a second slower than the best of the MotoGP boys earlier in the year. Not bad for a 39-year-old rider and his positively arcane 'street bike'. Notch up another new 2003 Superpole winner.

The weather on race day was foggy and less than hopeful, another reason for Hodgson to be somewhat wary.

With the World Championship itself at stake, prudence and the long view could have been expected from Hodgson during the first 16-lapper. On the evidence of the early exchanges in that contest, the nerves of the heir apparent were jangling a bit, but certainly he and his only possible assailant, Xaus, rode like a pair of recklessly unsure novices – one lap tentative, the next explosive, frequently making mistakes and trying too hard to outdo each other.

It was a four-rider first run at the front in any case, with Toseland and eventual third-placed Chili hanging on to the tantalisingly close exhausts of the works bikes. The large crowd was treated to a full-on display of aggression and only ephemeral race craft from the top two, and the contest increased in desperation at the tail end, as Xaus ran out the winner by 0.609 second.

It made no difference, however, as Hodgson secured his first World Championship with fully five races remaining. Not a scenario Xaus would have predicted pre-season, but one Hodgson may have envisaged in private.

The new champion's slow-down-lap celebrations – wearing the cheeky T-shirt message, 'Who's Your Daddy?' – put the many Brits in the crowd in nostalgic mood for the numerous post-race triumphs demonstrated by Carl

Fogarty in years past. The Lancashire sanction had scored another direct hit, although Hodgson was icing a cake that many were already saying wasn't as sweet or had fewer important ingredients.

In race two, it got even better, Hodgson taking revenge with his 12th full-pointer of the year. It proved to be a race ten seconds faster than the first, maybe thanks to 34-degree C track temperatures, up by fully ten degrees.

Xaus finished a close second to Hodgson, and a second Spanish flag came in useful for the podium celebrations, Lavilla having recovered from a crash to take third, seven seconds behind the warring Fila faction, but seven ahead of experienced Assen runner Laconi. The Frenchman's first race was a shambles, returning to the pit lane for repairs, but crossing the line into his pit box. This meant the black flag when he headed back out after the problem had been fixed.

In race one, aft of Toseland, Walker took fifth place. Behind him, an outstanding ride from Corser and the cooler running FP-1 triple took sixth, plus some much-needed self-respect and measurable progress for the team and its big-name sponsor.

Laconi scored fourth in race two, while Chili, again the hero of one race at least, was fifth. Young Brit Leon Haslam had an excellent ride to sixth, a contrast to Silverstone and Brands hero John Reynolds, who struggled all weekend with race suspension settings.

Round 10
ASSEN, Holland
7 September, 3.745-mile/6.027-km circuit

Race 1 16 laps, 59.920 miles/96.432 km

Pl.	Name	Nat.	Machine	No.	Time & gap	Laps
1	Ruben Xaus	E	Ducati	11	33m 07.249s	16
					108.548 mph/174.691 km/h	
2	Neil Hodgson	GB	Ducati	100	0.609s	16
3	Pierfrancesco Chili	I	Ducati	7	0.835s	16
4	James Toseland	GB	Ducati	52	1.062s	16
5	Chris Walker	GB	Ducati	9	14.737s	16
6	Troy Corser	AUS	Petronas	4	22.981s	16
7	Leon Haslam	GB	Ducati	90	23.118s	16
8	Ivan Clementi	I	Kawasaki	5	23.350s	16
9	Steve Martin	AUS	Ducati	99	45.862s	16
10	Mauro Sanchini	I	Kawasaki	6	54.164s	16
11	Alessandro Gramigni	I	Yamaha	39	1m 05.147s	16
12	Lucio Pedercini	I	Ducati	19	1m 39.774s	16
13	Horst Saiger	A	Yamaha	22	1m 51.449s	16
14	Gianmaria Liverani	I	Yamaha	98	1m 51.917s	16
15	Jiri Mrkvyka	CZ	Ducati	23	1m 52.416s	16
16	Robert Menzen	NL	Suzuki	41	1 lap	15
17	Paul Mooijman	NL	Suzuki	42	1 lap	15

DNF: Luca Pedersoli, I (Ducati) 26, 9 laps; Marco Borciani, I (Ducati) 20, 8 laps; Regis Laconi, F (Ducati) 55, 8 laps; Gregorio Lavilla, E (Suzuki) 10, 4 laps; John Reynolds, GB (Suzuki) 61, 3 laps; Walter Tortoroglio, I (Honda) 91, 3 laps; Stefan Nebel, D (Suzuki) 44, 3 laps; Juan Borja, E (Ducati) 33, 1 lap; Karl Truchsess, A (Yamaha) 69, 1 lap; Sergio Fuertes, E (Suzuki) 16, 1 lap.

Fastest lap: Lavilla, 2m 03.081s, 109.538 mph/176.284 km/h.

Race 2 16 laps, 59.920 miles/96.432 km

Pl.	Name	Nat.	Machine	No.	Time & gap	Laps
1	Neil Hodgson	GB	Ducati	100	32m 57.759s	16
					109.069 mph/175.530 km/h	
2	Ruben Xaus	E	Ducati	11	0.466s	16
3	Gregorio Lavilla	E	Suzuki	10	7.799s	16
4	Regis Laconi	F	Ducati	55	14.884s	16
5	Pierfrancesco Chili	I	Ducati	7	19.868s	16
6	Leon Haslam	GB	Ducati	90	27.997s	16
7	Ivan Clementi	I	Kawasaki	5	39.006s	16
8	Chris Walker	GB	Ducati	9	41.568s	16
9	Troy Corser	AUS	Petronas	4	43.155s	16
10	John Reynolds	GB	Suzuki	61	48.883s	16
11	Steve Martin	AUS	Ducati	99	57.319s	16
12	Mauro Sanchini	I	Kawasaki	6	1m 06.208s	16
13	Marco Borciani	I	Ducati	20	1m 08.487s	16
14	Lucio Pedercini	I	Ducati	19	1m 15.103s	16
15	Alessandro Gramigni	I	Yamaha	39	1m 27.128s	16
16	Juan Borja	E	Ducati	33	1m 40.984s	16
17	Stefan Nebel	D	Suzuki	44	1m 48.254s	16
18	Robert Menzen	NL	Suzuki	41	2m 00.048s	16
19	Gianmaria Liverani	I	Yamaha	98	2m 03.548s	16
20	Karl Truchsess	A	Yamaha	69	2m 13.852s	16
21	Paul Mooijman	NL	Suzuki	42	1 lap	15

DNF: James Toseland, GB (Ducati) 52, 14 laps; Luca Pedersoli, I (Ducati) 26, 14 laps; Horst Saiger, A (Yamaha) 22, 13 laps; Sergio Fuertes, E (Suzuki) 16, 6 laps; Jiri Mrkyvka, CZ (Ducati) 23, 0 laps.

DNS: Walter Tortoroglio, I (Honda) 91.

Fastest lap: Hodgson, 2m 02.649s, 109.924 mph/176.905 km/h.

Superpole: Chili, 2m 00.874s, 111.538 mph/179.503 km/h.

Lap record: Colin Edwards, USA (Honda), 2m 02.395s, 110.152 mph 177.272 km/h (2002).

Championship points: 1 Hodgson, 431; 2 Xaus, 291; 3 Toseland, 240; 4 Laconi, 221; 5 Lavilla, 201; 6 Walker, 191; 7 Chili, 186; 8 Martin, 109; 9 Borciani, 98; 10 Pedercini, 97; 11 Corser, 81; 12 Sanchini, 80; 13 Clementi, 62; 14 Borja, 59; 15 Bussei, 52.

Above left: Lavilla overcame a first-race spill to regain the rostrum in the second.

Left: Newly crowned champion Neil Hodgson took '99' off his number for Assen's race two. Team-mate Xaus leads the pursuit.

Both photographs: Gold & Goose

173

Round 11
IMOLA, Italy
28 September, 3.065-mile/4.933-km circuit

Race 1 21 laps, 64.365 miles/103.593 km

Pl.	Name	Nat.	Machine	No.	Time & gap	Laps
1	Ruben Xaus	E	Ducati	11	38m 30.586s	21
					100.291 mph/161.403 km/h	
2	Neil Hodgson	GB	Ducati	100	2.793s	21
3	Regis Laconi	F	Ducati	55	8.778s	21
4	Gregorio Lavilla	E	Suzuki	10	32.344s	21
5	Pierfrancesco Chili	I	Ducati	7	37.382s	21
6	Steve Martin	AUS	Ducati	99	39.576s	21
7	Troy Corser	AUS	Petronas	4	50.840s	21
8	Mauro Sanchini	I	Kawasaki	6	1m 00.616s	21
9	Ivan Clementi	I	Kawasaki	5	1m 01.306s	21
10	Marco Borciani	I	Ducati	20	1m 09.525s	21
11	Juan Borja	E	Ducati	33	1m 10.844s	21
12	David Garcia	E	Ducati	48	1m 21.015s	21
13	Alessandro Gramigni	I	Yamaha	39	1m 29.975s	21
14	Sergio Fuertes	E	Suzuki	16	1m 33.884s	21
15	Luca Pini	I	Suzuki	96	1m 44.014s	21
16	Giuseppe Zannini	I	Ducati	29	1 lap	20
17	Horst Saiger	A	Yamaha	22	1 lap	20
18	Walter Tortoroglio	I	Honda	91	1 lap	20
19	Luca Pedersoli	I	Ducati	26	1 lap	20
20	Gianmaria Liverani	I	Yamaha	98	1 lap	20
21	Simone Conti	I	Suzuki	57	1 lap	20

DNF: Lucio Pedercini, I (Ducati) 19, 13 laps; Lorenzo Mauri, I (Ducati) 82, 13 laps; Chris Walker, GB (Ducati) 9, 11 laps; James Haydon, GB (Petronas) 8, 5 laps; James Toseland, GB (Ducati) 52, 1 lap; Jiri Mrkyvka, CZ (Ducati) 23, 1 lap.

Fastest lap: Hodgson, 1m 49.317s, 100.943 mph/162.452 km/h.

Race 2 21 laps, 64.365 miles/103.593 km

Pl.	Name	Nat.	Machine	No.	Time & gap	Laps
1	Ruben Xaus	E	Ducati	11	38m 29.867s	21
					100.322 mph/161.453 km/h	
2	Regis Laconi	F	Ducati	55	12.038s	21
3	Gregorio Lavilla	E	Suzuki	10	15.741s	21
4	Neil Hodgson	GB	Ducati	100	24.846s	21
5	Chris Walker	GB	Ducati	9	25.952s	21
6	Lucio Pedercini	I	Ducati	19	51.778s	21
7	Troy Corser	AUS	Petronas	4	55.582s	21
8	Mauro Sanchini	I	Kawasaki	6	1m 00.859s	21
9	Juan Borja	E	Ducati	33	1m 03.424s	21
10	David Garcia	E	Ducati	48	1m 17.924s	21
11	Marco Borciani	I	Ducati	20	1m 31.807s	21
12	Alessandro Gramigni	I	Yamaha	39	1m 34.712s	21
13	Sergio Fuertes	E	Suzuki	16	1m 43.592s	21
14	Horst Saiger	A	Yamaha	22	1 lap	20
15	Luca Pini	I	Suzuki	96	1 lap	20
16	Walter Tortoroglio	I	Honda	91	1 lap	20
17	Simone Conti	I	Suzuki	57	1 lap	20

DNF: James Toseland, GB (Ducati) 52, 15 laps; Gianmaria Liverani, I (Yamaha) 98, 14 laps; Pierfrancesco Chili, I (Ducati) 7, 12 laps; Giuseppe Zannini, I (Ducati) 29, 11 laps; Lorenzo Mauri, I (Ducati) 82, 9 laps; Ivan Clementi, I (Kawasaki) 5, 14 laps; Luca Pedersoli, I (Ducati) 26, 6 laps; James Haydon, GB (Petronas) 8, 5 laps; Jiri Mrkyvka, CZ (Ducati) 23, 1 lap; Steve Martin, AUS (Ducati) 99, 1 lap.

Fastest lap: Xaus, 1m 49.181s, 101.069 mph/162.655 km/h.

Superpole: Xaus, 1m 48.636s, 101.576 mph/163.471 km/h.

Lap record: Troy Bayliss, AUS (Ducati), 1m 48.389s, 101.807 mph 163.843 km/h (2002).

Championship points: 1 Hodgson, 464; 2 Xaus, 341; 3 Laconi, 257; 4 Toseland, 240; 5 Lavilla, 230; 6 Walker, 202; 7 Chili, 197; 8 Martin, 119; 9 Borciani, 109; 10 Pedercini, 107; 11 Corser, 99; 12 Sanchini, 96; 13 Borja, 71; 14 Clementi, 69; 15 Bussei, 52.

Above right: Hodgson leads Xaus through Imola's crucial last chicane. At the finish, the positions were reversed.

Photograph: Gold & Goose

IMOLA

XAUS was finally finding his racing boots to be the right size and shape to kick down all barriers to another pair of wins, this time at the scene of one of his first ever SBK race victories, in 2001.

With the championship finished and Xaus almost safe in second, the first race was a real arm-wrestle between Fila team-mates Xaus and Hodgson, the gallant but outfoxed new champion.

Did we mention the determined Hodgson? A pass by Xaus was riposted with some vigour, as Hodgson block-passed entering Tosa, but it was Xaus in the lead as the last lap approached.

In the downhill luge run approaching the double lefts of Rivazza, the raging bull and the rabid bulldog squeezed themselves impossibly close to a pair of backmarkers, by necessity. Xaus cleverly used his line to block Hodgson's last-corner lunges, but choosing potential disaster before dishonour, Hodgson attempted to make up for his imperfect tight line with an early throttle application and almost highsided out, leaving Xaus enough of a gap to escape to victory.

A similarly ruthless second race led Hodgson into an error as he outbraked himself into Tosa, chattering across the gravel as three riders went past. Hodgson did reel in Walker shortly before the end, and to his credit had shown he was determined to put on a win-or-bust display.

The shadowing Laconi, slipping back by eight seconds at the end of race one, was third; rival Chili had the ride of his life to fifth after starting from the pit lane when his machine stalled on the line.

Laconi whipped himself into second in race two, Lavilla taking third, but the former's double podium gained him third overall, after rival Toseland left Italy with no additional points. The young Briton had suffered a broken gear linkage in race one and a big highside in the second while attempting a rash pass on his tormentor, Laconi.

Corser proved that the upturn in Foggy Petronas fortunes was more than one race deep, securing two sevenths among the plethora of Imola chicanes.

The biggest story of the weekend, however, was not Xaus's double win or Hodgson's double error, or even the unexpected swap of third overall from Toseland to Laconi. It was the rubber wars, for the umpteenth time in the season.

In race two, Michelin lined up their big guns, Xaus and Hodgson, along with their key rivals, with what appeared to be cut slicks on the rear of the 999s, even though there was no real change in the dry track conditions. What were they up to?

According to the tyre manufacturer, it was the first use of the kind of tyres they had intended to run in Supersport in 2004, had they not been denied the chance by the FGSport/Pirelli tie-up. Production tyres of a sort, if you like.

Later, a Pirelli spokesman said that they looked more like cut slicks, made to resemble DOT Michelin tread patterns, but with tell-tale chalk marks applied to guide the blade when cutting the grooves.

Whatever the facts of the matter, it was a well-directed message that achieved maximum impact, especially as in a pre-race press conference, Pirelli spokesmen had stated that using DOT-spec tyres in Superbike was not an option.

MAGNY-COURS

CONTRARY to much pre-race publicity, France had hosted SBK in the past, at Magny-Cours even, way back in the first development cycle of the series. Maybe it was appropriate that the send-off to what FGSport described as the old life of World Superbike would take place at a nominally new track, in a country with every reason to embrace FGSport and kiss both SBK and Supersport cheeks with Gallic warmth. After all, nearly half the Supersport field speaks French as a first or close second language.

The wisdom of running a race in mid-France in October had been questioned the second the idea had been mentioned. The possibility of rain was not the problem, but rather the bone-chilling overnight temperatures, which hardly improved until the afternoon sun drove them to lurk in the shadows of the impressively proportioned Magny-Cours facility.

Nice function, shame about the form, said many through chattering teeth. The cold surface in qualifying sent crash numbers soaring after a period of sense and sensibility.

On race day, the early morning mists looked as ominous as those at Assen, but it all went ahead almost on schedule. With tyre warmers working overtime, the track temperature a positively Antarctic 17 degrees C, rising to a race-two high of 21, there was a plethora of punt-offs, and only 15 finishers in race one.

The first of them was Hodgson, reasserting his authority over the proceedings, despite the bizarre experience of his boot coming loose half-way through the race. He crashed a couple of hours later while tailing sparring partner Xaus, who went on to win race two at a ten-second canter from Toseland and Walker.

Xaus had secured second in race one, and a bout of last-meeting adrenalin (with a weekend of fast laps behind him) put Walker on the podium twice, with two thirds.

Toseland had better reason to be happy with a race-two second, not only winning a wonderful battle with Walker, but also out-pointing Laconi on the day and in the championship overall, securing his third place after appearing to have lost it at Imola. Was he happy? Was he happier than he had been with his first Superpole for his departing GSE Racing Team? Was he even happier than being given a factory Ducati contract for 2004 (alongside Laconi, of course) the day before qualifying started?

We can only assume that his first-race fifth with a fading tyre and that second were enough to leave him on a high until the 2004 season-opener at Valencia on 29 February.

Rides of the day, however, came from Xaus, who had qualified eighth. He ripped up the track to a close second behind Hodgson in race one, then went a second faster overall in race two. Seven wins in the last 12 attempts, but where had he been in the previous 12, when Hodgson was effectively winning the title on the same bike? Xaus's enigma code remained unbroken.

For Laconi, so keen to hold on to second place and have at least a podium on home soil, race one proved a disaster; he blamed his rear Dunlop for dropping him to sixth after running up front for a while. He stopped for a new rear in race two, and 16th left him four points behind Toseland in the final standings.

Lavilla also ended his season with no podiums and fifth overall, ahead of Walker and double-DNF man Chili.

Round 12
MAGNY-COURS, France
19 October, 2.741-mile/4.411-km circuit

Race 1 23 laps, 63.043 miles/101.453 km

Pl.	Name	Nat.	Machine	No.	Time & gap	Laps
1	Neil Hodgson	GB	Ducati	100	39m 03.738s	23
					96.830 mph/155.833 km/h	
2	Ruben Xaus	E	Ducati	11	0.348s	23
3	Chris Walker	GB	Ducati	9	13.711s	23
4	Gregorio Lavilla	E	Suzuki	10	13.950s	23
5	James Toseland	GB	Ducati	52	21.480s	23
6	Regis Laconi	F	Ducati	55	32.420s	23
7	Steve Martin	AUS	Ducati	99	41.098s	23
8	Troy Corser	AUS	Petronas	4	41.204s	23
9	Juan Borja	E	Ducati	33	1m 18.737s	23
10	Mauro Sanchini	I	Kawasaki	6	1m 30.317s	23
11	Sergio Fuertes	E	Suzuki	16	1m 46.534s	23
12	Christian Zaiser	A	Suzuki	70	1m 48.154s	23
13	Bertrand Stey	F	Honda	68	1 lap	22
14	Frédéric Protat	F	Yamaha	92	1 lap	22
15	Horst Saiger	A	Yamaha	22	1 lap	22

DNF: Pierfrancesco Chili, I (Ducati) 7, 20 laps; Marco Borciani, I (Ducati) 20, 19 laps; Alessandro Gramigni, I (Yamaha) 39, 18 laps; Leon Haslam, GB (Ducati) 90, 9 laps; Lucio Pedercini, I (Ducati) 19, 2 laps; David Garcia, E (Ducati) 48, 2 laps; Sébastien Gimbert, F (Suzuki) 93, 1 lap; Ivan Clementi, I (Kawasaki) 5, 0 laps; James Haydon, GB (Ducati) 8, 0 laps.

Fastest lap: Hodgson, 1m 41.227s, 97.475 mph/156.871 km/h (record).

Race 2 23 laps, 63.043 miles/101.453 km

Pl.	Name	Nat.	Machine	No.	Time & gap	Laps
1	Ruben Xaus	E	Ducati	11	39m 02.330s	23
					96.888 mph/155.926 km/h	
2	James Toseland	GB	Ducati	52	10.435s	23
3	Chris Walker	GB	Ducati	9	10.582s	23
4	Gregorio Lavilla	E	Suzuki	10	22.253s	23
5	Steve Martin	AUS	Ducati	99	35.564s	23
6	Leon Haslam	GB	Ducati	90	35.865s	23
7	Juan Borja	E	Ducati	33	56.719s	23
8	Sébastien Gimbert	F	Suzuki	93	1m 00.813s	23
9	Ivan Clementi	I	Kawasaki	5	1m 02.307s	23
10	Mauro Sanchini	I	Kawasaki	6	1m 03.456s	23
11	Lucio Pedercini	I	Ducati	19	1m 33.537s	23
12	Alessandro Gramigni	I	Yamaha	39	1m 41.234s	23
13	Bertrand Stey	F	Honda	68	1 lap	22
14	Marco Borciani	I	Ducati	20	1 lap	22
15	Frédéric Protat	F	Yamaha	92	1 lap	22
16	Regis Laconi	F	Ducati	55	1 lap	22
17	Horst Saiger	A	Yamaha	22	1 lap	22

DNF: Neil Hodgson, GB (Ducati) 100, 20 laps; Sergio Fuertes, E (Suzuki) 16, 20 laps; Pierfrancesco Chili, I (Ducati) 7, 4 laps; James Haydon, GB (Petronas) 8, 4 laps; David Garcia, E (Ducati) 48, 4 laps; Christian Zaiser, A (Suzuki) 70, 0 laps; Troy Corser, AUS (Petronas) 4, 0 laps.

Fastest lap: Hodgson, 1m 41.219s, 97.483 mph/156.884 km/h (record).

Superpole: Toseland, 1m 40.965s, 97.728 mph/157.278 km/h.

Previous circuit record: Doug Polen, USA (Ducati), 1m 44.98s (1991).

Final World Championship points: See page 177.

Above left: Laconi had a disastrous day at home, losing second overall with tyre problems.

Left: Ducati cup? Toseland leads Xaus and Walker.
Both photographs: Gold & Goose

WORLD SUPERBIKE CHAMPIONSHIP RESULTS 2003

Position	Rider	Nationality	Machine	Valencia/1	Valencia/2	Phillip Island/1	Phillip Island/2	Sugo/1	Sugo/2	Monza/1	Monza/2	Oschersleben/1	Oschersleben/2	Silverstone/1	Silverstone/2	Misano/1	Misano/2	Laguna Seca/1	Laguna Seca/2	Brands Hatch/1	Brands Hatch/2	Assen/1	Assen/2	Imola/1	Imola/2	Magny-Cours/1	Magny-Cours/2	Points total
1	Neil Hodgson	GB	Ducati	25	25	25	25	25	25	25	25	25	20	25	25	–	20	20	20	20	11	20	25	20	13	25	–	489
2	Ruben Xaus	E	Ducati	20	20	20	20	13	13	9	–	–	11	16	16	25	25	–	25	–	13	25	20	25	25	20	25	386
3	James Toseland	GB	Ducati	13	16	–	11	16	11	13	11	16	25	20	13	20	–	16	–	10	16	13	–	–	–	11	20	271
4	Regis Laconi	F	Ducati	11	–	10	13	20	9	20	13	13	13	13	10	16	13	–	13	13	8	–	13	16	20	10	–	267
5	Gregorio Lavilla	E	Suzuki	9	10	16	9	11	20	16	20	–	–	–	20	13	11	–	11	9	10	–	16	13	16	13	13	256
6	Chris Walker	GB	Ducati	16	13	9	10	–	–	10	10	11	16	7	8	11	8	11	16	16	–	11	8	–	11	16	16	234
7	Pierfrancesco Chili	I	Ducati	–	–	–	16	–	16	11	16	20	5	9	9	–	16	25	–	7	9	16	11	11	–	–	–	197
8	Steve Martin	AUS	Ducati	10	11	13	7	1	–	7	9	10	10	–	–	10	7	–	–	2	–	7	5	10	–	9	11	139
9	Lucio Pedercini	I	Ducati	8	7	6	2	9	–	6	6	7	6	5	5	8	10	–	6	–	–	4	2	–	10	–	5	112
10	Marco Borciani	I	Ducati	7	6	7	6	3	3	8	8	9	7	6	3	5	2	6	7	–	2	–	3	6	5	–	2	111
11	Mauro Sanchini	I	Kawasaki	–	3	3	4	5	6	2	4	5	4	3	2	7	5	7	8	1	1	6	4	8	8	6	6	108
12	Troy Corser	AUS	Petronas	–	9	11	8	–	4	3	–	4	2	–	–	9	6	8	9	–	–	10	7	9	8	–	–	107
13	Juan Borja	E	Ducati	2	8	4	1	6	7	–	–	–	9	–	–	4	5	9	4	–	–	–	5	7	7	9	–	87
14	Ivan Clementi	I	Kawasaki	5	2	5	5	–	8	–	–	3	2	–	6	3	–	–	3	3	8	9	7	–	–	–	7	76
15	Giovanni Bussei	I	Yamaha	–	5	2	–	4	5	–	3	6	–	4	4	–	–	9	10	–	–	–	–	–	–	–	–	52
16	Shane Byrne	GB	Ducati	–	–	–	–	–	–	–	–	–	–	–	–	–	–	–	–	25	25	–	–	–	–	–	–	50
17	John Reynolds	GB	Suzuki	–	–	–	–	–	–	–	–	10	6	–	–	–	–	–	–	20	–	6	–	–	–	–	–	42
18=	Alessandro Gramigni	I	Yamaha	–	–	–	–	–	–	5	5	–	–	–	4	1	–	–	–	–	–	5	5	1	3	4	4	37
18=	Vittorio Iannuzzo	I	Suzuki	–	–	–	–	–	–	4	7	8	8	–	1	–	9	–	–	–	–	–	–	–	–	–	–	37
20=	Leon Haslam	GB	Ducati	–	–	–	–	–	–	–	–	–	–	–	–	–	–	–	–	6	9	10	–	–	–	–	10	35
20=	Yukio Kagayama	J	Suzuki	–	–	–	–	–	–	–	–	11	11	–	–	–	–	–	–	–	6	7	–	–	–	–	–	35
22	David Garcia	E	Ducati	6	4	8	–	–	–	–	–	–	–	–	–	–	–	–	–	–	–	–	–	4	6	–	–	28
23	Michael Rutter	GB	Ducati	–	–	–	–	–	–	–	–	8	7	–	–	–	–	–	–	8	–	–	–	–	–	–	–	23
24	Hitoyasu Izutsu	J	Honda	–	–	–	–	10	10	–	–	–	–	–	–	–	–	–	–	–	–	–	–	–	–	–	–	20
25	Mat Mladin	AUS	Suzuki	–	–	–	–	–	–	–	–	–	–	–	–	–	–	13	–	–	–	–	–	–	–	–	–	13
26=	Sergio Fuertes	E	Suzuki	1	–	–	–	–	–	–	–	–	–	–	1	–	–	–	–	–	–	–	–	2	3	5	–	12
26=	James Haydon	GB	Petronas	4	–	1	–	7	–	–	–	–	–	–	–	–	–	–	–	–	–	–	–	–	–	–	–	12
28=	Sean Emmett	GB	Ducati	–	–	–	–	–	–	–	–	–	–	–	–	–	–	–	–	–	11	–	–	–	–	–	–	11
28=	Nello Russo	I	Ducati	3	1	–	3	–	–	–	3	–	–	1	–	–	–	–	–	–	–	–	–	–	–	–	–	11
30	Aaron Yates	USA	Suzuki	–	–	–	–	–	–	–	–	–	–	–	–	–	–	10	–	–	–	–	–	–	–	–	–	10
31	Dean Ellison	GB	Ducati	–	–	–	–	–	–	–	–	–	–	–	–	–	–	–	–	–	–	5	4	–	–	–	–	9
32=	Serafino Foti	I	Ducati	–	–	–	–	–	–	1	2	2	1	–	–	2	–	–	–	–	–	–	–	–	–	–	–	8
32=	Sébastien Gimbert	F	Suzuki	–	–	–	–	–	–	–	–	–	–	–	–	–	–	–	–	–	–	–	–	–	–	–	8	8
32=	Atsushi Watanabe	J	Suzuki	–	–	–	–	8	–	–	–	–	–	–	–	–	–	–	–	–	–	–	–	–	–	–	–	8
35=	Horst Saiger	A	Yamaha	–	–	–	–	–	–	–	–	–	–	–	–	–	–	–	–	–	–	3	–	2	1	–	–	6
35=	Bertrand Stey	F	Honda	–	–	–	–	–	–	–	–	–	–	–	–	–	–	–	–	–	–	–	–	–	–	3	3	6
35=	Walter Tortoroglio	I	Honda	–	–	–	–	–	–	1	–	1	–	–	–	4	–	–	–	–	–	–	–	–	–	–	–	6
38=	Kenichiro Nakamura	J	Honda	–	–	–	–	2	2	–	–	–	–	–	–	–	–	–	–	–	–	–	–	–	–	–	–	4
38=	Christian Zaiser	A	Aprilia/Suzuki	–	–	–	–	–	–	–	–	–	–	–	–	–	–	–	–	–	–	–	–	–	–	4	–	4
40=	Paolo Blora	I	Ducati	–	–	–	–	–	–	–	–	–	–	–	–	3	–	–	–	–	–	–	–	–	–	–	–	3
40=	Luca Pedersoli	I	Ducati	–	–	–	–	–	–	–	–	–	–	–	–	–	3	–	–	–	–	–	–	–	–	–	–	3
40=	Frédéric Protat	F	Yamaha	–	–	–	–	–	–	–	–	–	–	–	–	–	–	–	–	–	–	–	–	–	–	2	1	3
43=	Gianmaria Liverani	I	Yamaha	–	–	–	–	–	–	–	–	–	–	–	–	–	–	–	–	–	–	2	–	–	–	–	–	2
43=	Jiri Mrkyvka	CZ	Ducati	–	–	–	–	–	–	1	–	–	–	–	–	–	–	–	–	–	–	1	–	–	–	–	–	2
43=	Luca Pini	I	Suzuki	–	–	–	–	–	–	–	–	–	–	–	–	–	–	–	–	–	–	–	–	1	1	–	–	2

YELLOW PERIL

By GORDON RITCHIE

EVERY year since the start of the World Supersport Championship there have been improvements in the calibre of the teams, machines, riders and tyres – the four horsemen of the racing apogee in any class. Given 2002's full-throttle action and factory interest, 2003 was going to be absolutely the most competitive World Supersport season ever, a truly apocalyptic fight between the real heavy hitters in racing, the Japanese factories, and a galaxy of Supersport champions in the making.

It didn't turn out quite like that, but not for the want of trying on everyone's part.

Reigning champs Honda, with the 'RC211V replica' CBR600RR, ran no fewer than eight supported riders with Ten Kate (Chris Vermeulen and Karl Muggeridge), Klaffi (Robert Ulm and Gianluigi Scalvini – sacked early on), van Zon (Iain Macpherson and Werner Daemen) and BKM (Broc Parkes and Christophe Cogan). The last named didn't last the year due to loss of sponsors.

Yamaha, with a 90-per-cent new and much racier R6, ran six-and-a-half works supported riders in four teams, from official subsidiary Belgarda (Jurgen van den Goorberg and Simone Sanna – eventually), Motor Germany (Jörg Teuchert and Christian Kellner), new outfit Motor France (World Supermotard Champion Thierry van den Bosch and Matthieu Lagrive) and the Team Italia mono rider effort with Alessio Corradi.

Suzuki stuck to the creaking, but cracking, GSX-R600, and a faithful duo of Stéphane Chambon and Katsuaki Fujiwara in Francis Batta's Alstare Team – on the only machine that was not brand new for the start of the testing season.

Kawasaki, middleweight stalwarts and champions in 2001, wheeled out an all-new ZX-6RR, with a radical chassis spec and the ministrations of a new French-based team. Big money and factory status lured 2002 champion Fabien Foret into the green spider's lair, and Pere Riba attempted to erase his errant MotoGP experiences as Foret's high-profile team-mate.

That made 19 factory bikes, swollen to a cool 20 if you count the Bertocchi Kawasaki of Stefano Cruciani, which talked the works-bike talk, but didn't threaten the podium walk.

Some legendary names in WSS never got the chance to saunter back down the pit lane in 2003. The Yamaha Belgarda team were planning to continue with their winning riders Paolo Casoli and James Whitham, but a big crash and head trauma for Casoli, and eyesight problems due to glaucoma for Whitham kiboshed that idea.

The winter tests, mainly in Spain, had demonstrated that the Ten Kate Hondas would be quick, that Kawasaki wouldn't be, that the Yamahas would be top all-rounders, and that the Suzukis wouldn't necessarily have their tail sections kicked with any degree of regularity.

The Valencia tests also showed that Pirelli were continuing their good work in their rubber war with Dunlop, eventually taking more wins and podiums. The war was real, however, so real in the treaded world of Supersport that Michelin made plans and tested in readiness to return to the euphemistically DOT-equipped class in 2004. That, among many other aspects of WSS, was to have an unexpected outcome.

No real surprise that Fujiwara won by a 4.5-second margin at Valencia, more of a surprise that Vermeulen was beaten back into a secondary role at Pirelli's and Ten Kate's favoured test track. Corradi pulled off his own minor magic trick by holding off Cogan and Teuchert to take his first, and last, podium of the season.

Van den Goorbergh, in a surprising ninth place, fought off starting and mid-race bike problems in his WSS induction, and remembered to take thicker elbow armour and a proximity sensor to detect other riders' improper advances to Australia.

The meaner, wiser VDG took a lonely third place in Australia, behind second-place Fujiwara and almost 15 seconds adrift of the disappearing symphony in yellow that was Chris Vermeulen. The rising Australian's first race win came at home, ironically the place he had to leave to become good enough to win in the first place. A win and a pole as well; thank you, cobber.

Just as it looked like there might have been some predictability on the horizon, Sugo triggered one of its mini-earthquakes, Kellner holding off wild-card BKM Honda youngster Ryuichi Kiyonari for the win; the veteran Chambon took third. Vermeulen squeezed out a fifth after taking a seventh in qualifying, a result he was relieved to snare in the lair of the dragons. Tekkyu Kayo was another surprising Japanese Supersportster, riding a factory Belgarda bike into fourth. A further indication of quite how seriously the Japanese are taking Supersport now.

Back in Europe, the disgruntled Muggeridge, bemused by his team's inability to set up his bike to the same winning ways as Vermeulen's, secured pole, but retired, leaving the Monza city expressway – the Autodromo Nazionale – free for pole man Vermeulen to paint the podium with a single yellow line. Van den Goorbergh achieved a clever second, ahead of the usual Monza mix of slip-streaming spectres, headed by single podium apparition Macpherson.

The next two events, however, belonged to Vermeulen alone, his three-in-a-row success moving swiftly on from Monza to Oschersleben and Silverstone. He was merciless, beating the Suzukis of Chambon and Fujiwara in Germany, trouncing van den Goorbergh and Muggeridge in England. Chris, still only 21 at the time, had a 131- to 84-point advantage over van den Goorbergh, and the impossible had indeed happened.

This just wasn't Supersport anymore. The best rider really had found the best team, bike, consistency and the best run of unbroken form in the history of the division. It made Foret's brilliant 2002 season look almost unconvincing. It would be all over by Brands at this rate, with three rounds left.

Then came Misano, the result of which could not be believed, even after it had been confirmed officially. Vermeulen crashed out of the lead, while defending champion Foret and his slow new Kawasaki won the race on undiluted and puckish willpower. VDG, Muggeridge and Riba failed to finish, and the world momentarily returned to Supersport bedlam. Fujiwara was an expected second, Parkes a career-best third.

Missing Laguna, the Supersport crew gathered at Brands Hatch, where Chambon took his only win of the year, with VDG second and Sébastien Charpentier (a superb Klaffi team replacement for the sacked-in-Oz Scalvini) third.

Vermeulen was only sixth, not that it mattered much with a 37-point lead going into his ancestors' and team's home race in Holland.

The utter dominance of the Ten Kate machine in the hands of Vermeulen would see him post two poles in the last three meetings, but the mantle of triple race winner was to pass to his team-mate, Muggeridge. With a change of on-track organisation in his side of the garage, Muggeridge made the most of it to secure the last three race wins on the hop – closely in Assen, clearly in Imola, and comprehensively in France. Vermeulen was thrice runner-up, with Fujiwara third at Assen and VDG taking the last two podiums.

With Muggeridge's late charge up the charts, the closest battle was always for second and only second, such was the pace of Vermeulen. The Misano aberration was forgivable for a 22-year-old, but nonetheless he became the only champion to break the 200-point barrier, by one.

Sixty-four points behind, Chambon held off VDG by one point, the late charging Muggeridge two points adrift in fourth overall.

The winning combination for 2003 was largely the same as 2002's: Ten Kate and Pirelli now with a very different Honda to run, and a whole new breed of WSS hero to rely on – an almost unerringly reliable one.

No one, not even Vermeulen, had expected this elitism in such a theoretically competitive year. We may not see its like again for a long time.

Facing page: **Chris Vermeulen powers his Honda to a win at Monza, his second of the year.**

Below: **Supersport veteran Stéphane Chambon (Suzuki) won a close battle for second overall.**
Both photographs: Mark Wernham

Below centre: **Jurgen van den Goorbergh found the going tough, but defended Yamaha's honour.**

Bottom: **Suzuki's Katsuaki Fujiwara won the first round, but never stood on the top step again.**
Both photographs: Gold & Goose

ONE TO THREE

By KEL EDGE

Above: Dean Ellison in action on the victorious Phase One Suzuki.

Photograph: Kel Edge

BRITISH team Phase One topped a superb season by taking the Endurance World Championship title after a nail-biting climax in the final round at Vallelunga. The Vallelunga 200-miler took place in varied conditions, and although Phase One held a 23-point lead going into the final round, one slip-up would have cost them the title. But the team, excellently organised as usual by former racer Russell Benney, did exactly what they had to do and deservedly took the crown. It was their third championship win in ten years and a fitting reward for all the hard graft they had put in over the decade.

Once again, there were three classes in the championship, but as usual all the 'big boys' opted to compete in the Superproduction class. Team Zongshen (from China, but based in France) were arguably the best funded and strongest on paper, but Phase One matched them in professionalism – if not budget. Zongshen fielded two teams of equal level on the venerable GSX-R1000 Suzuki, and Phase One (also Suzuki GSX-R1000) got in on the act by running two teams as well, their second squad called Junior Phase One. Other strong contenders included French outfits Team GMT 94, Moto 38 (Yamaha) and 22 Police Nationale (GSX-R1000 Suzuki); the Italian team D.R.E.5 (Ducati); Yamaha Austria; and Team Bolliger (Kawasaki ZX-9). A wide spread of manufacturers, and not a Honda in sight – until Suzuka of course.

Zongshen 1 won the season opener at Imola in May, with Phase One second, ahead of Yamaha Austria, but could only manage third in the next round at Assen. However, their team-mates (Zongshen 2) won the race, Phase One again being runners-up, so going into the third round there was just one point between the two great rivals. That round took place at Brno in the Czech Republic, and Zongshen 1 again emerged winners, with GMT 94 second and Phase One third, which meant that Zongshen had a ten-point advantage over Phase One as the teams headed off to the Albacete 12 hours.

Team Zongshen had a perfect day, scoring both first and second places, with Zongshen 1 gaining their third win of the season. Local team Folch Endurance took a superb third place, but Phase One could only manage sixth and now were 25 points behind Zongshen 1. Round five of the season, at the A1-Ring in Austria, saw Zongshen once again in command, with another 1-2 finish. GMT 94 were third, but Phase One's fourth kept them in the hunt – although the gap was now 37 points.

And so to round six, and the hardest race of the year for the regulars – the Suzuka Eight Hours. Suzuka used to be one the biggest motor cycle races of the year, with crowds of up to 300,000, but since the top GP and Superbike stars began to give it a miss, and Japanese youngsters discovered soccer and other activities, it has lost some of its appeal. It is still of huge significance to the home market, though, and all the Big Four factories in Japan spend vast sums of money trying to win it.

Suzuka is owned by Honda, and Honda normally win there, but this year they got the fright of their life when Suzuki led and seemed in control. At the very last pit stop, however, the Suzuki failed to fire up after refuelling and victory was snatched away. Local Honda riders won, but more importantly – for the championship – Phase One took a magnificent second place, while Zongshen failed to finish, reducing the deficit between them to just 17 points.

If that result was the turning point of the season, the next round at Oschersleben, with double points at stake, was where Phase One took command. The Oschersleben race is the only 24-hour event on the calendar, but it has become well established and the attendance is very good. This year, a Yamaha (GMT 94) took the glory, with Phase One second and another Yamaha (Moto 38) third. Zongshen 1 had their second DNF in a row, but their number-two team scored fourth. In the space of just two races, the whole championship had been turned upside-down for Zongshen, and what had been a 17-point lead over Phase One before Suzuka had become a 23-point deficit!

With one round left, it was hard to imagine how Phase One could lose, but endurance racing is nothing if not unpredictable, and the British team were not counting their chickens. The downpour just before the start of the race did nothing to calm their nerves, but by then team manager Benney had instructed his three riders (James and Dean Ellison and Andi Notman) to stay out of trouble and bring their GSX-R1000 Suzuki safely home and in the points. Although their twelfth place was their worst result of the season, it was enough to take the title; Zongshen 1 finished fifth.

Phase One had employed a variety of riders (James Ellison, Dean Ellison, Andi Notman, Jason Pridmore, Olivier Four, Jimmy Lindstrom and Josh Hayes) throughout the eight-race season, and each had played a vital part in the title chase. It was also a remarkable victory because the team had managed to score points in every round, a tremendous feat of endurance in itself.

Left: Rostrum overload at Vallelunga as the British Phase One team celebrate their third title win in ten years.

Below: The France-based Chinese Zongshen team take on fuel and riders. They led for the first part of a close-fought year.

Both photographs: Kel Edge

SPRINT OR MARATHON?

The endurance championship is a genuine world championship, but it is still seen as something of a sub-category by many race fans. However, while the crowds are not as big as those at World Superbike (or even British Superbike) events, there are signs that the series is beginning to grow.

FGSport are now in their fourth year of running the championship and, although the pace of growth may not be as fast as those within the series would like, progress is being made. When FGSport (originally the Flammini Group) took over the promotion and organisation of the series at the end of 1999, they decided to revamp the format and put some 'short' endurance races on the calendar. As a result, the 200-miler was born. This was not an original idea because, until the eighties, there had been been some famous 200-mile races – the Imola 200, the Moto Journal 200 and the Daytona 200 for example. None of these races formed part of any championship, but they were very popular thanks to the participation of the grand prix stars of the day (Barry Sheene, Kenny Roberts Snr, Marco Lucchinelli, Patrick Pons, etc). The Imola and Moto Journal 200-milers disappeared, although Daytona carries on. However, it is very much an American affair, as GP and World Superbike stars have given it a miss for some years.

The Imola 200 has now been reborn and forms part of the World Endurance Championship. It is one of three 200-mile races in the series, which also has two six-hour races, one eight-hour, one 12-hour and one 24-hour. This variation is actually part of the current problem with the series, many teams feeling that 200-mile races are not so much a test of endurance, more a short sprint. After all, 200 miles is only a bit longer than what the regular World Superbike riders do on a Sunday – albeit split into two races!

Before Flammini's involvement, there were three 24-hour races – Le Mans, Spa Francorchamps and the Bol d'Or – on the calendar. But the organisers of these races failed, or were unwilling, to agree terms with Flammini and opted out of the World Championship. With endurance being very much a 'French affair', they felt that they did not need outside help to put on a good show. They ran their own mini-series of three races, and the fans attended in significant numbers because all three were more than just races – they were 'events'. It did not matter if there were no stars racing, the fans came anyway. This is the problem that FGSport now have to address – how do they promote a race so that the fans feel they *must* attend?

Interestingly, apart from the Suzuka Eight Hours (which has always been regarded as something of a one-off), the best attended round is the Oschersleben 24-hour. The local organisation has worked hard over the years to make the round an event, providing amusements at the track to keep the spectators entertained, and they have succeeded.

Many riders and teams feel that there should be either one or two more 24-hour races – preferably at Le Mans or Spa Francorchamps. For endurance fans, a 24-hour race means making a weekend of it, the race being just part of the whole experience. A 200-miler, on the other hand, means just going on race day – and maybe not if the weather is bad in the morning. This year, there were eight races in five different formats, and for many fans this is not what endurance is all about. By all means have some different race formats, but why not a couple more marathons in the mix?

What has been a great benefit over the past few years, though, has been the Superproduction class, which has reduced the cost of competing and brought in more teams. However, there are changes to the Superbike class rules for 2004, and some teams may switch classes as a result. If that happens, it would be a shame, because Superproduction is a success story and one on which the championship should build. Keep the class, change the race formats, and endurance fans everywhere will be happy.

SIDECAR REVIEW

RECORD BREAKER

By JOHN McKENZIE

Top: Webster and his Suzuki-powered outfit in familiar form – leading at Brands Hatch. His closest challenger, Steinhausen, is chasing hard.

Above centre: Steve Webster and passenger Paul Woodhead. Webbo added a ninth world championship to his collection in 2003, having missed out in the previous two years.

Above: Jörg Steinhausen, son of former champion Rolf, and passenger Hopkinson took three wins and emerged as a credible threat.

All photographs: John McKenzie

AFTER missing the title for the last two years, Steve Webster and Paul Woodhead set out to regain the world crown with new sponsorship from Castrol Suzuki. Challengers were to be Q8-sponsored Jörg Steinhausen – who emerged as the only contender with the ability to test Webster – Klaus Klaffenböck (signed with Team Readymix after his previous OPCM sponsorship disappeared) and, of course, 2002 World Champions Steve Abbott and Jamie Biggs. Snapping at their heels would be fast-improving pair Tom Hanks and Phil Biggs. The planned Malaysian race having been cancelled, an extra race was put on at Assen on the Sunday afternoon, the first time the sidecars had had two races in one weekend.

Round 1, Valencia, Spain, 1 March 2003

Webster posted his intent with a resounding debut win for his new Team Castrol Suzuki set-up, serving up a textbook race plan executed with utter precision. After a lightning start, he was never headed over the 18 laps.

Early challenges from Klaffenböck and Hanks had been dispensed with by lap seven, Webster already nearly six seconds in front.

'We knew we had to get a good start and get away to build up a good lead. We wanted to fire a warning shot to the rest that we really mean business this year, and that result should have done it,' said a delighted Webster, winner by 11 seconds.

An intriguing battle for second was curtailed when Hanks collided with Klaffenböck's back wheel while braking hard at the end of the main straight after eight laps. Hanks lost control and slewed on to the gravel trap, leaving Klaffenböck clear until Abbott's heroic charge through the field.

Abbott produced a superb performance to steal second place from nowhere. With four laps to go, Klaffenböck was still 3.5 seconds up on Abbott and should have been able to hold him off, but the World Champions managed to pip him on the very last lap.

Round 2, Monza, Italy, 17 May 2003

What had promised to be an epic battle petered out when early-race pace-setter Webster's charge was halted at Curve Grande on lap eight by fuel-pump failure, leaving 2001 World Champion Klaffenböck a

clear track to sweep to victory, his third consecutive win at the ultra-fast Italian venue.

Having romped to an unchallenged 12-second win, Klaffenböck took a 16-point lead in the series after two rounds. Eventual second-place finisher was birthday boy Jörg Steinhausen, who'd battled long and hard with Steve Abbott before the latter slowed dramatically with fuel-starvation problems, eventually coming home 14th. The final rostrum place went to Dutch father-and-son pairing of Martien and Tonnie Van Gils.

Round 3, Oschersleben, Germany, 31 May 2003

It was back to business as usual for Webster and Woodhead, who gave a textbook demonstration of race technique as they blasted to a 13.2-second win over Klaffenböck. The latter had been hampered by an oiled visor after Steinhausen's seventh-lap blow-up. Third and final rostrum place went to Abbott, who'd overcome Hanks after a race-long battle.

Webster had been overwhelmed briefly in the starting flurry as Van Gils and Steinhausen rocketed away, but by the end of the first lap, he had his race head truly in place, wrenching back control and never to be headed for the duration of the 22 twisting laps.

'We did what we planned – good start, some fast laps and stay out of trouble. We've caught up a few points now on Klaffenböck. It's been a good day's work,' said Webster.

Fastest race lap also went to Webster at 1m 32.874s, marginally under his pole qualifying time, and the only rider to break the 1m 33s barrier.

Round 4, Silverstone, Great Britain, 14 June 2003

In perfect sunshine – notably rare at Silverstone! – Webster had to battle hard to overcome his customary poor start. Steinhausen shot into an early lead, shadowed by Hanks, with Webster in third. On lap two, Webster tried a brave move on the inside at Brooklands, but overcooked it, allowing Hanks back up the inside. But another lap was all that was needed for Webster to take second place from Hanks, and soon he was pressuring race leader Steinhausen. By the end of lap four, Webster had grabbed control of the race and immediately set about building a gap that, within three laps, had grown to three seconds.

The lead continued to increase until Webster had achieved his favoured five-second comfort zone. Then it was a matter of getting to the chequered flag, giving himself the chance to celebrate 20 years of world championship racing – it had been 1983 when he had made his GP debut at the Northamptonshire track. The result trimmed Klaffenböck's championship lead to just six points, the Austrian having shrugged off a last-lap challenge from Steinhausen.

Webster's main problem had come with three laps to go, when Andy Peach flipped his outfit in the middle of Woodcote, seconds before the former arrived; Peach was left feeling more foolish than hurt after the low-speed tumble.

Round 5, Misano, Italy, 21 June 2003

Extreme temperatures – 53 degrees C on the tarmac and mid-30s air temperature – combined with a new abrasive track surface proved to be the leveller in what was the closest race of the season so far.

Webster led from the third lap, but was never quite able to shake off Jörg Steinhausen, and with just five laps to go, he was forced to yield. Steinhausen went on to take his fourth career win.

'We had to go too fast, too early on. When Jörg came past, there was nothing I could do. It was very, very hard work with the heat, and there was nothing left at the end when we needed it,' said Webster.

On harder rubber, Steinhausen was soon able to forge a two-second lead on Webster, and with two laps to go, Tom Hanks demoted the latter to third.

Hanks's brilliant efforts from sixth on lap one nearly paid off; he just missed out on the win by less than half a second. With Webster's tyres fading, it even appeared as though fourth-place Klaus Klaffenböck might also catch him, but as the Austrian 2001 World Champion had also made the same tyre selection as Webster, he was unable to take the advantage.

Said a joyous Steinhausen, 'We have been working very hard, and it's satisfying when it all comes together. I was a bit surprised to see Webster's rear tyre go, but we kept plugging away.'

Passenger Hopkinson echoed his driver's words: 'This is our first genuine win – it was a long time coming.'

Abbott retired on lap four with an ignition problem; Klaffenböck finished in fourth place to stay in the top spot.

Below left: Steinhausen in his GSX-R outfit, fitted with trunk-like air scoop.
Photograph: John McKenzie

Round 6, Brands Hatch, Great Britain, 26 July 2003

In a commanding performance, Webster shrugged off torrential rain to record his 55th career victory and move into a six-point championship lead, despite suffering from a slow puncture for the last two laps.

'We were lucky to finish at all. Jörg really drove well and pushed us all the way, but I knew if we could keep going at the same pace, he couldn't pass because of the spray,' said Webster.

At the off, Hanks led into Druids, and despite spray from the fat 13-in tyres making vision almost impossible, by the end of the first lap, Steinhausen was out in front. By lap three, Webster was through to second, taking the lead from Steinhausen as the outfits streaked across the start/finish line. Steinhausen retook Webster at Hawthorn and led for a further lap until the latter once again forced a way through. From then on, Webster was never headed, doing just enough to hold off Steinhausen, who was tucked in never much more than a second behind, trying to pressurise Webster into making an error.

'In these conditions, there is one fast line around the track, and if you get one inch off it, you're out of control,' said Webster. 'I knew Jörg was right behind us, but I also knew he couldn't see to get past us because of the spray – and it's hard to race when someone is pressing you like that all the time – but we hung on, and Paul was magnificent in the chair!'

Woodhead explained, 'Apart from getting cold and wet, it's much more technical: you have much greater influence and control on moving the bike around, and you have to be very smooth and ensure your weight is giving the best grip for the conditions. But Steve drove really well and we kept them at just the right distance all the way through.'

Steinhausen was gracious in defeat: 'We were really pleased with second, because we couldn't use our race engine after some problems. It was a difficult race, but we had more grip than I expected, so it was quite fast for the conditions. We pushed

hard from the first lap, but Webbo knows more lines around here than me. I was surprised because I thought I knew the track quite well. We nearly caught him a couple of times, but it was impossible to see a way past because of the spray. I was waiting for him to make a mistake – but he didn't make one!'

A distant third place went to Klaffenböck, who just held off Abbott.

Round 7, Assen, Holland, 6 September 2003

After extending his astonishing run of pole qualifications to 25 on the trot, Webster got under way with his usual less-than-brilliant start, while Steinhausen dashed into the lead. Webster found himself in third place, boxed in behind Steve Abbott and Jamie Biggs, and his determination to get through caused a brief coming together on the first lap.

'I went for the gap, got in a bit too fast and bumped into the back of Abbo, catching Jamie on the backside! It dented the nose of our bike, but I apologised after,' said Webster.

With Webster not immediately able to find a way through, Steinhausen tried to make good his escape and soon pulled out a 3.5-second lead. Then Webster managed to squeeze under Abbott going into the chicane at the end of the first lap, and set off in hot pursuit. It took four determined laps for him to get right back on Steinhausen's rear wheel, smashing his own lap record in the process. Then he commandeered the lead at the end of the sixth lap, diving inside at the fast right-hander at the end of the start/finish straight.

With a clear road in front, Webster turned up the wick to stay just far enough in front to prevent Steinhausen from slipstreaming him. The lead built until, at the flag, he took the honours with a comfortable 6.86-second advantage. But the real battle of the race was for third. Abbott had seemed to have it sewn up, but found Klaffenböck all over him on the last lap. Somehow, the Austrian managed to dupe Abbott at the final chicane, diving inside and grabbing the last podium spot.

Round 8, Assen, Holland, 7 September 2003

In race two on Sunday afternoon, Abbott was the fast starter, leaving Webster in third behind Steinhausen. But this time, Webster was minded to get clear of the mêlée early, and by lap two he had taken the lead, running away with it on his favourite circuit. By the sixth lap, the gap was five seconds and still climbing. Eventually, he eased the pace slightly, taking his second race win in 24 hours by some 6.4 seconds.

'A perfect weekend! The bike was just great – all we did was change the oil between races, and it went perfectly. I thought having two races in two days would be hard work, but we prepared well for it and got the wins we so badly wanted,' said Webster, having notched up his 57th world championship race win.

Early challenger in race two, Steinhausen had to pit mid-race, but rejoined to finish sixth, while Abbott and Klaffenböck fought another desperate last-lap battle for the runner-up spot. Abbott had seemed comfortable in second place, but with two laps to go his engine started to overheat, allowing Klaffenböck to catch and pass him again on the last lap.

Round 9, Imola, Italy, 27 September 2003

Jörg Steinhausen, learning every race from Webster, grabbed the lead on the first lap and was never headed. For a while mid-race, it had seemed as though Webster, sitting on Steinhausen's back wheel, might be able to pressurise him into a mistake, but the German drove the most mature ride of his career to hold on to the lead.

Coming on to backmarkers at the chicane on lap ten, Steinhausen used the traffic to his advantage, quickly opening up a three-second gap on Webster.

'We were comfortable in second, just behind Jörg, and waiting for the opportunity to try to get past. Then the backmarkers got in the way. Jörg got past, but we got baulked, and really that was it.'

Though we tried hard for a couple of laps to catch him, I realised it would be better to go for a safe second place and 20 points. It would have been nice to win the championship today, but we at least get another bite at the cherry,' explained Webster, who now needed only a 15th in the final round.

In a distant third place, Klaffenböck completed the podium and went into the final race knowing that Webster had to retire and he had to win to stand any chance of the title.

Klaffenböck said, 'We have a slim chance, but we have to sort out the problems we have had in the last two races. Anyway, we will try hard.'

Abbott crashed out on the first lap, flipping his outfit in the process, after becoming caught up in the mid-field jostling.

Round 10, Magny-Cours, France, 18 October 2003

A careful fifth place at Magny-Cours was enough for Webster and Woodhead to lift the title. It was his ninth world crown and his second with Woodhead, and it extended his record and reputation as the most successful sidecar racer in the history of the sport.

Needing a single point to clinch the championship, the pair's fifth place and 11 points saw them winning the series by 19 points from Klaffenböck. The race win went to the season's most improved rider, and surely Webster's main rival-to-be, Jörg Steinhausen, son of 1975 and '76 World Champion Rolf Steinhausen.

Said Webster, 'We had two plans before the race – Plan A: get pole, get a good start and clear off; and Plan B: stay out of the way. As I made a mess of the start, Plan A was binned before the end of the first lap! I thought about having a go, but we just didn't need to do it. I got close to Abbo at one stage, but got showered with stones from his back wheel, and I realised we could easily get a holed radiator or something, so I thought, "Just back off, be sensible!"'

While pole-man (27th consecutive!) Webster held steady in fifth, Steinhausen surged to a decisive third win of the campaign, after taking the lead from Klaffenböck on the second lap. 'In the end, it was quite easy. We had no problems and I am very pleased for the team,' he said.

Outgoing World Champions Steve Abbott and Jamie Biggs put up a good showing, reeling in the leading group one by one to take a well-earned second place, and fourth in the final table.

As for Klaffenböck, he had to settle for third. 'We tried, but it was too hard. We are happy with second overall, given the tough season that we have had,' he said.

So Steve Webster extended his previous record of eight titles, gained in 1987, '88 and '89 with Tony Hewitt; in 1991 with Gavin Simmons; in 1997, '98 and '99 with David James; and in 2000 with Paul Woodhead.

Webbo's passenger, Woodhead, was overjoyed: 'It feels better than when we won it in 2000, but it hasn't really sunk in yet. I expect it will tomorrow with the hangover though!'

A happy Webster added, 'It's been a long, tough season, and we just couldn't have done it without the support of many people, particularly our main sponsors, Suzuki and Castrol. It's the first time for six years that I've run my own team, but there has also been more help behind the scenes than ever, with so many people all doing little bits and pieces that have helped the team achieve this.'

Webbo has already stated he wants title number ten – and who is going to stop him?

TOUGH TO BEAT

By PAUL CARRUTHERS

IF you didn't have time to review the entire AMA Superbike series from Mat Mladin's perspective, you could just take a look at the two-race Road Atlanta round for a quick summary of the Australian's season. In short: Mladin earns pole position; a tyre failure costs him victory in race one; Mladin comes back to handily win race two.

This sort of thing played out more than once as the AMA series criss-crossed the country. What occurred in Georgia, however, was a bit more graphic than the rest.

Starting from pole, Mladin appeared to be headed for his fifth victory in a row when all hell broke loose on the fastest section of Road Atlanta. The Yoshimura Suzuki GSX-R1000 was travelling at well over 150 mph when its rear Dunlop exploded. Miraculously, Mladin rode through the ensuing tankslapper, manhandling the out-of-control motor cycle to the nearest gravel trap before finally tipping over. It was harrowing to watch.

'I got lucky. If it would have happened a hundred yards up the race-track, I probably would have been dead. Or in a bad way,' Mladin explained afterward. 'I got lucky that it happened just as I was getting it straight.' While most would have spent the night in a cold sweat seriously considering another line of work, Mladin came back the next day undaunted, winning by over five seconds for a fifth time in the season.

He would go on to win a record tying ten races over the course of the season – a total that would have been higher if not for tyre problems that cost him certain victories along the way. Still, he was totally dominant, and at season's end he was crowned as the AMA Superbike Champion for a record fourth time. He headed home to Australia to be with his pregnant wife, Janine. The couple's first baby, a daughter, Emily Jean, was born on 19 October. Mladin was a happy man, and eager to get on with the business at hand – title number five.

But first, let's see how number four was earned.

Above: Australian Mat Mladin made history as the first ever four-times AMA Superbike winner.

Left: Mladin looks over his shoulder for the opposition. He was beaten more often by tyre mishaps than any other rider.

Both photographs: Tom Riles

As always, the season began at Daytona International Speedway, this time with some changes to the rules. This meant that the Yoshimura Suzuki team showed up in Florida with the all-mighty GSX-R1000s instead of the trusty old 750s, bikes that had started to show their age in the class the season before. Suzuki had shed one rider for a two-rider team – Mladin and Georgian Aaron Yates – the pair confident from an off-season of successful tests, which even included a jaunt to Malaysia for a shared session with the Suzuki MotoGP and World Superbike teams.

Mladin was served (again) by a team within a team, his mostly Australian crew forming a tightly-knit bunch that would (again) pick him up when he was down. And vice versa. The envy of most in the paddock, Mladin's mini-Yosh team works extremely well together, and that would show more in 2003 than perhaps in any other season. Perhaps 'the Australians' (as they are often referred to by others in the paddock) ended up showing too much of their hand, because by season's end, all the talk from the competition about Mladin's GSX-R1000 having an unfair advantage seemed to fall on ears that weren't so deaf. Now there are rules in place that will attempt to prevent the team from dominating again. But that's a story for 2004's MOTOCOURSE...

Yates ended up having a good season with three wins; although, to be fair, two were handed to him by Mladin's tyres. Still, he ended up second overall, and he was there to pick up the slop when others weren't.

Nicky Hayden having departed for MotoGP, Mladin's main competition was expected to come from Kawasaki's Eric Bostrom, the 'nearly man' of the series, who'd finished second in the points tally the previous two seasons. Bostrom wouldn't have the benefit of a new bike, but the rules did allow his ZX-7R to have a bit more displacement. Again, Eric was the lone man in the Kawasaki Superbike team, and he ended up winning two races along the way. But his season derailed at Laguna Seca, where he was injured in the second-turn mêlée in race one. Bostrom didn't race again in 2003 because of his surgically repaired shoulder and the back injuries that also came from the crash.

Even without Hayden, Honda's effort looked strong. Hayden had been replaced by Ducati World Superbike rider (and former AMA Superbike Champion) Ben Bostrom, the Californian returning to his home series full of promise and picked by many as Hayden's heir apparent. Bostrom showed glimpses of brilliance, but they were only glimpses, and it wasn't until very late in the year that he looked comfortable and aggressive on the RC51. By then, it was too late. He ended up fourth in the series but – surprisingly – was winless.

Bostrom's factory Honda team-mate, Miguel DuHamel, was everyone's hero. The French Canadian was as grizzled as ever and still showed that on his day he could run with whomever he lined up against. DuHamel somehow found a way to rise to the occasion, and if he did absolutely nothing else the entire year, winning the Daytona 200 was enough to make his season.

Kurtis Roberts was back for another year on the RC51, riding in the 'factory' satellite team of Erion Racing. The younger Roberts ended up winning his first AMA Superbike National only late in the season, at Virginia International Raceway, then followed up with another at the next round at the new Barber Motorsports Park. By the end of the year, he looked like the only man truly capable of coming close to Mladin's speed. Somewhat surprisingly, the Honda team didn't have a place for Roberts for 2004 (having already promised a ride to Superstock/600 cc Supersport Erion rider Jake Zemke), and he was left looking for work.

Oh, the woes of Ducati. Doug Polen where art thou...?

Two Ducati teams started the 2003 AMA season. One ended it, although with a different rider from the one they had started with. The 'Days Of Our Lives' Ducati soap opera continued.

The big team, Ducati Austin, came to Daytona with Anthony Gobert, the Australian looking fresh and full of promise. He was joined on the Italian V-twins by Larry Pegram, the Ohio man riding in a team owned by two rich Californians, aptly dubbed the Dream Team. It had turned into a nightmare by mid-season, and by the end of the year they were nowhere to be found; Pegram became a Supermoto rider for the KTM factory, while the owners returned to their original, more lucrative business ventures.

Gobert wasn't around by season's end either. The fresh promise that the Daytona sunshine always brings didn't last long for the Australian. The results never came, although the excuses often did. Gobert blamed the team for everything, citing a lack of testing, and a lack of support (blah, blah, blah) for his lack of results. The team mostly kept their mouths shut as Gobert seemed to go off the deep end again, smoking and drinking his way to yet another sacking, the Aussie having been fired more often than Lee Harvey Oswald's gun. As it turned out, Road America was the last we'd see of him.

The team would continue, replacing Gobert with Giovanni Bussei. The Italian was like a breath of fresh air for them, and by the end of the year, the World Superbike rider was running near the front, even getting on the podium in the final race by taking second.

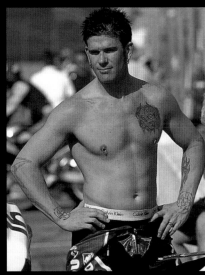

With Suzuki GSX-R1000s mostly the motor cycles of choice, a strong pack of privateers ended up supporting the seven factory riders. They were led at season's end by Millennium Motorsports' Shawn Higbee, the Wisconsinite sneaking into sixth in the series standings. Attack Suzuki's Jason Pridmore ended up eighth, while fellow privateers Vincent Haskovec and Jordan Szoke rounded out the top ten scorers.

Who needs Nicky Hayden, anyway? At Daytona, Honda didn't. Call it the Honda steamroller. Call it short-lived.

At Daytona, DuHamel, Bostrom and Roberts had Honda smiling like a teenager after his final visit to the orthodontist. The trio stormed away from everyone (except Yates, who stayed with them until running off the track late in the race; he ended up fourth and first non-Honda) and the victory was fought out among the three RC51s, with Daytona hero DuHamel inching ahead of Bostrom and Roberts on the run to the flag to claim his fourth 200.

With Eric Bostrom and Mladin fifth and sixth, the Honda team must have been licking their chops on the long flight home from Daytona.

The licking stopped with a violent slap to the head by Mladin at the next round at California Speedway, now in its second year of hosting the AMA event. The meeting began with a lively exchange between Mladin and Roberts in the post-qualifying press conference, a verbal jab-fest that was probably mistake number one for Roberts. After all, Mladin thrives on verbal warfare. It makes him tougher to beat, and no one was tougher to beat from that point on than Mladin. The war of words between the two would escalate, then drop off to turn into a virtual love-fest by mid-season, and then turn ugly again by the end. Good drama, at least off the track.

On the track, Mladin was dominant. He qualified on pole and won both races, ending a 623-day winless drought and giving the GSX-R1000 its first AMA Superbike victory. Yates was second in race one; Eric Bostrom in race two, the pair posting fourth-place finishes in their other two results. Roberts was sixth and fifth; Ben Bostrom third and sixth; DuHamel fifth and third. Honda's smile suddenly wasn't as big.

The Mladin steamroller continued when the series headed to Northern California and the Infineon Raceway (née Sears Point) for the most abbreviated weekend of action in the recent history of AMA road racing. Two races, two wins for Mladin, the Aussie besting team-mate Yates both times out – and all on the same day, as rain washed out both Friday and Saturday.

When the racing did take place, DuHamel put his Honda on the rostrum for the first time since Daytona. It went sour after that, however, as he broke his collar-bone in a 600 cc Supersport crash between the two Superbike finals. His team-mates, Roberts (who was nursing a shoulder injury suffered in a dirt-bike training accident) and Ben Bostrom, ended up seventh and fourth, then fifth and third respectively. Eric Bostrom posted a fourth and a fifth.

Again, Gobert wasn't a factor. He didn't finish the first race when a cam belt stretched, and he simply pulled out of race two with a motor cycle he said was unrideable. His best result of the year would come a race later, fourth at Road Atlanta, the only thing remotely close to a highlight for the Aussie.

With Mladin now leading the points standings by 24 after five rounds, it appeared as though it was getting close to 'game over'. But then came Road Atlanta and the first of Mladin's tyre problems. This allowed everyone back in. With seven races in the can, it was Yates in the lead by two points; Eric Bostrom was third, 12 behind Yates. The battle was on.

Eric Bostrom's first victory of the season came at the next round in Colorado – round eight. Already known as the man to beat at Pikes Peak International Raceway, Bostrom only added to the legend in 2003. After being off the pace throughout practice, he won the race in the Rockies for the fourth time, holding off Roberts for the victory. Yates was third ahead of Ben Bostrom and Gobert.

Mladin? He was ninth, another tyre-wear problem forcing him to pit for new rubber. 'Honestly, at the moment we can't figure out why we're wearing tyres out,' Mladin said.

Yates still led the series standings leaving Colorado, five ahead of Eric Bostrom and nine clear of Mladin.

Weather played a role in the next round at Road America. On Saturday, it was dry and Mladin was the man. After a race-long battle, he beat DuHamel by a scant 0.280 second, Roberts just as close in third. A day later, the weather was drastically different. With the track surface ever changing, Eric Bostrom left the others in his wake, winning by over 32 seconds. A bad tyre choice forced Mladin to change mid-way through, and the best he could muster was tenth place.

With Wisconsin behind them, suddenly Eric Bostrom led on points, just one ahead of Mladin, who had six wins to Bostrom's two.

Round 11 was at Brainerd International Raceway in Minnesota. Like the mosquitoes that continually pester the lakeside residents, tyre problems again brought down Mladin. Failure number four led to his demise, the Australian being forced to pit for a new rear and dropping from second to seventh, and from a tie in the championship (he'd earned a point for pole the day before) to second again.

'I think it's fair to say that he's clearly the fastest rider on the race-track when he's out there,' Dunlop's Jim Allen said of Mladin. 'The long and short of it is we haven't done a good job of keeping him out there all year.'

Mladin's loss was Yates's gain, the Georgian's second win of the season. DuHamel ended up second, with Roberts third and Eric Bostrom fourth. Bussei, replacing Gobert, made a memorable AMA debut with fifth. Mladin finished seventh; Ben Bostrom 12th, also victim of a chunked rear Dunlop.

Mladin went to Laguna Seca Raceway hell-bent on showing exactly who was in control of this championship. From the time a wheel was turned at the famous facility on the Monterey Peninsula of California, he was quick. It resulted in win number seven for the Yoshimura Suzuki man, this one by some eight seconds over team-mate Yates. Eric Bostrom was third, losing the points lead to Mladin in the process. The Laguna round would be Bostrom's last hurrah, as he suffered his shoulder injury the next day in the World Superbike round, ending his season.

Mladin's lead was six over the departed Eric Bostrom and, more importantly, 11 over Yates.

At Mid-Ohio for rounds 13 and 14, Mladin drove the dagger deep into the barely beating heart of his competition. It was also at Mid-Ohio that one Kurtis Roberts started to come good, his much-ballyhooed talent starting to fulfil its promise on the race-track.

Mladin ended up winning both races, but Roberts was tough both times too. In the first race, the pair were never separated by more than a second and battled to the end, swapping the lead five times on the final lap alone. It ended with Mladin winning and Roberts in the gravel trap, remounting to finish seventh. But he'd been there, finally threatening Mladin at the front.

A day later, they went at it again. This time, Mladin was stronger, changes to his bike making him better in the spots that Roberts had used to his advantage the day before. Mladin went on to score the win, while Roberts suffered a transmission problem that put him out of the race.

The man who ended up second in both races was none other than Pridmore, the Suzuki privateer putting in quite an effort over the course of the weekend. DuHamel was third on day one; Ben Bostrom on day two. Yates could do no better than fifth and fourth over the two days, and when the paddock cleared on Sunday night, Mladin was 33 points ahead of his team-mate. It looked like Easy Street from here on out.

Now it was Roberts's turn to suffer heartbreak. With victory in hand in race one at Virginia International Raceway, he was denied the win when his rear tyre came apart. That handed the race to Mladin, who had worked his way cautiously through the pack to be there when Roberts had his problems. It was his tenth win of the season and it put him in the catbird seat to take the title.

In race two, delayed by rain until Monday, Roberts got his long-overdue first victory. Mladin rode to a safe fifth-place finish. With Yates sixth and second over the two days, Mladin went to the final race needing only to survive to take the title.

That last round was held at the immaculate Barber Motorsports Park in Alabama, without a doubt the finest facility the AMA visits. The races themselves turned out to be just as good as the race-track.

Saturday's race was won by Yates, his third and final win of the year coming after a race-long battle with Roberts. The Honda rider held on to second, with Ben Bostrom and Mladin finishing third and fourth respectively. The title was almost in the bag.

The final race looked to be a *déjà vu* replay of the very first, the three Hondas pulling away from the rest to do battle as a trio. But unlike Daytona, it all went wrong. With three laps remaining, Bostrom crashed in turn four, taking two lapped riders and team-mate DuHamel with him. Fortunately for Roberts (and Honda), he was clear of the mêlée and was able to cruise to his second win of the season.

Behind him, Mladin resisted the urge to chase. His patience paid off with fourth place and a fourth AMA Superbike title. He is the first to win four, moving ahead of triple winners Reg Pridmore, Fred Merkel and Doug Chandler.

'For what this team has done, it's pretty amazing,' Mladin said. 'You can be a good rider, you can have a good bike, you can be the best rider and have the best bike. But without a good team, you're not going to win anything. I've got to give all four of these wins to my team. Because if I was on any other team, it wouldn't have happened. And that's for sure.'

In the support classes, Yamaha's Jamie Hacking won his first ever AMA title, taking the all-important 600 cc Supersport crown over his team-mate, Damon Buckmaster. The Formula Xtreme title went to Yoshimura Suzuki's teenage phenomenon, Ben Spies – again over oh-so-close Buckmaster (for the fourth straight year, Bucky had lost a title by just a handful of points). Attack Suzuki's Josh Hayes earned the Superstock crown.

In the last and final season of AMA 250 cc Grand Prix racing, the king of the class, Rich Oliver, took the title, the old man winning all 11 rounds for the third perfect season of his career. His win in the last race, at Barber, was his 72nd in the class – 47 more than the next best US 250 rider, Jimmy Filice.

For race fans, the abiding memory of the 2003 TT races will have nothing to do with laurels or records, but the tragic death of lap record holder David Jefferies during practice on Thursday, 29 May. The 30-year-old Yorkshireman, winner of three races in each of the last three TT meetings, was killed instantly after crashing his 1000 cc TAS Suzuki at over 160 mph in the village of Crosby, four miles into the 37.73-mile TT course.

Jefferies was unquestionably the TT's finest current exponent, and never before has the TT lost an outright lap record holder, let alone one so popular as big Dave. The loss cast a pall over everything, and shook DJ's erstwhile rivals to their boots. Perhaps fittingly, the week's greatest honours went to Adrian Archibald, Jefferies's team-mate in the TAS Suzuki squad. But few riders, Archibald included, left the Isle of Man feeling good about the fortnight they had endured.

ISLE OF MAN TT REVIEW

FROM UNDER A CLOUD

By MAC McDIARMID

...

PRACTICE

Even prior to Thursday's tragedy, many of the top riders had experienced a troubled practice week, made worse by changeable weather. John McGuinness, riding the MonsterMob Ducati F02, on which Shakey Byrne was romping away with the British Superbike championship, was still finding his way, albeit relieved that his crew had cured the instability problems that had blighted his efforts at the North-West 200 two weeks before.

Less confident, despite buoyant pronouncements to the contrary, was Ian Lougher, riding the same ex-Colin Edwards factory Honda Britain SP-2 that Steve Plater was struggling to control on British short circuits. 'I suspect Honda are going the wrong way,' suggested MonsterMob mechanic Stuart Bland. 'The answer's in geometry and tyres, not suspension. And we've got a secret – but I'm not telling you what it is.'

Whatever it was, McGuinness liked it, lapping at 122 mph from a standing start on Tuesday evening, then putting in a flying lap at 124.47 mph, just 23 seconds off the outright lap record. 'It's good,' he grinned afterward, 'dry all the way round, just a bit foggy on top.'

Twenty-four seconds behind, at 121.84 mph, came Lougher. As it rumbled into the paddock, his SP-2 was mobbed by Honda personnel. Afterward, 'Lucky' stood eyeing the Honda ruefully. The body language spoke of heavy problems, but his mechanic, Martin Gerrish, was more upbeat: 'It's not perfect, but an improvement. We've got a base setting, now we can fine-tune it.'

It didn't happen. When all other efforts at taming the SP-2's weaves failed, the team made a late and embarrassing switch from Dunlop to Pirelli tyres. Whatever their shortcomings in World Superbikes, the Italian products are the rubber of choice for high-speed road circuits. By week's end, they had notched wins in all six classes in which they were used, scoring no less than 54 out of 60 top-ten places along the way. For Lougher, however, the switch came too late to permit adequate testing.

Even the TAS Suzukis, which seemed to have been ready to go straight out of the van a year before, were experiencing handling problems. The new GSX-R1000 was certainly faster than the old machine, but not so easy to set up. 'No, I'm not happy,' admitted team boss Hector Neill half-way through practice week. 'We haven't got the handling right. Maybe it's the extra power, but last year we seemed to hit it right from the beginning – I almost wish I'd brought last year's bikes.'

By his own high standards, Archibald has underperformed in recent TTs. Yet despite these problems, the 33-year-old Ballymoney man was quietly impressive throughout qualifying. Early in the week, he'd had the edge on Jefferies, who was experiencing a fitful time, made worse by two breakdowns. Ironically, the fastest lap of the week was DJ's 125.20 mph from a standing start, on the lap before he died. He also led the 1000 Production standings at 122.57 mph,

narrowly ahead of Archibald, both on Suzuki GSX-R1000s. Archibald had the compensation of topping the 600 Production leaderboard at 118.06 mph, admittedly some way off Lougher's 2002 record of 120.25 mph.

It was the hugely competitive Junior (600 cc) class that sprang the greatest surprise. Twenty-eight years after the company had last won a TT, things were looking good for Triumph, fresh from Bruce Anstey's second place for the Val-Moto (formerly V&M) squad at the NW200. In Junior (Supersports) trim, the Hinckley fours have the speed to be genuine contenders, while the minor handling gremlins they suffer on short circuits aren't a factor on the Isle of Man. Between them, their three riders – Moodie, John McGuinness and Anstey – could muster 11 TT wins. From the outset, the Triumphs were on the pace, Anstey heading the eventual leaderboard with a lap at 121.04 mph during the final session, compared to Archibald's 2000 lap record of 121.15 mph.

In the Lightweight 400 division, John Barton's Yamaha topped the leaderboard at 109.07 mph, narrowly outside Richard Quayle's record. Another Isle of Man-based rider, former British champion Chris Palmer, led the 125 cc class at 110.48 mph, precisely equalling Lougher's 2002 lap record.

In the absence of Rob Fisher, last year's double winner, on Superside duty, one man utterly dominated the sidecars – and you didn't need a stopwatch to tell. After throwing a con-rod on his GSX-R600 at Appledene on Saturday, Dave Jefferies settled down to watch the sidecar action.

'Molly's in a different class,' he whistled later. 'You could hear the rest of the sidecars rolling it, but he seemed to be right on the gas.' Even Molyneux himself was impressed. Other than a few runs at Jurby airfield, this was his first lap of any circuit on the DMR outfit he had just finished building. His second lap, 111.60 mph, was only 12.5 seconds outside his 1999 lap record and allowed him to opt out of much of the rest of practice.

Second, and even more chuffed, was Ian Bell, who had written off his own new DMR at Croft a few weeks earlier. Riding his four-year-old spare machine, the Northumbrian put in his fastest ever TT lap at 111.27 mph.

FORMULA ONE

By the time racing finally got under way after a delayed start to the six-lap Formula One TT, Archibald and his TAS Suzuki team had wrestled with their natural misgivings and decided to compete. 'It's what DJ would have wanted,' was the prevailing mood. If he had been available for comment, big Dave would probably also have wanted his TAS colleague to win, and that's precisely what happened.

To no one's surprise, the Ulsterman dedicated his emotional win to his late team-mate, in a muted garlanding ceremony notable for the absence of sprayed champagne. Debut TT win or not, neither Archibald nor anyone else seemed to feel remotely triumphant. This was DJ's day, not theirs. To make

matters worse, local favourite Richard Quayle was badly injured when he crashed heavily at Ballaspur.

The early pace was set by the V-twins of McGuinness and Lougher. The MonsterMob rider led for two laps until overhauled by Archibald during a slow pit stop. Later, his Ducati succumbed to gear-selection problems caused by a bent selector fork, necessitating an unscheduled pit stop, which dropped him to third place, narrowly ahead of Jason Griffiths.

Once at the front, Archibald, a notoriously slow starter at the best of times, drew ahead to win by 75 seconds from Lougher's SP-2. Given the fearful time he had endured in practice, second place was the grittiest of performances from the Welsh veteran. 'I'm happy with that,' he said later. 'After a hard practice week, we achieved a good set-up and hopefully we can do a bit more work on the suspension before the Senior. I'll be out to win that.'

Archibald, however, summed up the prevailing mood with the admission that he 'just wanted to win this one for David and his family. I was very nervous to begin with – it took me a few laps to settle in.'

SIDECARS

When Dave Molyneux's DMR Honda chewed up a wheel bearing and ground to a halt at Ramsey on lap one of the sidecar 'A' race, it left the way clear for Ian Bell and Neil Carpenter to score a maiden TT victory. The Bedlington duo led throughout to win by over 50 seconds on their elderly DMR Yamaha – ironically built by Molyneux himself. 'That was good reward for a hard week's work,' enthused the likeable veteran after the race. 'I thought this moment would never happen, I thought that Molly would romp away with it.'

Molly's problem was tracked down to a faulty batch of bearings that had already afflicted several other crews in practice. Paradoxically, if his new outfit hadn't worked quite so well out of the box, he'd have suffered the failure in practice rather than the race.

After Gary Horspole and Kevin Leigh trundled to a halt at Laurel Bank on the last lap, second place went to the Ireson of local pairing Nick Crowe and Darren Hope, racing for only the second time over the Mountain course. Steve Norbury and Andrew Smith brought their Yamaha home in third place, a further 24 seconds behind.

The form book was restored in the sidecar 'B' race, but not without more drama than most competitors liked. It was dry in Douglas when they declared the second sidecar event a wet race. Within moments, a light rain began falling, although conditions around the course were reportedly much worse. Riders and mechanics fretted to fit the right tyres. Pre-race favourite Dave Molyneux had no hesitation in fitting slicks. 'Inters just don't work,' he explained brusquely.

At Glen Helen on the first lap, Molly lay fifth, then began his charge. By Ballaugh, he had moved up to second, just 3.2 seconds behind Nick Crowe and Darren Hope, and by Ramsey his lead was five seconds and rising. From then

on, the TT master extended his lead inexorably to win by 50 seconds from Crowe and Hope, with Greg Lambert and Daniel Sayle an additional minute behind in third.

'I just took it steady on cold tyres on the first lap,' said the Manxman afterward. 'It was scary through Crosby – flat in top at 14,000 rpm, and the tyres still freezing cold. On the last lap, the fog really came down over the Mountain and we were passing backmarkers. Some were doing about 50 mph less than us, so it took a lot of concentration. The new outfit was superb, practically steered itself. But we just don't have tyres for these conditions.'

'That was the most dangerous TT I've ever ridden in,' added Craig Hallam. 'It was wet – soaking wet – from Union Mills to beyond Ballaugh. I thought Dave was going to pull in at Westwood, we seemed to be going that slow. We tried to signal for the race to be stopped, but they took no notice.'

Saturday's winner, Ian Bell, placed fifth.

ULTRA-LIGHTWEIGHT 125 cc

Chris Palmer, originally from Carlisle, but now a Manx resident, took his first TT win in the Ultra-Lightweight event dominated, as ever, by RS125 Hondas. Having topped the practice leaderboard, the veteran set off cautiously in tricky, blustery conditions, overhauling early leader Michael Wilcox on the notoriously rough run down to Ramsey on lap two and posting a 110.41-mph lap record along the way. 'I couldn't catch Michael on the first lap, but on the second, through the bumpy section, our suspension changes from yesterday paid off. This is absolutely fantastic.'

Wilcox placed second, 40 seconds in arrears, having struggled to control his Honda on the more windswept Mountain sections. Ian Lougher, three times a Lightweight winner, was third, ahead of four-times winner Robert Dunlop.

LIGHTWEIGHT 400 cc

Having cheekily borrowed a 400 Honda only on the eve of the TT, John McGuinness was an unlikely winner of the Lightweight event, his third TT victory. After resisting early challenges from Ulstermen Richard Britton and Ryan Farquhar, the Lancashire rider led from start to finish on a bike he'd ridden for only a couple of practice laps. His fastest race lap, 111.36 mph, was the best for a decade, but Jim Moodie's 1993 lap speed clings stubbornly to the record books. Britton took second, 16 seconds ahead of compatriot Farquhar, with local veteran David Madsen-Mygdal in fourth.

A tragic postscript to the race occurred during the classic parade, held on the same afternoon. Peter Jarmann, a motor cycle mechanic from Switzerland, was killed when he lost control of a TSS Bultaco less than half a mile from the start. Earlier in the day, he had finished ninth, earning a bronze replica, in the Lightweight TT.

Above: Triumph wins a TT, after more than three decades – Bruce Anstey wheels his 600 Daytona to victory in the Junior.

Top: Archibald is all tucked in on his way to the Formula One win.

Both photographs: Dave Collister/www.photocycles.com

1000 cc PRODUCTION

In what was becoming a good year for New Zealand, Shaun Harris gained his second TT victory (his first had been a 750 cc class win in the 1000 cc Production event of 2000) with an emphatic performance on the all-conquering GSX-R1000. The big Suzuki grabbed no fewer than 16 of the first 17 places.

Despite an early challenge from Bruce Anstey, third in the same event last year, the ebullient Harris led throughout to win by 16 seconds from his compatriot. In turn, Anstey was 15 seconds ahead of slow-starting Ryan Farquhar, who had battled to turn the tables on Richard Britton. For TAS Suzuki, so dominant last year, it was a race to forget. Luckless Adrian Archibald finished eighth after holding third until he ran out of fuel, within moments of making a scheduled pit stop.

JUNIOR TT

Nearly three decades since they last scored a TT win with the legendary 'Slippery Sam', Triumph won the Junior (Supersport 600) event. Riding a ValMoto 600 Daytona, normally raced by Craig Jones in the British Supersport championship, Bruce Anstey led from start to finish of the four-lap race. His winning margin was 11 seconds from Ian Lougher's CBR600 Honda, while Adrian Archibald's GSX-R600 Suzuki was another six seconds behind in third.

Aided by good signals, Anstey was able to hold an edge of around ten seconds for most of the race. Even when Ryan Farquhar repassed him on the road at Ramsey Hairpin, he could tell from his boards that the Irishman's pace was more than adequate. Indeed, Farquhar, still a relative novice, set a new lap record of 122.30 mph on his final lap. Lougher, equally, could tell from his signals that he was making no impact on the Triumph man, and settled for consolidating second place.

There was nothing fluky about a victory at race-record speed, the first Junior to be won at over 120 mph. Triumph also took the team prize, through the ninth and tenth places of Jim Moodie and John McGuinness, both clearly 'detuned' after David Jefferies's tragic death.

In the 250 cc class, now largely moribund and run alongside the 600s, Chris Palmer took a borrowed four-year-old Honda to victory.

600 cc PRODUCTION

After a much delayed start, New Zealand's third win of the week, and Shaun Harris's second, came in the 600 cc Production event, introduced last year. Begun in sunny conditions and scheduled for three laps, the race was reduced to two when the Cloak of Mannanan – or mist if you prefer – rolled in from the Irish Sea.

In second place by 16 seconds, Ian Lougher was one of many to endorse

the decision to halt the race early. 'The fog really came in and the organisers did the right thing by stopping the race…I dread to think what it was like farther down the field with the lads who started ten minutes after us.'

Ryan Farquhar took third, narrowly ahead of fellow Ulsterman Adrian Archibald, while Jason Griffiths and Richard Britton completed the top six. The Triumphs, so impressive in Supersport trim, could place no higher than eighth.

SENIOR TT

The final race of the week, the 'blue riband' Senior TT, was reduced from six laps to four and postponed to Saturday because of the same weather conditions that had cut short the Production event. In the early stages, McGuinness's F02 Ducati again led narrowly from Lougher's SP-2 and Archibald's GSX-R. But by Ramsey on lap one, the Irishman had forged a narrow lead, which he increased all the way to the end.

'I wasn't pushing too hard,' grinned Archibald after the race, 'and didn't have any moments. The bike was perfect and the pit stop went well. The wind really got up on the Mountain on the last lap and pushed me wide a few times, but other than that it was perfect.'

'I think I was too tense and trying too hard,' admitted McGuinness after finishing second again. 'I outbraked myself at Parliament Square, had a few big slides and missed a few apexes. By the time I got my composure back, my signals were saying "+6", then Adrian put in a blinding lap two. There was nothing I could do to catch him. He's been riding well and deserves his wins.'

Lougher placed third, from Griffiths, Farquhar and Harris. By winning both the Formula One and Senior races, Archibald also claimed the Joey Dunlop Trophy, presented in memory of his former friend and mentor from his home town of Ballymoney.

Hector Neill, manager of Archibald's TAS Suzuki team, was almost lost for words. 'I'm so delighted for Adrian after a sad, sad start to the TT. But I'm glad in a way that he didn't take the lap record – that still belongs to David.'

Above: Dave Molyneux and Craig Hallam were unbeatable in the second sidecar race.
Photograph: Dave Collister/www.photocycles.com

Left: Chris Palmer took a borrowed Honda to victory in the 250 cc class of the Junior TT.
Photograph: Dave Purves

BRITISH SUPERBIKES REVIEW

HIGHS AND LOWS

By GARY PINCHIN

SHANE Byrne came of age as a Superbike star by ripping the formbook apart in BSB to clinch his first major title with the MonsterMob Ducati team. In the 12-round series, Shakey won 12 of the 24 races – eight on the trot – and finished on the podium no fewer than 21 times. Not surprisingly, he wrapped up the title with two rounds still remaining after winning the first race at Cadwell Park on Bank Holiday Monday.

As soon as the title was decided, the unassuming Byrne revealed a burning ambition to race at a higher level in 2004. 'I've had a great season in BSB, and by winning at Cadwell I clinched the title just how I always dreamed of. We gelled well as a team, but I think both myself and the crew reached a stage where we needed a new challenge.

'I want to race in WSB for the next couple of years as a stepping-stone to MotoGP. I know it's not going to be easy, but I need to push myself and become a better rider. Winning the BSB is just the first step. If I can race in Moto-GP and beat someone like Rossi, only then will I start thinking that I've actually achieved something a bit special.'

In fact, he bypassed Superbikes altogether. At Valencia, the final GP, Aprilia presented him with a two-year deal to race in MotoGP. He grabbed the opportunity with both hands.

Byrne was anything but a BSB pre-season favourite. Everyone knew he had the pace. He'd shown that in 2002 with race-winning rides on a Renegade Ducati, but there was no hint of the consistency required to put a championship season together.

There was also a question mark over his ability to get his head around the problems of setting up his bike in the very short practice sessions at BSB races. When he raced with Renegade, he often relied on the settings of team-mate Michael Rutter – and if they didn't suit him, he had to ride around any problems. Not the ideal way to compete in one of the world's toughest domestic Superbike championships.

The difference for 2003 was the people around him. Paul Bird's MonsterMob Ducati team had the necessary experience to help their new rider. Stacks of it. They had won the title with Steve Hislop in 2002, and probably would have won it the year before, had Hizzy not been seriously injured in the penultimate round of the series at the controversial new Rockingham circuit.

Hizzy had the damper put on his 41st birthday celebrations when he was ditched by Bird during the winter of 2002, in favour of the 26-year-old Byrne. The restructuring process, allegedly at the behest of team backers, was designed to take the team forward into WSB in 2004.

The beauty of Bird's team has always been its stark functionality, only four regular crew members being required to keep things ticking over smoothly. Crew chief Phil Borley is a meticulous genius of an engineer whose CV includes British Superbike and Supersport successes as a rider. Not only does he continue to build incredibly reliable motor cycles, but also he has an uncanny empathy with his riders when it comes to fine-tuning both chassis and engine set-up. He was backed up by co-ordinator Stuart Bland, data technician Mark 'Mr Bean' Richardson and tyre man/truckie Garry Matthews. Such is their experience that rarely are any words exchanged between them during routine pit stops – each instinctively knows his own job.

Shakey learned a lot about set-up in 2003, but didn't really have to worry too much with Borley looking out for him. Even he admitted as such. 'I come in sometimes and speak to Phil, and he already knows what the bike is doing,' said Shakey at one meeting. 'It's great having him in my garage. Imagine how bloody hard it would be racing against someone with that much knowledge.'

As a result, Byrne was able to develop his own game. He found the true meaning of consistency and became a complete package for the first time in his career, one of the most highly rated riders in BSB.

MonsterMob started the season with the best two bikes in the championship for Byrne. Both were brand-new factory F02 Ducatis, identical in spec to the bike that Troy Bayliss raced to second place in WSB in 2002. Renegade also had two F02s, second-hand bikes that had logged a season's mileage with Bayliss and Xaus.

Byrne was on the pace from the moment he straddled his bike in Valencia for the BSB Dunlop tyre test. The team nonchalantly arrived a day later than anyone else, then left a day early, but only after Byrne and his crew had found an effective base setting that would give them a good start to the season.

And when the season got under way at Silverstone, on 30 March, Shakey jumped into an immediate points lead, winning the first race and finishing second in race two behind Rutter.

Rutter beat Byrne again in the first race at Snetterton two weeks later, but Shakey's second-leg victory was the start of an eight-race unbeaten streak that set him well on his way to the title by the mid-point of the season at Brands in June.

That round was held on the Grand Prix circuit, using the reconfigured Dingle Dell section for the first time in advance of the WSB round in August. Shakey was in sensational form, coming out on top after one of the best scraps of the year with Rizla Suzuki's John Reynolds.

It was JR's first race at full fitness after breaking his collar-bone during Superpole in the very first round of the series. Reynolds turned the tables in race two, thus spoiling Shakey's opportunity to establish a new record of scoring double race wins in four successive BSB rounds.

Shakey's second half of the season wasn't as strong as his first – if you discount his astounding race-winning double at the Brands WSB round in August, when he again had to do battle with Reynolds. The WSB regulars never got a look in. But in BSB, he won only three more races, taking his season tally to 12 when he wrapped up the title with a race-one victory at Cadwell.

If Reynolds hadn't suffered that injury right at the start, the championship might have been much closer fought. He was back in the saddle two weeks later at Snetterton, and ignored the agony to claim a pair of thirds. A week later, the high-speed bumps of Thruxton were simply too punishing, but he still scored four points – points that might have been vital later in the year.

As it turned out, Shakey was long gone in the championship race, and Reynolds had to be content with second overall. It was largely due to his gritty brand of determination, as he became the man to beat in the second half of the year and actually outscored the eventual champion over the last five rounds (191–173).

In addition to getting the better of Byrne at Brands, Reynolds took the GSX-R1000 to a double at Mondello, and stood on the rostrum in every one of the final seven races of the year, including a win on the tight little Brands Hatch Indy circuit.

It was the second season of the GSX-R1000, and by the end of the year it was definitely the bike to beat. The ex-factory Ducatis remained a formidable all-round package, but the Suzukis of Reynolds and Japanese team-mate Yukio Kagayama were often faster, and still had the grunt to out-accelerate almost

Facing page: Shane Byrne came of age as a BSB rider in 2003, winning the title convincingly and earning a GP slot.

Below: But for early injury, John Reynolds would have been a serious contender for the title. By year's end, he and his Suzuki were the combination to beat.

Bottom: Michael Rutter was stymied by problems within the Renegade Ducati team.
All photographs: Clive Challinor Motor Sport Photography

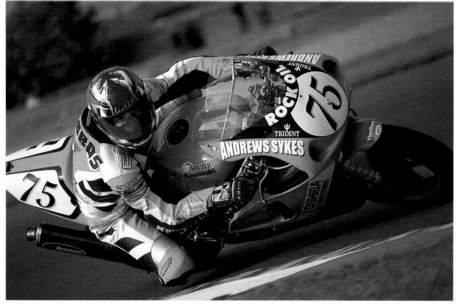

Top: Steve Plater finally got the ex-Edwards title-winning Honda Superbike working to his liking – here he is en route to victory at Oulton Park.

Above: Glenn Richards consistently achieved the impossible on the outpaced 750 Kawasaki.

Right: Byrne gave centre stage to John Reynolds at Brands in September.

All photographs: Clive Challinor Motor Sport Photography

anything on the track. The bike was better overall than it had been in 2002, suspension tweaks having improved its tendency to drop off toward the end of a race once the tyres started to lose grip.

Reynolds also suffered from a lack of strength to flick the bike from side to side – not because of his injured shoulder, but because he had the pegs mounted very high to improve ground clearance. The problem really came to light at Rockingham, which requires several fast changes of direction. Lowering the pegs by 7 mm after that meeting gave him the manoeuvrability he had been lacking up to that point.

Michael Rutter finished third in the series, after being tipped as pre-season favourite by many. In 2002, the rookie Renegade team had become a force to be reckoned with, after Rutter finished runner-up to Steve Hislop, and team-mate Byrne was fourth. But for 2003, the team that had promised so much became a farce. A catalogue of mechanical disasters, team sackings (including that of Rutter's new team-mate, Sean Emmett) and general misguided management contrived to ruin Rutter's season.

Team boss Mark Griffiths secured a pair of F02 Ducatis, originally for Rutter, while Emmett was to have two of the team's 2002 998R Testastrettas. But Griffiths wilted under pressure from Emmett and decided to split the factory bikes, giving each rider an F02 and 998R.

That virtually rendered the 998Rs redundant and placed high mileage on the F02s. The team was short of spares and, after several very public mechanical disasters – including Rutter's expensive blow-up at Knockhill – the F02s were parked and both riders continued the season on the less-competitive 998Rs.

The F02s had arrived late anyway – just in time for the pre-season media test day at Donington. That gave Rutter and Emmett just two hours to get dialled in for the season ahead. As it turned out, they were very competitive out of the box, and Rutter won two of the first four races and was on the podium in the next four. But things started to go awry for the team at Knockhill, where his engine exploded spectacularly in the second race.

By Thruxton, the riders themselves had decided it was a fruitless exercise trying to work with just one factory bike each, and Emmett gave up his F02 to Rutter in favour of the two 998Rs. The bigger problem was getting the best out of the bike. Unlike the MonsterMob team, who seemed to have an endless supply of spares and an experienced crew, Renegade had no data technician, which is vital to get the most out of any Ducati – and especially a factory Ducati.

Rutter's crew did their best, but while the rider made some blinding starts and ran up front for a lap or so, his bike was invariably blown away by Byrne's 'identical' Ducati – and the Suzukis.

Eventually, Emmett was sacked after Brands, but instead of cutting his losses and putting all the team's effort behind Rutter, Griffiths moved young Leon Haslam up to the Superbike ranks, ditching the team's British Supersport programme completely.

Rutter, to his credit, never spoke out publicly about the team's internal strife, but that was more out of fear of losing his job and wages than any real loyalty to his team boss. It was no surprise when Griffiths announced in October, after the season had ended, that Leon Haslam was confirmed for 2004, and that he was allowing Rutter to enter into talks with other teams – this just a few short months after stating publicly on two separate occasions that Rutter had 'a job with Renegade for life'.

What Glen Richards did on the Hawk Kawasaki ZX7-RR should not have been possible. To put an ageing 750 cc Superbike at the front of BSB races against the latest factory Ducatis and 1000 cc fours was simply outrageous. The Australian never won a race, but to the delight of Kawasaki fans everywhere, he got on to the podium with third places at Silverstone (twice), Thruxton and Mondello, and secured fourth overall ahead of a bunch of more well-equipped riders.

The quietly-spoken, but ever smiling Richards did it by maximising the positive traits of the old bike – he kept the motor buzzing at the red line, used fearsome corner speeds and relied on the nimble chassis to get him out of trouble. Richards became one of the BSB crowd favourites with his Super-moto-style antics, backing the green bike into corners and then lighting up the rear tyre on the exits.

His ZX-R had started life as a Chris Walker factory bike, but the small, yet efficient, Hawk Kawasaki squad had ditched the stiff works chassis and used their own more flexible street-bike version, which gave Richards infinitely more feel. The team also used the best parts of the gear-driven DOHC factory motors, but built their own spec engines. It's fair to say that, by the end of the year, theirs were probably the best examples of the marque the world has ever seen.

Emmett suffered a second successive year of turmoil. He'd been a 2002 title contender until his Ducati team went bust and he was forced to seek a ride elsewhere. Virgin Yamaha boss Rob McElnea snapped him up and he did a sterling job of keeping his title hopes alive, until he crashed and broke his right wrist in the penultimate race of the year.

Fully fit and raring to go, Emmett joined the Renegade team for 2003, but failed to recapture his 2002 form in the early part of the year. A string of bike problems saw him scoring only one podium finish in 12 races, before being ditched by the team. Lack of results wasn't the reason. A minor disagreement with team boss Mark Griffiths over being late for a pit-lane walkabout erupted into a full-scale row at Brands, and Emmett was given his marching orders the next day.

His salvation was linking up with the Scottish-based ETI Ducati team. John Crawford had struggled to get to grips with the ex-Hizzy 2002 title-winning bikes, so team boss Alistair Flanagan replaced him with Emmett from Rockingham on. Emmett was bang on the pace at Mondello, if not a little over-exuberant. He finished second in the first race – the team's first podium – but then overshot corners in race two and narrowly missed taking out rival competitors several times. But there was no faulting his commitment, and he finally gave the team its first ever BSB win in the second race on the Brands Indy course. Second place in race one made it his best weekend of the season.

Emmett finished the season in style with second and third places in the final meeting of the year at Donington, underlining his potential as one of the most competitive riders in BSB.

Steve Plater was another rider to find form late in the year. Signed by Honda Racing to ride the ex-Colin Edwards WSB title-winning SP1 V-twin, Plater was thought to have an easy shot at the title. The reality was something quite different.

First, the bike had been built for Edwards – a world-class rider. Second, it had been developed on Michelin tyres, not the Dunlops the team was forced to use in BSB (Michelin had no presence in the BSB paddock). And finally, the bike had been designed for the fast, open world circuits, not the tight, bumpy little tracks on which the majority of BSB races are held.

Plater's job was even under threat early in the year, when he was struggling to come to terms with a bike that had so much torque it pushed the front end in every corner at the merest whiff of the throttle. Unhappy with his results in testing and in the first meetings of the year, Honda brought in Mark Heckles, who had been impressive in a post-2002 test on the bike at Brands – but at that time, it had been on Michelins.

Heckles gave it his best shot, but he also struggled with the bike. Plater kept plugging away and eventually got it working to his liking, well enough to win at Oulton and Cadwell Parks. He might even have celebrated a double at Cadwell, but for the chain derailing when the bike landed heavily after the Mountain jump in race one.

Such is the importance placed on BSB by the Japanese factories that Suzuki asked Paul Denning's Rizla team to run factory tester and occasional GP racer Yukio Kagayama in Britain. Yukio was the find of the series. The fun loving Japanese star was such good value on and off the track. On the bike, he was a joy to watch, with his aggressive, unconventional riding style. Off track, he embraced the British lifestyle totally, was always ready for a good laugh, and brought a refreshing brand of humour – and humility – to the paddock.

Before every round, Yukio did either a track day or an official practice day in an effort to learn the tracks, and he coped admirably with virtually everything our unique little circuits threw at him – at least until he reached Cadwell. Not only that, but also he showed his world-class ability by subbing for the injured Kenny Roberts on the lacklustre GSV-R in MotoGP and riding selected rounds of the WSB on Rizla's bike, plus the Suzuka Eight Hours.

Yukio finished second and fourth in his very first meeting of the year at Silverstone, but it was later on, at Rockingham, that he really came good with a double victory. He was strong the following weekend at Mondello, a track where no one had any previous experience. Third there in race one, he was battling with team-mate Reynolds for the lead when he dumped it on the final lap. Undeterred, he bounced back for two more brilliant rides at Oulton, netting second and first places. Then the crash in the very next round at Cadwell sidelined him for the remainder of the year.

And it was a horrible crash. Yukio was on a fast lap in race-morning warm-up, approaching the bottom of the Mountain, when a slower rider, Chris Heath, acknowledging the blue overtaking flags, unwittingly moved over into his path. Yuki, with nowhere to go, crashed headlong into a tyre wall, suffering a badly broken pelvis and serious internal injuries. As *MOTOCOURSE* went to press, he was back in Japan recuperating, and was expected to make a full recovery to return to racing at the start of the 2004 season with Denning's Suzuki team.

Gary Mason had a difficult season in the Virgin Yamaha team. He was signed as a number two, and no one really expected too much of him after his difficult 2002 rookie season on an uncompetitive FireBlade. But as his vastly experienced team-mate, Steve Hislop, struggled with the R1, so Mason shouldered more and more responsibilities – of development and carrying the team in terms of getting results.

Hislop went out of his way to help Mason get to grips with a top-level Superbike, and he responded well to become one of the front-runners in the series. Although he never quite managed to get on to the podium, he did score four fourth places.

Scott Smart and Leon Haslam also paid their dues in 2003, and could become big names in the Superbike class in future. Former 250 British Champion Smart secured a ride with Hawk Kawasaki and spent the year getting the hang of a Superbike after finishing runner-up in the national Supersport class the previous year. He proved his pace by getting on to the front row at Mondello, and managed to score in every round of the series – except the final one at Donington, where he was side-swiped at the Esses by a rival competitor.

Haslam gamely raced an uncompetitive Ducati 749 in British Supersport until Renegade team boss Griffiths promoted him to BSB to replace Emmett. Ex-GP racer Leon acquitted himself well: fourth in the second Cadwell race, plus a couple of fifths at Brands and Donington. He also scored well in two WSB races for the team and secured a ride with them for 2004.

The saddest story of 2003 was Steve Hislop's. After winning the title in 2002, Hizzy was dumped by the MonsterMob team and never really got to grips with the Virgin Yamaha R1.

Hizzy's biggest asset had always been his high corner speed, but he was never able to use it on the R1. The heavy crank of the in-line 1000 cc four always wanted to push the front end in corners, which left Hizzy struggling to adapt his style to make the bike work. Only once did the fans get a glimpse of his potential, at Thruxton, where he finished a sparkling second in the first race – just a week after he'd been threatened with the sack following a dismal outing at Snetterton.

Hizzy did eventually get the push after Rockingham, but he was quickly snapped up by ETI for the Oulton Park race. He saw it as his big chance to finish the season with a flourish. ETI boss Alistair Flanagan had even bought an ex-Doug Chandler 2002 998R for him to race.

Tragically, Steve Hislop never got the chance. The Isle of Man resident was killed in a helicopter crash in August, shortly after he had left his hometown of Hawick. British racing had lost one of the most talented racers it had ever known.

Above: Yukio Kagayama won friends and races before he was badly hurt at Cadwell Park.

Left: Garry Mason took over from Hislop as team leader for the Virgin Yamaha team.
Both photographs: Clive Challinor Motor Sport Photography

Above: Sean Emmett had another season of turmoil, but bounced back on the ETI Ducati to win at Brands late in the year.

Left: The late Steve Hislop never did come to terms with the Yamaha.
Both photographs: Clive Challinor Motor Sport Photography

MAJOR WORLDWIDE RESULTS

Compiled by Kay Edge

Endurance World Championship

200 MIGLIA DI IMOLA, Autodromo Enzo e Dino Ferrari, Imola, Italy, 4 May.
Endurance World Championship, round 1. 66 laps of the 3.065-mile/4.933-km circuit, 202.290 miles/325.578 km

1 Zongshen 1: Warwick Nowland/Stephane Mertens, AUS/B (Suzuki GSXR), 2h 09m 23.578s, 93.810 mph/150.972 km/h.

2 Phase One: James Ellison/Olivier Four, GB/F (Suzuki GSXR), 66 laps; **3** Yamaha Austria: Horst Saiger/Erwin Wilding, A/A (Yamaha YZF), 65; **4** 22 Police Nationale: Gwen Giabbani/Paolo Blora, F/I (Suzuki GSXR), 65; **5** Bolliger Team: Marcel Kellenberger/Benny Jerzenbech/Tobias Nyström, CH/D/S (Kawasaki ZXR), 65; **6** GMT 94: Sébastien Scarnato/Christophe Guyot, F/F (Yamaha YZF), 65; **7** Ducati DRE 91: Paolo Tessari/Lorenzo Mauri, I/I (Ducati 999), 65; **8** Fabi Corse: Fabio Capriotti/Patrizio Fabi, I/I (Suzuki 988), 64; **9** Team Bergamelli: Gianluca Battisti/Paolo Bosetti, I/I (Suzuki GSXR), 64; **10** KFM Herber: Hans Herber/Michal Bursa, D/CZ (Suzuki GSXR), 64; **11** Poland Position: Tomasz Kedzior/Adam Badziak, POL/POL (Suzuki 998), 64; **12** DMG 24: Andrea Giachino/Eric Marangon, I/I (Suzuki GSXR), 63; **13** Jet Team: Claude-Alain Jäggi/Eric Monot/Sylvain Waldmeier, CH/F/CH (Suzuki GSXR), 63; **14** Hofmann Racing: Frank Spenner/Lars Albrecht/Niggi Schmassmann, D/D/CH (Suzuki GSXR), 63; **15** No Limits: Roberto Ruozzi/Moreno Codeluppi, I/I (Suzuki GSXR), 62.

Fastest lap: Nowland, 1m 54.914s, 96.027 mph/154.540 km/h.

Championship points: **1** Zongshen 1, 25; **2** Phase One, 20; **3** Yamaha Austria, 16; **4** 22 Police Nationale, 13; **5** Bolliger Team, 11; **6** GMT 94, 10.

200 MILES ENDURANCE NETHERLANDS, Assen Circuit, Holland, 25 May.
Endurance World Championship, round 2. 83 laps of the 2.412-mile/3.881-km circuit, 200.196 miles/322.123 km

1 Zongshen 2: Igor Jerman/Bruno Bonhuil, SLO/F (Suzuki GSXR), 1h 59m 24.581s, 100.573 mph/161.857 km/h.

2 Phase One: James Ellison/Jason Pridmore, GB/USA (Suzuki GSXR), 83 laps; **3** Zongshen 1: Warwick Nowland/Stephane Mertens, AUS/B (Suzuki GSXR), 83; **4** Moto 38: Laurent Brian/Bernard Cuzin/David Morillon, F/F/F (Yamaha YZF), 82; **5** Lowlands Racing: John Bakker/Ivan Batens, NL/B (Suzuki GSXR), 81; **6** 22 Police Nationale: Gwen Giabbani/Paolo Blora/Jerome Chauchard, F/I/F (Suzuki GSXR), 81; **7** Trackdaze 11: James Hutchins/Mike Edwards/Kevin Falcke, GB/GB/GB (Suzuki GSXR), 81; **8** Fabi Corse: Fabio Capriotti/Patrizio Fabi, I/I (Suzuki GSXR), 80; **9** Junior Phase One: Henry Fincher/Martin Jessop, GB/GB (Suzuki GSXR), 80; **10** Bergmann & Sohne: Harald Kitsch/Claus Ehrenberger, D/D (Suzuki GSXR), 80; **11** CRT Suzuki: Leon Tijssen/Robert de Vries/Jean Paul Heindijk, NL/NL/NL (Suzuki 988), 79; **12** PS Schlesinger: Peter Meyer/Stefan Meyer, D/D (Suzuki GSXR), 79; **13** Team Fagersjo: Niklas Carlberg/Andi Notman, S/GB (Yamaha YZF), 79; **14** Rookie Endurance: Heinz Platacis/Thomas Roth, D/D (Suzuki GSXR), 79; **15** Jet Team: Claude-Alain Jäggi/Sylvain Waldmeier, CH/CH (Suzuki GSXR), 79.

Fastest lap: Ellison, 1m 23.376s, 104.125 mph/167.573 km/h.

Championship points: **1** Zongshen 1, 41; **2** Phase One, 40; **3** Zongshen 2, 25; **4** 22 Police Nationale, 23; **5** Fabi Corse and Yamaha Austria, 16.

6 HOURS OF BRNO, Autodrom Brno, Czech Republic, 15 June.
Endurance World Championship, round 3. 166 laps of the 3.357-mile/5.403-km circuit, 557.262 miles/896.898 km

1 Zongshen 1: Warwick Nowland/Stephane Mertens, AUS/B (Suzuki GSXR), 6h 01m 58.358s, 92.378 mph/148.668 km/h.

2 GMT 94: Sébastien Scarnato/William Costes/Christophe Guyot, F/F/F (Yamaha YZF), 165 laps; **3** Phase One: Jason Pridmore/Jimmy Lindstrom/Olivier Four, USA/S/F (Suzuki GSXR), 164; **4** Ducati DRE 5: Dario Marchetti/Marc Garcia/Stéphane Coutelle, I/F/F (Ducati 999), 163; **5** Trackdaze 11: Kevin Falcke/James Hutchins/Mike Edwards, GB/GB/GB (Suzuki GSXR), 162; **6** 22 Police Nationale: Gwen Giabbani/Paolo Blora/Jerome Cauchard, F/I/F (Suzuki GSXR), 162; **7** Bolliger Team: Marcel Kellenberger/Tobias Nyström/Roger Bantli, CH/S/CH (Kawasaki ZX9R), 161; **8** PS Schlesinger: Peter Mayer/Stefan Mayer, D/D (Suzuki GSX), 160; **9** Jet Team: Claude-Alain Jäggi/Eric Monot/Sébastien Pelleriti, CH/F/CH (Suzuki GSXR), 160; **10** Junior Phase One: Henry Fincher/Martin Jessop, GB/GB (Suzuki GSXR), 160; **11** Rookie Endurance: Thomas Roth/Christian Plantius, D/D (Suzuki GSXR), 158; **12** Hofmann Racing: Sandor Bitter/Niggi Schmassmann, H/CH (Suzuki GSXR), 158; **13** Motopol Racing: Ireneusz Sikora/Bartlomiej Wiczynski, POL/POL (Honda), 157; **14** KFM Herber: Hans Herber/Michal Bursa/Gustav Persson, D/CZ/S (Suzuki GSXR), 156; **15** Poland Position: Pawel Szkopek/Adam Badziak/Tomasz Kedzior, POL/POL/POL (Suzuki GSXR), 156.

Fastest lap: Scarnato, 2m 07.510s, 94.786 mph/152.543 km/h.

Championship points: **1** Zongshen 1, 66; **2** Phase One, 56; **3** 22 Police Nationale, 33; **4** GMT 94, 30; **5** Zongshen 2, 25; **6** Bolliger Team and Trackdaze 11, 20.

12 HOURS OF ALBACETE, Albacete, Spain, 29 June.
Endurance World Championship, round 4. 441 laps of the 2.199-mile/3.539-km circuit, 969.759 miles/1560.699 km

1 Zongshen 1: Warwick Nowland/Stephane Mertens/Igor Jerman, AUS/B/SLO (Suzuki GSXR), 12h 00m 37.437s, 80.741 mph/129.940 km/h.

2 Zongshen 2: Piergiorgio Bontempi/Bruno Bonhuil/Lerats Vanstaen, I/F/F (Suzuki GSXR), 440 laps; **3** Folch Endurance: Oriol Fernandez/Daivd Tomás/Javier Rodriguez, E/E/E (Yamaha YZF), 440; **4** GMT 94: Sébastien Scarnato/Ludovic Holon/Serafino Foti, F/F/I (Yamaha YZF), 437; **5** Moto 38: David Morillon/Bernard Cuzin/Laurent Brian, F/F/F (Yamaha YZF), 435; **6** Phase One: Jimmy Lindstrom/James Ellison/Dean Ellison, S/GB/GB (Suzuki GSXR), 429; **7** Yamaha Austria: Horst Saiger/Erwin Wilding/Karl Truchsess, A/A/A (Yamaha YZF), 428; **8** Bolliger Team: Marcel Kellenberger/Tobias Nyström/Roman Stamm, CH/S/CH (Kawasaki ZX9R), 426; **9** Junior Phase One: Andi Notman/Henry Fincher/Martin Jessop, GB/GB/GB (Suzuki GSXR), 421; **10** Trackdaze 11: Kevin Falcke/Nick Pilborough/James Hutchins, GB/GB/GB (Suzuki GSXR), 420; **11** Hofmann Racing: Frank Spenner/Niggi Schmassmann/Sandor Bitter, D/CH/H (Suzuki GSXR), 416; **12** Bemposta Vodafone Sendo: Rui Jorge Reigoto/Leite/Manuel da Costa, P/P/P (Suzuki GSXR), 414; **13** Yamaha Endurance Belgium: Danny Scheers/Koen Reymenants/Peter Ploemen, B/B/B (Yamaha), 413; **14** PS Schlesinger: Peter Meyer/Stefan Meyer/Hendrich Peuker, D/D/D (Suzuki GSXR), 412; **15** Würth: Antonio Gil/Martin Lopetegui/Mikel Zabaleta, E/E/E (Suzuki), 411.

Fastest lap: Bontempi, 1m 33.665s, 84.339 mph/135.731 km/h.

Championship points: **1** Zongshen 1, 91; **2** Phase One, 66; **3** Zongshen 2, 45; **4** GMT 94, 43; **5** 22 Police Nationale, 33; **6** Bolliger Team, 28.

A1-RING 6 HOURS, A1-Ring, Austria, 20 July.
Endurance World Championship, round 5. 225 laps of the 2.688-mile/4.326-km circuit, 604.800 miles/973.350 km

1 Zongshen 1: Warwick Nowland/Stephane Mertens, AUS/B (Suzuki GSXR), 6h 01m 25.635s, 100.221 mph/161.290 km/h.

2 Zongshen 2: Igor Jerman/Bruno Bonhuil/Piergiorgio Bontempi, SLO/F/I (Suzuki GSXR), 225 laps; **3** GMT 94: Christophe Guyot/Serafino Foti/Sébastien Scarnato, F/I/F (Yamaha YZF), 224; **4** Phase One: James Ellison/Jason Pridmore, GB/USA (Suzuki GSXR), 225*; **5** Moto 38: Brian Laurent/David Morillon/Bernard Cuzin, F/F/F (Yamaha YZF), 220; **6** 22 Police Nationale: Gwen Giabbani/Paolo Blora, F/I (Suzuki GSXR), 219; **7** Yamaha Austria: Karl Truchsess/Erwin Wilding/Horst Saiger, A/A/A (Yamaha YZF), 218; **8** Ducati DRE 5: Dario Marchetti/Marc Garcia/Mike Edwards, I/F/GB (Ducati 999), 218; **9** Rookie Racing: Thomas Roth/Christian Plantius, D/D (Suzuki GSXR), 215; **10** Bolliger Team: Tobias Nyström/Harald Kitsch, S/D (Kawasaki ZX9R), 215; **11** Hofmann Racing: Frank Spenner/Niggi Schmassmann/Lars Albrecht, D/CH/D (Suzuki GSXR), 215; **12** PS Schlesinger: Peter Meyer/Stefan Meyer, D/D (Suzuki GSXR), 214; **13** No Limits: Roberto Ruozzi/Moreno Codeluppi, I/I (Suzuki GSXR), 214; **14** Jet Team: Eric Monot/Sylvain Waldmeier, F/CH (Suzuki GSXR), 213; **15** Solandra: Andrea Clerici/Alex Barduzzo, I/I (Suzuki 1000), 209.

** demoted from 3rd place on a technicality.*

Fastest lap: Bontempi, 1m 33.604s.

Championship points: **1** Zongshen 1, 116; **2** Phase One, 79; **3** Zonghsen 2, 65; **4** GMT 94, 59; **5** 22 Police Nationale, 43; **6** Moto 38, 35.

SUZUKA EIGHT HOURS, Suzuka International Circuit, Japan, 3 August.
Endurance World Championship, round 6. 212 laps of the 3.617-mile/5.821-km circuit, 766.804 miles/1234.052 km

1 Sakurai Honda 71: Yukio Nukumi/Gaku Kamada, J/J (Honda SPW), 8h 00m 38.909s, 95.722 mph/154.050 km/h.

2 Phase One: Jason Pridmore/James Ellison/Jimmy Lindstrom, USA/GB/S (Suzuki GSXR), 208 laps; **3** 22 Police Nationale: Gwen Giabbani/Takaharu Kishida, F/J (Suzuki GSXR), 207; **4** Corona Light TiForce: Alex Fergusson/Anthony Gobert, AUS/AUS (Suzuki GSXR), 206; **5** RS Itoh & Kaze: Isami Higashimura/Syohei Karita, J/J (Kawasai ZX7RR), 204; **6** Blue Helmets MSC: Kenichiro Nakamura/Noriyoshi Sasaki, J/J (Honda VTR), 202; **7** Sofukai Suzuka: Tomoki Arakawa/Kazuhiro Matsushita, J/J (Honda VTR), 202; **8** Hammamatsu Escargot: Norikazu Odagiri/H. Senmyo, J/J (Honda VTR), 201; **9** RS Itoh & Kaze: Izumi Matsubara/Masakatsu Murakami, J/J (Kawasaki ZX7RR), 199; **10** Team TKM Xyna: Yuki Okuda/Tomohiro Kimura, J/J (Suzuki GSXR), 198; **11** Yamashina: Takeshi Kawarabayashi/Tamotsu Mizusawa, J/J (Kawasaki ZX7RR), 196; **12** Honda Kumamoto Racing: Takaomi Ryu/Tsutomu Maeda, J/J (Honda SPW), 192; **13** Driver Stand: Tamotsu Nakamura/Takumi Shimizu, J/J (Suzuki GSXR), 191; **14** Team Little Wing: Fumihisa Asano/Takeshi Kimura, J/J (Honda CBR), 191; **15** Team MO2 Motosport Hirose: Masayuki Tokunaga/Katsushi Sakai, J/J (Kawasaki ZX7RR), 180.

Fastest lap: not givon.

Championship points: **1** Zongshen 1, 116; **2** Phase One, 99; **3** Zongshen 2, 65; **4** 22 Police Nationale and GMT 94, 59; **6** Moto 38, 35.

24 STUNDEN VON OSCHERSLEBEN, Oschersleben Circuit, Germany, 23–24 August.
Endurance World Championship, round 7. 896 laps of the 2.279-mile/3.667-km circuit, 2041.984 miles/3285.632 km

1 GMT 94: Serafino Foti/David Checa/Sébastien Scarnato, I/E/F (Yamaha YZF), 24h 01m 20.212s, 84.987 mph/136.774 km/h.

2 Phase One: Jason Pridmore/James Ellison/Josh Hayes, USA/GB/USA (Suzuki GSXR), 891 laps; **3** Moto 38: Christian Hacquin/David Morillon/Bernard Cuzin, F/F/F (Yamaha YZF), 889; **4** Zongshen 2: Piergiorgio Bontempi/Bruno Bonhuil/Lerats Vanstaen, I/F/F (Suzuki GSXR), 888; **5** Bolliger Team: Marcel Kellenberger/Roman Stamm/Tobias Nyström, CH/CH/S (Kawasaki ZX9R), 882; **6** 22 Police Nationale: Gwen Giabbani/Paolo Blora/Takaharu Kishida, F/I/J (Suzuki GSXR), 876; **7** Yamaha Austria: Karl Truchsess/Erwin Wilding/Horst Saiger, A/A/A (Yamaha YZF), 873; **8** Jet Team: Claude-Alain Jäggi/Eric Monot/Sylvain Waldmeier, CH/F/CH (Suzuki GSXR), 870; **9** PS Schlesinger: Peter Meyer/Stefan Meyer/Ronny Wehran, D/D/D (Suzuki GSXR), 864; **10** Yamaha OBI-Shell: Rico Penzkofer/Phillipp Ludwig/Rene Knöfler, D/D/D (Yamaha YZF), 862; **11** Junior Phase One: Henry Fincher/Martin Jessop/Damian Codlin, GB/GB/AUS (Suzuki GSXR), 858; **12** Bridgestone Bikers Profit: Stefan Strauch/Tim Röthig/Thomas Czyborra, D/D/D (Suzuki GSXR), 849; **13** Ducati Rheinhessen: Toni Heiler/Peter Hecker/Harry Gres, D/D/D (Ducati 998), 833; **14** Team Fagersjo: Niklas Carlberg/Lars Carlbark/Tobias Andersson, S/S/S (Yamaha YXF), 830; **15** Yamaha Endurance Belgium: Danny Scheers/Koen Reymenants/Peter Ploeman, B/B/B (Yamaha R1), 829.

Fastest lap: Bontempi/Bonhuil/Vanstaen, 1m 31.296s, 89.849 mph/144.598 km/h.

Championship points: **1** Phase One, 139; **2** Zongshen 1, 116; **3** GMT 94, 109; **4** Zonghsen 2, 91; **5** 22 Police Nationale, 79; **6** Moto 38, 67.

200 MIGLIA DI VALLELUNGA, Vallelunga Circuit, Italy, 6 October.
Endurance World Championship, round 8. 100 laps of the 2.006-mile/3.228-km circuit, 200.600 miles/322.800 km

1 22 Police Nationale: Gwen Giabbani/Frédéric Moreira/Paolo Blora, F/F/I (Suzuki GSXR), 2h 26m 45.696s, 82.383 mph/132.582 km/h.

2 GMT 94: Serafino Foti/Sébastien Scarnato, I/F (Yamaha YZF), 100 laps; **3** Ducati DRE 5: Dario Marchetti/Mike Edwards/Marc Garcia, I/GB/F (Ducati 998), 100; **4** KFM Herber: Hans Herber/Arne Tode, D/D (Suzuki GSXR), 99; **5** Zongshen 1: Warwick Nowland/Piergiorgio Bontempi, AUS/I (Suzuki GSXR), 98; **6** Yamaha Austria: Horst Saiger/Erwin Wilding/Karl Truchsess, A/A/A (Yamaha YZF), 98; **7** Jet Team: Eric Monot/Sylvain Waldmeier, F/CH (Suzuki GSXR), 98; **8** Diablo GB: James Hutchins/Kevin Falcke/Shaun Harris, GB/GB/GB (Suzuki GSXR), 98; **9** Trackdaze 11: Nick Pilborough/Damian Codlin/Jeff Collins, GB/AUS/GB (Suzuki GSXR), 98; **10** Ducati DRE 101: Paolo Tessari/Lorenzo Mauri, I/I (Ducati 999), 98; **11** Moto 38: Laurent Brian/David Morillon/Jean-François Cortinovis, F/F/F (Yamaha YZF), 98; **12** Phase One: James Ellison/Dean Ellison/Andi Notman, GB/GB/GB (Suzuki GSXR), 97; **13** Team Fagersjo: Pete Jennings/Thomas Sykes, GB/S (Yamaha YZF), 96; **14** Celani Team: Alex Martinez/Walter Tortoroglio/Ilario Dionisi, E/I/I (Suzuki GSXR), 96; **15** PS Schlesinger: Peter Meyer/Stefan Meyer, D/D (Suzuki GSXR), 96.

Fastest lap: Nowland/Bontempi, 1m 20.341s, 90.296 mph/145.317 km/h.

Final World Championship points

1	Phase One, GB	143
2	GMT 94, F	129
3	Zongshen 1, CHN	127
4	22 Police Nationale, F	104
5	Zongshen 2, CHN	91

6 Moto 38, F, 72; **7** Yamaha Austria, A, 62; **8** Bolliger Team, CH, 56; **9** Jet Team, CH, 38; **10** Ducati DRE 5, I, 37; **11** Trackdaze 11, GB, 33; **12** PS Schlesinger, D, 32; **13** Junior Phase One, GB, 30; **14** Team Sakurai Honda, J, 71, 25; **15** KFM Herber, D, 21.

Superside World Championship

VALENCIA, Spain, 1 March. 2.489-mile/4.005-km circuit.
Superside World Championship, round 1 (18 laps, 44.802 miles/72.090 km)

1 Steve Webster/Paul Woodhead, GB/GB (Suzuki), 30m 55.539s, 86.907 mph/139.864 km/h.

2 Steve Abbott/Jamie Biggs, GB/GB (Yamaha); **3** Klaus Klaffenböck/Christian Parzer, A/A (Yamaha); **4** Jock Skene/Neil Miller, GB/GB (Suzuki); **5** Mike Roscher/Heidenreich, D/D (Suzuki); **6** Bill Philp/Gary Yendell, GB/GB (Suzuki); **7** Dan Morrissey/Darren Harper, GB/GB (Yamaha); **8** Sepp Doppler/Bernhard Wagner, A/A (Yamaha); **9** Duncan Hendry/Peter Wilson, GB/GB (Suzuki); **10** Gerhard Hauzenberger/Ian Simons, A/GB (Suzuki); **11** Bryan Pedder/Scott Parnell, GB/GB (Yamaha); **12** Andy Peach/Dudley Tomkinson, GB/GB (Suzuki); **13** Jean-Nöel Minguet/Nicolas Bidault, F/F (Suzuki); **14** Barry Fleury/Jane Fleury, NZ/NZ (Yamaha).

Fastest lap: Webster/Woodhead, 1m 41.365s, 88.383 mph/142.238 km/h.

Championship points: **1** Webster, 25; **2** Abbott, 20; **3** Klaffenböck, 16; **4** Skene, 13; **5** Roscher, 11; **6** Philp, 10.

MONZA, Italy, 17 May. 3.600-mile/5.793-km circuit.
Superside World Championship, round 2 (14 laps, 50.400 miles/81.102 km)

1 Klaus Klaffenböck/Christian Parzer, A/A (Yamaha), 27m 38.583s, 109.382 mph/176.034 km/h.

2 Jörg Steinhausen/Trevor Hopkinson, D/GB (Suzuki); **3** Martien Van Gils/Tonnie Van Gils, NL/NL (Suzuki); **4** Mike Roscher/Adolf Hänni, D/CH (Suzuki); **5** Rob Fisher/Rick Long, GB/GB (Yamaha); **6** Gerhard Hauzenberger/Ian Simons, A/GB (Suzuki); **7** Billy Gallrös/Peter Berglund, S/S (Suzuki); **8** Philippe Le Bail/Christian Chaigneau, F/F (Yamaha); **9** Dan Morrissey/Vince Biggs, GB/GB (Yamaha); **10** Richard Gatt/Paul Randall, GB/GB (Yamaha); **11** Bryan Pedder/Scott Parnell, GB/GB (Yamaha); **12** Jean-Nöel Minguet/Nicolas Bidault, F/F (Suzuki); **13** Chris Founds/Stuart Muldoon, GB/GB (Yamaha); **14** Steve Abbott/Jamie Biggs, GB/GB (Yamaha); **15** Barry Fleury/Jane Fleury, NZ/NZ (Yamaha).

Fastest lap: Steve Webster/Paul Woodhead, GB/GB (Suzuki), 1m 57.251s, 110.520 mph/177.865 km/h.

Championship points: **1** Klaffenböck, 41; **2** Webster, 25; **3** Roscher, 24; **4** Abbott, 22; **5** Steinhausen, 20; **6** Van Gils, 16.

OSCHERSLEBEN, Germany, 31 May. 2.279-mile/3.667-km circuit.
Superside World Championship, round 3 (22 laps, 50.138 miles/80.674 km)

1 Steve Webster/Paul Woodhead, GB/GB (Suzuki), 34m 45.872s, 86.517 mph/139.235 km/h.

2 Klaus Klaffenböck/Christian Parzer, A/A (Yamaha); **3** Steve Abbott/Jamie Biggs, GB/GB (Yamaha); **4** Tom Hanks/Phil Biggs, GB/GB (Yamaha); **5** Martien Van Gils/Tonnie Van Gils, NL/NL (Suzuki); **6** Mike Roscher/Adolf Hänni, D/CH (Suzuki); **7** Billy Gallrös/Peter Berglund, S/S (Suzuki); **8** Gerhard Hauzenberger/Ian Simons, A/GB (Suzuki); **9** Bill Philp/Gary Yendell, GB/GB (Suzuki); **10** Sepp Doppler/Bernhard Wagner, A/A (Yamaha); **11** Chris Founds/Heidenreich, GB/D (Yamaha); **12** Dan Morrissey/Darren Harper, GB/GB (Yamaha); **13** Jean-Nöel Minguet/Nicolas Bidault, F/F (Suzuki); **14** Barry Fleury/Jane Fleury, NZ/NZ (Yamaha); **15** Peter Lindström-Riedel/Carolina Riedel, S/S (Yamaha).

Fastest lap: Webster/Woodhead, 1m 32.874s, 88.322 mph/142.141 km/h.

Championship points: **1** Klaffenböck, 61; **2** Webster, 50; **3** Abbott, 38; **4** Roscher, 34; **5** Van Gils, 27; **6** Hauzenberger, 24.

SILVERSTONE, Great Britain, 14 June. 3.129-mile/5.036-km circuit.
Superside World Championship, round 4 (16 laps, 50.064 miles/80.576 km)

1 Steve Webster/Paul Woodhead, GB/GB (Suzuki), 32m 19.005s, 92.957 mph/149.599 km/h.

2 Klaus Klaffenböck/Christian Parzer, A/A (Yamaha); 3 Jörg Steinhausen/Trevor Hopkinson, D/GB (Suzuki); 4 Tom Hanks/Phil Biggs, GB/GB (Yamaha); 5 Steve Abbott/Jamie Biggs, GB/GB (Suzuki); 6 Martien Van Gils/Tonnie Van Gils, NL/NL (Suzuki); 7 Mike Roscher/Adolf Hänni, D/CH (Suzuki); 8 Bill Philp/Gary Yendell, GB/GB (Yamaha); 9 Jock Skene/Neil Miller, GB/GB (Suzuki); 10 Dan Morrissey/Darren Harper, GB/GB (Yamaha); 11 Richard Gatt/Paul Randall, GB/GB (Yamaha); 12 Duncan Hendry/Peter Wilson, GB/GB (Suzuki); 13 Stuart Woodard/Steve English, GB/GB (Yamaha); 14 Barry Fleury/Jane Fleury, NZ/NZ (Yamaha); 15 Billy Gallrös/Peter Berglund, S/S (Suzuki).
Fastest lap: Webster/Woodhead, 1m 59.481s, 94.284 mph/151.736 km/h (record).
Championship points: 1 Klaffenböck, 81; **2** Webster, 75; **3** Abbott, 49; **4** Roscher, 43; **5** Van Gils, 37; **6** Steinhausen, 36.

MISANO, Italy, 21 June. 2.523-mile/4.060-km circuit.
Superside World Championship, round 5 (20 laps, 50.460 miles/81.200 km)
1 Jörg Steinhausen/Trevor Hopkinson, D/GB (Suzuki), 33m 50.862s, 89.440 mph/143.939 km/h.
2 Tom Hanks/Phil Biggs, GB/GB (Yamaha); 3 Steve Webster/Paul Woodhead, GB/GB (Suzuki); 4 Klaus Klaffenböck/Christian Parzer, A/A (Yamaha); 5 Martien Van Gils/Tonnie Van Gils, NL/NL (Suzuki); 6 Mike Roscher/Adolf Hänni, D/CH (Suzuki); 7 Bill Philp/Gary Yendell, GB/GB (Yamaha); 8 Jean-Nöel Minguet/Nicolas Bidault, F/F (Suzuki); 9 Richard Gatt/Paul Randall, GB/GB (Yamaha); 10 Gerhard Hauzenberger/Trevor Simons, A/GB (Yamaha); 11 Jock Skene/Neil Miller, GB/GB (Suzuki); 12 Billy Gallrös/Peter Berglund, S/S (Suzuki); 13 Sepp Doppler/Bernhard Wagner, A/A (Yamaha); 14 Chris Founds/Heidenreich, GB/D (Yamaha); 15 Barry Fleury/Jane Fleury, NZ/NZ (Yamaha).
Fastest lap: Steinhausen/Hopkinson, 1m 39.739s, 91.057 mph/146.542 km/h.
Championship points: 1 Klaffenböck, 94; **2** Webster, 91; **3** Steinhausen, 61; **4** Roscher, 53; **5** Abbott, 49; **6** Van Gils, 48.

BRANDS HATCH, Great Britain, 26 July. 2.608-mile/4.197-km circuit.
Superside World Championship, round 6 (19 laps, 49.552 miles/79.743 km)
1 Steve Webster/Paul Woodhead, GB/GB (Suzuki), 32m 54.191s, 90.356 mph/145.414 km/h.
2 Jörg Steinhausen/Trevor Hopkinson, D/GB (Suzuki); 3 Klaus Klaffenböck/Christian Parzer, A/A (Yamaha); 4 Steve Abbott/Jamie Biggs, GB/GB (Suzuki); 5 Tom Hanks/Phil Biggs, GB/GB (Yamaha); 6 Richard Gatt/Paul Randall, GB/GB (Yamaha); 7 Martien Van Gils/Tonnie Van Gils, NL/NL (Suzuki); 8 Bill Philp/Gary Yendell, GB/GB (Yamaha); 9 Gerhard Hauzenberger/Trevor Simons, A/GB (Yamaha); 10 Roger Lovelock/Dawna Holloway, GB/GB (Suzuki); 11 Mike Roscher/Adolf Hänni, D/CH (Suzuki); 12 Dan Morrissey/Darren Harper, GB/GB (Yamaha); 13 Billy Gallrös/Peter Berglund, S/S (Suzuki); 14 Jean-Nöel Minguet/Nicolas Bidault, F/F (Suzuki); 15 Chris Founds/Peter Founds, GB/GB (Yamaha).
Fastest lap: Webster/Woodhead, 1m 41.688s, 92.326 mph/148.584 km/h (record).
Championship points: 1 Webster, 116; **2** Klaffenböck, 110; **3** Steinhausen, 81; **4** Abbott, 62; **5** Roscher, 58; **6** Hanks and Van Gils, 57.

ASSEN, Holland, 6–7 September. 3.745-mile/6.027-km circuit.
Superside World Championship, rounds 7 and 8 (2 x 13 laps, 48.685 miles/78.351 km)
Race 1
1 Steve Webster/Paul Woodhead, GB/GB (Suzuki), 28m 19.356s, 103.137 mph/165.983 km/h.
2 Jörg Steinhausen/Trevor Hopkinson, D/GB (Suzuki); 3 Klaus Klaffenböck/Christian Parzer, A/A (Yamaha); 4 Steve Abbott/Jamie Biggs, GB/GB (Suzuki); 5 Tom Hanks/Phil Biggs, GB/GB (Yamaha); 6 Bill Philp/Gary Yendell, GB/GB (Yamaha); 7 Jock Skene/Neil Miller, GB/GB (Suzuki); 8 Richard Gatt/Paul Randall, GB/GB (Yamaha); 9 Martien Van Gils/Tonnie Van Gils, NL/NL (Suzuki); 10 Tim Reeves/Tristan Reeves, GB/GB (Suzuki); 11 Billy Gallrös/Peter Berglund, S/S (Suzuki); 12 Mike Roscher/Adolf Hänni, D/CH (Suzuki); 13 Paul Steenbergen/Rene Steenbergen, NL/NL (Yamaha); 14 Barry Fleury/Jane Fleury, NZ/NZ (Yamaha); 15 Trevor Stafford/Rick Long, GB/GB (Yamaha).
Fastest lap: Webster/Woodhead, 2m 08.392s, 105.007 mph/168.992 km/h (record).

Race 2
1 Steve Webster/Paul Woodhead, GB/GB (Suzuki), 28m 33.867s.
2 Klaus Klaffenböck/Christian Parzer, A/A (Yamaha); 3 Steve Abbott/Jamie Biggs, GB/GB (Suzuki); 4 Tom Hanks/Phil Biggs, GB/GB (Yamaha); 5 Martien Van Gils/Tonnie Van Gils, NL/NL (Suzuki); 6 Jörg Steinhausen/Trevor Hopkinson, D/GB (Suzuki); 7 Tim Reeves/Tristan Reeves, GB/GB (Suzuki); 8 Billy Gallrös/Peter Berglund, S/S (Suzuki); 9 Bill Philp/Gary Yendell, GB/GB (Yamaha); 10 Chris Founds/Peter Founds, GB/GB (Yamaha); 11 Dan Morrissey/Darren Harper, GB/GB (Yamaha); 12 Paul Steenbergen/Rene Steenbergen, NL/NL (Yamaha); 13 Trevor Stafford/Rick Long, GB/GB (Yamaha); 14 Barry Fleury/Jane Fleury, NZ/NZ (Yamaha); 15 Mike Roscher/Adolf Hänni, D/CH (Suzuki).
Fastest lap: Webster/Woodhead, 2m 09.925s.
Championship points: 1 Webster, 166; **2** Klaffenböck, 146; **3** Steinhausen, 111; **4** Abbott, 91; **5** Hanks, 81; **6** Van Gils, 75.

IMOLA, Italy, 27 September. 3.065-mile/4.933-km circuit.
Superside World Championship, round 9 (16 laps, 49.040 miles/78.928 km)
1 Jörg Steinhausen/Trevor Hopkinson, D/GB (Suzuki), 31m 33.153s, 93.261 mph/150.089 km/h.

Pegram (Ducati); 7 Jordan Szoke (Suzuki); 8 Michael Barnes (Suzuki); 9 Geoff May (Suzuki); 10 Shawn Higbee (Suzuki).

Race 2
1 Mat Mladin (Suzuki).
2 Eric Bostrom (Kawasaki); 3 Kurtis Roberts (Honda); 4 Aaron Yates (Suzuki); 5 Ben Bostrom (Honda); 6 Jason Pridmore (Suzuki); 7 Larry Pegram (Ducati); 8 Anthony Gobert (Ducati); 9 Miguel DuHamel (Honda); 10 Shawn Higbee (Suzuki).

PIKES PEAK INTERNATIONAL RACEWAY, Fountain, Colorado, 1 June. 52.600 miles/84.160 km
1 Eric Bostrom (Kawasaki).
2 Kurtis Roberts (Honda); 3 Aaron Yates (Suzuki); 4 Ben Bostrom (Honda); 5 Anthony Gobert (Ducati) 6 Jason Pridmore (Suzuki); 7 Miguel DuHamel (Honda); 8 Jordan Szoke (Suzuki); 9 Mat Mladin (Suzuki); 10 Steve Rapp (Suzuki).

ROAD AMERICA, Elkhart Lake, Wisconsin, 7–8 June. 64.000 miles/102.998 km
Race 1
1 Mat Mladin (Suzuki).
2 Miguel DuHamel (Honda); 3 Kurtis Roberts (Honda); 4 Ben Bostrom (Honda); 5 Anthony Gobert (Ducati); 6 Jason Pridmore (Suzuki); 7 Shawn Higbee (Suzuki); 8 Jordan Szoke (Suzuki); 9 Mike Ciccotto (Suzuki); 10 Geoff May (Suzuki).

Race 2
1 Eric Bostrom (Kawasaki).
2 Aaron Yates (Suzuki); 3 Larry Pegram (Ducati); 4 Miguel DuHamel (Honda); 5 Ben Bostrom (Honda); 6 Jason Pridmore (Suzuki); 7 Shawn Higbee (Suzuki); 8 Michael Barnes (Suzuki); 9 Kurtis Roberts (Honda); 10 Mat Mladin (Suzuki).

BRAINERD INTERNATIONAL RACEWAY, Brainerd, Minnesota, 29 June. 63.000 miles/100.800 km
1 Mat Mladin (Suzuki).
2 Miguel DuHamel (Honda); 3 Kurtis Roberts (Honda); 4 Eric Bostrom (Kawasaki); 5 Giovanni Bussei (Ducati); 6 Jason Pridmore (Suzuki); 7 Mat Mladin (Suzuki); 8 Jordan Szoke (Suzuki); 9 Shawn Higbee (Suzuki); 10 Vincent Haskovec (Suzuki).

MAZDA RACEWAY LAGUNA SECA, Monterey, California, 12 July. 61.600 miles/98.560 km
1 Mat Mladin (Suzuki).
2 Aaron Yates (Suzuki); 3 Eric Bostrom (Kawasaki); 4 Ben Bostrom (Honda); 5 Jason Pridmore (Suzuki); 6 Miguel DuHamel (Honda); 7 Jordan Szoke (Suzuki); 8 Shawn Higbee (Suzuki); 9 Michael Barnes (Suzuki); 10 James Randolph (Suzuki).

MID-OHIO SPORTS CAR COURSE, Lexington, Ohio, 26–27 July. 62.400 miles/99.840 km
Race 1
1 Mat Mladin (Suzuki).
2 Jason Pridmore (Suzuki); 3 Miguel DuHamel (Honda); 4 Ben Bostrom (Honda); 5 Aaron Yates (Suzuki); 6 Giovanni Bussei (Ducati); 7 Kurtis Roberts (Honda); 8 Shawn Higbee (Suzuki); 9 Geoff May (Suzuki); 10 Mike Ciccotto (Suzuki).

Race 2
1 Mat Mladin (Suzuki).
2 Jason Pridmore (Suzuki); 3 Ben Bostrom (Honda); 4 Aaron Yates (Suzuki); 5 Jordan Szoke (Suzuki); 6 Giovanni Bussei (Ducati); 7 Shawn Higbee (Suzuki); 8 Geoff May (Suzuki); 9 Vincent Haskovec (Suzuki); 10 Mike Ciccotto (Suzuki).

VIRGINIA INTERNATIONAL RACEWAY, Alton, Virginia, 30 August–1 September. 62.300 miles/99.680 km
Race 1
1 Mat Mladin (Suzuki).
2 Miguel DuHamel (Honda); 3 Ben Bostrom (Honda); 4 Giovanni Bussei (Ducati); 5 Jordan Szoke (Suzuki); 6 Aaron Yates (Suzuki); 7 Shawn Higbee (Suzuki); 8 Geoff May (Suzuki); 9 Jacob Holden (Suzuki); 10 Mike Ciccotto (Suzuki).

Race 2
1 Kurtis Roberts (Honda).
2 Aaron Yates (Suzuki); 3 Miguel DuHamel (Honda); 4 Ben Bostrom (Honda); 5 Mat Mladin (Suzuki); 6 Giovanni Bussei (Ducati); 7 Jason Pridmore (Suzuki); 8 Shawn Higbee (Suzuki); 9 Jordan Szoke (Suzuki); 10 Steve Rapp (Suzuki).

BARBER MOTORSPORTS PARK, Birmingham, Alabama, 20–21 September. 64.400 miles/103.040 km
Race 1
1 Aaron Yates (Suzuki).
2 Kurtis Roberts (Honda); 3 Ben Bostrom (Honda); 4 Mat Mladin (Suzuki); 5 Giovanni Bussei (Ducati); 6 Shawn Higbee (Suzuki); 7 Miguel DuHamel (Honda); 8 Jordan Szoke (Suzuki); 9 Tom Kipp (Suzuki); 10 Vincent Haskovec (Suzuki).

Race 2
1 Kurtis Roberts (Honda).
2 Giovanni Bussei (Ducati); 3 Mat Mladin (Suzuki); 4 Aaron Yates (Suzuki); 5 Steve Rapp (Suzuki); 6 Shawn Higbee (Suzuki); 7 Tom Kipp (Suzuki); 8 Vincent Haskovec (Suzuki); 9 Eric Wood (Suzuki); 10 Michael Barnes (Suzuki).

Final Championship Points
1	Mat Mladin	550
2	Aaron Yates	519
3	Kurtis Roberts	474
4	Ben Bostrom	462
5	Miguel DuHamel	417

6 Shawn Higbee, 396; 7 Eric Bostrom, 350; 8 Jason Pridmore, 339; 9 Vincent Haskovec, 285; 10 Jordan Szoke, 339.

---

2 Steve Webster/Paul Woodhead, GB/GB (Suzuki); 3 Klaus Klaffenböck/Christian Parzer, A/A (Yamaha); 4 Martien Van Gils/Tonnie Van Gils, NL/NL (Suzuki); 5 Bill Philp/Gary Yendell, GB/GB (Yamaha); 6 Tim Reeves/Tristan Reeves, GB/GB (Yamaha); 7 Jock Skene/Neil Miller, GB/GB (Suzuki); 8 Tom Hanks/Phil Biggs, GB/GB (Yamaha); 9 Richard Gatt/Paul Randall, GB/GB (Yamaha); 10 Renaud Dernoncourt/Alain Lailheugue, F/F (Suzuki); 11 Mike Roscher/Adolf Hänni, D/CH (Suzuki); 12 Billy Gallrös/Peter Berglund, S/S (Suzuki); 13 Chris Founds/Rick Long, GB/GB (Yamaha); 14 Jean-Nöel Minguet/Nicolas Bidault, F/F (Suzuki); 15 Dan Morrissey/Darren Harper, GB/GB (Yamaha).
Fastest lap: Steinhausen/Hopkinson, 1m 56.954s, 94.351 mph/151.844 km/h (record).

MAGNY-COURS, France, 18 October. 2.741-mile/4.411-km circuit.
Superside World Championship, round 10 (18 laps, 49.338 miles/79.398 km)
1 Jörg Steinhausen/Trevor Hopkinson, D/GB (Suzuki), 32m 48.255s, 90.236 mph/145.221 km/h.
2 Steve Abbott/Jamie Biggs, GB/GB (Suzuki); 3 Klaus Klaffenböck/Christian Parzer, A/A (Yamaha); 4 Martien Van Gils/Tonnie Van Gils, NL/NL (Suzuki); 5 Steve Webster/Paul Woodhead, GB/GB (Suzuki); 6 Bill Philp/Gary Yendell, GB/GB (Yamaha); 7 Renaud Dernoncourt/Alain Lailheugue, F/F (Suzuki); 8 Mike Roscher/Adolf Hänni, D/CH (Suzuki); 9 Richard Gatt/Paul Randall, GB/GB (Yamaha); 10 Jean-Nöel Minguet/Nicolas Bidault, F/F (Suzuki); 11 Sepp Doppler/Bernhard Wagner, A/A (Yamaha); 12 Rob Cameron/Mark Cox, GB/GB (Suzuki); 13 Jock Skene/Neil Miller, GB/GB (Suzuki); 14 Philippe Le Bail/Christian Chaigneau, F/F (Yamaha); 15 Dan Morrissey/Darren Harper, GB/GB (Yamaha).
Fastest lap: Steinhausen/Hopkinson, 1m 47.674s, 91.639 mph/147.478 km/h (record).

Final World Championship points
1	Steve Webster/Paul Woodhead, GB/GB	197
2	Klaus Klaffenböck/Christian Parzer, A/A	178
3	Jörg Steinhausen/Trevor Hopkinson, D/GB	161
4	Steve Abbott/Jamie Biggs, GB/GB	111
5	Martien Van Gils/Tonnie Van Gils, NL/NL	101

6 Tom Hanks/Phil Biggs, GB/GB, 89; 7 Bill Philp/Gary Yendell, GB/GB, 80; 8 Mike Roscher/Adolf Hänni, D/CH, 76; 9 Richard Gatt/Paul Randall, GB/GB, 50; 10 Jock Skene/Neil Miller, GB/GB, 37; 11 Billy Gallrös/Peter Berglund, S/S, 43; 12= Gerhard Hauzenberger/Ian Simons, A/GB and Dan Morrissey/Darren Harper, GB/GB, 37; 14 Jean-Nöel Minguet/Nicolas Bidault, F/F, 28; 15 Tim Reeves/Tristan Reeves, GB/GB, 25.

AMA National Championship Road Race Series (Superbike)

DAYTONA INTERNATIONAL SPEEDWAY, Daytona Beach, Florida, 9 March. 200.000 miles/321.869 km
1 Miguel DuHamel (Honda).
2 Ben Bostrom (Honda); 3 Kurtis Roberts (Honda); 4 Aaron Yates (Suzuki); 5 Eric Bostrom (Kawasaki); 6 Mat Mladin (Suzuki); 7 Ben Spies (Suzuki); 8 Michael Barnes (Suzuki); 9 Jason Pridmore (Suzuki); 10 Shawn Higbee (Suzuki).

CALIFORNIA SPEEDWAY, Fontana, California, 5–6 April. 66.080 miles/106.345 km
Race 1
1 Mat Mladin (Suzuki).
2 Aaron Yates (Suzuki); 3 Ben Bostrom (Honda); 4 Eric Bostrom (Kawasaki); 5 Miguel DuHamel (Honda); 6 Kurtis Roberts (Honda); 7 Larry Pegram (Ducati); 8 Jason Pridmore (Suzuki); 9 Steve Crevier (Suzuki); 10 Shawn Higbee (Suzuki).

Race 2
1 Mat Mladin (Suzuki).
2 Eric Bostrom (Kawasaki); 3 Miguel DuHamel (Honda); 4 Aaron Yates (Suzuki); 5 Kurtis Roberts (Honda); 6 Ben Bostrom (Honda); 7 Anthony Gobert (Ducati); 8 Jordan Szoke (Suzuki); 9 Shawn Higbee (Suzuki); 10 Andy Deatherage (Suzuki).

INFINEON RACEWAY, Sonoma, California, 3–4 May. 60.320 miles/97.060 km
Race 1
1 Mat Mladin (Suzuki).
2 Aaron Yates (Suzuki); 3 Miguel DuHamel (Honda); 4 Eric Bostrom (Kawasaki); 5 Ben Bostrom (Honda); 6 Steve Rapp (Suzuki); 7 Kurtis Roberts (Honda); 8 Larry Pegram (Ducati); 9 Jason Pridmore (Suzuki); 10 Lee Acree (Suzuki).

Race 2
1 Mat Mladin (Suzuki).
2 Aaron Yates (Suzuki); 3 Ben Bostrom (Honda); 4 Kurtis Roberts (Honda); 5 Eric Bostrom (Kawasaki); 6 Larry Pegram (Ducati); 7 Jason Pridmore (Suzuki); 8 Steve Rapp (Suzuki); 9 Steve Crevier (Suzuki); 10 Shawn Higbee (Suzuki).

ROAD ATLANTA, Braselton, Georgia, 17–18 May. 63.500 miles/101.389 km
Race 1
1 Aaron Yates (Suzuki).
2 Eric Bostrom (Kawasaki); 3 Kurtis Roberts (Honda); 4 Anthony Gobert (Ducati); 5 Ben Bostrom (Honda); 6 Larry

---

Isle of Man Tourist Trophy Races

ISLE OF MAN TOURIST TROPHY COURSE, 31 May–7 June. 37.730-mile/60.720-km course.
Duke Formula One TT (6 laps, 226.380 miles/364.320 km)
1 Adrian Archibald (Suzuki 1000), 1h 50m 15.7s, 123.18 mph/198.24 km/h.
2 Ian Lougher (Honda 1000), 1h 51m 30.5s; 3 John McGuinness (Ducati 998), 1h 52m 35.5s; 4 Jason Griffiths (Yamaha 1000), 1h 52m 37.4s; 5 Ryan Farquhar (Suzuki 1000), 1h 53m 07.8s; 6 Shaun Harris (Suzuki 1000), 1h 53m 41.8s; 7 Gordon Blackley (Suzuki 1000), 1h 53m 43.1s; 8 Chris Heath (Suzuki 1000), 1h 54m 53.2s; 9 Paul Hunt (Suzuki 1000), 1h 55m 11.3s.
Fastest lap: Archibald, 18m 02.9s, 125.43 mph/201.86 km/h.

Lightweight TT (4 laps, 150.920 miles/242.880 km)
1 John McGuinness (Honda 400), 1h 22m 40.97s, 109.52 mph/176.26 km/h.
2 Richard Britton (Honda 400), 1h 23m 07.29s; 3 Ryan Farquhar (Kawasaki 400), 1h 23m 23.21s; 4 David Madsen-Mygdal (Honda 400), 1h 24m 28.96s; 5 Robert Price (Yamaha 399), 1h 26m 00.42s.
Fastest lap: McGuinness, 20m 19.68s, 111.36 mph/179.22 km/h.

Ultra-Lightweight TT (4 laps, 150.920 miles/242.880 km)
1 Chris Palmer (Honda 125), 1h 23m 20.57s, 108.65 mph/174.86 km/h.
2 Michael Wilcox (Honda 125), 1h 24m 00.46s; 3 Ian Lougher (Honda 125), 1h 24m 21.04s; 4 Robert Dunlop (Honda 125), 1h 24m 47.25s; 5 Nigel Beattie (Honda 125), 1h 27m 15.22s.
Fastest lap: Palmer, 20m 30.25s, 110.41 mph/177.69 km/h.

Scottish Life International Production 1000 TT (3 laps, 113.190 miles/182.160 km)
1 Shaun Harris (Suzuki 1000), 55m 39.38s, 122.02 mph/196.37 km/h.
2 Bruce Anstey (Suzuki 1000), 55m 55.42s; 3 Ryan Farquhar (Suzuki 1000), 56m 10.50s; 4 Richard Britton (Suzuki 1000), 56m 20.87s; 5 Chris Heath (Suzuki 1000), 56m 52.84s; 6 Jason Griffiths (Yamaha 1000), 57m 07.66s; 7 Paul Hunt (Suzuki 1000), 57m 26.07s; 8 Adrian Archibald (Suzuki 1000), 57m 27.51s; 9 Martin Finnegan (Suzuki 1000), 57m 42.87s.
Fastest lap: Harris, 18m 19.37s, 123.55 mph/198.83 km/h.

Isle of Man Steam Packet Junior/250 cc TT (4 laps, 150.920 miles/242.880 km)
1 Bruce Anstey (Triumph 600), 1h 15m 13.98s, 120.36 mph/193.70 km/h.
2 Ian Lougher (Honda 600), 1h 15m 24.94s; 3 Adrian Archibald (Suzuki 600), 1h 15m 30.00s; 4 Ryan Farquhar (Kawasaki 600), 1h 15m 31.15s; 5 Shaun Harris (Suzuki 600), 1h 15m 48.42s; 6 Jason Griffiths (Yamaha 600), 1h 15m 54.72s; 7 Richard Britton (Kawasaki 600), 1h 16m 09.02s; 8 Gordon Blackley (Yamaha 600), 1h 16m 35.90s; 9 Jim Moodie (Triumph 600), 1h 16m 38.46s; 10 John McGuinness (Triumph 600), 1h 16m 04.81s; 12 Chris Heath (Honda 600), 1h 17m 27.75s; 13 Mark Parrett (Yamaha 600), 1h 18m 24.65s.
Fastest lap: Farquhar, 18m 30.65s, 122.30 mph/196.82 km/h.

Production 600 TT (2 laps, 75.460 miles/121.440 km)
1 Shaun Harris (Suzuki 600), 34m 49.79s, 119.68 mph/192.61 km/h.
2 Ian Lougher (Honda 600), 38m 06.10s; 3 Ryan Farquhar (Kawasaki 600), 38m 10.17s; 4 Adrian Archibald (Suzuki 600), 38m 13.25s; 5 Jason Griffiths (Yamaha 600), 38m 17.08s; 6 Richard Britton (Honda 600), 38m 31.89s; 7 Martin Finnegan (Honda 600), 38m 36.64s; 8 Bruce Anstey (Triumph 600), 38m 50.74s; 9 Chris Heath (Yamaha 600), 38m 51.01s; 10 Roy Richardson (Kawasaki 600), 39m 14.30s; 11 Davy Morgan (Yamaha 600), 39m 20.09s; 12 Jim Moodie (Triumph 600), 39m 27.01s; 13 Mark Parrett (Yamaha 600), 39m 30.91s; 14 Philip Gilder (Honda 600), 39m 40.29s; 15 Iain Duffus (Honda 600), 39m 04m 21.2s.
Fastest lap: Harris, 18m 54.28s, 119.75 mph/192.72 km/h.

Standard Bank Offshore Senior TT (4 laps, 150.920 miles/242.880 km)
1 Adrian Archibald (1000 Suzuki), 1h 12m 42.9s, 124.53 mph/200.41 km/h.
2 John McGuinness (998 Ducati), 1h 13m 03.7s; 3 Ian Lougher (1000 Honda), 1h 13m 29.5s; 4 Jason Griffiths (1000 Yamaha), 1h 13m 44.1s; 5 Ryan Farquhar (1000 Suzuki), 1h 14m 00.1s; 6 Shaun Harris (1000 Suzuki), 1h 14m 15.0s; 7 Bruce Anstey (1000 Suzuki), 1h 14m 25.8s; 8 Richard Britton (1000 Suzuki), 1h 14m 45.2s; 9 Mark Parrett (750 Kawasaki), 1h 15m 15.1s; 10 Gary Carswell (1000 Suzuki), 1h 16m 06.3s.
Fastest lap: Archibald, 17m 51.0s, 126.82 mph/204.10 km/h.

Hilton Hotel & Casino Sidecar TT: Race A (3 laps, 113.190 miles/182.160 km)
1 Ian Bell/Neil Carpenter (Yamaha 600), 1h 01m 39.0s, 110.16 mph/177.29 km/h.
2 Nick Crowe/Darren Hope (Ireson 600), 1h 02m 30.6s; 3 Steve Norbury/Andrew Smith (Yamaha 600), 1h 02m 54.3s; 4 Andrew Laidlow/Patrick Farrance (Yamaha 600), 1h 03m 13.8s; 5 Tony Baker/Mark Hegarty (Yamaha 600), 1h 04m 12.3s; 6 Allan Schofield/Mark Cox (Jacobs 600), 1h 04m 13.6s; 7 Geoff Bell/Jake Beckworth (Yamaha 600), 1h 04m 21.2s.
Fastest lap: Bell/Carpenter, 20m 25.7s, 110.81 mph/178.33 km/h.

Hilton Hotel & Casino Sidecar TT: Race B (3 laps, 113.190 miles/182.160 km)
1 David Molyneux/Craig Hallam (Honda 600), 1h 04m 25.17s, 105.42 mph/169.66 km/h.
2 Nick Crowe/Darren Hope (Ireson 600), 1h 05m 15.67s; 3 Gregory Lambert/Daniel Sayle (Molyneux 600), 1h 06m

17.31s; **4** Ben Dixon/Mark Lambert (Molyneux 600), 1h 06m 37.02s; **5** Geoff Bell/Jake Beckworth (Yamaha 600), 1h 06m 48.06s; **6** John Holden/Colin Hardman (Yamaha 600), 1h 07m 15.87s; **7** Andrew Laidlow/Patrick Farrance (Yamaha 600), 1h 07m 33.42s; **8** Roy Hanks/David Wells (Molyneux 599), 1h 07m 35.35s.
Fastest lap: Molyneux/Hallam, 20m 46.19s, 108.99 mph/175.40 km/h.

British Championships

SILVERSTONE INTERNATIONAL CIRCUIT, 30 March. 2.213-mile/3.561-km circuit.
British Superbike Championship powered by Halls, rounds 1 and 2 (2 x 22 laps, 48.686 miles/78.342 km)
Race 1
1 Shane Byrne (Ducati), 32m 28.749s, 89.80 mph/144.52 km/h.
2 Yukio Kagayama (Suzuki); **3** Glen Richards (Kawasaki); **4** Michael Rutter (Ducati); **5** Gary Mason (Yamaha); **6** Scott Smart (Kawasaki); **7** Dean Ellison (Ducati); **8** Steve Hislop (Yamaha); **9** Lee Jackson (Kawasaki); **10** Dean Thomas (Yamaha); **11** Paul Jones (Suzuki).
Fastest lap: Kagayama, 1m 27.573s, 90.97 mph/146.40 km/h.

Race 2
1 Michael Rutter (Ducati), 32m 21.299s, 90.14 mph/145.07 km/h.
2 Shane Byrne (Ducati); **3** Glen Richards (Kawasaki); **4** Yukio Kagayama (Suzuki); **5** Steve Hislop (Yamaha); **6** John Crawford (Ducati); **7** Scott Smart (Kawasaki); **8** Gary Mason (Yamaha); **9** Dean Thomas (Yamaha); **10** Steve Plater (Honda); **11** Lee Jackson (Kawasaki); **12** Paul Jones (Suzuki).
Fastest lap: Rutter, 1m 27.435s, 91.11 mph/146.63 km/h.
Championship points: **1** Byrne, 45; **2** Rutter, 38; **3** Kagayama, 33; **4** Richards, 32; **5** Hislop, Mason and Smart, 19.

British Supersport Championship, round 1 (15 laps, 33.195 miles/53.415 km)
1 Karl Harris (Honda), 22m 54.507s, 86.74 mph/139.59 km/h.
2 John Crockford (Honda); **3** Stuart Easton (Ducati); **4** Leon Haslam (Ducati); **5** Adrian Coates (Honda); **6** Tom Sykes (Yamaha); **7** Simon Andrews (Yamaha); **8** Michael Laverty (Honda); **9** Craig Jones (Triumph); **10** Kieran Murphy (Kawasaki); **11** Jamie Robinson (Yamaha); **12** Mark Burr (Yamaha); **13** Jim Moodie (Triumph); **14** Tom Tunstall (Yamaha); **15** Craig Sproston (Honda).
Fastest lap: Haslam, 1m 30.820s, 87.72 mph/141.17 km/h.
Championship points: **1** Harris, 25; **2** Crockford, 20; **3** Easton, 16; **4** Haslam, 13; **5** Coates, 11; **6** Sykes, 10.

National 125GP Championship, round 1 (16 laps, 35.408 miles/56.976 km)
1 John Pearson (Honda), 25m 46.805s, 82.23 mph/132.34 km/h.
2 Christian Elkin (Honda); **3** Chester Lusk (Honda); **4** Guy Farbrother (Honda); **5** Paul Robinson (Honda); **6** Daniel Cooper (Honda); **7** Sam Owens (Honda); **8** Thomas Bridewell (Honda); **9** Kris Weston (Honda); **10** Jon Vincent (Honda); **11** Steven Neate (Honda); **12** Jonathan Rea (Honda); **13** Joe Dickinson (Honda); **14** James Ford (Honda); **15** Lee Longden (Honda).
Fastest lap: Cooper, 1m 35.566s, 83.36 mph/134.16 km/h.
Championship points: **1** Pearson, 25; **2** Elkin, 20; **3** Lusk, 16; **4** Farbrother, 13; **5** Robinson, 11; **6** Cooper, 10.

National Superstock Championship, round 1 (18 laps, 39.834 miles/64.098 km)
1 Lorenzo Lanzi (Ducati), 27m 23.217s, 87.100 mph/140.170 km/h.
2 David Jefferies (Suzuki); **3** Andy Tinsley (Suzuki); **4** Luke Quigley (Suzuki); **5** Matt Llewellyn (Suzuki); **6** Tristan Palmer (Suzuki); **7** Steve Allan (Kawasaki); **8** Steve Brogan (Suzuki); **9** David Johnson (Yamaha); **10** Jamie Morley (Suzuki); **11** Marshall Neill (Suzuki); **12** Ben Wilson (Suzuki); **13** Dennis Hobbs (Suzuki); **14** Kelvin Reilly (Suzuki); **15** Malcolm Ashley (Ducati).
Fastest lap: Jefferies, 1m 30.566s, 87.96 mph/141.56 km/h.
Championship points: **1** Lanzi, 25; **2** Jefferies, 20; **3** Tinsley, 16; **4** Quigley, 13; **5** Llewellyn, 11; **6** Palmer, 10.

SNETTERTON CIRCUIT, 13 April. 1.952-mile/3.141-km circuit.
British Superbike Championship powered by Halls, rounds 3 and 4
Race 1 (25 laps, 48.800 miles/78.525 km)
1 Michael Rutter (Ducati), 28m 09.817s, 103.96 mph/167.31 km/h.
2 Shane Byrne (Ducati); **3** John Reynolds (Suzuki); **4** Steve Plater (Honda); **5** Glen Richards (Kawasaki); **6** John Crawford (Ducati); **7** Paul Young (Yamaha); **8** Gary Mason (Yamaha); **9** Scott Smart (Kawasaki); **10** Jon Kirkham (Yamaha); **11** Lee Jackson (Kawasaki); **12** Nick Medd (Ducati); **13** Paul Jones (Suzuki).
Fastest lap: Byrne, 1m 06.364s, 105.88 mph/170.41 km/h.

Race 2 (20 laps, 39.040 miles/62.820 km)
1 Shane Byrne (Ducati), 22m 18.701s, 104.98 mph/168.95 km/h.
2 Sean Emmett (Ducati); **3** John Reynolds (Suzuki); **4** Gary Mason (Yamaha); **5** Yukio Kagayama (Suzuki); **6** John Crawford (Ducati); **7** Mark Heckles (Honda); **8** Steve Plater (Honda); **9** Paul Young (Yamaha); **10** Scott Smart (Kawasaki); **11** Jon Kirkham (Yamaha); **12** Lee Jackson (Kawasaki); **13** Nick Medd (Ducati); **14** Paul Jones (Suzuki); **15** Dean Ellison (Ducati).
Fastest lap: Byrne, 1m 06.049s, 106.39 mph/171.22 km/h (record).
Championship points: **1** Byrne, 90; **2** Rutter, 63; **3** Kagayama, 44; **4** Richards, 43; **5** Mason, 40; **6** Reynolds and Smart, 32.

British Supersport Championship, round 2 (22 laps, 42.944 miles/69.102 km)
1 Michael Laverty (Honda), 25m 42.368s, 100.23 mph/161.30 km/h.
2 Karl Harris (Honda); **3** Rob Frost (Kawasaki); **4** Adrian Coates (Honda); **5** Simon Andrews (Yamaha); **6** John McGuinness (Honda); **7** Craig Jones (Triumph); **8** Jim Moodie (Triumph); **9** Tom Tunstall (Yamaha); **10** Callum Ramsay (Honda); **11** Les Shand (Honda); **12** Danny Beaumont (Kawasaki); **13** Mark Burr (Yamaha); **14** John Barnett (Suzuki); **15** Leon Haslam (Ducati).
Fastest lap: John Crockford (Honda), 1m 09.363s, 101.31 mph/163.04 km/h (record).
Championship points: **1** Harris, 45; **2** Laverty, 33; **3** Coates, 24; **4** Andrews and Crockford, 20; **6** Easton, Frost and Jones, 16.

National 125GP Championship, round 2 (18 laps, 35.136 miles/56.538 km)
1 Michael Wilcox (Honda), 22m 42.307s, 92.85 mph/149.43 km/h.
2 Thomas Bridewell (Honda); **3** Danny Coutts (Honda); **4** Paul Robinson (Honda); **5** Eugene Laverty (Honda); **6** Christian Elkin (Honda); **7** Paul Veazey (Honda); **8** John Pearson (Honda); **9** Kris Weston (Honda); **10** Chester Lusk (Honda); **11** Lee Longden (Honda); **12** Jon Boy Lee (Honda); **13** Sam Owens (Honda); **14** Steve Neate (Honda); **15** Midge Smart (Honda).
Fastest lap: Robert Guiver (Honda), 1m 14.442s, 94.39 mph/151.91 km/h.
Championship points: **1** Pearson, 33; **2** Elkin, 30; **3** Bridewell, 28; **4** Wilcox, 25; **5** Robinson, 24; **6** Lusk, 22.

National Superstock Championship, rounds 2 and 3 (2 x 20 laps, 39.040 miles/62.820 km)
Race 1
1 Matt Llewellyn (Suzuki), 23m 01.926s, 101.70 mph/163.67 km/h.
2 Jamie Morley (Suzuki); **3** Steve Brogan (Suzuki); **4** David Jefferies (Suzuki); **5** Andy Tinsley (Suzuki); **6** Jason Davis (Suzuki); **7** Luke Quigley (Suzuki); **8** Tristan Palmer (Suzuki); **9** John Laverty (Suzuki); **10** Stephen Thompson (Suzuki); **11** Marshall Neill (Suzuki); **12** Marty Nutt (Suzuki); **13** Kierran Blair (Suzuki); **14** Dennis Hobbs (Suzuki); **15** Ian Hutchinson (Suzuki).
Fastest lap: Brogan, 1m 08.373s, 102.77 mph/165.40 km/h (record).

Race 2
1 Steve Brogan (Suzuki), 24m 16.928s, 96.46 mph/155.24 km/h.
2 Matt Llewellyn (Suzuki); **3** Tristan Palmer (Suzuki); **4** Jamie Morley (Suzuki); **5** David Jefferies (Suzuki); **6** Andy Tinsley (Suzuki); **7** Ben Wilson (Suzuki); **8** Luke Quigley (Suzuki); **9** Marty Nutt (Suzuki); **10** John Laverty (Suzuki); **11** Dennis Hobbs (Suzuki); **12** Ian Hutchinson (Suzuki); **13** Jason Davis (Suzuki); **14** Jonti Hobday (Suzuki); **15** Kelvin Reilly (Suzuki).
Fastest lap: Morley, 1m 08.469s, 102.63 mph/165.17 km/h.
Championship points: **1** Llewellyn, 56; **2** Brogan, 49; **3** Jefferies, 44; **4** Morley, 39; **5** Tinsley, 37; **6** Palmer, 34.

THRUXTON CIRCUIT, 20 April. 2.356-mile/3.792-km circuit.
British Superbike Championship powered by Halls, rounds 5 and 6
Race 1 (21 laps, 49.476 miles/79.632 km)
1 Shane Byrne (Ducati), 26m 58.706s, 110.03 mph/177.08 km/h.
2 Steve Hislop (Yamaha); **3** Michael Rutter (Ducati); **4** Glen Richards (Kawasaki); **5** Steve Plater (Honda); **6** Sean Emmett (Ducati); **7** Gary Mason (Yamaha); **8** Mark Heckles (Honda); **9** Yukio Kagayama (Suzuki); **10** John Crawford (Ducati); **11** Lee Jackson (Kawasaki); **12** John Reynolds (Suzuki); **13** Scott Smart (Kawasaki); **14** Paul Young (Yamaha); **15** Paul Jones (Suzuki).
Fastest lap: Byrne, 1m 16.335s, 111.11 mph/178.81 km/h.

Race 2 (22 laps, 51.832 miles/83.424 km)
1 Shane Byrne (Ducati), 28m 11.120s, 110.33 mph/177.56 km/h.
2 Michael Rutter (Ducati); **3** Glen Richards (Kawasaki); **4** Steve Plater (Honda); **5** Steve Hislop (Yamaha); **6** Gary Mason (Yamaha); **7** Sean Emmett (Ducati); **8** Mark Heckles (Honda); **9** Yukio Kagayama (Suzuki); **10** Dean Ellison (Ducati); **11** Scott Smart (Kawasaki); **12** Lee Jackson (Kawasaki); **13** John Crawford (Ducati); **14** Paul Young (Yamaha); **15** Paul Jones (Suzuki).
Fastest lap: Plater, 1m 16.126s, 111.41 mph/179.30 km/h.
Championship points: **1** Byrne, 140; **2** Rutter, 99; **3** Richards, 72; **4** Mason, 59; **5** Kagayama, 58; **6** Plater, 51.

British Supersport Championship, round 3 (20 laps, 47.120 miles/75.840 km)
1 Stuart Easton (Ducati), 26m 13.654s, 107.79 mph/173.47 km/h.
2 Karl Harris (Honda); **3** John Crockford (Honda); **4** Simon Andrews (Yamaha); **5** Tom Sykes (Yamaha); **6** Adrian Coates (Honda); **7** Rob Frost (Kawasaki); **8** Kieran Murphy (Kawasaki); **9** Tom Tunstall (Yamaha); **10** Shane Norval (Yamaha); **11** Jamie Robinson (Yamaha); **12** Danny Beaumont (Kawasaki); **13** John McGuinness (Honda); **14** Jim Moodie (Triumph); **15** Craig McLelland (Suzuki).
Fastest lap: Easton, 1m 17.841s, 108.96 mph/175.35 km/h (record).
Championship points: **1** Harris, 65; **2** Easton, 41; **3** Crockford, 36; **4** Coates, 34; **5** Andrews and Laverty, 33.

National 125GP Championship, round 3 (16 laps, 37.696 miles/60.672 km)
1 Michael Wilcox (Honda), 22m 01.604s, 102.68 mph/165.25 km/h.
2 Danny Coutts (Honda); **3** John Pearson (Honda); **4** Lee Longden (Honda); **5** Paul Veazey (Honda); **6** Kris Weston (Honda); **7** Eugene Laverty (Honda); **8** Thomas Bridewell (Honda); **9** Sam Owens (Honda); **10** Chester Lusk (Honda); **11** Jonathan Rea (Honda); **12** Jon Boy Lee (Honda); **13** Leon Morris (Aprilia); **14** Midge Smart (Honda); **15** Brian Clark (Honda).
Fastest lap: Coutts, 1m 21.675s, 103.84 mph/167.12 km/h.
Championship points: **1** Wilcox, 50; **2** Pearson, 49; **3** Bridewell and Coutts, 36; **5** Elkin, 30; **6** Lusk, 28.

National Superstock Championship, round 4 (17 laps, 40.052 miles/64.464 km)
1 David Jefferies (Suzuki), 22m 26.505s, 107.08 mph/172.33 km/h.
2 Matt Llewellyn (Suzuki); **3** Steve Brogan (Suzuki); **4** Andy Tinsley (Suzuki); **5** Jason Davis (Suzuki); **6** John Laverty (Suzuki); **7** David Johnson (Yamaha); **8** Ben Wilson (Suzuki); **9** Kelvin Reilly (Suzuki); **10** Malcolm Ashley (Ducati); **11** Jonti Hobday (Suzuki); **12** Magnus Houston (Suzuki); **13** Ben Wylie (Suzuki); **14** Gary May (Suzuki); **15** Donald MacFadyen (Suzuki).
Fastest lap: Llewellyn, 1m 18.015s, 108.71 mph/174.96 km/h (record).
Championship points: **1** Llewellyn, 76; **2** Jefferies, 69; **3** Brogan, 65; **4** Tinsley, 50; **5** Morley, 39; **6** Palmer, 34.

OULTON PARK INTERNATIONAL, 5 May. 2.692-mile/4.332-km circuit.
British Superbike Championship powered by Halls, rounds 7 and 8 (2 x 18 laps, 48.456 miles/77.976 km)
Race 1
1 Shane Byrne (Ducati), 29m 37.968s, 98.11 mph/157.89 km/h.
2 Michael Rutter (Ducati); **3** Steve Hislop (Yamaha); **4** Steve Plater (Honda); **5** Yukio Kagayama (Suzuki); **6** John Crawford (Ducati); **7** Gary Mason (Yamaha); **8** John Reynolds (Suzuki); **9** Glen Richards (Kawasaki); **10** Mark Heckles (Honda); **11** Jon Kirkham (Yamaha); **12** Scott Smart (Kawasaki); **13** Lee Jackson (Kawasaki); **14** Paul Young (Yamaha); **15** Nick Medd (Ducati).
Fastest lap: Byrne, 1m 38.104s, 98.78 mph/158.97 km/h (record).

Race 2
1 Shane Byrne (Ducati), 29m 30.799s, 98.51 mph/158.54 km/h.
2 John Reynolds (Suzuki); **3** Michael Rutter (Ducati); **4** Yukio Kagayama (Suzuki); **5** Steve Hislop (Yamaha); **6** Mark Heckles (Honda); **7** Dean Ellison (Ducati); **8** Glen Richards (Kawasaki); **9** Gary Mason (Yamaha); **10** John Crawford (Ducati); **11** Paul Young (Yamaha); **12** Lee Jackson (Kawasaki); **13** Scott Smart (Kawasaki); **14** Nick Medd (Ducati); **15** Paul Jones (Suzuki).
Fastest lap: Byrne, 1m 37.722s, 99.17 mph/159.60 km/h (record).
Championship points: **1** Byrne, 190; **2** Rutter, 135; **3** Richards, 87; **4** Kagayama, 82; **5** Hislop, 77; **6** Mason, 75.

British Supersport Championship, round 4 (16 laps, 43.072 miles/69.312 km)
1 Karl Harris (Honda), 27m 26.193s, 94.19 mph/151.58 km/h.
2 Dean Thomas (Honda); **3** Simon Andrews (Yamaha); **4** Leon Haslam (Ducati); **5** Michael Laverty (Honda); **6** Stuart Easton (Ducati); **7** Adrian Coates (Honda); **8** Craig Jones (Triumph); **9** Jamie Robinson (Yamaha); **10** Kieran Murphy (Kawasaki); **11** John McGuinness (Honda); **12** Jim Moodie (Triumph); **13** John Crockford (Honda); **14** Craig McLelland (Suzuki); **15** Tom Tunstall (Yamaha).
Fastest lap: Thomas, 1m 41.826s, 95.17 mph/153.16 km/h (record).
Championship points: **1** Harris, 90; **2** Easton, 51; **3** Andrews, 49; **4** Laverty, 44; **5** Coates, 43; **6** Crockford, 39.

National 125GP Championship, round 4 (14 laps, 37.688 miles/60.648 km)
1 Midge Smart (Honda), 25m 41.558s, 88.01 mph/141.64 km/h.
2 Michael Wilcox (Honda); **3** Kris Weston (Honda); **4** Eugene Laverty (Honda); **5** Christian Elkin (Honda); **6** Thomas Bridewell (Honda); **7** Chester Lusk (Honda); **8** Sam Owens (Honda); **9** Danny Coutts (Honda); **10** Lee Longden (Honda); **11** Steve Neate (Honda); **12** John Pearson (Honda); **13** Joe Dickinson (Honda); **14** Paul Veazey (Honda); **15** Jon Boy Lee (Honda).
Fastest lap: Bridewell, 1m 47.602s, 90.06 mph/144.94 km/h (record).
Championship points: **1** Wilcox, 70; **2** Pearson, 53; **3** Bridewell, 46; **4** Coutts, 43; **5** Elkin, 41; **6** Weston, 40.

National Superstock Championship, round 5 (15 laps, 40.380 miles/64.980 km)
1 David Jefferies (Suzuki), 25m 33.058s, 94.82 mph/152.60 km/h.
2 Steve Brogan (Suzuki); **3** Andy Tinsley (Suzuki); **4** Jamie Morley (Suzuki); **5** Luke Quigley (Suzuki); **6** Matt Llewellyn (Suzuki); **7** Darren Mitchell (Suzuki); **8** Jason Davis (Suzuki); **9** Jonti Hobday (Suzuki); **10** Steve Allan (Kawasaki); **11** John Laverty (Suzuki); **12** Ben Wilson (Suzuki); **13** Kelvin Reilly (Suzuki); **14** Ian Hutchinson (Suzuki); **15** Malcolm Ashley (Ducati).
Fastest lap: Brogan, 1m 41.450s, 95.52 mph/153.73 km/h (record).
Championship points: **1** Jefferies, 94; **2** Llewellyn, 86; **3** Brogan, 85; **4** Tinsley, 66; **5** Morley, 52; **6** Quigley, 41.

KNOCKHILL CIRCUIT, 18 May. 1.299-mile/2.091-km circuit.
British Superbike Championship powered by Halls, rounds 9 and 10
Race 1 (30 laps, 38.970 miles/62.730 km)
1 Shane Byrne (Ducati), 29m 13.549s, 79.98 mph/128.72 km/h.
2 Paul Young (Yamaha); **3** John Reynolds (Suzuki); **4** Steve Plater (Honda); **5** Sean Emmett (Ducati); **6** Glen Richards (Kawasaki); **7** Gary Mason (Yamaha); **8** John McGuinness (Ducati); **9** John Crawford (Ducati); **10** Yukio Kagayama (Suzuki); **11** Lee Jackson (Kawasaki); **12** Scott Smart (Kawasaki); **13** Steve Hislop (Yamaha); **14** Paul Jones (Suzuki); **15** Michael Rutter (Ducati).
Fastest lap: Rutter, 55.400s, 84.38 mph/135.80 km/h.

Race 2 (20 laps, 25.980 miles/41.820 km)
1 Shane Byrne (Ducati), 17m 04.035s, 91.30 mph/146.93 km/h.
2 John Reynolds (Suzuki); **3** Steve Plater (Honda); **4** Glen Richards (Kawasaki); **5** Steve Hislop (Yamaha); **6** Gary Mason (Yamaha); **7** Yukio Kagayama (Suzuki); **8** Sean Emmett (Ducati); **9** Paul Young (Yamaha); **10** John McGuinness (Ducati); **11** Scott Smart (Kawasaki); **12** Lee Jackson (Kawasaki); **13** Jon Kirkham (Yamaha); **14** Nick Medd (Ducati); **15** Paul Jones (Suzuki).
Fastest lap: Reynolds, 50.511s, 92.55 mph/148.95 km/h.
Championship points: **1** Byrne, 240; **2** Rutter, 136; **3** Richards, 110; **4** Reynolds, 100, **5** Kagayama, 97; **6** Mason, 94.

British Supersport Championship, round 5 (28 laps, 36.372 miles/58.548 km)
1 Karl Harris (Honda), 25m 53.477s, 84.26 mph/135.60 km/h.
2 Leon Haslam (Ducati); **3** Rob Frost (Kawasaki); **4** Stuart Easton (Ducati); **5** Jamie Robinson (Yamaha); **6** Adrian Coates (Honda); **7** Craig Jones (Triumph); **8** Tom Sykes (Yamaha); **9** Dean Thomas (Honda); **10** John Crockford (Honda); **11** Tom Tunstall (Yamaha); **12** Jonnie Ekerold (Honda); **13** Michael Laverty (Honda); **14** Bob Grant (Suzuki); **15** Simon Andrews (Yamaha).
Fastest lap: Easton, 53.976s, 86.61 mph/139.38 km/h.
Championship points: **1** Harris, 115; **2** Easton, 64; **3** Coates, 53; **4** Andrews, 50; **5** Haslam and Laverty, 47.

National 125GP Championship, round 5 (24 laps, 31.176 miles/50.184 km)
1 Lee Longden (Honda), 24m 21.074s, 76.79 mph/123.58 km/h.
2 Midge Smart (Honda); **3** Michael Wilcox (Honda); **4** Jonathan Rea (Honda); **5** John Pearson (Honda); **6** Thomas Bridewell (Honda); **7** Paul Veazey (Honda); **8** Jon Vincent (Honda); **9** Joe Dickinson (Honda); **10** Ryan Saxelby (Honda); **11** Danny Coutts (Honda); **12** Oliver Bridewell (Honda); **13** James Ford (Honda), **14** Brian Clark (Honda); **15** Ashley Beech (Honda).
Fastest lap: Longden, 59.690s, 78.32 mph/126.04 km/h.
Championship points: **1** Wilcox, 86; **2** Pearson, 64; **3** T. Bridewell, 56; **4** Longden, 50; **5** Coutts and Smart, 48.

National Superstock Championship, round 6 (26 laps, 33.774 miles/54.366 km)
1 Steve Brogan (Suzuki), 25m 46.282s, 78.60 mph/126.49 km/h.
2 Steve Allan (Kawasaki); **3** Jonti Hobday (Suzuki); **4** Donald MacFadyen (Suzuki); **5** David Jefferies (Suzuki); **6** Jason Davis (Suzuki); **7** David Johnson (Yamaha); **8** Roger Bennett (Suzuki); **9** Chris Miller (Suzuki); **10** Norman MacLeod (Suzuki); **11** Ben Wylie (Suzuki); **12** Mark Buckley (Suzuki); **13** Aaron Zanotti (Suzuki); **14** Magnus Houston (Suzuki); **15** Darren Mitchell (Suzuki).
Fastest lap: Andy Tinsley (Suzuki), 56.244s, 83.11 mph/133.76 km/h.
Championship points: **1** Brogan, 110; **2** Jefferies, 105; **3** Llewellyn, 86; **4** Tinsley, 66; **5** Morley, 52; **6** Davis, 42.

BRAND HATCH GRAND PRIX CIRCUIT, 22 June. 2.608-mile/4.197-km circuit.
British Superbike Championship powered by Halls, rounds 11 and 12 (2 x 20 laps, 52.160 miles/83.940 km)
Race 1
1 Shane Byrne (Ducati), 30m 54.420s, 101.30 mph/163.03 km/h.
2 John Reynolds (Suzuki); **3** Steve Plater (Honda); **4** Gary Mason (Yamaha); **5** Steve Hislop (Yamaha); **6** Glen Richards (Kawasaki); **7** Scott Smart (Kawasaki); **8** John McGuinness (Ducati); **9** John Crawford (Ducati); **10** Lee Jackson (Kawasaki); **11** Nick Medd (Ducati).
Fastest lap: Byrne, 1m 27.332s, 107.51 mph/173.02 km/h (record).

Race 2
1 John Reynolds (Suzuki), 29m 08.941s, 107.41 mph/172.86 km/h.
2 Shane Byrne (Ducati); **3** Michael Rutter (Ducati); **4** Sean Emmett (Ducati); **5** Glen Richards (Kawasaki); **6** Gary Mason (Yamaha); **7** Steve Hislop (Yamaha); **8** Steve Plater (Honda); **9** Scott Smart (Kawasaki); **10** Yukio Kagayama (Suzuki); **11** John Crawford (Ducati); **12** John McGuinness (Ducati); **13** Lee Jackson (Kawasaki); **14** Nick Medd (Ducati); **15** Jon Kirkham (Yamaha).
Fastest lap: Reynolds, 1m 26.800s, 108.17 mph/174.08 km/h (record).
Championship points: **1** Byrne, 285; **2** Rutter, 152; **3** Reynolds, 145; **4** Richards, 131; **5** Mason and Plater, 117.

British Supersport Championship, round 6 (18 laps, 46.944 miles/75.546 km)
1 Dean Thomas (Honda), 27m 18.358s, 103.20 mph/166.08 km/h.
2 Karl Harris (Honda); **3** Stuart Easton (Ducati); **4** Leon Haslam (Ducati); **5** Simon Andrews (Yamaha); **6** Tom Sykes (Yamaha); **7** Takeshi Tsujimura (Honda); **8** Jamie Robinson (Yamaha); **9** Rob Frost (Kawasaki); **10** Craig Jones (Triumph); **11** Jonnie Ekerold (Honda); **12** Danny Beaumont (Kawasaki); **13** Shane Norval (Yamaha); **14** Tom Tunstall (Yamaha); **15** Kieran Murphy (Kawasaki).
Fastest lap: Easton, 1m 30.207s, 104.08 mph/167.51 km/h (record).
Championship points: **1** Harris, 135; **2** Easton, 80; **3** Andrews, 61; **4** Haslam, 60; **5** Coates, 53; **6** Thomas, 52.

National 125GP Championship, round 6 (10 laps, 26.080 miles/41.970 km)
1 Michael Wilcox (Honda), 16m 10.743s, 96.79 mph/155.77 km/h.

2 Thomas Bridewell (Honda); 3 John Pearson (Honda); 4 Paul Veazey (Honda); 5 Sam Owens (Honda); 6 Midge Smart (Honda); 7 Brian Clark (Honda); 8 Joe Dickinson (Honda); 9 Chester Lusk (Honda); 10 Ryan Saxelby (Honda); 11 James Ford (Honda); 12 Robert Guiver (Honda); 13 Jon Vincent (Honda); 14 Leon Morris (Aprilia); 15 James Rose (Honda).
Fastest lap: Wilcox, 1m 35.374s, 98.44 mph/158.43 km/h.
Championship points: 1 Wilcox, 111; 2 Pearson, 80; 3 T. Bridewell, 76; 4 Smart, 58; 5 Longden, 50; 6 Coutts, 48.

National Superstock Championship, round 7 (15 laps, 39.120 miles/62.955 km)
1 Darren Mitchell (Suzuki), 24m 30.306s, 95.83 mph/154.22 km/h.
2 Matt Llewellyn (Suzuki); 3 Andy Tinsley (Suzuki); 4 Luke Quigley (Suzuki); 5 Tristan Palmer (Suzuki); 6 Steve Brogan (Suzuki); 7 Ben Wilson (Suzuki); 8 Jamie Morley (Suzuki); 9 Magnus Houston (Suzuki); 10 David Johnson (Yamaha); 11 Andrew Weymouth (Yamaha); 12 Jason Davis (Suzuki); 13 Ben Wylie (Suzuki); 14 Chris Miller (Suzuki); 15 Marty Nutt (Suzuki).
Fastest lap: Quigley, 1m 33.365s, 100.56 mph/161.84 km/h.
Championship points: 1 Brogan, 120; 2 Llewellyn 106; 3 Jefferies, 105; 4 Tinsley, 82; 5 Morley, 60; 6 Quigley, 54.

ROCKINGHAM CIRCUIT, 6 July. 1.736-mile/2.794-km circuit.
British Superbike Championship powered by Halls, rounds 13 and 14 (2 x 22 laps, 38.192 miles/61.468 km)
Race 1
1 Yukio Kagayama (Suzuki), 26m 05.661s, 87.81 mph/141.32 km/h.
2 Shane Byrne (Ducati); 3 Steve Plater (Honda); 4 Michael Rutter (Ducati); 5 John Reynolds (Suzuki); 6 Glen Richards (Kawasaki); 7 Sean Emmett (Ducati); 8 Leon Haslam (Ducati); 9 Scott Smart (Kawasaki); 10 Steve Hislop (Yamaha); 11 Jon Kirkham (Yamaha); 12 Lee Jackson (Kawasaki).
Fastest lap: Kagayama, 1m 10.035s, 89.23 mph/143.61 km/h.

Race 2
1 Yukio Kagayama (Suzuki), 26m 00.078s, 88.13 mph/141.83 km/h.
2 Shane Byrne (Ducati); 3 Michael Rutter (Ducati); 4 Steve Plater (Honda); 5 John Reynolds (Suzuki); 6 Scott Smart (Kawasaki); 7 Gary Mason (Yamaha); 8 Sean Emmett (Ducati); 9 Leon Haslam (Ducati); 10 Mark Heckles (Honda); 11 Steve Hislop (Yamaha); 12 Paul Young (Yamaha); 13 Lee Jackson (Kawasaki); 14 Paul Jones (Suzuki).
Fastest lap: Kagayama, 1m 09.893s, 89.41 mph/143.90 km/h (record).
Championship points: 1 Byrne, 325; 2 Rutter, 181; 3 Reynolds, 167; 4 Kagayama, 153; 5 Plater, 146; 6 Richards, 141.

British Supersport Championship, round 7 (20 laps, 34.720 miles/55.880 km)
1 Karl Harris (Honda), 24m 21.280s, 85.53 mph/137.65 km/h.
2 Stuart Easton (Ducati); 3 Dean Thomas (Honda); 4 John Crockford (Honda); 5 Simon Andrews (Yamaha); 6 Michael Laverty (Honda); 7 Adrian Coates (Honda); 8 Craig Jones (Triumph); 9 Jamie Robinson (Yamaha); 10 Shane Norval (Yamaha); 11 Mark Burr (Yamaha); 12 Tom Tunstall (Yamaha); 13 Andi Notman (Honda); 14 Kieran Murphy (Kawasaki); 15 Kim Ashkenazi (Yamaha).
Fastest lap: Harris, 1m 11.969s, 86.83 mph/139.75 km/h.
Championship points: 1 Harris, 160; 2 Easton, 100; 3 Andrews, 72; 4 Thomas, 68; 5 Coates, 62; 6 Haslam, 60.

MONDELLO PARK, 20 July. 2.176-mile/3.502-km circuit.
British Superbike Championship powered by Halls, rounds 15 and 16
Race 1 (17 laps, 36.992 miles/59.534 km)
1 John Reynolds (Suzuki), 29m 04.650s, 76.35 mph/122.87 km/h.
2 Sean Emmett (Ducati); 3 Yukio Kagayama (Suzuki); 4 Glen Richards (Kawasaki); 5 Michael Rutter (Ducati); 6 Steve Plater (Honda); 7 Gary Mason (Yamaha); 8 Scott Smart (Kawasaki); 9 Shane Byrne (Ducati); 10 Leon Haslam (Ducati); 11 Mark Heckles (Honda); 12 Jon Kirkham (Yamaha); 13 Lee Jackson (Kawasaki); 14 Paul Jones (Suzuki.
Fastest lap: Emmett, 1m 41.738s, 77.01 mph/123.95 km/h (record).

Race 2 (18 laps, 39.168 miles/63.036 km)
1 John Reynolds (Suzuki), 30m 43.350s, 76.51 mph/123.13 km/h.
2 Shane Byrne (Ducati); 3 Glen Richards (Kawasaki); 4 Gary Mason (Yamaha); 5 Michael Rutter (Ducati); 6 Steve Plater (Honda); 7 Leon Haslam (Ducati); 8 Sean Emmett (Ducati); 9 Mark Heckles (Honda); 10 Paul Young (Yamaha); 11 Jon Kirkham (Yamaha); 12 Lee Jackson (Kawasaki); 13 Scott Smart (Kawasaki); 14 Paul Jones (Suzuki).
Fastest lap: Reynolds, 1m 41.234s, 77.40 mph/124.56 km/h (record).
Championship points: 1 Byrne, 352; 2 Reynolds, 217; 3 Rutter, 203; 4 Richards, 170; 5 Kagayama, 169; 6 Plater, 166.

British Supersport Championship, round 8 (16 laps, 34.816 miles/56.032 km)
1 Stuart Easton (Ducati), 28m 01.740s, 74.54 mph/119.96 km/h.
2 Tom Sykes (Yamaha); 3 Michael Laverty (Honda); 4 John Crockford (Honda); 5 Simon Andrews (Yamaha); 6 Craig Jones (Triumph); 7 Kieran Murphy (Kawasaki); 8 Rob Frost (Kawasaki); 9 Adrian Coates (Honda); 10 Jamie Robinson (Yamaha); 11 Karl Harris (Honda); 12 Mark Burr (Yamaha); 13 Dean Thomas (Honda); 14 Jonnie Ekerold (Honda); 15 Jim Moodie (Triumph).
Fastest lap: Easton, 1m 44.304s, 75.12 mph/120.90 km/h (record).
Championship points: 1 Harris, 165; 2 Easton, 125; 3 Andrews, 83; 4 Laverty, 73; 5 Crockford and Thomas, 71.

National 125GP Championship, round 7 (14 laps, 30.464 miles/49.028 km)
1 Thomas Bridewell (Honda), 25m 24.305s, 71.96 mph/115.81 km/h.
2 John Pearson (Honda); 3 Midge Smart (Honda); 4 Lee Longden (Honda); 5 Robert Guiver (Honda); 6 Sam Owens (Honda); 7 Kris Weston (Honda); 8 Allan O'Connor (Honda); 9 Tim Stott (Honda); 10 James Ford (Honda); 11 Paul Veazey (Honda); 12 Daniel Cooper (Honda); 13 Brian Clark (Honda); 14 Ashley Beech (Honda); 15 Nathan Pallett (Honda).
Fastest lap: Bridewell, 1m 48.011s, 72.54 mph/116.75 km/h.
Championship points: 1 Wilcox, 111; 2 T. Bridewell, 101; 3 Pearson, 100; 4 Smart, 74; 5 Longden, 63; 6 Veazey and Weston, 49.

OULTON PARK INTERNATIONAL, 10 August. 2.692-mile/4.332-km circuit.
British Superbike Championship powered by Halls, rounds 17 and 18
Race 1 (12 laps, 32.304 miles/51.984 km)
1 Steve Plater (Honda), 20m 26.439s, 94.82 mph/152.60 km/h.
2 Yukio Kagayama (Suzuki); 3 Sean Emmett (Ducati); 4 Michael Rutter (Ducati); 5 Glen Richards (Kawasaki); 6 Scott Smart (Kawasaki); 7 Mark Heckles (Honda); 8 Leon Haslam (Ducati); 9 Dean Ellison (Ducati); 10 Paul Young (Yamaha); 11 Lee Jackson (Kawasaki); 12 Jason Vincent (Yamaha); 13 Nick Medd (Ducati).
Fastest lap: Reynolds, 1m 39.059s, 97.83 mph/157.44 km/h.

Race 2 (18 laps, 48.456 miles/77.976 km)
1 Yukio Kagayama (Suzuki), 29m 29.099s, 98.60 mph/158.68 km/h.
2 John Reynolds (Suzuki); 3 Sean Emmett (Ducati); 4 Shane Byrne (Ducati); 5 Steve Plater (Honda); 6 Michael Rutter (Ducati); 7 Leon Haslam (Ducati); 8 Glen Richards (Kawasaki); 9 Mark Heckles (Honda); 10 Scott Smart (Kawasaki); 11 Dean Ellison (Ducati); 12 Paul Young (Yamaha); 13 Jason Vincent (Yamaha); 14 Lee Jackson (Kawasaki); 15 Paul Jones (Suzuki).
Fastest lap: Reynolds, 1m 37.449s, 99.44 mph/160.04 km/h (record).
Championship points: 1 Byrne, 365; 2 Reynolds, 237; 3 Rutter, 226; 4 Kagayama, 214; 5 Plater, 202; 6 Richards, 189.

British Supersport Championship, round 9 (16 laps, 43.072 miles/69.312 km)
1 Karl Harris (Honda), 28m 16.418s, 91.40 mph/147.09 km/h.
2 Stuart Easton (Ducati); 3 Simon Andrews (Yamaha); 4 Rob Frost (Kawasaki); 5 John Crockford (Honda); 6 Tom Sykes (Yamaha); 7 Michael Laverty (Honda); 8 Dean Thomas (Honda); 9 Craig Jones (Triumph); 10 Tom Tunstall (Yamaha); 11 Kim Ashkenazi (Yamaha); 12 Jonnie Ekerold (Honda); 13 Shane Norval (Yamaha); 14 Les Shand (Honda); 15 John Crawford (Honda).
Fastest lap: Harris, 1m 40.833s, 96.11 mph/154.67 km/h (record).
Championship points: 1 Harris, 190; 2 Easton, 145; 3 Andrews, 99; 4 Crockford and Laverty, 82; 6 Thomas, 79.

National 125GP Championship, round 8 (13 laps, 34.996 miles/56.316 km)
1 Eugene Laverty (Honda), 23m 43.446s, 88.50 mph/142.43 km/h.
2 Chris Martin (Honda); 3 Thomas Bridewell (Honda); 4 Michael Wilcox (Honda); 5 Sam Owens (Honda); 6 John Pearson (Honda); 7 Christian Elkin (Honda); 8 Lee Longden (Honda); 9 Paul Veazey (Honda); 10 Ryan Saxelby (Honda); 11 Kris Weston (Honda); 12 Robert Guiver (Honda); 13 Jon Boy Lee (Honda); 14 Steven Neate (Honda); 15 Chester Lusk (Honda).
Fastest lap: Elkin, 1m 47.221s, 90.38 mph/145.46 km/h (record).
Championship points: 1 Wilcox, 124; 2 T. Bridewell, 117; 3 Pearson, 110; 4 Smart, 74; 5 Longden, 71; 6 Owens, 59.

National Superstock Championship, round 8 (15 laps, 40.380 miles/64.980 km)
1 Steve Brogan (Suzuki), 25m 40.123s, 94.38 mph/151.89 km/h.
2 Andy Tinsley (Suzuki); 3 Luke Quigley (Suzuki); 4 Jason Davis (Suzuki); 5 John Laverty (Suzuki); 6 Tristan Palmer (Suzuki); 7 David Johnson (Yamaha); 8 Darren Mitchell (Suzuki); 9 Ian Hutchinson (Suzuki); 10 Jonti Hobday (Suzuki); 11 Gary May (Suzuki); 12 Les Shand (Suzuki); 13 Ben Wylie (Suzuki); 14 Chris Miller (Suzuki); 15 Doug Cowie (Suzuki).
Fastest lap: Tinsley, 1m 41.730s, 95.26 mph/153.31 km/h.
Championship points: 1 Brogan, 145; 2 Llewellyn, 106; 3 Jefferies, 105; 4 Tinsley, 102; 5 Quigley, 70; 6 Morley, 60.

CADWELL PARK CIRCUIT, 25 August. 2.173-mile/3.497-km circuit.
British Superbike Championship powered by Halls, rounds 19 and 20 (2 x 18 laps, 39.114 miles/62.946 km)
Race 1
1 Shane Byrne (Ducati), 27m 26.156s, 85.53 mph/137.65 km/h.
2 John Reynolds (Suzuki); 3 Michael Rutter (Ducati); 4 Gary Mason (Yamaha); 5 Glen Richards (Kawasaki); 6 Scott Smart (Kawasaki); 7 Sean Emmett (Ducati); 8 Lee Jackson (Kawasaki); 9 Nick Medd (Ducati); 10 Paul Jones (Suzuki).
Fastest lap: Reynolds, 1m 25.181s, 91.83 mph/147.79 km/h.

Race 2
1 Steve Plater (Honda), 25m 52.771s, 90.68 mph/145.94 km/h.
2 John Reynolds (Suzuki); 3 Shane Byrne (Ducati); 4 Leon Haslam (Ducati); 5 Gary Mason (Yamaha); 6 Glen Richards (Kawasaki); 7 Sean Emmett (Ducati); 8 Chris Burns (Yamaha); 9 Lee Jackson (Kawasaki); 10 Dean Ellison (Ducati); 11 Jon Kirkham (Yamaha); 12 Nick Medd (Ducati); 13 Paul Jones (Suzuki); 14 Scott Smart (Kawasaki); 15 Michael Rutter (Ducati).
Fastest lap: Byrne, 1m 25.307s, 91.70 mph/147.57 km/h.
Championship points: 1 Byrne, 406; 2 Reynolds, 277; 3 Rutter, 243; 4 Plater, 227; 5 Kagayama, 214; 6 Richards, 210.

British Supersport Championship, round 10 (16 laps, 34.768 miles/55.952 km)
1 Karl Harris (Honda), 23m 36.486s, 88.36 mph/142.20 km/h.
2 Michael Laverty (Honda); 3 Simon Andrews (Yamaha); 4 Stuart Easton (Ducati); 5 Tom Sykes (Yamaha); 6 Adrian Coates (Honda); 7 Rob Frost (Kawasaki); 8 Dean Thomas (Honda); 9 Kim Ashkenazi (Yamaha); 10 Tom Tunstall (Yamaha); 11 John Crawford (Honda); 12 Jim Moodie (Triumph); 13 Craig Jones (Triumph); 14 Jonnie Ekerold (Honda); 15 Glyn Ormerod (Honda).
Fastest lap: Harris, 1m 27.745s, 89.15 mph/143.47 km/h (record).
Championship points: 1 Harris, 215; 2 Easton, 158; 3 Andrews, 115; 4 Laverty, 102; 5 Thomas, 87; 6 Crockford, 82.

National 125GP Championship, round 9 (12 laps, 26.076 miles/41.964 km)
1 Chris Martin (Honda), 18m 26.480s, 84.84 mph/136.54 km/h.
2 John Pearson (Honda); 3 Michael Wilcox (Honda); 4 Midge Smart (Honda); 5 Kris Weston (Honda); 6 Eugene Laverty (Honda); 7 Thomas Bridewell (Honda); 8 Ryan Saxelby (Honda); 9 Lee Longden (Honda); 10 Joe Dickinson (Honda); 11 Steven Neate (Honda); 12 Ashley Beech (Honda); 13 Daniel Cooper (Honda); 14 Paul Veazey (Honda); 15 Brian Clark (Honda).
Fastest lap: Wilcox, 1m 30.991s, 85.97 mph/138.36 km/h.

National 125GP Championship, round 10 (13 laps, 28.249 miles/45.461 km)
1 Chris Martin (Honda), 20m 06.123s, 84.31 mph/135.68 km/h.
2 Midge Smart (Honda); 3 Michael Wilcox (Honda); 4 Eugene Laverty (Honda); 5 Danny Coutts (Honda); 6 Kris Weston (Honda); 7 John Pearson (Honda); 8 Ryan Saxelby (Honda); 9 Sam Owens (Honda); 10 Joe Dickinson (Honda); 11 Daniel Cooper (Honda); 12 Ashley Beech (Honda); 13 Steven Neate (Honda); 14 Chester Lusk (Honda); 15 James Westmoreland (Honda).
Fastest lap: Martin, 1m 30.900s, 86.05 mph/138.49 km/h.
Championship points: 1 Wilcox, 156; 2 Pearson, 139; 3 T. Bridewell, 126; 4 Smart, 107; 5 Laverty, 81; 6 Longden, 78.

National Superstock Championship, round 9 (15 laps, 32.595 miles/52.455 km)
1 Ben Wilson (Suzuki), 22m 28.066s, 87.04 mph/140.08 km/h.
2 Andy Tinsley (Suzuki); 3 Jamie Morley (Suzuki); 4 Luke Quigley (Suzuki); 5 Matt Llewellyn (Suzuki); 6 Steve Brogan (Suzuki); 7 Darren Mitchell (Suzuki); 8 Marty Nutt (Suzuki); 9 Tristan Palmer (Suzuki); 10 Les Shand (Suzuki); 11 David Johnson (Yamaha); 12 Matt Layt (Suzuki); 13 Gary May (Suzuki); 14 Aaron Zanotti (Suzuki); 15 Chris Miller (Suzuki).
Fastest lap: Wilson, 1m 28.973s, 87.92 mph/141.49 km/h (record).
Championship points: 1 Brogan, 155; 2 Tinsley, 122; 3 Llewellyn, 117; 4 Jefferies, 105; 5 Quigley, 83; 6 Morley, 76.

BRANDS HATCH INDY CIRCUIT, 14 September. 1.226-mile/1.973-km circuit.
British Superbike Championship powered by Halls, rounds 21 and 22 (2 x 30 laps, 36.780 miles/59.190 km)
Race 1
1 John Reynolds (Suzuki), 24m 28.732s, 90.21 mph/145.18 km/h.
2 Sean Emmett (Ducati); 3 Shane Byrne (Ducati); 4 Michael Rutter (Ducati); 5 Glen Richards (Kawasaki); 6 Gary Mason (Yamaha); 7 Steve Plater (Honda); 8 Scott Smart (Kawasaki); 9 Leon Haslam (Ducati); 10 Chris Burns (Yamaha); 11 Mark Heckles (Honda); 12 Jon Kirkham (Yamaha); 13 Lee Jackson (Kawasaki); 14 Dean Ellison (Ducati); 15 Paul Jones (Suzuki).
Fastest lap: Reynolds, 46.397s, 95.14 mph/153.11 km/h.

Race 2
1 Sean Emmett (Ducati), 23m 26.076s, 94.23 mph/151.65 km/h.
2 John Reynolds (Suzuki); 3 Shane Byrne (Ducati); 4 Glen Richards (Kawasaki); 5 Leon Haslam (Ducati); 6 Steve Plater (Honda); 7 Gary Mason (Yamaha); 8 Scott Smart (Kawasaki); 9 Michael Rutter (Ducati); 10 Mark Heckles (Honda); 11 Jon Kirkham (Yamaha); 12 Chris Burns (Yamaha); 13 Dean Ellison (Ducati); 14 Tom Sykes (Suzuki).
Fastest lap: Richards, 46.274s, 95.39 mph/153.52 km/h.
Championship points: 1 Byrne, 438; 2 Reynolds, 322; 3 Rutter, 263; 4 Plater, 246; 5 Richards, 234; 6 Kagayama, 214.

British Supersport Championship, round 11 (28 laps, 34.328 miles/55.244 km)
1 Stuart Easton (Ducati), 22m 30.781s, 91.55 mph/147.34 km/h.
2 Simon Andrews (Yamaha); 3 Dean Thomas (Honda); 4 John Crockford (Honda); 5 Kim Ashkenazi (Yamaha); 6 Tom Tunstall (Yamaha); 7 Shane Norval (Yamaha); 8 Craig Jones (Triumph); 9 John Crawford (Honda); 10 Danny Beaumont (Kawasaki); 11 Andi Notman (Honda); 12 Craig Sproston (Honda); 13 Les Shand (Honda); 14 Ryan Rainey (Honda); 15 Nathan Flanagan (Ducati).
Fastest lap: Andrews, 47.782s, 92.38 mph/148.67 km/h (record).
Championship points: 1 Harris, 215; 2 Easton, 183; 3 Andrews, 135; 4 Thomas, 103; 5 Laverty, 102; 6 Crockford, 95.

National 125GP Championship, round 11 (24 laps, 29.424 miles/47.352 km)
1 Midge Smart (Honda), 20m 07.358s, 87.80 mph/141.30 km/h.
2 Steven Neate (Honda); 3 Jonathan Rea (Honda); 4 Thomas Bridewell (Honda); 5 Michael Wilcox (Honda); 6 Lee Longden (Honda); 7 Robert Guiver (Honda); 8 Paul Veazey (Honda); 9 Daniel Cooper (Honda); 10 Ryan Saxelby (Honda); 11 James Westmoreland (Honda); 12 John Pearson (Honda); 13 Chris Martin (Honda); 14 James Ford (Honda); 15 Jon Vincent (Honda).
Fastest lap: Neate, 49.292s, 89.55 mph/144.12 km/h.
Championship points: 1 Wilcox, 167; 2 Pearson, 143; 3 T. Bridewell, 139; 4 Smart, 132; 5 Longden, 88; 6 Laverty, 81.

National Superstock Championship, round 10 (26 laps, 31.876 miles/51.298 km)
1 Luke Quigley (Suzuki), 21m 06.648s, 90.66 mph/145.90 km/h.
2 Ben Wilson (Suzuki); 3 Tristan Palmer (Suzuki); 4 Jamie Morley (Suzuki); 5 Andy Tinsley (Suzuki); 6 Marty Nutt (Suzuki); 7 Darren Mitchell (Suzuki); 8 Stephen Thompson (Suzuki); 9 David Johnson (Yamaha); 10 Steve Brogan (Suzuki); 11 Matt Layt (Suzuki); 12 Aaron Zanotti (Suzuki); 13 Steve Booker (Suzuki); 14 Ben Wylie (Suzuki); 15 Les Shand (Suzuki).
Fastest lap: Palmer, 48.274s, 91.44 mph/147.16 km/h (record).
Championship points: 1 Brogan, 161; 2 Tinsley, 133; 3 Llewellyn, 117; 4 Quigley, 108; 5 Jefferies, 105; 6 Morley, 89.

DONINGTON PARK GRAND PRIX CIRCUIT, 28 September. 2.500-mile/4.023-km circuit.
British Superbike Championship powered by Halls, rounds 23 and 24 (2 x 20 laps, 50.000 miles/80.460 km)
Race 1
1 Shane Byrne (Ducati), 31m 35.018s, 94.92 mph/152.76 km/h.
2 Sean Emmett (Ducati); 3 John Reynolds (Suzuki); 4 Michael Rutter (Ducati); 5 Glen Richards (Kawasaki); 6 Scott Smart (Kawasaki); 7 Leon Haslam (Ducati); 8 Gary Mason (Yamaha); 9 Dean Ellison (Ducati); 10 Jon Kirkham (Yamaha); 11 Mark Heckles (Honda); 12 Lee Jackson (Kawasaki).
Fastest lap: Byrne, 1m 33.883s, 95.86 mph/154.27 km/h.

Race 2
1 Shane Byrne (Ducati), 31m 24.167s, 95.47 mph/153.64 km/h.
2 John Reynolds (Suzuki); 3 Sean Emmett (Ducati); 4 Michael Rutter (Ducati); 5 Leon Haslam (Ducati); 6 Glen Richards (Kawasaki); 7 Gary Mason (Yamaha); 8 Jon Kirkham (Yamaha); 9 Mark Heckles (Honda); 10 Paul Jones (Suzuki).
Fastest lap: Byrne, 1m 33.324s, 96.43 mph/155.20 km/h.

British Supersport Championship, round 12 (18 laps, 45.000 miles/72.414 km)
1 Michael Laverty (Honda), 30m 31.390s, 88.39 mph/142.25 km/h.
2 Karl Harris (Honda); 3 Craig Jones (Triumph); 4 Dean Thomas (Honda); 5 Simon Andrews (Yamaha); 6 Tom Sykes (Yamaha); 7 Stuart Easton (Ducati); 8 Jamie Robinson (Yamaha); 9 Kim Ashkenazi (Yamaha); 10 Tom Tunstall (Yamaha); 11 Shane Norval (Yamaha); 12 John Crawford (Honda); 13 Danny Beaumont (Kawasaki); 14 Leon Camier (Honda); 15 Les Shand (Honda).
Fastest lap: Laverty, 1m 37.205s, 92.58 mph/149.00 km/h.

National 125GP Championship, round 12 (15 laps, 37.500 miles/60.345 km)
1 Chris Martin (Honda), 25m 43.694s, 87.38 mph/140.62 km/h.
2 John Pearson (Honda); 3 Michael Wilcox (Honda); 4 Midge Smart (Honda); 5 Sam Owens (Honda); 6 Lee Longden (Honda); 7 Ryan Saxelby (Honda); 8 Brian Clark (Honda); 9 Jonathan Rea (Honda); 10 Paul Veazey (Honda); 11 Chester Lusk (Honda); 12 Ashley Beech (Honda); 13 Robert Guiver (Honda); 14 James Westmoreland (Honda); 15 James Rose (Honda).
Fastest lap: Clark, 1m 42.017s, 88.22 mph/141.97 km/h.

National Superstock Championship, rounds 11 and 12 (2 x 15 laps, 37.500 miles/60.345 km)
Race 1
1 Luke Quigley (Suzuki), 24m 45.298s, 90.81 mph/146.14 km/h.
2 Andy Tinsley (Suzuki); 3 Ben Wilson (Suzuki); 4 Danny Beaumont (Suzuki); 5 Darren Mitchell (Suzuki); 6 Tristan Palmer (Suzuki); 7 Rob Frost (Kawasaki); 8 David Johnson (Yamaha); 9 Stephen Thompson (Suzuki); 10 Ben Wylie (Suzuki); 11 Shaun Harris (Suzuki); 12 Jonti Hobday (Suzuki); 13 Matt Llewellyn (Suzuki); 14 Ian Hutchinson (Suzuki); 15 James Hurrell (Suzuki).
Fastest lap: Tinsley, 1m 37.828s, 91.99 mph/148.05 km/h.

Race 2
1 Andy Tinsley (Suzuki), 24m 40.393s, 91.11 mph/146.63 km/h.
2 Luke Quigley (Suzuki); 3 Ben Wilson (Suzuki); 4 Darren Mitchell (Suzuki); 5 Danny Beaumont (Suzuki); 6 Shaun Harris (Suzuki); 7 John McGuinness (Suzuki); 8 Marty Nutt (Suzuki); 9 Craig Fitzpatrick (Suzuki); 10 Ben Wylie (Suzuki); 11 Stephen Thompson (Suzuki); 12 Les Shand (Suzuki); 13 Aaron Zanotti (Suzuki); 14 Jonti Hobday (Suzuki); 15 Ian Hutchinson (Suzuki).
Fastest lap: Quigley, 1m 37.564s, 92.24 mph/148.45 km/h.

Final British Superbike Championship points

1	Shane Byrne	488
2	John Reynolds	358
3	Michael Rutter	289
4	Glen Richards	255
5	Sean Emmett	247

6 Steve Plater, 246; 7 Yukio Kagayama, 214; 8 Gary Mason, 208; 9 Scott Smart, 154; 10 Steve Hislop, 122; 11 Leon Haslam, Mark Heckles and Lee Jackson, 98; 14 John Crawford and Paul Young, 74.

Final British Supersport Championship points

1 Karl Harris — 235
2 Stuart Easton — 192
3 Simon Andrews — 146
4 Michael Laverty — 127
5 Dean Thomas — 116

6 John Crockford, 95; 7 Craig Jones, 91; 8 Tom Sykes, 90; 9 Adrian Coates, 79; 10 Rob Frost, 78; 11 Leon Haslam, 60; 12 Jamie Robinson, 57; 13 Tom Tunstall, 56; 14 Kieran Murphy and Shane Norval, 32.

Final National 125GP Championship points

1 Michael Wilcox — 183
2 John Pearson — 159
3 Midge Smart — 145
4 Thomas Bridewell — 139
5= Lee Longden — 98
5= Chris Martin — 98

7 Eugene Laverty, 81; 8 Sam Owens, 77; 9 Kris Weston, 75; 10 Paul Veazey, 72; 11 Danny Coutts, 59; 12 Chester Lusk, 52; 13 Christian Elkin, 50; 14 Ryan Saxelby, 49; 15 Jonathan Rea, 45.

Final National Superstock Championship points

1 Andy Tinsley — 178
2 Steve Brogan — 161
3 Luke Quigley — 153
4 Matt Llewellyn — 120
5 Ben Wilson — 111

6 David Jefferies, 105; 7 Jamie Morley, 89; 8 Tristan Palmer, 88; 9 Darren Mitchell, 85; 10 David Johnson, 60; 11 Jason Davis, 59; 12 Jonti Hobday, 42; 13 John Laverty, 39; 14 Marty Nutt, 38; 15 Steve Allan, 35.

Supersport World Championship

VALENCIA, Spain, 2 March. 2.489-mile/4.005-km circuit.
Supersport World Championship, round 1 (23 laps, 57.247 miles/92.115 km)
1 Katsuaki Fujiwara, J (Suzuki), 38m 10.992s, 89.942 mph/144.747 km/h.

2 Chris Vermeulen, AUS (Honda); 3 Alessio Corradi, I (Yamaha); 4 Christophe Cogan, F (Honda); 5 Jörg Teuchert, D (Yamaha); 6 Karl Muggeridge, AUS (Honda); 7 Broc Parkes, AUS (Honda); 8 Christian Kellner, D (Yamaha); 9 Jurgen van den Goorbergh, NL (Yamaha); 10 Werner Daemen, B (Honda); 11 Pere Riba, E (Kawasaki); 12 Simone Sanna, I (Yamaha); 13 Michael Schulten, D (Honda); 14 Fabien Foret, F (Kawasaki); 15 Matthieu Lagrive, F (Yamaha).
Fastest lap: Corradi, 1m 38.874s, 90.609 mph/145.822 km/h (record).
Championship points: 1 Fujiwara, 25; 2 Vermeulen, 20; 3 Corradi, 16; 4 Cogan, 13; 5 Teuchert, 11; 6 Muggeridge, 10.

PHILLIP ISLAND, Australia, 30 March. 2.762-mile/4.445-km circuit.
Supersport World Championship, round 2 (21 laps, 58.002 miles/93.345 km)
1 Chris Vermeulen, AUS (Honda), 34m 03.675s, 102.172 mph/164.430 km/h.

2 Katsuaki Fujiwara, J (Suzuki); 3 Jurgen van den Goorbergh, NL (Yamaha); 4 Stéphane Chambon, F (Suzuki); 5 Kevin Curtain, AUS (Yamaha); 6 Jörg Teuchert, D (Yamaha); 7 Karl Muggeridge, AUS (Honda); 8 Pere Riba, E (Kawasaki); 9 Alessio Corradi, I (Yamaha); 10 Robert Ulm, A (Honda); 11 Fabien Foret, F (Kawasaki); 12 Christian Kellner, D (Yamaha); 13 Christophe Cogan, F (Honda); 14 Werner Daemen, B (Honda); 15 Simone Sanna, I (Yamaha).
Fastest lap: Fujiwara, 1m 36.642s, 102.887 mph/165.580 km/h (record).
Championship points: 1 Fujiwara and Vermeulen, 45; 3 Corradi and van den Goorbergh, 23; 5 Teuchert, 21; 6 Muggeridge, 19.

SUGO, Japan, 27 April. 2.322-mile/3.737-km circuit.
Supersport World Championship, round 3 (25 laps, 58.050 miles/93.425 km)
1 Christian Kellner, D (Yamaha), 39m 19.896s, 88.557 mph/142.519 km/h.

2 Ryuichi Kiyonari, J (Honda); 3 Stéphane Chambon, F (Suzuki); 4 Tekkyu Kayo, J (Yamaha); 5 Chris Vermeulen, AUS (Honda); 6 Karl Muggeridge, AUS (Honda); 7 Broc Parkes, AUS (Honda); 8 Jurgen van den Goorbergh, NL (Yamaha); 9 Pere Riba, E (Kawasaki); 10 Alessio Corradi, I (Yamaha); 11 Christophe Cogan, F (Honda); 12 Werner Daemen, B (Honda); 13 Simone Sanna, I (Yamaha); 14 Gianluca Nannelli, I (Yamaha); 15 Katsuaki Fujiwara, J (Suzuki).
Fastest lap: Kellner, 1m 33.244s, 89.651 mph/144.280 km/h.
Championship points: 1 Vermeulen, 56; 2 Fujiwara, 46; 3 Kellner, 37; 4 van den Goorbergh, 31; 5 Chambon, Corradi and Muggeridge, 29.

MONZA, Italy, 18 May. 3.600-mile/5.793-km circuit.
Supersport World Championship, round 4 (16 laps, 57.600 miles/92.688 km)
1 Chris Vermeulen, AUS (Honda), 30m 16.092s, 114.166 mph/183.733 km/h.

2 Jurgen van den Goorbergh, NL (Yamaha); 3 Iain Macpherson, GB (Honda); 4 Stéphane Chambon, F (Suzuki); 5 Fabien Foret, F (Kawasaki); 6 Sébastien Charpentier, F (Honda); 7 Christian Kellner, D (Yamaha); 8 Alessio Corradi, I (Yamaha); 9 Pere Riba, E (Kawasaki); 10 Katsuaki Fujiwara, J (Suzuki); 11 Robert Ulm, A (Honda); 12 Christophe Cogan, F (Honda); 13 Barry Veneman, NL (Honda); 14 Simone Sanna, I (Yamaha); 15 Broc Parkes, AUS (Honda).
Fastest lap: Vermeulen, 1m 52.635s, 115.049 mph/185.154 km/h (record).
Championship points: 1 Vermeulen, 81; 2 Fujiwara, 52; 3 van den Goorbergh, 51; 4 Kellner, 46; 5 Chambon, 42; 6 Corradi, 37.

OSCHERSLEBEN, Germany, 1 June. 2.279-mile/3.667-km circuit.
Supersport World Championship, round 5 (28 laps, 63.812 miles/102.676 km)
1 Chris Vermeulen, AUS (Honda), 42m 51.384s, 89.321 mph/143.749 km/h.

2 Stéphane Chambon, F (Suzuki); 3 Katsuaki Fujiwara, J (Suzuki); 4 Jurgen van den Goorbergh, NL (Yamaha); 5 Broc Parkes, AUS (Honda); 6 Pere Riba, E (Kawasaki); 7 Jörg Teuchert, D (Yamaha); 8 Christian Kellner, D (Yamaha); 9 Sébastien Charpentier, F (Honda); 10 Gianluca Nannelli, I (Yamaha); 11 Robert Ulm, A (Honda); 12 Matthieu Lagrive, F (Yamaha); 13 Dean Thomas, AUS (Honda); 14 Barry Veneman, NL (Honda); 15 Karl Muggeridge, AUS (Honda).

Fastest lap: Fujiwara, 1m 30.858s, 90.282 mph/145.295 km/h.
Championship points: 1 Vermeulen, 106; 2 Fujiwara, 68; 3 van den Goorbergh, 64; 4 Chambon, 62; 5 Kellner, 54; 6 Corradi, 37.

SILVERSTONE, Great Britain, 15 June. 3.129-mile/5.036-km circuit.
Supersport World Championship, round 6 (19 laps, 59.451 miles/95.684 km)
1 Chris Vermeulen, AUS (Honda), 37m 21.429s, 95.492 mph/153.680 km/h.

2 Jurgen van den Goorbergh, NL (Yamaha); 3 Karl Muggeridge, AUS (Honda); 4 Thierry van den Bosch, F (Yamaha); 5 Alessio Corradi, I (Yamaha); 6 Christophe Cogan, F (Honda); 7 Pere Riba, E (Kawasaki); 8 Katsuaki Fujiwara, J (Suzuki); 9 Matthieu Lagrive, F (Yamaha); 10 Robert Ulm, A (Honda); 11 Christian Kellner, D (Yamaha); 12 Takeshi Tsujimura, J (Honda); 13 Dean Thomas, AUS (Honda); 14 Gianluca Nannelli, I (Yamaha); 15 Werner Daemen, B (Honda).
Fastest lap: Vermeulen, 1m 56.459s, 96.731 mph/155.674 km/h (record).
Championship points: 1 Vermeulen, 131; 2 van den Goorbergh, 84; 3 Fujiwara, 76; 4 Chambon, 62; 5 Kellner, 59; 6 Corradi, 48.

MISANO, Italy, 22 June. 2.523-mile/4.060-km circuit.
Supersport World Championship, round 7 (23 laps, 58.029 miles/93.380 km)
1 Fabien Foret, F (Kawasaki), 37m 55.497s, 91.798 mph/147.734 km/h.

2 Katsuaki Fujiwara, J (Suzuki); 3 Broc Parkes, AUS (Honda); 4 Stéphane Chambon, F (Suzuki); 5 Jörg Teuchert, D (Yamaha); 6 Christian Kellner, D (Yamaha); 7 Alessio Corradi, I (Yamaha); 8 Simone Sanna, I (Yamaha); 9 Christophe Cogan, F (Honda); 10 Stefano Cruciani, I (Kawasaki); 11 Matthieu Lagrive, F (Yamaha); 12 Sébastien Charpentier, F (Honda); 13 Alessandro Polita, I (Yamaha); 14 Iain Macpherson, GB (Honda); 15 Ivan Goi, I (Yamaha).
Fastest lap: Fujiwara, 1m 37.924s, 92.745 mph/149.259 km/h (record).
Championship points: 1 Vermeulen, 131; 2 Fujiwara, 96; 3 van den Goorbergh, 84; 4 Chambon, 75; 5 Kellner, 69; 6 Corradi, 57.

BRANDS HATCH, Great Britain, 27 July. 2.608-mile/4.197-km circuit.
Supersport World Championship, round 8 (21 laps, 54.768 miles/88.137 km)
1 Stéphane Chambon, F (Suzuki), 31m 28.121s, 104.420 mph/168.047 km/h.

2 Jurgen van den Goorbergh, NL (Yamaha); 3 Sébastien Charpentier, F (Honda); 4 Karl Muggeridge, AUS (Honda); 5 Fabien Foret, F (Kawasaki); 6 Chris Vermeulen, AUS (Honda); 7 Christian Kellner, D (Yamaha); 8 Jörg Teuchert, D (Yamaha); 9 Katsuaki Fujiwara, J (Suzuki); 10 Alessio Corradi, I (Yamaha); 11 Tom Sykes, GB (Yamaha); 12 Pere Riba, E (Kawasaki); 13 Christophe Cogan, F (Honda); 14 Broc Parkes, AUS (Honda).
Fastest lap: Chambon, 1m 29.149s, 105.312 mph/169.483 km/h (record).
Championship points: 1 Vermeulen, 141; 2 van den Goorbergh, 104; 3 Fujiwara, 103; 4 Chambon, 100; 5 Kellner, 78; 6 Corradi, 63.

ASSEN, Holland, 7 September. 3.745-mile/6.027-km circuit.
Supersport World Championship, round 9 (16 laps, 59.920 miles/96.432 km)
1 Karl Muggeridge, AUS (Honda), 34m 05.948s, 105.434 mph/169.679 km/h.

2 Chris Vermeulen, AUS (Honda); 3 Katsuaki Fujiwara, J (Suzuki); 4 Stéphane Chambon, F (Suzuki); 5 Sébastien Charpentier, F (Honda); 6 Fabien Foret, F (Kawasaki); 7 Jörg Teuchert, D (Yamaha); 8 Gianluca Nannelli, I (Yamaha); 9 Werner Daemen, B (Honda); 10 Barry Veneman, NL (Yamaha); 11 Michael Laverty, IRL (Honda); 12 Dean Thomas, AUS (Honda); 13 Jan Hanson, S (Honda); 14 Jan Hanson, S (Yamaha); 15 Robert Ulm, A (Honda).
Fastest lap: Fujiwara, 2m 06.922s, 106.223 mph/170.949 mph (record).
Championship points: 1 Vermeulen, 161; 2 Fujiwara, 119; 3 Chambon, 113; 4 van den Goorbergh, 104; 5 Muggeridge, 84; 6 Kellner, 78.

IMOLA, Italy, 28 September. 3.065-mile/4.933-km circuit.
Supersport World Championship, round 10 (21 laps, 64.365 miles/103.593 km)
1 Karl Muggeridge, AUS (Honda), 39m 48.471s, 97.021 mph/156.140 km/h.

2 Chris Vermeulen, AUS (Honda); 3 Jurgen van den Goorbergh, NL (Yamaha); 4 Stéphane Chambon, F (Suzuki); 5 Sébastien Charpentier, F (Honda); 6 Gianluca Nannelli, I (Yamaha); 7 Tekkyu Kayo, J (Yamaha); 8 Iain Macpherson, GB (Honda); 9 Antonio Carlacci, I (Yamaha); 10 Simone Sanna, I (Yamaha); 11 Matthieu Lagrive, F (Yamaha); 12 Christian Kellner, D (Yamaha); 13 Robert Ulm, A (Honda); 14 Jörg Teuchert, D (Yamaha); 15 Alessandro Polita, I (Yamaha).
Fastest lap: Kevin Curtain, AUS (Yamaha), 1m 53.122s, 97.548 mph/156.988 km/h (record).
Championship points: 1 Vermeulen, 181; 2 Chambon, 126; 3 van den Goorbergh, 120; 4 Fujiwara, 119; 5 Muggeridge, 109; 6 Kellner, 82.

MAGNY-COURS, France, 19 October. 2.741-mile/4.411-km circuit.
Supersport World Championship, round 11 (23 laps, 63.043 miles/101.453 km)
1 Karl Muggeridge, AUS (Honda), 40m 24.892s, 93.589 mph/150.617 km/h.

2 Chris Vermeulen, AUS (Honda); 3 Jurgen van den Goorbergh, NL (Yamaha); 4 Sébastien Charpentier, F (Honda); 5 Stéphane Chambon, F (Suzuki); 6 Pere Riba, E (Kawasaki); 7 Matthieu Lagrive, F (Yamaha); 8 Christian Kellner, D (Yamaha); 9 Christophe Cogan, F (Honda); 10 Werner Daemen, B (Honda); 11 Simone Sanna, I (Yamaha); 12 Julien da Costa, F (Yamaha); 13 Gianluca Nannelli, I (Yamaha); 14 Michael Schulten, D (Honda); 15 Ludovic Holon, F (Yamaha).
Fastest lap: Muggeridge, 1m 44.643s, 94.293 mph/151.750 km/h (record).

Final World Championship points

1 Chris Vermeulen, AUS — 201
2 Stéphane Chambon, F — 137
3 Jurgen van den Goorbergh, NL — 136
4 Karl Muggeridge, AUS — 134
5 Katsuaki Fujiwara, J — 119

6 Christian Kellner, D, 90; 7 Sébastien Charpentier, F, 72; 8 Alessio Corradi, I, 68; 9 Fabien Foret, F, 64; 10 Jörg Teuchert, D, 60; 11 Pere Riba, E, 59; 12 Christophe Cogan, F, 51; 13 Broc Parkes, AUS, 47; 14= Matthieu Lagrive, F, Iain Macpherson, GB and Gianluca Nannelli, I, 31.